Methods for Achieving Your Purpose in Writing

The Bedford Reader centers on common ways of thinking and writing about all kinds of subjects, from everyday experiences to complex scientific theories. Whatever your purpose in writing, one or more of these ways of thinking—or methods of development—can help you discover and shape your ideas. You will find the methods useful in developing individual paragraphs or entire papers.

The following list connects various purposes you may have for writing and the methods for achieving those purposes. We explain the methods generally on pages 37–38 and then give detailed guidelines and numerous examples in Chapters 4 through 13.

- If you want to tell a story about your subject, possibly to enlighten readers or to explain something to them, use *narration* (Chap. 4).

- If you want readers to understand your subject through the evidence of their senses—sight, hearing, touch, smell, taste—use *description* (Chap. 5).

- If you want to explain your subject with instances that show readers its nature or character, use *example* (Chap. 6).

- If you want to explain or evaluate your subject by helping readers see the similarities and differences between it and another subject, use *comparison and contrast* (Chap. 7).

- If you want readers to understand how to do something or how something works—how a sequence of actions leads to a particular result—use *process analysis* (Chap. 8).

- If you want to explain a conclusion about your subject by showing readers the subject's parts or elements, use *division or analysis* (Chap. 9).

- If you want readers to see order in your subject by understanding the kinds or groups it can be sorted into, use *classification* (Chap. 10).

- If you want to tell readers the reasons for or consequences of your subject, explaining why or what if, use *cause and effect* (Chap. 11).

- If you want readers to grasp the meaning of your subject—its boundaries and its distinctions from other subjects—use *definition* (Chap. 12).

- If you want readers to consider your opinion about your subject or your proposal for it, use *argument and persuasion* (Chap. 13).

THE BEDFORD READER

EIGHTH EDITION

X. J. Kennedy • Dorothy M. Kennedy

Jane E. Aaron

BEDFORD/ST. MARTIN'S   BOSTON • NEW YORK

FOR BEDFORD/ST. MARTIN'S

Developmental Editors: Genevieve Hamilton, Maura Shea
Production Editor: Arthur Johnson
Production Supervisor: Maria Gonzalez
Marketing Manager: Brian Wheel
Editorial Assistants: Karin Halbert, Erin Durkin
Production Assistant: Kendra LeFleur
Copyeditor: Mary Lou Wilshaw-Watts
Cover Design: Donna Lee Dennison
Cover Art: Eric Sealine, *Arabesque,* mixed media. Courtesy of Chase Gallery, Boston.
Composition: Stratford Publishing Services, Inc.
Printing and Binding: Haddon Craftsmen, Inc., an R.R. Donnelley & Sons Company

President: Joan E. Feinberg
Editor in Chief: Karen S. Henry
Director of Marketing: Karen Melton
Director of Editing, Design, and Production: Marcia Cohen
Managing Editor: Elizabeth M. Schaaf

Library of Congress Control Number: 2002102538

For information, write: Bedford/St. Martin's, 75 Arlington Street, Boston, MA 02116
(617-399-4000)

ISBN: 0–312–39500–0

Acknowledgments

Sherman Alexie. "Indian Education" from *The Lone Ranger and Tonto Fistfight in Heaven* by Sherman Alexie. Used by permission of Grove/Atlantic, Inc. Copyright © 1993 by Sherman Alexie. "Sherman Alexie on Writing," excerpt from "Poetry and Three-pointers" by Pam Lambert from *People Weekly,* May 8, 1995. Copyright © 1995 by Time, Inc. Reprinted by permission of Time, Inc. Excerpt from "Sherman Alexie: A Reservation of the Mind" by Doug Marx from *Publishers Weekly,* September 16, 1996. Reprinted by permission of *Publishers Weekly.* Excerpt from "Interview: Sherman Alexie" from *Dreaming the Dawn* by E. K. Caldwell. Reprinted by permission of University of Nebraska Press. Excerpt from "Profile: Sherman Alexie" by Joel McNally from *Writermag.com.*

Acknowledgments and copyrights are continued at the back of the book on pages 719–25, which constitute an extension of the copyright page. It is a violation of the law to reproduce these selections by any means whatsoever without the written permission of the copyright holder.

PREFACE
FOR INSTRUCTORS

"A writer," says Saul Bellow, "is a reader moved to emulate." In a nutshell, the aim of *The Bedford Reader* is to move students to be writers, through reading and emulating the good writing of others.

Like its predecessor, this eighth edition of *The Bedford Reader* works toward its aim both rhetorically and thematically. We present the rhetorical methods realistically, as we ourselves use them — as natural forms that assist invention and fruition and as flexible forms that mix easily for any purpose a writer may have. Further, we forge scores of thematic connections among selections, both in paired selections in each rhetorical chapter and in writing topics after all the selections.

Filling in this outline is a wealth of features, new and old.

NEW VISUAL DIMENSION.   Dramatically extending its range, the new *Bedford Reader* adds an element that will be obvious to anyone thumbing the pages: an emphasis on the visual. The purpose is far from cosmetic, for reading visual images is often just as important as reading words.

In Chapter 1, *The Bedford Reader* provides a short course in thinking critically about the visual, with an advertisement serving as a case study. Then a range of visuals — ads, cartoons, photographs, paintings — open the ten rhetorical chapters. Along with accompanying text and questions, these openers invite students' own critical reading and show how the rhetorical methods work visually. Finally, several of the book's selections take visual images as their focal points and model the close reading encouraged of students.

VARIED SELECTIONS BY WELL-KNOWN AUTHORS.   The selections in *The Bedford Reader* vary in authorship, topics, even length. We offer clear models of the methods of development by noted writers such as Amy Tan, Joan Didion, E. B. White, and Dave Barry. Half the selections are by women, and a quarter touch on cultural diversity. They range in subject from family to science, from language to disability.

As always, freshening the book's selections engrossed us. Twenty-six new selections include works by Sherman Alexie, Jhumpa Lahiri, Bill Bryson, William Safire, David Sedaris, Shelby Steele, George F. Will, Cornel West, and Terry Tempest Williams. New literary selections by Joyce Carol Oates, Alice Walker, Don DeLillo, and C. Day Lewis raise the total to four short stories and two poems. And two new student essays increase student contributions to sixteen, including the case studies discussed below.

UNIQUE COMMENTS BY WRITERS ON WRITING.   After their essays, poems, or stories, fifty-seven of the book's writers offer comments on everything from grammar to revision to how they developed the reprinted piece. Besides providing rock-solid advice, these comments also prove that for the pros, too, writing is usually a challenge. Twenty Writers on Writing are new to this edition, including those by Don DeLillo, David Sedaris, and Joyce Carol Oates.

For easy access, the Writers on Writing are listed in the book's index under the topics they address. Look up "Revision," for instance, and find that Dave Barry, Russell Baker, and Maxine Hong Kingston, among others, have something to say about this crucial stage of the writing process.

REALISTIC TREATMENT OF THE RHETORICAL METHODS.   At the core of *The Bedford Reader*, ten chapters treat ten methods of development not as boxes to be stuffed full of verbiage but as tools for inventing, for shaping, and, ultimately, for accomplishing a purpose. Clear, practical chapter introductions link the methods to the range of purposes they can serve and give step-by-step guidance for writing and revising in the method. (For quick reference, the purpose–method links also appear inside the book's front cover.) In addition, a case study in every rhetorical chapter, appearing on gray-bordered pages, shows how a student arrived at the method to achieve a practical writing goal, such as reporting an accident, crafting a résumé, or advertising an apartment for sublet.

Taking this realistic approach to the methods even further, we show how writers freely combine the methods to achieve their purposes: Each rhetorical introduction discusses how that method might work with others, and at least one "Other Methods" question after every selection helps students analyze how methods work together. Most significantly, Part Three provides an anthology of classic works by well-known writers that specifically illustrate mixed methods. The headnotes for these selections point to where each method comes into play.

EXTENSIVE THEMATIC CONNECTIONS. *The Bedford Reader* provides substantial topics for class discussion and writing. A pair of essays in each rhetorical chapter addresses the same subject, from the ordinary (housekeeping) to the controversial (the death penalty). At least one "Connections" writing topic after every selection suggests links to other selections. And an alternate thematic table of contents arranges the book's selections under more than two dozen topics.

THOROUGH COVERAGE OF CRITICAL READING AND WRITING. *The Bedford Reader* offers detailed advice on the kinds of reading and writing that students are expected to do in college and beyond. We have broken the long general introduction into smaller, more accessible chapters. Chapter 1 covers critical reading, including a sample of a student's annotations on a text and practical guidelines for summarizing, analyzing, and interpreting texts. The new introduction to reading visual images also appears in this chapter. Then Chapter 2 covers writing, from ideas through editing, illustrated with a student work-in-progress.

EXPANDED TREATMENT OF RESEARCH WRITING. A new Chapter 3, "Using and Documenting Sources," greatly expands the appendix of former editions. The chapter offers advice on evaluating sources (including online sources), summarizing and paraphrasing, avoiding plagiarism, integrating sources, and documenting sources in MLA style. A new student research paper, with marginal annotations, provides a model.

ABUNDANT EDITORIAL APPARATUS. As always, we've surrounded the selections with a wealth of material designed to get students reading, thinking, and writing. To help structure students' critical approach to the selections, each one comes with two headnotes (on the author and the selection itself), three sets of questions (on meaning, writing strategy, and language), and at least four writing topics. One writing topic, now immediately following the selection, encourages students to explore their responses in their journals. Another topic then suggests how to develop the journal writing into an essay, while two others emphasize critical writing and draw connections to other selections.

Besides the aids with every selection, the book also includes additional writing topics for every rhetorical chapter, a glossary ("Useful Terms") that defines all terms used in the book (including all those printed in SMALL CAPITAL LETTERS), and an index that alphabetizes authors and titles and important topics (including, as noted earlier, those covered in the Writers on Writing).

INSTRUCTOR'S MANUAL AND COMPANION WEB SITE. Bound into the Instructor's Edition, *Notes and Resources for Teaching The Bedford Reader* suggests ways to integrate journal writing and collaboration into writing classes, ways to use the book's Chapters 1 and 2 on reading and writing (including the new material on visual literacy), and ways to work the student case studies into a course. In addition, *Notes and Resources* discusses every method, every selection (with possible answers to all questions), and every Writer on Writing.

Instructors and students have access to a range of resources at the companion Web site for *The Bedford Reader* (*http://www.bedfordstmartins.com/thebedfordreader*). Annotated links direct students to further reading on authors in the book and on topics covered by the book's selections. In addition, direct links lead to two Bedford/St. Martin's sites—*The English Research Room* and *Research and Documentation Online*—that provide advice on research writing and documentation, practice tutorials, and links to Internet research sources.

TWO VERSIONS. *The Bedford Reader* has a sibling. A shorter edition, *The Brief Bedford Reader*, features forty-eight selections instead of seventy-three, including five rather than fifteen essays in Part Three.

ACKNOWLEDGMENTS

Hundreds of the teachers and students using *The Bedford Reader* over the years have helped us shape the book. For this edition, the following teachers offered insights from their experiences that encouraged worthy changes: Christopher Baker, Armstrong Atlantic State University; Kelly R. Bober, Elgin Community College; Ellen Burke, Casper College; Mary Paniccia Carden, Southeastern Oklahoma State University; Elisabeth Cobb, Chapman University; Kathryn Cowan, Cabrillo College; Sarah T. Coyne, West Liberty State University; Pamela Cross, Stockton College; Dana B. Crotwell, El Camino College; Christine Cucciarre, Lakeland Community College; Natalie S. Daley, Linn-Benton Community College; Maria Dintino, Keene State College; Teresa Dunn, Clemson University; J. Arthur Faber, Wittenberg University; Mary E. Fakler, Mount St. Mary College; Jolly Kay Faught, Cumberland College; Kathy Griffith Fish, Cumberland College; Thomas E. Fish, Cumberland College; Jefferson Hancock, Cabrillo College; Frederick Jeffrey Karem, Cleveland State University; Jocelyn Ladner, St. Louis Community College; Frances Lozano, Gavilan College; William B. Martin, Armstrong Atlantic State University; Todd McCann, Bay de Noc Community College; Devonee McDonald, Kirkwood Community College; Kathy McWilliams, Cuyamaca College; Alan Merickel, Tallahassee Community College; Stephanie Mood, Grossmont College; Julie R. Morgan, Volunteer State Community College; Mary Murray, Cleveland State University; Bill O'Boyle, Nashville Community College; Vicki Lynn Samson, Grossmont College; Nancy E. Sherrod, Georgia Southern University; Carol Treadwell, Santa Monica College; Sandia Tuttle, Grossmont College; James E. Van Sickle, Grand Valley State University; Debra Vazquez, Central Florida Community College; Michael J. Volz, University of New Mexico; Cliff Wakeman, Columbia Basin College; Ping'an Wang, Cleveland State University; and Christian Wiman, Lynchburg College.

Once again, we owe a huge debt to the creative people at and around Bedford/St. Martin's. Charles Christensen, Joan Feinberg, and Karen Henry contributed their customary insight and support. Developing the book, Genevieve Hamilton and Maura Shea served in sequence as both hand holders and gentle prods, idea factories and sounding boards. Karin Halbert, their assistant, provided first-rate research and responded nimbly to any request. Mark Gallaher and Karla Saari Kitalong helped to shape the book's apparatus and instructor's manual. Donna Dennison created the striking cover. And Arthur Johnson produced a book from a difficult manuscript on a tight schedule with uncommon thoroughness and grace.

CONTENTS

An incident in the writer's childhood proves the occasion for a revelation about her
father's past and a lesson in the nature of violence.

2   WRITING EFFECTIVELY   33

A student questions M. F. K. Fisher's acceptance of physical punishment as a justifiable
form of violence.

3   USING AND DOCUMENTING SOURCES   49

Even the best baseball players have trouble hitting a knuckleball pitch. Citing scientific research, a student writer explains why.

PART TWO
THE METHODS
71

She didn't dare ring up a sale while that epic battle was on. A noted African American writer remembers from her early childhood the night when a people's fate hung on a pair of boxing gloves.

**PAIRED
SELECTIONS**

The writer remembers her teenaged angst when the minister and his cute blond son attended her family's Christmas Eve dinner, an elaborate Chinese feast.

5   DESCRIPTION: Writing with Your Senses   127

PAIRED
SELECTIONS

6   EXAMPLE: Pointing to Instances   175

PAIRED
SELECTIONS

PAIRED
SELECTIONS

8   PROCESS ANALYSIS: Explaining Step by Step   267

VISUAL IMAGES: *Eagle in Flight, 1884–86,* photographs by Eadweard Muybridge

Analyzing hip-hop music, the writer finds its appeal in the "myths and images that compensate for a sense of alienation."

A missile designer helped create the hard, highly molded Barbie doll. What are the implications for the millions of girls who grow up with this sexy toy?

Your car will make you feel sexy, loved, and powerful. At least that's what many car companies want you to believe, says a well-known media critic. We reprint several of the numerous advertisements she cites.

In this fictional exchange, a daughter can barely insert two sentences into her mother's litany of instructions on how to become a lady, not a slut.

The goal of inanimate objects, declares the renowned humorist, is nothing short of the destruction of the human race.

PART THREE
MIXING THE METHODS
565

THEMATIC TABLE OF CONTENTS

AUTOBIOGRAPHY

BIOGRAPHY

CAPITAL PUNISHMENT

CHILDHOOD AND FAMILY

CLASS

READING, WRITING, AND LANGUAGE

SCIENCE AND TECHNOLOGY

SELF-DISCOVERY

SEXUALITY

SOCIAL CUSTOMS

SPORTS AND LEISURE

VIOLENCE

WOMEN AND MEN

WORK

INTRODUCTION

WHY READ? WHY WRITE?
WHY NOT PHONE?

Many prophets have forecast the doom of the word on paper. Soon, they have argued, books and magazines will be read on pocket computers. Newspapers will be found only in attics, supplanted by interactive television. The mails will be replaced by electronic message boards.

The prophets have been making such forecasts for many decades, but book sales remain high, magazines and newspapers keep publishing, and mailing services have trouble keeping up with volume. In the electronic office, the computer workstation is often an island in a sea of paper. Evidently, the permanent, word-on-paper record still has its advantages.

Even if the day comes when we throw away pens and paper, it is doubtful that the basic aims and methods of writing will completely change. Whether on paper or on screens, we will need to arrange our thoughts in a clear order. We will still have to explain them to others plainly and forcefully.

That is why, in almost any career or profession you may enter, you will be expected to read continually and also to write. This book assumes that reading and writing are a unity. Deepen your mastery of one, and you deepen your mastery of the other. The experience of carefully reading an excellent writer,

1

noticing not only what the writer has to say but also the quality of its saying, rubs off (if you are patient and perceptive) on your own writing. "We go to college," said the poet Robert Frost, "to be given one more chance to learn to read in case we haven't learned in high school. Once we have learned to read, the rest can be trusted to add itself *unto us*."

For any writer, reading is indispensable. It turns up fresh ideas; it stocks the mind with information, understanding, examples, and illustrations; it instills critical awareness of one's surroundings. When you have a well-stocked and girded mental storehouse, you tell truths, even small and ordinary truths. Instead of building shimmering spires of words in an attempt to make a reader think, "Wow, what a grade A writer," you write what most readers will find worth reading. Thornton Wilder, playwright and novelist, put this advice memorably: "If you write to *impress* it will always be bad, but if you write to *express* it will be good."

USING *THE BEDFORD READER*

The Selections

In this book, we trust, you'll find at least a few selections you will enjoy and care to remember. *The Bedford Reader* features work by many of the finest nonfiction writers and even a few sterling fiction writers and poets.

The selections deal with more than just writing and literature and such usual concerns of English courses; they cut broadly across a college curriculum. You'll find writings on science, history, business, popular culture, sociology, education, communication, the environment, technology, sports, politics, the media, and minority experience. Some writers recall their childhoods, their families, their problems and challenges. Some explore matters likely to spark controversy: drug use, funerals, sex roles, race relations, the death penalty. Some writers are intently serious; others, funny. In all, these seventy-three selections—including four stories and two poems—reveal kinds of reading you will meet in other college courses. Such reading is the usual diet of well-informed people with lively minds—who, to be sure, aren't found only on campuses.

The selections have been chosen with one main purpose in mind: to show you how good writers write. Don't feel glum if at first you find an immense gap in quality between E. B. White's writing and yours. Of course there's a gap: White is an immortal with a unique style that he perfected over half a century. You don't have to judge your efforts by comparison. The idea is to gain whatever writing techniques you can. If you're going to learn from other writers, why not go to the best of them? Do you want to know how to define an idea so that the definition is vivid and clear? Read Marie Winn's "TV Addiction." Do you want to know how to tell a story about your childhood and make it stick in someone's memory? Read Maya Angelou. Incidentally, not all the selections in this book are the work of professional writers: Students, too, write essays worth studying, as Christine D'Angelo, Greg Tartaglia, Brad Manning, Linnea Saukko, Christine Leong, and Colleen Wenke prove.

Not all the selections in this book are solely verbal, either, for much of what we "read" in the world is visual information, such as in photographs and paintings, or visual-with-verbal information, such as in advertisements, films, and Web sites. In all, we include seventeen visual works. Some of them are subjects of writing, as when a poet comments on a painting or a critic comments on an advertisement. Other visual works stand free, offering themselves to be understood, interpreted, and perhaps enjoyed, just as prose and poetry do.

We combine visual material with written texts to further a key aim of *The Bedford Reader:* to encourage you to think critically about what you see, hear, and read, that is, to think with an open, questioning mind. Like everyone else, you face a daily barrage of words and pictures—from the media, from your courses, from relatives and friends. Mulling over the views of the writers, artists, and others represented in this book—figuring out their motives and strategies, agreeing or disagreeing with their ideas—will help you learn to manage, digest, and use, in your own writing, what you read and hear.

The Organization

As a glance over the table of contents will show, the selections in *The Bedford Reader* fall into two parts. In Part Two each of the ten chapters explains a familiar method of developing ideas, such as DESCRIPTION or CLAS-SIFICATION or DEFINITION, and the selections illustrate the method. Then Part Three offers an anthology of selections by well-known writers that illustrate how, most often, the methods work together.

These methods of development aren't empty jugs to pour full of any old, dull words. Neither are they straitjackets woven by fiendish English teachers to pin your writing arm to your side and keep you from expressing yourself naturally. The methods are tools for achieving your PURPOSE in writing, whatever that purpose may be. They can help you discover what you know, what you need to know, how to think critically about your subject, and how to shape your writing.

Suppose, for example, that you set out to explain what makes a certain popular singer unique. You want to discuss her voice, her music, her lyrics, her style. While putting your ideas down on paper, it strikes you that you can best illustrate the singer's distinctions by showing the differences between her and another popular singer, one she is often compared with. To achieve your purpose, then, you draw on the method of COMPARISON AND CONTRAST, and as you proceed the method prompts you to notice differences between the two singers that you hadn't dreamed of noticing. Using the methods, such little miracles of focusing and creating take place with heartening regularity. Give the methods a try. See how they help you reach your writing goals by giving you more to say, more that you think is worth saying.

To demonstrate the many uses of the methods of development, each chapter includes not only essays illustrating a method but more as well. A photograph, advertisement, cartoon, or other image shows how the method can contribute to the visual representation of an idea. And a case study shows how a student used a method to solve an actual writing problem, from crafting a cover letter and a résumé for a job application to composing an ad to sublet an apartment. Further, half a dozen works of literature — stories or poems — show how the methods can guide authors' explorations of subjects as diverse as the feelings depicted in a painting, the experiences of a young girl, or the compulsion to watch real-life crime.

Examining *The Bedford Reader*'s selections, you'll discover two important facts about the methods of development. First, they are flexible: Two people can use the same method for quite different ends, and just about any method can point a way into just about any subject. To prove this flexibility, in every method chapter we offer a pair of essays on the same general subject but with different purposes, and we provide two sample paragraphs, one about television and one drawn from a college textbook.

The sample paragraphs illustrate another point about the methods of development: A writer never sticks to just one method all the way through a piece of writing. Even when one method predominates, as in all the essays in Part Two, you'll see the writer pick up another method, let it shape a paragraph or more, and then move on to yet another method — all to achieve some overriding aim. In "TV Addiction," Marie Winn mainly defines the term in her title, but she also compares TV addiction with drug and alcohol addiction, gives EXAMPLES of TV addiction that include description, and examines the CAUSES AND EFFECTS of the addiction. The point is that Winn employs whatever methods suit her dual purpose of explaining what TV addiction is and convincing readers that it is, in fact, an addiction.

So the methods are like oxygen, iron, and other elements that make up substances in nature: all around us, indispensable to us, but seldom found alone and isolated, in laboratory-pure states. When you read an essay in a chapter called "Description" or "Classification," don't expect it to describe or classify in every line, but do notice how the method is central to the writer's purpose. Then, when you read the selections in Part Three, notice how the "elements" of description, example, comparison, definition, and so on rise to prominence and recede as the writer's need dictates.

The Journal Prompts, Questions, Writing Topics, and Glossary

Immediately after every selection, you'll find a suggestion for responding in your journal to what you've just read. (See p. 36 for more on journal writing.) Then you'll find questions on meaning, writing strategy, and language that can help you analyze the selection and learn from it. (You can see a sample of how these questions work when we analyze M. F. K. Fisher's "The Broken Chain," starting on p. 21.) These questions are followed by at least four suggestions for writing, including one that proposes turning your journal entry into an essay, one that links the selection with one or two others in the book, and one that asks you to read the selection and write about it with your critical faculties alert (more on this in Chap. 1). More writing topics conclude each chapter.

In this Introduction and throughout the following chapters, certain terms appear in CAPITAL LETTERS. These are words helpful in discussing both the selections in this book and the reading and writing you do. If you'd like to see such a term defined and illustrated, you can find it in the glossary, Useful Terms, at the back of this book. This section offers more than just brief definitions. It is there to provide you with further information and support.

Writers on Writing

We have tried to give this book another dimension. We want to show that the writers represented here do not produce their readable and informative text on the first try, as if by magic, leaving the rest of us to cope with writer's block, awkward sentences, and all the other difficulties of writing. Take comfort and cheer: These writers, too, struggled to make themselves interesting and clear. In proof, we visit their workshops littered with crumpled paper and forgotten coffee cups. In Chapter 2, when we discuss the writing process briefly and include an essay by a student, Christine D'Angelo, we also include her drafts and her thoughts about them. Then following most of the other selections are statements by the writers, revealing how they write (or wrote), offering their tricks, setting forth things they admire about good writing.

No doubt you'll soon notice some contradictions in these statements: The writers disagree about when and how to think about their readers, about whether outlines have any value, about whether style follows subject or vice versa. The reason for the difference of opinion is, simply, that no two writers follow the same path to finished work. Even the same writer may take the left instead of the customary right fork if the writing situation demands a change. A key aim of providing D'Angelo's drafts and the other writers' statements on writing, then, is to suggest the sheer variety of routes open to you, the many approaches to writing and strategies for succeeding at it. At the very end of the book, an index points you toward the writers' comments on such practical matters as drafting, finding your point, and revising sentences.

PART ONE

READING, WRITING, AND RESEARCH

1

READING CRITICALLY

Whatever career you enter, much of the reading you will do—for business, not for pleasure—will probably be hasty. You'll skim: glance at words here and there, find essential facts, catch the drift of an argument. To cross oceans of print, you won't have time to paddle: You'll need to hop a jet. By skimming, you'll be able to tear through screens full of electronic mail or quickly locate the useful parts of a long report.

But other reading that you do for work, most that you do in college, and all that you do in this book call for closer attention. You may be trying to understand a new company policy, seeking the truth in a campaign ad, researching a complicated historical treaty, or (in using this book) looking for pointers to sharpen your reading and writing skills. To learn from the selections here how to write better yourself, expect to spend an hour or two in the company of each one. Does the essay assigned for today remain unread, and does class start in five minutes? "I'll just breeze through this little item," you might tell yourself. But no, give up. You're a goner.

Good writing, as every writer knows, demands toil, and so does CRITICAL READING—reading that looks beneath the surface of a work, whether written or visual, seeking to understand the creator's intentions, the strategies for achieving them, and their worthiness. Never try to gulp down a rich and potent work without chewing; all it will give you is indigestion. When you're going to read an essay or study a visual image in depth, seek out some quiet place—a library, a study cubicle, your room (provided it doesn't also hold a cranky baby or two roommates playing poker). Flick off the radio, stereo, or television. What writer or artist can outsing Aretha Franklin or outshout a kung fu movie? The fewer the distractions, the easier your task will be and the more you'll enjoy it.

How do you read critically? Exactly how, that is, do you see beneath the surface of a work, master its complexities, gauge its intentions and techniques, judge its value? To find out, we'll model critical-thinking processes that you can apply to the selections in this book, taking a close look at an essay, M. F. K. Fisher's "The Broken Chain" (p. 13), and at an insurance advertisement that mingles the visual and the verbal (p. 29).

READING AN ESSAY

The Preliminaries

Critical reading starts before you read the first word of a piece of writing. Like a pilot circling an airfield, you take stock of what's before you, locating clues to the work's content and the writer's biases.

The Title

Often the title will tell you the writer's subject, as in Lucinda Rosenfeld's "How to Dump a Friend" or H. L. Mencken's "The Penalty of Death." Sometimes the title immediately states the THESIS, the main point the writer will make: "I Want a Wife." The title may set forth the subject as a question: "Why Don't We Complain?" Some titles spell out the method a writer proposes to follow: "Grant and Lee: A Study in Contrasts." The TONE of the title may also reveal the writer's attitude toward the material, as "The Cancer-Cluster Myth" or "Marrying Absurd" does.

Some titles reveal more than others. M. F. Fisher's title, "The Broken Chain," is a bit mysterious. We may suspect that the author does not mean "chain" literally (a bicycle chain) but figuratively (like a chain of events or a chain reaction). The essay's title hints at change (a chain breaks), so we may guess that this broken chain lies at the heart of a story. The rest is for us to find out.

Whatever it does, a title sits atop its essay like a neon sign. It tells you what's inside or makes you want to venture in. To pick an alluring title for an essay of your own is a skill worth cultivating.

The Author

Whatever you know about a writer—background, special training, previous works, outlook, or ideology—often will help you guess something about the essay before you read a word of it. Is the writer on new taxes a political conservative? Expect an argument against added "revenue enhancement." Is the writer a liberal? Expect an argument that new social programs are worth the price. Is the writer a feminist? an athlete? an internationally renowned philosopher? a popular television comedian? By knowing something about a writer's background or beliefs, you may know beforehand a little of what he or she will say.

To help provide such knowledge, this book supplies biographical notes. The one on M. F. K. Fisher before "The Broken Chain" (p. 13) tells us that Fisher often wrote about food but that she told other stories as well. You won't know until you read it whether "The Broken Chain" is about food. But if you guess from the note that the essay will be thought provoking, enjoyable, and readily understandable, you will be right.

Where the Work Was Published

Clearly, it matters to a writer's credibility whether an article called "Living Mermaids: An Amazing Discovery" appears in *Scientific American*, a magazine for scientists and interested nonscientists, or in a popular tabloid weekly, sold at supermarket checkout counters, that is full of eye-popping sensations. But no less important, examining where a work appears can tell you for whom the writer was writing.

In this book we'll strongly urge you as a writer to think of your AUDIENCE, your readers, and to try looking at what you write as if through their eyes. To help you develop this ability, we tell you something about the sources and thus the original readers of each essay you study, in a note just before the essay. (Such a note precedes "The Broken Chain" on p. 13.) After you have read the sample essay, we'll further consider how having a sense of your readers helps you write.

When the Work Was Published

Knowing in what year a work appeared may give you another key to understanding it. A 1988 essay on mermaids will contain statements of fact more recent and more reliable than an essay printed in 1700—although the older essay might contain valuable information, too, and perhaps some delectable language, folklore, and poetry. In *The Bedford Reader* the introductory note on every essay tells you not only where but also when the essay was originally printed. If you're reading an essay elsewhere—say, in one of the writer's books—you can usually find this information on the copyright page.

The First Reading

On first reading an essay, you don't want to bog down over every troublesome particular. "The Broken Chain" is written for an educated audience, and that means the author may use a few large words when they seem necessary. If you meet any words that look intimidating, take them in your stride. When, in reading a rich essay, you run into an unfamiliar word or name, see if you can figure it out from its surroundings. If a word stops you cold and you feel lost, circle it in pencil; you can always look it up later. (In a little while we'll come back to the helpful habit of reading with a pencil. Indeed, some readers feel more confident with pencil in hand from the start.)

The first time you read an essay, size up the forest; later, you can squint at the acorns all you like. Glimpse the essay in its entirety. When you start to read "The Broken Chain," don't even think about dissecting it. Just see what Fisher has to say.

M. F. K. FISHER

MARY FRANCES KENNEDY FISHER was born in 1908 and began telling stories at age four. Raised in California and educated there and in Illinois and France, Fisher became renowned for her writing about food. Her first book, *Serve It Forth* (1937), was followed by more than sixteen others before her death at eighty-three in 1992. Not all of them concerned eating, and even those on food, such as *How to Cook a Wolf* (1942), expanded the subject to encompass needs and pleasures of all sorts. Besides writing her books, Fisher produced essays, poetry, and a screenplay, kept house, tended a vineyard in Switzerland, and translated a French gastronomical classic, Brillat-Savarin's *The Physiology of Taste*. Her works reveal a keen sense of story, a sharply observant, independent mind, and a search for the truths in her own and others' lives.

The Broken Chain

"The Broken Chain" was written in 1983 and first published in Fisher's last book, *To Begin Again* (1992). Taking her lead from news headlines, Fisher flashes back to an incident in 1920 that transformed her and her father, Rex, and could perhaps help others as well.

There has been more talk than usual lately about the abuse and angry 1 beating of helpless people, mostly children and many women. I think about it. I have never been beaten, so empathy is my only weapon against the ugliness I know vicariously. On the radio someone talks about a chain of violence. When is it broken? he asks. How?

When I was growing up, I was occasionally spanked and always by my 2 father. I often had to go upstairs with him when he came home from the *News* for lunch, and pull down my panties and lay myself obediently across his long bony knees, and then steel my emotions against the ritualistic whack of five or eight or even ten sharp taps from a wooden hairbrush. They were counted by my age, and by nine or ten he began to use his hand, in an expert upward slap that stung more than the hairbrush. I often cried a little, to prove that I had learned my lesson.

I knew that Rex disliked this duty very much, but that it was part of being 3 Father. Mother could not or would not punish us. Instead, she always said, by agreement with him and only when she felt that things were serious enough to drag him into it, that she would have to speak with him about the ugly matter when he came home at noon.

This always left me a cooling-off period of thought and regret and conditioned dread, even though I knew that I had been the cause, through my own stupidity, of involving both my parents in the plot. 4

Maybe it was a good idea. I always felt terrible that it was dragged out. I   5
wished that Mother would whack me or something and get it over with. And
as I grew older I resented having to take several undeserved blows because I
was the older child and was solemnly expected to be a model to my younger
sister, Anne. She was a comparatively sickly child, and spoiled and much clev-
erer than I, and often made it bitterly clear to me that I was an utter fool to
take punishment for her own small jaunty misdoings. I continued to do this,
far past the fatherly spankings and other parental punishments, because I
loved her and agreed that I was not as clever as she.

Once Rex hit me. I deserved it, because I had vented stupid petulance on   6
my helpless little brother David. He was perhaps a year old, and I was twelve.
We'd all left the lunch table for the living room and had left him sitting alone
in his high chair, and Father spotted him through the big doors and asked me
to get him down. I felt sulky about something, and angered, and I stamped
back to the table and pulled up the wooden tray that held the baby in his
chair, and dumped him out insolently on the floor. David did not even cry out,
but Rex saw it and in a flash leapt across the living room toward the dining
table and the empty high chair and gave me a slap across the side of my head
that sent me halfway across the room against the big old sideboard. He picked
up David and stood staring at me. Mother ran in. A couple of cousins came,
looking flustered and embarrassed at the sudden ugliness.

I picked myself up from the floor by the sideboard, really raging with   7
insulted anger, and looked disdainfully around me and then went silently up
the stairs that rose from the dining room to all our sleeping quarters. Behind
me I could hear Mother crying, and then a lot of talk.

I sat waiting for my father to come up to the bedroom that Anne and I   8
always shared, from her birth until I was twenty, in our two family homes in
Whittier, and in Laguna in the summers, and then when we went away to
three different schools. I knew I was going to be punished.

Finally Father came upstairs, looking very tired. "Daughter," he said, "your   9
mother wants you to be spanked. You have been bad. Pull down your panties
and lie across my knees."

I was growing very fast and was almost as tall as I am now, with small   10
growing breasts. I looked straight at him, not crying, and got into the old position, all long skinny arms and legs, with my bottom bared to him. I felt
insulted and full of fury. He gave me twelve expert upward stinging whacks. I
did not even breathe fast, on purpose. Then I stood up insolently, pulled up
my sensible Munsingwear panties, and stared down at him as he sat on the
edge of my bed.

"That's the last time," he said.   11
"Yes," I said. "And you hit me."   12

"I apologize for that," he said, and stood up slowly, so that once again I had   13
to look up into his face as I had always done. He went out of the room and
downstairs, and I stayed alone in the little room under the eaves of the Ranch
house, feeling my insult and anger drain slowly out and away forever. I knew
that a great deal had happened, and I felt ashamed of behaving so carelessly
toward my helpless little brother and amazed at the way I had simply blown
across the room and into the sideboard under my own father's wild stinging
blow across my cheek. I wished that I would be maimed, so that he would feel
shame every time he looked at my poor face. I tried to forget how silly I'd felt,
baring my pubescent bottom to his heavy dutiful slaps across it. I was full of
scowling puzzlements.

My mother came into the room, perhaps half an hour later, and wrapped   14
her arms around me with a tenderness I had never felt from her before,
although she had always been quietly free with her love and her embraces.
She had been crying but was very calm with me, as she told me that Father
had gone back to the *News* and that the cousins were playing with the
younger children. I wanted to stay haughty and abused with her, but sat there
on the bed quietly, while she told me about Father.

She said that he had been beaten when he was a child and then as a grow-   15
ing boy, my age, younger, older. His father beat him, almost every Saturday,
with a long leather belt. He beat all four of his boys until they were big enough
to tell him that it was the last time. They were all of them tall strong people,
and Mother said without any quivering in her voice that they were all about
sixteen before they could make it clear that if it ever happened again, they
would beat their father worse than he had ever done it to them.

He did it, she said, because he believed that he was ridding them of the   16
devil, of sin. Grandfather, she said quietly, was not a brute or a beast, not sin-
ful, not a devil. But he lived in the wild prairies and raised strong sons to survive, as he had, the untold dangers of frontier life. When he was starting his
family, as a wandering newspaperman and printer of political broadsides, he
got religion. He was born again. He repented of all his early wildness and tried
to keep his four sons from "sinning," as he came to call what he had done
before he accepted God as his master.

I sat close to Mother as she explained to me how horrible it had been only   17
a few minutes or hours before in my own short life, when Rex had broken a
long vow and struck his own child in unthinking anger. She told me that
before they married, he had told her that he had vowed when he was sixteen
to break the chain of violence and that never would he strike anyone in anger.
She must help him. They promised each other that they would break the
chain. And then today he had, for the first time in his whole life, struck out,
and he had struck his oldest child.

I could feel my mother trembling. I was almost overwhelmed by pity 18
for the two people whom I had betrayed into this by my stupidity. "Then
why did he hit me?" I almost yelled suddenly. She said that he hardly remembered doing it, because he was so shocked by my dumping the helpless baby
out onto the floor. "Your father does not remember," she repeated. "He simply
had to stop you, stop the unthinking way you acted toward a helpless baby.
He was . . . He suddenly acted violently. And it is dreadful for him now to
see that, after so long, he can be a raging animal. He thought it would never
happen. That is why he has never struck any living thing in anger. Until
today."

We talked for a long time. It was a day of spiritual purging, obviously. I 19
have never been the same—still stupid but never unthinking, because of
the invisible chains that can be forged in all of us, without our knowing it.
Rex knew of the chain of violence that was forged in him by his father's whippings, brutal no matter how mistakenly committed in the name of God. I
learned of what violence could mean as I sat beside my mother, that day when
I was twelve, and felt her tremble as she put her arm over my skinny shoulders
and pulled me toward her in an embrace that she was actually giving to her
husband.

It is almost certain that I stayed aloof and surly, often, in the next years 20
with my parents. But I was never spanked again. And I know as surely as I do
my given name that Rex no longer feared the chain of violence that had
bound him when he was a boy. Perhaps it is as well that he hit me, the one
time he found that it had not been broken for him.

❋

Writing While Reading

In giving an essay a going-over, many readers find a pencil in hand as good as a currycomb for a horse's mane. The pencil (or pen or computer keyboard) concentrates the attention wonderfully, and, as often happens with writing, it can lead you to unexpected questions and connections. (Some readers favor markers that roll pink or yellow ink over a word or line, making the eye jump to that spot, but you can't use a highlighter to note *why* a word or idea is important.) You can annotate your own books, underlining essential ideas, scoring key passages with vertical lines, writing questions in the margins about difficult words or concepts, venting feelings ("Bull!" "Yes!" "Says who?"). Here, as an example, are the jottings of one student, Christine D'Angelo, on a paragraph of Fisher's essay:

"I apologize for that," he said, and stood up slowly, so that once again I had to look up into his face as I had always done. He went out of the room and downstairs, and I stayed alone in the little room under the eaves of the Ranch house, feeling my insult and anger drain slowly out and away forever. I knew that a great deal had happened, and I felt ashamed of behaving so carelessly toward my helpless little brother and amazed at the way I had simply blown across the room and into the sideboard under my own father's wild stinging blow across my cheek. I wished that I would be maimed, so that he would feel shame every time he looked at my poor face. I tried to forget how silly I'd felt, baring my pubescent bottom to his heavy dutiful slaps across it. I was full of scowling puzzlements.

Annotations:
- *What was his expression?*
- *already forgives father?*
- *difference in blow and spanking (to author and father)*
- *Good phrase for child's mixed emotions*
- ?

If a book is borrowed, you can accomplish the same thing by making notes on a separate sheet of paper or on your computer.

Whether you own the book or not, you'll need separate notes for responses that are lengthier and more substantial than the margins can contain, such as the informal responses, summaries, detailed analyses, and evaluations discussed below. For such notes, you may find a JOURNAL handy. It can be a repository of your ideas, a comfortable place to record meandering or direct thoughts about what you read. You may be surprised to find that the more you write in an unstructured way, the more you'll have to say when it's time to write a structured essay. (For more on journals, see p. 36.)

Writing and reading help you behold the very spine of an essay, as if in an X-ray view, so that you, as much as any expert, can judge its curves and connections. You'll develop an opinion about what you read, and you'll want to express it. While reading this way, you're being a writer. Your pencil tracks or keystrokes will jog your memory, too, when you review for a test, when you take part in class discussion, or when you want to write about what you've read.

Summarizing

It's usually good practice, especially with more difficult essays, to SUMMA-RIZE the content in writing to be sure you understand it or, as often happens, to come to understand it. We use summary all the time to fill friends in on the gist of a story—shrinking a two-hour movie to a single sentence, "This woman is recruited to be a spy, and she stops a ring of double agents." In summarizing a work of writing, you digest, *in your own words*, what the author says: You take the essence of the author's meaning, without the supporting evidence and other details that make that gist convincing or interesting. When you are practicing reading and the work is short (the case with the reading you do in this book), you may want to make this a two-step procedure: First write a summary sentence for every paragraph or related group of paragraphs; then summarize those sentences in two or three others that capture the heart of the author's meaning.

Here is a two-step summary of "The Broken Chain." (The numbers in parentheses refer to paragraph numbers in the essay.) First, the longer version:

> (1) Fisher wonders about the "chain of violence" against children and women. (2–3) As a child, she was sometimes spanked on her bare bottom by her father, who carried out the job reluctantly as a father's responsibility. (4–5) The spanking did not occur immediately after the bad behavior, and the delay left Fisher feeling sorry and afraid and often resentful of her younger sister, who escaped such punishment. (6) Then once Fisher peevishly dropped her baby brother on the floor, and her father struck her suddenly and violently in anger. (7–13) She was simply furious at first, but she became remorseful, vindictive, and embarrassed as well when her father later spanked her for her deed and apologized for striking her. (14–16) Her mother then comforted her and explained that her father had been regularly beaten by his own father. (17–18) Her father had sworn that he would "break the chain of violence" by never hitting another person out of anger, and now he was horrified to discover that he, too, could be violent. (19) The incident helped Fisher understand her father and violence. (20) It also broke the chain by releasing her father from his fear that any violence in him must control him as it had his own father.

Now the short summary:

> Fisher's father sometimes reluctantly spanked her as punishment, but once when she deliberately dropped her baby brother he struck her suddenly and

violently. Her father had not escaped the "chain of violence" begun by his own father's regular beatings, but the incident released him from his fear that the chain must control him.

(We're suggesting that you write summaries for yourself, but the technique is also useful when you discuss other people's works in your writing. Then you must use your own words or use quotation marks for the author's words, and either way you must acknowledge the source in a citation. See pp. 52–54.)

Thinking Critically

Summarizing will start you toward understanding the author's meaning, but it won't take you as far as you're capable of going, or as far as you'll need to go in school or work or just to live well in our demanding Information Age. Passive, rote learning (such as memorizing the times tables in arithmetic) won't do. You require techniques for comprehending what you encounter. But more: You need tools for discovering the meaning and intentions of an essay or case study or business letter or political message. You need ways to discriminate between the trustworthy and the not so and to apply what's valid in your own work and life.

We're talking here about critical thinking—not "negative," the common conception of *critical,* but "thorough, thoughtful, question-asking, judgment-forming." When you approach something critically, you harness your faculties, your fund of knowledge, and your experiences to understand, appreciate, and evaluate the object. Using this book—guided by questions on meaning, writing strategy, and language—you'll read an essay and ask what the author's purpose and main idea are, how clear they are, and how well supported. You'll isolate which writing techniques the author has used to special advantage, what hits you as particularly fresh, clever, or wise—and what *doesn't* work, too. You'll discover exactly what the writer is saying, how he or she says it, and whether, in the end, it was worth saying. In class discussions and in writing, you'll tell others what you think and why.

Critical thinking is a process involving several overlapping operations: analysis, inference, synthesis, and evaluation.

Analysis

Say you're listening to a new album by a band called the Alley Cats. Without thinking much about it, you isolate melodies, song lyrics, and instrumentals—in other words, you ANALYZE the album by separating it into its parts. Analysis is a way of thinking so basic to us that it has its own chapter (9) in this book. For reading in this book, you'll consciously analyze essays by looking at the author's main idea, support for the idea, special writing strate-gies, and other elements.

Analysis underlies many of the other methods of development discussed in this book, so that while you are analyzing a subject you might also (even unconsciously) begin classifying it, or comparing it with something else, or fig-uring out what caused it. For instance, you might compare the Alley Cats' new instrumentals with those on their earlier albums, or you might notice that the lyrics seem to be influenced by another band's. Similarly, in analyzing a poem you might compare several images of water, or in analyzing a journal article in psychology you might consider how the author's theories affect her interpre-tations of behavior.

Inference

Say that after listening to the Alley Cats' new album, you conclude that it reveals a preoccupation with traditional blues music and themes. Now you are using INFERENCE, drawing conclusions about a work based on your store of information and experience, your knowledge of the creator's background and biases, and your analysis. When you infer, you add to the work, making explicit what was only implicit.

In critical thinking, inference is especially important in discovering a writer's ASSUMPTIONS: opinions or beliefs, often unstated, that direct the writer's choices of ideas, support, writing strategies, and language. A writer who favors gun control may assume without saying so that some individual rights (such as the right to bear arms) may be infringed for the good of the community. A writer who opposes gun control may assume the opposite — that in this case the individual's right is superior to the community's.

Synthesis

What are the Alley Cats trying to accomplish with their new album? Is it different from their previous album in its understanding of the blues? Answer-ing such questions leads you into SYNTHESIS, linking elements into a whole, or linking two or more wholes. During synthesis, you use your special aptitudes, interests, and training to reconstitute the work so that it now contains not just the original elements but also your sense of their underpinnings and relation-ships. About an essay you might ask why the author elicits contradictory feel-ings from readers, or what this essay has to do with that other essay, or what this essay has to do with your life.

Analysis, inference, and synthesis overlap—so much so that it's often impossible to distinguish one from the other during critical thinking. To stave off confusion, in this book we use the word *analysis* to cover all of these operations: identifying elements, drawing conclusions about them, *and* reconstituting them.

Evaluation

Not all critical thinking involves EVALUATION, or judging the quality of the work. You'll probably form a judgment of the Alley Cats' new album (is the band getting better or just standing still?), but often you (and your teachers) will be satisfied with a nonjudgmental reading of a work. ("Nonjudgmental" does not mean "uncritical": You will still be expected to analyze, infer, and synthesize.) When you *do* evaluate, you determine adequacy, significance, value. You answer a question such as whether an essay moves you as it was intended to, or whether the author has proved a case, or whether the argument is even worthwhile.

Analyzing "The Broken Chain"

The following comments on M. F. K. Fisher's "The Broken Chain" show how a critical reading can work. The headings "Meaning," "Writing Strategy" (p. 24), and "Language" (p. 25) correspond to those organizing the questions at the end of each essay.

Meaning

"No man but a blockhead," declared Samuel Johnson, "ever wrote except for money." Perhaps the eighteenth-century critic, journalist, and dictionary maker was remembering his own days as a literary drudge in London's Grub Street; but surely most people who write often do so for other reasons.

When you read an essay, you'll find it rewarding to ask, "What is this writer's PURPOSE?" By purpose, we mean the writer's apparent reason for writing: what he or she was trying to achieve with readers. A purpose is as essential to a good, pointed essay as a destination is to a trip. It affects every choice or decision the writer makes. (On vacation, of course, carefree people sometimes climb into a car without a thought and go happily rambling around; but if a writer rambles like that in an essay, the reader may plead, "Let me out!")

In making a simple statement of a writer's purpose, we might say that the writer writes *to entertain* readers, or *to explain* something to them, or *to persuade* them. To state a purpose more fully, we might say that a writer writes not just to persuade but "to tell readers a story to illustrate the point that when you are being cheated it's a good idea to complain," or not just to entertain but "to tell a horror story to make chills shoot down readers' spines." If the essay is an argument meant to convince, a fuller statement of its writer's purpose might be "to win readers over to the writer's opinion that San Antonio is the most livable city in the United States," or "to persuade readers to take action by writing their representatives and urging more federal spending for the reha-bilitation of criminals."

"But," the skeptic might object, "how can I know a writer's purpose? I'm no mind reader, and even if I were, how could I tell what E. B. White was trying to do? He's dead and buried." And yet writers living and dead have revealed their purposes in their writing, just as visibly as a hiker leaves foot-prints.

What is M. F. K. Fisher's purpose in writing? If you want to be more exact, you can speak of her *main purpose* or *central purpose*, for "The Broken Chain" fulfills more than one. Fisher clearly wants to tell her readers something about her parents and herself as a child. She is not averse to entertaining readers with details capturing the fierce moodiness of a twelve-year-old. But Fisher's main purpose is larger than these and encompasses them. She has heard much lately of child abuse, and a recollection from her own childhood might throw some light on the problem. She wants to help.

How can you tell a writer's purpose? This is where analysis, inference, and synthesis come in. Fisher hints at her purpose in the first paragraph, asking "When is [the chain of violence] broken? [. . .] How?" The rest of her essay answers these questions: At least for her father, the chain broke when he no longer feared it (par. 20). The opening questions and last paragraph form the THESIS of the essay—the point made for a purpose, the overwhelming idea that the writer communicates. Some writers will come right out and sum up this central idea in a sentence or two (the THESIS SENTENCE). In her response to M. F. K. Fisher's essay titled "Has the Chain Been Broken?" (p. 47), the stu-dent Christine D'Angelo states her gist in her opening paragraph:

> The answer [to the difference Fisher sees between spanking and hitting] lies
> in her distinction between justified and unjustified violence.

D'Angelo's thesis is obvious early on. Sometimes, however, like Fisher, a writer will introduce and conclude the thesis at the beginning and end. Other writers won't come out and state their theses in any neat capsule at all. Even so, the main point of a well-written essay will make itself clear to you—so clear that you can sum it up in a sentence or two of your own. What might that sentence be for Fisher's essay? Perhaps this: The chain of violence against children may be broken when a former victim understands that violence need not take control even when it is expressed.

It's part of your job as an active reader to answer questions like these: What is the writer's purpose? How does it govern the writer's choices? Is it actually achieved? Does the thesis come through? How is it supported? Is the support adequate to convince you of the author's sincerity and truthfulness? (Such conviction is a basic transaction between writer and reader, even when the writer isn't seeking the reader's outright agreement or action.) Sometimes you'll be confused by a writer's point—"What *is* this about?"—and sometimes your confusion won't yield to repeated careful readings. That's when you'll want to toss the book or magazine aside in exasperation, but you won't always have the choice: A school or work assignment or just an urge to figure out the writer's problem may keep you at it. Then it'll be up to you to figure out why the writer fails—in essence, to clarify what's unclear—by, say, digging for buried assumptions that you may not agree with or by spotting where facts and examples fall short.

With some reservations, we think M. F. K. Fisher achieves her purpose. Her essay is engaging. She gives plenty of details to place us in her shoes, to experience what she experienced. Her story about her father rings true, as does the lesson to be learned from it. The story and the lesson do lean on certain assumptions, though, and these are bound to influence a reader's response. One is that the father's spankings are justified and, because they are reluctant and unemotional, do not constitute violence—at least not the abusive violence that concerns Fisher. (This is the assumption that D'Angelo examines in "Has the Chain Been Broken?") Even if the spankings are justified, a second, more ticklish assumption is that their manner is appropriate. Fisher describes herself merely as feeling "silly [. . .] baring my pubescent bottom" for the spanking (par. 13), but these days many readers might condemn her father for expecting her to undress. If you are one of these readers, the essay may be hard to accept. For us, such objections are understandable but ultimately irrelevant because Fisher was writing of a time (1920) when spankings and whippings (even on bare bottoms) were common methods of disciplining children.

Analyzing writers' purposes and their successes and failures makes you an alert and critical reader. Applied to your own writing, this analysis also gives you a decided advantage, for when you write with a clear-cut purpose in mind, aware of your assumptions, you head toward a goal. Of course, sometimes you just can't know what you are going to say until you say it, to echo the English novelist E. M. Forster. In such a situation, your purpose emerges as you write. But the earlier and more exactly you define your purpose, the easier you'll find it to fulfill.

Writing Strategy

To the extent that M. F. K. Fisher holds our interest and engages our sympathies, it pays to ask, "How does she succeed?" (When a writer bores or angers us, we ask why he or she fails.) As we've already hinted, success and failure lie in the eye of the beholder: The reader knows. Almost all writing is a *transaction* between a writer and an audience, maybe one reader, maybe millions. Conscious writers make choices intended to get their audience on their side so that they can achieve their purpose. These choices are what we mean by STRATEGY in writing.

Fisher's audience was the readers of her memoir, *To Begin Again*. She might have assumed that many of these readers would be familiar with her earlier writing and predisposed to like her work. But even for such an appreciative audience, and certainly for newcomers, Fisher would have to be interesting and focused, making readers (us) care about *this* piece. She grabs our attention right at the start by connecting with the disturbing and controversial issue of physical abuse. She doesn't oversell, though—she hasn't been abused herself—so she whets our appetites without setting us up for disappointment. When she begins her story, she keeps involving us by referring to common feelings and experiences in memorably specific terms. Even if we've never been spanked, we can feel her father's "long bony knees" and the "sharp taps" of the brush (par. 2). We share Fisher's resentment of her sister, who "made it bitterly clear to me that I was an utter fool to take punishment for her own small jaunty misdoings" (5). We know that adolescent feeling of "stupid petulance" that caused Fisher to drop her brother (6) and her "raging with insulted anger" at being struck by her father (7). We see that "little room under the eaves" where Fisher found herself "full of scowling puzzlements" (13). We submit as her mother "wrapped her arms around me with a tenderness I had never felt from her before" (14), "an embrace that she was actually giving to her husband" (19). We believe Fisher because of how vivid and precise she is all along.

Part of a writer's strategy—Fisher's, too—is in the methods used to elicit and arrange details such as these. Fisher draws mainly on two methods: narration (telling a story) and description (conveying the evidence of the senses). But she also gives examples of spankings and her feelings about them (2–5), contrasts the "heavy dutiful slaps" of a spanking with the "wild stinging blow" of being struck (13), analyzes her own reactions (13), defines the "chain of violence" (17, 19), and examines the causes and effects of child abuse (15–20). In short, Fisher uses nearly every method discussed in this book, asking each one to perform the work it's best suited for. As we noted earlier, one method or another may predominate in an essay (as narration and description do in Fisher's), but other methods will help the writer explore the subject in paragraphs or shorter passages.

Aside from the details and the methods used to develop them, probably no writing strategy is as crucial to success as finding an appropriate structure. Writing that we find interesting and clear and convincing almost always has UNITY (everything relates to the main idea) and COHERENCE (the relations between parts are clear). When we find an essay wanting, it may be because the writer got lost in digressions or couldn't make the parts fit together.

Sometimes structure almost takes care of itself. When she chose the method of narration, for instance, Fisher also chose a chronological sequence (reporting events as they occurred in time). But she still had to emphasize certain events and de-emphasize others. She lingers over the important moments: dropping her brother and being struck by her father (6–7), the following encounters with her father (8–13) and her mother (14–18). She compresses all the events that contribute background but are not the heart of the story, notably the previous spankings (2–4) and taking the blame for her sister (5).

This kind of handiwork will be even more evident in essays where the method of development doesn't dictate an overall structure. Then the writer must mold and shape ideas and details to pique, hold, and direct our interest. One writer may hit us with the big idea right at the start and then fill us in on the details. Another writer may gradually unfold the idea, leading to a surprise. One writer may arrange information in order of increasing importance; another may do the opposite. Like all other choices in writing, these come out of the writer's purpose: What is the aim? What do I want readers to think or feel? What's the best way to achieve that? As you'll see in this book, there are as many options as there are writers.

Language

To examine the element of language is often to go even more deeply into an essay and how it was made. Fisher, you'll notice, is a writer whose language is rich and varied. It isn't bookish. Many expressions from common speech lend her prose vigor and naturalness. "I always felt terrible that it was dragged out," she writes (par. 5). Her father "gave me a slap across the side of my head that sent me halfway across the room against the big old sideboard" (6). When spanked, she says, "I did not even breathe fast, on purpose" (10). "I have never been the same —" she concludes, "still stupid but never unthinking" (19). These relaxed sentences suit the material: Fisher's recollections of herself as a fresh, moody adolescent. At the same time, Fisher is an adult addressing adults, and her vocabulary reflects as much. Consult a dictionary if you need help defining *vicariously* (1), *ritualistic* (2), *conditioned* (4), *petulance, insolently* (6), *disdainfully* (7), *pubescent* (13), or *haughty* (14).

Fisher's words and sentence structures not only sharpen and animate her meaning but also convey her attitudes and elicit them from readers. They create a TONE, the equivalent of tone of voice in speaking. Whether it's angry, sarcastic, or sad, joking or serious, tone carries almost as much information about a writer's purpose as the words themselves do. Fisher's tone is sincere, matter-of-fact. In true adolescent fashion, she occasionally veers into indignation or embarrassment or compassion; but she never indulges in histrionics, which would overwhelm the sensations and make her account untrustworthy.

With everything you read, as with "The Broken Chain," it's instructive to study the writer's tone so that you are aware of whether and how it affects you. Pay particular attention to the CONNOTATIONS of words—their implied meanings, their associations. We sympathize when Fisher takes those "twelve expert upward stinging whacks" (10)—stinging whacks *hurt*. We identify with her "scowling puzzlements" (13)—the anger and hurt are there and also the confusion. When one writer calls the homeless "society's downtrodden" and another calls them "human refuse," we know something of their attitudes and can use that knowledge to analyze and evaluate what they say about homelessness.

One other use of language is worth noting in Fisher's essay and in many others in this book: FIGURES OF SPEECH, bits of colorful language not meant to be taken literally. In one instance, Fisher makes her adolescent gangliness vivid with *hyperbole*, or exaggeration, describing herself as "all skinny arms and legs" (10). Most memorable is the extended *metaphor* of the "chain of violence" (17, 19–20)—not an actual, physical chain, of course, but a pattern of behavior passed from generation to generation. This chain is "invisible"; it had "bound" Fisher's father since childhood; and finally, as the title tells us, it was "broken." Such a colorful comparison—a chain and a destructive behavior—gives Fisher's essay flavor and force. (More examples of figures of speech can be found under Useful Terms, p. 705.)

Many questions in this book point to such figures, to oddities of tone, or to troublesome or unfamiliar words. We don't wish to swamp you in details or make you a slave to your dictionary; we only want to get you thinking about how meaning and effect begin at the most basic level, with the word. As a writer, you can have no traits more valuable to you than a fondness and respect for words and a yen to experiment with them.

THINKING CRITICALLY
ABOUT VISUAL IMAGES

Does a particular billboard always catch your eye when you drive by it? Does a certain television commercial irritate you or make you smile? Do you look at the pictures in a magazine before you read the articles? If so, you're like everyone else in that you are subject to the visual representations coming at you continually, unbidden, from all around.

Much of the flood of visual information just washes over us, like noise to the eyes. Sometimes we do focus on an image or a whole sequence that interests us—maybe it tweaks our emotions or tells us something we want to know. But even then we aren't always thinking that an image, just as much as a sentence of words, was created by somebody for a reason. No matter what it is—Web advertisement, TV commercial, painting, music video, photograph, cartoon—a visual image originated with a creator or creators who had a purpose, an intention for how the image should look and how we, the viewers, should respond to it.

In their purposefulness, then, visual images are not much different from written texts, and they are no less open to critical thinking that will uncover their meanings and effects. To a great extent, the method for critically "reading" visuals parallels the one for essays outlined on pages 10–21. In short:

- *Get the big picture:* As when scoping out a written work, survey the image or sequence for a view of the whole and clues about its origins and purposes.
- *Analyze:* Discern the elements of the image or sequence.
- *Infer:* Interpret the underlying meanings of the elements and the ASSUMP-TIONS and intentions of the work's creators.
- *Synthesize:* Understand how the elements function together to produce a whole and to deliver a message.
- Often, *evaluate:* Judge the quality, significance, or value of the work.

One other important parallel with critical reading of written works: Always write while examining a visual image or images. Jotting down responses, questions, and other notes will not only help you remember what you were thinking but also jog further thoughts into being.

To show the critical method in action, we'll look closely at the advertisement on page 29, which appeared in the magazine *US News & World Report.* Further examples of analyzing visual works appear elsewhere in *The Bedford Reader* as well. See pages 165 (a painting), 285 (an advertisement for flowers), 340 (advertisements for cars), and 586 (a fresco). In addition, Chapters 4–13 each open with a visual image that gives you a chance to try out the method yourself.

The Big Picture

To examine any visual representation, it helps first to get an overview, a sense of the whole. Try making some inquiries of the work:

- What is the source of the work? Who created it—for instance, a painter, a teacher, an advertiser—and when?
- What does the work show overall? What appears to be happening?
- At a glance, why was the work created—for instance, to educate, to sell, to shock, to entertain?

The example on the facing page is obviously an advertisement, which we can assume was created by an advertising agency to suit the client, the St. Paul Companies. Like most advertisements, this one has a clear purpose: to encourage readers of *US News & World Report* to consider St. Paul for insurance. (Grasping the purpose of visual images is not always this easy. Sometimes you'll have to proceed through layers of thinking to grasp it.) The main selling tools in the ad, each occupying about half the page, are a photograph and a block of text. The photograph shows a young girl petting a huge rhinoceros. The text emphasizes the word *Trust*.

Analysis

After you've gained an overview of the visual work, begin focusing on the elements that contribute to the whole—not just the people, animals, or objects depicted but the background and what might be called the artistic elements of lighting, color, shape, and balance.

- Which elements of the image stand out? What is distinctive about each one?
- What does the composition of the image emphasize?
- If spoken or written words accompany the work, what do they say? How are they sized and placed in relation to the visual elements?

In the insurance advertisement, three elements are especially prominent: the improbable image of a little girl and a rhinoceros and the words *Trust* and *St. Paul*. In this context, we notice details as well: the girl wearing what seems to be a homespun dress, her head bent affectionately, her smooth hand against the rhinoceros's rough face; the relatively huge size of the rhinoceros, the dangerous upward thrust of its horn, the bright look of its eye; the waving grass at the figures' feet, receding to the stormy-looking horizon; the direct connection between the image and the word *Trust*; the small and sedate italic type for the rest of the written copy, which requires the viewer to concentrate on reading in order to get more information.

Trust is not being afraid even if you're vulnerable.

Is there someone who understands how frightening a situation can be? Someone who

believes fear can be dismantled when we are armed with confidence? Is there an insurance

company that is consistently rated superior by independent rating services – a company

with a 148 year history of providing strength in the face of uncertainty? Without Question.

Without Question. **The St Paul**

Property and Liability Insurance

Inference

Identifying the elements of the visual representation leads you to consider what they mean and how the image's creator has selected and arranged them so that viewers will respond in certain ways. As when reading a written text critically, you make explicit what may only be implicit in the work.

- What do the elements of the work say about the creator's intentions and assumptions? In particular, what does the creator seem to assume about viewers' backgrounds, needs, interests, and values?
- If the work includes written or spoken words, how do they interact with the visual components?

We can guess at the intentions of the St. Paul ad's creators: Use an arresting image to grab the attention of *US News* readers, link image to copy so they'll read the copy, encourage them to look into buying St. Paul insurance so that ultimately they'll invest in it. We can infer the basic meaning of the ad without difficulty: Trust = St. Paul; St. Paul = Trust. But the message is also more complicated than that. In the photograph, the girl's homespun dress, the grassy savannah-like setting, the beastly rhino, and the very idea of a rhino responding tamely to a girl all suggest a primitive feeling or experience. The small-type copy elaborates on the message Trust = St. Paul by introducing another primitive feeling, fear. Trust = fearlessness despite vulnerability and uncertainty = confidence = St. Paul. The ad's creators seem to assume that viewers are well heeled (they read *US News*; they have assets to insure) and that they're anxious and cautious about their assets (they understand fear; they want insurance; they need trust).

Synthesis

Linking the elements and your inferences about them, you'll move into a new conception of the visual representation, a sense of its overall intentions and effect.

- What general appeal does the work make to viewers? For instance, does it emphasize logical argument, emotion, or the creator's or subject's worthiness?
- What feelings, memories, moods, or ideas does the work seem intended to summon from viewers' own store of experiences? Why, given the purpose of the work, would its creator try to establish these associations?

The St. Paul ad appeals mainly to viewers' emotions—most obviously, their need for trust, less obviously (but more interestingly) their fear. Look again at the rhino's great size and its prominent and scary horn: The animal represents a clear threat to physical security and by extension to financial security. The girl—representing St. Paul—disarms the fearsome beast. The small-type copy asks its readers to act in part from logic (the company has a superior rating and performance history), but it and the photograph work hardest to stir up fear so that the audience will take refuge in St. Paul insurance. Backed up, no doubt, by plenty of market research, the ad's creators see strong anxiety among the prosperous readers of *US News*.

When using synthesis, you may often go outside the work itself to explore its cultural context. For instance, the St. Paul ad might be compared with other ads that use images of tamed nature or that play to fear.

Evaluation

Often in criticizing visual works, you'll take one step beyond synthesis to evaluate success or significance or value.

- Does the work seem to fulfill its creator's intentions? Does it do what the creator wanted?
- Apart from the creator's intentions, how does the work affect you? Does it move you? amuse you? bore you? offend you?
- Was the work worth creating?

The St. Paul ad seems to fulfill at least one of its creators' intentions: The image of the girl and the rhino is arresting. To us, the message of fear is culturally interesting—a typical insurance sales pitch, here worked especially hard. Whether it's successful, though, only the company can say. It doesn't sell us, but then we're not in the market for insurance.

2

WRITING EFFECTIVELY

The CRITICAL THINKING discussed in the previous chapter will serve you in just about every role you'll play in life — consumer, voter, friend, parent. As a student and a worker, though, you'll find critical thinking especially important as the foundation for writing. Whether to demonstrate your competence or to contribute to discussions and projects, writing will be the main way you communicate with teachers, supervisors, and peers.

Like critical thinking, writing is no snap: As this book's Writers on Writing attest, even professionals do not produce thoughtful, detailed, attention-getting prose in a single draft. Writing well demands, and rewards, a willingness to work recursively — to begin tentatively, perhaps, and then to double back, to welcome change and endure frustration, to recognize and exploit progress. The path can be rocky and confusing, but you'll find it was worth following when your readers respond just as you hoped they would.

THE WRITING SITUATION

Any writing you do will occur in a specific situation: What are you writing about? Whom are you writing to? Why are you writing about this subject to these people? Subject, AUDIENCE, and PURPOSE are the main components in the writing situation, but others may figure as well, such as length or deadline.

The elements of a writing situation may be specified in the assignment that starts you writing in the first place. In many cases, though, you'll have to infer whom you're writing to (instructor? instructor and classmates? boss? colleagues?), why you're writing (to show mastery of material? provide information? propose a solution?), and even, if the assignment has left room for choice, what your specific subject is.

In *The Bedford Reader* we've provided ideas for writing about the selections that will also give you practice in working with writing assignments. Immediately after each selection, a "Journal Writing" prompt encourages you to respond to the selection just for yourself. (See page 36 for a discussion of journal writing.) Then, in "Suggestions for Writing," one assignment proposes turning that journal writing into an essay for others to read. Of the three or four other suggestions, one labeled "Critical Writing" asks you to take a deliberate, critical look at the selection, and another labeled "Connections" helps you relate the selection to one or two others in the book. You may not wish to take any of our suggestions as worded; they may merely urge your own thoughts toward what you want to say.

To give you an idea of the writing suggestions we provide, here are possibilities for M. F. K. Fisher's "The Broken Chain," the essay reprinted in the preceding chapter (p. 13):

Journal Writing

Write about a moment in your childhood or adolescence that changed you or someone you know or both. Try to capture the details of the incident: where, why, and how it happened; how the participants looked and behaved; what the participants said and how they spoke.

Suggestions for Writing

1. **FROM JOURNAL TO ESSAY.** Following M. F. K. Fisher's example, shape your journal writing into an essay full of concrete, specific details so that your readers understand the incident and its effects. Use a chronological organization, and take advantage of your distance from the incident to evaluate how it changed you or someone else.
2. If you have had some experience with physical abuse (as a counselor, bystander, victim, abuser) and you care to write about it, compose an essay that develops a thesis about the problem. You do not have to write in the first person (*I*) unless you want to. Draw on personal experience, observation, or reading as needed to support your thesis. (If you draw on reading, be sure to acknowledge your sources.)
3. **CRITICAL WRITING.** Write an essay in which you analyze and evaluate Fisher's attitudes toward physical punishment. Consider what Fisher actually says about spanking and what her words convey about her feelings. (You will have to infer

some of her assumptions.) When you are sure you understand Fisher's point of view, explain it and then evaluate it, using specific evidence from the essay and from your own sources (experience, observation, reading). Do you agree with Fisher? Does she omit any important considerations? In your view, do her attitudes toward physical punishment weaken or strengthen the essay? Why?

4. **CONNECTIONS.** Both Fisher's "The Broken Chain" and Brad Manning's "Arm Wrestling with My Father" (p. 136) address the ways love and standards of behavior are passed from one generation to another. Compare and contrast these two essays, looking closely at how Fisher's and Manning's parents love and educate their children. Be specific in your analysis, using evidence from the essays and, if you wish, your own experience. (If you need help with the method of comparison and contrast, see Chap. 7.)

THE WRITING PROCESS

"The writing process" is not really a single process at all, not even for an individual writer. Some people work out meticulous plans before beginning to compose sentences; others find plans stifling and prefer to just start writing; still others will work one way for one project and a different way for another. Generally, though, writers do move through three rough stages between assignment or initial idea and finished work: discovery, drafting, and revision.

In examining these stages, we'll have the help of a student, Christine D'Angelo. D'Angelo wrote an essay for *The Bedford Reader* responding to M. F. K. Fisher's essay "The Broken Chain." Along with the final draft of her essay (pp. 47–48), D'Angelo also provided her notes and earlier drafts and her comments on her progress at each stage.

Discovery

During the first phase of the writing process, DISCOVERY, you'll feel your way into an assignment. This is the time when you critically examine any text or image that is part of the assignment and begin to generate ideas for writing. When writing about selections in this book, you'll be reading and rereading and writing, coming to understand the work, figuring out what you think of it, figuring out what you have to *say* about it. From notes during reading to jotted phrases, lists, or half-finished paragraphs after reading, this stage should always be a writing stage. You may even produce a rough draft. The important thing is to let yourself go: Do not, above all, concern yourself with making beautiful sentences or correcting errors. Such self-consciousness at this stage will only jam the flow of thoughts. If your idea of "audience" is "teacher with sharp pencil" (not, by the way, a fair picture), then temporarily blank out your audience, too.

Several techniques can help you let go and open up during the discovery stage, among them writing in a journal, freewriting, and using the methods of development.

Journal Writing

A JOURNAL is a notebook or tablet or computer file where you record your thoughts *for yourself*. (Teachers sometimes assign journals and periodically collect them to see how students are doing, but even in these situations the journal is for yourself.) In keeping a journal, you don't have to worry about being understood by a reader or making mistakes: You are free to write however you want to get your thoughts down.

Kept faithfully—say, for ten or fifteen minutes a day—a journal can limber up your writing muscles, giving you more confidence and flexibility as a writer. It can also provide a place to work out personal difficulties, explore half-formed ideas, make connections between courses, or respond to reading. Here, for instance, is Christine D'Angelo's initial journal entry on M. F. K. Fisher's "The Broken Chain":

> *I liked this—the writer makes me remember what it's like to be really mad at my parents for being mean, even when part of me knows they might be right (like the time I stole the car and got grounded!). But I don't get why Fisher makes such a big deal about the difference between a slap from her father when she dropped the baby and the regular spankings she got from him. She's getting hit either way, right? Got to get at the difference Fisher sees.*

Freewriting

Another technique for limbering up, but more in response to specific writing assignments than as a regular habit, is *freewriting*. When freewriting, you write without stopping for ten or fifteen minutes, not halting to reread, criticize, edit, or admire. You can use partial sentences, abbreviations, question marks for uncertain words. If you can't think of anything to write about, jot "can't think" over and over until new words come (they will).

You can use this technique to find a subject for writing or to explore ideas on a subject you already have. Of course, when you've finished, you'll need to separate the promising passages from the dead ends, using those promising bits as the starting place for more freewriting or perhaps a freely written first draft.

The Methods of Development

Since each method of development provides a different perspective on your subject, you can use the methods singly or together to discover possible ideas or directions. Say you already have a sense of your purpose for writing: Then you can search the methods for one or more that will help you achieve that purpose by revealing and focusing your ideas. Or say you're still in the dark about your purpose: Then you can apply each method of development systematically to throw light on your subject, as a headlight illuminates a midnight road, so that you see its possible angles.

The introductions to Chapters 4–13 suggest the purposes each method is suited for and some specific ways the method can open up your subject. For now, we've given some examples of how the methods can reveal responses, either direct or indirect, to Fisher's "The Broken Chain."

- *Narration:* Tell a story about the subject, possibly to enlighten or entertain readers or to explain something to them. Answer the journalist's questions: who, what, when, where, why, how? For instance, consider an incident in your own life that changed you, as Fisher's experience changed her and her father.
- *Description:* To explain or evoke the subject, focus on its look, sound, feel, smell, taste—the evidence of the senses. For instance, examine Fisher's use of language to evoke sensation.
- *Example:* Point to instances, or illustrations, of the subject that clarify and support your idea about it. For instance, give examples that illustrate Fisher's use of language to portray herself as an adolescent.
- *Comparison and contrast:* Set the subject beside something else, noting similarities or differences or both, for the purpose of either explaining or evaluating. For instance, compare and contrast Fisher's views of spanking and hitting.
- *Process analysis:* Explain step by step how to do something or how something works—in other words, how a sequence of actions leads to a particular result. For instance, explain a process for disciplining children that does not involve physical punishment.
- *Division or analysis:* Slice the subject into its parts or elements in order to show how they relate and to explain your conclusions about the subject. For instance, analyze Fisher's tone and its relation to her purpose.
- *Classification:* To show resemblances and differences among many related subjects, or the many forms of a subject, sort them into kinds or groups. For example, classify different kinds of family discipline, physical and otherwise.
- *Cause and effect:* Explain why or what if, showing reasons for or consequences of the subject. For instance, explain why parents strike their children.
- *Definition:* Trace a boundary around the subject to pin down its meaning. For instance, define *violence* or *child abuse.*

- *Argument and persuasion:* Formulate an opinion or make a proposal about the subject. For instance, argue that Fisher's father did (or did not) abuse her by spanking her.

Drafting

Sooner or later, the discovery stage yields to DRAFTING: writing out sentences and paragraphs, linking ideas, focusing them.

Methods of Drafting

For most writers, drafting is the occasion for exploring the relations among ideas, filling in the details to support them, beginning to work out the shape and aim of the whole. During drafting, you may clarify your purpose, try out different arrangements of material, or experiment with tone. Sometimes, though, you may find that just spelling out thoughts into complete sentences is challenge enough for a first draft, and you'll leave issues of purpose, structure, and tone for another round.

A few suggestions for drafting:

- Give yourself time, at least a couple of hours.
- Work in a place where you won't be disturbed.
- Stay loose so that you can wander down intriguing avenues or consider changing direction altogether.
- Don't feel compelled to follow a straight path from beginning to end. If the introduction is giving you fits, skip it until later.
- Keep your eyes on what's ahead, not on the pebbles underfoot — the possible mistakes, "wrong" words, and bumpy sentences that you can attend to later. This is an important message that many inexperienced writers miss: It's okay to make mistakes. You can fix them later.

The Thesis and the Thesis Sentence

One important element that should receive some attention during drafting, or shortly after, is the THESIS, often stated in a THESIS SENTENCE or two. The thesis, to recap page 22, is the main idea of a piece of writing, its focus. Without a focus, either expressed or implied, an essay wanders and irritates and falls flat. With a focus, an essay is much more likely to click.

On page 22 we gave one example of a thesis sentence from Christine D'Angelo's "Has the Chain Been Broken?" Here are some other examples from the essays in this book:

These were two strong men, these oddly different generals [Ulysses S. Grant and Robert E. Lee], and they represented the strengths of two conflicting currents that, through them, had come into final collision. (Bruce Catton, "Grant and Lee: A Study in Contrasts")

Inanimate objects are classified into three major categories — those that don't work, those that break down and those that get lost. (Russell Baker, "The Plot Against People")

It is possible to stop most drug addiction in the United States within a very short time. Simply make all drugs available and sell them at cost. (Gore Vidal, "Drugs")

These three diverse examples share a few important qualities:

- The authors assert opinions, taking positions on their subjects. They do not merely state facts, as in "Grant and Lee both signed the document ending the Civil War" or "Grant and Lee were different men."
- Each thesis sentence projects a single idea. The thesis may have parts (such as Baker's three categories of objects), but the parts fit under a single umbrella idea.
- As you will see when you read the essays themselves, each thesis sentence accurately forecasts the scope of its essay, neither taking on too much nor leaving out essential parts.
- Each thesis statement hints about the writer's purpose — we can tell that Catton and Baker want to explain, whereas Vidal wants mainly to persuade. (Explaining and persuading overlap a great deal; we're talking here about the writer's *primary* purpose.)

Every single essay in this book has a *thesis* because a central, controlling idea is a requirement of good writing. But we can give no rock-hard rules about the *thesis sentence* — how long it must be or where it must appear in an essay or even whether it must appear. Indeed, the essays in this book demonstrate that writers have great flexibility in these areas. For your own writing, we advise stating your thesis explicitly and putting it near the beginning of your essay — at least until you've gained experience as a writer. The stated thesis will help you check that you have that necessary focus, and the early placement will tell your readers what to expect from your writing.

Revision

If it helps you produce writing, you may want to view your draft as a kind of dialogue with readers, fulfilling their expectations, answering the questions you imagine they would ask. But some writers save this kind of thinking for the next stage, REVISION. Literally "re-seeing," revision is the price you pay for the freedom to experiment and explore. Initially the work centers on you and your material, but gradually it shifts into that transaction we spoke of earlier between you and your reader. And that means stepping outside the intense circle of you-and-the-material to see the work as a reader will, with whatever qualities you imagine that reader to have. Questions after most essays in this book ask you to analyze how the writers' ideas of their readers have influenced their writing strategies, and how you as a reader react to the writers' choices. These analyses will teach you much about responding to your own readers.

Like many writers, you will be able to concentrate better if you approach revision as at least a two-step process. First you question fundamental matters, using a checklist like this one:

QUESTIONS FOR REVISION

Will my purpose be clear to readers? Have I achieved it?
What is my thesis? Have I proved it?
Is the essay unified (all parts relate to the thesis)?
Is the essay coherent (the parts relate clearly)?
Will readers be able to follow the organization?
Have I given enough details, examples, and other specifics for readers to
    understand me and stay with me?
Is the tone appropriate for my purpose?
Have I used the methods of development to full advantage?

When these deeper issues are resolved, you then look at the surface of the writing in the step called *editing*:

QUESTIONS FOR EDITING

Do PARAGRAPH breaks help readers grasp related information?
Do TRANSITIONS tell readers where I am making connections, additions,
    and other changes?
Are sentences smooth and concise? Do they use PARALLELISM, EMPHASIS,
    and other techniques to clarify meaning?
Do words say what I mean, and are they as vivid as I can make them?
Are my grammar and punctuation correct?
Are any words misspelled?

Two-step revision is like inspecting a ship before it sails. First check under the water for holes to make sure the boat will stay afloat. Then look above the water at what will move the boat and please the passengers: intact sails, sparkling hardware, gleaming decks.

A Note on Collaboration

Your writing teacher may ask you to spend some time talking with your classmates, as a whole class or in small groups or pairs. You may analyze the essays in this book (perhaps answering the end-of-essay questions), read each other's journals or drafts, or plot revision strategies. Such conversation and collaboration—voicing, listening to, and arguing about ideas—can help you develop more confidence in your writing and give you a clearer sense of audience. One classmate may show you that your introduction, which you thought was lame, really worked to get her involved in your essay. Another classmate may question you in a way that helps you see how the introduction sets up expectations in the reader, expectations you're obliged to fulfill.

You may at first be anxious about collaboration: How can I judge others' writing? How can I stand others' criticism of my own writing? These are natural worries, and your teacher will try to help you with both of them—for instance, by providing a checklist to guide your critique of your classmates' writing. (The first checklist on the opposite page works for reading others' drafts as well as your own.) With practice and plentiful feedback, you'll soon appreciate how much you're learning about writing and what a good effect that knowledge has on your work. You're writing for an audience, after all, and you can't beat the immediate feedback of a live one.

AN ESSAY-IN-PROGRESS

In the following pages, you have a chance to watch Christine D'Angelo as she develops an essay through journal notes and several drafts. Her topic is the third one on page 34, about M. F. K. Fisher's attitudes toward physical punishment—a topic she had already started exploring in her journal (p. 36). D'Angelo's journal notes during each stage enlighten us about her thinking as she proceeds through the writing process.

Reading and Drafting

Journal Notes on Reading

"I have never been beaten"—she doesn't consider her father's punishment as beating. (¶ 1)

Very conscious of how to play role of victim (excellent description of kids that age).

> *—"I often cried a little, to prove that I had learned my lesson" (¶ 2)*
> *—wishes she were maimed (¶ 13)*
> *—"I wanted to stay haughty and abused with her" (¶ 14)*

"Your mother wants you to be spanked" (¶ 9): typical of fathers' tendency not to take responsibility for feelings. More common when trying to express tenderness: *"Your mother was worried sick about you," "Your mother and I are going to miss you," "You know we love you,"* etc. The potentially embarrassing feelings are diluted.

She doesn't seem to consider spankings as violent:

> *"Once Rex hit me" (¶ 6)*
> *"And you hit me" (¶ 12)*

Calling father by first name: distancing?
("Father" vs. "Rex")

Justifies father's actions

> —he *"disliked this duty very much" (¶ 3)*
> —*"fatherly spankings" (¶ 5)*
> —*"two people whom I had betrayed into this" (¶ 18)*

Is father's reaction justified by narrator's act? Both are acts of violence. It's easy to understand his anger.

"Once Rex hit me" and *"And you hit me"* literally confusing until you become aware that she doesn't count spanking as *"hitting."*

Mother shares same refusal to see spanking as violent.

Fisher's ideas about physical punishment outdated. These days many people would consider spanking abusive.

I think I have a lot of evidence here to answer question 3, about Fisher's attitudes toward physical punishment and whether they weaken or strengthen the essay.

It's clear that she doesn't think of the spankings as violent. I like the idea of talking about how Fisher's assumptions confuse the reader who doesn't share them. I was confused that she opened with *"I have never been beaten"* and then recounted many spankings. (This could be a good introduction.)

Even though they're interesting ideas, I don't think I'll be able to use anything about the narrator knowing how to play the victim or fathers' inability to express their emotions. (Not in this paper at least.)

First Draft

How is the reader of "The Broken Chain" to reconcile the narrator's account of the physical punishment she suffered from her father up to the age of twelve with her assumption in the very first paragraph that "I have never been beaten"?

Knowing that the father has a history of spanking the narrator, the reader has a hard time interpreting her statement "Once Rex hit me." Why does she say "once" if he actually hit her quite often? In the key scene in which the narrator is spanked for having dropped her baby brother on the floor, her father says "That's the last time," after he has finished spanking her. To which she responds, "And you hit me." "Once" and "And" make no sense. Until we realize that spanking seems to fall under the realm of just punishment but on the other hand violence outside the clear realm of punishment is unjustifiable.

The narrator's mother shares this distinction. Describing her husband's history of violence in the family, she maintains that up until now he had succeeded in breaking the chain. "He has never struck any living thing in anger," she says, "Until today." In other words, the spankings have never counted as part of the chain of violence.

It is interesting to note that the narrator never questions why it should be the father who struggles constantly to keep his violence in check, who has this "duty" rather than the mother. After all, isn't such a choice rather like putting a dieter in charge of guarding the refrigerator?

When we understand that the narrator does not consider her father's spankings to be violent, we can only call this assumption into question, in fact it is easier to justify the father's response to the dumping of the baby on the floor, itself a violent act that could have been deadly, than his more calculated, repeated capital punishment. If the father is so concerned with breaking the "chain of violence" in his family, why can he not look to alternative methods of punishment? And again, why is it him and not the mother who must carry out this punishment?

I can only speculate on Fisher's reasons for not classifying her father's spankings as violent. But capital punishment is no longer considered an acceptable form of punishment--it is recognized as violence in its own right. In writing this essay, Fisher's purpose was to expose in a family the "chain of violence" against children passed down from generation to generation. But she herself is too blind to see that spanking is a form of violence too.

Revising

Journal Notes on First Draft

This gets at what I want to say pretty well, but there are some big holes. I need an explicit thesis sentence—an answer to the question I pose in the first paragraph—to tie the whole thing together. The last sentence of the second paragraph is really my thesis: that the narrator makes a distinction between two kinds of violence—one kind (the spankings) being OK, the other (the slap) unjustified. The rest of the paper goes on to explain this distinction and call it into question. I just need to make this thesis clearer and bring it up into the first paragraph.

The second paragraph needs to be developed more, probably expanded into two paragraphs. I think the first paragraph can pretty much stay the way it is, talking about readers' confusion. But the idea of the last sentence—now the thesis—needs to be fleshed out, expanded into an entire paragraph. Need to define the narrator's distinction between justified and unjustified violence.

What to do with the fourth paragraph asking why only the father, not the mother, has the duty of spanking? It's an interesting point, but it goes nowhere and doesn't fit in with the rest of the paper. Think it's going to have to be cut. (Same for last sentence of the next paragraph.)

The last sentence of the conclusion is too angry and judgmental. Instead, I could say something about how the very fact that Fisher doesn't see the spankings as violent just goes to show how subtle the "chain" is.

Title??? It should work in the thesis somehow.

Big mistake: spanking is corporal, not capital, punishment.

Revised Draft

Has the Chain Been Broken?
Two Ideas of Violence in "The Broken Chain"

How is the reader of "The Broken Chain" to reconcile the narrator's account

of the physical punishment she suffered from her father up to the age of twelve

with her assumption in the very first paragraph that "I have never been beaten"? *The answer lies in the difference she makes between what is in her view justified and unjustified violence.*

⁋ *This distinction is never made explicit in the essay and is apt to lead to confusion on the readers' part.*

∧ Knowing that the father has a history of spanking the narrator, the reader

has a hard time interpreting her statement "Once Rex hit me." ~~Why does she say~~
Likewise, i
~~"once" if he actually hit her quite often?~~ Ĭn the key scene in which the narrator

is spanked for having dropped her baby brother on the floor, her father says

"That's the last time," after he has finished spanking her. To which she responds,
What does she mean by "And"?
"And you hit me." ~~"Once" and "And" make no sense. Until we realize that spanking~~

~~seems to fall under the realm of just punishment but on the other hand violence~~
~~outside the clear realm of punishment is unjustifiable.~~

The "Once" and "And" make no sense until we realize that they do not refer to the fathers spankings. They refer to his violent, immediate reaction to the narrator's dropping the baby. It becomes clear that "spanking" and "hitting" have different values for the narrator depending on the intention behind it. Spanking, in her eyes, falls under the realm of just punishment, unpleasant though it may be, she sees it as an appropriate response to her own crime. On the other hand, violence outside the clear realm of punishment, in this case the blow, is unjustifiable, despite the fact that both are responses to the same wrongdoing (and each probably hurts about as much as the other!).

between "just" and "unjust" violence.

The narrator's mother shares this distinction, Describing her husband's history of violence in the family, she maintains that up until now he had succeeded in breaking the chain. "He has never struck any living thing in anger," she says, "Until today." In other words, the spankings have never counted as part of the chain of violence.

~~It is~~ interesting to note that the narrator never questions why it ~~should be~~ the father who struggles ~~constantly~~ to keep his ~~violence in~~ check, who has this "duty" rather than the ~~mother. After all, isn't such a choice~~ rather like putting a ~~dieter in~~ charge of guarding the refrigerator?

When we understand that the narrator does not consider her father's spankings to be violent, we can only call this assumption into question, in fact it is easier to justify the father's response to the dumping of the baby on the floor, itself a
corporal
violent act that could have been deadly, than his more calculated, repeated ~~capital~~ punishment. If the father is so concerned with breaking the "chain of violence" in his family, why can he not look to alternative methods of punishment? ~~And again,~~ *In law, a premeditated crime is more serious than one committed on the spur of the moment.* ~~why is it him and not the mother who must carry out this punishment?~~

I can only speculate on Fisher's reasons for not classifying her father's spankings as violent. *Perhaps she loved and respected her parents too much to judge them objectively, even sixty years after the events of the essay.*
corporal
But ~~capital~~ punishment is no longer considered an acceptable form of punishment-- it is recognized as violence in its own right. In writing this essay, Fisher's purpose was to expose in a family the "chain of violence" against children passed down
her refusal to recognize corporal punishment as
from generation to generation. But ~~she herself is too blind to see that spanking is~~ *a form of violence is a good example of how subtle the chain is, and why it is so hard* ~~a form of violence too.~~
to break.

Editing

Journal Notes on Revised Draft

This hangs together much better now; more coherent. Every paragraph has something to do with the distinction between "good" and "bad" violence. The new title incorporates both the thesis (the two standards of violence) and the hint in the conclusion about the chain not necessarily being broken.

The first sentence is abrupt. Need a "cushion" to ease the reader into the paper.

I think saying "the narrator" is too impersonal for an autobiographical essay. Since this is a personal essay, not fiction, I could just say "Fisher." And since the events in the essay really happened, I should change them to the past tense, keeping present tense when referring to Fisher as writer, in 1983. This will help make it clear that there are really two "Fishers" in question.

Conclusion: Last sentence is still too angry. I could change "refusal" to "inability," taking some of the blame off Fisher.

Need to edit for rough or awkward sentences, spelling and grammar mistakes, and poor word choice.

Edited Paragraph

The "Once" and "And" make no sense until we realize that they ~~do not~~
not   ,   *but*
referₐto the fathers spankingsₐ ~~They refer~~ to his violent, immediate reaction to
Fisher's
~~the narrator's~~ dropping the baby. It becomes clear that "spanking" and "hitting"
                         Fisher   *them.*
have different values for ~~the narrator~~ depending on the intention behind ~~it.~~ Spank-
                                                        . *U*
ing, in her eyes, falls under the realm of just punishment,/ npleasant though it
        have been,   *misconduct.*
may ~~be;~~ she sees it as an appropriate response to her own ~~crime. On the other~~
But   *well-defined*   —   —
~~hand,~~ violence outside the ~~clear~~ realm of punishment,/ in this case the blow,/ is

unjustifiable, despite the fact that both are responses to the same wrongdoing,/
                        the same!).
(and ~~each~~ probably hurt$ ~~about as much as the other!).~~

Final Draft

We have annotated D'Angelo's final draft to show you something of how it works. D'Angelo's purpose is to explain and dispute the contradiction she sees in Fisher's essay. For this purpose, she draws heavily on DIVISION or ANALYSIS, examining the elements of the essay (especially Fisher's words) and how they work together. Throughout, D'Angelo provides EXAMPLES from Fisher's essay to illustrate her points.

Within the two primary methods of division or analysis and example, D'Angelo also uses other methods to develop her ideas, especially CAUSE AND EFFECT, DEFINITION, and COMPARISON AND CONTRAST.

Has the Chain Been Broken?

Two Ideas of Violence in "The Broken Chain"

There is a problem of definition in "The Broken Chain." How is the reader to reconcile M. F. K. Fisher's account of the physical punishment she suffered from her father up to the age of twelve with her assertion in the very first paragraph that "I have never been beaten" (13)? The answer lies in her distinction between justified and unjustified violence.

This distinction is never made explicit in the essay. Knowing that the father had a history of spanking Fisher, the reader has a hard time interpreting her statement "Once Rex hit me" (14). Then after Fisher was spanked for dropping her baby brother on the floor and her father said, "That's the last time," she responded, "And you hit me" (14). What did she mean by "And"?

The "Once" and "And" make no sense until we realize that they refer not to the father's spankings but to his violent, immediate reaction to Fisher's dropping the baby. It becomes clear that "spanking" and "hitting" have different values for Fisher depending on the intention behind them. Spanking, in her eyes, falls under the realm of just punishment. Unpleasant though it may have been, she sees it as an appropriate response to her own misconduct. But violence outside the well-defined realm of punishment--in this case the blow--is unjustifiable, despite the fact that both are responses to the same wrongdoing (and probably hurt the same!).

The mother shared Fisher's distinction between "just" and "unjust" violence. Describing the "chain of violence" passed down from generation to generation in her husband's family, she maintained that up until then he had succeeded in breaking the chain. "[H]e has never struck any living thing in anger," she said. "Until today" (16). In other words, the spankings never counted.

Once we understand that Fisher does not consider her father's spankings to be violent, we can only call this assumption into question. In fact, it is easier to justify the father's heated response to the dumping of the baby on the floor, a violent act that could have been deadly, than his more calculated, repeated corporal punishment. In law, a premeditated crime is more serious than one committed on the spur of the moment. If the father was so concerned with breaking the "chain of violence," why didn't he look into alternative methods of punishment?

One can only speculate on Fisher's reasons for not classifying her father's spankings as violent. Perhaps she loves and respects her parents too much to judge them objectively, even sixty years after the events of the essay. But physical punishment is no longer universally considered acceptable; it is recognized as violence in its own right. In writing this essay, Fisher intends to expose the "chain of violence" against children passed from generation to generation in a family. But her inability to recognize corporal punishment as a form of violence is a good example of how subtle the chain is, and why it is so hard to break.

Cause and effect proposes a reason for Fisher's view.

Comparison and contrast distinguishes past and present attitudes.

Conclusion ties together elements of Fisher's essay and D'Angelo's critique, ending with implications for the present.

Work Cited

Fisher, M. F. K. "The Broken Chain." The Bedford Reader. Ed. X. J. Kennedy, Dorothy M. Kennedy, and Jane E. Aaron. 8th ed. Boston: Bedford/St. Martin's, 2002. 13-16.

3

USING AND
DOCUMENTING
SOURCES

When you write about them, the selections in this book serve as your sources: Either you ANALYZE them or you use them to support your own ideas. Writing with sources will occupy you for much of your academic career, as you rely on books, periodical articles, interviews, Web sites, electronic databases, and other materials to establish and extend your own ideas.

This chapter introduces the essentials of using sources: evaluating them (below), summarizing and paraphrasing (p. 52), avoiding plagiarism (p. 53), integrating quotations into your own prose (p. 54), and documenting sources using the style of the Modern Language Association, or MLA (p. 55).

CRITICAL THINKING ABOUT SOURCES

Working with sources, you have an opportunity and an obligation to think critically—to analyze, infer, synthesize, and evaluate as described on pages 19–21 and 27–31. Of course, you want every potential source to be relevant to your subject and your approach. But you also want it to be reliable—that is, based on good evidence, carefully reasoned. If a source's evidence is shaky or its opinions are strongly biased, you may still be able to use the source, but you'll want to balance it with others that are more reliable.

The following guidelines apply to both print and online sources. Special guidelines for online sources begin on the facing page.

Relevance and Reliability

To determine a source's relevance and reliability, ask yourself a series of questions:

- What is the PURPOSE of the source, and who is its intended AUDIENCE?
- Is the material a primary or a secondary source?
- Is the author an expert? What are his or her credentials?
- Does the author's bias affect the reliability of his or her argument?
- Does the author support his or her argument with EVIDENCE that is complete and up to date?

Purpose and Audience

You may find material that was written for a variety of reasons—for instance, to inform the public, to publish new research, to promote a product or service, to influence readers' opinions about a particular issue. While the first two of these purposes might lead to a balanced approach to the subject, the second two should raise yellow caution flags: Watch for bias that undermines the source's reliability.

A source's intended audience can suggest relevance. Was the work written for general readers? Then it may provide a helpful overview but not much detail. Was the work written for specialists? Then it will probably cover the topic in depth, but it may be difficult to understand.

Primary Versus Secondary Sources

Primary sources are works by people who conducted or saw events firsthand. They include research reports, eyewitness accounts, diaries, and personal essays as well as novels, poems, and other works of literature. Secondary sources, in contrast, present and analyze the information in primary sources and include histories, reviews, and surveys of a field. Both types of source can be useful in research writing. For example, if you were writing about the debate over John F. Kennedy's assassination, you might seek an overview in books that discuss the evidence and propose theories about what happened—secondary sources. But you would be remiss not to read eyewitness accounts and law-enforcement documents—the primary sources.

Author's Credentials and Bias

Before you use a source to support your ideas, investigate the author's background to be sure that he or she is trustworthy. Look for biographical information in the introduction or preface of a book or in a note at the beginning or end of an article. Is the author an expert on the topic? Do other writers cite the author of your source in their work?

Investigating the author's background and credentials will probably uncover any bias as well—that is, the author's preference for a particular view of an issue. Actually, bias itself is not a problem: Everyone has a unique outlook created by experience, training, and even research techniques. What does matter is whether the author deals frankly with his or her bias and argues reasonably despite it. (See Chap. 13 for a discussion of reasoning.)

Evidence

Look for strong and convincing evidence to support the ideas in a source: facts, examples, reported experience, expert opinions. A source that doesn't muster convincing evidence, or much evidence at all, is not a reliable source. For very current topics, such as in medicine or technology, the source's ideas and evidence should be as up to date as possible.

Online Sources

The Internet makes it fairly quick and easy to find numerous sources on just about any topic. Unlike print sources, though, many online sources are not published or released by an organization that checks for reliability. Just about anyone can put just about anything on the Internet, so you're as likely to find the rantings of an extremist or an advertisement posing as research as you are to find reasonable opinions and scholarly research.

Stringently evaluating online sources is thus crucial to sound research writing. You should use the criteria discussed above—gauging purpose and audience, bias, and other factors—but you'll frequently need to broaden your evaluation, too.

Authorship or Sponsorship

Often, you won't be able to tell easily, or at all, who put a potential source on the Internet and thus whether that author or sponsor is credible and reliable. Sometimes an abbreviation in an electronic address contains a clue to the origin of a source: *edu* for educational institution, *gov* for government body, *org* for nonprofit organization, *com* for commercial organization. More specific background on the author or sponsor may require digging. On Web sites look for pages that have information about the author or sponsor or links to such information on other sites. In discussion groups ask anonymous authors for information about themselves. If you can't identify an author or a sponsor at all, you probably should not use the source.

Links or References to Sources

Most print sources will acknowledge borrowed evidence and ideas and tell you where you can find them. Some but not all online sources will do the same: A Web site, for instance, may provide links to its sources. Check out source citations that you find to be sure they represent a range of views. Be suspicious of any online work that doesn't acknowledge sources at all.

Currency

Online sources tend to be more current than print sources, which can actually be a disadvantage: The most current information may not have been tested by others and so may not be reliable. Always seek to verify recent information in other online sources or in print sources.

If they aren't tended regularly by their authors or sponsors, online sources can also be deceptive—that is, they may seem current but actually be out of date. Look for a date of copyright, publication, or last revision to gauge currency. If you don't find a date (and often you won't), compare the source with others you know to be recent before using its information.

SUMMARY AND PARAPHRASE

To summarize or paraphrase is to express the ideas from a source in your own words. A SUMMARY condenses an entire passage, article, or even a book into a few lines that convey the source's essential meaning. We discuss summary as a reading technique on pages 18–19, and the advice and examples there apply here as well. For another example, here is a summary of Barbara Lazear Ascher's "On Compassion," which appears on pages 183–85.

> Ascher shows how contact with the homeless can be unsettling and depressing. Yet she also suggests that these encounters are useful because they can teach others to be more compassionate (183–85).

Notice how the summary identifies the source author and page numbers and uses words that are *not* the author's. (Any of Ascher's distinctive phrasing would have to be placed in quotation marks.)

In contrast to a summary, a PARAPHRASE usually restates a single idea, again in words different from those of the original author. Here is a quotation from Ascher's essay and a paraphrase of it:

> QUOTATION: "Could it be that the homeless, like [Greek dramatists], are reminding us of our common humanity? Of course, there is a difference. This play doesn't end—and the players can't go home."

> PARAPHRASE: Ascher points out an important distinction between the New York City homeless and the characters in Greek tragedies: The homeless are living real lives, not performing on a stage (185).

As with the summary, note that the paraphrase cites the original author and page number. Here is another example of paraphrase, this from an essay about immigration by David Cole.

> QUOTATION: "If we are collectively judged by how we treat immigrants—those who appear to be 'other' but will in a generation be 'us'—we are not in very good shape."

> PARAPHRASE: Cole argues that the way native-born Americans deal with immigrants reflects badly on the native-born citizens themselves. He also points out that today's immigrants will be part of tomorrow's mainstream society (110).

PLAGIARISM

Take a look at another attempt to paraphrase the sentence above by David Cole.

> Cole argues that if we are judged as a group by how we treat immigrants—those who seem to be different but eventually will be the same—we are in bad shape (110).

This is PLAGIARISM—the theft of someone's ideas or written work. Even though the writer identifies Cole as the source of the information, the language essentially remains the same. It is not enough to change a few words—"collectively" to "as a group," "in a generation" to "eventually," "not in very good shape" to "in bad shape." A paraphrase or summary must express the original idea in an entirely new way, both in word choice and in sentence structure. (Even more blatant plagiarism, of course, would have repeated Cole's statement exactly as he wrote it, without quotation marks *or* a source citation.) Plagiarism also occurs when a writer neglects to cite a source at all—if, for example, a writer paraphrased Ascher's comparison of the homeless with actors in a Greek drama, as above, but did not mention Ascher's name.

Not all information from sources must be cited. Some falls under the category of common knowledge—facts so widely known or agreed upon that they are not attributable to a specific source. The statement "World War II ended after the United States dropped atomic bombs on Hiroshima and Nagasaki, Japan" is an obvious example: Most people recognize this statement as true. But some lesser-known information is also common knowledge. You may not know that President Dwight Eisenhower coined the term *military-industrial complex* during his 1961 farewell address; still, you could easily discover the information in encyclopedias, in books and articles about Eisenhower, and in contemporary newspaper accounts. The prevalence of the information and the fact that it is used elsewhere without source citation tell you that it's common knowledge.

In contrast, a scholar's argument that Eisenhower waited too long to criticize the defense industry, or the president's own comments on the subject in his diary, or an opinion from a Defense Department report in 1959—any of these needs to be credited. Unlike common knowledge, each of them remains the property of its author.

INTEGRATION OF QUOTATIONS

Quotations from your sources can serve as EVIDENCE for your own ideas (see p. 502) and can enliven your subject—*if* they are well chosen. Too many quotations can clutter an essay and detract from your own voice. Choose quotations that are relevant to the point you are making, that are concise and pithy, and that use lively, bold, or original language. Sentences that lack distinction—for example, a statement providing statistics on economic growth between 1985 and 1995—should almost always be paraphrased.

When you do quote from a source, you want to integrate the quotation into your own sentences and also set it up so that readers know what you expect them to make of it. In the passage below, the writer drops the quotation awkwardly into her sentence and doesn't clarify how the quotation relates to her idea.

> NOT INTEGRATED: The problem of homelessness is not decreasing, and "It is impossible to insulate ourselves against what is at our very doorstep" (Ascher 185).

In the following revision, however, the writer indicates with "As Ascher says" that she is using the quotation to reinforce her point. These words also link the quotation to the writer's sentence.

> INTEGRATED: The problem of homelessness is not decreasing, nor is our awareness of it, however much we wish otherwise. As Ascher says, "It is impossible to insulate ourselves against what is at our very doorstep" (185).

You can integrate a quotation into your sentence by interpreting the quotation and by mentioning the author in your text—both techniques illustrated above. The introductory phrase "As Ascher says" has a number of variations:

According to one authority . . .

John Eng maintains that . . .

The author of an important study, Hilda Brown, observes that . . .

Ascher, the author of "On Compassion," has a different view, claiming . . .

For variety, such a phrase can also fall elsewhere in the quotation.

"It is impossible," Ascher says, "to insulate ourselves against what is at our very doorstep" (185).

When you omit something from a quotation, signal the omission with three spaced periods (an ellipsis mark) surrounded by brackets:

"It is impossible to insulate ourselves [. . .]," says Ascher (185).

In Ascher's view, "Compassion [. . .] must be learned" (185).

SOURCE CITATION USING MLA STYLE

On the following pages we explain the documentation style of the Modern Language Association, as described in the *MLA Handbook for Writers of Research Papers,* 5th edition (1999). This style—used in English, foreign languages, and some other humanities—involves a brief parenthetical citation in the text that refers to an entry in a list of works cited at the end of the text.

PARENTHETICAL TEXT CITATION

The homeless may be to us what tragic heroes were to the ancient Greeks (Ascher 185).

ENTRY IN LIST OF WORKS CITED

Ascher, Barbara Lazear. "On Compassion." The Bedford Reader. Ed. X. J. Kennedy, Dorothy M. Kennedy, and Jane E. Aaron. 8th ed. Boston: Bedford/St. Martin's, 2002. 183-85.

By providing the author's name and page number in your text citation, you're giving the reader just enough information to find the source in the list of works cited and then find the place in the source where the borrowed material appears.

MLA Parenthetical Citations

When citing sources in your text, you have two options:

- You can identify both the author and the page number within parentheses, as in the example on the preceding page.
- You can introduce the author's name into your own sentence and use the parentheses only for the page number, as here:

Wilson points out that sharks, which have existed for 350 million years, are now more diverse than ever (301).

A work with two or three authors

More than 90 percent of the hazardous waste produced in the United States comes from seven major industries, all energy-intensive (Romm and Curtis 70).

A work with more than three authors

With more than three authors, name all the authors, or name only the first author followed by "et al." ("and others"). Use the same form in your list of works cited.

Gilman herself created the misconception that doctors tried to ban her story "The Yellow Wallpaper" when it appeared in 1892 (Dock, Allen, Palais, and Tracy 61).

Gilman herself created the misconception that doctors tried to ban her story "The Yellow Wallpaper" when it appeared in 1892 (Dock et al. 61).

An entire work

Reference to an entire work does not require a page number.

Postman argues that television is destructive because of the nature of the medium itself.

An electronic source

Most electronic sources can be cited like print sources, by author's name or, if there is no author, by title. If a source numbers screens or paragraphs instead of pages, give the reference number as in the following model, after "par." (one paragraph), "pars." (more than one paragraph), "screen," or "screens." For a source with no reference numbers at all, use the model on the facing page for an entire work.

> One nurse questions whether doctors are adequately trained in tending patients' feelings (Van Eijk, pars. 6-7).

A work in more than one volume

If you cite two or more volumes of the same work, identify the volume number before the page number. Separate volume number and page number with a colon.

> According to Gibbon, during the reign of Gallienus "every province of the Roman world was afflicted by barbarous invaders and military tyrants" (1: 133).

Two or more works by the same author(s)

If you cite more than one work by the same author or authors, include the work's title. If the title is long, shorten it to the first one or two main words. (The full title for the first citation below is Death at an Early Age.)

> In the 1960s Kozol was reprimanded by his principal for teaching the poetry of Langston Hughes (Death 83).

> Kozol believes that most people do not understand the effect that tax and revenue policies have on the quality of urban public schools (Savage Inequalities 207).

An unsigned work

Cite an unsigned work by using a full or shortened version of the title.

> In 1995 concern about Taiwan's relationship with China caused investors to transfer large amounts of capital to the United States ("How the Missiles Help" 45).

An indirect source

Use "qtd. in" ("quoted in") to indicate that you found the source you quote within another source.

> Despite his tendency to view human existence as an unfulfilling struggle, Schopenhauer disparaged suicide as "a vain and foolish act" (qtd. in Durant 248).

A literary work

Because novels, poems, and plays may be published in various editions, the page number may not be enough to lead readers to the quoted line or passage. For a novel, specify the chapter number after the page number and a semicolon.

> Among South Pacific islanders, the hero of Conrad's Lord Jim found "a totally new set of conditions for his imaginative faculty to work upon" (160; ch. 21).

For a verse play or a poem, omit the page number in favor of line numbers.

> In "Dulce Et Decorum Est," Wilfred Owen undercuts the heroic image of warfare by comparing suffering soldiers to "beggars" and "hags" (lines 1-2) and describing a man dying in a poison-gas attack as "guttering, choking, drowning" (17).

If the work has parts, acts, or scenes, cite those as well (below: act 1, scene 5, lines 16–17).

> Lady Macbeth worries about her husband's ambition: "Yet I do fear thy nature; / It is too full o' the milk of human kindness" (1.5.16-17).

More than one work

> In the post-Watergate era, journalists have often employed aggressive reporting techniques not for the good of the public but simply to advance their careers (Gopnik 92; Fallows 64).

MLA List of Works Cited

Your list of works cited is a complete record of your sources. Follow these guidelines for the list:

- Title the list "Works Cited." Do not enclose the title in quotation marks.
- Double-space the entire list.
- Arrange the sources alphabetically by the last name of the first author.
- Begin the first line of each entry at the left margin. Indent the subsequent lines of the entry one-half inch or five spaces.

Following are the essentials of a works-cited entry:

- Reverse the names of the author, last name first, with a comma between. If there is more than one author, give the others' names in normal order.

- Give the full title of the work, capitalizing all important words. Underline the titles of books and periodicals; use quotation marks for the titles of parts of books and articles in periodicals.
- Give publication information. For books, this information includes city of publication, publisher, date of publication. For periodicals, this information includes volume number, date of publication, and page numbers for the article you cite. For online sources such as Web sites, this information includes the electronic address and the date you consulted the source.
- Use periods between parts of each entry.

You may need to combine the models below for a given source—for instance, combine "A book with two or three authors" and "A book with an editor" for a book with two or three editors.

Books

A book with one author

Tuchman, Barbara W. <u>The March of Folly: From Troy to Vietnam</u>. New
    York: Knopf, 1984.

A book with two or three authors

Silverstein, Olga, and Beth Rashbaum. <u>The Courage to Raise Good Men</u>.
    New York: Viking, 1994.

Trevor, Sylvia, Joan Hapgood, and William Leumi. <u>Women Writers of the</u>
    <u>1920s</u>. New York: Columbia UP, 1998.

A book with more than three authors

You may list all authors or only the first author followed by "et al." ("and others"). Use the same form in your parenthetical text citation.

Kippax, Susan, R. W. Connel, G. W. Dowsett, and June Crawford. <u>Gay</u>
    <u>Communities Respond to Change</u>. London: Falmer, 2000.

Kippax, Susan, et al. <u>Gay Communities Respond to Change</u>. London:
    Falmer, 2000.

More than one work by the same author(s)

Kozol, Jonathan. <u>Death at an Early Age: The Destruction of the Hearts</u>
    <u>and Minds of Negro Children in the Boston Public Schools</u>. Boston:
    Houghton, 1967.

---. Savage Inequalities: Children in America's Schools. New York: Crown,
    1991.

A book with an editor

Gwaltney, John Langston, ed. Drylongso: A Self-Portrait of Black America.
    New York: Random, 1980.

A book with an author and an editor

Orwell, George. The Collected Essays, Journalism and Letters of George
    Orwell. Ed. Sonia Orwell and Ian Angus. New York: Harcourt, 1968.

A later edition

Mumford, Lewis. Herman Melville: A Study of His Life and Vision. 2nd ed.
    New York: Harcourt, 1956.

A work in a series

Hall, Donald. Poetry and Ambition. Poets on Poetry. Ann Arbor: U of
    Michigan P, 1988.

An anthology

Glantz, Michael H., ed. Societal Responses to Regional Climatic Change.
    London: Westview, 1998.

A selection from an anthology

The numbers at the end of this entry are the page numbers on which the
entire cited selection appears.

Kellog, William D. "Human Impact on Climate: The Evolution of an Aware-
    ness." Societal Responses to Regional Climatic Change. Ed. Michael
    H. Glantz. London: Westview, 1998. 283-96.

If you cite more than one selection from the same anthology, you may give
the anthology as a separate entry and cross-reference it by the editor's or editors' last names in the selection entries.

Ascher, Barbara Lazear. "On Compassion." Kennedy, Kennedy, and Aaron
    183-85.
Kennedy, X. J., Dorothy M. Kennedy, and Jane E. Aaron, eds. The
    Bedford Reader. 8th ed. Boston: Bedford/St. Martin's, 2002.
Quindlen, Anna. "Homeless." Kennedy, Kennedy, and Aaron 188-90.

A reference work

Cheney, Ralph Holt. "Coffee." <u>Collier's Encyclopedia</u>. 2001 ed.

"Versailles, Treaty of." <u>The New Encyclopaedia Britannica: Macropaedia</u>.
    15th ed. 1990.

Periodicals:
Journals, Magazines, and Newspapers

An article in a journal with continuous pagination
throughout the annual volume

In many journals the pages are numbered consecutively for an entire
annual volume of issues, so that the year's fourth issue might run from pages
240 to 320. For this type of journal, give the volume number after the journal
title, followed by the year of publication in parentheses, a colon, and the page
numbers of the article.

Clayton, Richard R., and Carl G. Leukefeld. "The Prevention of Drug
    Use Among Youth: Implications of Legalization." <u>Journal of Primary</u>
    <u>Prevention</u> 12 (2000): 289-301.

An article in a journal that pages issues separately

Some journals begin page numbering at 1 for each issue. For this kind of
journal, give the issue number after the volume number and a period.

Vitz, Paul C. "Back to Human Dignity: From Modern to Postmodern Psy-
    chology." <u>Intercollegiate Review</u> 31.2 (1999): 15-23.

An article in a monthly or bimonthly magazine

Fallows, James. "Why Americans Hate the Media." <u>Atlantic Monthly</u> Feb.
    1996: 45-64.

An article in a weekly magazine

Gopnik, Adam. "Read All About It." <u>New Yorker</u> 12 Dec. 2000: 84-102.

An article in a newspaper

Gorman, Peter. "It's Time to Legalize." <u>Boston Sunday Globe</u> 28 Aug.
    1999, late ed.: 69+.

The page number "69+" means that the article begins on page 69 and continues on a later page. If the newspaper is divided into lettered sections, give both section letter and page number, as in "A7."

An unsigned article

"How the Missiles Help California." Time 1 Apr. 1996: 45.

A review

Bergham, V. R. "The Road to Extermination." Rev. of Hitler's Willing
    Executioners, by Daniel Jonah Goldhagen. New York Times Book
    Review 14 Apr. 1996: 6.

CD-ROMs, Diskettes, and
Magnetic Tapes

For portable databases (CD-ROMs, diskettes, magnetic tapes), the content of the citation depends on whether the database is a periodical and whether it is also published in print.

For a periodical that is also published in print, provide full print information (following the models given earlier), the title of the electronic source, the medium (for instance, "CD-ROM"), the name of the distributor, and the date of electronic publication:

Rausch, Janet. "So Late in the Day." Daily Sun 10 Dec. 1998, late ed.: C1.
    Daily Disk. CD-ROM. Cybernews. Jan. 1999.

If the periodical is published only as a CD-ROM, omit the publication information for a print version.

Treat a portable database that is not a periodical as if it were a book, but provide the version or release number and the medium after the title.

Hardy, Joel P. Rose Quartz: A Study in Geology. Magnetic tape. Ver. 2.
    New York: Hestas, 1996.

Online Sources

Online sources vary greatly, and they may be and often are updated. Your aim in citing such sources should be to tell what version you used and how readers can find it for themselves. The basic MLA format for an online source includes (1) author's name, (2) the title of the work you used, (3) the title of the online site, (4) the date of electronic publication, (5) the date you consulted the source, and (6) the source's complete electronic address in angle brackets (<>).

①   ②   ③   ④
Valesquez, Joel. "Wearing Out the Internet." Internet Concerns. 15 Apr.
⑤   ⑥
2002. 23 May 2002 <http://downtown.centaur.com/new/conc/

internet/essay/valesquez.htm>.

The following models show various kinds of additional information to be inserted between these basic elements. If some information is unavailable, list what you can find.

A scholarly project or database

Include the names, if any, of the editor and of the institution or organization that sponsors the project or database.

Bartleby Library. Ed. Steven van Leeuwan. 1999. Academic Information
    Systems, Columbia U. 3 Mar. 1999 <http://www.columbia.edu/acis/
    bartleby.html>.

A personal or professional site

Provide the date of electronic publication if it differs from the date of your access. If there is a sponsoring institution or organization, insert its name after the publication date.

McClure, Mark. "Speakers." Online Calendar of Shakespeare Conferences.
    18 Apr. 1999. 23 May 1999 <http://www.mwc.edu/~mcclure/
    sa_spkrs.html>.

A book

For a book published independently, after the title add any editor's or translator's name, either the publication information for a print version (as in the following model) or the date of electronic publication, and any sponsoring institution or organization.

Murphy, Bridget. Fictions of the Irish Emigration. Cambridge: Harvard
    UP, 1992. 5 Apr. 1999 <http://www.historicalfictions.unv.edu/
    irel_murph.html>.

For a book published as part of a scholarly project, give any information about print publication and then add the publication information for the project (including the date of publication). See above for a model of a scholarly project.

Frost, Robert. <u>Mountain Interval</u>. New York: Holt, 1920. <u>Bartleby Library</u>.
Ed. Steven van Leeuwan. 1999. Academic Information Systems,
Columbia U. 16 June 2002 <http://www.columbia.edu/acis/bartleby/
frost/index3.html>.

An article in a journal

Base an entry for an online journal article on one of the models on
page 61 for a print journal article.

Zurbrugg, Nicholas. "Poetry, Entertainment, and the Mass Media."
<u>The Chicago Review</u> 40.2 (1995): 52-60. 7 July 2001 <http://
bug.chicago.edu:8080/CR4023/4023giorno.html>.

If the journal does not number pages in sequence but does provide some indi-
cation of length (pages, sections, paragraphs), provide the total for the article
(for instance, "6 pp." or "15 pars.").

An article in a newspaper

Base an entry for an online newspaper article on the model on page 61 for
a print newspaper article.

Grady, Denise. "Trapped at the South Pole, Doctor Becomes a Patient."
<u>New York Times on the Web</u> 13 July 1999. 14 July 1999
<http://www.nytimes.com/library/national/science/
071399hth-southpole-cancer.html>.

An article in a magazine

Base an entry for an online magazine article on one of the models on
pages 61–62 for a print magazine article.

Brus, Michael. "Proxy War." <u>Slate</u> 9 July 1999. 12 July 1999
<http://www.slate.com/Features/profile/profile.html>.

A work from an online service

For a personal service, such as America Online, or a library service, such
as Lexis-Nexis, give an electronic address if one is available. Otherwise, give
the keyword or topic path you used to reach the source, as in the following
example.

"Morpheus." <u>Encyclopedia Mythica</u>. 2002. America Online. 3 July 2002.
Path: Research & Learn; Encyclopedia; More Encyclopedias.

Electronic mail

Give as the title the text of the e-mail's subject line, in quotation marks. "To the author" in the example means to you, the author of the paper.

> Dove, Chris. "Re: Bishop's Poems." E-mail to the author. 7 May 2002.

A posting to a discussion group

For a posting to a discussion group, give the posting's subject line as the title, and follow the title with "Online posting," the date of the posting, and the title of the group (without underlining or quotation marks).

> Forrester, Jane. "Embracing Mathematics." Online posting. 21 Sept. 1998. Math Teaching Discussion List. 22 Sept. 1998 <http://www.acc.edu/ gargantuan/smart/mathteach.html>.

A synchronous communication

Cite a contribution to a MOO, MUD, or other form of synchronous communication with the name of the speaker, a description of the event, the date of the event, and the name of the forum.

> Marvell, Peter. Interview. 20 May 2000. JeffersonMOO. 20 May 2000 <telnet://jefferson.village.virginia.edu.osheim:8888>.

Other Sources

A film or video recording

> Achbar, Mark, and Peter Wintonick, dirs. Manufacturing Consent: Noam Chomsky and the Media. Zeitgeist, 1992.

A television or radio program

> Irving, John, guest. "Movies into Books." Talk of the Nation. PBS. KQED, San Francisco. 20 Nov. 2001.

A recording

> Mendelssohn, Felix. A Midsummer Night's Dream. Cond. Erich Leinsdorf. Boston Symphony Orch. RCA, 1982.

A letter

List a published letter under the author's name, and provide full publication information.

Hemingway, Ernest. Letter to Grace Hemingway. 15 Jan. 1920. In
Ernest Hemingway: Selected Letters. Ed. Carlos Baker. New York:
Scribner's, 1981. 44.

For a letter that you receive, list the source under the writer's name, add "to
the author," and provide the date of the correspondence.

Dove, Chris. Letter to the author. 7 May 1999.

An interview

Kesey, Ken. Interview. "The Art of Fiction." Paris Review 130 (1994):
59-94.

Macedo, Donaldo. Personal interview. 13 May 2002.

SAMPLE RESEARCH PAPER

Greg Tartaglia wrote the following paper for his freshman writing course.
We reprint it here for two reasons: It illustrates many techniques of using and
documenting sources, which are highlighted in marginal comments; and it
shows a writer working with a topic that interests him in a way that arouses
the reader's interest as well.

The Elusive Butterfly

When I was a young boy, maybe about four years old, I
tried to catch a butterfly. Actually, my mother helped me because
I was always a little wary around insects, even pretty, colorful
ones. We got a net and went out to the backyard to try to catch a
monarch dining in Mom's flower bed. We never actually caught
it--it would flutter out of the way as soon as the net came near it.
It kept us busy for a while, until we finally gave up. Did everyone
have this much trouble catching a simple, defenseless butterfly?

*Introduction sets up
"butterfly" image for
knuckleball.*

Later in life, I found out that some of the toughest men in
America--major-league baseball batters--occasionally have the
same problem. The only difference is they are equipped with a
large wooden bat instead of a net and the fluttering object of their
frustration is not a motley winged insect but the knuckleball.
The knuckler is a near-impossible pitch to hit; former New York
Yankee Bobby Murcer once said that trying to get a hit off
knuckleballer Phil Niekro was "like eating Jell-O with chopsticks"

(qtd. in Cohen). Big-leaguers approach it the way I approached butterflies as a child--with the utmost wariness.

Unlike "normal" pitches, where the spin determines how the ball moves, a knuckleball is thrown with very little spin. The pitcher grips the ball with the fingertips or fingernails (not with the knuckles, as the name would indicate), keeps the wrist stiff, and "pushes" it forward with almost no spin. Dennis Springer, a major-league knuckleball pitcher for the Tampa Bay Devil Rays, offers this advice relative to gripping and throwing a knuckler: "I grab the baseball like I am throwing a palm ball, then I raise my first two fingers [forefinger and middle finger], putting my fingertips into the ball. I try to keep a stiff wrist when throwing the ball so that when I release the ball, it comes out of my hand without spin." It is also thrown very slowly, sometimes at almost half the speed of a fastball. The sportswriter John Romano, writing about Springer's pitching, says, "Thrown softly, the knuckleball is incapable of breaking anything. Except maybe a batter's spirit." Springer throws it at only about fifty to sixty-five miles per hour. In comparison, Nolan Ryan's fastball has been clocked at upwards of a hundred miles per hour.

The idea behind the knuckler is that if it is thrown with little or no spin, it will be more susceptible to forces in the air on its way to the plate. The physicist Robert Watts explains that "as a knuckleball approaches home plate, it changes directions erratically in an apparently random manner" (960). Because of this random approach, a batter has difficulty predicting the ball's movement and making contact. Unfortunately, the pitcher and catcher often don't know what it's going to do either, leading to wild pitches and passed balls. As Dennis Springer says, "I have played catch with guys who throw good [knuckleballs] and I hate it. [. . .] Some guys really do have a good one that will move all over the place."

But is this theory of a knuckleball's susceptibility to every gust of wind true? Scientists have studied a baseball's aerodynamics in order to figure out what makes a knuckler "dance" the way it does. A baseball is not an entirely smooth sphere: Its stitches give it rough edges. Scientists focus on "the role of the baseball's stitches in creating turbulence in the airflow"

Citation of an indirect source. The online Cohen source has no page or other reference numbers.

Brackets surround addition to quotation.

No parenthetical citation because author is named in text and source (an e-mail interview) has no page or other reference numbers.

Quotation integrated into writer's text.

Author named in text, so citation includes just page number.

Bracketed ellipsis mark indicates omission from quotation.

("Why Does the Knuckleball" 364). According to Robert Adair in The Physics of Baseball, turbulence results when imperfections disrupt air flowing over a smooth surface. With pitches that spin, turbulence is not a factor because the ball moves forward and spins fast enough to overcome the effects of turbulence on its way to home plate. However, when a baseball is not rotating much, the stitches can unbalance it and greatly alter its trajectory (29).

Unsigned source cited with a shortened version of its title.

Introduction of author's name at beginning and parenthetical page number at end make clear the source of a three-sentence paraphrase.

In other words, the stitches cause the air around a knuckleball to become turbulent, which in turn causes it to bounce around in the air: "At first the seams' aerodynamic influence might be pushing the ball outside, away from the plate; then, suddenly, a small shift in the seams might reverse the force, causing the ball to plunge back across the inside corner" ("Why Does the Knuckleball" 366). The slight rotation of a knuckler causes that "small shift." So a knuckleball thrown without any spin is useless. Through wind-tunnel testing, Robert Watts says, scientists have found that

> if the knuckleball is thrown in such a fashion that it has no spin at all, it can only curve laterally in one direction. [. . .] The single exception can occur in the remote possibility that the strings are initially positioned so that they disturb the point of boundary layer separation and bring about the oscillating wake phenomenon. (963)

Quotation of more than four typed lines is set off and indented 10 spaces or 1 inch.

Watts means that a nonspinning baseball will move only one way, unless the seams are perfectly aligned in a way that causes turbulence regardless of spin. In baseball speak, a nonspinning knuckler is said to behave like a "batting practice fastball," meaning it travels straight and is easy to hit. "Too much spin could prove disastrous, however," says Watts, "since the inertia of the ball would not allow a significant deflection" (963). A knuckleball that spins too much will also behave like a very slow fastball and most likely end up in the front row of the outfield bleachers. The most effective way to throw a knuckler is with just a slight rotation.

Different temperatures and air pressures also affect the way a knuckleball behaves. Springer observes,

> I have always loved pitching in hot and humid weather. For some reason the ball just works better in those conditions. [. . .] I do not at all enjoy pitching in high altitudes such as Albuquerque or Denver. [. . .] There is no air in those high altitudes that will help the ball move.

In humid weather, the moisture in the air magnifies the effects of turbulence on a baseball. The exact opposite is true in high altitudes, where the thin air reduces turbulence. The lower the air pressure, the less effect the air has on the seams of the ball that disturb the airflow. If pitched in a vacuum, a knuckleball would move straight through the air.

Writer's explanation of quotation does not require quotation marks or source citation.

One of the most important factors in considering how a knuckleball moves, though, is the pitcher. The knuckler is a tough pitch to get the hang of, and not everyone can throw it well. Only three knuckleball pitchers play in the major leagues today: Springer, Tom Candiotti of the Athletics, and Tim Wakefield of the Red Sox. Three is also the number of knuckleballers in the Baseball Hall of Fame: Phil Niekro, Hoyt Wilhelm, and Jesse Haines. This is a testament to how difficult it is to be a successful knuckleball pitcher. Springer comments, "I think just the fact that it took me almost nine years to make it to the big leagues proves that it is indeed a tough pitch to master. [. . .] It took me a long time to learn and I am still learning." Because of its unpredictable nature, one can never throw a knuckleball and expect consistent results. Springer's manager, the Devil Rays' Larry Rothschild, says, "You have to realize with a knuckleball pitcher that on bad days, they're going to be bad. On good days, they're able to beat anybody" (qtd. in Romano). It's a hit-or-miss situation. Even the best knuckleball pitchers have bad days.

No source citation for common knowledge.

Citation of an indirect source. Romano is an online source with no page or other numbering.

Perhaps the knuckleball should be renamed the screwball--not just because you don't throw it off the knuckles, but because it's such an unusual pitch. Most ballpark visitors want to see a pitcher who can throw ninety-eight miles per hour or who baffles batters with a pinpoint curveball. They often write off the knuckleball pitchers, thinking, "I could throw a pitch that slow." Perhaps they just don't understand all the factors that go into a knuckleball. For sure they never stood in the batter's box, flailed at, missed, and were completely embarrassed by the ever-elusive butterfly of pitches, the knuckler.

Works Cited

Adair, Robert K. The Physics of Baseball. New York: Harper, 1990.   *A book.*

Cohen, Eliot. "Baseball Lore: Knuckleballs." Total Baseball. 1996.   *A page on a Web site.*
6 Mar. 1998 <http://www.totalbaseball.com/story~person/
player/lore/knuckle.ht~>.

Romano, John. "Devil Rays Love Their Knucklehead." Nando
Sportserver. 1998. 8 Mar. 1998 <http://
www.archive.sportserver.com/newsroom/sports/bbo/1998/
mlb/tam/feat/archive/032798/tam64861.html>.

                                                                                 An e-mail interview
Springer, Dennis. E-mail interview. 27 Mar. 1998.   *conducted by the writer.*

Watts, Robert G. "Aerodynamics of a Knuckleball." American   *A journal that pages*
Journal of Physics 43.11 (1975): 960-63.   *issues separately.*

"Why Does the Knuckleball Behave That Way?" The New York   *An unsigned selection*
Times Book of Science Literacy. Ed. Richard Flaste. New   *from an anthology, listed*
York: Times, 1991. 364-68.   *last because "Why" falls*
                                                                                 last alphabetically.

PART TWO

THE METHODS

Narration in a comic strip

Boondocks, a newspaper comic strip by Aaron McGruder, focuses on two
African American brothers who find themselves transplanted from Chicago's
South Side to the leafy, mostly white suburb of Woodcrest. Resisting their new
environment, the boys sometimes have fun letting their mere presence scare
the inhabitants. In the sequence shown here, McGruder tells a brief narrative,
or story. What happens in the narrative? What does each panel of the sequence
tell us about the characters or otherwise contribute to the narrative? What is
the point of the narrative?

4

NARRATION

Telling a Story

WELL, THAT OUGHTA KEEP **HIM** AWAKE TONIGHT ...

THE METHOD

"What happened?" you ask a friend who sports a luminous black eye. Unless he merely grunts, "A golf ball," he may answer you with a narrative—a story, true or fictional.

"Okay," he sighs, "you know The Tenth Round? That nightclub down by the docks that smells of formaldehyde? Last night I heard they were giving away $500 to anybody who could stand up for three minutes against this karate expert, the Masked Samurai. And so . . ."

You lean forward. At least, you lean forward *if* you love a story. Most of us do, particularly if the story tells us of people in action or in conflict, and if it is told briskly, vividly, and with insight into the human heart. NARRATION, or storytelling, is therefore a powerful method by which to engage and hold the attention of listeners—readers as well. A little of its tremendous power flows to the public speaker who starts off with a joke, even a stale joke ("A funny thing happened to me on my way over here . . ."), and to the preacher who at the beginning of a sermon tells of some funny or touching incident. In its opening paragraph, an article in a popular magazine ("Vampires Live Today!") will give us a brief, arresting narrative: perhaps the case history of a car dealer who noticed, one moonlit night, his incisors strangely lengthening.

The term *narrative* takes in abundant territory. A narrative may be short or long, factual or imagined, as artless as a tale told in a locker room or as artful as a novel by Henry James. A narrative may instruct and inform, or simply divert and regale. It may set forth some point or message, or it may be no more significant than a horror tale that aims to curdle your blood.

At least a hundred times a year, you probably resort to narration, not always for the purpose of telling an entertaining story, but often to explain, to illustrate a point, to report information, to argue, or to persuade. That is, although a narrative can run from the beginning of an essay to the end, more often in your writing (as in your speaking) a narrative is only a part of what you have to say. It is there because it serves a larger purpose. In truth, because narration is such an effective way to put across your ideas, the ability to tell a compelling story—on paper, as well as in conversation—may be one of the most useful skills you can acquire.

A novel is a narrative, but a narrative doesn't have to be long. Sometimes an essay will include several brief stories. See, for instance, "Why Don't We Complain?" by William F. Buckley, Jr. (p. 543). A type of story often used to illustrate a point is the ANECDOTE, a short, entertaining account of a single incident. Anecdotes add color and specifics to history and to every issue of *People* magazine, and they often help support an ARGUMENT by giving it the flesh and blood of real life. Besides being vivid, an anecdote can be deeply revealing. In a biography of Samuel Johnson, the great eighteenth-century critic and scholar, W. Jackson Bate uses an anecdote to show that his subject was human and lovable. As Bate tells us, Dr. Johnson, a portly and imposing gentleman of fifty-five, had walked with some friends to the crest of a hill, where the great man,

> delighted by its steepness, said he wanted to "take a roll down." They tried to stop him. But he said he "had not had a roll for a long time," and taking out of his pockets his keys, a pencil, a purse, and other objects, lay down parallel at the edge of the hill, and rolled down its full length, "turning himself over and over till he came to the bottom."

However small the event it relates, this anecdote is memorable—partly because of its attention to detail, such as the exact list of the contents of Johnson's pockets. In such a brief story, a superhuman figure comes down to human size. In one stroke, Bate reveals an essential part of Johnson: his boisterous, hearty, and boyish sense of fun.

An anecdote may be used to explain a point. Asked why he had appointed to a cabinet post Josephus Daniels, the harshest critic of his policies, President Woodrow Wilson replied with an anecdote of a woman he knew. On spying a strange man urinating through her picket fence into her flower garden, she invited the offender into her yard because, as she explained to him, "I'd a whole lot rather have you inside pissing out than have you outside pissing in." By telling this story, Wilson made clear his situation in regard to his political enemy more succinctly and pointedly than if he had given a more abstract explanation.

THE PROCESS

Purpose and Shape

Every good story has a purpose, and we've suggested several on the preceding pages. A narrative without a purpose is bound to irritate readers, as a young child's rambling can vex an unsympathetic adult.

Whatever the reason for its telling, an effective story holds the attention of readers or listeners; and to do so, the storyteller shapes that story to appeal to its audience. If, for instance, you plan to tell a few friends of an embarrassing moment you had on your way to campus—you tripped and spilled a load of books into the arms of a passing dean—you know how to proceed. Simply to provide a laugh is your purpose, and your listeners, who need no introduction to you or the dean, need to be told only the bare events of the story. Perhaps you'll use some vivid words to convey the surprise on the dean's face when sixty pounds of literary lumber hit her. Perhaps you'll throw in a little surprise of your own. At first, you didn't take in the identity of this passerby on whom you'd dumped a load of literary lumber. Then you realized: It was the dean!

The Narrator in the Story

Such simple, direct storytelling is so common and habitual that we do it without planning in advance. The NARRATOR (or teller) of such a personal experience is the speaker, the one who was there. (All the selections in this chapter tell of such experiences. All use the first-PERSON *I*.) The telling is usually SUBJECTIVE, with details and language chosen to express the writer's feelings. Of course, a personal experience told in the first person can use some artful telling and some structuring. (In the course of this discussion, we'll offer advice on telling stories of different kinds.)

When a story isn't your own experience but a recital of someone else's, or of events that are public knowledge, then you proceed differently as narrator. Without expressing opinions, you step back and report, content to stay invisible. Instead of saying, "I did this; I did that," you use the third person, *he, she, it,* or *they:* "The runner did this; he did that." You may have been on the scene; if so, you will probably write as a spectator, from your own POINT OF VIEW (or angle of seeing). If you put together what happened from the testimony of others, you tell the story from the point of view of a nonparticipant (a witness who didn't take part). Generally, a nonparticipant is OBJECTIVE in setting forth events: unbiased, as accurate and dispassionate as possible.

When you narrate a story in the third person, you aren't a character central in the eyes of your audience. Unlike the first-person writer of a personal experience, you aren't the main actor; you are the camera operator, whose job is to focus on what transpires. Most history books and news stories are third-person narratives, and so is much fiction. In narrating actual events, writers stick to the facts and do not invent the thoughts of participants (historical novels, though, do mingle fact and fancy in this way). And even writers of fiction and anecdote imagine the thoughts of their characters only if they want to explore psychology. Note how much Woodrow Wilson's anecdote would lose if the teller had gone into the thoughts of his characters: "The woman was angry and embarrassed at seeing the stranger. . . ."

A final element of the narrator's place in the story is verb tense, whether present (*I stare, he stares*) or past (*I stared, he stared*). Telling a story in the present tense (instead of the past, traditionally favored) gives events a sense of immediacy. Presented as though everything were happening right now, Wilson's story might have begun, "Peering out her window, a woman spies a strange man. . . ." You can try the present tense, if you like, and see how immediate it seems to you. Be warned, however, that it can seem artificial (because we're used to reading stories in the past tense), and it can be difficult to sustain throughout an entire narrative. The past tense may be more removed, but it is still powerful: Just look at Edgar Allan Poe's toe-curling story "The Tell-Tale Heart," at the end of this chapter.

What to Emphasize

Discovery and Choice of Details

Whether you tell of your own experience or of someone else's, even if it is brief, you need a whole story to tell. If the story is complex, do some searching and discovering in writing. One trusty method to test your memory (or to make sure you have all the necessary elements of a story) is that of a news reporter. Ask yourself:

1. *What* happened?
2. *Who* took part?
3. *When?*
4. *Where?*
5. *Why* did this event (or these events) take place?
6. *How* did it (or they) happen?

That last *how* isn't merely another way of asking what happened. It means: In exactly what way or under what circumstances? If the event was a murder, how was it done—with an ax or with a bulldozer? Journalists call this handy list of questions "the five W's and the H."

Well-prepared storytellers, those who first search their memories (or do some research and legwork), have far more information on hand than they can use. The writing of a good story calls for careful choice. In choosing, remember your purpose and your audience. If you're writing that story of the dean and the books to give pleasure to readers who are your friends, delighted to hear about the discomfort of a pompous administrator, you will probably dwell lovingly on each detail of her consternation. You would tell the story differently if your audience were strangers who didn't know the dean from Eve. They would need more information on her background, reputation for stiffness, and appearance. If, suspected of having deliberately contrived the dean's humiliation, you were writing a report of the incident for the campus police, you'd want to give the plainest possible account of the story—without drama, without adornment, without background, and certainly without any humor whatsoever.

Scene Versus Summary

Your purpose and your audience, then, clearly determine which of the two main strategies of narration you're going to choose: to tell a story by SCENE or to tell it by SUMMARY. When you tell a story in a scene, or in scenes, you visualize each event as vividly and precisely as if you were there—as though it were a scene in a film, and your reader sat before the screen. This is the strategy of most fine novels and short stories—and of much excellent nonfiction as well. Instead of just mentioning people, you portray them. You recall dialogue as best you can, or you invent some that could have been spoken. You include DESCRIPTION (a mode of writing to be dealt with fully in our next chapter).

For a lively example of a well-drawn scene, see Maya Angelou's account of a tense crowd's behavior as, jammed into a small-town store, they listen to a fight broadcast (in "Champion of the World," beginning on p. 86). Angelou prolongs one scene for almost her entire essay. Sometimes, though, a writer will draw a scene in only two or three sentences. This is the brevity we find in W. Jackson Bate's glimpse of the hill-rolling Johnson (p. 75). Unlike Angelou, Bate evidently seeks not to weave a tapestry of detail but to show, in telling of one brief event, a trait of his hero's character.

When, on the other hand, you tell a story by the method of summary, you relate events concisely. Instead of depicting people and their surroundings in great detail, you set down just the essentials of what happened. Most of us employ this method in most stories we tell, for it takes less time and fewer words. A summary is to a scene, then, as a simple stick figure is to a portrait in oils. This is not to dismiss simple stick figures as inferior. The economy of a story told in summary may be as effective as the lavish detail of a story told in scenes.

Again, your choice of a method depends on your answer to the questions you ask yourself: What is my purpose? Who is my audience? How fully to flesh out a scene, how much detail to include—these choices depend on what you seek to do, and on how much your audience needs to know to follow you. Read the life of some famous person in an encyclopedia, and you will find the article telling its story in summary form. Its writer's purpose, evidently, is to recount the main events of a whole life in a short space. But glance through a book-length biography of the same celebrity, and you will probably find scenes in it. A biographer writes with a different purpose: to present a detailed portrait roundly and thoroughly, bringing the subject vividly to life.

To be sure, you can use both methods in telling a single story. Often, summary will serve a writer who passes briskly from one scene to the next, or hurries over events of lesser importance. Were you to write, let's say, the story of a man's fiendish passion for horse racing, you might decide to give short shrift to most other facts of his life. To emphasize what you consider essential, you might begin a scene with a terse summary: "Seven years went by, and after three marriages and two divorces, Lars found himself again back at Hialeah." (A detailed scene might follow.)

Good storytellers know what to emphasize. They do not fall into a boring drone: "And then I went down to the club and I had a few beers and I noticed this sign, Go 3 Minutes with the Masked Samurai and Win $500, so I went and got knocked out and then I had pizza and went home." In this lazily strung-out summary, the narrator reduces all events to equal unimportance. A more adept storyteller might leave out the pizza and dwell in detail on the big fight.

In *The Bedford Reader* we are concerned with the kind of writing you do every day in college: nonfiction writing in which you generally explain ideas, organize information you have learned, analyze other people's ideas, or argue a case. In fiction, though, we find an enormously popular and appealing use of narration and certain devices of storytelling from which all storytellers can learn. For these reasons, this chapter includes one celebrated short story by a master storyteller, Edgar Allan Poe. But fiction and fact barely separate Poe's story and the equally compelling true memoirs in this chapter. All the authors strive to make people and events come alive for us. All of them also use a tool that academic writers generally do not: dialogue. Reported speech, in quotation marks, is invaluable for revealing characters' feelings.

Organization

In any kind of narration, the simplest approach is to set down events in CHRONOLOGICAL ORDER, the way they happened. To do so is to have your story already organized for you. A chronological order is therefore an excellent sequence to follow unless you can see some special advantage in violating it. Ask: What am I trying to do? If you are trying to capture your readers' attention right away, you might begin *in medias res* (Latin, "in the middle of things") and open with a colorful, dramatic event, even though it took place late in the chronology. If trying for dramatic effect, you might save the most exciting or impressive event for last, even though it actually happened early. By this means, you can keep your readers in suspense for as long as possible. (You can return to earlier events by a FLASHBACK, an earlier scene recalled.) Let your purpose be your guide.

The writer Calvin Trillin has recalled why, in a narrative titled "The Tunica Treasure," he deliberately chose not to follow a chronology:

I wrote a story on the discovery of the Tunica treasure which I couldn't begin by saying, "Here is a man who works as a prison guard in Angola State Prison, and on his weekends he sometimes looks for buried treasure that is rumored to be around the Indian village." Because the real point of the story centered around the problems caused when an amateur wanders onto professional territory, I thought it would be much better to open with how momentous the discovery was, that it was the most important archeological discovery about Indian contact with the European settlers to date, and *then* to say that it was discovered by a prison guard. So I made a conscious choice *not* to start with Leonard Charrier working as a prison guard, not to go back to his boyhood in Bunkie, Louisiana, not to talk about how he'd always been interested in treasure hunting—hoping that the reader would assume I was about to say that the treasure was found by an archeologist from the Peabody Museum at Harvard.

Trillin, by saving the fact that a prison guard made the earthshaking discovery, effectively took his reader by surprise.

No matter what order you choose, either following chronology or departing from it, make sure your audience can follow it. The sequence of events has to be clear. This calls for TRANSITIONS of time, whether they are brief phrases that point out exactly when each event happened ("Seven years later," "A moment earlier"), or whole sentences that announce an event and clearly locate it in time ("If you had known Leonard Charrier ten years earlier, you would have found him voraciously poring over every archeology text he could lay his hands on in the public library"). See *Transitions* in Useful Terms for a list of possibilities.

The Point

In writing a news story, a reporter often begins with the conclusion, placing the main event in the opening paragraph (called the lead) so that readers get the essentials up front. Similarly, in using an anecdote to explain something or to argue a point, you'll want to tell readers directly what you think the story demonstrates. But in most other kinds of narration, whether fiction or nonfiction, whether to entertain or to make an idea clear, the storyteller refrains from revealing the gist of the story, its point, right at the beginning. In fact, many narratives do not contain a THESIS SENTENCE, a statement of the idea behind the story, because such a statement can rob the reader of the very pleasure of narration, the excitement of seeing a story build. That doesn't mean the story lacks a focal point—far from it. The writer has every obligation to construct the narrative as if a thesis sentence showed the way at the start, even when it didn't.

By the end of the story, that focal point should become obvious, as the writer builds toward a memorable CONCLUSION. In a story Mark Twain liked to tell aloud, a woman's ghost returns to claim her artificial arm made of gold, which she wore in life and which her greedy husband had unscrewed from her corpse. Carefully, Twain would build up suspense as the ghost pursued the husband upstairs to his bedroom, stood by his bed, breathed her cold breath on him, and intoned, *"Who's got my golden arm?"* Twain used to end his story by suddenly yelling at a member of the audience, *"You've got it!"*—and enjoying the victim's shriek of surprise. That final punctuating shriek may be a technique that will work only in oral storytelling; yet, like Twain, most storytellers like to end with a bang if they can. For another example, take specific notice of Edgar Allan Poe's ending for "The Tell-Tale Heart" (*after* you've read the whole story, that is). The final impact need not be as dramatic as Twain's and Poe's, either. As Maya Angelou and Barbara Huttmann demonstrate in their narratives in this chapter, you can achieve a lot just by leading to your point, stating your thesis sentence at the very end. You can sometimes make your point just by saving the best incident—the most dramatic or the funniest—for last.

CHECKLIST FOR REVISING A NARRATIVE

✔ **POINT OF VIEW.** Is your narrator's position in the story appropriate for your purpose and consistent throughout the story? Check for awkward or confusing shifts in point of view (participant or nonparticipant; first, second, or third person) and in the tenses of verbs (present to past or vice versa).

✔ **SELECTION OF EVENTS.** Have you selected and emphasized events to suit your audience and fulfill your purpose? Tell the important parts of the story in the greatest detail. Summarize the less important, connective events.

✔ **ORGANIZATION.** If your organization is not strictly chronological (first event to last), do you have a compelling reason for altering it? If you start somewhere other than the beginning of the story or use flashbacks at any point, will your readers benefit from your creativity?

✔ **TRANSITIONS.** Have you used transitions to help clarify the order of events and their duration?

✔ **DIALOGUE.** If you have used dialogue, quoting participants in the story, is it appropriate for your purpose? Is it concise, telling only the important, revealing lines? Does the language sound like spoken English?

✔ **THE POINT.** What is the point of your narrative? Will it be clear to readers by the end? Even if you haven't stated it in a thesis sentence, your story should focus on a central idea. If you can't risk readers' misunderstanding—if, for instance, you're using narration to support an argument or explain a concept—then have you stated your thesis outright?

NARRATION IN A PARAGRAPH:
TWO ILLUSTRATIONS

Using Narration to Write About Television

The following paragraph was written for *The Bedford Reader* as a kind of mini-essay. But it is easy to see how it might have worked in the context of a full essay about, say, the emotional effects of television on children. Recounting events vividly, moment by moment, the writer gives evidence for a rather dramatic effect on one little girl.

Oozing menace from beyond the stars or from the deeps, televised horror powerfully stimulates a child's already frisky imagination. As parents know, a "Creature Double Feature" has an impact that lasts long after the click of the *off* button. Recently a neighbor reported the strange case of her eight-year-old. Discovered late at night in the game room watching *The Exorcist*, the girl was promptly sent to bed. An hour later, her parents could hear her chanting something in the darkness of her bedroom. On tiptoe, they stole to her door to listen. The creak of springs told them that their daughter was swaying rhythmically to and fro, and the smell of acrid smoke warned them that something was burning. At once, they shoved open the door to find the room flickering with shadows cast by a lighted candle. Their daughter was sitting in bed, rocking back and forth as she intoned over and over, "Fiend in human form . . . Fiend in human form . . ." This case may be unique; still, it seems likely that similar events take place each night all over the screen-watching world.

Claim to be supported by narrative

Transitions (underlined) clarify sequence and pace of events

Anecdote builds suspense:

  Mystery

  Warnings

  Crisis

Conclusion broadens claim

Using Narration in an Academic Discipline

In this paragraph from a geology textbook, the authors use narration to illustrate a powerful geological occurrence. Following another paragraph that explains landslides more generally, the narrative places the reader at an actual event.

The news media periodically relate the terrifying and often grim details of landslides. On May 31, 1970, one such event occurred when a gigantic rock avalanche buried more than 20,000 people in Yungay and Ranrahirca, Peru. There was little warning of the impending disaster; it began and ended in just a matter of a few minutes. The avalanche started 14 kilometers from Yungay, near the summit of 6,700-meter-high Nevados Huascaran, the loftiest peak in the Peruvian Andes. Triggered by the ground motion from a strong offshore earthquake, a huge mass of rock and ice broke free from the precipitous north face of the mountain. After plunging

Generalization illustrated by narrative

Anecdote helps explain landslides:

  Sudden beginning

nearly one kilometer, <u>the material pulverized on impact and imme-</u>
diately began rushing down the mountainside, made fluid by trapped
air and melted ice. The initial mass ripped loose additional millions
of tons of debris <u>as it roared downhill.</u> The shock waves produced
by the event created thunderlike noise and stripped nearby hillsides
of vegetation. Although the material followed a previously eroded
gorge, a portion of the debris jumped a 200–300-meter-high bed-
rock ridge that had protected Yungay from past rock avalanches and
buried the entire city. <u>After inundating another town in its path,</u>
Ranrahirca, the mass of debris <u>finally</u> reached the bottom of the valley where its momentum carried it across the Rio Santa and tens of
meters up the opposite bank.

—Edward J. Tarbuck and Frederick K. Lutgens,
The Earth: An Introduction to Physical Geology

Fast movement

Irresistible force

Transitions (underlined) clarify sequence and pace of events

CASE STUDY
Using Narration

Robert Guzman was on his way to class at Cañada College when his car was hit at an intersection. He reported the accident to his insurance company, and the claims adjuster asked him to supplement the standard police report with a letter explaining what happened.

"What happened?" prompted Guzman to write the following narrative. Since the accident was uncomplicated, he had little difficulty getting the events down in chronological order. In editing, though, he did add some clarifying TRANSITIONS, such as "After the light turned green" and "When I was midway through the intersection."

Robert Guzman
415 Washington St., Apt. 5
San Carlos, CA 94070
June 7, 2001

David McClure
MDN Insurance
2716 El Camino Real
San Carlos, CA 94072

Dear Mr. McClure:

Thanks for your call about my claim. Here is the report you requested about the accident I was involved in.

At about 7:30 on the morning of June 4, I was driving south on Laurel Street in San Carlos. The traffic light at the corner of Laurel and San Carlos Avenue was red and I stopped at it, the first car in the stop line.

After the light turned green, I looked to my left and right. Although I saw a car approaching from the right on San Carlos, it seemed to be slowing for the light. Since my light was green, I proceeded through the intersection.

The car, which I later found out was driven by Mr. Henry, did not stop for its red light. When I was midway through the intersection, I heard its tires squeal and felt an impact. Mr. Henry's car hit the rear fender and bumper on my passenger side. My car spun clockwise and came to a stop facing north, in the northbound lane of Laurel.

Mr. Henry parked in a lot across the street, and I pulled in after him. I called the police on my cell phone, and we waited for the police to arrive.

No one was injured, but my passenger-side rear fender is severely dented and my bumper is twisted like a pretzel.

As you can see, I was not at fault in this accident. I believe Mr. Henry will confirm as much. Please let me know if you have any questions or if I can help my claim in any other way.

Sincerely,

Robert Guzman

Robert Guzman

MAYA ANGELOU

MAYA ANGELOU was born Marguerite Johnson in Saint Louis in 1928. After an unpleasantly eventful youth by her account ("from a broken family, raped at eight, unwed mother at sixteen"), she went on to join a dance company, star in an off-Broadway play (*The Blacks*), write six books of poetry, produce a series on Africa for PBS-TV, act in the television-special series *Roots*, serve as a coordinator for the Southern Christian Leadership Conference, and accept several honorary doctorates. She may be best known, however, for the six books of her searching, frank, and joyful autobiography — beginning with *I Know Why the Caged Bird Sings* (1970), which she adapted for television, through *A Song Flung Up to Heaven* (2002). Her books also include the essay collections *Wouldn't Take Nothing for My Journey Now* (1993) and *Even the Stars Look Lonesome* (1997). In 1998 Angelou directed her first feature film, *Down in the Delta*. She is Reynolds Professor of American Studies at Wake Forest University.

Champion of the World

"Champion of the World" is the nineteenth chapter in *I Know Why the Caged Bird Sings;* the title is a phrase taken from the chapter. Remembering her childhood, the writer tells how she and her older brother, Bailey, grew up in a town in Arkansas. The center of their lives was Grandmother and Uncle Willie's store, a gathering place for the black community. On the night when this story takes place, Joe Louis, the "Brown Bomber" and the hero of his people, defends his heavyweight boxing title against a white contender. Angelou's telling of the event both entertains us and explains what it was like to be African American in a certain time and place.

Amy Tan's "Fish Cheeks," following Angelou's essay, also explores the experience of growing up an outsider in mainly white America.

The last inch of space was filled, yet people continued to wedge them-   1
selves along the walls of the Store. Uncle Willie had turned the radio up to its last notch so that youngsters on the porch wouldn't miss a word. Women sat on kitchen chairs, dining-room chairs, stools, and upturned wooden boxes. Small children and babies perched on every lap available and men leaned on the shelves or on each other.

The apprehensive mood was shot through with shafts of gaiety, as a black   2
sky is streaked with lightning.

"I ain't worried 'bout this fight. Joe's gonna whip that cracker like it's open   3
season."

"He gone whip him till that white boy call him Momma."   4

At last the talking finished and the string-along songs about razor blades   5
were over and the fight began.

"A quick jab to the head." In the Store the crowd grunted. "A left to the   6
head and a right and another left." One of the listeners cackled like a hen and
was quieted.

"They're in a clinch, Louis is trying to fight his way out."   7

Some bitter comedian on the porch said, "That white man don't mind   8
hugging that niggah now, I betcha."

"The referee is moving in to break them up, but Louis finally pushed the   9
contender away and it's an uppercut to the chin. The contender is hanging on,
now he's backing away. Louis catches him with a short left to the jaw."

A tide of murmuring assent poured out the door and into the yard.   10

"Another left and another left. Louis is saving that mighty right . . ."   11
The mutter in the Store had grown into a baby roar and it was pierced by the
clang of a bell and the announcer's "That's the bell for round three, ladies and
gentlemen."

As I pushed my way into the Store I wondered if the announcer gave any   12
thought to the fact that he was addressing as "ladies and gentlemen" all the
Negroes around the world who sat sweating and praying, glued to their "Master's voice."[1]

There were only a few calls for RC Colas, Dr Peppers, and Hires root beer.   13
The real festivities would begin after the fight. Then even the old Christian
ladies who taught their children and tried themselves to practice turning the
other cheek would buy soft drinks, and if the Brown Bomber's victory was a
particularly bloody one they would order peanut patties and Baby Ruths also.

Bailey and I laid the coins on top of the cash register. Uncle Willie didn't   14
allow us to ring up sales during a fight. It was too noisy and might shake up the
atmosphere. When the gong rang for the next round we pushed through the
near-sacred quiet to the herd of children outside.

"He's got Louis against the ropes and now it's a left to the body and a right   15
to the ribs. Another right to the body, it looks like it was low . . . Yes, ladies
and gentlemen, the referee is signaling but the contender keeps raining the
blows on Louis. It's another to the body, and it looks like Louis is going down."

My race groaned. It was our people falling. It was another lynching, yet   16
another Black man hanging on a tree. One more woman ambushed and raped.
A Black boy whipped and maimed. It was hounds on the trail of a man running through slimy swamps. It was a white woman slapping her maid for being
forgetful.

The men in the Store stood away from the walls and at attention. Women   17
greedily clutched the babes on their laps while on the porch the shufflings and

---

[1] "His master's voice," accompanied by a picture of a little dog listening to a phonograph,
was a familiar advertising slogan. (The picture still appears on some RCA recordings.) —EDS.

smiles, flirtings and pinching of a few minutes before were gone. This might be the end of the world. If Joe lost we were back in slavery and beyond help. It would all be true, the accusations that we were lower types of human beings. Only a little higher than apes. True that we were stupid and ugly and lazy and dirty and, unlucky and worst of all, that God Himself hated us and ordained us to be hewers of wood and drawers of water, forever and ever, world without end.

We didn't breathe. We didn't hope. We waited.   18

"He's off the ropes, ladies and gentlemen. He's moving towards the   19
center of the ring." There was no time to be relieved. The worst might still happen.

"And now it looks like Joe is mad. He's caught Carnera with a left hook to   20
the head and a right to the head. It's a left jab to the body and another left to the head. There's a left cross and a right to the head. The contender's right eye is bleeding and he can't seem to keep his block up. Louis is penetrating every block. The referee is moving in, but Louis sends a left to the body and it's an uppercut to the chin and the contender is dropping. He's on the canvas, ladies and gentlemen."

Babies slid to the floor as women stood up and men leaned toward the   21
radio.

"Here's the referee. He's counting. One, two, three, four, five, six,   22
seven . . . Is the contender trying to get up again?"

All the men in the store shouted, "NO."   23

"—eight, nine, ten." There were a few sounds from the audience, but they   24
seemed to be holding themselves in against tremendous pressure.

"The fight is all over, ladies and gentlemen. Let's get the microphone over   25
to the referee . . . Here he is. He's got the Brown Bomber's hand, he's holding it up . . . Here he is . . ."

Then the voice, husky and familiar, came to wash over us—"The win-   26
nah, and still heavyweight champeen of the world . . . Joe Louis."

Champion of the world. A Black boy. Some Black mother's son. He was   27
the strongest man in the world. People drank Coca-Colas like ambrosia and ate candy bars like Christmas. Some of the men went behind the Store and poured white lightning in their soft-drink bottles, and a few of the bigger boys followed them. Those who were not chased away came back blowing their breath in front of themselves like proud smokers.

It would take an hour or more before the people would leave the Store   28
and head for home. Those who lived too far had made arrangements to stay in town. It wouldn't do for a Black man and his family to be caught on a lonely country road on a night when Joe Louis had proved that we were the strongest people in the world.

Journal Writing

How do you respond to the group identification and solidarity that Angelou writes about in this essay? What groups do you belong to, and how do you know you're a member? Consider groups based on race, ethnic background, religion, sports, hobbies, politics, friendship, kinship, or any other ties. (To take your journal writing further, see "From Journal to Essay" below.)

Questions on Meaning

1. What do you take to be the author's PURPOSE in telling this story?
2. What connection does Angelou make between the outcome of the fight and the pride of African Americans? To what degree do you think the author's view is shared by the others in the store listening to the broadcast?
3. To what extent are the statements in paragraphs 16 and 17 to be taken literally? What function do they serve in Angelou's narrative?
4. Primo Carnera was probably *not* the Brown Bomber's opponent on the night Maya Angelou recalls. Louis fought Carnera only once, on June 25, 1935, and it was not a title match; Angelou would have been no more than seven years old at the time. Does the author's apparent error detract from her story?

Questions on Writing Strategy

1. What details in the opening paragraphs indicate that an event of crucial importance is about to take place?
2. How does Angelou build up SUSPENSE in her account of the fight? At what point were you able to predict the winner?
3. Comment on the IRONY in Angelou's final paragraph.
4. What EFFECT does the author's use of direct quotation have on her narrative?
5. **OTHER METHODS.** Besides narration, Angelou also relies heavily on the method of DESCRIPTION. Analyze how narration depends on description in paragraph 27 alone.

Questions on Language

1. Explain what the author means by "string-along songs about razor blades" (par. 5).
2. How does Angelou's use of NONSTANDARD ENGLISH contribute to her narrative?
3. Be sure you know the meanings of these words: apprehensive (par. 2); assent (10); ambushed, maimed (16); ordained (17); ambrosia, white lightning (27).

Suggestions for Writing

1. **FROM JOURNAL TO ESSAY.** From your journal entry, choose one of the groups you belong to and explore your sense of membership through a narrative that tells of

an incident that occurred when that sense was strong. Try to make the incident come alive for your readers with vivid details, dialogue, and tight sequencing of events.

2. Write an essay based on some childhood experience of your own, still vivid in your memory.

3. **CRITICAL WRITING.** Angelou does not directly describe relations between African Americans and whites, yet her essay implies quite a lot. Write a brief essay about what you can INFER from the exaggeration of paragraphs 16–17 and the obliqueness of paragraph 28. Focus on Angelou's details and the language she uses to present them.

4. **CONNECTIONS.** Angelou's "Champion of the World" and the next essay, Amy Tan's "Fish Cheeks," both tell stories of children who felt like outsiders in predominantly white America. COMPARE AND CONTRAST the two writers' perceptions of what sets them apart from the dominant culture. How does the event each reports affect that sense of difference? Use specific examples from both essays as your EVIDENCE.

Maya Angelou on Writing

Maya Angelou's writings have shown great variety: She has done notable work as an autobiographer, poet, short-story writer, screenwriter, journalist, and song lyricist. Asked by interviewer Sheila Weller, "Do you start each project with a specific idea?" Angelou replied:

It starts with a definite subject, but it might end with something entirely different. When I start a project, the first thing I do is write down, in longhand, everything I know about the subject, every thought I've ever had on it. This may be twelve or fourteen pages. Then I read it back through, for quite a few days, and find—given that subject—what its rhythm is. 'Cause everything in the universe has a rhythm. So if it's free form, it still has a rhythm. And once I hear the rhythm of the piece, then I try to find out what are the salient points that I must make. And then it begins to take shape.

I try to set myself up in each chapter by saying: "This is what I want to go from—from B to, say, G-sharp. Or from D to L." And then I find the hook. It's like the knitting, where, after you knit a certain amount, there's one thread that begins to pull. You know, you can see it right along the cloth. Well, in writing, I think: "Now where is that one hook, that one little thread?" It may be a sentence. If I can catch that, then I'm home free. It's the one that tells me where I'm going. It may not even turn out to be in the final chapter. I may throw it out later or change it. But if I follow it through, it leads me right out.

For Discussion

1. How would you define the word *rhythm* as Maya Angelou uses it?
2. What response would you give a student who said, "Doesn't Angelou's approach to writing waste more time and thought than it's worth?"

AMY TAN

AMY TAN is a gifted storyteller whose first novel, *The Joy Luck Club* (1989), met with critical acclaim and huge success. The relationships it details between immigrant Chinese mothers and their Chinese American daughters came from Tan's firsthand experience. She was born in 1952 in Oakland, California, the daughter of immigrants who had fled China's Cultural Revolution in the late 1940s. She majored in English and linguistics at San Jose State University, where she received a BA in 1973 and an MA in 1974. After two more years of graduate work, Tan became a consultant in language development for disabled children and then started her own company writing reports and speeches for business corporations. Tan began writing fiction to explore her ethnic ambivalence and to find a voice for herself. Since *The Joy Luck Club*, she has published three more novels: *The Kitchen God's Wife* (1991), *The Hundred Secret Senses* (1995), and *The Bonesetter's Daughter* (2001). Tan has also written children's books and contributed essays to *McCall's*, *Life*, *Glamour*, *The Atlantic Monthly*, and other magazines.

Fish Cheeks

"Fish Cheeks" is a very brief narrative, almost an anecdote, but still it deftly portrays the contradictory feelings and the advantages of a girl with feet in different cultures. The essay first appeared in *Seventeen*, a magazine for teenage girls and young women, in 1987.

For a complementary view of growing up "different," read the preceding essay, Maya Angelou's "Champion of the World."

I fell in love with the minister's son the winter I turned fourteen. He was 1 not Chinese, but as white as Mary in the manger. For Christmas I prayed for this blond-haired boy, Robert, and a slim new American nose.

When I found out that my parents had invited the minister's family over 2 for Christmas Eve dinner, I cried. What would Robert think of our shabby Chinese Christmas? What would he think of our noisy Chinese relatives who lacked proper American manners? What terrible disappointment would he feel upon seeing not a roasted turkey and sweet potatoes but Chinese food?

On Christmas Eve I saw that my mother had outdone herself in creating 3 a strange menu. She was pulling black veins out of the backs of fleshy prawns. The kitchen was littered with appalling mounds of raw food: A slimy rock cod with bulging eyes that pleaded not to be thrown into a pan of hot oil. Tofu, which looked like stacked wedges of rubbery white sponges. A bowl soaking dried fungus back to life. A plate of squid, their backs crisscrossed with knife markings so they resembled bicycle tires.

And then they arrived—the minister's family and all my relatives in a   4
clamor of doorbells and rumpled Christmas packages. Robert grunted hello,
and I pretended he was not worthy of existence.

Dinner threw me deeper into despair. My relatives licked the ends of their   5
chopsticks and reached across the table, dipping them into the dozen or so
plates of food. Robert and his family waited patiently for platters to be passed
to them. My relatives murmured with pleasure when my mother brought out
the whole steamed fish. Robert grimaced. Then my father poked his chopsticks just below the fish eye and plucked out the soft meat. "Amy, your
favorite," he said, offering me the tender fish cheek. I wanted to disappear.

At the end of the meal my father leaned back and belched loudly, thank-   6
ing my mother for her fine cooking. "It's a polite Chinese custom to show you
are satisfied," explained my father to our astonished guests. Robert was looking down at his plate with a reddened face. The minister managed to muster
up a quiet burp. I was stunned into silence for the rest of the night.

After everyone had gone, my mother said to me, "You want to be the same   7
as American girls on the outside." She handed me an early gift. It was a
miniskirt in beige tweed. "But inside you must always be Chinese. You must be
proud you are different. Your only shame is to have shame."

And even though I didn't agree with her then, I knew that she understood   8
how much I had suffered during the evening's dinner. It wasn't until many
years later—long after I had gotten over my crush on Robert—that I was able
to fully appreciate her lesson and the true purpose behind our particular menu.
For Christmas Eve that year, she had chosen all my favorite foods.

Journal Writing

Do you sympathize with the shame Tan feels because of her family's differences from
their non-Chinese guests? Or do you think she should have been more proud to share
her family's customs? Think of an occasion when, for whatever reason, you were
acutely aware of being different. How did you react? Did you try to hide your difference in order to fit in, or did you reveal or celebrate your uniqueness? (To take your
journal writing further, see "From Journal to Essay" on the next page.)

Questions on Meaning

1. Why does Tan cry when she finds out that the boy she is in love with is coming
   to dinner?
2. Why does Tan's mother go out of her way to prepare a disturbingly traditional
   Chinese dinner for her daughter and guests? What one sentence best sums up the
   lesson Tan was not able to understand until years later?

3. How does the fourteen-year-old Tan feel about her Chinese background? about her mother?
4. What is Tan's PURPOSE in writing this essay? Does she just want to entertain readers, or might she have a weightier goal?

Questions on Writing Strategy

1. How does Tan draw the reader into her story right from the beginning?
2. How does Tan use TRANSITIONS both to drive and to clarify her narrative?
3. What is the IRONY of the last sentence of the essay?
4. **OTHER METHODS.** Paragraph 3 is a passage of pure DESCRIPTION. Why does Tan linger over the food? What is the EFFECT of this paragraph?

Questions on Language

1. The simile about Mary in the second sentence of the essay is surprising. Why? Why is it amusing? (See *Figures of speech* in Useful Terms for a definition of *simile*.)
2. How does the narrator's age affect the TONE of this essay? Give EXAMPLES of language particularly appropriate to a fourteen-year-old.
3. Make sure you know the meanings of the following words: prawns, tofu (par. 3); clamor (4); grimaced (5); muster (6).

Suggestions for Writing

1. **FROM JOURNAL TO ESSAY.** Using Tan's essay as a model, write a brief narrative based on your journal sketch about a time when you felt different from others. Try to imitate the way Tan integrates the external events of the dinner with her own feelings about what is going on. Your story may be humorous, like Tan's, or more serious.
2. Take a perspective like that of the minister's son, Robert: Write a narrative essay about a time when you had to adjust to participating in a culture different from your own. It could be a meal, a wedding or other rite of passage, a religious ceremony, a trip to another country. What did you learn from your experience, about yourself and others?
3. **CRITICAL WRITING.** From this essay one can INFER two very different sets of ASSUMPTIONS about the extent to which immigrants should seek to integrate themselves into the culture of their adopted country. Take either of these positions, in favor of or against assimilation (cultural integration), and make an ARGUMENT for your case.
4. **CONNECTIONS.** Both Tan and Maya Angelou, in "Champion of the World" (p. 86), write about difference from white Americans, but their POINTS OF VIEW are not the same: Tan's is a teenager's lament about not fitting in; Angelou's is an oppressed child's excitement about proving the injustice of oppression. In an essay, ANALYZE the two authors' uses of narration to convey their perspectives. What details do they focus on? What internal thoughts do they report? Is one essay more effective than the other? Why, or why not?

Amy Tan on Writing

In 1989 Amy Tan delivered a lecture titled "Mother Tongue" at the State of the Language Symposium in San Francisco. The lecture, later published in *The Threepenny Review* in 1990, addresses Tan's own experience as a bilingual child speaking both Chinese and English. "I do think that the language spoken in the family, especially in immigrant families, which are more insular, plays a large role in shaping the language of the child. And I believe that it affected my results on achievement tests, IQ tests, and the SAT. While my English skills were never judged as poor, compared to math English could not be considered my strong suit. [. . .] This was understandable. Math is precise; there is only one correct answer. Whereas, for me at least, the answers on English tests were always a judgment call, a matter of opinion and personal experience."

Tan goes on to say that the necessity of adapting to different styles of expression may affect other children from bilingual households. "I've been asked, as a writer, why there are not more Asian-Americans represented in American literature. Why are there few Asian-Americans enrolled in creative-writing programs? Why do so many Chinese students go into engineering? Well, these are broad sociological questions I can't begin to answer. But I have noticed in surveys [. . .] that Asian students, as a whole, always do significantly better on math achievement tests than in English. And this makes me think that there are other Asian-American students whose English spoken in the home might also be described as 'broken' or 'limited.' And perhaps they also have teachers who are steering them away from writing and into math and science, which is what happened to me."

Tan admits that when she first began writing fiction, she wrote "what I thought to be wittily crafted sentences, sentences that would finally prove I had mastery over the English language." But they were awkward and self-conscious, so she changed her tactic. "I later decided I should envision a reader for the stories I would write. And the reader I decided upon was my mother, because these were stories about mothers. So with this reader in mind—and in fact, she did read my early drafts—I began to write stories using all the Englishes I grew up with: the English I spoke to my mother, [. . .] the English she used with me, [. . .] my translation of her Chinese, [. . .] and what I imagined to be her translation of her Chinese if she could speak in perfect English, her internal language, and for that I sought to preserve the essence, but not either an English or a Chinese structure. I wanted to capture what language ability tests can never reveal: her intent, her passion, her imagery, the rhythms of her speech and the nature of her thoughts.

"Apart from what any critic had to say about my writing, I knew I had succeeded where it counted when my mother finished reading my book and gave
me her verdict: 'So easy to read.'"

For Discussion

1. How could growing up in a household of "broken" English be a handicap for a student taking an achievement test?
2. What does the author suggest is the reason why more Asian Americans major in
   engineering than major in writing?
3. Why did Amy Tan's mother make a good reader?

ANNIE DILLARD

ANNIE DILLARD is accomplished as a prose writer, poet, and literary critic. Born in 1945, she earned a BA (1967) and an MA (1968) from Hollins College in Virginia. Dillard's first published prose, *Pilgrim at Tinker Creek* (1974), is a work alive with close, intense, and poetic descriptions of the natural world. It won her a Pulitzer Prize and comparison with Thoreau. Since then, Dillard's entranced and entrancing writing has appeared regularly in *Harper's, American Scholar, The Atlantic Monthly*, and other magazines and in her books: *Tickets for a Prayer Wheel* (1975), poems; *Holy the Firm* (1978), a prose poem; *Living by Fiction* (1982), literary criticism; *Teaching a Stone to Talk* (1982), nonfiction; *Encounters with Chinese Writers* (1984), an account of a trip to China; *An American Childhood* (1987), an autobiography; *The Writing Life* (1989), anecdotes and metaphors about writing; *The Living* (1992), a historical novel set in the Pacific Northwest; *Mornings Like This: Found Poems* (1995); and *For the Time Being* (1999), an exploration of how God and evil can coexist. In 1999 Dillard was inducted into the American Academy of Arts and Letters.

The Chase

In this chapter from her autobiography, An American Childhood, Dillard leads us running desperately through snow-filled backyards. Like all of Dillard's writing, this romp shows an unparalleled enthusiasm for life and skill at expressing it.

Some boys taught me to play football. This was fine sport. You thought up   1
a new strategy for every play and whispered it to the others. You went out for a pass, fooling everyone. Best, you got to throw yourself mightily at someone's running legs. Either you brought him down or you hit the ground flat on your chin, with your arms empty before you. It was all or nothing. If you hesitated in fear, you would miss and get hurt: you would take a hard fall while the kid got away, or you would get kicked in the face while the kid got away. But if you flung yourself wholeheartedly at the back of his knees—if you gathered and joined body and soul and pointed them diving fearlessly—then you likely wouldn't get hurt, and you'd stop the ball. Your fate, and your team's score, depended on your concentration and courage. Nothing girls did could compare with it.

Boys welcomed me at baseball, too, for I had, through enthusiastic prac-   2
tice, what was weirdly known as a boy's arm. In winter, in the snow, there was neither baseball nor football, so the boys and I threw snowballs at passing cars. I got in trouble throwing snowballs, and have seldom been happier since.

On one weekday morning after Christmas, six inches of new snow had   3
just fallen. We were standing up to our boot tops in snow on a front yard on
trafficked Reynolds Street, waiting for cars. The cars traveled Reynolds Street
slowly and evenly; they were targets all but wrapped in red ribbons, cream
puffs. We couldn't miss.

I was seven; the boys were eight, nine, and ten. The oldest two Fahey boys   4
were there—Mikey and Peter—polite blond boys who lived near me on
Lloyd Street, and who already had four brothers and sisters. My parents
approved Mikey and Peter Fahey. Chickie McBride was there, a tough kid,
and Billy Paul and Mackie Kean too, from across Reynolds, where the boys
grew up dark and furious, grew up skinny, knowing, and skilled. We had all
drifted from our houses that morning looking for action, and had found it here
on Reynolds Street.

It was cloudy but cold. The cars' tires laid behind them on the snowy   5
street a complex trail of beige chunks like crenellated castle walls. I had
stepped on some earlier; they squeaked. We could have wished for more traffic. When a car came, we all popped it one. In the intervals between cars we
reverted to the natural solitude of children.

I started making an iceball—a perfect iceball, from perfectly white snow,   6
perfectly spherical, and squeezed perfectly translucent so no snow remained
all the way through. (The Fahey boys and I considered it unfair actually to
throw an iceball at somebody, but it had been known to happen.)

I had just embarked on the iceball project when we heard tire chains   7
come clanking from afar. A black Buick was moving toward us down the
street. We all spread out, banged together some regular snowballs, took aim,
and, when the Buick drew nigh, fired.

A soft snowball hit the driver's windshield right before the driver's face. It   8
made a smashed star with a hump in the middle.

Often, of course, we hit our target, but this time, the only time in all of   9
life, the car pulled over and stopped. Its wide black door opened; a man got
out of it, running. He didn't even close the car door.

He ran after us, and we ran away from him, up the snowy Reynolds side-   10
walk. At the corner, I looked back; incredibly, he was still after us. He was
in city clothes: a suit and tie, street shoes. Any normal adult would have
quit, having sprung us into flight and made his point. This man was gaining
on us. He was a thin man, all action. All of a sudden, we were running for our
lives.

Wordless, we split up. We were on our turf; we could lose ourselves in the   11
neighborhood backyards, everyone for himself. I paused and considered.
Everyone had vanished except Mikey Fahey, who was just rounding the cor-

ner of a yellow brick house. Poor Mikey, I trailed him. The driver of the Buick sensibly picked the two of us to follow. The man apparently had all day.

He chased Mikey and me around the yellow house and up a backyard path   12 we knew by heart: under a low tree, up a bank, through a hedge, down some snowy steps, and across the grocery store's delivery driveway. We smashed through a gap in another hedge, entered a scruffy backyard and ran around its back porch and tight between houses to Edgerton Avenue; we ran across Edgerton to an alley and up our own sliding woodpile to the Halls' front yard; he kept coming. We ran up Lloyd Street and wound through mazy backyards toward the steep hilltop at Willard and Lang.

He chased us silently, block after block. He chased us silently over picket   13 fences, through thorny hedges, between houses, around garbage cans, and across streets. Every time I glanced back, choking for breath, I expected he would have quit. He must have been as breathless as we were. His jacket strained over his body. It was an immense discovery, pounding into my hot head with every sliding, joyous step, that this ordinary adult evidently knew what I thought only children who trained at football knew: that you have to fling yourself at what you're doing, you have to point yourself, forget yourself, aim, dive.

Mikey and I had nowhere to go, in our own neighborhood or out of it, but   14 away from this man who was chasing us. He impelled us forward; we compelled him to follow our route. The air was cold; every breath tore my throat. We kept running, block after block; we kept improvising, backyard after backyard, running a frantic course and choosing it simultaneously, failing always to find small places or hard places to slow him down, and discovering always, exhilarated, dismayed, that only bare speed could save us—for he would never give up, this man—and we were losing speed.

He chased us through the backyard labyrinths of ten blocks before he   15 caught us by our jackets. He caught us and we all stopped.

We three stood staggering, half blinded, coughing, in an obscure hilltop   16 backyard: a man in his twenties, a boy, a girl. He had released our jackets, our pursuer, our captor, our hero: He knew we weren't going anywhere. We all played by the rules. Mikey and I unzipped our jackets. I pulled off my sopping mittens. Our tracks multiplied in the backyard's new snow. We had been breaking new snow all morning. We didn't look at each other. I was cherishing my excitement. The man's lower pants legs were wet; his cuffs were full of snow, and there was a prow of snow beneath them on his shoes and socks. Some trees bordered the little flat backyard, some messy winter trees. There was no one around: a clearing in a grove, and we the only players.

It was a long time before he could speak. I had some difficulty at first   17 recalling why we were there. My lips felt swollen; I couldn't see out of the sides of my eyes; I kept coughing.

"You stupid kids," he began perfunctorily.   18

We listened perfunctorily indeed, if we listened at all, for the chewing out   19
was redundant, a mere formality, and beside the point. The point was that he
had chased us passionately without giving up, and so he had caught us. Now
he came down to earth. I wanted the glory to last forever.

But how could the glory have lasted forever? We could have run through   20
every backyard in North America until we got to Panama. But when he
trapped us at the lip of the Panama Canal, what precisely could he have done
to prolong the drama of the chase and cap its glory? I brooded about this for
the next few years. He could only have fried Mikey Fahey and me in boiling
oil, say, or dismembered us piecemeal, or staked us to anthills. None of which
I really wanted, and none of which any adult was likely to do, even in the
spirit of fun. He could only chew us out there in the Panamanian jungle, after
months or years of exalting pursuit. He could only begin, "You stupid kids,"
and continue in his ordinary Pittsburgh accent with his normal righteous
anger and the usual common sense.

If in that snowy backyard the driver of the black Buick had cut off our   21
heads, Mikey's and mine, I would have died happy, for nothing has required
so much of me since as being chased all over Pittsburgh in the middle of
winter—running terrified, exhausted—by this sainted, skinny, furious redheaded man who wished to have a word with us. I don't know how he found
his way back to his car.

Journal Writing

Why do you suppose Dillard, after so many years, remembers in such vivid detail the
rather insignificant event she describes? What incidents from your childhood seem to
you momentous even now? List these significant incidents, along with some notes
about their importance. (To take your journal writing further, see "From Journal to
Essay" on the facing page.)

Questions on Meaning

1. What is Dillard's PURPOSE in this essay? Obviously, she wants to entertain readers,
   but does she have another purpose as well?
2. Does the persistence of the pursuer seem reasonable to you, given the children's
   prank?
3. What does the pursuer represent for the narrator? How do her feelings about him
   change after the chase is over, and why?

4. Why does Dillard describe the "chewing out," seemingly the object of the chase, as "redundant, a mere formality, and beside the point" (par. 19)?

Questions on Writing Strategy

1. Why does Dillard open her story with a discussion of football? In what way does the game of football serve as a metaphor in the story? (Hint: Look at par. 13, as well as the sentence "It was all or nothing" in par. 1.) (See *Figures of speech* in Useful Terms for a definition of *metaphor*.)
2. Identify the two rapid TRANSITIONS in paragraph 2. Do they contribute to or detract from the COHERENCE of the essay?
3. Why does Dillard interrupt the story of the chase with an "immense discovery" (par. 13)? Does this interruption weaken the narrative?
4. Discuss Dillard's POINT OF VIEW. Is her perspective that of a seven-year-old girl, or that of an adult writer reflecting on her childhood experience?
5. **OTHER METHODS.** Dillard's story implicitly COMPARES AND CONTRASTS a child's and an adult's way of looking at life. What are some of the differences that Dillard implies?

Questions on Language

1. Look up the meaning of any of the following words you don't already know: crenellated (par. 5); translucent (6); nigh (7); impelled, compelled (14); prow (16); perfunctorily (18); redundant (19); dismembered, piecemeal, exalting, righteous (20).
2. Explain the contradiction in this statement: "I got in trouble throwing snowballs, and have seldom been happier since" (par. 2). Can you find other examples of paradox in what the narrator says? How is this paradox related to the narrator's apparent view of children? (See *Figures of speech* in Useful Terms for a definition of *paradox*.)
3. What is the EFFECT of the last sentence of the essay?

Suggestions for Writing

1. **FROM JOURNAL TO ESSAY.** Choose one significant incident from the list of childhood experiences you wrote in your journal, and narrate the incident as vividly as you can. Include the details: Where did the event take place? What did people say? How were they dressed? What was the weather like? Follow Dillard's model in putting CONCRETE IMAGES to work for an idea, in this case an idea about the significance of the incident to you then and now.
2. From what you have seen of children and adults, do you agree with Dillard's characterization of the two groups (see "Writing Strategy" question 5)? Write an essay comparing and contrasting children's and adults' attitudes toward play. (You will

have to GENERALIZE, of course, but try to keep your broad statements grounded in a reality your readers will share.)

3. **CRITICAL WRITING.** Dillard's narration of the chase is only six paragraphs long (pars. 10–15), but it seems longer, as if almost in real time. What techniques does Dillard use in these paragraphs to hold our attention and re-create the breathlessness of the chase? Look at concrete details, repetition, PARALLELISM, and the near absence of time-marking transitions. In ANALYZING Dillard's techniques, use plenty of quotations from the essay.

4. **CONNECTIONS.** Dillard's essay and Brad Manning's "Arm Wrestling with My Father" (p. 136) both deal with childhood values and how they are transformed as one grows older. In an essay, compare and contrast the two writers' treatment of this subject. How does the TONE of each essay contribute to its effect?

Annie Dillard on Writing

Writing for *The Bedford Reader,* Dillard has testified to her work habits. Rarely satisfied with an essay until it has gone through many drafts, she sometimes goes on correcting and improving it even after it has been published. "I always have to condense or toss openings," she affirms; "I suspect most writers do. When you begin something, you're so grateful to have begun you'll write down anything, just to prolong the sensation. Later, when you've learned what the writing is really about, you go back and throw away the beginning and start over."

Often she replaces a phrase or sentence with a shorter one. In one essay, to tell how a drop of pond water began to evaporate on a microscope slide, she first wrote, "Its contours pulled together." But that sentence seemed to suffer from "tortured abstraction." She made the sentence read instead, "Its edges shrank." Dillard observes, "I like short sentences. They're forceful, and they can get you out of big trouble."

For Discussion

1. Why, according to Dillard, is it usually necessary for writers to revise the opening paragraphs of what they write?

2. Dillard says that short sentences "can get you out of big trouble." What kinds of "big trouble" do you suppose she means?

SHERMAN ALEXIE

SHERMAN ALEXIE is a poet, fiction writer, and filmmaker known for witty and frank explorations of the lives of contemporary Native Americans. A Spokane/Coeur d'Alene Indian, Alexie was born in 1966 and grew up on the Spokane Indian Reservation in Wellpinit, Washington. He spent two years at Gonzaga University before transferring to Washington State University in Pullman. The same year he graduated, 1991, Alexie published *The Business of Fancydancing*, a book of poetry that led the *New York Times Book Review* to call him "one of the major lyric voices of our time." Since then Alexie has published many more books of poetry, including *I Would Steal Horses* (1993) and *One Stick Song* (2000); the novels *Reservation Blues* (1995) and *Indian Killer* (1996); and the story collections *The Lone Ranger and Tonto Fistfight in Heaven* (1993) and *The Toughest Indian in the World* (2000). Alexie also wrote and produced *Smoke Signals*, a film that won awards at the 1998 Sundance Film Festival, and he wrote and directed *The Business of Fancydancing* (2002), a film about the paths of two young men from the Spokane reservation. Living in Seattle with his wife and children, Alexie occasionally performs as a stand-up comic and holds the record for the most consecutive years as World Heavyweight Poetry Bout Champion.

Indian Education

Alexie attended the tribal school on the Spokane reservation through the seventh grade, when he decided to seek a better education at an off-reservation all-white high school. As this year-by-year account of his schooling makes clear, he was not firmly at home in either setting. The essay first appeared in Alexie's *The Lone Ranger and Tonto Fistfight in Heaven*.

First Grade

My hair was too short and my US Government glasses were horn-rimmed, ugly, and all that first winter in school, the other Indian boys chased me from one corner of the playground to the other. They pushed me down, buried me in the snow until I couldn't breathe, thought I'd never breathe again.

They stole my glasses and threw them over my head, around my outstretched hands, just beyond my reach, until someone tripped me and sent me falling again, facedown in the snow.

I was always falling down; my Indian name was Junior Falls Down. Sometimes it was Bloody Nose or Steal-His-Lunch. Once, it was Cries-Like-a-White-Boy, even though none of us had seen a white boy cry.

Then it was a Friday morning recess and Frenchy SiJohn threw snowballs at me while the rest of the Indian boys tortured some other *top-yogh-yaught* kid, another weakling. But Frenchy was confident enough to torment me all by himself, and most days I would have let him.

But the little warrior in me roared to life that day and knocked Frenchy to 5 the ground, held his head against the snow, and punched him so hard that my knuckles and the snow made symmetrical bruises on his face. He almost looked like he was wearing war paint.

But he wasn't the warrior. I was. And I chanted *It's a good day to die, it's a* 6 *good day to die*, all the way down to the principal's office.

Second Grade

Betty Towle, missionary teacher, redheaded and so ugly that no one ever 7 had a puppy crush on her, made me stay in for recess fourteen days straight.

"Tell me you're sorry," she said. 8

"Sorry for what?" I asked. 9

"Everything," she said and made me stand straight for fifteen minutes, 10 eagle-armed with books in each hand. One was a math book; the other was English. But all I learned was that gravity can be painful.

For Halloween I drew a picture of her riding a broom with a scrawny cat 11 on the back. She said that her God would never forgive me for that.

Once, she gave the class a spelling test but set me aside and gave me a test 12 designed for junior high students. When I spelled all the words right, she crumpled up the paper and made me eat it.

"You'll learn respect," she said. 13

She sent a letter home with me that told my parents to either cut my 14 braids or keep me home from class. My parents came in the next day and dragged their braids across Betty Towle's desk.

"Indians, indians, indians." She said it without capitalization. She called 15 me "indian, indian, indian."

And I said, *Yes, I am. I am Indian. Indian, I am.* 16

Third Grade

My traditional Native American art career began and ended with my very 17 first portrait: *Stick Indian Taking a Piss in My Backyard.*

As I circulated the original print around the classroom, Mrs. Schluter 18 intercepted and confiscated my art.

Censorship, I might cry now. *Freedom of expression*, I would write in edito- 19 rials to the tribal newspaper.

In third grade, though, I stood alone in the corner, faced the wall, and 20 waited for the punishment to end.

I'm still waiting. 21

Fourth Grade

"You should be a doctor when you grow up," Mr. Schluter told me, even   22
though his wife, the third grade teacher, thought I was crazy beyond my years.
My eyes always looked like I had just hit-and-run someone.

"Guilty," she said. "You always look guilty."   23

"Why should I be a doctor?" I asked Mr. Schluter.   24

"So you can come back and help the tribe. So you can heal people."   25

That was the year my father drank a gallon of vodka a day and the same   26
year that my mother started two hundred different quilts but never finished
any. They sat in separate, dark places in our HUD[1] house and wept savagely.

I ran home after school, heard their Indian tears, and looked in the mir-   27
ror. *Doctor Victor,* I called myself, invented an education, talked to my reflection. *Doctor Victor to the emergency room.*

Fifth Grade

I picked up a basketball for the first time and made my first shot. No. I   28
missed my first shot, missed the basket completely, and the ball landed in the
dirt and sawdust, sat there just like I had sat there only minutes before.

But it felt good, that ball in my hands, all those possibilities and angles. It   29
was mathematics, geometry. It was beautiful.

At that same moment, my cousin Steven Ford sniffed rubber cement from   30
a paper bag and leaned back on the merry-go-round. His ears rang, his mouth
was dry, and everyone seemed so far away.

But it felt good, that buzz in his head, all those colors and noises. It was   31
chemistry, biology. It was beautiful.

Oh, do you remember those sweet, almost innocent choices that the   32
Indian boys were forced to make?

Sixth Grade

Randy, the new Indian kid from the white town of Springdale, got into a   33
fight an hour after he first walked into the reservation school.

Stevie Flett called him out, called him a squawman, called him a pussy,   34
and called him a punk.

Randy and Stevie, and the rest of the Indian boys, walked out into the   35
playground.

---

[1] Housing and Urban Development, a US government department. —EDS.

"Throw the first punch," Stevie said as they squared off.   36

"No," Randy said.   37

"Throw the first punch," Stevie said again.   38

"No," Randy said again.   39

"Throw the first punch!" Stevie said for the third time, and Randy reared   40
back and pitched a knuckle fastball that broke Stevie's nose.

We all stood there in silence, in awe.   41

That was Randy, my soon-to-be first and best friend, who taught me the   42
most valuable lesson about living in the white world: *Always throw the first
punch*.

Seventh Grade

I leaned through the basement window of the HUD house and kissed the   43
white girl who would later be raped by her foster-parent father, who was also
white. They both lived on the reservation, though, and when the headlines
and stories filled the papers later, not one word was made of their color.

Just Indians being Indians, someone must have said somewhere and they   44
were wrong.

But on the day I leaned through the basement window of the HUD   45
house and kissed the white girl, I felt the good-byes I was saying to my entire
tribe. I held my lips tight against her lips, a dry, clumsy, and ultimately stupid kiss.

But I was saying good-bye to my tribe, to all the Indian girls and women I   46
might have loved, to all the Indian men who might have called me cousin,
even brother.

I kissed that white girl and when I opened my eyes, she was gone from the   47
reservation, and when I opened my eyes, I was gone from the reservation, living in a farm town where a beautiful white girl asked my name.

"Junior Polatkin," I said, and she laughed.   48

After that, no one spoke to me for another five hundred years.   49

Eighth Grade

At the farm town junior high, in the boys' bathroom, I could hear voices   50
from the girls' bathroom, nervous whispers of anorexia and bulimia. I could
hear the white girls' forced vomiting, a sound so familiar and natural to me
after years of listening to my father's hangovers.

"Give me your lunch if you're just going to throw it up," I said to one of   51
those girls once.

I sat back and watched them grow skinny from self-pity.   52

Back on the reservation, my mother stood in line to get us commodities.   53
We carried them home, happy to have food, and opened the canned beef that
even the dogs wouldn't eat.

But we ate it day after day and grew skinny from self-pity.   54

There is more than one way to starve.   55

Ninth Grade

At the farm town high school dance, after a basketball game in an over-   56
heated gym where I had scored twenty-seven points and pulled down thirteen
rebounds, I passed out during a slow song.

As my white friends revived me and prepared to take me to the emergency   57
room where doctors would later diagnose my diabetes, the Chicano teacher
ran up to us.

"Hey," he said. "What's that boy been drinking? I know all about these   58
Indian kids. They start drinking real young."

Sharing dark skin doesn't necessarily make two men brothers.   59

Tenth Grade

I passed the written test easily and nearly flunked the driving, but still   60
received my Washington State driver's license on the same day that Wally Jim
killed himself by driving his car into a pine tree.

No traces of alcohol in his blood, good job, wife and two kids.   61

"Why'd he do it?" asked a white Washington State trooper.   62

All the Indians shrugged their shoulders, looked down at the ground.   63

"Don't know," we all said, but when we look in the mirror, see the history   64
of our tribe in our eyes, taste failure in the tap water, and shake with old tears,
we understand completely.

Believe me, everything looks like a noose if you stare at it long enough.   65

Eleventh Grade

Last night I missed two free throws which would have won the game   66
against the best team in the state. The farm town high school I play for is
nicknamed the "Indians," and I'm probably the only actual Indian ever to play
for a team with such a mascot.

This morning I pick up the sports page and read the headline: INDIANS   67
LOSE AGAIN.

Go ahead and tell me none of this is supposed to hurt me very much.   68

Twelfth Grade

I walk down the aisle, valedictorian of this farm town high school, and my   69
cap doesn't fit because I've grown my hair longer than it's ever been. Later, I
stand as the school-board chairman recites my awards, accomplishments, and
scholarships.

I try to remain stoic for the photographers as I look toward the future.   70

Back home on the reservation, my former classmates graduate: a few can't   71
read, one or two are just given attendance diplomas, most look forward to the
parties. The bright students are shaken, frightened, because they don't know
what comes next.

They smile for the photographer as they look back toward tradition.   72

The tribal newspaper runs my photograph and the photograph of my for-   73
mer classmates side by side.

Postscript: Class Reunion

Victor said, "Why should we organize a reservation high school reunion?   74
My graduating class has a reunion every weekend at the Powwow Tavern."

Journal Writing

Alexie mingles positive and negative school experiences, each seeming almost to
grow out of the other. Write down some of your own memorable school experiences,
positive or negative. Which kind of memories seem to dominate? Are the experiences
connected? (To take your journal writing further, see "From Journal to Essay" on the
facing page.)

Questions on Meaning

1. What overall impression does Alexie create of life on the reservation? Point to
   specific EXAMPLES in the text that contribute to this impression.
2. Notice those places in the essay where Alexie describes how Native Americans
   face prejudice and negative stereotyping. What does this focus suggest about his
   PURPOSE?

3. The title "Indian Education" refers here to more than just formal schooling. What are some other implications of the title?
4. Alexie refers to his hair in the opening sentence of the essay and in the sections on second grade and twelfth grade. How, and of what, is his hair a SYMBOL?

Questions on Writing Strategy

1. In this essay Alexie offers thirteen scenes: one for each school grade and a post-script reunion. Why do you think he set these scenes up in separate sections and labeled them with headings, instead of, say, running the sections together and introducing each with a phrase like "During first grade" or "When I was in second grade"? What is the EFFECT of Alexie's narrative technique?
2. Each section of the essay ends with a brief paragraph, usually a single sentence. What common function do all of these conclusions perform? How do their functions vary, and why?
3. How does the section on the seventh grade, almost exactly in the middle of the essay, serve as a thematic transition?
4. Why do you think Alexie ends with the section "Postscript: Class Reunion"? What is the effect of this final image?
5. **OTHER METHODS.** At several points in the essay, Alexie uses COMPARISON AND CONTRAST. Locate at least two examples, and explain what each contributes to the essay.

Questions on Language

1. In paragraph 15 Alexie writes that his teacher said of him and his parents "Indians, indians, indians [. . .] without capitalization." What is his point?
2. At the end of the seventh grade section (par. 49), Alexie writes that "no one spoke to me for another five hundred years." What does he mean? What is the effect of this hyperbole? (See *Figures of speech* in Useful Terms if you need a definition of *hyperbole*.)
3. Describe the IRONY in paragraphs 67 and 68.
4. Notice the similarities between the pairs of sentences composing paragraphs 29 and 31 and paragraphs 70 and 72. What point does Alexie make with the similarities?
5. If any of the following words are unfamiliar, be sure to look them up in a dictionary: horn-rimmed (par. 1); symmetrical (5); scrawny (11); circulated, intercepted, confiscated (18); ultimately (45); anorexia, bulimia (50); commodities (53); diabetes (57); valedictorian (69).

Suggestions for Writing

1. **FROM JOURNAL TO ESSAY.** Write an essay about a particularly memorable aspect of your life as a student, whether positive, negative, or a mix of both. You might focus on a single event, a series of events over years, or perhaps an entire school year. As you relate your story, try to give your personal experience meaning for your readers.

2. Using Alexie's essay as a model, write an essay about significant moments that occurred in your life and that had in common a challenge or a struggle or an achievement that is or was important to you. You need not organize according to school years, nor need the events be school related. Do make sure that the common theme in the events and the significance of each event is clear to readers.

3. **CRITICAL WRITING.** Alexie is well known for injecting humor, sometimes very dark humor, into tales that might otherwise be unrelievedly bleak. Where do you see humor in "Indian Education"? Who or what, if anything, does Alexie poke fun at? How effective is the humor? Write an essay analyzing Alexie's use of humor, focusing your analysis on a single central idea of your own and supporting it with plenty of examples from Alexie's essay.

4. **CONNECTIONS.** Like Alexie's "Indian Education," Maya Angelou's "Champion of the World" (p. 86) and Amy Tan's "Fish Cheeks" (p. 92) also report experiences of being culturally and racially different from mainstream white America. Earlier "Connections" writing topics ask you to compare and contrast Angelou's and Tan's perceptions of what sets them apart from the dominant culture (p. 90) or their uses of narration to convey their differing POINTS OF VIEW (p. 94). Now bring Alexie into one of these comparisons with Angelou or Tan or both. Be sure to use examples from the essays to support your main idea.

Sherman Alexie on Writing

The humor woven into his work sometimes surprises first-time readers of Sherman Alexie. "One of the biggest misconceptions about Indians is that we're stoic," Alexie told Pam Lambert of *People Weekly*. "But humor is an essential part of our culture." The humor in Alexie's writing reflects its role in the lives of contemporary Native Americans, for whom, Alexie told Doug Marx of *Publishers Weekly*, "laughter is a ceremony. It's the way people cope."

Alexie does not avoid depicting the poverty, alcoholism, and despair faced by many Indians. Sometimes criticized by other Indians for portraying reservation life as hopeless, Alexie responded to Doug Marx: "I write what I know and I don't try to mythologize myself, which is what some seem to want, and which some Indian women and men writers are doing, this Earth Mother and Shaman Man thing, trying to create these 'authentic, traditional' Indians. We don't live our lives that way."

Alexie believes that as an American Indian writer he has a special responsibility "to tell the truth," as he put it to E. K. Caldwell in another interview. But, he continued, "Part of the danger in being an artist of whatever color is that you fall in love with your wrinkles. The danger is that if you fall in love with your wrinkles then you don't want to get rid of them. You start to glorify them and perpetuate them. If you write about pain, you can end up searching for more pain to write about, that kind of thing, that self-destructive route. We need to get away from that. We can write about pain and anger without having it consume us."

Alexie doesn't mind being typecast as a Native American writer. Speaking to Joel McNally of *The Writer* magazine, Alexie said, "If you object to being defined by your race and culture, you are saying there is something wrong with writing about your race and your culture. I'm not going to let others define me. [. . .] If I write it, it's an Indian novel. If I wrote about Martians, it would be an Indian novel. If I wrote about the Amish, it would be an Indian novel. That's who I am."

For Discussion

1. What do you think Alexie means by the "Earth Mother and Shaman Man thing" that he disparages in the work of some Indian writers? Why does he disapprove of it?
2. Judging from his essay "Indian Education," how would you say Alexie follows his own advice to "write about the pain and anger without having it consume us"?

BARBARA HUTTMANN

BARBARA HUTTMANN is a registered nurse, a health-care administrator, and a writer on health-care issues. Born in 1935, she received a BS in nursing and an MS in nursing administration. She has directed a consulting firm for hospitals, nursing organizations, and health-care consumers, and she is currently a technical writer for a medical software company. Huttmann has also published two books, *The Patient's Advocate* (1981) and *Code Blue: A Nurse's True-Life Story* (1982). She lives in California.

A Crime of Compassion

As a nurse, Huttmann has had to care for many people who are dying. In this essay from a 1983 *Newsweek*, Huttmann tells of one such patient, Mac, whose rapid decline she witnessed and whose death she finally did nothing to prevent. She uses narration to explain herself and to argue that patients like Mac have the right to choose death.

"Murderer," a man shouted. "God help patients who get *you* for a nurse." 1

"What gives you the right to play God?" another one asked. 2

It was the Phil Donahue show where the guest is a fatted calf and the audi- 3
ence a two-hundred-strong flock of vultures hungering to pick at the bones. I had told them about Mac, one of my favorite cancer patients. "We resuscitated him fifty-two times in just one month. I refused to resuscitate him again. I simply sat there and held his hand while he died."

There wasn't time to explain that Mac was a young, witty, macho cop who 4
walked into the hospital with thirty-two pounds of attack equipment, looking as if he could single-handedly protect the whole city, if not the entire state. "Can't get rid of this cough," he said. Otherwise, he felt great.

Before the day was over, tests confirmed that he had lung cancer. And 5
before the year was over, I loved him, his wife, Maura, and their three kids as if they were my own. All the nurses loved him. And we all battled his disease for six months without ever giving death a thought. Six months isn't such a long time in the whole scheme of things, but it was long enough to see him lose his youth, his wit, his macho, his hair, his bowel and bladder control, his sense of taste and smell, and his ability to do the slightest thing for himself. It was also long enough to watch Maura's transformation from a young woman into a haggard, beaten old lady.

When Mac had wasted away to a sixty-pound skeleton kept alive by liq- 6
uid food we poured down a tube, i.v. solutions we dripped into his veins, and oxygen we piped to a mask on his face, he begged us: "Mercy . . . for God's sake, please just let me go."

The first time he stopped breathing, the nurse pushed the button that 7 calls a "code blue" throughout the hospital and sends a team rushing to resuscitate the patient. Each time he stopped breathing, sometimes two or three times in one day, the code team came again. The doctors and technicians worked their miracles and walked away. The nurses stayed to wipe the saliva that drooled from his mouth, irrigate the big craters of bedsores that covered his hips, suction the lung fluids that threatened to drown him, clean the feces that burned his skin like lye, pour the liquid food down the tube attached to his stomach, put pillows between his knees to ease the bone-on-bone pain, turn him every hour to keep the bedsores from getting worse, and change his gown and linen every two hours to keep him from being soaked in perspiration.

At night I went home and tried to scrub away the smell of decaying flesh 8 that seemed woven into the fabric of my uniform. It was in my hair, the upholstery of my car—there was no washing it away. And every night I prayed that Mac would die, that his agonized eyes would never again plead with me to let him die.

Every morning I asked his doctor for a "no-code" order. Without that 9 order, we had to resuscitate every patient who stopped breathing. His doctor was one of several who believe we must extend life as long as we have the means and knowledge to do it. To not do it is to be liable for negligence, at least in the eyes of many people, including some nurses. I thought about what it would be like to stand before a judge, accused of murder, if Mac stopped breathing and I didn't call a code.

And after the fifty-second code, when Mac was still lucid enough to beg 10 for death again, and Maura was crumbled in my arms again, and when no amount of pain medication stilled his moaning and agony, I wondered about a spiritual judge. Was all this misery and suffering supposed to be building character or infusing us all with the sense of humility that comes from impotence?

Had we, the whole medical community, become so arrogant that we 11 believed in the illusion of salvation through science? Had we become so self-righteous that we thought meddling in God's work was our duty, our moral imperative and our legal obligation? Did we really believe that we had the right to force "life" on a suffering man who had begged for the right to die?

Such questions haunted me more than ever early one morning when 12 Maura went home to change her clothes and I was bathing Mac. He had been still for so long, I thought he at last had the blessed relief of coma. Then he opened his eyes and moaned, "Pain . . . no more . . . Barbara . . . do something . . . God, let me go."

The desperation in his eyes and voice riddled me with guilt. "I'll stop," I 13 told him as I injected the pain medication.

I sat on the bed and held Mac's hands in mine. He pressed his bony fingers   14
against my hand and muttered, "Thanks." Then there was one soft sigh and I
felt his hands go cold in mine. "Mac?" I whispered, as I waited for his chest to
rise and fall again.

A clutch of panic banded my chest, drew my finger to the code button,   15
urged me to do something, anything . . . but sit there alone with death. I kept
one finger on the button, without pressing it, as a waxen pallor slowly transformed his face from person to empty shell. Nothing I've ever done in my forty-
seven years has taken so much effort as it took *not* to press that code button.

Eventually, when I was as sure as I could be that the code team would fail   16
to bring him back, I entered the legal twilight zone and pushed the button.
The team tried. And while they were trying, Maura walked into the room and
shrieked, "No . . . don't let them do this to him . . . for God's sake . . . please,
no more."

Cradling her in my arms was like cradling myself, Mac, and all those   17
patients and nurses who had been in this place before, who do the best they
can in a death-denying society.

So a TV audience accused me of murder. Perhaps I am guilty. If a doctor   18
had written a no-code order, which is the only *legal* alternative, would he have
felt any less guilty? Until there is legislation making it a criminal act to code
a patient who has requested the right to die, we will all of us risk the same fate
as Mac. For whatever reason, we developed the means to prolong life, and
now we are forced to use it. We do not have the right to die.

Journal Writing

Respond to Huttmann's essay. Consider: Did Huttmann do the right thing? Does a
terminally ill patient have a right to choose death? Should a doctor or anyone else be
legally empowered to overrule a patient's wish for death? (To take your journal writing further, see "From Journal to Essay" on the facing page.)

Questions on Meaning

1. Is Huttmann's PURPOSE in this essay personal (wanting to justify her act) or social
   (wanting to establish the right to die) or both? Explain.
2. What is the contradiction in the title of the essay?
3. What personal risk does Huttmann assume when she decides not to press the button? What does she mean by "legal twilight zone" (par. 16)?
4. Is Huttmann confident that she made the right decision?
5. Where does Huttmann state her THESIS?

Questions on Writing Strategy

1. Why does Huttmann begin the essay the way she does? What do we ASSUME about the nurse referred to in the first sentence, and at what point do we begin to question that assumption?
2. What is the TONE of this piece? How does Huttmann manage to avoid the SENTI-MENTALITY one might expect of an essay on this subject? (Cite specific EXAMPLES from the text.)
3. How does the detail about resuscitating Mac fifty-two times in one month (par. 3) contribute to the effectiveness of Huttmann's ARGUMENT?
4. **OTHER METHODS.** This essay illustrates how narrative can help promote an argument. Summarize Huttmann's argument. What does she gain by supporting it with a story?

Questions on Language

1. Consult a dictionary for any of the following words whose meanings you are un-sure of: resuscitate (par. 3); haggard (5); irrigate, suction, feces, lye, bedsores (7); lucid, infusing, impotence (10); imperative (11); riddled (13); banded, pallor (15).
2. Some of the words in the vocabulary list above are medical terminology, but per-haps fewer than one would expect, given the subject. What about her AUDIENCE (originally readers of *Newsweek* magazine) would influence Huttmann's use of terms?
3. Find words in the essay that illustrate Huttmann's particular fondness for Mac. What difference does the closeness of their relationship make to her argument?
4. Explain the metaphor in paragraph 3. (See *Figures of speech* in Useful Terms for a definition of *metaphor*.)

Suggestions for Writing

1. **FROM JOURNAL TO ESSAY.** Elaborating on the opinions and beliefs you expressed in your journal, write an essay arguing for or against the right of a terminally ill patient to choose death. You may, like Huttmann, support your argument with a personal narrative. Or you may argue on other grounds—religious, moral, humanitarian, medical, and so on. In your argument, be sure to acknowledge the views of those who might oppose you, as you understand those views. This acknowledgment will help show your fairness and reach out to more readers.
2. Think back to a moment in your life when you had to make a difficult choice, one with important consequences. (The stakes need not have been as high as in Huttmann's essay.) What were the circumstances? What was the result of the decision you made? In a narrative essay, start by stating the choice you had to make and its implications; then go back and relate the circumstances; and, finally, conclude by explaining the results of your choice and its effectiveness.
3. Huttmann presents two opposed ideas of God's role in human life and death. For the member of Phil Donahue's audience, only God can decide to stop someone's life; anyone who tries to make that decision is "play[ing] God" (par. 2). For Huttmann, in contrast, sustaining life artificially is "meddling in God's work"

(par. 11). Which view do you agree with, and why? (If you'd rather not debate the role of God, try "nature" instead.)

4. **CRITICAL WRITING.** When they take the Hippocratic oath, physicians promise to "do no harm." It could be argued that neither choice available to Huttmann avoids harm to her patient. Given the circumstances of the patient she describes, did she choose the less harmful alternative? Why, or why not? Can your argument be generalized: Is it applicable in every case?

5. **CONNECTIONS.** Barbara Huttmann and Barbara Lazear Ascher, in "On Compassion" (p. 183), both examine, as Ascher puts it, "the conditions that finally give birth to empathy, the mother of compassion." Write a well-detailed narrative about a time when you helped someone or were helped by someone. Use this essay as an opportunity to examine your own ideas about compassion: How do you define the word? What causes compassionate feelings?

EDGAR ALLAN POE

EDGAR ALLAN POE (1809–49) was the first American writer to gain a reputation outside the United States. His short stories and poems, famously mysterious or frightening, were popular both at home and in Europe, and his literary criticism helped shape the course of French poetry. Poe was born in Boston, grew up in England and Virginia, and died in Baltimore at only forty years of age. His short life was often clouded by family troubles, disciplinary problems (he was expelled from West Point), and heavy drinking; yet he held jobs on magazines, wrote volumes of criticism, published collections of poetry, and crafted immortal stories. Poe is perhaps best known for such stories as "The Tell-Tale Heart" (printed here), "The Pit and the Pendulum" (1843), and "The Cask of Amontillado" (1846), as well as for his poems "Annabel Lee" (1849, addressed to his recently deceased wife) and "The Raven" (1845). In honor of the famous poet who died there, the city of Baltimore in 1996 named its football team the Baltimore Ravens, thus making Poe, as the humorist Russell Baker observed, "the first literary man to break into professional sports."

The Tell-Tale Heart

This masterpiece of paranoid terror, first published in 1843, uses narration not only to entertain us but also to tell us something of human nature. If you've never read the story before, bear with the occasionally old-fashioned style until you swing into the narrator's groove (as you certainly will). If you have read the story, read it again just for the pleasure, noticing how Poe's narrative technique pulls you in and along.

True!—nervous—very, very dreadfully nervous I had been and am; but why *will* you say that I am mad? The disease had sharpened my senses—not destroyed—not dulled them. Above all was the sense of hearing acute. I heard all things in the heaven and in the earth. I heard many things in hell. How, then, am I mad? Hearken! and observe how healthily—how calmly I can tell you the whole story.

It is impossible to say how first the idea entered my brain; but once conceived, it haunted me day and night. Object there was none. Passion there was none. I loved the old man. He had never wronged me. He had never given me insult. For his gold I had no desire. I think it was his eye! yes, it was this! One of his eyes resembled that of a vulture—a pale blue eye, with a film over it. Whenever it fell upon me, my blood ran cold; and so by degrees—very gradually—I made up my mind to take the life of the old man, and thus rid myself of the eye for ever.

Now this is the point. You fancy me mad. Madmen know nothing. But 3
you should have seen *me*. You should have seen how wisely I proceeded —
with what caution — with what foresight — with what dissimulation I went to
work! I was never kinder to the old man than during the whole week before I
killed him. And every night, about midnight, I turned the latch of his door
and opened it — oh, so gently! And then, when I had made an opening sufficient for my head, I put in a dark lantern, all closed, closed, so that no light
shone out, and then I thrust in my head. Oh, you would have laughed to see
how cunningly I thrust it in! I moved it slowly — very, very slowly, so that I
might not disturb the old man's sleep. It took me an hour to place my whole
head within the opening so far that I could see him as he lay upon his bed.
Ha — would a madman have been so wise as this? And then, when my head
was well in the room, I undid the lantern cautiously — oh, so cautiously —
cautiously (for the hinges creaked) — I undid it just so much that a single thin
ray fell upon the vulture eye. And this I did for seven long nights — every
night just after midnight — but I found the eye always closed; and so it was
impossible to do the work; for it was not the old man who vexed me, but his
Evil Eye. And every morning, when the day broke, I went boldly into the
chamber, and spoke courageously to him, calling him by name in a hearty
tone, and inquiring how he had passed the night. So you see he would have
been a very profound old man, indeed, to suspect that every night, just at
twelve, I looked in upon him while he slept.

Upon the eighth night I was more than usually cautious in opening the 4
door. A watch's minute hand moves more quickly than did mine. Never
before that night had I *felt* the extent of my own powers — of my sagacity. I
could scarcely contain my feelings of triumph. To think that there I was, opening the door, little by little, and he not even to dream of my secret deeds or
thoughts. I fairly chuckled at the idea; and perhaps he heard me; for he moved
on the bed suddenly, as if startled. Now you may think that I drew back — but
no. His room was as black as pitch with the thick darkness (for the shutters
were close fastened, through fear of robbers), and so I knew that he could not
see the opening of the door, and I kept pushing it on steadily, steadily.

I had my head in, and was about to open the lantern, when my thumb 5
slipped upon the tin fastening, and the old man sprang up in the bed, crying
out — "Who's there?"

I kept quite still and said nothing. For a whole hour I did not move a 6
muscle, and in the meantime I did not hear him lie down. He was still sitting
up in the bed listening; — just as I have done, night after night, hearkening to
the death watches in the wall.

Presently I heard a slight groan, and I knew it was the groan of mortal 7
terror. It was not a groan of pain or of grief — oh, no! — it was the low stifled

sound that arises from the bottom of the soul when overcharged with awe. I knew the sound well. Many a night, just at midnight, when all the world slept, it has welled up from my own bosom, deepening with its dreadful echo, the terrors that distracted me. I say I knew it well. I knew what the old man felt, and pitied him, although I chuckled at heart. I knew that he had been lying awake ever since the first slight noise, when he had turned in the bed. His fears had been ever since growing upon him. He had been trying to fancy them causeless, but could not. He had been saying to himself—"It is nothing but the wind in the chimney—it is only a mouse crossing the floor," or "it is merely a cricket which has made a single chirp." Yes, he has been trying to comfort himself with these suppositions; but he had found all in vain. *All in vain*; because Death, in approaching him, had stalked with his black shadow before him, and enveloped the victim. And it was the mournful influence of the unperceived shadow that caused him to feel—although he neither saw nor heard—to *feel* the presence of my head within the room.

When I had waited a long time, very patiently, without hearing him lie down, I resolved to open a little—a very, very little crevice in the lantern. So I opened it—you cannot imagine how stealthily, stealthily—until, at length, a single dim ray, like the thread of the spider, shot from out the crevice and full upon the vulture eye. 8

It was open—wide, wide open—and I grew furious as I gazed upon it. I saw it with perfect distinctness—all a dull blue, with a hideous veil over it that chilled the very marrow in my bones, but I could see nothing else of the old man's face or person: for I had directed the ray as if by instinct, precisely upon the damned spot. 9

And now have I not told you that what you mistake for madness is but over-acuteness of the senses?—now, I say, there came to my ears a low, dull, quick sound, such as a watch makes when enveloped in cotton. I knew *that* sound well too. It was the beating of the old man's heart. It increased my fury, as the beating of a drum stimulates the soldier into courage. 10

But even yet I refrained and kept still. I scarcely breathed. I held the lantern motionless. I tried how steadily I could maintain the ray upon the eye. Meantime the hellish tattoo of the heart increased. It grew quicker and quicker, and louder and louder every instant. The old man's terror *must* have been extreme! It grew louder, I say, louder every moment!—do you mark me well? I have told you that I am nervous: so I am. And now at the dead hour of the night, amid the dreadful silence of that old house, so strange a noise as this excited me to uncontrollable terror. Yet, for some minutes longer I refrained and stood still. But the beating grew louder, louder! I thought the heart must burst. And now a new anxiety seized me—the sound would be heard by a neighbor! The old man's hour had come! With a loud yell, I threw open the 11 lantern and leaped into the room. He shrieked once—once only. In an instant I dragged him to the floor, and pulled the heavy bed over him. I then smiled gaily, to find the deed so far done. But, for many minutes, the heart beat on with a muffled sound. This, however, did not vex me; it would not be heard through the wall. At length it ceased. The old man was dead. I removed the bed and examined the corpse. Yes, he was stone, stone dead. I placed my hand upon the heart and held it there many minutes. There was no pulsation. He was stone dead. His eye would trouble me no more.

If still you think me mad, you will think so no longer when I describe the   12
wise precautions I took for the concealment of the body. The night waned, and I worked hastily, but in silence. First of all I dismembered the corpse. I cut off the head and the arms and the legs.

I then took up three planks from the flooring of the chamber, and   13
deposited all between the scantlings. I then replaced the boards so cleverly, so cunningly, that no human eye—not even *his*—could have detected anything wrong. There was nothing to wash out—no stain of any kind—no blood-spot whatever. I had been too wary for that. A tub had caught all—ha! ha!

When I had made an end of these labors, it was four o'clock—still dark   14
as midnight. As the bell sounded the hour, there came a knocking at the street door. I went down to open it with a light heart—for what had I *now* to fear? There entered three men, who introduced themselves, with perfect suavity, as officers of the police. A shriek had been heard by a neighbor during the night; suspicion of foul play had been aroused; information had been lodged at the police office, and they (the officers) had been deputed to search the premises.

I smiled—for *what* had I to fear? I bade the gentlemen welcome. The   15
shriek, I said, was my own in a dream. The old man, I mentioned, was absent in the country. I took my visitors all over the house. I bade them search—search *well*. I led them, at length, to *his* chamber. I showed them his treasures, secure, undisturbed. In the enthusiasm of my confidence, I brought chairs into the room, and desired them *here* to rest from their fatigues, while I myself, in the wild audacity of my perfect triumph, placed my own seat upon the very spot beneath which reposed the corpse of the victim.

The officers were satisfied. My *manner* had convinced them. I was sin-   16
gularly at ease. They sat, and while I answered cheerily, they chatted famil-iar things. But, ere long, I felt myself getting pale and wished them gone. My head ached, and I fancied a ringing in my ears: but still they sat and still chatted. The ringing became more distinct:—it continued and became more distinct: I talked more freely to get rid of the feeling: but it continued and gained definitiveness—until, at length, I found that the noise was *not* within my ears.

No doubt I now grew *very* pale;—but I talked more fluently, and with a   17
heightened voice. Yet the sound increased—and what could I do? It was *a
low, dull, quick sound—much such a sound as a watch makes when enveloped in
cotton*. I gasped for breath—and yet the officers heard it not. I talked more
quickly—more vehemently; but the noise steadily increased. I arose and
argued about trifles, in a high key and with violent gesticulations, but the
noise steadily increased. Why *would* they not be gone? I paced the floor to and
fro with heavy strides, as if excited to fury by the observation of the men—but
the noise steadily increased. Oh God! what *could* I do? I foamed—I raved—
I swore! I swung the chair upon which I had been sitting, and grated it upon
the boards, but the noise arose over all and continually increased. It grew
louder—louder—*louder!* And still the men chatted pleasantly, and smiled.
Was it possible they heard not? Almighty God—no, no! They heard!—they
suspected!—they *knew!*—they were making a mockery of my horror—this
I thought, and this I think. But any thing was better than this agony! Any
thing was more tolerable than this derision! I could bear those hypocritical
smiles no longer! I felt that I must scream or die—and now—again!—hark!
louder! louder! louder! *louder!*—

"Villains!" I shrieked, "dissemble no more! I admit the deed!—tear up   18
the planks—here, here!—it is the beating of his hideous heart!"

Journal Writing

Poe's story of madness and criminality is a classic of American literature. How would
you account for its appeal? Why do you think so many people are drawn to stories of
crime, whether from fiction or from life? Write about an actual crime that interests
you, setting down the facts as completely and OBJECTIVELY as you can. If you need ideas
for crimes, try looking in a tabloid newspaper or watching a true-crime program on
television. (To take your journal writing further, see "From Journal to Essay" on the
next page.)

Questions on Meaning

1. On what basis does the narrator claim to be sane? Is he convincing?
2. In paragraph 7 the narrator empathizes with his victim's fears. How does he know
   so much of what the old man feels?
3. Why does the narrator choose to sit directly above the buried heart during his
   interview with the police?
4. Why does the narrator unnecessarily give himself away in the end?
5. What, in your opinion, was Poe's PURPOSE in writing this story?

Questions on Writing Strategy

1. What is the purpose of the opening paragraph? Why does Poe delay the opening of the story?
2. What is the EFFECT of the narrator's addressing the reader directly as *you* (for example, par. 3)?
3. What is the IRONY in the fact that the old man's shutters were always closed (par. 4)?
4. Note the conciseness of the narration in the second half of paragraph 14. From whose POINT OF VIEW is the story being told here? How do you know?
5. **OTHER METHODS.** The narrator complains that he suffers from "over-acuteness of the senses" (par. 10), an affliction that gives Poe an opportunity for rich DESCRIPTION. ANALYZE Poe's treatment of the sense of sound in paragraph 11. How does Poe play on the contrast between sound and silence, stillness and movement, in this paragraph?

Questions on Language

1. What effect is created by Poe's frequent use of repetition—for instance, "slowly—very, very slowly" (par. 3); "stealthily, stealthily" (8); "The old man was dead. [. . .] Yes, he was stone, stone dead. [. . .] He was stone dead" (11)? Is this bad prose? Why, or why not?
2. Poe is a master of forceful FIGURES OF SPEECH. In paragraph 4 he writes, "A watch's minute hand moves more quickly than did mine." Substitute the word *hour* for *minute*. Which is more effective, and why? What other powerful figures of speech can you find in the story?
3. What is the effect of Poe's use of italics throughout the story, especially in paragraph 17? Do any of the choices of italicized words seem strange or arbitrary?
4. This story contains a number of words that may be unfamiliar, including a couple of familiar words used in unfamiliar ways (these are asterisked). Look up any words you're unsure of: hearken (par. 1); foresight, dissimulation, cunningly, vexed (3); sagacity (4); stifled, suppositions, mournful (7); crevice, stealthily (8); refrained, tattoo,* mark* (11); dismembered (12); scantlings (13); suavity, deputed (14); bade, fatigues, audacity (15); ere (16); vehemently, gesticulations, derision, hypocritical, hark (17); dissemble (18).

Suggestions for Writing

1. **FROM JOURNAL TO ESSAY.** Retell the events of the crime you wrote about in your journal, taking the point of view of the criminal. Choose any psychology you like for the criminal: articulate but mad (like the narrator of Poe's story), guilt-ridden, unjustly accused—use your imagination. Like Poe, you will need to add IMAGES and details to spice up the objective account in your journal.
2. Look up the clinical DEFINITIONS of *obsessive-compulsive disorder* and *paranoia* in an encyclopedia or a psychology textbook. How well does Poe's narrator fit either of these definitions? Make a case for a clinical basis to the narrator's madness,

drawing on both the narrator's own descriptions of his mental states and faculties and the textbook definitions of the two mental disorders.

3. **CRITICAL WRITING.** Notice how much effort Poe devotes to recounting an event as simple as the opening of a door or lantern. How does Poe manage to keep readers on the edge of their seats while working on such a microscopic level? How does he indicate the passing of time? How does he create SUSPENSE? In a brief essay, analyze the rhythm of Poe's narrative, paying close attention to TRANSITIONS.

4. **CONNECTIONS.** In "Safe-Sex Lies" (p. 442) Meghan Daum writes about a very different kind of paranoia from that of Poe's narrator—what she sees as the unreasonable fear of AIDS among low-risk groups. Although it will be easier to CONTRAST than to COMPARE the two selections, try to find as many common points as you can between the paranoia of Poe's narrator and that described by Daum.

Edgar Allan Poe on Writing

Writing in *Graham's Magazine* in 1842, Edgar Allan Poe commented on the stories of his contemporary Nathaniel Hawthorne and in the process revealed much about his own views of narration. What he says could apply equally to fiction and to nonfiction. (It could also apply equally to female and to male writers. Poe uses the generalized *he,* once universally understood to mean "he or she.")

Poe emphasizes that "in almost all classes of composition, the unity of effect or impression is a point of the greatest importance," something achievable in "the short prose narrative, requiring from a half-hour to one or two hours in its perusal. [. . .] In the brief tale, [. . .] the author is enabled to carry out the fullness of his intention, be it what it may. During the hour of perusal the soul of the reader is at the writer's control. [. . .]

"A skillful literary artist has constructed a tale. If wise, he has not fashioned his thoughts to accommodate his incidents; but having conceived, with deliberate care, a certain unique or single *effect* to be wrought out, [. . .] he then combines such events as may best aid him in establishing this preconceived effect. If his very initial sentence tends not to the outbringing of this effect, then he has failed in his first step. In the whole composition there should be no word written, of which the tendency, direct or indirect, is not to the one pre-established design. And by such means, with such care and skill, a picture is at length painted which leaves in the mind of him who contemplates it with a kindred art, a sense of the fullest satisfaction."

For Discussion

1. Why, according to Poe, is the "unity of effect" so important to a narrative?
2. What role do you see for revision in Poe's narrative process? Do you think he means that the first sentence must be perfect the first time it's written? Why, or why not?

ADDITIONAL WRITING TOPICS

Narration

1. Write a narrative with one of the following as your subject. It may be (as your instructor may advise) either a first-PERSON memoir or a story written in the third person, observing the experience of someone else. Decide before you begin what your PURPOSE is and whether you are writing (1) an anecdote; (2) an essay consisting mainly of a single narrative; or (3) an essay that includes more than one story.

   A memorable experience from your early life
   A lesson you learned the hard way
   A trip into unfamiliar territory
   An embarrassing moment that taught you something
   A monumental misunderstanding
   An accident
   An unexpected encounter
   A story about a famous person, or someone close to you
   A conflict or contest
   A destructive storm
   An assassination attempt
   A historical event of significance

2. Tell a true story of your early or recent school days, either humorous or serious, relating a struggle you experienced (or still experience) in school.

Note: Writing topics combining narration and description appear on pages 172–73.

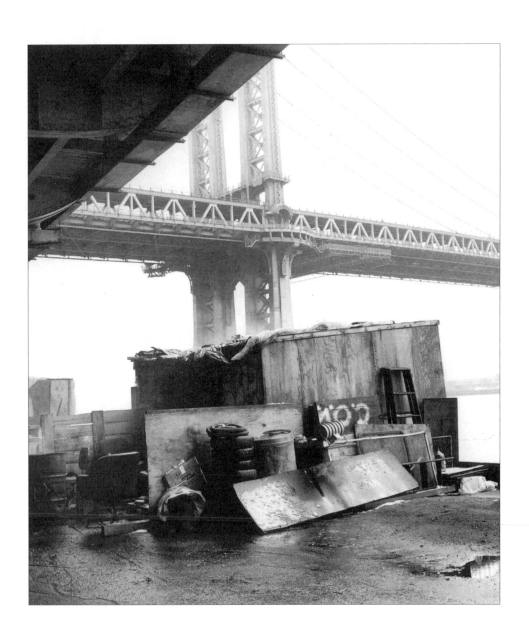

5

DESCRIPTION
Writing with Your Senses

Description in a photograph

Margaret Morton photographs homeless communities in New York City. This photograph, titled *Doug and Mizan's House, East River, 1993,* depicts a make-shift dwelling on a Manhattan riverbank. Consider Morton's photograph as a work of description—revealing a thing through the perceptions of the senses. What do you see through her eyes? What is the house made of? What do the overhanging structure on the upper left and the bridge behind the house add to the impression of the house? If you were standing in the picture, in front of the house, what might you hear or smell? If you touched the house, what textures might you feel? What main idea do you think Morton wants this photograph to convey?

THE METHOD

Like narration, DESCRIPTION is a familiar method of expression, already a working part of you. In any talk-fest with friends, you probably do your share of describing. You depict in words someone you've met by describing her clothes, the look on her face, the way she walks. You describe somewhere you've been, something you admire, something you just can't abide. In a diary or in e-mail to a friend, you describe your college (cast concrete buildings, crowded walks, pigeons rattling their wings); or perhaps you describe your brand-new secondhand car, from the snakelike glitter of its hubcaps to the odd antiques in its trunk, bequeathed by its previous owner. You hardly can live a day without describing (or hearing described) some person, place, or thing. Small wonder that, in written discourse, description is almost as indispensable as paper.

Description reports the testimony of your senses. It invites your readers to imagine that they, too, not only see but perhaps also hear, taste, smell, and touch the subject you describe. Usually, you write a description for either of two PURPOSES: (1) to convey information without bias or emotion; or (2) to convey it with feeling.

In writing with the first purpose in mind, you write an OBJECTIVE (or *impartial, public,* or *functional*) description. You describe your subject so clearly and exactly that your reader will understand it or recognize it, and you leave your emotions out. Technical or scientific descriptive writing is usually objective: a manual detailing the parts of an internal combustion engine, a biology report on a species of frog. You write this kind of description in sending a friend directions for finding your house: "Look for the green shutters on the windows and a new garbage can at the front door." Although in a personal letter describing your house you might very well become emotionally involved with it (and call it, perhaps, a "fleabag"), in writing an objective description your purpose is not to convey your feelings. You are trying to make the house easily recognized.

The other type of descriptive writing is SUBJECTIVE (or *emotional, personal,* or *impressionistic*). This is the kind included in a magazine advertisement for a new car. It's what you write in your e-mail to a friend setting forth what your college is like—whether you are pleased or displeased with it. In this kind of description, you may use biases and personal feelings—in fact, they are essential. Let us consider a splendid example: a subjective description of a storm at sea. Charles Dickens, in his memoir *American Notes,* conveys his passenger's-eye view of an Atlantic steamship on a morning when the ocean is wild:

> Imagine the ship herself, with every pulse and artery of her huge body swollen and bursting [. . .] sworn to go on or die. Imagine the wind howling, the sea roaring, the rain beating; all in furious array against her. Picture the

sky both dark and wild, and the clouds in fearful sympathy with the waves, making another ocean in the air. Add to all this the clattering on deck and down below; the tread of hurried feet; the loud hoarse shouts of seamen; the gurgling in and out of water through the scuppers; with every now and then the striking of a heavy sea upon the planks above, with the deep, dead, heavy sound of thunder heard within a vault; and there is the head wind of that January morning.

    I say nothing of what may be called the domestic noises of the ship; such as the breaking of glass and crockery, the tumbling down of stewards, the gambols, overhead, of loose casks and truant dozens of bottled porter, and the very remarkable and far from exhilarating sounds raised in their various staterooms by the seventy passengers who were too ill to get up to breakfast.

Notice how many *sounds* are included in this primarily ear-minded description. We can infer how Dickens feels about the storm. It is a terrifying event that reduces the interior of the vessel to chaos; and yet the writer (in hearing the loose barrels and beer bottles merrily gambol, in finding humor in the seasick passengers' plight) apparently delights in it. Writing subjectively, he intrudes his feelings. Think of what a starkly different description of the very same storm the captain might set down—objectively—in the ship's log: "At 0600 hours, watch reported a wind from due north of 70 knots. White-caps were noticed, in height two ells above the bow. Below deck, much gear was reported adrift, and ten casks of ale were broken and their staves strewn about. Mr. Liam Jones, chief steward, suffered a compound fracture of the left leg. . . ." But Dickens, not content simply to record information, strives to ensure that the mind's eye is dazzled and the mind's ear regaled.

    Description is usually found in the company of other methods of writing. Often, for instance, it will enliven NARRATION and make the people in the story and the setting unmistakably clear. Writing an ARGUMENT in his essay "Why Don't We Complain?" (p. 543), William F. Buckley, Jr., begins with a description of eighty suffering commuters perspiring in an overheated train; the description makes the argument more powerful. Description will help a writer in examining the EFFECTS of a flood, or in COMPARING AND CONTRAST-ING two towns. Keep the method of description in mind when you come to try expository and argumentative writing.

THE PROCESS

Purpose, Audience, and Dominant Impression

    Understand, first of all, why you are writing about your subject and thus what kind of description is called for. Is it appropriate to perceive and report without emotion or bias—and thus write an objective description? Or is it appropriate to express your personal feelings as well as your perceptions—and thus write a subjective description?

Give a little thought to your AUDIENCE. What do your readers need to be told, if they are to share the perceptions you would have them share, if they are clearly to behold what you want them to? If, let's say, you are describing a downtown street on a Saturday night for an audience of fellow students who live in the same city and know it well, then you need not dwell on the street's familiar geography. What must you tell? Only those details that make the place different on a Saturday night. But if you are remembering your home city, and writing for readers who don't know it, you'll need to establish a few central landmarks to sketch (in their minds) an unfamiliar street on a Saturday night.

Before you begin to write a description, go look at your subject. If that is not possible, your next best course is to spend a few minutes imagining the subject until, in your mind's eye, you can see every flyspeck on it.

Then, having fixed your subject in mind, ask yourself which of its features you'll need to report to your particular audience, for your particular purpose. Ask, "What am I out to accomplish? What main impression of my subject am I trying to give?" Let your description, as a whole, convey this one DOMINANT IMPRESSION. If you plan to write a subjective description of an old house, lay-ing weight on its spooky atmosphere for readers you wish to make shiver, then you might mention its squeaking bats and its shadowy halls, leaving out any reference to its busy swimming pool and the stomping dance music that bil-lows from its interior. If, however, you are describing the house in a classified ad, for an audience of possible buyers, you might focus instead on its eat-in kitchen, working fireplace, and proximity to public transportation. Details have to be carefully selected. Feel no grim duty to include every perceptible detail. To do so would only invite chaos—or perhaps, for the reader, mere tedium. Pick out the features that matter most.

Your dominant impression is like the THESIS of your description—the main idea about your subject that you want readers to take away with them. When you use description to explain or to argue, it's usually a good strategy to state that dominant impression outright, tying it to your essay's thesis or a part of it. In a biology report on a species of frog, for instance, you might preface your description with a statement like this one:

> A number of unique features distinguish this frog from others in the order Anura.

Or in an argument in favor of cleaning a local toxic-waste site, you might begin with a description of the site and then state your point about it:

> This landscape is as poisonous as it looks, for underneath its barren crust are enough toxic chemicals to sicken a small village.

When you use subjective description more for its own sake—to show the reader a place or a person, to evoke feelings—you needn't always state your dominant impression as a THESIS SENTENCE, as long as the impression is there dictating the details.

Organization

You can organize a description in several ways. In depicting the storm at sea—a subjective description—Charles Dickens sorts out the pandemonium for us. He groups the various sounds into two classes: those of sea and sailors, and the "domestic noises" of the ship's passengers—their smashing dishes, their rolling bottles, the crashing of stewards who wait on them.

Other writers of description rely on their POINT OF VIEW to help them arrange details—the physical angle from which they're perceiving and describing. In the previous chapter, on narration, we spoke of point of view: how essential it is for a story to have a narrator—one who, from a certain position, reports what takes place. A description, too, needs a consistent point of view: that of an observer who stays put and observes steadily. From this point of view, you can make a carefully planned inspection tour of your subject, moving spatially (from left to right, from near to far, from top to bottom, from center to periphery), or perhaps moving from prominent objects to tiny ones, from dull to bright, from commonplace to extraordinary—or vice versa.

The plan for you is the one that best fulfills your purpose, arranging details so that the reader firmly receives the impression you mean to convey. If you were to describe, for instance, a chapel in the middle of a desert, you might begin with the details of the lonely terrain. Then, as if approaching the chapel with the aid of a zoom lens, you might detail its exterior and then go on inside. That might be a workable method to write a description *if* you wanted to create the dominant impression of the chapel as an island of beauty and feeling in the midst of desolation. Say, however, that you had a different impression in mind: to emphasize the spirituality of the chapel's interior. You might then begin your description inside the structure, perhaps with its most prominent feature, the stained glass windows. You might mention the surrounding desert later in your description, but only incidentally.

Whatever method you follow in arranging details, stick with it all the way through. Don't start out describing a group of cats by going from old cats to kittens, then switch in the middle of your description and line up the cats according to color. If your arrangement would cause any difficulty for the reader, you need to rearrange your details. If a writer, in describing a pet shop, should skip about wildly from clerks to cats to customers to cat food to customers to cat food to clerks, the reader may quickly be lost. Instead, the writer might group clerks together with customers, and cats together with cat food (or in some other clear order). But suppose (the writer might protest) it's a wildly confused pet shop I'm trying to describe? No matter—the writer nevertheless has to write in an orderly manner, if the reader is to understand. Dickens describes a scene of shipboard chaos, yet his prose is orderly.

Details

Luckily, to write a memorable description, you don't need a storm at sea or any other awe-inspiring subject. As Sarah Vowell demonstrates in "Shooting Dad" later in this chapter, you can write about your family as effectively as you write about a tornado. The secret is in the vividness, the evocativeness of the details. Like most good describers, Vowell uses many IMAGES (language calling up concrete sensory experiences), including FIGURES OF SPEECH (expressions that do not mean literally what they say, often describing one thing in terms of another). For instance, using *metaphor* Vowell writes that "the respective work spaces governed by my father and me were jealously guarded totalitarian states in which each of us declared ourselves dictator." Another writer, the humorist S. J. Perelman, uses metaphor to convey the garish brightness of a certain low-rent house. Notice how he makes clear the spirit of the place: "After a few days, I could have sworn that our faces began to take on the hue of Kodachromes, and even the dog, an animal used to bizarre surroundings, developed a strange, off-register look, as if he were badly printed in overlapping colors."

When you, too, write an effective description, you'll convey your sensory experience as exactly as possible. Find vigorous, specific words, and you will enable your reader to behold with the mind's eye—and to feel with the mind's fingertips.

CHECKLIST FOR REVISING A DESCRIPTION

✔ **SUBJECTIVE OR OBJECTIVE.** Given your purpose and audience, is your description appropriately subjective (emphasizing feelings) or objective (unemotional)?

✔ **DOMINANT IMPRESSION.** What is the dominant impression of your subject? If you haven't stated it, will your readers be able to express it accurately to themselves?

✔ **POINT OF VIEW AND ORGANIZATION.** Do your point of view and organization work together to make your subject clear in readers' minds? Are they consistent?

✔ **DETAILS.** Have you provided all the details—and just those—needed to convey your dominant impression? What needs expanding? What needs condensing or cutting?

✔ **CONCRETE LANGUAGE.** Have you used words that appeal to the senses of sight, hearing, touch, taste, and smell? A vague word such as *loud* does little for readers; a concrete word such as *screeching* works harder, and a fresh figure of speech such as *a screech like a missile directly overhead* does even more.

DESCRIPTION IN A PARAGRAPH: TWO ILLUSTRATIONS

Using Description to Write About Television

In this paragraph written especially for *The Bedford Reader,* description works with narration to create suspense. Without even knowing the cause of the suspense, we gather tension from the details. Such a paragraph might pull us into an essay on the subject that is finally revealed only in the last sentence.

At 2:59 this Monday afternoon, a thick hush settles like cigarette smoke inside the sweat-scented TV room of Harris Hall. First to arrive, freshman Lee Ann squashes down into the catbird seat in front of the screen. Soon she is flanked by roommates Lisa and Kate, silent, their mouths straight lines, their upturned faces lit by the nervous flicker of a detergent ad. To the left and right of the couch, Pete and Anse crouch on the floor, leaning forward like runners awaiting a starting gun. Behind them, stiff standees line up at attention. Farther back still, English majors and jocks compete for an unobstructed view. Fresh from class, shirttail flapping, arm crooking a bundle of books, Dave barges into the room demanding, "Has it started? Has it started yet?" He is shushed. Somebody shushes a popped-open can of Dr Pepper whose fizz is distractingly loud. What do these students so intently look forward to—the announcement of World War III? A chord of music signals the opening of a soap opera.

Dominant impression (not stated): tense expectation of something vital

Details (underlined) contribute to dominant impression

Organization proceeds from front of room (at TV) to back

Using Description in an Academic Discipline

Description interprets a familiar painting in the following paragraph from a text on art history. The details "translate" the painting, creating a bridge between the reader and the text's reproduction of the great work.

While working on *The Battle of Anghiari,* Leonardo painted his most famous portrait, the *Mona Lisa.* The delicate *sfumato* already

(Sfumato: soft gradations of light and dark)

noted in the *Madonna of the Rocks* is here so perfected that it seemed miraculous to the artist's contemporaries. The forms are built from layers of glazes so gossamer-thin that the entire panel seems to glow with a gentle light from within. But the fame of the *Mona Lisa* comes not from this pictorial subtlety alone; even more intriguing is the psychological fascination of the sitter's personality. Why, among all the smiling faces ever painted, has this particular one been singled out as "mysterious"? Perhaps the reason is that, as a portrait, the picture does not fit our expectations. The features are too individual for Leonardo to have simply depicted an ideal type, yet the element of idealization is so strong that it blurs the sitter's character. Once again the artist has brought two opposites into harmonious balance. The smile, too, may be read in two ways: as the echo of a momentary mood, and as a timeless, symbolic expression (somewhat like the "Archaic smile" of the Greeks [. . .]). Clearly, the *Mona Lisa* embodies a quality of maternal tenderness which was to Leonardo the essence of womanhood. Even the landscape in the background, composed mainly of rocks and water, suggests elemental generative forces.

—H. W. Janson, *History of Art*

Main idea (topic sentence) of the paragraph, supported by description of "pictorial subtlety" (above) and "psychological fascination" (below)

Details (underlined) contribute to dominant impression

CASE STUDY
Using Description

Edward Johnson was leaving campus for the summer and wanted to sublet his apartment. Scouting around, he discovered that the best place to advertise his apartment was with his college's online "Housing Connection," which served as a network for students, staff, and faculty seeking short- or long-term rentals.

Johnson looked through many of the ads at "The Housing Connection," especially in his category of one-bedrooms, to see how he could make his place seem irresistible compared with the others listed. He noticed that other ads tended to be bare-bones, just the basics on rooms and rent, so he decided to use the twelve lines allotted to him to portray the special qualities of his apartment. In just a couple of drafts, he summoned the descriptive details that would attract a tenant. Here is the actual online posting:

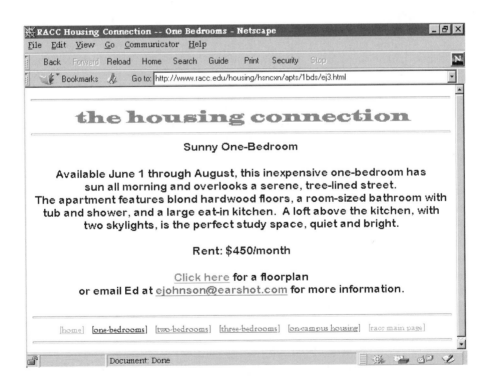

BRAD MANNING

Brad Manning was born in Little Rock, Arkansas, in 1967 and grew up near Charlottesville, Virginia. He attended Harvard University, graduating in 1990 with a BA in history and religion. At Harvard he played intramural sports and wrote articles and reviews for the *Harvard Independent*. After graduation Manning wrote features and news stories for the *Charlotte Observer* and then attended law school at the University of Virginia, graduating in 1995. Now living in Charlottesville with his wife and three children, Manning is finishing medical school at the University of Virginia, training to be a child and family psychiatrist.

Arm Wrestling with My Father

In this essay written for his freshman composition course, Manning explores his physical contact with his father over the years, perceiving gradual changes that are, he realizes, inevitable. For Manning, description provides a way to express his feelings about his father and to comment on relations between sons and fathers. In the essay after Manning's, Sarah Vowell uses description for similar ends, but her subject is the relationship between a daughter and her father.

Manning's essay has been published in a Harvard collection of students' writing; in *Student Writers at Work: The Bedford Prizes*; and in *Montage*, a collection of Russian and American stories published in Russian.

"Now you say when" is what he always said before an arm-wrestling   1
match. He liked to put the responsibility on me, knowing that he would always control the outcome. "When!" I'd shout, and it would start. And I would tense up, concentrating and straining and trying to push his wrist down to the carpet with all my weight and strength. But Dad would always win; I always had to lose. "Want to try it again?" he would ask, grinning. He would see my downcast eyes, my reddened, sweating face, and sense my intensity. And with squinting eyes he would laugh at me, a high laugh, through his perfect white teeth. Too bitter to smile, I would not answer or look at him, but I would just roll over on my back and frown at the ceiling. I never thought it was funny at all.

That was the way I felt for a number of years during my teens, after I had   2
lost my enjoyment of arm wrestling and before I had given up that same intense desire to beat my father. Ours had always been a physical relationship, I suppose, one determined by athleticism and strength. We never communicated as well in speech or in writing as in a strong hug, battling to make the other gasp for breath. I could never find him at one of my orchestra concerts.

But at my lacrosse games, he would be there in the stands, with an angry look, ready to coach me after the game on how I could do better. He never helped me write a paper or a poem. Instead, he would take me outside and show me a new move for my game, in the hope that I would score a couple of goals and gain confidence in my ability. Dad knew almost nothing about lacrosse and his movements were all wrong and sad to watch. But at those times I could just feel how hard he was trying to communicate, to help me, to show the love he had for me, the love I could only assume was there.

His words were physical. The truth is, I have never read a card or a letter   3
written in his hand because he never wrote to me. Never. Mom wrote me all the cards and letters when I was away from home. The closest my father ever came, that I recall, was in a newspaper clipping Mom had sent with a letter. He had gone through and underlined all the important words about the dangers of not wearing a bicycle helmet. Our communication was physical, and that is why we did things like arm wrestle. To get down on the floor and grapple, arm against arm, was like having a conversation.

This ritual of father-son competition in fact had started early in my life,   4
back when Dad started the matches with his arm almost horizontal, his wrist an inch from defeat, and still won. I remember in those battles how my tiny shoulders would press over our locked hands, my whole upper body pushing down in hope of winning that single inch from his calm, unmoving forearm. "Say when," he'd repeat, killing my concentration and causing me to squeal, "I did, I did!" And so he'd grin with his eyes fixed on me, not seeming to notice his own arm, which would begin to rise slowly from its starting position. My greatest efforts could not slow it down. As soon as my hopes had disappeared I'd start to cheat and use both hands. But the arm would continue to move steadily along its arc toward the carpet. My brother, if he was watching, would sometimes join in against the arm. He once even wrapped his little legs around our embattled wrists and pulled back with everything he had. But he did not have much and, regardless of the opposition, the man would win. My arm would lie at rest, pressed into the carpet beneath a solid, immovable arm. In that pinned position, I could only giggle, happy to have such a strong father.

My feelings have changed, though. I don't giggle anymore, at least not   5
around my father. And I don't feel pressured to compete with him the way I thought necessary for years. Now my father is not really so strong as he used to be and I am getting stronger. This change in strength comes at a time when I am growing faster mentally than at any time before. I am becoming less my father and more myself. And as a result, there is less of a need to be set apart from him and his command. I am no longer a rebel in the household, wanting to stand up against the master with clenched fists and tensing jaws, trying to impress him with my education or my views on religion. I am no longer a

challenger, quick to correct his verbal mistakes, determined to beat him whenever possible in physical competition.

I am not sure when it was that I began to feel less competitive with my father, but it all became clearer to me one day this past January. I was home in Virginia for a week between exams, and Dad had stayed home from work because the house was snowed in deep. It was then that I learned something I never could have guessed.

I don't recall who suggested arm wrestling that day. We hadn't done it for a long time, for months. But there we were, lying flat on the carpet, face to face, extending our right arms. Our arms were different. His still resembled a fat tree branch, one which had leveled my wrist to the ground countless times before. It was hairy and white with some pink moles scattered about. It looked strong, to be sure, though not so strong as it had in past years. I expect that back in his youth it had looked even stronger. In high school he had played halfback and had been voted "best-built body" of the senior class. Between college semesters he had worked on road crews and on Louisiana dredges. I admired him for that. I had begun to row crew in college and that accounted for some small buildup along the muscle lines, but it did not seem to be enough. The arm I extended was lanky and featureless. Even so, he insisted that he would lose the match, that he was certain I'd win. I had to ignore this, however, because it was something he always said, whether or not he believed it himself.

Our warm palms came together, much the same way we had shaken hands the day before at the airport. Fingers twisted and wrapped about once again, testing for a better grip. Elbows slid up and back making their little indentations on the itchy carpet. My eyes pinched closed in concentration as I tried to center as much of my thought as possible on the match. Arm wrestling, I knew, was a competition that depended less on talent and experience than on one's mental control and confidence. I looked up into his eyes and was ready. He looked back, smiled at me, and said softly (did he sound nervous?), "You say when."

It was not a long match. I had expected him to be stronger, faster. I was conditioned to lose and would have accepted defeat easily. However, after some struggle, his arm yielded to my efforts and began to move unsteadily toward the carpet. I worked against his arm with all the strength I could find. He was working hard as well, straining, breathing heavily. It seemed that this time was different, that I was going to win. Then something occurred to me, something unexpected. I discovered that I was feeling sorry for my father. I wanted to win but I did not want to see him lose.

It was like the thrill I had once experienced as a young boy at my grandfather's lake house in Louisiana when I hooked my first big fish. There was that sudden tug that made me leap. The red bobber was sucked down beneath the surface and I pulled back against it, reeling it in excitedly. But when my cousin caught sight of the fish and shouted out, "It's a keeper," I realized that I would be happier for the fish if it were let go rather than grilled for dinner. Arm wrestling my father was now like this, like hooking "Big Joe," the old fish that Lake Quachita holds but you can never catch, and when you finally think you've got him, you want to let him go, cut the line, keep the legend alive.

Perhaps at that point I could have given up, letting my father win. But it was so fast and absorbing. How could I have learned so quickly how it would feel to have overpowered the arm that had protected and provided for me all of my life? His arms have always protected me and the family. Whenever I am near him I am unafraid, knowing his arms are ready to catch me and keep me safe, the way they caught my mother one time when she fainted halfway across the room, the way he carried me, full grown, up and down the stairs when I had mononucleosis, the way he once held my feet as I stood on his shoulders to put up a new basketball net. My mother may have had the words or the touch that sustained our family, but his were the arms that protected us. And his were the arms now that I had pushed to the carpet, first the right arm, then the left. 11

I might have preferred him to be always the stronger, the one who carries me. But this wish is impossible now; our roles have begun to switch. I do not know if I will ever physically carry my father as he has carried me, though I fear that someday I may have that responsibility. More than once this year I have hesitated before answering the phone late at night, fearing my mother's voice calling me back to help carry his wood coffin. When I am home with him and he mentions a sharp pain in his chest, I imagine him collapsing onto the floor. And in that second vision I see me rushing to him, lifting him onto my shoulders, and running. 12

A week after our match, we parted at the airport. The arm-wrestling match was by that time mostly forgotten. My thoughts were on school. I had been awake most of the night studying for my last exam, and by that morning I was already back into my college-student manner of reserve and detachment. To say goodbye, I kissed and hugged my mother and I prepared to shake my father's hand. A handshake had always seemed easier to handle than a hug. His hugs had always been powerful ones, intended I suppose to give me strength. They made me suck in my breath and struggle for control, and the way he would pound his hand on my back made rumbles in my ears. So I offered a handshake; but he offered a hug. I accepted it, bracing myself for the impact. Once our arms were wrapped around each other, however, I sensed a different message. His embrace was softer, longer than before. I remember how it surprised me and how I gave an embarrassed laugh as if to apologize to anyone watching. 13

I got on the airplane and my father and mother were gone. But as the   14
plane lifted my throat was hurting with sadness. I realized then that Dad must
have learned something as well, and what he had said to me in that last hug
was that he loved me. Love was a rare expression between us, so I had denied
it at first. As the plane turned north, I had a sudden wish to go back to Dad
and embrace his arms with all the love I felt for him. I wanted to hold him for
a long time and to speak with him silently, telling him how happy I was,
telling him all my feelings, in that language we shared.

In his hug, Dad had tried to tell me something he himself had discovered.   15
I hope he tries again. Maybe this spring, when he sees his first crew match,
he'll advise me on how to improve my stroke. Maybe he has started doing
pushups to rebuild his strength and challenge me to another match—if this
were true, I know I would feel less challenged than loved. Or maybe, rather
than any of this, he'll just send me a card.

Journal Writing

Manning expresses conflicting feelings about his father. How do you respond to his
conflict? When have you felt strongly conflicting emotions about a person or an
event, such as a relative, friend, breakup, ceremony, move? Write a paragraph or two
exploring your feelings. (To take your journal writing further, see "From Journal to
Essay" on the facing page.)

Questions on Meaning

1. In paragraph 3 Manning says that his father's "words were physical." What does
   this mean?
2. After his most recent trip home, Manning says, "I realized then that Dad must
   have learned something as well" (par. 14). What is it that father and son have
   each learned?
3. Manning says in the last paragraph that he "would feel less challenged than
   loved" if his father challenged him to a rematch. Does this statement suggest that
   he did not feel loved earlier? Why, or why not?
4. What do you think is Manning's PURPOSE in this essay? Does he want to express
   love for his father, or is there something more as well?

Questions on Writing Strategy

1. Why does Manning start his essay with a match that leaves him "too bitter to
   smile" and then move backward to earlier bouts of arm wrestling?

2. In the last paragraph Manning suggests that his father might work harder at competing with him and pushing him to be competitive, or he might just send his son a card. Why does Manning present both of these options? Are we supposed to know which will happen?
3. Explain the fishing ANALOGY Manning uses in paragraph 10.
4. **OTHER METHODS.** Manning's essay is as much a NARRATIVE as a description: The author gives brief stories, like video clips, to show the dynamic of his relationship with his father. Look at the story in paragraph 4. How does Manning mix elements of both methods to convey his powerlessness?

Questions on Language

1. Manning uses the word *competition* throughout this essay. Why is this a more accurate word than *conflict* to describe Manning's relationship with his father?
2. What is the EFFECT of "the arm" in this line from paragraph 4: "But the arm would continue to move steadily along its arc toward the carpet"?
3. In paragraph 9 Manning writes, "I wanted to win but I did not want to see him lose." What does this apparent contradiction mean?
4. If any of these words is unfamiliar, look it up in a dictionary: embattled (par. 4); dredges, crew (7); conditioned (9); mononucleosis (11).

Suggestions for Writing

1. **FROM JOURNAL TO ESSAY.** Expand your journal entry into a descriptive essay that brings to life your mixed feelings about a person or an event. Focus less on the circumstances and events than on emotions, both positive and negative.
2. Write an essay that describes your relationship with a parent or another close adult. You may want to focus on just one aspect of your relationship, or one especially vivid moment, in order to give yourself the space and time to build many sensory details into your description.
3. **CRITICAL WRITING.** In paragraph 12 Manning writes, "our roles have begun to switch." Does this seem like an inevitable switch, or one that this father and son have been working to achieve? Use EVIDENCE from Manning's essay to support your answer. Also consider whether Manning and his father would respond the same way to this question.
4. **CONNECTIONS.** Like "Arm Wrestling with My Father," the next essay, Sarah Vowell's "Shooting Dad," depicts a struggle for communication between child and parent. In an essay, COMPARE AND CONTRAST the two essays on this point. What impedes positive communication between the two authors and their fathers? In what circumstances are they able to communicate?

Brad Manning on Writing

For *The Bedford Reader*, Brad Manning offered some valuable concrete advice on writing as a student.

You hear this a lot, but writing takes a long time. For me, this is especially true. The only difference between the "Arm Wrestling" essay and all the other essays I wrote in college (and the only reason it's in this book and not thrown away) is that I rewrote it six or seven times over a period of weeks.

If I have something to write, I need to start early. In college, I had a bad habit of putting off papers until 10 PM the night before they were due and spending a desperate night typing whatever ideas the coffee inspired. But putting off papers didn't just lower my writing quality; it robbed me of a good time.

I like starting early because I can jot down notes over a stretch of days; then I type them up fast, ignoring typos; I print the notes with narrow margins, cut them up, and divide them into piles that seem to fit together; then it helps to get away for a day and come back all fresh so I can throw away the corny ideas. Finally, I sit on the floor and make an outline with all the cutouts of paper, trying at the same time to work out some clear purpose for the essay.

When the writing starts, I often get hung up most on trying to "sound" like a good writer. If you're like me and came to college from a shy family that never discussed much over dinner, you might think your best shot is to sound like a famous writer like T. S. Eliot and you might try to sneak in words that aren't really your own like *ephemeral* or *the lilacs smelled like springtime*. But the last thing you really want a reader thinking is how good or bad a writer you are.

Also, in the essay on arm wrestling, I got hung up thinking I had to make my conflict with my father somehow "universal." So in an early draft I wrote in a classical allusion — Aeneas lifting his old father up onto his shoulders and carrying him out of the burning city of Troy.[1] I'd read that story in high school and guessed one classical allusion might make the reader think I knew a lot more. But Aeneas didn't help the essay much, and I'm glad my teacher warned me off trying to universalize. He told me to write just what was true for me.

But that was hard, too, and still is — especially in the first draft. I don't know anyone who enjoys the first draft. If you do, I envy you. But in my early drafts, I always get this sensation like I have to impress somebody and I end up overanalyzing the effects of every word I am about to write. This self-consciousness may be unavoidable (I get self-conscious calling L. L. Bean to

[1] In the *Aeneid*, by the Roman poet Vergil (70–19 BC), the mythic hero Aeneas escaped from the city of Troy when it was sacked by the Greeks and went on to found Rome. — EDS.

order a shirt), but, in this respect, writing is great for shy people because you can edit all you want, all day long, until it finally sounds right. I never feel that I am being myself until the third or fourth draft, and it's only then that it gets personal and starts to be fun.

When I said that putting off papers robbed me of a good time, I really meant it. Writing the essay about my father turned out to be a high point in my life. And on top of having a good time with it, I now have a record of what happened. And my ten-month-old son, when he grows up, can read things about his grandfather and father that he'd probably not have learned any other way.

For Discussion

1. What did Manning miss by writing his college papers at the last minute?
2. Why does Manning say that "writing is great for shy people"? Have you ever felt that you could express yourself in writing better than in speech?

SARAH VOWELL

SARAH VOWELL is best known for the smart, witty spoken essays she delivers on public radio. Born in Muskogee, Oklahoma, in 1969, Vowell grew up in Oklahoma and Montana. After graduating from Montana State University, she earned an MA in art history and criticism from the School of the Art Institute of Chicago. Radio has played a large part in Vowell's life: She worked as a DJ for her college station in Montana; she published a day-by-day diary of one year spent listening to the radio, *Radio On: A Listener's Diary* (1996); and in 1996 she became a contributing editor for *This American Life* on Public Radio International. Many of her essays from *This American Life* appear in her book *Take the Cannoli: Stories from the New World* (2000), commentaries on everything from the *Godfather* movies to the forced migration of Native Americans to her makeover as a "goth." Her most recent book is *See America* (2002). Vowell is also a regular columnist for the online magazine *Salon*, and her writing has appeared in numerous print periodicals, including *Esquire, GQ,* the *Los Angeles Times,* and *Spin.* She lives in New York City.

Shooting Dad

Like the previous essay, Brad Manning's "Arm Wrestling with My Father," Vowell's "Shooting Dad" explores the relationship between child and father. Engaged in a lifelong opposition to her father's politics, interests, and even his work, Vowell discovers with a jolt how much she has in common with him. Vowell read this essay, in slightly different form, on *This American Life* and then included it in *Take the Cannoli.*

If you were passing by the house where I grew up during my teenage years and it happened to be before Election Day, you wouldn't have needed to come inside to see that it was a house divided. You could have looked at the Democratic campaign poster in the upstairs window and the Republican one in the downstairs window and seen our home for the Civil War battleground it was. I'm not saying who was the Democrat or who was the Republican—my father or I—but I will tell you that I have never subscribed to *Guns & Ammo*, that I did not plaster the family vehicle with National Rifle Association stickers, and that hunter's orange was never my color. 1

About the only thing my father and I agree on is the Constitution, though I'm partial to the First Amendment, while he's always favored the Second. 2

I am a gunsmith's daughter. I like to call my parents' house, located on a quiet residential street in Bozeman, Montana, the United States of Firearms. Guns were everywhere: the so-called pretty ones like the circa 1850 walnut muzzleloader hanging on the wall, Dad's clients' fixer-uppers leaning into cor- 3 ners, an entire rack right next to the TV. I had to move revolvers out of my way to make room for a bowl of Rice Krispies on the kitchen table.

I was eleven when we moved into that Bozeman house. We had never lived in town before, and this was a college town at that. We came from Oklahoma—a dusty little Muskogee County nowhere called Braggs. My parents' property there included an orchard, a horse pasture, and a couple of acres of woods. I knew our lives had changed one morning not long after we moved to Montana when, during breakfast, my father heard a noise and jumped out of his chair. Grabbing a BB gun, he rushed out the front door. Standing in the yard, he started shooting at crows. My mother sprinted after him screaming, "Pat, you might ought to check, but I don't think they do that up here!" From the look on his face, she might as well have told him that his American citizenship had been revoked. He shook his head, mumbling, "Why, shooting crows is a national pastime, like baseball and apple pie." Personally, I preferred baseball and apple pie. I looked up at those crows flying away and thought, I'm going to like it here.

Dad and I started bickering in earnest when I was fourteen, after the 1984 Democratic National Convention. I was so excited when Walter Mondale chose Geraldine Ferraro as his running mate that I taped the front page of the newspaper with her picture on it to the refrigerator door. But there was some sort of mysterious gravity surge in the kitchen. Somehow, that picture ended up in the trash all the way across the room.

Nowadays, I giggle when Dad calls me on Election Day to cheerfully inform me that he has once again canceled out my vote, but I was not always so mature. There were times when I found the fact that he was a gunsmith horrifying. And just *weird.* All he ever cared about were guns. All I ever cared about was art. There were years and years when he hid out by himself in the garage making rifle barrels and I holed up in my room reading Allen Ginsberg poems, and we were incapable of having a conversation that didn't end in an argument.

Our house was partitioned off into territories. While the kitchen and the living room were well within the DMZ,[1] the respective work spaces governed by my father and me were jealously guarded totalitarian states in which each of us declared ourselves dictator. Dad's shop was a messy disaster area, a labyrinth of lathes. Its walls were hung with the mounted antlers of deer he'd bagged, forming a makeshift museum of death. The available flat surfaces were buried under a million scraps of paper on which he sketched his mechanical inventions in blue ballpoint pen. And the floor, carpeted with spiky metal shavings, was a tetanus shot waiting to happen. My domain was the cramped,

---

[1] Abbreviation for "demilitarized zone," an area off-limits to war making. —EDS.

cold space known as the music room. It was also a messy disaster area, an obstacle course of musical instruments—piano, trumpet, baritone horn, valve trombone, various percussion doodads (bells!), and recorders. A framed portrait of the French composer Claude Debussy was nailed to the wall. The available flat surfaces were buried under piles of staff paper, on which I penciled in the pompous orchestra music given titles like "Prelude to the Green Door" (named after an O. Henry short story by the way, not the watershed porn flick *Behind the Green Door*) I started writing in junior high.

It has been my experience that in order to impress potential suitors, skip the teen Debussy anecdotes and stick with the always attention-getting line "My dad makes guns." Though it won't cause the guy to like me any better, it will make him handle the inevitable breakup with diplomacy—just in case I happen to have any loaded family heirlooms lying around the house.   8

But the fact is, I have only shot a gun once and once was plenty. My twin sister, Amy, and I were six years old—six—when Dad decided that it was high time we learned how to shoot. Amy remembers the day he handed us the gun for the first time differently. She liked it.   9

Amy shared our father's enthusiasm for firearms and the quick-draw cowboy mythology surrounding them. I tended to daydream through Dad's activities—the car trip to Dodge City's Boot Hill, his beloved John Wayne Westerns on TV. My sister, on the other hand, turned into Rooster Cogburn Jr., devouring Duke movies with Dad. In fact, she named her teddy bear Duke, hung a colossal John Wayne portrait next to her bed, and took to wearing one of those John Wayne shirts that button on the side. So when Dad led us out to the backyard when we were six and, to Amy's delight, put the gun in her hand, she says she felt it meant that Daddy trusted us and that he thought of us as "big girls."   10

But I remember holding the pistol only made me feel small. It was so heavy in my hand. I stretched out my arm and pointed it away and winced. It was a very long time before I had the nerve to pull the trigger and I was so scared I had to close my eyes. It felt like it just went off by itself, as if I had no say in the matter, as if the gun just had this *need*. The sound it made was as big as God. It kicked little me back to the ground like a bully, like a foe. It hurt. I don't know if I dropped it or just handed it back over to my dad, but I do know that I never wanted to touch another one again. And, because I believed in the devil, I did what my mother told me to do every time I felt an evil presence. I looked at the smoke and whispered under my breath, "Satan, I rebuke thee."   11

It's not like I'm saying I was traumatized. It's more like I was decided. Guns: Not For Me. Luckily, both my parents grew up in exasperating households where children were considered puppets and/or slaves. My mom and dad were hell-bent on letting my sister and me make our own choices. So if I decided   12 that I didn't want my father's little death sticks to kick me to the ground again, that was fine with him. He would go hunting with my sister, who started calling herself "the loneliest twin in history" because of my reluctance to engage in family activities.

Of course, the fact that I was allowed to voice my opinions did not mean   13
that my father would silence his own. Some things were said during the Reagan administration that cannot be taken back. Let's just say that I blamed Dad for nuclear proliferation and Contra aid. He believed that if I had my way, all the guns would be confiscated and it would take the commies about fifteen minutes to parachute in and assume control.

We're older now, my dad and I. The older I get, the more I'm interested in   14
becoming a better daughter. First on my list: Figure out the whole gun thing.

Not long ago, my dad finished his most elaborate tool of death yet. A can-   15
non. He built a nineteenth-century cannon. From scratch. It took two years.

My father's cannon is a smaller replica of a cannon called the Big Horn   16
Gun in front of Bozeman's Pioneer Museum. The barrel of the original has been filled with concrete ever since some high school kids in the '50s pointed it at the school across the street and shot out its windows one night as a prank. According to Dad's historical source, a man known to scholars as A Guy at the Museum, the cannon was brought to Bozeman around 1870, and was used by local white merchants to fire at the Sioux and Cheyenne Indians who blocked their trade access to the East in 1874.

"Bozeman was founded on greed," Dad says. The courthouse cannon,   17
he continues, "definitely killed Indians. The merchants filled it full of nuts, bolts, and chopped-up horseshoes. Sitting Bull could have been part of these engagements. They definitely ticked off the Indians, because a couple of years later, Custer wanders into them at Little Bighorn. The Bozeman merchants were out to cause trouble. They left fresh baked bread with cyanide in it on the trail to poison a few Indians."

Because my father's sarcastic American history yarns rarely go on for   18
long before he trots out some nefarious ancestor of ours—I come from a long line of moonshiners, Confederate soldiers, murderers, even Democrats—he cracks that the merchants hired some "community-minded Southern soldiers from North Texas." These soldiers had, like my great-great-grandfather John Vowell, fought under pro-slavery guerrilla William C. Quantrill. Quantrill is most famous for riding into Lawrence, Kansas, in 1863 flying a black flag and commanding his men pharaohlike to "kill every male and burn down every house."

"John Vowell," Dad says, "had a little rep for killing people." And since he   19
abandoned my great-grandfather Charles, whose mother died giving birth to him in 1870, and wasn't seen again until 1912, Dad doesn't rule out the

possibility that John Vowell could have been one of the hired guns on the Bozeman Trail. So the cannon isn't just another gun to my dad. It's a map of all his obsessions—firearms, certainly, but also American history and family history, subjects he's never bothered separating from each other.

After tooling a million guns, after inventing and building a rifle barrel boring machine, after setting up that complicated shop filled with lathes and blueing tanks and outmoded blacksmithing tools, the cannon is his most ambitious project ever. I thought that if I was ever going to understand the ballistic bee in his bonnet, this was my chance. It was the biggest gun he ever made and I could experience it and spend time with it with the added bonus of not having to actually pull a trigger myself.

I called Dad and said that I wanted to come to Montana and watch him shoot off the cannon. He was immediately suspicious. But I had never taken much interest in his work before and he would take what he could get. He loaded the cannon into the back of his truck and we drove up into the Bridger Mountains. I was a little worried that the National Forest Service would object to us lobbing fiery balls of metal onto its property. Dad laughed, assuring me that "you cannot shoot fireworks, but this is considered a firearm."

It is a small cannon, about as long as a baseball bat and as wide as a coffee can. But it's heavy—110 pounds. We park near the side of the hill. Dad takes his gunpowder and other tools out of this adorable wooden box on which he has stenciled "PAT G. VOWELL CANNONWORKS." Cannonworks: So that's what NRA members call a metal-strewn garage.

Dad plunges his homemade bullets into the barrel, points it at an embankment just to be safe, and lights the fuse. When the fuse is lit, it resembles a cartoon. So does the sound, which warrants Ben Day dot words along the lines of *ker-pow!* There's so much Fourth of July smoke everywhere I feel compelled to sing the national anthem.

I've given this a lot of thought—how to convey the giddiness I felt when the cannon shot off. But there isn't a sophisticated way to say this. It's just really, really cool. My dad thought so, too.

Sometimes, I put together stories about the more eccentric corners of the American experience for public radio. So I happen to have my tape recorder with me, and I've never seen levels like these. Every time the cannon goes off, the delicate needles which keep track of the sound quality lurch into the bad, red zone so fast and so hard I'm surprised they don't break.

The cannon was so loud and so painful, I had to touch my head to make sure my skull hadn't cracked open. One thing that my dad and I share is that we're both a little hard of hearing—me from Aerosmith, him from gunsmith.

He lights the fuse again. The bullet knocks over the log he was aiming at.

I instantly utter a sentence I never in my entire life thought I would say. I tell him, "Good shot, Dad."

Just as I'm wondering what's coming over me, two hikers walk by. Apparently, they have never seen a man set off a homemade cannon in the middle of the wilderness while his daughter holds a foot-long microphone up into the air recording its terrorist boom. One hiker gives me a puzzled look and asks, "So you work for the radio and that's your dad?"

Dad shoots the cannon again so that they can see how it works. The other hiker says, "That's quite the machine you got there." But he isn't talking about the cannon. He's talking about my tape recorder and my microphone—which is called a *shotgun* mike. I stare back at him, then I look over at my father's cannon, then down at my microphone, and I think, Oh. My. God. My dad and I are the same person. We're both smart-alecky loners with goofy projects and weird equipment. And since this whole target practice outing was my idea, I was no longer his adversary. I was his accomplice. What's worse, I was liking it.

I haven't changed my mind about guns. I can get behind the cannon because it is a completely ceremonial object. It's unwieldy and impractical, just like everything else I care about. Try to rob a convenience store with this 110-pound Saturday night special, you'd still be dragging it in the door Sunday afternoon.

I love noise. As a music fan, I'm always waiting for that moment in a song when something just flies out of it and explodes in the air. My dad is a one-man garage band, the kind of rock 'n' roller who slaves away at his art for no reason other than to make his own sound. My dad is an artist—a pretty driven, idiosyncratic one, too. He's got his last *Gesamtkunstwerk*[2] all planned out. It's a performance piece. We're all in it—my mom, the loneliest twin in history, and me.

When my father dies, take a wild guess what he wants done with his ashes. Here's a hint: It requires a cannon.

"You guys are going to love this," he smirks, eyeballing the cannon. "You get to drag this thing up on top of the Gravellies on opening day of hunting season. And looking off at Sphinx Mountain, you get to put me in little paper bags. I can take my last hunting trip on opening morning."

I'll do it, too. I will have my father's body burned into ashes. I will pack these ashes into paper bags. I will go to the mountains with my mother, my sister, and the cannon. I will plunge his remains into the barrel and point it into a hill so that he doesn't take anyone with him. I will light the fuse. But I will not cover my ears. Because when I blow what used to be my dad into the earth, I want it to hurt.

---

[2] German, "total work of art," specifically a work that seeks to unify all the arts. —EDS.

Journal Writing

How do you respond to Vowell's eccentric, even obsessive, father? Do you basically come to sympathize with him or not? Who in your life has quirky behavior that you find charming or annoying or a little of both? Write a paragraph or two about this person, focusing on his or her particular habits or obsessions. (To take your journal writing further, see "From Journal to Essay" on the facing page.)

Questions on Meaning

1. In her opening sentence, Vowell describes growing up in "a house divided." What does she mean? Where in the essay does she make the divisions in her household explicit?
2. Why, given Vowell's father's love of guns, was it "fine" with him that his daughter decided as a young child that she wanted nothing to do with guns (par. 12)? What does this attitude suggest about his character?
3. What motivated Vowell to come home to watch her father shoot off his homemade cannon? Why, given her aversion to guns, does she regard this cannon positively?
4. What do paragraphs 18–19, about her father's family history, contribute to Vowell's portrait of him?
5. What seems to be Vowell's PURPOSE in writing here? What DOMINANT IMPRESSION of her father does she create?

Questions on Writing Strategy

1. Why is the anecdote Vowell relates in paragraph 4 an effective introduction both to her father and to their relationship?
2. Paragraph 8 is sort of an aside in this essay—not entirely on the main topic. What purpose does it serve?
3. What does Vowell's final sentence mean? Do you find it a satisfying conclusion to her essay? Why, or why not?
4. **OTHER METHODS.** Throughout her essay, Vowell relies on COMPARISON AND CONTRAST to express her relationship with her father (and with her twin sister in pars. 9–12). Find examples of comparison and contrast. Why is the method important to the essay? How does the method help reinforce Vowell's main point about her relationship with her father?

Questions on Language

1. In paragraph 4 Vowell shows her father "mumbling" that "shooting crows is a national pastime, like baseball and apple pie," while she notes that she herself "preferred baseball and apple pie." How does the language here illustrate IRONY?

2. In paragraph 9 Vowell writes, "My twin sister, Amy, and I were six years old—six—when Dad decided that it was high time we learned how to shoot. Amy remembers the day he handed us the gun for the first time differently. She liked it." What are the EFFECTS of the repetition of the word *six* in the first sentence and of the three-word final sentence?

3. Study the FIGURES OF SPEECH Vowell uses in paragraph 11 to describe the gun she shot. What is their effect?

4. Consult a dictionary if you need help in defining the following: muzzleloader (par. 3); revoked (4); bickering (5); partitioned, respective, totalitarian, labyrinth, lathes, pompous (7); colossal (10); traumatized (12); proliferation, confiscated (13); cyanide (17); nefarious, moonshiners, guerrilla, pharaohlike (18); ballistic (20); giddiness (24); adversary, accomplice (29); unwieldy (30); idiosyncratic (31).

Suggestions for Writing

1. **FROM JOURNAL TO ESSAY.** Based on your journal writing, compose an essay that uses description to portray your subject and his or her personal quirks. Be sure to include specific incidents you've witnessed and specific details to create a vivid dominant impression of the person. You may, like Vowell, focus on the evolution of your relationship with this person—whether mainly positive or mainly negative.

2. Conflict between generations is common in many families—whether over music, clothing, hair styles, friends, or larger issues of politics, values, and religion. Write an essay about generational conflicts you have experienced in your family or that you have witnessed in other families. Are such conflicts inevitable? How can they be resolved?

3. **CRITICAL WRITING.** Vowell's essay divides into several fairly distinct sections: paragraphs 1–4, 5–7, 8, 9–12, 13, 14–31 (which includes an aside in pars. 17–19), and 32–34. In an essay, analyze what happens in each of these sections. How do they fit together to help develop Vowell's dominant impression? How does the relative length of each section contribute to your understanding of her evolving relationship with her father?

4. **CONNECTIONS.** Both Vowell and Brad Manning, in "Arm Wrestling with My Father" (p. 136), describe their fathers. In an essay, examine words Manning and Vowell use to convey their feelings of distance from their fathers and also their feelings of closeness. Use quotations from both essays to support your analysis.

Sarah Vowell on Writing

Writing for both radio and print, Sarah Vowell has discovered differences in listening and reading audiences. On Transom.org's Internet discussion board, she explained how she writes differently for the two media.

[S]ometimes I feel like I'm so much more manipulative on the radio. I know how to use my voice to make you feel a certain way. And that's not writing—that's acting. I get tired of acting sometimes. Which is why it's nice to be able to go back to the cold old page. Also, real time is an unforgiving medium. I still maintain a little academic streak, and any time I read something on the air or out loud, I have to cut back on the abstract, thinky bits. I have to read a story out loud in front of an audience this week and I had to lop it off by half, to prune it of its dull information and, sometimes, its very point. Those things for you the listener, are bonuses—the listener doesn't get as much filler, the listener gets to feel more. Readers are more patient. [. . .]

The only real drawback I think from moving between verbal and print media is punctuation. I'm working on another book right now, and there are so many things I want to say that I have to normalize on the page because I do not think in complete, fluid sentences. I seem to think in stopgaps and asides. Which the listener doesn't notice. But the reader, I think, becomes antsy when there are too many dashes and parentheses. So that is a constant battle—(dash!) trying to retain my casual, late twentieth-century (it's where I'm from), American-girl cadences, but without driving the reader crazy with a bunch of marks all over the place. Also, I love the word *and*. And I start too many sentences with *and*. Again, no one notices out loud because that's normative speech. But do that too much on the page and it's distracting and stupid.

For Discussion

1. What does Vowell mean by having to "normalize [her thoughts] on the page"?
2. What difficulties or rewards have you encountered trying to put ideas into written words for others to read?
3. In your experience as a speaker and a writer, what are the advantages of each form of communication? What are the disadvantages of each?

JHUMPA LAHIRI

JHUMPA LAHIRI was born in London, England, in 1967, the child of parents born and raised in India. The family moved to Rhode Island when Lahiri was two but made frequent trips to India. After graduating with a BA from Barnard College, Lahiri attended Boston University, eventually receiving MAs in English, comparative literature, and creative writing and a PhD in Renaissance studies. Despite the degrees, Lahiri felt she "was not meant to be a scholar" and instead pursued her "passion for writing." She soon sold a story to *The New Yorker,* which has since published more of her work and placed her on its list of "twenty best young fiction writers in America." In 2000 Lahiri won the Pulitzer Prize for fiction for *Interpreter of Maladies,* a collection of stories about characters who live in the United States or in India and who struggle to communicate across cultural and emotional barriers. The title story received the O. Henry Award and was published in *Best American Short Stories 1999.* Lahiri lives in New York City and is working on her first novel.

Indian Takeout

Lahiri published the following essay in *Food and Wine* magazine in April 2000, and it was later collected in *Best Food Writing 2000.* Drawing on the fiction writer's descriptive power, Lahiri tells truths about mingled experiences of the senses and the emotions.

I am the daughter of former pirates, of a kind. Our loot included gold, silver, even a few precious gems. Mainly though, it was food, so much that throughout my childhood I was convinced my parents were running the modern equivalent of the ancient spice trade. They didn't exactly plunder this food; they bought it in the bazaars of Calcutta, where my mother was born and to which we returned as a family every couple of years. The destination was Rhode Island, where we lived, and where, back in the Seventies, Indian groceries were next to impossible to come by.

Our treasure chest, something we called the Food Suitcase, was an elegant relic from the Fifties with white stitching and brass latches that fastened shut with satisfying clicks. The inside was lined in peach-colored satin, had shirred lingerie pockets on three sides and was large enough to house a wardrobe for a long journey. Leave it to my parents to convert a vintage portmanteau into a portable pantry. They bought it one Saturday morning at a yard sale in the neighborhood, and I think it's safe to say that it had never been to India before.

Trips to Calcutta let my parents eat again, eat the food of their childhood,   3
the food they had been deprived of as adults. As soon as he hit Indian soil, my
father began devouring two or three yellow-skinned mangoes a day, sucking
the pits lovingly smooth. My mother breakfasted shamelessly on sticky orange
sweets called *jelebis*. It was easy to succumb. I insisted on accompanying each
of my meals with the yogurt sold at confectioners in red clay cups, their lids
made of paper, and my sister formed an addiction to *Moghlai parathas*, flatbread
folded, omelet-style, over mincemeat and egg.

As the end of each visit neared, our focus shifted from eating to shopping.   4
My parents created lists on endless sheets of paper, and my father spent days
in the bazaars, haggling and buying by the kilo. He always insisted on packing
the goods himself, with the aura of a man possessed: bare-chested, seated
cross-legged on the floor, determined, above all, to make everything fit. He
bound the Food Suitcase with enough rope to baffle Houdini and locked it up
with a little padlock, a scheme that succeeded in intimidating the most assiduous customs inspectors. Into the suitcase went an arsenal of lentils and every
conceivable spice, wrapped in layers of cloth ripped from an old sari and
stitched into individual packets. In went white poppy seeds, and resin made
from date syrup, and as many tins of Ganesh mustard oil as possible. In went
Lapchu tea, to be brewed only on special occasions, and sacks of black-
skinned Gobindovog rice, so named, it is said, because it's fit for offering to the
god Govinda. In went six kinds of *dalmoot*, a salty, crunchy snack mix bought
from big glass jars in a tiny store at the corner of Vivekananda Road and Corn-
wallis Street. In, on occasion, went something fresh, and therefore flagrantly
illegal: a bumpy, bright green bitter melon, or bay leaves from my uncle's garden. My parents weren't the only ones willing to flout the law. One year my
grandmother secretly tucked *parvals*, a vaguely squashlike vegetable, into the
Food Suitcase. My mother wept when she found them.

My parents also bought utensils: bowl-shaped iron *karhais*, which my   5
mother still prefers to ordinary pots and pans, and the areca-nut cracker that's
now somewhere in the back of the silverware drawer, and even a *boti*, a large
curved blade that sits on the floor in Bengali kitchens and is used instead of
handheld knives. The most sensational gadget we ever transported was a
sil-nora, an ancient food processor of sorts, which consists of a massive club-
like pestle and a slab the size, shape and weight of a headstone. Bewildered
relatives shook their heads, and airport workers in both hemispheres must
have cursed us. For a while my mother actually used it, pounding garlic
cloves by hand instead of pressing a button on the Osterizer. Then it turned
into a decorative device, propped up on the kitchen counter. It's in the basement now.

The suitcase was full during the trip from Rhode Island to Calcutta too,   6
with gifts for family. People there seldom asked for any food from America;
instead they requested the stuff of duty-free, Dunhills or Johnnie Walker. We
brought them Corning Ware plates and bowls, which, in their eyes, were
exotic alternatives to the broad, gleaming stainless steel dishes they normally
used. The only food we packed for ourselves was a big jar of Tang, which my
father carried with him at all times and stirred obsessively into the bitter puri-
fied water.

In spite of everything we managed to haul back, the first meal we ate after   7
returning from India was always a modest affair. My mother prepared the simplest of things: rice, some quartered potatoes, eggs if she was motivated, all
boiled together in a single pot. That first meal was never an occasion to celebrate but rather to mourn for the people and the city we had, once again, left
behind. And so my mother made food to mirror our mood, food for the weary
and melancholy. I remember thinking how strangely foreign our own kitchen
felt that first night back, with its giant, matching appliances, water we could
safely drink straight from the tap and rice which bore no stray stones. Just
before we ate, my mother would ask my father to untie the ropes and unlock
the suitcase. A few pappadams quickly fried and a drop of mustard oil drizzled
over the potatoes would convert our survivalist meal into a delicacy. It was
enough, that first lonely evening, not only to satisfy our hunger but to make
Calcutta seem not so very far away.

My parents returned last August from their thirteenth visit to India in   8
their thirty-odd years abroad. When I asked my mother what foods they'd
brought back she replied, with some sadness, "Nothing, really." My father
observed matter-of-factly that most everything was sold here these days. It's
true. Saffron and cardamom grace supermarket shelves, even in the small
towns of Rhode Island. The world, the culinary world in particular, has shrunk
considerably. Still, when my cousin's mother recently visited New York City,
she packed several pieces of fried *ruhi*, the everyday fish of Bengal, into her
bags. Of course, the Indian markets of Jackson Heights, Queens, were only a
subway ride away, but the fish had been sliced, salted and fried in Calcutta.
This was what mattered.

Today the Food Suitcase sits in our basement, neglected, smelling of   9
cumin. When I opened it on my last trip home, a few stray lentils rolled
around in one corner. Yet the signs were still visible, in the cupboards and the
refrigerator, that my parents have not abandoned their pirating ways. You
would know as much, were you to visit them yourself, by the six kinds of *dalmoot* my mother would set out with tea and the mustard oil she would offer to
drizzle on your potatoes at dinner.

Journal Writing

Lahiri evokes the sight, feel, smell, and taste of Indian foods for readers who may be unfamiliar with them. In a paragraph, do the same for one of your favorite foods, using details of the senses. (To take your journal writing further, see "From Journal to Essay" on the facing page.)

Questions on Meaning

1. In her first sentence, Lahiri refers to her parents as "pirates, of a kind" and also to their "loot." What does she mean?
2. Why was bringing food home from India so important to Lahiri's parents?
3. Lahiri writes in paragraph 7 that the family's first meal on their return from visits to India was always a modest one. Why does she find this appropriate?
4. Why do Lahiri's parents no longer use their "Food Suitcase"? How does the family regard the unused suitcase?
5. What would you say is Lahiri's PURPOSE in this essay? Writing for *Food and Wine* magazine, what could she assume about her readers' interests and concerns?

Questions on Writing Strategy

1. What is the EFFECT of Lahiri's opening sentence?
2. Most of Lahiri's essay moves in chronological order, beginning with the purchase of the "Food Suitcase" (par. 2), then describing the foods the family ate on arriving in Calcutta (3), their purchases and preparations for the trip back to the United States (4–5), and their first night after their return (7). Paragraph 6, however, does not follow this chronological order. Why do you think Lahiri chose to use this paragraph and to place it where she did?
3. How does Lahiri's conclusion echo her introduction? What is the effect of this echo?
4. **OTHER METHODS.** Is paragraph 4 an example of NARRATION or of PROCESS ANALYSIS? Why do you think so? What does the paragraph add to the essay?

Questions on Language

1. What is the double meaning of Lahiri's title? How do you respond to this title?
2. Does Lahiri describe Indian foods and cooking utensils in enough detail to make them clear for non-Indian readers? Do you find any foods or utensils that she does not adequately describe?
3. Lahiri's vocabulary includes some words that may be unfamiliar to you, especially food terms. Check a dictionary for any of the following: equivalent, bazaars (par. 1); shirred, portmanteau (2); succumb, confectioners, mincemeat (3); kilo, aura, assiduous, arsenal, lentils, sari, resin, flout (4); pestle, hemispheres (5); melancholy, pappadams, survivalist (7); saffron, cardamom, culinary (8); cumin (9).

Suggestions for Writing

1. **FROM JOURNAL TO ESSAY.** Using your journal entry as a springboard, write an essay about at least one of your favorite foods, describing its look, taste, smell, feel, and even sound if it has one. If, like Lahiri, you'd rather describe several foods that are related in some way, do so. Describe the food lavishly even if you think readers will already be familiar with it. The point is to exercise your descriptive powers to show how the food affects you.

2. Many families have unique traditions, like Lahiri's family tradition of carrying loads of food back from India. Think of a tradition that is unique to your family or to another group you belong to—for instance, a holiday celebration, a vacation activity, a way of resolving or avoiding disagreement. In an essay, describe that tradition, focusing on the objects used, the activities involved, and the feelings associated with it.

3. **CRITICAL WRITING.** Typically for a fiction writer, Lahiri subtly shifts her TONE to convey the different feelings aroused by memories. For instance, she is sometimes swaggering ("I am the daughter of former pirates," par. 1), sometimes empathetic ("Trips to Calcutta let my parents eat again," 3), and sometimes gloomy ("I remember thinking how strangely foreign our own kitchen felt," 7). Where do such shifts occur, and how does Lahiri use particular language to match mood and reflection?

4. **CONNECTIONS.** In "Fish Cheeks" (p. 92) Amy Tan also writes about foods traditional to her immigrant family during her childhood. COMPARE AND CONTRAST the ways Tan and Lahiri describe foods and how each uses food for a larger purpose.

Jhumpa Lahiri on Writing

In a 1999 interview for *Newsweek*, Vibhuti Patel asked Jhumpa Lahiri why she started writing. "I was a shy child," she explained, "uncomfortable in groups, so I sought out those with a similar sensibility—quiet girls who like stories. When I learned to read, I felt the need to copy. I started writing ten-page 'novels' during recess, with my friends. Sitting around the sandbox, we'd say things out loud. At playtime, we'd be princesses in a castle in France. Writing allowed me to observe and make sense of things without having to participate. I didn't belong. I looked different and felt like an outsider."

As a child of Indian immigrants, Lahiri felt like an outsider not only in the United States but also in India, where she traveled frequently with her parents. She told Gaiutra Bahudur of the *Philadelphia City Paper*, "I was expected to be Indian by Indians and American by Americans. [. . .] In the act of writing, it was more justified to withdraw into myself and have that be a vital experience, rather than just feeling neglected or left out." Lahiri said that being Indian American contributed to her desire to write: "It didn't make me want to be a writer so much as it made me want to write. To seek solace through observation and recording my impressions in a space that was very much my own, on the page. That's the place where I answered only to myself, from a very young age."

For Discussion

1. What motivated Lahiri to begin writing as a child?
2. What role has solitude played in Lahiri's development as a writer?
3. How do you think Lahiri's tendency "to observe and make sense of things" contributed to her development as a writer?

JOAN DIDION

A writer whose fame is fourfold—as novelist, essayist, journalist, and screen-writer—JOAN DIDION was born in 1934 in California, where her family has lived for five generations. After graduation from the University of California, Berkeley, she spent a few years in New York, working as a feature editor for *Vogue*, a fashion magazine. In 1964 she returned to California, where she worked as a freelance journalist and wrote four much-discussed novels: *River Run* (1963), *Play It As It Lays* (1971), *A Book of Common Prayer* (1977), and *Democracy* (1984). *Salvador* (1983), her book-length essay based on a visit to war-torn El Salvador, and *Miami* (1987), a study of Cuban exiles in Florida, also received wide attention. With her husband, John Gregory Dunne, Didion has coauthored screenplays, notably for *A Star Is Born* (1976), *True Confessions* (1981), and, most recently, *Up Close and Personal* (1996). Didion's latest books are *After Henry* (1992), a collection of essays; *The Last Thing He Wanted* (1996), a novel; and *Political Fictions* (2001), a collection of writings about the American political system.

Marrying Absurd

"Marrying Absurd" appeared originally in 1967 in the *Saturday Evening Post*, a general-interest magazine, and was reprinted in a book of Didion's essays, *Slouching Towards Bethlehem* (1968). As you will see, the essay is no aged relic of the 1960s. Didion's descriptions of Las Vegas and the people who marry there are enduringly fresh and funny.

To be married in Las Vegas, Clark County, Nevada, a bride must swear   1
that she is eighteen or has parental permission and a bridegroom that he is twenty-one or has parental permission. Someone must put up five dollars for the license. (On Sundays and holidays, fifteen dollars. The Clark County Courthouse issues marriage licenses at any time of the day or night except between noon and one in the afternoon, between eight and nine in the evening, and between four and five in the morning.) Nothing else is required. The State of Nevada, alone among these United States, demands neither a premarital blood test nor a waiting period before or after the issuance of a marriage license. Driving in across the Mojave from Los Angeles, one sees the signs way out on the desert, looming up from the moonscape of rattlesnakes and mesquite even before the Las Vegas lights appear like a mirage on the horizon: "GETTING MARRIED? Free License Information First Strip Exit." Perhaps the Las Vegas wedding industry achieved its peak operational efficiency between 9:00 PM and midnight of August 26, 1965, an otherwise unremarkable

Thursday which happened to be, by Presidential order, the last day on which anyone could improve his draft status merely by getting married. One hundred and seventy-one couples were pronounced man and wife in the name of Clark County and the State of Nevada that night, sixty-seven of them by a single justice of the peace, Mr. James A. Brennan. Mr. Brennan did one wedding at the Dunes and the other sixty-six in his office, and charged each couple eight dollars. One bride lent her veil to six others. "I got it down from five to three minutes," Mr. Brennan said later of his feat. "I could've married them *en masse*, but they're people, not cattle. People expect more when they get married."

What people who get married in Las Vegas actually do expect—what, in   2
the largest sense, their "expectations" are—strikes one as curious and self-contradictory business. Las Vegas is the most extreme and allegorical of American settlements, bizarre and beautiful in its venality and in its devotion to immediate gratification, a place the tone of which is set by mobsters and call girls and ladies' room attendants with amyl nitrate poppers in their uniform pockets. Almost everyone notes that there is no "time" in Las Vegas, no night and no day and no past and no future (no Las Vegas casino, however, has taken the obliteration of the ordinary time sense quite so far as Harold's Club in Reno, which for a while issued, at odd intervals in the day and night, mimeographed "bulletins" carrying news from the world outside); neither is there any logical sense of where one is. One is standing on a highway in the middle of a vast hostile desert looking at an eighty-foot sign which blinks "STARDUST" or "CAESAR'S PALACE." Yes, but what does that explain? This geographical implausibility reinforces the sense that what happens there has no connection with "real" life; Nevada cities like Reno and Carson are ranch towns, Western towns, places behind which there is some historical imperative. But Las Vegas seems to exist only in the eye of the beholder. All of which makes it an extraordinarily stimulating and interesting place, but an odd one in which to want to wear a candlelight satin Priscilla of Boston wedding dress with Chantilly lace insets, tapered sleeve and a detachable modified train.

And yet the Las Vegas wedding business seems to appeal to precisely that   3
impulse. "Sincere and Dignified Since 1954," one wedding chapel advertises. There are nineteen such wedding chapels in Las Vegas, intensely competitive, each offering better, faster, and, by implication, more sincere services than the next: Our Photos Best Anywhere, Your Wedding on a Phonograph Record, Candlelight with Your Ceremony, Honeymoon Accommodations, Free Transportation from Your Motel to Courthouse to Chapel and Return to Motel, Religious or Civil Ceremonies, Dressing Rooms, Flowers, Rings, Announcements, Witnesses Available, and Ample Parking. All of these services, like

most others in Las Vegas (sauna baths, payroll-check cashing, chinchilla coats for sale or rent), are offered twenty-four hours a day, seven days a week, presumably on the premise that marriage, like craps, is a game to be played when the table seems hot.

But what strikes one most about the Strip chapels, with their wishing   4
wells and stained-glass paper windows and their artificial bouvardia, is that so much of their business is by no means a matter of simple convenience, of late-night liaisons between show girls and baby Crosbys. Of course there is some of that. (One night about eleven o'clock in Las Vegas I watched a bride in an orange minidress and masses of flame-colored hair stumble from a Strip chapel on the arm of her bridegroom, who looked the part of the expendable nephew in movies like *Miami Syndicate*. "I gotta get the kids," the bride whimpered. "I gotta pick up the sitter, I gotta get to the midnight show." "What you gotta get," the bridegroom said, opening the door of a Cadillac Coupe de Ville and watching her crumple on the seat, "is sober.") But Las Vegas seems to offer something other than "convenience"; it is merchandising "niceness," the facsimile of proper ritual, to children who do not know how else to find it, how to make the arrangements, how to do it "right." All day and evening long on the Strip, one sees actual wedding parties, waiting under the harsh lights at a crosswalk, standing uneasily in the parking lot of the Frontier while the photographer hired by The Little Church of the West ("Wedding Place of the Stars") certifies the occasion, takes the picture: the bride in a veil and white satin pumps, the bridegroom usually in a white dinner jacket, and even an attendant or two, a sister or a best friend in hot-pink *peau de soie*, a flirtation veil, a carnation nosegay. "When I Fall in Love It Will Be Forever," the organist plays, and then a few bars of Lohengrin. The mother cries; the stepfather, awkward in his role, invites the chapel hostess to join them for a drink at the Sands. The hostess declines with a professional smile; she has already transferred her interest to the group waiting outside. One bride out, another in, and again the sign goes up on the chapel door: "One moment please—Wedding."

I sat next to one such wedding party in a Strip restaurant the last time I   5
was in Las Vegas. The marriage had just taken place; the bride still wore her dress, the mother her corsage. A bored waiter poured out a few swallows of pink champagne ("on the house") for everyone but the bride, who was too young to be served. "You'll need something with more kick than that," the bride's father said with heavy jocularity to his new son-in-law; the ritual jokes about the wedding night had a certain Panglossian character, since the bride was clearly several months pregnant. Another round of pink champagne, this time not on the house, and the bride began to cry. "It was just as nice," she sobbed, "as I hoped and dreamed it would be."

Journal Writing

Do you find the Las Vegas wedding industry and its clients, as described by Didion, to be ridiculous, depressing, amusing, harmless, or something else? Compose a one- or two-paragraph answer in your journal. (To take your journal writing further, see "From Journal to Essay" below.)

Questions on Meaning

1. Why do people from other states choose to get married in Nevada?
2. Why does Didion feel that in Las Vegas there is "no night and no day" (par. 2)?
3. What is Didion's *thesis* in this essay? Where is it stated?
4. Does Didion seem sympathetic to her subjects?

Questions on Writing Strategy

1. To which of our senses does Didion's description primarily appeal? Why might that be?
2. What kinds of EVIDENCE does Didion use to support her impressions?
3. How would you characterize Didion's POINT OF VIEW in this essay? Note her use of pronouns—she is "one" until the middle of paragraph 4, when she appears as "I."
4. What is the essay's DOMINANT IMPRESSION?
5. **OTHER METHODS.** Over the course of her essay, Didion offers a PROCESS ANALYSIS of the Las Vegas wedding. Outline this process.

Questions on Language

1. Is Didion's DICTION well matched to her subject matter? How would you describe it?
2. What is the TONE of this essay? Give EXAMPLES to support your opinion.
3. What is the EFFECT of Didion's use of brand names, place names, and business slogans? Look closely at paragraphs 3 and 4. How do strings of commercial phrases help reinforce Didion's thesis?
4. What does Didion ALLUDE to with the expression "Panglossian character" (par. 5)?
5. Check a dictionary for the meanings of the following words: allegorical, venality, implausibility, imperative (par. 2); chinchilla (3); bouvardia, *peau de soie* (4); jocularity (5).

Suggestions for Writing

1. **FROM JOURNAL TO ESSAY.** Write an essay, drawn from your journal entry, in which you spell out and explain your response to Didion's essay. If you find it depressing,

for instance, what depresses you—the marrying couples? the people who marry them? both? Why do you think these people do what they do? *Why* do they depress you? What do you think these people say about American culture?

2. Didion's description of Las Vegas weddings illustrates some contemporary attitudes toward marriage. Along the same lines, write an essay describing another ritual or social custom (for example, a graduation, military induction, presidential inauguration, religious service). What does the conduct of this custom tell us about our attitudes toward it? Try to convey a strong DOMINANT IMPRESSION.

3. Like Los Angeles, New York, and some other American cities, Las Vegas is a place with a reputation. What does Las Vegas mean to you? Base your answer on firsthand experience if you can, but also on information in the media (TV, movies, books, magazines). In an essay giving specific examples, describe the city as you understand it.

4. **CRITICAL WRITING.** Didion is well known for her detached, wryly IRONIC tone. Reread the essay, making note of how its tone is set. Write a brief essay analyzing Didion's use of words and sentence structures to create this tone.

5. **CONNECTIONS.** After reading Didion's essay, turn to Jessica Mitford's "Behind the Formaldehyde Curtain" (p. 290). How are the wedding and funeral industries similar or different? Use quotations from both essays to support your comparison. (If you need help with COMPARISON AND CONTRAST, see Chap. 7.)

Joan Didion on Writing

In "Why I Write," an essay published by the *New York Times Book Review*, adapted from her Regents' Lecture at the University of California at Berkeley, Joan Didion writes, "I stole the title for this talk, from George Orwell [see p. 637]. One reason I stole it was that I like the sound of the words: Why I Write. There you have three short unambiguous words that share a sound, and the sound they share is this:

I

I

I

In many ways writing is the act of saying *I*, of imposing oneself upon other people, of saying *listen to me, see it my way, change your mind* [. . .]."

Didion's "way," though, comes not from notions of how the world works or should work but from its observable details. She writes, "I am not in the least an intellectual, which is not to say that when I hear the word 'intellectual' I reach for my gun, but only to say that I do not think in abstracts. During the years when I was an undergraduate at Berkeley I tried, with a kind of hopeless late-adolescent energy, to buy some temporary visa into the world of ideas, to forge for myself a mind that could deal with the abstract. [. . .]

In short, I tried to think. I failed. My attention veered inexorably back to the specific, to the tangible, to what was generally considered, by everyone I knew then and for that matter have known since, the peripheral. I would try to contemplate the Hegelian dialectic and would find myself concentrating instead on the flowering pear tree outside my window and the particular way the petals fell on my floor."

Later in the essay, Didion writes, "During those years I was traveling on what I knew to be a very shaky passport, forged papers: I knew that I was no legitimate resident in any world of ideas. I knew I couldn't think. All I knew then was what I wasn't, and it took me some years to discover what I was.

"Which was a writer.

"By which I mean not a 'good' writer or a 'bad' writer but simply a writer, a person whose most absorbed and passionate hours are spent arranging words on pieces of paper. Had my credentials been in order I would never have become a writer. Had I been blessed with even limited access to my own mind there would have been no reason to write. I write entirely to find out what I'm thinking, what I'm looking at, what I see, and what it means. What I want and what I fear. [. . .] *What is going on in these pictures in my mind?*"

In the essay, Didion emphasizes that these mental pictures have a grammar. "Grammar is a piano I play by ear, since I seem to have been out of school the year the rules were mentioned. All I know about grammar is its infinite power. To shift the structure of a sentence alters the meaning of that sentence, as definitely and inflexibly as the position of a camera alters the meaning of the object photographed. Many people know about camera angles now, but not so many know about sentences. The arrangement of the words matters, and the arrangement you want can be found in the picture in your mind. The picture dictates the arrangement. The picture dictates whether this will be a sentence with or without clauses, a sentence that ends hard or a dying-fall sentence, long or short, active or passive. The picture tells you how to arrange the words and the arrangement of the words tells you, or tells me, what's going on in the picture."

For Discussion

1. What is Didion's definition of thinking? Do you agree with it?
2. To what extent does Didion's writing support her remarks about how and why she writes?
3. What does Didion mean when she says that grammar has "infinite power"? Power to do what?

JOYCE CAROL OATES

One of America's most respected and prolific contemporary authors, JOYCE CAROL OATES was born in 1938 in Lockport, New York. After graduating from Syracuse University in 1960, she earned a master's degree from the University of Wisconsin. In 1963 she published her first book, a collection of short stories, and she has published an average of two books a year since then. (To the charge that she publishes too much, Oates replies that her critics may be "secretly afraid that someone will accuse them of having done too little with their lives.") With the novel *them* (1969), Oates became one of the youngest writers to receive the National Book Award for fiction. Other notable novels include *Wonderland* (1971), *Because It Is Bitter, and Because It Is My Heart* (1990), and, most recently, *Beasts* (2001). Oates has also written more than a dozen volumes of poetry, a score of plays, and many works of nonfiction, including literary criticism and a study of boxing. In almost every novel, short story, poem, play, literary analysis, or essay, Oates remains, she says, "concerned with only one thing: the moral and social conditions of my generation." Since 1978 Oates has taught writing and literature at Princeton University.

Edward Hopper's Nighthawks, *1942*

First published in Oates's poetry collection *The Time Traveler* (1989), this poem responds to a well-known painting by the American Edward Hopper (1882–1967). The painting, *Nighthawks,* is reproduced on the next page, both in full view and in detail.

The three men are fully clothed, long sleeves,
even hats, though it's indoors, and brightly lit,
and there's a woman. The woman is wearing
a short-sleeved red dress cut to expose her arms,
a curve of her creamy chest; she's contemplating   5
a cigarette in her right hand, thinking that
her companion has finally left his wife but
can she trust him? Her heavy-lidded eyes,
pouty lipsticked mouth, she has the redhead's
true pallor like skim milk, damned good-looking   10
and she guesses she knows it but what exactly
has it gotten her so far, and where?—he'll start
to feel guilty in a few days, she knows
the signs, an actual smell, sweaty, rancid, like
dirty socks; he'll slip away to make telephone calls   15

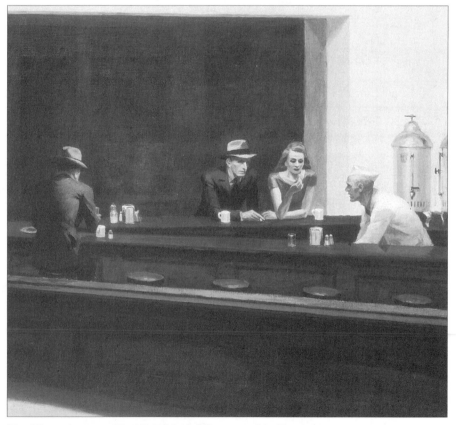

Edward Hopper, American, 1882–1967, *Nighthawks* (full painting and detail), 1942, oil on canvas, 84.1 × 152.4 cm, Friends of American Art Collection, 1942.51. © 2002 The Art Institute of Chicago. All rights reserved.

and she swears she isn't going to go through that
again, isn't going to break down crying or begging
nor is she going to scream at him, she's finished
with all that. And he's silent beside her,
not the kind to talk much but he's thinking   20
thank God he made the right move at last,
he's a little dazed like a man in a dream—
is this a dream?—so much that's wide, still,
mute, horizontal, and the counterman in white,
stooped as he is and unmoving, and the man   25
on the other stool unmoving except to sip
his coffee; but he's feeling pretty good,
it's primarily relief, this time he's sure
as hell going to make it work, he owes it to her
and to himself, Christ's sake. And she's thinking   30
the light in this place is too bright, probably
not very flattering, she hates it when her lipstick
wears off and her makeup gets caked, she'd like
to use a ladies' room but there isn't one here
and Jesus how long before a gas station opens?—   35
it's the middle of the night and she has a feeling
time is never going to budge. This time
though she isn't going to demean herself—
he starts in about his wife, his kids, how
he let them down, they trusted him and he let   40
them down, she'll slam out of the goddamned room
and if he calls her *Sugar* or *Baby* in that voice,
running his hands over her like he has the right,
she'll slap his face hard, *You know I hate that: Stop!*
And he'll stop. He'd better. The angrier   45
she gets the stiller she is, hasn't said a word
for the past ten minutes, not a strand
of her hair stirs, and it smells a little like ashes
or like the henna she uses to brighten it, but
the smell is faint or anyway, crazy for her   50
like he is, he doesn't notice, or mind—
burying his hot face in her neck, between her cool
breasts, or her legs—wherever she'll have him,
and whenever. She's still contemplating
the cigarette burning in her hand,   55
the counterman is still stooped gaping
at her, and he doesn't mind that, why not,

as long as she doesn't look back, in fact
he's thinking he's the luckiest man in the world
so why isn't he happier?   60

Journal Writing

In this poem Oates describes what she sees in Hopper's painting and also what she imagines, particularly about the woman. Most of us have unobtrusively observed strangers in a public place and imagined what they were thinking or what was going on between them. Write a paragraph or two on why such observation can be interesting or what it can (or can't) reveal. (To take your journal writing further, see "From Journal to Essay" on the facing page.)

Questions on Meaning

1. What story does Oates imagine about the couple in *Nighthawks*? How are the man's and the woman's thoughts different?
2. Line 23 of the poem asks, "*is* this a dream?" Who is posing this question? What about the painting is dreamlike?
3. Throughout the poem, Oates emphasizes the silence and stillness of the scene in the coffee shop—for instance, "The angrier / she gets the stiller she is, hasn't said a word / for the past ten minutes" (lines 45–47). What meanings about the painting and the people in it might Oates be emphasizing?

Questions on Writing Strategy

1. Where in the poem does Oates describe what can actually be seen in the painting, as opposed to what she imagines? How does she use the former to support the latter? What does the mixture suggest about Oates's PURPOSE?
2. The thoughts of the woman include some vivid sensory images. What are some examples? How do these thoughts contrast with the man's?
3. What techniques of sentence structure does Oates use in lines 12–19 and 30–45 to suggest the woman's rising anger?
4. **OTHER METHODS.** Where does Oates use NARRATION in the poem? Where does she imply a narrative? Why is narration important to her analysis of Hopper's painting?

Questions on Language

1. Oates uses just a few words that might be unfamiliar. Make sure you know the meanings of contemplating (line 5); rancid (14); budge (37); demean (38); henna (49).

2. The man's and woman's thoughts are peppered with strong language that some might find offensive. What does this suggest about how Oates sees the characters?
3. In lines 27–28 Oates writes that the man is "feeling pretty good, / primarily relief." How does the word "relief" undercut the notion of "feeling pretty good"?

Suggestions for Writing

1. **FROM JOURNAL TO ESSAY.** Find a public place where you can observe strangers unobtrusively from a distance—a park, for example, or a plaza, campus quad, dining hall, restaurant, bus, train. Take notes about what you observe—what your subject or subjects look like, how they behave, how they interact with each other. Then write an essay based on your notes that incorporates both actual description of your subjects and what the details lead you to imagine the subjects are thinking to themselves and saying to each other. Make sure the link between actual and imaginary is clear to your readers.
2. In a local gallery or museum, in a library art book, or on a Web site such as *WebMuseum* (*http://www.ibiblio.org/wm/paint*), find a painting that seems to you particularly intriguing or appealing. Then write a prose essay or a poem that expresses the painting's appeal to you. You may but need not imitate Oates by focusing on the thoughts of any figures in the painting. Describe the details of the painting and how they work together to create meaning for you. If you write a poem, don't worry about the technical aspects of poetry (meter, rhyme, and the rest). Think instead about your choice of words and IMAGES, building the poem through description.
3. **CRITICAL WRITING.** Throughout her poem, Oates interweaves description of the painting and its figures with what she imagines the figures are thinking. Mark each kind of material in the poem, and then analyze the shifts from one to the other. How does Oates make readers aware that she is moving from one to the other? Are the shifts always clear? If not, are the blurrings deliberate or a mistake? What do you think of this technique overall?
4. **CONNECTIONS.** In "Marrying Absurd" (p. 159), Joan Didion observes strangers and imagines their lives and feelings as a way of reporting on the phenomenon of the Las Vegas wedding. In an essay, COMPARE AND CONTRAST the way Didion presents her impressions of the actual people she observes with the way Oates presents her impressions of the figures in Edward Hopper's painting. Do the two writers exhibit a similar act of imagination, or do their different subjects require that they resort to different imaginative methods? Use quotations from both works to explain your comparison.

Joyce Carol Oates on Writing

For a 1997 book titled *Introspections: American Poets on One of Their Own Poems*, Joyce Carol Oates did us the valuable service of writing an essay about her poem "Edward Hopper's *Nighthawks*, 1942." She tells us why and how the painting sparked her own work of imagination.

The attempt to give concrete expression to a very amorphous impression is the insurmountable difficulty in painting.

These words of Edward Hopper's apply to all forms of art, of course. Certainly to poetry. How to evoke, in mere words, the powerful, inchoate flood of emotions that constitute "real life"? How to take the reader into the poet's innermost self, where the poet's language becomes the reader's, if only for a quicksilver moment? This is the great challenge of art, which even to fail in requires faith.

Insomniac nights began for me when I was a young teenager. Those long, lonely stretches of time when no one else in the house was awake (so far as I knew); the romance of solitude and self-sufficiency in which time seems not to pass or passes so slowly it will never bring dawn.

Always there was an air of mystery in the insomniac night. What profound thoughts and visions came to me! How strangely detached from the day-self I became! Dawn brought the familiar world, and the familiar self; a "self" that was obliged to accommodate others' expectations, and was, indeed, defined by others, predominantly adults. *Yes but you don't know me*, I would think by day, in adolescent secrecy and defiance. *You don't really know me!*

Many of Edward Hopper's paintings evoke the insomniac's uncanny vision, none more forcefully than *Nighthawks,* which both portrays insomniacs and evokes their solitude in the viewer. In this famous painting, "reality" has undergone some sort of subtle yet drastic alteration. The immense field of detail that would strike the eye has been reduced to smooth, streamlined surfaces; people and objects are enhanced, as on a lighted stage; not life but a nostalgia for life, a memory of life, is the true subject. Men and women in Hopper's paintings are somnambulists, if not mannequins, stiffly posed, with faces of the kind that populate our dreams, at which we dare not look too closely for fear of seeing the faces dissolve.

Here is, not the world, but a memory of it. For all dreams are memory: cobbled-together sights, sounds, impressions, snatches of previous experience. The dream-vision is the perpetual present, yet its contents relate only to the past.

There is little of Eros in Hopper's puritanical vision, *Nighthawks* being the rare exception. The poem enters the painting as a way of animating what cannot be animated; a way of delving into the painting's mystery. *Who are these people, what has brought them together, are they in fact together?* At the time of writing the poem I hadn't read Gail Levin's definitive biography of Hopper, and did not know how Hopper had made himself into the most methodical and premeditated of artists, continuously seeking, with his wife Jo (who would have posed for the redheaded nighthawk), scenes and tableaux to paint. Many of Hopper's canvases are elaborately posed, and their suggestion of movie stills is not accidental. This is a visual art purposefully evoking narrative, or at least the opening strategies of narrative, in which a scene is "set," "characters" are presented, often in ambiguous relationships.

Nighthawks is a work of silence. Here is an Eros of stasis, and of melancholy. It is an uncommonly beautiful painting of stark, separate, sculpted forms, in heightened juxtapositions, brightly lit and yet infinitely mysterious. The poem slips into it with no transition, as we "wake" in a dream, yearning to make the frozen narrative come alive; but finally thwarted by the painting's measured void of a world, in which silence outweighs the human voice, and the barriers between human beings are impenetrable. So the poem ends as it begins, circling upon its lovers' obsessions, achieving no crisis, no confrontation, no epiphany, no release, time forever frozen in the insomniac night.

For Discussion

1. For Oates, as well as for Hopper, what is the "great challenge of art"?
2. Why, according to Oates, did she write a poem about Hopper's painting?
3. Why is the poem circular, ending where it began?

ADDITIONAL WRITING TOPICS

Description

1. This is an in-class writing experiment. Describe another person in the room so clearly and unmistakably that when you read your description aloud, your subject will be recognized. (Be OBJECTIVE. No insulting descriptions, please!)

2. Write a paragraph describing one subject from *each* of the following categories. It will be up to you to make the general subject refer to a particular person, place, or thing. Write at least one paragraph as an objective description and at least one as a SUBJECTIVE description.

PERSON

A friend or roommate
A typical hip-hop, jazz, or country musician
One of your parents
An elderly person you know
A prominent politician
A historical figure

PLACE

An office
A classroom
A college campus
A vacation spot
A hospital emergency room
A forest

THING

A car
A dentist's drill
A painting or photograph
A foggy day
A season of the year
A musical instrument

3. In a brief essay, describe your ideal place: an apartment, a dorm room, a vacation spot, a restaurant, a gym, a store, a garden, a golf course. With concrete details, try to make the ideal seem actual.

Narration and Description

4. Use a combination of NARRATION and description to develop any one of the following topics:

Your first day on the job
Your first day at college

Returning to an old neighborhood
Getting lost
A brush with a celebrity
Delivering bad (or good) news

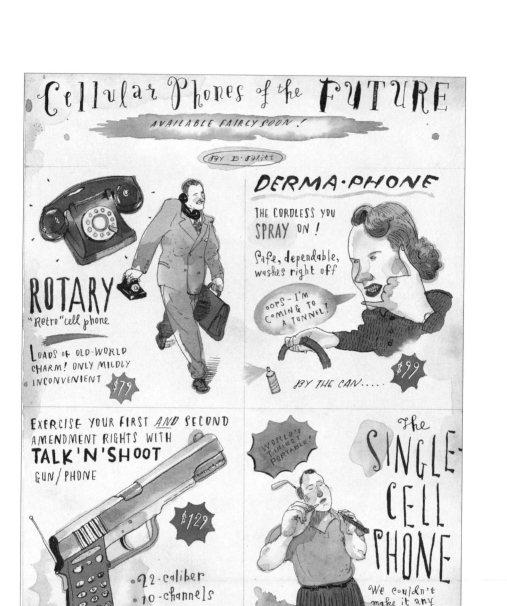

6

EXAMPLE

Pointing to Instances

Examples in a cartoon

This 2000 cartoon by Barry Blitt, from *Mother Jones* magazine, uses the method of example in a complex way. Most simply, the drawings-with-text propose instances or illustrations of the general category stated in the title—not every conceivable future cell phone but a few possibilities. At the same time, the humor of the examples reveals other, sharper observations by the artist—ideas about current and future uses of cell phones, our expectations for technology, and the results of technology whether we expect them or not. What are some of these general ideas? How, for instance, would you state the artist's opinion of the usefulness or necessity of innovations in telephone technology?

THE METHOD

"There have been many women runners of distinction," a writer begins, and quickly goes on, "among them Joan Benoit, Grete Waitz, Florence Griffith Joyner, and Marion Jones."

You have just seen examples at work. An EXAMPLE (from the Latin *exemplum:* "one thing selected from among many") is an instance that reveals a whole type. By selecting an example, a writer shows the nature or character of the group from which it is taken. In a written essay, examples will often serve to illustrate a general statement, or GENERALIZATION. Here, for instance, the writer Linda Wolfe makes a point about the food fetishes of Roman emperors (Domitian and Claudius ruled in the first century AD).

> The emperors used their gastronomical concerns to indicate their contempt of the country and the whole task of governing it. Domitian humiliated his cabinet by forcing them to attend him at his villa to help solve a serious problem. When they arrived he kept them waiting for hours. The problem, it finally appeared, was that the emperor had just purchased a giant fish, too large for any dish he owned, and he needed the learned brains of his ministers to decide whether the fish should be minced or whether a larger pot should be sought. The emperor Claudius one day rode hurriedly to the Senate and demanded they deliberate the importance of a life without pork. Another time he sat in his tribunal ostensibly administering justice but actually allowing the litigants to argue and orate while he grew dreamy, interrupting the discussions only to announce, "Meat pies are wonderful. We shall have them for dinner."

Wolfe might have allowed the opening sentence of her paragraph—the TOPIC SENTENCE—to remain a vague generalization. Instead, she supports it with three examples, each a brief story of an emperor's contemptuous behavior. With these examples, Wolfe not only explains and supports her generalization but also animates it.

The method of giving examples—of illustrating what you're saying with a "for instance"—is not merely helpful to practically all kinds of writing, it is indispensable. Bad writers—those who bore us, or lose us completely—often have an ample supply of ideas; their trouble is that they never pull their ideas down out of the clouds. A dull writer, for instance, might declare, "The emperors used food to humiliate their governments," and then, instead of giving examples, go on, "They also manipulated their families," or something—adding still another large, unillustrated idea. Specific examples are *needed* elements in effective prose. Not only do they make ideas understandable, but they also keep readers awake. (The previous paragraphs have tried—by giving examples from Linda Wolfe and from "a dull writer"—to illustrate this point.)

Example 177

THE PROCESS

The Generalization

Examples illustrate a generalization, such as Linda Wolfe's opening statement about the Roman emperors, and any example essay is bound to have a generalization as its THESIS STATEMENT. Here are a few examples from the essays in this chapter:

> Sometimes I think we would be better off [in dealing with social problems] if we forgot about the broad strokes and concentrated on the details. (Anna Quindlen, "Homeless")

> That first encounter, and those that followed, signified that a vast, unnerving gulf lay between nighttime pedestrians—particularly women—and me. (Brent Staples, "Black Men and Public Space")

Such a generalization forms the backbone, the central idea, of an essay developed by example. Then the specifics bring the idea down to earth for readers.

The Examples

An essay developed by example will often start with an example or two. That is, you'll see something—a man pilfering a quarter for bus fare from a child's Kool-Aid stand, a friend dating another friend's fiancé (or fiancée)—and your observation will suggest a generalization (perhaps a statement about how people mishandle ethical dilemmas). But a mere example or two probably won't demonstrate your generalization for readers and thus won't achieve your PURPOSE. For that you'll need a range of instances.

Where do you find more? In anything you know—or care to learn. Start close to home. Seek examples in your own immediate knowledge and experience. Explore your conversations with others, your studies, and the storehouse of information you have gathered from books, newspapers, radio, TV, and the Internet as well as from popular hearsay: proverbs and sayings, bits of wisdom you've heard voiced in your family, folklore, popular song.

Now and again, you may feel an irresistible temptation to make up an example out of thin air. This procedure is risky, but with imagination can work wonderfully. When Henry David Thoreau, in *Walden*, attacks Americans' smug pride in the achievements of nineteenth-century science and industry, he wants to illustrate that kind of invention or discovery "which distracts our attention from serious things." And so he makes up the examples— far-fetched at the time, but pointed—of a transatlantic speaking tube and what it might convey: "We are eager to tunnel under the Atlantic and bring the Old World some weeks nearer to the New; but perchance the first news that will leak through into the broad, flapping American ear will be that the

Princess Adelaide has the whooping cough." (Thoreau would be appalled at our immersion in the British Royal Family via just the sort of communication he imagined.)

Thoreau's examples (and the sarcastic phrase about the American ear) bespeak genius; but, of course, not every writer can be a Thoreau—or needs to be. A hypothetical example may well be better than no example at all; yet, as a rule, an example from fact or experience is likely to carry more weight. Suppose you have to write about the benefits—any benefits—that recent science has conferred upon the nation. You might imagine one such benefit: the prospect of one day being able to vacation in outer space and drift about in free-fall like a soap bubble. That imagined benefit would be all right, but it is obviously a conjecture that you dreamed up without going to the library. Do a little digging on the Internet or in recent books and magazines. Your reader will feel better informed to be told that science—specifically, the NASA space program—has produced useful inventions. You add:

> Among these are the smoke detector, originally developed as Skylab equipment; the inflatable air bag to protect drivers and pilots, designed to cushion astronauts in splashdowns; a walking chair that enables paraplegics to mount stairs and travel over uneven ground, derived from the moonwalkers' surface buggy; the technique of cryosurgery, the removal of cancerous tissue by fast freezing.

By using specific examples like these, you render the idea of "benefits to society" more concrete and more definite. Such examples are not prettifications of your essay; they are necessary if you are to hold your readers' attention and convince them that you are worth listening to.

When giving examples, you'll find other methods useful. Sometimes, as in the paragraph by Linda Wolfe, an example takes the form of a NARRATIVE (Chap. 4): a brief story, an ANECDOTE, or a case history. Sometimes an example embodies a vivid DESCRIPTION of a person, place, or thing (Chap. 5).

Lazy writers think, "Oh well, I can't come up with any example here—I'll just leave it to the reader to find one." The flaw in this ASSUMPTION is that the reader may be as lazy as the writer. As a result, a perfectly good idea may be left suspended in the stratosphere. The linguist and writer S. I. Hayakawa tells the story of a professor who, in teaching a philosophy course, spent a whole semester on the theory of beauty. When students asked him for a few examples of beautiful paintings, symphonies, or works of nature, he refused, saying, "We are interested in principles, not in particulars." The professor himself may well have been interested in principles, but it is a safe bet that his classroom resounded with snores. In written EXPOSITION, it is undoubtedly the particulars—the pertinent examples—that keep a reader awake and having a good time, and taking in the principles besides.

Example   **179**

> **CHECKLIST FOR REVISING AN EXAMPLE ESSAY**
>
> ✔ **GENERALIZATION.** What general statement do your examples illustrate? Will it be clear to readers what ties the examples together?
>
> ✔ **SUPPORT.** Do you have enough examples to establish your generalization, or will readers be left needing more?
>
> ✔ **SPECIFICS.** Are your examples detailed? Does each capture some aspects of the generalization?
>
> ✔ **RELEVANCE.** Do all your examples relate to your generalization? Should any be cut because they go off track?

EXAMPLE IN A PARAGRAPH: TWO ILLUSTRATIONS

Using Example to Write About Television

This paragraph appears in an essay maintaining that television merely simulates, or imitates, real problems, events, activities, and institutions. The essay offers many examples of programming that only seems to represent what's real, such as morning news shows, small-claims courts (*Judge Judy*), and wrestling. Here the author uses further examples of TV wrestling to show how it simulates televised football, basketball, and other sports.

To sustain the simulation, wrestling must construct and maintain a little universe of the simulated. To do this, its discourse refers in its every enunciation to the apparatus used to broadcast conventional sport. *[Generalization to be illustrated]* Wrestling features the same style of ringside commentary, the same interpolation of interviews, the same mystification of sporting expertise, the same freeze-frame and instant replay formats, the same faintly prurient interest in the wrestlers' private lives (not to mention parts), the same cults of personality, and so on. *[Six examples]* This system of understanding, however, is marshaled in the service of an event which is a parody of its originating source: "real" sport.
—Michael Sorkin, "Faking It,"
in *Watching Television*, ed. Todd Gitlin

Using Example in an Academic Discipline

The following paragraph from an economics textbook appears amid the author's explanation of how markets work. To dispel what might seem clouds of theory, the author here brings an abstract principle down to earth with a concrete and detailed example.

The primary function of the market is to bring together suppliers and demanders so that they can trade with one another. Buyers
and sellers do not necessarily have to be in face-to-face contact;   *Generalization to be*
they can signal their desires and intentions through various inter-   *illustrated*
mediaries. For example, the demand for green beans in California is
not expressed directly by the green bean consumers to the green
bean growers. People who want green beans buy them at a grocery
store; the store orders them from a vegetable wholesaler; the whole-
saler buys them from a bean cooperative, whose manager tells local   *Single extended example*
farmers of the size of the current demand for green beans. The de-
manders of green beans are able to signal their demand schedule to
the original suppliers, the farmers who raise the beans, without any
personal communication between the two parties.

—Lewis C. Solmon, *Microeconomics*

CASE STUDY
Using Examples

As a college sophomore, Kharron Reid was applying for a summer internship implementing computer networks for businesses. He put together a résumé structured to present his previous work experience and his education for this kind of job. (See the résumé on pp. 364–65.)

In drafting a cover letter for the résumé, Reid at first found himself repeating all his background in a very long letter. On the advice of his school's placement office, he rewrote the letter to emphasize just what the prospective employer would most need to know: the work, courses, and computer skills that qualified him for the opening it had. The rewritten letter, below, focuses on examples from the résumé to support the statement (in the second-to-last paragraph) that "my education and my hands-on experience with networking prepare me for the opening you have."

Kharron Reid
137 Chester St., Apt. E
Allston, MA 02134
February 23, 2001

Ms. Dolores Jackson
Human Resources Director
E-line Systems
75 Arondale Avenue
Boston, MA 02114

Dear Ms. Jackson:

I am applying for the networking internship in your information technology department, advertised in the career services office of Boston University.

I have considerable experience in networking from summer internships at NBS Systems and at Pioneer Networking. At NBS I planned and laid the physical platforms and configured the software for seven WANs on a Windows NT server. At Pioneer, I laid the physical platforms and configured the software to connect eight workstations into a LAN. Both internships gave me experience in every stage of networking.

In the fall I will be entering my third year in Boston University's School of Management, majoring in business administration and information systems. I have completed courses in computers (including programming), information systems, and business. In addition to my experience and coursework, I am proficient in Unix, NT, and Linux.

As the enclosed résumé indicates, my education and my hands-on experience with networking prepare me for the opening you have.

I am available for an interview at your convenience. Please call me at (617) 555-4009 or e-mail me at kreid@bu.edu.

Sincerely,

Kharron Reid

Kharron Reid

BARBARA LAZEAR ASCHER

BARBARA LAZEAR ASCHER was born in 1946 and educated at Bennington College and Cardozo School of Law. She practiced law for two years in a private firm, where she found herself part of a power structure in which those on top resembled "the two-year-old with the biggest plastic pail and shovel on the beach. It's a life of nervous guardianship." Ascher quit the law to devote herself to writing, to explore, as she says, "what really matters." Her essays have appeared in the *New York Times*, the *Yale Review, Vogue,* and other periodicals and have been collected in *Playing After Dark* (1986) and *The Habit of Loving* (1989). She is a contributing editor of *Self* magazine. Her most recent books are *Landscape Without Gravity: A Memoir of Grief* (1993), about her brother's death from AIDS; and *Dancing in the Dark: Romance, Yearning, and the Search for the Sublime* (1999), about our search for romance in our lives.

On Compassion

Ascher often writes about life in New York City, where human problems sometimes seem larger and more stubborn than in other places. In this essay Ascher uses examples from the city to address a universal need: compassion for those who require help. First published in *Elle* magazine in 1988, the essay was later reprinted in *The Habit of Loving.* The essay following this one, Anna Quindlen's "Homeless," addresses the same issue.

The man's grin is less the result of circumstance than dreams or madness. 1
His buttonless shirt, with one sleeve missing, hangs outside the waist of his baggy trousers. Carefully plaited dreadlocks bespeak a better time, long ago. As he crosses Manhattan's Seventy-ninth Street, his gait is the shuffle of the forgotten ones held in place by gravity rather than plans. On the corner of Madison Avenue, he stops before a blond baby in an Aprica stroller. The baby's mother waits for the light to change and her hands close tighter on the stroller's handle as she sees the man approach.

The others on the corner, five men and women waiting for the crosstown 2
bus, look away. They daydream a bit and gaze into the weak rays of November light. A man with a briefcase lifts and lowers the shiny toe of his right shoe, watching the light reflect, trying to catch and balance it, as if he could hold and make it his, to ease the heavy gray of coming January, February, and March. The winter months that will send snow around the feet, calves, and knees of the grinning man as he heads for the shelter of Grand Central or Pennsylvania Station.

But for now, in this last gasp of autumn warmth, he is still. His eyes fix on 3 the baby. The mother removes her purse from her shoulder and rummages through its contents: lipstick, a lace handkerchief, an address book. She finds what she's looking for and passes a folded dollar over her child's head to the man who stands and stares even though the light has changed and traffic navigates about his hips.

His hands continue to dangle at his sides. He does not know his part. He 4 does not know that acceptance of the gift and gratitude are what make this transaction complete. The baby, weary of the unwavering stare, pulls its blanket over its head. The man does not look away. Like a bridegroom waiting at the altar, his eyes pierce the white veil.

The mother grows impatient and pushes the stroller before her, bearing 5 the dollar like a cross. Finally, a black hand rises and closes around green.

Was it fear or compassion that motivated the gift? 6

Up the avenue, at Ninety-first Street, there is a small French bread shop 7 where you can sit and eat a buttery, overpriced croissant and wash it down with rich cappuccino. Twice when I have stopped here to stave hunger or stay the cold, twice as I have sat and read and felt the warm rush of hot coffee and milk, an old man has wandered in and stood inside the entrance. He wears a stained blanket pulled up to his chin, and a woolen hood pulled down to his gray, bushy eyebrows. As he stands, the scent of stale cigarettes and urine fills the small, overheated room.

The owner of the shop, a moody French woman, emerges from the 8 kitchen with steaming coffee in a Styrofoam cup, and a small paper bag of . . . of what? Yesterday's bread? Today's croissant? He accepts the offering as silently as he came, and is gone.

Twice I have witnessed this, and twice I have wondered, what compels 9 this woman to feed this man? Pity? Care? Compassion? Or does she simply want to rid her shop of his troublesome presence? If expulsion were her motivation she would not reward his arrival with gifts of food. Most proprietors do not. They chase the homeless from their midst with expletives and threats.

As winter approaches, the mayor of New York City is moving the home- 10 less off the streets and into Bellevue Hospital. The New York Civil Liberties Union is watchful. They question whether the rights of these people who live in our parks and doorways are being violated by involuntary hospitalization.

I think the mayor's notion is humane, but I fear it is something else as 11 well. Raw humanity offends our sensibilities. We want to protect ourselves from an awareness of rags with voices that make no sense and scream forth in inarticulate rage. We do not wish to be reminded of the tentative state of our own well-being and sanity. And so, the troublesome presence is removed from the awareness of the electorate.

Like other cities, there is much about Manhattan now that resembles   12
Dickensian London. Ladies in high-heeled shoes pick their way through
poverty and madness. You hear more cocktail party complaints than usual, "I
just can't take New York anymore." Our citizens dream of the open spaces of
Wyoming, the manicured exclusivity of Hobe Sound.

And yet, it may be that these are the conditions that finally give birth to   13
empathy, the mother of compassion. We cannot deny the existence of the
helpless as their presence grows. It is impossible to insulate ourselves against
what is at our very doorstep. I don't believe that one is born compassionate.
Compassion is not a character trait like a sunny disposition. It must be
learned, and it is learned by having adversity at our windows, coming through
the gates of our yards, the walls of our towns, adversity that becomes so familiar that we begin to identify and empathize with it.

For the ancient Greeks, drama taught and reinforced compassion within   14
a society. The object of Greek tragedy was to inspire empathy in the audience so that the common response to the hero's fall was: "There, but for the
grace of God, go I." Could it be that this was the response of the mother who
offered the dollar, the French woman who gave the food? Could it be that the
homeless, like those ancients, are reminding us of our common humanity? Of
course, there is a difference. This play doesn't end—and the players can't go
home.

Journal Writing

Using Ascher's essay as a springboard, consider a personal experience that involved
misfortune. Have you ever needed to beg on the street, been evicted from an apartment, or had to scrounge for food? Have you ever been asked for money by beggars,
worked in a soup kitchen, or volunteered at a shelter or public hospital? Write about
such an experience in your journal. (To take your journal writing further, see "From
Journal to Essay" on the next page.)

Questions on Meaning

1. What do the two men in Ascher's essay exemplify?
2. What is Ascher's THESIS? What is her PURPOSE?
3. What solution to homelessness is introduced in paragraph 10? What does Ascher
   think of this possibility?
4. How do you interpret Ascher's last sentence? Is she optimistic or pessimistic
   about whether people will learn compassion?

Questions on Writing Strategy

1. Which comes first, the GENERALIZATIONS or the supporting examples? Why has Ascher chosen this order?
2. What assumptions does the author make about her AUDIENCE?
3. Why do the other people at the bus stop look away (par. 2)? What does Ascher's DESCRIPTION of their activities say about them?
4. **OTHER METHODS.** Ascher explores CAUSES AND EFFECTS. Do you agree with her that exposure to others' helplessness increases our compassion? Why, or why not?

Questions on Language

1. What is the difference between empathy and compassion? Why does Ascher say that "empathy [is] the mother of compassion" (par. 13)?
2. Find definitions for the following words: plaited, dreadlocks, bespeak (par. 1); stave, stay (7); expletives (9); inarticulate, electorate (11).
3. What are the implications of Ascher's ALLUSION to "Dickensian London" (par. 12)?
4. Examine the language Ascher uses to describe the two homeless men. Is it OBJECTIVE? sympathetic? negative?

Suggestions for Writing

1. **FROM JOURNAL TO ESSAY.** Write an essay on the experience you explored in your journal, using examples to convey the effect the experience had on you.
2. Write an essay on the problem of homelessness in your town or city. Use examples to support your view of the problem and a possible solution.
3. In paragraph 10 Ascher refers to the involuntary hospitalization of homeless people and the concerns such government action raises among supporters of individual rights, such as the American Civil Liberties Union. What is your opinion of the rights of homeless people to live on the streets? How do you distinguish among the individual's rights, the community's responsibilities to the individual, and the community's rights? (For instance, what if a homeless person seems sick? What if he or she seems unstable, if not violent?) You may work solo on this assignment—stating your ideas and supporting them with EVIDENCE from your own observations and experience—or you may conduct research to discover legal and other arguments and data to support your ideas.
4. **CRITICAL WRITING.** In her last paragraph, Ascher mentions but does not address another key difference between the characters in Greek tragedy and the homeless on today's streets: The former were "heroes"—gods and goddesses, kings and queens—whereas the latter are placeless, poor, anonymous, even reviled. Does this difference negate Ascher's comparison between Greek theatergoers and ourselves or her larger point about how compassion is learned? Answer in a brief essay, saying why or why not.
5. **CONNECTIONS.** The next essay, Anna Quindlen's "Homeless," also uses examples to make a point about homelessness. What are some of the differences in the examples each writer uses? In a brief essay, explore whether and how these differences create different TONES in the two works.

Barbara Lazear Ascher on Writing

A lawyer before she was a full-time writer, Barbara Lazear Ascher thinks that her legal training helped her become a stronger writer.

"I believe there is a kind of legal thinking that becomes part of your own thinking," she told Jean W. Ross of *Contemporary Authors*. "What it did for me was help me to become quite a tight writer. My pieces are very short, and I think a lot of that has to do with the training in law, which is to tell the facts and the theories, and then put it all together and close it up. I might have been a more excessive writer if I hadn't had the legal training."

For Ascher, the essay is the ideal form of expression. "I'm quite impatient, so it's very satisfying to have a small space in which to tell what it was you wanted to tell. You get to the point right away instead of having to drag it out and slowly reveal it."

For Discussion

1. How did her legal training help Ascher when she became a writer? How does a "tight writer" help readers as well?
2. How might an "excessive writer" have trouble with the essay form? What, in your view, is "excessive" writing?

ANNA QUINDLEN

ANNA QUINDLEN was born in 1952 and graduated from Barnard College in 1974. She worked as a reporter for the *New York Post* and the *New York Times* before taking over the *Times*'s "About New York" column, serving as the paper's deputy metropolitan editor, and in 1986 creating her own weekly column, "Life in the Thirties." Many of the essays from this popular column were collected in *Living Out Loud* (1988). Between 1989 and 1994 Quindlen wrote a twice-weekly op-ed column for the *Times*, on social and political issues. The columns earned her the Pulitzer Prize in 1992, and many of them were collected in *Thinking Out Loud: On the Personal, the Political, the Public, and the Private* (1993). In 1999 Quindlen began writing a biweekly "My Turn" column for *Newsweek* magazine. She has also published two books about children, two for children, and three successful novels: *Object Lessons* (1991), *One True Thing* (1994), and *Black and Blue: A Novel* (1998).

Homeless

In this essay from *Living Out Loud,* Quindlen uses examples to explore the same topic as Barbara Lazear Ascher (p. 183), but with a different slant. Typically for Quindlen, she mingles a reporter's respect for details with a passionate regard for life.

Her name was Ann, and we met in the Port Authority Bus Terminal several Januarys ago. I was doing a story on homeless people. She said I was wasting my time talking to her; she was just passing through, although she'd been passing through for more than two weeks. To prove to me that this was true, she rummaged through a tote bag and a manila envelope and finally unfolded a sheet of typing paper and brought out her photographs.

They were not pictures of family, or friends, or even a dog or cat, its eyes brown-red in the flashbulb's light. They were pictures of a house. It was like a thousand houses in a hundred towns, not suburb, not city, but somewhere in between, with aluminum siding and a chain-link fence, a narrow driveway running up to a one-car garage and a patch of backyard. The house was yellow. I looked on the back for a date or a name, but neither was there. There was no need for discussion. I knew what she was trying to tell me, for it was something I had often felt. She was not adrift, alone, anonymous, although her bags and her raincoat with the grime shadowing its creases had made me believe she was. She had a house, or at least once upon a time had had one. Inside were curtains, a couch, a stove, potholders. You are where you live. She was somebody.

I've never been very good at looking at the big picture, taking the global view, and I've always been a person with an overactive sense of place, the legacy of an Irish grandfather. So it is natural that the thing that seems most wrong with the world to me right now is that there are so many people with no homes. I'm not simply talking about shelter from the elements, or three square meals a day or a mailing address to which the welfare people can send the check—although I know that all these are important for survival. I'm talking about a home, about precisely those kinds of feelings that have wound up in cross-stitch and French knots on samplers over the years.

Home is where the heart is. There's no place like it. I love my home with   4
a ferocity totally out of proportion to its appearance or location. I love dumb things about it: the hot-water heater, the plastic rack you drain dishes in, the roof over my head, which occasionally leaks. And yet it is precisely those dumb things that make it what it is—a place of certainty, stability, pre-dictability, privacy, for me and for my family. It is where I live. What more can you say about a place than that? That is everything.

Yet it is something that we have been edging away from gradually during   5
my lifetime and the lifetimes of my parents and grandparents. There was a time when where you lived often was where you worked and where you grew the food you ate and even where you were buried. When that era passed, where you lived at least was where your parents had lived and where you would live with your children when you became enfeebled. Then, suddenly where you lived was where you lived for three years, until you could move on to something else and something else again.

And so we have come to something else again, to children who do not   6
understand what it means to go to their rooms because they have never had a room, to men and women whose fantasy is a wall they can paint a color of their own choosing, to old people reduced to sitting on molded plastic chairs, their skin blue-white in the lights of a bus station, who pull pictures of houses out of their bags. Homes have stopped being homes. Now they are real estate.

People find it curious that those without homes would rather sleep sitting   7
up on benches or huddled in doorways than go to shelters. Certainly some pre-fer to do so because they are emotionally ill, because they have been locked in before and they are damned if they will be locked in again. Others are afraid of the violence and trouble they may find there. But some seem to want some-thing that is not available in shelters, and they will not compromise, not for a cot, or oatmeal, or a shower with special soap that kills the bugs. "One room," a woman with a baby who was sleeping on her sister's floor, once told me, "painted blue." That was the crux of it; not size or location, but pride of own-ership. Painted blue.

This is a difficult problem, and some wise and compassionate people are   8
working hard at it. But in the main I think we work around it, just as we walk around it when it is lying on the sidewalk or sitting in the bus terminal—the

problem, that is. It has been customary to take people's pain and lessen our own participation in it by turning it into an issue, not a collection of human beings. We turn an adjective into a noun: the poor, not poor people; the homeless, not Ann or the man who lives in the box or the woman who sleeps on the subway grate.

Sometimes I think we would be better off if we forgot about the broad 9 strokes and concentrated on the details. Here is a woman without a bureau. There is a man with no mirror, no wall to hang it on. They are not the homeless. They are people who have no homes. No drawer that holds the spoons. No window to look out upon the world. My God. That is everything.

Journal Writing

What does the word *home* mean to you? Does it involve material things, privacy, family, a sense of permanence? In your journal, explore your ideas about this word. (To take your journal writing further, see "From Journal to Essay" on the facing page.)

Questions on Meaning

1. What is Quindlen's THESIS?
2. What distinction is Quindlen making in her CONCLUSION with the sentences "They are not the homeless. They are people who have no homes"?
3. Why does Quindlen believe that having a home is important?

Questions on Writing Strategy

1. Why do you think Quindlen begins with the story of Ann? How else might Quindlen have begun her essay?
2. What is the EFFECT of Quindlen's examples of her own home?
3. What key ASSUMPTIONS does the author make about her AUDIENCE? Are the assumptions reasonable? Where does she specifically address an assumption that might undermine her view?
4. **OTHER METHODS.** Quindlen uses examples to support an ARGUMENT. What position does she want readers to recognize and accept?

Questions on Language

1. What is the effect of "My God" in the last paragraph?
2. How might Quindlen be said to give new meaning to the old CLICHÉ "Home is where the heart is" (par. 4)?
3. What is meant by "crux" (par. 7)? Where does the word come from?

Suggestions for Writing

1. **FROM JOURNAL TO ESSAY.** Write an essay that gives a detailed DEFINITION of *home* by using your own home(s), hometown(s), or experiences with home(s) as supporting examples. (See Chap. 12 if you need help with definition.)
2. Have you ever moved from one place to another? What sort of experience was it? Write an essay about leaving an old home and moving to a new one. Was there an activity or a piece of furniture that helped ease the transition?
3. Address Quindlen's contention that turning homelessness into an issue avoids the problem, that we might "be better off if we forgot about the broad strokes and concentrated on the details."
4. **CRITICAL WRITING.** Write a brief essay in which you agree or disagree with Quindlen's assertion that a home is "everything." Can one, for instance, be a fulfilled person without a home? In your answer, take account of the values that might underlie an attachment to home; Quindlen mentions "certainty, stability, predictability, privacy" (par. 4), but there are others, including some (such as fear) that are less positive.
5. **CONNECTIONS.** COMPARE AND CONTRAST the views of homelessness and its solution in Quindlen's "Homeless" and Barbara Lazear Ascher's "On Compassion" (p. 183). Use specific passages from each essay to support your comparison.

Anna Quindlen on Writing

Anna Quindlen started her writing career as a newspaper reporter. "I had wanted to be a writer for most of my life," she recalls in the introduction to her book *Living Out Loud*, "and in the service of the writing I became a reporter. For many years I was able to observe, even to feel, life vividly, but at second-hand. I was able to stand over the chalk outline of a body on a sidewalk dappled with black blood; to stand behind the glass and look down into an operating theater where one man was placing a heart in the yawning chest of another; to sit in the park on the first day of summer and find myself professionally obligated to record all the glories of it. Every day I found answers: who, what, when, where, and why."

Quindlen was a good reporter, but the business of finding answers did not satisfy her personally. "In my own life," she continues, "I had only questions." Then she switched from reporter to columnist at the *New York Times*. It was "exhilarating," she says, that "my work became a reflection of my life. After years of being a professional observer of other people's lives, I was given the opportunity to be a professional observer of my own. I was permitted—and permitted myself—to write a column, not about my answers, but about my questions. Never did I make so much sense of my life as I did then, for it was inevitable that as a writer I would find out most clearly what I thought, and what I only thought I thought, when I saw it written down. [. . .] After years of feeling secondhand, of feeling the pain of the widow, the joy of the winner, I was able to allow myself to feel those emotions for myself."

For Discussion

1. What were the advantages and disadvantages of news reporting, according to Quindlen?
2. What did Quindlen feel she could accomplish in a column that she could not accomplish in a news report? What evidence of this difference do you see in her essay "Homeless"?

BILL BRYSON

BILL BRYSON, known for both travel memoirs and language studies, was born in Des Moines, Iowa, in 1951. After graduating from Drake College, Bryson moved to England, where he lived for almost twenty years. He worked in a psychiatric hospital and then embarked on a journalism career in the British press. In 1987 he left regular newspaper work to write books, notably volumes on language such as *Mother Tongue: English and How It Got That Way* (1990), and perceptive and amusing travel writing, such as *The Lost Continent* (1989), recounting a search for the perfect small American town; *Notes from a Small Island* (1995), telling of a farewell tour of Great Britain; and *A Walk in the Woods* (1998), detailing an 870-mile hike along the Appalachian Trail. Bryson's latest work, *In a Sunburned Country* (2000), chronicles his travels in Australia. He lives in New Hampshire with his wife and four children.

Design Flaws

Bryson is at his witty, peevish best in this essay from his book *I'm a Stranger Here Myself: Notes on Returning to America After Twenty Years* (1999). What examples can you add to his?

I have a teenage son who is a runner. He has, at a conservative estimate, sixty-one hundred pairs of running shoes, and every one of them represents a greater investment of cumulative design effort than, say, the Verrazano Narrows Bridge. These shoes are amazing. I was just reading a review in one of his running magazines of the latest in "Sport Utility Sneakers," as they are evidently called, and it was full of passages like this: "A dual density EVA midsole with air units fore and aft provides stability while a gel heel-insert absorbs shock, but the shoe makes a narrow footprint, a characteristic that typically suits only the biomechanically efficient runner." Alan Shepard[1] went into space with less science at his disposal than that.

So here is my question. If my son can have his choice of a seemingly limitless range of scrupulously engineered, biomechanically efficient footwear, why does my computer keyboard suck? This is a serious inquiry.

My computer keyboard has 102 keys, almost double what my old manual typewriter had, which on the face of it seems awfully generous. Among other typographical luxuries, I can choose between three styles of bracket and two kinds of colon. I can dress my text with carets (∧) and cedillas (~). I can have slashes that fall to the left or to the right, and goodness knows what else.

---

[1] An astronaut, Alan Shepard in 1961 became the first American to be launched into space and in 1971 was the fourth person to walk on the moon. — EDS.

I have so many keys, in fact, that over on the right-hand side of the key-   4
board there are whole communities of buttons of whose function I haven't the
tiniest inkling. Occasionally I hit one by accident and subsequently discover
that several paragraphs of my w9rk n+w look l*ke th?s, or that I have written the last page and a half in an interesting but unfortunately nonalphabetic
font called Wingdings, but otherwise I haven't the faintest idea what those
buttons are there for.

Never mind that many of these keys duplicate the functions of other keys,   5
while others apparently do nothing at all (my favorite in this respect is one
marked "Pause," which when pressed does absolutely nothing, raising the
interesting metaphysical question of whether it is therefore doing its job), or
that several keys are arrayed in slightly imbecilic places. The delete key, for
instance, is right beside the overprint key so that often I discover, with a trill
of gay laughter, that my most recent thoughts have been devouring, PacMan-
like, everything I had previously written. Quite often, I somehow hit a combination of keys that summons a box that says, in effect, "This Is a Pointless
Box. Do You Want It?" which is followed by another that says "Are You *Sure*
You Don't Want the Pointless Box?" Never mind all that. I have known for a
long time that the computer is not my friend.

But here is what gets me. Out of all the 102 keys at my disposal, there   6
is no key for the fraction ½. Typewriter keyboards always used to have a key
for ½. Now, however, if I wish to write ½, I have to bring down the font menu
and call up a directory called "WP Characters," then hunt through a number
of subdirectories until I remember, or more often blunder on, the particular
one, "Typographic Symbols," in which hides the furtive ½ sign. This is irksome and pointless, and it doesn't seem right to me.

But then most things in the world don't seem right to me. On the dash-   7
board of our family car is a shallow indentation about the size of a paperback
book. If you are looking for somewhere to put your sunglasses or spare change,
it is the obvious place, and it works extremely well, I must say, so long as the
car is not actually moving. However, as soon as you put the car in motion, and
particularly when you touch the brakes, turn a corner, or go up a gentle slope,
everything slides off. There is, you see, no lip around this dashboard tray. It is
just a flat space with a dimpled bottom. It can hold nothing that has not been
nailed to it.

So I ask you: What then is it *for*? Somebody had to design it. It didn't just   8
appear spontaneously. Some person—perhaps, for all I know, a whole committee of people in the Dashboard Stowage Division—had to invest time and
thought in incorporating into the design of this vehicle (it's a Dodge Excreta,
if you're wondering) a storage tray that will actually hold nothing. That is
really quite an achievement.

But it is nothing, of course, compared with the manifold design achieve-   9
ments of those responsible for the modern video recorder. Now I am not going
to prattle on about how impossible it is to program the typical VCR because
you know that already. Nor will I observe how irritating it is that you must
cross the room and get down on your stomach to confirm that it is actually
recording. But I will just make one small passing observation. I recently
bought a VCR, and one of the selling points—one of the things the manufacturer boasted about—was that it was capable of recording programs up
to twelve months in advance. Now think about this for a moment and tell
me any circumstance—and I mean any circumstance at all—in which you
can envision wanting to set a video machine to record a program one year
from now.

I don't want to sound like some old guy who is always moaning. I freely   10
acknowledge that there are many excellent, well-engineered products that
didn't exist when I was a boy—the pocket calculator and Post-it notes are
two that fill me yet with gratitude and wonder—but it does seem to me that
an awful lot of things out there have been designed by people who cannot possibly have stopped to think how they will be used.

Just think for a moment of all the everyday items you have to puzzle   11
over—fax machines, scanners, photocopiers, hotel showers, hotel alarm
clocks, airline tickets, television remote control units, microwave ovens,
almost any electrical product owned by someone other than you—because
they are ill thought out.

And why are they so ill thought out? Because all the best designers are   12
making running shoes. Either that or they are just idiots. In either case, it
really isn't fair.

Journal Writing

Do you share Bryson's irritation with user-unfriendly consumer products? What product or other object of design do you have complaints about—a bicycle? a computer
program? a building on campus? Explore these complaints in your journal. (To take
your journal writing further, see "From Journal to Essay" on the next page.)

Questions on Meaning

1. What is Bryson's PURPOSE in this essay? What is his THESIS?
2. What is Bryson's point in opening and closing with references to the design of
   running shoes?

3. What are Bryson's specific complaints about his computer keyboard? Which of these seem to bother him the most?

Questions on Writing Strategy

1. How many examples of poorly designed products does Bryson discuss? Do they adequately support the generalization of his thesis? Why, or why not?
2. What ASSUMPTIONS does Bryson seem to make about his AUDIENCE? How do these assumptions affect the way he presents his ideas?
3. What does Bryson accomplish by acknowledging "that there are many excellent, well-engineered products that didn't exist when I was a boy" (par. 10)?
4. **OTHER METHODS.** How does Bryson's presentation of his three main examples rely on CAUSE AND EFFECT?

Questions on Language

1. Bryson says, "I don't want to sound like some old guy who is always moaning" (par. 10). Does he succeed in avoiding such a TONE? How would you characterize his tone?
2. How does Bryson's DICTION shift in paragraph 2? What is the effect of this shift?
3. In paragraph 8 how does Bryson have some fun with the names car manufacturers give their products?
4. Consult a dictionary if you need help defining the following: cumulative (par. 1); scrupulously (2); inkling (4); metaphysical, imbecilic (5); disposal, furtive (6); spontaneously (8); manifold, prattle (9).

Suggestions for Writing

1. **FROM JOURNAL TO ESSAY.** Based on your earlier journal writing, write an essay about one or more products, buildings, or other designed objects with flaws that impede, frustrate, or irritate users. Use plenty of examples to support a clear generalization about the object or objects.
2. In paragraph 10 Bryson writes that certain technological innovations, such as the pocket calculator and Post-it notes, cause him to feel "gratitude and wonder." Write an essay about a recent technological innovation that you see as indispensable to your life—the cell phone, for example. Alternatively, you might focus your essay on an innovation you find so annoying that you wish it had never been invented—the cell phone, for example. In either case, explain *why* it is indispensable or *why* it is annoying. Like Bryson, you may wish to approach your topic humorously.
3. **CRITICAL WRITING.** Write an essay in which you ANALYZE Bryson's use of humor in "Design Flaws." In your view does humor help the author support his case, or does it do more to undercut his case? Explain why you think so, using quotations from the essay to support your analysis.
4. **CONNECTIONS.** In "The Plot Against People" (p. 366), Russell Baker also writes humorously about his frustration with inanimate objects. In an essay, COMPARE

AND CONTRAST "Design Flaws" with "The Plot Against People." Do the two writers use humor in basically the same way, or can you point to specific differences? Which essay do you prefer, and why?

Bill Bryson on Writing

In "Lost in Cyberspace," another essay in the collection *I'm a Stranger Here Myself,* Bryson expands on his difficulties with computers. This passage from the essay zeros in on his word processor's spelling checker.

Like nearly everything else to do with computers, a spell checker is marvelous in principle. When you have done a piece of work, you activate it and it goes through the text looking for words that are misspelled. Actually, since a computer doesn't understand what words are, it looks for letter clusters it isn't familiar with, and here is where the disappointment begins.

First, it doesn't recognize any proper nouns—names of people, places, corporations, and so on—or nonstandard spellings like *kerb* and *colour*. Nor does it recognize many plurals or other variant forms (like *steps* or *stepped*), or abbreviations or acronyms. Nor, evidently, any word coined since Eisenhower was president. Thus, it recognizes *sputnik* and *beatnik* but not *Internet, fax, cyberspace,* or *butthead,* among many others.

But the really distinctive feature of my spell checker—and here is the part that can provide hours of entertainment for anyone who doesn't have anything approaching a real life—is that it has been programmed to suggest alternatives. These are seldom less than memorable. For this column, for instance, for *Internet* it suggested *internat* (a word that I cannot find in any dictionary, American or British), *internode, interknit,* and *underneath. Fax* prompted no fewer than thirty-three suggested alternatives, including *fab, fays, feats, fuzz, feaze, phase,* and at least two more that are unknown to lexicography: *falx* and *phose. Cyberspace* drew a blank, but for *cyber* it came up with *chubbier* and *scabbier.*

I have tried without success to discern the logic by which a computer and programmer working in tandem could decide that someone who typed *f-a-x* would really have intended to write *p-h-a-s-e,* or why *cyber* might suggest *chubbier* and *scabbier* but not, say, *watermelon* or *full-service gas station,* to name two equally random alternatives. Still less can I explain how nonexistent words like *phose* and *internat* would get into the program. Call me exacting, but I would submit that a computer program that wants to discard a real word in favor of one that does not exist is not ready to be offered for public use.

For Discussion

1. What does Bryson find objectionable about spelling checkers?
2. Have you shared some of Bryson's problems with spelling checkers? Have you had other problems he doesn't mention — for instance, a checker's inability to distinguish among *not* and *now* and *no* or among *their* and *there* and *they're*?
3. What do you think is the remedy for spelling errors when the checking program is flawed? Use the program and hope for the best? Stop using the program and hope for the best? Something else?

WILLIAM SAFIRE

Born in New York City in 1929, WILLIAM SAFIRE is best known for his writing about two subjects, American politics and the English language. Safire studied at Syracuse University for two years and then became by turns a reporter for the *New York Herald Tribune*, a US Army correspondent, a radio and television producer, a public-relations executive, and a speechwriter for President Richard Nixon. In 1973 Safire joined the *New York Times*, beginning as a political columnist on the op-ed page and then, in 1979, taking on the additional role of language columnist in the paper's Sunday magazine. Often he merges his two interests in columns on the language of politics. Safire's many books include collections of his language columns, such as *I Stand Corrected* (1984) and *Spread the Word* (1999); works on politics, such as *Before the Fall* (1988) and *The First Dissident* (1992); and the novels *Full Disclosure* (1977), *Freedom* (1987), *Sleeper Spy* (1995), and *Scandalmonger* (2000). In 1978 Safire received the Pulitzer Prize for distinguished commentary. He lives in Washington, DC.

Fulminations

William Safire's "On Language" column in the *New York Times Magazine* takes on tricky or controversial issues of grammar, usage, and word origin. In this essay from May 2001 he provides a forum for scientists and other specialists who are upset at the general public's misuse of their terminology.

1   The specialists are in open rebellion at the theft of their vocabularies. Egged on by sly agitation in this space to fulminate about raids by the general public on their fields' linguistic larders, the specialists have at last found an outlet for their ire at the twisting of their favorite terms.

2   "I cannot resist the invitation to rail against the boneheaded misuse of *organic*," fulminates Stephen Slatin, at the department of physiology and biophysics of the Albert Einstein College of Medicine in the Bronx. "It does not, or certainly should not, mean 'vegetables grown without fertilizers' or 'fruit produced without pesticides.'"

3   Right on, says Richard Fireman of Chicago: "*Organic* used to mean 'carbon based.' An 'inorganic food' would be an oxymoron"—prescriptive usagists would insist on the more specific "contradiction in terms"—"unless someone knows a way to get nourishment from stones."

4   Chemists think of an "organized body" as an animal or plant containing compounds derived from hydrocarbons; they call that kind of chemistry *organic* and bristle at the "unscientific" extension of meaning into food "grown without chemical additives or genetic manipulation."

Geologists, too, excoriate lay writers with rocks in their heads. When I   5
wrote that San Jose was "the *epicenter* of the California computer industry's
power consumption," Julian Stone of Rumson, New Jersey, noted: "*Epicenter* is
a scientific term referring to the point on the surface of the earth above the
underground focus of an earthquake. Do you mean that the center of power
consumption in California is underground?"

The geophysicist Joseph D. Sides adds, "Writers should be advised that   6
epi- no more intensifies the meaning of *center* than does *pen-* intensify the
meaning of *ultimate*."[1] (The prefix *epi-* most often means "on" or "over"; *pen*,
not a prefix, is from the Latin *paene*, "almost.") Sides defines *epicenter* as "the
point on the surface of the earth vertically above the center of an earthquake,
the quake's 'hypocenter.'" It is also, he says, "the point on the earth's surface
vertically below the atmospheric detonation of a bomb, the 'hypercenter' of
the explosion." He finds "misuse of the offending term attributable to spurious
erudition on the part of the writers combined with scientific illiteracy on the
part of copy editors."

Is your understanding of these terms growing exponentially? No! thunders   7
a totality of mathematicians. "I'm vexed to hear some trend described as
'growing *exponentially*' when the writer means it is growing rapidly," writes
Maurice Fox of Arlington, Virginia. "*Exponential* growth is not necessarily
rapid. The mathematical term merely describes something whose rate of
growth is proportional to its size. My savings account grows *exponentially* but
not rapidly."

Geometric, or compound, growth can be fast or slow; if our economy   8
grows by 0.1 percent a year, that's *exponential*, but the stock market tanks. A
professor of physics at Tufts University, Roger Tobin, is equally annoyed at the
lay misuse of *exponential* to mean "a whole lot," referring to quantity rather
than rate of growth, "but to say my annoyance is *exponentially* greater today
than yesterday is gibberish."

Tobin is not offended, however, by a general use of *quantum* to mean "sud-   9
den," provided we don't use it to mean "huge": "The crucial characteristic of
a *quantum jump* isn't its size but its abruptness—something goes from one
state to another without passing through any intermediate states in between."
That's one of the "stolen meanings" that started this specialist agitation,
which is growing fast if not exponentially.

Those intellectuals who name their companion animals Peeve (to be able   10
to say "This is my pet, Peeve") have as their ally Jacques Barzun, America's

---

[1] The word *penultimate* means "next to last" but is often misused to mean something like
"most ultimate."—EDS.

only best-selling nonagenarian. "A couple of misplaced technicalities," he writes from San Antonio. "*Synergy*, which belongs to physiology and relates to the working together of muscles, etc. Applied to the merger of two clothing firms (actual), it is ridiculous, especially since technically the meaning is 'greater effect than the sum of the efforts.'"

A semantic theft by educators is *module*, which Professor Barzun says "is   11
used ambiguously to mean 'a class period' and 'a portion of program.' (Years ago, it was 'nucleus.') A *module* in architecture or building generally is a part that does not change size, character or function and thus serves as a measure of a larger whole. In a column, it is the measurement itself—half the diameter of the base."

Architects, too, have their linguistic *bêtes noires*.[2] ("Peeve, meet my *bête,*   12
Noire.") "I am very annoyed at the current usage of the term *architect*," writes Fran Read, who is one. "Examples include '*architect* of the peace plan,' 'software *architect*' and in the phrase spoken by several CEOs and commentators on CNBC, 'We *rearchitected* the software.'"

Read's pique is superstructured by Tim Groninger, a project engineer.   13
"Word thievery in engineering has become especially acute," he seethes, "due to the ever-growing hunger for words in the world of computers. I can no longer use the word *architecture* in the traditional sense. The word now implies the design and construction of computer networks, not buildings."

The architect Edwin Elias-Narvaez piles on with "It is particularly galling   14
to perform an Internet search for *architect* only to find thousands of references having nothing to do with the traditional meaning of the word."

(The magazine *Architectural Record* recently interviewed Richard Saul   15
Wurman, who said: "I invented the term *information architect* in 1975, when I was national chairman of the AIA convention in Philadelphia. It was called 'The Architecture of Information.' Now I would say that somewhere between 20,000 and 100,000 people in the US have *information architect* on their business cards.")

Fulminations from other fields are still coming in. Ophthalmologists nar-   16
row their eyes at the nearsighted semantic theft of their *myopic*. Yoga practitioners in rooster position cock-a-doodle mellowly but firmly about the extension of *guru* from "revered teacher and spiritual leader" to a sarcastic "self-appointed cult figure." And most of all, logicians everywhere pose the query, What are the philistines doing to our *beg the question?*

The specialists are not going to take it anymore.   17

---

[2] French, meaning literally "beasts black" or, in English word order, "black beasts": unpleasant or unlucky things or people to be avoided.—EDS.

Journal Writing

When have you found offense or humor in the misuse of a word or expression you know well—perhaps a technical term like the ones Safire cites, a term from a hobby or other favorite activity, or a slang term? In your journal, write the word or expression's true meaning and the misuses you've heard. (To take your journal writing further, see "From Journal to Essay" on the facing page.)

Questions on Meaning

1. Safire states his THESIS early on. What is it?
2. What does *fulmination* mean? Why does Safire use this word in his title? Do you think he means it seriously?
3. PARAPHRASE the misuses and accurate meanings of Safire's first four examples.
4. In paragraph 16 Safire piles on several last examples. He hints at the true meaning of one of them, *myopic*, and leaves another one, *begs the question*, undefined. Check a dictionary for *myopic* and page 509 of this book for *begs the question*. What can you add to fill in Safire's references? What might the specialists object to in the use of these terms?

Questions on Writing Strategy

1. Almost all of Safire's examples come in the form of quotations from others. Why are such quotations appropriate for the author's PURPOSE?
2. What are some of the TRANSITIONS Safire uses to shift his discussion from one term to the next in his essay?
3. Considering that he first published this piece in the *New York Times Magazine*, what ASSUMPTIONS do you think Safire made about his readers' education and their interest in language? How do the essay's TONE and examples support your INFERENCE?
4. **OTHER METHODS.** How does Safire use COMPARISON AND CONTRAST throughout this essay?

Questions on Language

1. The vocabulary of Safire and of the people he quotes is sometimes quite sophisticated. Be sure you understand the meaning of the following words: linguistic, larders, ire (par. 1); rail (2); prescriptive, usagists (3); genetic, manipulation (4); excoriate (5); spurious, erudition, illiteracy (6); vexed (7); gibberish (8); nonagenarian (10); semantic (11); pique, acute (13); galling (14); ophthalmologists, yoga, philistines (16).
2. What is the nature of Safire's wordplay—the jokes using language—in the first sentence of paragraph 5, the second sentence of 7, the first sentence of 13, and the second sentence of 16?

3. What is the verbal joke in Safire's parenthetical "Peeve, meet my *bête, Noire*" (par. 12)? How does it relate to "This is my pet, Peeve" in paragraph 10?

Suggestions for Writing

1. **FROM JOURNAL TO ESSAY.** Expand your journal entry into a brief essay that explains the meaning of your misused word or expression and how and why it's important to you. Give examples of its misuses, explaining why they are inappropriate.
2. People tend to have pet peeves about the ways others drive, watch television, view movies in theaters, eat, or talk. Choose one of these subjects or another one and ask at least six people to describe their pet peeve about it. Then write an essay in which you explain these irritations, relying at least partly on direct quotations from your interviewees.
3. **CRITICAL WRITING.** Respond to Safire's essay, focusing on the specialists' concerns about the misuses of their terminology. Do you think the specialists' reactions are justified, or not? Does a group have an exclusive right to a word it coined? Do you see virtue, or not, in restricting specialized terms to their specialized meanings?
4. **CONNECTIONS.** Safire's "Fulminations" and William Lutz's "The World of Doublespeak" (p. 399) both detail complaints about the use of language, using examples to clarify the problems. The authors' basic attitudes toward their subjects differ markedly, however. COMPARE AND CONTRAST the two authors' TONES, giving examples to illustrate your generalizations. Also consider the appropriateness of each author's tone for the importance and seriousness of his subject.

William Safire on Writing

In the introduction to *On Language* (1980), the first collection of his language columns, William Safire explained how someone with no apparent qualifications—"not even a college degree"—could become a judge of language.

Where do I come off, tossing about such terms as "permissible," "correct," and "wrong" [. . .]? Who is to say what is "permissible" and what is not? Russell Baker[1] wrote of the Great Mentioner, the secret source responsible for candidates being "mentioned for President"—on that analogy, where is the Great Permitter [. . .]? What, other than sheer chutzpah, gives authority to any language "authority"—or, as my correspondents put it, "Who the hell are you to say?"

---

[1] A colleague of Safire's at the *New York Times*. See page 366.—EDS.

I'm a working writer, that's who. (That's *whom*? No. *Who* is correct.) I write because I enjoy expressing myself, and writing forces me to think more coherently than I do when just shooting off my mouth. Because I both write to live and live to write, I have taken an interest in the implements of my craft. (Why *implements*? Why not the shorter and more understandable *tools*? Because that would draw me into "tools of my trade," a cliché. But isn't it better to use a convenient cliché than to seem to labor to get away from it? Yes; I should have written "tools of my trade.") [. . .]

There is a big difference between being conscious of your language and being self-conscious about the way you write and speak. To be conscious of language is to be proud of the magnificent and subtle instrument in your hands; to be self-conscious about the possibility of error, or fearful of the derision of your listener at your experiments with the instrument, is to be a nerd, a schnook, and a wimp.

Who are the Great Permitters? We are the people who care about clarity and precision, who detest fuzziness of expression that reveals sloppiness or laziness of thought. [. . .] We live the life of the mindful, and we intend each utterance to say a mouthful. We are not fuddy-duddies: If we want to carefully and deliberately split an infinitive, we do so with zest, knowing that the most fun in breaking a rule is in knowing what rule you're breaking. (That's why I can get away with all these parentheses.)

Rules? Who the hell are you and I, then, to arrogate the right to make or defend rules, to assume responsibility for deciding what is "correct," to dictate what is to be embraced as good, preferred, or "standard" usage—and what is to be ridiculed and reviled as vulgar, barbaric, or confusing?

We are the people who care; we've registered for the linguistic primary. Our interest is our power.

For Discussion

1. Why do you think Safire calls himself and other language authorities the "Great Permitters"? What does this label suggest? Why does Safire capitalize it?
2. Safire reports that his readers ask, "Who the hell are you to say [what's correct or not in language]?" How does Safire answer this question? Do you find the answers satisfactory?
3. What, according to Safire, is the difference between "being conscious" and "being self-conscious" about one's language use? Do you fall into one camp or the other? Do you find Safire's distinction accurate and fair?

BRENT STAPLES

BRENT STAPLES is a member of the editorial board of the *New York Times*.
Born in 1951 in Chester, Pennsylvania, Staples has a BA in behavioral science from Widener University in Chester and a PhD in psychology from the
University of Chicago. Before joining the *New York Times* in 1985, he
worked for the *Chicago Sun-Times*, the *Chicago Reader*, *Chicago* magazine,
and *Down Beat* magazine. At the *Times*, Staples writes on culture and politics. He has also contributed to the *New York Times Magazine*, *New York
Woman*, *Ms.*, *Harper's*, and other magazines. His memoir, *Parallel Time:
Growing Up in Black and White*, appeared in 1994. He is currently writing a
book about the Associated Negro Press, a service that for much of the twentieth century supplied news stories, commentary, and other material for
African American newspapers.

Black Men and Public Space

"Black Men and Public Space" appeared in the December 1986 issue of
Harper's magazine and was then published, in a slightly different version, in
Staples's memoir, *Parallel Time*. To explain a recurring experience of African
American men, Staples relates incidents when he has been "a night walker
in the urban landscape."

My first victim was a woman—white, well dressed, probably in her late   1
twenties. I came upon her late one evening on a deserted street in Hyde Park,
a relatively affluent neighborhood in an otherwise mean, impoverished section of Chicago. As I swung onto the avenue behind her, there seemed to be
a discreet, uninflammatory distance between us. Not so. She cast back a worried glance. To her, the youngish black man—a broad six feet two inches with
a beard and billowing hair, both hands shoved into the pockets of a bulky military jacket—seemed menacingly close. After a few more quick glimpses, she
picked up her pace and was soon running in earnest. Within seconds she disappeared into a cross street.

That was more than a decade ago. I was twenty-two years old, a graduate   2
student newly arrived at the University of Chicago. It was in the echo of that
terrified woman's footfalls that I first began to know the unwieldy inheritance
I'd come into—the ability to alter public space in ugly ways. It was clear that
she thought herself the quarry of a mugger, a rapist, or worse. Suffering a bout
of insomnia, however, I was stalking sleep, not defenseless wayfarers. As a
softy who is scarcely able to take a knife to a raw chicken—let alone hold one
to a person's throat—I was surprised, embarrassed, and dismayed all at once.
Her flight made me feel like an accomplice in tyranny. It also made it clear

that I was indistinguishable from the muggers who occasionally seeped into
the area from the surrounding ghetto. That first encounter, and those that
followed, signified that a vast, unnerving gulf lay between nighttime pedestrians—particularly women—and me. And I soon gathered that being perceived as dangerous is a hazard in itself. I only needed to turn a corner into a
dicey situation, or crowd some frightened, armed person in a foyer somewhere,
or make an errant move after being pulled over by a policeman. Where fear
and weapons meet—and they often do in urban America—there is always
the possibility of death.

In that first year, my first away from my hometown, I was to become thor-   3
oughly familiar with the language of fear. At dark, shadowy intersections, I
could cross in front of a car stopped at a traffic light and elicit the *thunk, thunk,*
thunk, thunk of the driver—black, white, male, or female—hammering down
the door locks. On less traveled streets after dark, I grew accustomed to but
never comfortable with people crossing to the other side of the street rather
than pass me. Then there were the standard unpleasantries with policemen,
doormen, bouncers, cabdrivers, and others whose business it is to screen out
troublesome individuals *before* there is any nastiness.

I moved to New York nearly two years ago and I have remained an avid   4
night walker. In central Manhattan, the near-constant crowd cover minimizes
tense one-on-one street encounters. Elsewhere—in SoHo, for example, where
sidewalks are narrow and tightly spaced buildings shut out the sky—things
can get very taut indeed.

After dark, on the warrenlike streets of Brooklyn where I live, I often see   5
women who fear the worst from me. They seem to have set their faces on neutral, and with their purse straps strung across their chests bandolier-style, they
forge ahead as though bracing themselves against being tackled. I understand,
of course, that the danger they perceive is not a hallucination. Women are
particularly vulnerable to street violence, and young black males are drastically overrepresented among the perpetrators of that violence. Yet these
truths are no solace against the kind of alienation that comes of being ever the
suspect, a fearsome entity with whom pedestrians avoid making eye contact.

It is not altogether clear to me how I reached the ripe old age of twenty-   6
two without being conscious of the lethality nighttime pedestrians attributed
to me. Perhaps it was because in Chester, Pennsylvania, the small, angry
industrial town where I came of age in the 1960s, I was scarcely noticeable
against a backdrop of gang warfare, street knifings, and murders. I grew up one
of the good boys, had perhaps a half-dozen fistfights. In retrospect, my shyness
of combat has clear sources.

As a boy, I saw countless tough guys locked away; I have since buried sev-   7
eral, too. They were babies, really—a teenage cousin, a brother of twenty-

two, a childhood friend in his mid-twenties—all gone down in episodes of bravado played out in the streets. I came to doubt the virtues of intimidation early on. I chose, perhaps unconsciously, to remain a shadow—timid, but a survivor.

The fearsomeness mistakenly attributed to me in public places often has a 8 perilous flavor. The most frightening of these confusions occurred in the late 1970s and early 1980s, when I worked as a journalist in Chicago. One day, rushing into the office of a magazine I was writing for with a deadline story in hand, I was mistaken for a burglar. The office manager called security and, with an ad hoc posse, pursued me through the labyrinthine halls, nearly to my editor's door. I had no way of proving who I was. I could only move briskly toward the company of someone who knew me.

Another time I was on assignment for a local paper and killing time before 9 an interview. I entered a jewelry store on the city's affluent Near North Side. The proprietor excused herself and returned with an enormous red Doberman pinscher straining at the end of a leash. She stood, the dog extended toward me, silent to my questions, her eyes bulging nearly out of her head. I took a cursory look around, nodded, and bade her good night.

Relatively speaking, however, I never fared as badly as another black male 10 journalist. He went to nearby Waukegan, Illinois, a couple of summers ago to work on a story about a murderer who was born there. Mistaking the reporter for the killer, police officers hauled him from his car at gunpoint and but for his press credentials would probably have tried to book him. Such episodes are not uncommon. Black men trade tales like this all the time.

Over the years, I learned to smother the rage I felt at so often being taken 11 for a criminal. Not to do so would surely have led to madness. I now take precautions to make myself less threatening. I move about with care, particularly late in the evening. I give a wide berth to nervous people on subway platforms during the wee hours, particularly when I have exchanged business clothes for jeans. If I happen to be entering a building behind some people who appear skittish, I may walk by, letting them clear the lobby before I return, so as not to seem to be following them. I have been calm and extremely congenial on those rare occasions when I've been pulled over by the police.

And on late-evening constitutionals I employ what has proved to be an 12 excellent tension-reducing measure: I whistle melodies from Beethoven and Vivaldi and the more popular classical composers. Even steely New Yorkers hunching toward nighttime destinations seem to relax, and occasionally they even join in the tune. Virtually everybody seems to sense that a mugger wouldn't be warbling bright, sunny selections from Vivaldi's *Four Seasons*. It is my equivalent of the cowbell that hikers wear when they know they are in bear country.

Journal Writing

Staples explains how he perceives himself altering public space. Write in your journal about a time when you felt as if *you* altered public space—in other words, you changed people's attitudes or behavior just by being in a place or entering a situation. If you haven't had this experience, write about a time when you saw someone else alter public space in this way. (To take your journal writing further, see "From Journal to Essay" on the facing page.)

Questions on Meaning

1. What is the PURPOSE of this essay? Do you think Staples believes that he (or other African American men) will cease "to alter public space in ugly ways" in the near future? Does he suggest any long-term solution for "the kind of alienation that comes of being ever the suspect" (par. 5)?
2. In paragraph 5 Staples says he understands that the danger women fear when they see him "is not a hallucination." Do you take this to mean that Staples perceives himself to be dangerous? Explain.
3. Staples says, "I chose, perhaps unconsciously, to remain a shadow—timid, but a survivor" (par. 7). What are the usual CONNOTATIONS of the word *survivor*? Is "timid" one of them? How can you explain this apparent discrepancy?

Questions on Writing Strategy

1. The concept of altering public space is relatively abstract. How does Staples convince you that this phenomenon really takes place?
2. The author employs a large number of examples in a fairly small space. He cites three specific instances that involved him, several general situations, and one incident involving another African American man. How does Staples avoid having the piece sound like a list? How does he establish COHERENCE among all these examples? (Look, for example, at details and TRANSITIONS.)
3. **OTHER METHODS.** Many of Staples's examples are actually ANECDOTES—brief NARRATIVES. The opening paragraph is especially notable. Why is it so effective?

Questions on Language

1. What does the author accomplish by using the word *victim* in the essay's first paragraph? Is the word used literally? What TONE does it set for the essay?
2. Be sure you know how to define the following words, as used in this essay: affluent, uninflammatory (par. 1); unwieldy, tyranny, pedestrians (2); intimidation (7); congenial (11); constitutionals (12).
3. The word *dicey* (par. 2) comes from British slang. Without looking it up in your dictionary, can you figure out its meaning from the context in which it appears?

Suggestions for Writing

1. **FROM JOURNAL TO ESSAY.** Write an essay narrating either your experience of altering public space yourself or your experience of being a witness when someone else altered public space. What changes did you observe in the behavior of the people around you? Was your behavior similarly affected? In retrospect, do you think your reactions were justified?

2. Write an essay using examples to show how a trait of your own or of someone you know well always seems to affect people, whether positively or negatively.

3. **CRITICAL WRITING.** Consider, more broadly than Staples does, what it means to alter public space. Staples would rather not have the power to do so, but it *is* a power, and it could perhaps be positive in some circumstances (wielded by a street performer, for instance, or the architect of a beautiful new building on campus). Write an essay expanding on Staples's essay in which you examine the pros and cons of altering public space. Use specific examples as your EVIDENCE.

4. **CONNECTIONS.** Like Staples, Barbara Lazear Ascher, in "On Compassion" (p. 183), considers how people regard and respond to "the Other," the one who is viewed as different. In an essay, COMPARE AND CONTRAST the POINTS OF VIEW of these two authors. How does point of view affect each author's selection of details and tone?

Brent Staples on Writing

In comments written especially for *The Bedford Reader,* Brent Staples talks about the writing of "Black Men and Public Space." "I was only partly aware of how I felt when I began this essay. I knew only that I had this collection of experiences (facts) and that I felt uneasy with them. I sketched out the experiences one by one and strung them together. The bridge to the essay — what I wanted to say, but did not know when I started — sprang into life quite unexpectedly as I sat looking over these experiences. The crucial sentence comes right after the opening anecdote, in which my first 'victim' runs away from me: 'It was in the echo of that terrified woman's footfalls that I first began to know the unwieldy inheritance I'd come into — the ability to alter public space in ugly ways.' 'Aha!' I said. 'This is why I feel bothered and hurt and frustrated when this happens. I don't want people to think I'm stalking them. I want some fresh air. I want to stretch my legs. I want to be as anonymous as any other person out for a walk in the night.'"

A news reporter and editor by training and trade, Staples sees much similarity between the writing of a personal essay like "Black Men and Public Space" and the writing of, say, a murder story for a daily newspaper. "The newspaper murder," he says, "begins with standard newspaper information:

the fact that the man was found dead in an alley in such-and-such a section of the city; his name, occupation, and where he lived; that he died of gunshot wounds to such-and-such a part of his body; that arrests were or were not made; that such-and-such a weapon was found at the scene; that the police have established no motive; etc.

"Personal essays take a different tack, but they, too, begin as assemblies of facts. In 'Black Men and Public Space,' I start out with an anecdote that crystallizes the issue I want to discuss—what it is like to be viewed as a criminal all the time. I devise a sentence that serves this purpose and also catches the reader's attention: 'My first victim was a woman—white, well dressed, probably in her late twenties.' The piece gives examples that are meant to illustrate the same point and discusses what those examples mean.

"The newspaper story stacks its details in a specified way, with each piece taking a prescribed place in a prescribed order. The personal essay begins often with a flourish, an anecdote, or the recounting of a crucial experience, then goes off to consider related experiences and their meanings. But both pieces rely on reporting. Both are built of facts. Reporting is the act of finding and analyzing facts.

"A fact can be a state of the world—a date, the color of someone's eyes, the arc of a body that flies through the air after having been struck by a car. A fact can also be a feeling—sorrow, grief, confusion, the sense of being pleased, offended, or frustrated. 'Black Men and Public Space' explores the relationship between two sets of facts: (1) the way people cast worried glances at me and sometimes run away from me on the streets after dark, and (2) the frustration and anger I feel at being made an object of fear as I try to go about my business in the city."

Personal essays and news stories share one other quality as well, Staples thinks: They affect the writer even when the writing is finished. "The discoveries I made in 'Black Men and Public Space' continued long after the essay was published. Writing about the experiences gave me access to a whole range of internal concerns and ideas, much the way a well-reported news story opens the door onto a given neighborhood, situation, or set of issues."

For Discussion

1. In recounting how his essay developed, what does Staples reveal about his writing process?
2. How, according to Staples, are essay writing and news writing similar? How are they different?
3. What does Staples mean when he says that "writing about the experiences gave me access to a whole range of internal concerns and ideas"?

ADDITIONAL WRITING TOPICS

Example

1. Select one of the following general statements, or set forth a general statement of your own that one of these inspires. Making it your central idea (or THESIS), support it in an essay full of examples. Draw your examples from your reading, your studies, your conversation, or your own experience.

Voice mail is a great convenience (or a great inconvenience) for the caller.

Electronic mail provides a form of communication that letters and the telephone don't.

People one comes to admire don't always at first seem likable.

Fashions this year are loonier than ever before.

Good (or bad) habits are necessary to the nation's economy.

Each family has its distinctive lifestyle.

Certain song lyrics, closely inspected, promote violence.

Comic books are going to the dogs.

At some point in life, most people triumph over crushing difficulties.

Churchgoers aren't perfect.

TV commercials suggest that buying the advertised product will improve your love life like crazy.

Home cooking can't win over fast food.

Ordinary lives sometimes give rise to legends.

Some people I know are born winners (or losers).

Books can change our lives.

Certain machines *do* have personalities.

Some road signs lead drivers astray.

2. In a brief essay, make a GENERALIZATION about either the terrors or the joys that members of minority groups seem to share. To illustrate your generalization, draw examples from personal experience, from outside reading, or from two or three of the essays in this book by the following authors: Maya Angelou (p. 86), Amy Tan (p. 92), Sherman Alexie (p. 103), Jhumpa Lahiri (p. 153), Brent Staples (p. 205), Nancy Mairs (p. 249), Shelby Steele (p. 328), Gloria Naylor (p. 468), Christine Leong (p. 474), Sandra Cisneros (p. 568), Judith Ortiz Cofer (p. 575), Martin Luther King, Jr. (p. 603), Richard Rodriguez (p. 639), and Cornel West (p. 664).

Comparison and contrast in a painting and a photograph

Created just five years apart, these works relate in time as well as subject. Below, the painting *American Gothic,* by the Iowan Grant Wood (1892–1942), depicts farmers in 1930, before the Great Depression was fully underway. Opposite, the photograph *Rural Rehabilitation Client,* by the Lithuanian-born New Jerseyan Ben Shahn (1899–1969), depicts recipients of a federal aid program in Arkansas in 1935, at the Depression's low point. Closely examine the people in each image (clothes, postures, expressions) and their settings. What striking and not-so-striking similarities do you notice? What is the most obvious difference? What are some more subtle differences? What does the medium of each work (painting versus photography) contribute to the differences? How would you summarize the visions of rural folk conveyed by Wood and Shahn?

7

COMPARISON
AND CONTRAST
Setting Things Side by Side

THE METHOD

Should we pass laws to regulate pornography or just let pornography run wild? Which team do you place your money on, the Cowboys or the Forty-Niners? To go to school full-time or part-time: What are the rewards and drawbacks of each way of life? How do the Republican and the Democratic platforms stack up against each other? How is the work of Picasso like or unlike that of Matisse? These are questions that may be addressed by the dual method of COMPARISON AND CONTRAST. In comparing, you point to similar features of the subjects; in contrasting, to different features. (The features themselves you identify by the method of DIVISION or ANALYSIS; see Chap. 9.)

With the aid of comparison and contrast, you can show why you prefer one thing to another, one course of action to another, one idea to another. In an argument in which you support one of two possible choices, a careful and detailed comparison and contrast of the choices may be extremely convincing. In an expository essay, it can demonstrate that you understand your subjects thoroughly. That is why, on exams that call for essay answers, often you will be asked to compare and contrast. Sometimes the examiner will come right out and say, "Compare and contrast nineteenth-century methods of treating drug addiction with those of the present day." Sometimes, however, comparison and contrast won't even be mentioned by name; instead, the examiner will ask, "What resemblances and differences do you find between John Updike's short story 'A & P' and the Grimm fairy tale 'Godfather Death'?" Or, "Explain the relative desirability of holding a franchise as against going into business as an independent proprietor." But those—as you realize when you begin to plan your reply—are just other ways of asking you to compare and contrast.

In practice, the two methods are usually inseparable. A little reflection will show you why you need both. Say you intend to write a portrait-in-words of two people. No two people are in every respect exactly the same or entirely dissimilar. Simply to compare them or to contrast them would not be true to life. To set them side by side and portray them accurately, you must consider both similarities and differences.

A good essay in comparing and contrasting serves a PURPOSE. Most of the time, the writer of such an essay has one of two purposes in mind:

1. *The purpose of showing each of two subjects distinctly by considering both, side by side.* Writing with such a purpose, the writer doesn't necessarily find one of the subjects better than the other. In "Grant and Lee" in this chapter, Bruce Catton examines the characters of two Civil War generals. His

conclusion is not that either was a better man but that each reflected strong currents of American society.

2. *The purpose of choosing between two things.* In daily life, we often EVALUATE two possibilities to choose between them: which college course to elect, which movie to see, which luncheon special to take — chipped beef over green noodles or fried smelt on a bun? Our thinking on a matter such as the last is quick and informal: "Hmmmm, the smelt *looks* better. Red beef, green noodles — ugh, what a sight! Smelt has bones, but the beef is rubbery. Still, I don't like the smell of that smelt. I'll go for the beef (or maybe just grab a hamburger after class)." In essays, too, a writer, by comparing and evaluating points, decides which of two things is more admirable: "Organic Gardening, Yes; Gardening with Chemical Fertilizers, No!" — or "Skydiving Versus the Safe, Sane Life." In writing, as in thinking, you need to consider the main features of both subjects, the positive features and the negative, and to choose the subject whose positive features more clearly predominate.

THE PROCESS

Subjects for Comparison

When you find yourself considering two subjects side by side or preferring one subject over another, you have already embarked on comparison and contrast. Just be sure that your two subjects display a clear basis for comparison. In other words, they should have something significant in common. Comparison usually works best with two of a kind: two means of reading for the visually impaired, two ways of gardening, two California wines, two mystery writers, two schools of political thought.

It can sometimes be effective to find similarities between evidently unlike subjects — a city and a country town, say — and a special form of comparison, ANALOGY, always equates two very unlike things, explaining one in terms of the other. (In an analogy you might explain how the human eye works by comparing it to a simple camera, or you might explain the forces in a thunderstorm by comparing them to armies in battle.) In any comparison of unlike things, you must have a valid reason for bringing the two together. In "Grant and Lee," Bruce Catton compares two Civil War generals. But in an essay called "General Grant and Mick Jagger" you would be hard-pressed to find any real basis for comparison. Although you might wax ingenious and claim, "Like Grant, Jagger posed a definite threat to Nashville," the ingenuity would wear thin and soon the yoking together of general and rock star would fall apart.

Basis for Comparison

Beginning to identify the shared and dissimilar features of your subjects will get you started, but the comparison won't be manageable for you or interesting to your readers unless you also limit it. You would be overly ambitious to try to compare and contrast the Russian way of life with the American way of life in five hundred words; you couldn't include all the important similarities and differences. In a brief paper, you would be wise to select a single basis for comparison: to show, for instance, how day-care centers in Russia and the United States are both like and unlike each other.

This basis for comparison will eventually underpin the THESIS of your essay—the claim you have to make about the similarities and dissimilarities of two things or about one thing's superiority over another. Here, from essays in this chapter, are THESIS SENTENCES that clearly lay out what's being compared and why:

> Neat people are lazier and meaner than sloppy people. (Suzanne Britt, "Neat People vs. Sloppy People")

> These were two strong men, these oddly different generals, and they represented the strengths of two conflicting currents that, through them, had come into collision. (Bruce Catton, "Grant and Lee: A Study in Contrasts")

Notice that each author not only identifies his or her subjects (neat and sloppy people, two generals) but also previews the purpose of the comparison, whether to evaluate (Britt) or to explain (Catton).

Organization

Even with a limited basis for comparison, the method of comparison and contrast can be tricky without some planning. We suggest that you make an outline (preferably in writing), using one of two organizations described below. Say you're writing an essay on two banjo-pickers, Jed and Jake. Your purpose is to explain the distinctive identities of the two players, and your thesis sentence might be the following:

> Jed and Jake are both excellent banjo-pickers whose differences reflect their training.

Here are the two ways you might arrange your comparison:

1. *Subject by subject.* Set forth all your facts about Jed, then do the same for Jake. Next, sum up their similarities and differences. In your conclusion, state what you think you have shown.

1. *Jed*
   Training
   Choice of material
   Technical dexterity
   Playing style

2. *Jake*
   Training
   Choice of material
   Technical dexterity
   Playing style

SUMMARY
CONCLUSION

This procedure works for a paper of a few paragraphs, but for a longer one, it has a built-in disadvantage: Readers need to remember all the facts about subject 1 while they read about subject 2. If the essay is long and lists many facts, this procedure may be burdensome.

2. *Point by point.* Usually more workable in writing a long paper than the first method, the second scheme is to compare and contrast as you go. You consider one point at a time, taking up your two subjects alternately. In this way, you continually bring the subjects together, perhaps in every paragraph. Notice the differences in the outline:

1. *Training*
   Jed: studied under Earl Scruggs
   Jake: studied under Bela Fleck

2. *Choice of material*
   Jed: bluegrass
   Jake: jazz-oriented

3. *Technical dexterity*
   Jed: highly skilled
   Jake: highly skilled

4. *Playing style*
   Jed: rapid-fire
   Jake: impressionistic

For either the subject-by-subject or the point-by-point scheme, your conclusion might be: Although similar in skill, the two differ greatly in aims and in personalities. Jed is better suited to the Grand Ol' Opry and Jake to a concert hall.

No matter how you group your points, they have to balance; you can't discuss Jed's on-stage manner without discussing Jake's too. If you have nothing to say about Jake's on-stage manner, then you might as well omit the point. A surefire loser is the paper that proposes to compare and contrast two subjects but then proceeds to discuss quite different elements in each: Jed's playing style and Jake's choice of material, Jed's fondness for smelt on a bun and Jake's hobby of antique-car collecting. The writer of such a paper doesn't compare and contrast the two musicians at all, but provides two quite separate discussions.

By the way, a subject-by-subject organization works most efficiently for a *pair* of subjects. If you want to write about *three* banjo-pickers, you might first consider Jed and Jake, then Jake and Josh, then Josh and Jed—but it would probably be easiest to compare and contrast all three point by point.

Flexibility

As you write, an outline will help you see the shape of your paper and keep your procedure in mind. But don't be the simple tool of your outline. Few essays are more boring to read than the long comparison and contrast written mechanically. The reader comes to feel like a weary tennis spectator whose head has to swivel from side to side: now Jed, now Jake; now Jed again, now back to Jake. You need to mention the same features of both subjects, it is true, but no law decrees *how* you must mention them. You need not follow your outline in lockstep order, or cover similarities and differences at precisely the same length, or spend a hundred words on Jed's banjo-picking skill just because you spend a hundred words on Jake's. Your essay, remember, doesn't need to be as symmetrical as a pair of salt and pepper shakers. What is your outline but a simple means to organize your account of a complicated reality? As you write, keep casting your thoughts upon a living, particular world—not twisting and squeezing that world into a rigid scheme, but moving through it with open senses, being patient and faithful and exact in your telling of it.

CHECKLIST FOR REVISING A COMPARISON AND CONTRAST

✔ **PURPOSE.** What is the aim of your comparison: to explain two subjects or to evaluate them? Will the purpose be clear to readers from the start?

✔ **SUBJECTS.** Are the subjects enough alike, sharing enough features, to make comparison worthwhile?

✔ **THESIS.** Does your thesis establish a limited basis for comparison so that you have room and time to cover all the relevant similarities and differences?

✔ **ORGANIZATION.** Does your arrangement of material, whether subject by subject or point by point, do justice to your subjects and help readers follow the comparison?

✔ **BALANCE AND FLEXIBILITY.** Have you covered the same features of both subjects? At the same time, have you avoided a rigid back-and-forth movement that could bore or exhaust a reader?

COMPARISON AND CONTRAST IN A PARAGRAPH: TWO ILLUSTRATIONS

Using Comparison and Contrast to Write About Television

The following example, written especially for *The Bedford Reader,* uses point-by-point comparison for a clear purpose: to evaluate television drama then and now, and to express a preference for one over the other. Notice that the writer is fair—acknowledging (toward the end) that today's dramas also have fine actors and have none of the primitiveness of yesterday's dramas.

Though written to be freestanding, this paragraph on drama might do good work in a full essay about, say, the chief differences between TV programming in the medium's early days and programming now.

Seen on aged 16-millimeter film, the original production of Paddy Chayevsky's *Marty* makes clear the differences between television drama of 1953 and that of today. <u>Today</u> there's no weekly Goodyear Playhouse to showcase original one-hour plays by important authors; most scriptwriters collaborate, all but anonymously, on serials about familiar characters. *Marty* features no bodice ripping, no drug busts, no deadly illness, no laugh track. <u>Instead,</u> it simply shows the awakening of love between a heavyset butcher and a mousy high-school teacher: both single, lonely, and shy, never twice dating the same person. <u>Unlike the writer of today,</u> Chayevsky couldn't set scenes outdoors or on location. In one small studio, in slow lingering takes (some five minutes long—not eight to twelve seconds, <u>as we now expect</u>), the camera probes the faces of two seated characters as Marty and his pal Angie plan Saturday night ("What do you want to do?"—"I dunno, what do *you*?"). Oddly, the effect is spellbinding. To bring such scenes to life, the actors must project with vigor; and <u>like the finer actors of today,</u> Rod Steiger as Marty exploits each moment. <u>In 1953,</u> plays were telecast live. Today, well-edited videotape may eliminate blown lines, but a chill slickness prevails. Technically, *Marty* is primitive, yet it probes souls. Most televised drama <u>today</u> displays a physically larger world—only to nail a box around it.

Point-by-point comparison supporting this topic sentence

1. *Original plays vs. serials*

2. *Simple love story vs. violence and sex*

3. *Studio sets with long takes vs. locations with short takes*

4. *Good acting vs. good acting*

5. *Live vs. videotaped*

6. *Primitive and probing vs. big and limited*

Transitions (underlined) clarify the comparison

Using Comparison and Contrast
in an Academic Discipline

Taken from a textbook on architectural history, this subject-by-subject comparison explains the differences between two competing theories of architecture in Russia in the 1920s and 1930s. The paragraph is one of several in which the author shows how modernist architects divided into those concerned mainly with form and those concerned mainly with social progress.

In Russia, too, modernists fell into two camps. They squared off against each other in public debate and in Vkhutemas, a school of architecture organized in 1920 along lines parallel to the Bauhaus. "The measure of architecture is architecture," went the motto of one camp. They believed in an unfettered experimentalism of form. The rival camp had a problem-solving orientation. The architect's main mission, in their view, was to share in the common task of achieving the transformation of society promised by the October Revolution [of 1917]. They were keen on standardization, user interviews, and ideological prompting. They worked on new building programs that would consolidate the social order of communism. These they referred to as "social condensers."

Subject-by-subject comparison supporting this topic sentence

1. First camp: experimental

2. Second camp: problem-solving (receives more attention because it eventually prevailed)

— Spiro Kostof, *A History of Architecture*

CASE STUDY
Using Comparison and Contrast

In the fall of her sophomore year in college, Susan Wheeler was running for president of her dormitory. She prepared a campaign statement for the student newspaper's coverage of the election, and she also created the flier on the next page for posting throughout the dorm.

Wheeler believed that her campaign platform was much stronger than her opponent's, and she decided to highlight the differences by showing her ideas alongside her opponent's (in a point-by-point arrangement). But her draft needed work to make the points more concise and to give them PARALLEL wording that would clarify and stress the contrasts. Originally, the first three points read as follows:

Susan Wheeler	*Matt Parker*
• A supporter of all extra-curricular activities	• Supports mainly sports and cheerleading
• Actively participates in student government association	• He is not in the student government association
• The food plans should be more flexible for all students	• Does not mention the food plans

In Wheeler's final draft (next page), the parallel wording (each point beginning with a verb) is both easier to read and more emphatic.

Susan Wheeler
for
Dorm President

Here are the reasons why:

Susan Wheeler

- Supports all extracurricular activities
- Participates actively in student government association
- Wants to make food plans more flexible for all students
- Wants to extend bookstore hours
- Wants to increase quantity and accessibility of copiers
- Wants a 24-hour computer lab in the dorm
- Has made Dean's List every semester

Matt Parker

- Supports mainly sports and cheerleading
- Does not participate in student government association
- Does not mention the food plans
- Does not mention extending bookstore hours
- Does not mention copier problems
- Does not mention a computer lab
- Has not made Dean's List

Vote May 2

SUSAN WHEELER FOR PRESIDENT . . . WE'LL DO IT TOGETHER!

SUZANNE BRITT

SUZANNE BRITT was born in Winston-Salem, North Carolina, and studied at Salem College and Washington University, where she earned an MA in English. She writes a regular column for a newsletter, *Authors Ink*. Britt has written for *Sky Magazine*, the *New York Times*, *Newsweek*, the *Boston Globe*, and many other publications. She teaches English part-time at Meredith College in North Carolina and has published a history of the college and two English textbooks. Her other books are collections of her essays: *Skinny People Are Dull and Crunchy like Carrots* (1982) and *Show and Tell* (1983).

Neat People
vs.
Sloppy People

"Neat People vs. Sloppy People" appears in Britt's collection *Show and Tell*. Mingling humor with seriousness (as she often does), Britt has called the book a report on her journey into "the awful cave of self: You shout your name and voices come back in exultant response, telling you their names." In this essay, Britt uses comparison mainly to entertain by showing us aspects of our own selves, awful or not. For another approach to a similar subject, see the next essay, by Dave Barry.

I've finally figured out the difference between neat people and sloppy people. The distinction is, as always, moral. Neat people are lazier and meaner than sloppy people. 1

Sloppy people, you see, are not really sloppy. Their sloppiness is merely the unfortunate consequence of their extreme moral rectitude. Sloppy people carry in their mind's eye a heavenly vision, a precise plan, that is so stupendous, so perfect, it can't be achieved in this world or the next. 2

Sloppy people live in Never-Never Land. Someday is their métier. Someday they are planning to alphabetize all their books and set up home catalogs. Someday they will go through their wardrobes and mark certain items for tentative mending and certain items for passing on to relatives of similar shape and size. Someday sloppy people will make family scrapbooks into which they will put newspaper clippings, postcards, locks of hair, and the dried corsage from their senior prom. Someday they will file everything on the surface of their desks, including the cash receipts from coffee purchases at the snack shop. Someday they will sit down and read all the back issues of *The New Yorker*. 3

For all these noble reasons and more, sloppy people never get neat. They aim too high and wide. They save everything, planning someday to file, order, 4 and straighten out the world. But while these ambitious plans take clearer and clearer shape in their heads, the books spill from the shelves onto the floor, the clothes pile up in the hamper and closet, the family mementos accumulate in every drawer, the surface of the desk is buried under mounds of paper, and the unread magazines threaten to reach the ceiling.

Sloppy people can't bear to part with anything. They give loving atten-   5
tion to every detail. When sloppy people say they're going to tackle the surface of a desk, they really mean it. Not a paper will go unturned; not a rubber
band will go unboxed. Four hours or two weeks into the excavation, the desk
looks exactly the same, primarily because the sloppy person is meticulously
creating new piles of papers with new headings and scrupulously stopping to
read all the old book catalogs before he throws them away. A neat person
would just bulldoze the desk.

Neat people are bums and clods at heart. They have cavalier attitudes   6
toward possessions, including family heirlooms. Everything is just another
dust-catcher to them. If anything collects dust, it's got to go and that's that.
Neat people will toy with the idea of throwing the children out of the house
just to cut down on the clutter.

Neat people don't care about process. They like results. What they want   7
to do is get the whole thing over with so they can sit down and watch the
rasslin' on TV. Neat people operate on two unvarying principles: Never handle
any item twice, and throw everything away.

The only thing messy in a neat person's house is the trash can. The   8
minute something comes to a neat person's hand, he will look at it, try to
decide if it has immediate use and, finding none, throw it in the trash.

Neat people are especially vicious with mail. They never go through their   9
mail unless they are standing directly over a trash can. If the trash can is
beside the mailbox, even better. All ads, catalogs, pleas for charitable contributions, church bulletins, and money-saving coupons go straight into the trash
can without being opened. All letters from home, postcards from Europe, bills,
and paychecks are opened, immediately responded to, then dropped in the
trash can. Neat people keep their receipts only for tax purposes. That's it. No
sentimental salvaging of birthday cards or the last letter a dying relative ever
wrote. Into the trash it goes.

Neat people place neatness above everything, even economics. They are   10
incredibly wasteful. Neat people throw away several toys every time they walk
through the den. I knew a neat person once who threw away a perfectly good
dish drainer because it had mold on it. The drainer was too much trouble to
wash. And neat people sell their furniture when they move. They will sell a
La-Z-Boy recliner while you are reclining in it.

Neat people are no good to borrow from. Neat people buy everything in   11 expensive little single portions. They get their flour and sugar in two-pound bags. They wouldn't consider clipping a coupon, saving a leftover, reusing plastic nondairy whipped cream containers, or rinsing off tin foil and draping it over the unmoldy dish drainer. You can never borrow a neat person's newspaper to see what's playing at the movies. Neat people have the paper all wadded up and in the trash by 7:05 AM.

Neat people cut a clean swath through the organic as well as the inorganic   12
world. People, animals, and things are all one to them. They are so insensitive. After they've finished with the pantry, the medicine cabinet, and the attic, they will throw out the red geranium (too many leaves), sell the dog (too many fleas), and send the children off to boarding school (too many scuff-marks on the hardwood floors).

Journal Writing

Britt suggests that grouping people according to oppositions, such as neat versus sloppy, reveals other things about them. Write about the oppositions you use to evaluate people. Smart versus dumb? Fit versus out of shape? Hip versus clueless? Rich versus poor? Outgoing versus shy? Open-minded versus narrow-minded? (To take your journal writing further, see "From Journal to Essay" on the next page.)

Questions on Meaning

1. "Suzanne Britt believes that neat people are lazy, mean, petty, callous, wasteful, and insensitive." How would you respond to this statement?
2. Is the author's main PURPOSE to make fun of neat people, to assess the habits of neat and sloppy people, to help neat and sloppy people get along better, to defend sloppy people, to amuse and entertain, or to prove that neat people are morally inferior to sloppy people? Discuss.
3. What is meant by "as always" in the sentence "The distinction is, as always, moral" (par. 1)? Does the author seem to be suggesting that any and all distinctions between people are moral?

Questions on Writing Strategy

1. What is the general TONE of this essay? What words and phrases help you determine that tone?
2. Britt mentions no similarities between neat and sloppy people. Does that mean this is not a good comparison and contrast essay? Why might a writer deliberately focus on differences and give very little or no time to similarities?
3. Consider the following GENERALIZATIONS: "For all these noble reasons and more, sloppy people never get neat" (par. 4) and "The only thing messy in a neat person's

house is the trash can" (8). How can you tell that these statements are generalizations? Look for other generalizations in the essay. What is the EFFECT of using
so many?

4. **OTHER METHODS.** Although filled with generalizations, Britt's essay does not lack
for EXAMPLES. Study the examples in paragraph 11, and explain how they do and
don't work the way examples are supposed to, to bring the generalizations about
people down to earth.

Questions on Language

1. Consult your dictionary for definitions of these words: rectitude (par. 2); métier,
tentative (3); accumulate (4); excavation, meticulously, scrupulously (5); salvaging (9).
2. How do you understand the use of the word *noble* in the first sentence of paragraph 4? Is it meant literally? Are there other words in the essay that appear to be
written in a similar tone?

Suggestions for Writing

1. **FROM JOURNAL TO ESSAY.** From your journal entry (previous page), choose your
favorite opposition for evaluating people, and write an essay in which you compare and contrast those who pass your "test" with those who fail it. You may
choose to write your essay tongue-in-cheek, as Britt does, or seriously.
2. Write an essay in which you compare and contrast two apparently dissimilar
groups of people: for example, blue-collar workers and white-collar workers,
people who write a lot of e-mail and people who don't bother with it, runners and
football players, readers and TV watchers, or any other variation you choose.
Your approach may be either lighthearted or serious, but make sure you come to
some conclusion about your subjects. Which group do you favor? Why?
3. ANALYZE the similarities and differences between two characters in your favorite
novel, story, film, or television show. Which aspects of their personalities make
them work well together, within the context in which they appear? Which characteristics work against each other, and therefore provide the necessary conflict
to hold the reader's or viewer's attention?
4. **CRITICAL WRITING.** Britt's essay is remarkable for its exaggeration of the two
types. Write a brief essay analyzing and contrasting the ways Britt characterizes
sloppy people and neat people. Be sure to consider the CONNOTATIONS of the
words, such as "moral rectitude" for sloppy people (par. 2) and "cavalier" for neat
people (6).
5. **CONNECTIONS.** Neither Suzanne Britt nor the author of the next essay, Dave
Barry, seems to have much sympathy for neat people. Write a brief essay in which
you explain why neatness matters. Or if you haven't a clue why, then write a brief
essay in which you explain the benefits of dirt and disorder.

Suzanne Britt on Writing

Asked to tell how she writes, Suzanne Britt contributed the following comment to The Bedford Reader.

The question "How do you write?" gets a snappy, snappish response from me. The first commandment is "Live!" And the second is like unto it: "Pay attention!" I don't mean that you have to live high or fast or deep or wise or broad. And I certainly don't mean you have to live true and upright. I just mean that you have to suck out all the marrow of whatever you do, whether it's picking the lint off the navy-blue suit you'll be wearing to Cousin Ione's funeral or popping an Aunt Jemimah frozen waffle into the toaster oven or lying between sand dunes, watching the way the sea oats slice the azure sky. The ominous question put to me by students on all occasions of possible accountability is "Will this count?" My answer is rock bottom and hard: "Everything counts," I say, and silence falls like prayers across the room.

The same is true of writing. Everything counts. Despair is good. Numbness can be excellent. Misery is fine. Ecstasy will work — or pain or sorrow or passion. The only thing that won't work is indifference. A writer refuses to be shocked and appalled by anything going or coming, rising or falling, singing or soundless. The only thing that shocks me, truth to tell, is indifference. How dare you not fight for the right to the crispy end piece on the standing-rib roast? How dare you let the fragrance of Joy go by without taking a whiff of it? How dare you not see the old woman in the snap-front housedress and the rolled-down socks, carrying her Polident and Charmin in a canvas tote that says, simply, elegantly, Le Bag?

After you have lived, paid attention, seen connections, felt the harmony, writhed under the dissonance, fixed a Diet Coke, popped a big stick of Juicy Fruit in your mouth, gathered your life around you as a mother hen gathers her brood, as a queen settles the folds in her purple robes, you are ready to write. And what you will write about, even if you have one of those teachers who makes you write about, say, Guatemala, will be something very exclusive and intimate — something just between you and Guatemala. All you have to find out is what that small intimacy might be. It is there. And having found it, you have to make it count.

There is no rest for a writer. But there is no boredom either. A Sunday morning with a bottle of extra-strength aspirin within easy reach and an ice bag on your head can serve you very well in writing. So can a fly buzzing at

your ear or a heart-stopping siren in the night or an interminable afternoon in
a biology lab in front of a frog's innards.

All you need, really, is the audacity to believe, with your whole being,
that if you tell it right, tell it truly, tell it so we can all see it, the "it" will play
in Peoria, Poughkeepsie, Pompeii, or Podunk. In the South we call that conviction, that audacity, an act of faith. But you can call it writing.

For Discussion

1. What advice does Britt offer a student assigned to write a paper about, say,
   Guatemala? If you were that student, how would you go about taking her advice?
2. Where in her comment does the author use colorful and effective FIGURES OF
   SPEECH?
3. What is the TONE of Britt's remarks? Sum up her attitude toward her subject,
   writing.

DAVE BARRY

DAVE BARRY is a humorist whom the *New York Times* has called "the funniest man in America." Barry was born in 1947 in Armonk, New York, and graduated from Haverford College in 1969. He worked as a journalist for five years and lectured businesspeople on writing for eight years while he began to establish himself as a columnist. His humor writing now appears in several hundred newspapers and has been collected in more than twenty books, including *Bad Habits: A 100% Fact Free Book* (1985), *The World According to Dave Barry* (1994), *Dave Barry in Cyberspace* (1996), and *Dave Barry Hits Below the Beltway* (2001), the last about American politics. In 1988 Barry received the Pulitzer Prize for "distinguished commentary," although, he says, "nothing I've ever written fits the definition." (He thinks he won because his columns stood out from the "earthshakingly important" competition.) Barry lives in Miami with his family.

Batting Clean-Up and Striking Out

This essay from *Dave Barry's Greatest Hits* (1988) illustrates Barry's gift, in the words of critic Alison Teal, "for taking things at face value and rendering them funny on those grounds alone, for rendering every ounce of humor out of a perfectly ordinary experience." Like Suzanne Britt in the previous essay, Barry contrasts two styles of dealing with a mess.

The primary difference between men and women is that women can see extremely small quantities of dirt. Not when they're babies, of course. Babies of both sexes have a very low awareness of dirt, other than to think it tastes better than food.

But somewhere during the growth process, a hormonal secretion takes place in women that enables them to see dirt that men cannot see, dirt at the level of *molecules,* whereas men don't generally notice it until it forms clumps large enough to support agriculture. This can lead to tragedy, as it did in the ill-fated ancient city of Pompeii, where the residents all got killed when the local volcano erupted and covered them with a layer of ash twenty feet deep.[1] Modern people often ask, "How come, when the ashes started falling, the Pompeii people didn't just *leave?*" The answer is that in Pompeii, it was the custom for the men to do the housework. They never even *noticed* the ash until it had for the most part covered the children. "Hey!" the men said (in Latin). "It's mighty quiet around here!" This is one major historical reason why, to this very day, men tend to do extremely little in the way of useful housework.

[1] Pompeii, in what is now southern Italy, was buried in the eruption of Mount Vesuvius in AD 79. —EDS.

What often happens in my specific family unit is that my wife will say to   3
me: "Could you clean Robert's bathroom? It's filthy." So I'll gather up the
Standard Male Cleaning Implements, namely a spray bottle of Windex and a
wad of paper towels, and I'll go into Robert's bathroom, and it *always looks perfectly fine*. I mean, when I hear the word "filthy" used to describe a bathroom,
I think about this bar where I used to hang out called Joe's Sportsman's
Lounge, where the men's room had bacteria you could enter in a rodeo.

Nevertheless, because I am a sensitive and caring kind of guy, I "clean" the   4
bathroom, spraying Windex all over everything including the six hundred
action figures each sold separately that God forbid Robert should ever take a
bath without, and then I wipe it back off with the paper towels, and I go back
to whatever activity I had been engaged in, such as doing an important project on the Etch-a-Sketch, and a little while later my wife will say: "I hate to
rush you, but could you do Robert's bathroom? It's really *filthy*." She is in there
looking at the very walls I *just Windexed*, and she is seeing *dirt! Everywhere!*
And if I tell her I already *cleaned* the bathroom, she gives me this look that she
has perfected, the same look she used on me the time I selected Robert's out-
fit for school and part of it turned out to be pajamas.

The opposite side of the dirt coin, of course, is sports. This is an area   5
where men tend to feel very sensitive and women tend to be extremely callous. I have written about this before and I always get irate letters from women
who say they are the heavyweight racquetball champion of some place like
Iowa and are sensitive to sports to the point where they could crush my skull
like a ripe grape, but I feel these women are the exception.

A more representative woman is my friend Maddy, who once invited   6
some people, including my wife and me, over to her house for an evening of
stimulating conversation and jovial companionship, which sounds fine except
that this particular evening occurred *during a World Series game*. If you can
imagine such a social gaffe.

We sat around the living room and Maddy tried to stimulate a conver-   7
sation, but we males could not focus our attention on the various suggested
topics because we could actually *feel* the World Series television and radio
broadcast rays zinging through the air, penetrating right into our bodies, causing our dental fillings to vibrate, and all the while the women were behaving
as though nothing were wrong. It was exactly like that story by Edgar Allan Poe
where the murderer can hear the victim's heart beating louder and louder
even though he (the murder victim) is dead, until finally he (the murderer)
can't stand it anymore, and he just *has* to watch the World Series on television.[2] That was how we felt.

---

[2] Barry refers to Poe's story "The Tell-Tale Heart" (1843). The story (minus Barry's World
Series ending) appears on page 117 of this book. —EDS.

Maddy's husband made the first move, coming up with an absolutely bril- 8
liant means of escape: *He used their baby.* He picked up Justine, their seven-
month-old daughter, who was fussing a little, and announced: "What this
child needs is to have her bottle and watch the World Series." And just like
that he was off to the family room, moving very quickly for a big man holding
a baby. A second male escaped by pretending to clear the dessert plates. Soon
all four of us were in there, watching the Annual Fall Classic, while the
women prattled away about human relationships or something. It turned out
to be an extremely pivotal game.

Journal Writing

Are you ever baffled by the behavior of members of the opposite sex — or members of
your own sex, if you often find yourself behaving differently from most of them? List
traits of men or women that you find foreign or bewildering, such as that they do or
do not want to talk about their feelings or that they can spend countless hours watching sports on television or shopping. (To take your journal writing further, see "From
Journal to Essay" on the next page.)

Questions on Meaning

1. What is the PURPOSE of Barry's essay? How do you know?
2. How OBJECTIVE is Barry's portrayal of men and women? Does he seem to understand one sex better than the other? Does he seek to justify and excuse male sloppiness and antisocial behavior?
3. What can you INFER about Barry's attitude toward the differences between the
   sexes? Does he see a way out?

Questions on Writing Strategy

1. Barry's comparison is organized point by point — differences in sensitivity to dirt,
   then differences in sensitivity to sports. What is the EFFECT of this organization?
   Or, from another angle, what would have been the effect of a subject-by-subject
   organization — just men, then just women (or vice versa)?
2. How does Barry set the TONE of this piece from the very first paragraph?
3. The first sentence looks like a THESIS SENTENCE but turns out not to be complete.
   Where does Barry finish his statement of the essay's thesis? Does it hurt or help
   the essay that the thesis is divided? Why?
4. How does Barry's ALLUSION to Poe's "The Tell-Tale Heart" (par. 7) enhance Barry's
   own story?
5. **OTHER METHODS.** How persuasive is the historical EXAMPLE cited in paragraph 2
   as EVIDENCE for Barry's claims about men's and women's differing abilities to perceive dirt? Must examples always be persuasive?

Questions on Language

1. Define these words: hormonal (par. 2); implements (3); callous, irate (5); jovial, gaffe (6); prattled, pivotal (8).
2. Paragraph 4 begins with a textbook example of a run-on sentence. Does Barry need a better copyeditor, or is he deliberately going for an effect here? If so, what is it?
3. What effect does Barry achieve through his frequent use of italics (for example, *just Windexed,*" par. 4) and capital letters ("Standard Male Cleaning Implements," 3)?
4. Why does Barry use the word *males* instead of *men* in paragraphs 7 and 8?

Suggestions for Writing

1. **FROM JOURNAL TO ESSAY.** From the list you compiled in your journal (previous page), choose the trait of men or women that seems to have the most potential for humor. Write an essay similar to Barry's, exaggerating the difference to the point where it becomes the defining distinction between men and women.
2. How well do you conform to Barry's GENERALIZATIONS about your gender? In what ways are you stereotypically male or female? Do such generalizations amuse or merely annoy you? Why?
3. **CRITICAL WRITING.** Barry is obviously not afraid of offending women: He claims to have already done so (par. 5), and yet he persists. Do you take offense at any of this essay's stereotypes of women and men? If so, explain the nature of the offense as coolly as you can. Whether you take offense or not, can you see any virtue in using such stereotypes for humor? For instance, does the humor help undermine the stereotypes or merely strengthen them? Write an essay in which you address these questions, using quotations from Barry as examples and evidence.
4. **CONNECTIONS.** Write an essay about the humor gained from exaggeration, relying on Barry's essay and the previous one, Suzanne Britt's "Neat People vs. Sloppy People." Consider why exaggeration is often funny and what qualities humorous exaggeration has. Use quotations and PARAPHRASES from Barry's and Britt's essays as your support.

Dave Barry on Writing

For Dave Barry, coming up with ideas for humorous writing is no problem. "Just about anything's a topic for a humor column," he told an interviewer for *Contemporary Authors* in 1990, "any event that occurs in the news, anything that happens in daily life — driving, shopping, reading, eating. You can look at just about anything and see humor in it somewhere."

Writing challenges, for Barry, occur after he has his idea. "Writing has always been hard for me," he says. "The hard part is getting the jokes to come, and it never happens all at once for me. I very rarely have any idea where a column is going to go when it starts. It's a matter of piling a little piece here and a little piece there, fitting them together, going on to the next part, then going back and gradually shaping the whole piece into something. I know what I want in terms of reaction, and I want it to have a certain feel. I know when it does and when it doesn't. But I'm never sure when it's going to get there. That's what writing is. That's why it's so painful and slow. But that's more technique than anything else. You don't rely on inspiration — I don't, anyway, and I don't think most writers do. The creative process is just not an inspirational one for most people. There's a little bit of that and a whole lot of polishing."

A humor writer must be sensitive to readers, trying to make them smile, but Barry warns against catering to an audience. "I think it's a big mistake to write humor for anybody but yourself, to try to adopt any persona other than your own. If I don't at some point think something is funny, then I'm not going to write it." Not that his own sense of humor will always make a piece fly. "Thinking of it in rough form is one thing," Barry confesses, "and shaping and polishing it so that you like the way it reads is so agonizingly slow that by the time you're done, you don't think anything is funny. You think this is something you might use to console a widow."

More often, though, the shaping and polishing — the constant revision — do work. "Since I know how to do that," Barry says, "since I do it every day of the week and have for years and years, I'm confident that if I keep at it I'll get something."

For Discussion

1. Do you agree with Barry that "[y]ou can look at just about anything and see humor in it somewhere"? What topics do you think would be off-limits for humor?
2. What does successful writing depend on, according to Barry? What role does inspiration play?
3. How might Barry's views on writing be relevant to your own experiences as a writer? What can a humor writer teach a college writer?

DAVID SEDARIS

Named Humorist of the Year 2001 by *Time* magazine, DAVID SEDARIS was born in 1957 and grew up in North Carolina. After graduating from the School of the Art Institute of Chicago in 1987, Sedaris taught writing there part-time and then moved to New York City, where he took various odd jobs. One of these jobs—a stint as a department-store Christmas elf—provided Sedaris with material for "The Santaland Diaries," the essay that launched his career as a humorist after he read it on National Public Radio's *Morning Edition* in 1993. Since then, Sedaris has contributed numerous commentaries to public radio's *Morning Edition* and *This American Life* and has published frequently in *The New Yorker, Esquire,* and other magazines. His essays are collected in *Barrel Fever* (1994), *Naked* (1996), *Holidays on Ice* (1997), and *Me Talk Pretty One Day* (2000). In 2001 Sedaris received the Thurber Prize for American Humor. He lives in Paris, France.

Remembering My Childhood on the Continent of Africa

Many of Sedaris's essays locate comedy in his basically normal North Carolina childhood. In this essay from *Me Talk Pretty One Day,* Sedaris highlights that normality by contrasting it with the distinctly unusual childhood of a friend.

When Hugh was in the fifth grade, his class took a field trip to an Ethiopian slaughterhouse. He was living in Addis Ababa at the time, and the slaughterhouse was chosen because, he says, "it was convenient." 1

This was a school system in which the matter of proximity outweighed such petty concerns as what may or may not be appropriate for a busload of eleven-year-olds. "What?" I asked. "Were there no autopsies scheduled at the local morgue? Was the federal prison just a bit too far out of the way?" 2

Hugh defends his former school, saying, "Well, isn't that the whole point of a field trip? To see something new?" 3

"Technically yes, but . . ." 4

"All right then," he says. "So we saw some new things." 5

One of his field trips was literally a trip to a field where the class watched a wrinkled man fill his mouth with rotten goat meat and feed it to a pack of waiting hyenas. On another occasion they were taken to examine the bloodied bedroom curtains hanging in the palace of the former dictator. There were tamer trips, to textile factories and sugar refineries, but my favorite is always the slaughterhouse. It wasn't a big company, just a small rural enterprise run 6 by a couple of brothers operating out of a low-ceilinged concrete building. Following a brief lecture on the importance of proper sanitation, a small white piglet was herded into the room, its dainty hooves clicking against the concrete floor. The class gathered in a circle to get a better look at the animal, who seemed delighted with the attention he was getting. He turned from face to face and was looking up at Hugh when one of the brothers drew a pistol from his back pocket, held it against the animal's temple, and shot the piglet, execution-style. Blood spattered, frightened children wept, and the man with the gun offered the teacher and bus driver some meat from a freshly slaughtered goat.

When I'm told such stories, it's all I can do to hold back my feelings of 7
jealousy. An Ethiopian slaughterhouse. Some people have all the luck. When I was in elementary school, the best we ever got was a trip to Old Salem or Colonial Williamsburg, one of those preserved brick villages where time supposedly stands still and someone earns his living as a town crier. There was always a blacksmith, a group of wandering patriots, and a collection of bonneted women hawking corn bread or gingersnaps made "the ol'-fashioned way." Every now and then you might come across a doer of bad deeds serving time in the stocks, but that was generally as exciting as it got.

Certain events are parallel, but compared with Hugh's, my childhood was 8
unspeakably dull. When I was seven years old, my family moved to North Carolina. When he was seven years old, Hugh's family moved to the Congo. We had a collie and a house cat. They had a monkey and two horses named Charlie Brown and Satan. I threw stones at stop signs. Hugh threw stones at crocodiles. The verbs are the same, but he definitely wins the prize when it comes to nouns and objects. An eventful day for my mother might have involved a trip to the dry cleaner or a conversation with the potato-chip deliveryman. Asked one ordinary Congo afternoon what she'd done with her day, Hugh's mother answered that she and a fellow member of the Ladies' Club had visited a leper colony on the outskirts of Kinshasa. No reason was given for the expedition, though chances are she was staking it out for a future field trip.

Due to his upbringing, Hugh sits through inane movies never realizing 9
that they're often based on inane television shows. There were no poker-faced sitcom martians in his part of Africa, no oil-rich hillbillies or aproned brides trying to wean themselves from the practice of witchcraft. From time to time a movie would arrive packed in a dented canister, the film scratched and faded from its slow trip around the world. The theater consisted of a few dozen folding chairs arranged before a bedsheet or the blank wall of a vacant hangar out near the airstrip. Occasionally a man would sell warm soft drinks out of a cardboard box, but that was it in terms of concessions.

When I was young, I went to the theater at the nearby shopping center 10 and watched a movie about a talking Volkswagen. I believe the little car had a taste for mischief but I can't be certain, as both the movie and the afternoon proved unremarkable and have faded from my memory. Hugh saw the same movie a few years after it was released. His family had left the Congo by this time and were living in Ethiopia. Like me, Hugh saw the movie by himself on a weekend afternoon. Unlike me, he left the theater two hours later, to find a dead man hanging from a telephone pole at the far end of the unpaved parking lot. None of the people who'd seen the movie seemed to care about the dead man. They stared at him for a moment or two and then headed home, saying they'd never seen anything as crazy as that talking Volkswagen. His father was late picking him up, so Hugh just stood there for an hour, watching the dead man dangle and turn in the breeze. The death was not reported in the newspaper, and when Hugh related the story to his friends, they said, "You saw the movie about the talking car?"

I could have done without the flies and the primitive theaters, but I wouldn't have minded growing up with a houseful of servants. In North Carolina it wasn't unusual to have a once-a-week maid, but Hugh's family had houseboys, a word that never fails to charge my imagination. They had cooks and drivers, and guards who occupied a gatehouse, armed with machetes. Seeing as I had regularly petitioned my parents for an electric fence, the business with the guards strikes me as the last word in quiet sophistication. Having protection suggests that you are important. Having that protection paid for by the government is even better, as it suggests your safety is of interest to someone other than yourself.

Hugh's father was a career officer with the US State Department, and every morning a black sedan carried him off to the embassy. I'm told it's not as glamorous as it sounds, but in terms of fun for the entire family, I'm fairly confident that it beats the sack race at the annual IBM picnic. By the age of three, Hugh was already carrying a diplomatic passport. The rules that applied to others did not apply to him. No tickets, no arrests, no luggage search: He was officially licensed to act like a brat. Being an American, it was expected of him, and who was he to deny the world an occasional tantrum?

They weren't rich, but what Hugh's family lacked financially they more than made up for with the sort of exoticism that works wonders at cocktail parties, leading always to the remark "That sounds fascinating." It's a compliment one rarely receives when describing an adolescence spent drinking Icees at the North Hills Mall. No fifteen-foot python ever wandered onto my school's basketball court. I begged, I prayed nightly, but it just never happened. Neither did I get to witness a military coup in which forces sympathetic to the colonel arrived late at night to assassinate my next-door neighbor. Hugh had been at the Addis Ababa teen club when the electricity was cut off and soldiers arrived to evacuate the building. He and his friends had to hide in the back of a jeep and cover themselves with blankets during the ride home. It's something that sticks in his mind for one reason or another.

Among my personal highlights is the memory of having my picture taken   14 with Uncle Paul, the legally blind host of a Raleigh children's television show. Among Hugh's is the memory of having his picture taken with Buzz Aldrin on the last leg of the astronaut's world tour. The man who had walked on the moon placed his hand on Hugh's shoulder and offered to sign his autograph book. The man who led Wake County schoolchildren in afternoon song turned at the sound of my voice and asked, "So what's your name, princess?"

When I was fourteen years old, I was sent to spend ten days with my   15 maternal grandmother in western New York State. She was a small and private woman named Billie, and though she never came right out and asked, I had the distinct impression she had no idea who I was. It was the way she looked at me, squinting through her glasses while chewing on her lower lip. That, coupled with the fact that she never once called me by name. "Oh," she'd say, "are you still here?" She was just beginning her long struggle with Alzheimer's disease, and each time I entered the room, I felt the need to reintroduce myself and set her at ease. "Hi, it's me. Sharon's boy, David. I was just in the kitchen admiring your collection of ceramic toads." Aside from a few trips to summer camp, this was the longest I'd ever been away from home, and I like to think I was toughened by the experience.

About the same time I was frightening my grandmother, Hugh and his   16 family were packing their belongings for a move to Somalia. There were no English-speaking schools in Mogadishu, so, after a few months spent lying around the family compound with his pet monkey, Hugh was sent back to Ethiopia to live with a beer enthusiast his father had met at a cocktail party. Mr. Hoyt installed security systems in foreign embassies. He and his family gave Hugh a room. They invited him to join them at the table, but that was as far as they extended themselves. No one ever asked him when his birthday was, so when the day came, he kept it to himself. There was no telephone service between Ethiopia and Somalia, and letters to his parents were sent to Washington and then forwarded on to Mogadishu, meaning that his news was more than a month old by the time they got it. I suppose it wasn't much different than living as a foreign-exchange student. Young people do it all the time, but to me it sounds awful. The Hoyts had two sons about Hugh's age who were always saying things like "Hey that's *our* sofa you're sitting on" and "Hands off that ornamental stein. It doesn't belong to you."

He'd been living with these people for a year when he overheard Mr. Hoyt   17 tell a friend that he and his family would soon be moving to Munich, Germany, the beer capital of the world.

"And that worried me," Hugh said, "because it meant I'd have to find 18
some other place to live."

Where I come from, finding shelter is a problem the average teenager 19
might confidently leave to his parents. It was just something that came with
having a mom and a dad. Worried that he might be sent to live with his grandparents in Kentucky, Hugh turned to the school's guidance counselor, who
knew of a family whose son had recently left for college. And so he spent
another year living with strangers and not mentioning his birthday. While I
wouldn't have wanted to do it myself, I can't help but envy the sense of fortitude he gained from the experience. After graduating from college, he moved
to France knowing only the phrase "Do you speak French?"—a question guaranteed to get you nowhere unless you also speak the language.

While living in Africa, Hugh and his family took frequent vacations, 20
often in the company of their monkey. The Nairobi Hilton, some suite of
high-ceilinged rooms in Cairo or Khartoum: These are the places his people
recall when gathered at a common table. "Was that the summer we spent in
Beirut or, no, I'm thinking of the time we sailed from Cyprus and took the *Ori-
ent Express* to Istanbul."

Theirs was the life I dreamt about during my vacations in eastern North 21
Carolina. Hugh's family was hobnobbing with chiefs and sultans while I ate
hush puppies at the Sanitary Fish Market in Morehead City, a beach towel
wrapped like a hijab[1] around my head. Someone unknown to me was very
likely standing in a muddy ditch and dreaming of an evening spent sitting
in a clean family restaurant, drinking iced tea and working his way through
an extra-large seaman's platter, but that did not concern me, as it meant I
should have been happy with what I had. Rather than surrender to my bitterness, I have learned to take satisfaction in the life that Hugh has led. His stories have, over time, become my own. I say this with no trace of a kumbaya.[2]
There is no spiritual symbiosis; I'm just a petty thief who lifts his memories the
same way I'll take a handful of change left on his dresser. When my own experiences fall short of the mark, I just go out and spend some of his. It is with
pleasure that I sometimes recall the dead man's purpled face or the report of
the handgun ringing in my ears as I studied the blood pooling beneath the
dead white piglet. On the way back from the slaughterhouse, we stopped for
Cokes in the village of Mojo, where the gas-station owner had arranged a few
tables and chairs beneath a dying canopy of vines. It was late afternoon by the
time we returned to school, where a second bus carried me to the foot of Cof-

---

[1] A headscarf worn by Muslim women.—EDS.

[2] From the gospel-folk song with the line "Kumbaya, my Lord, kumbaya," meaning "Come
by here." Probably because of its popularity in folk music, the word now also has negative connotations of passivity or touchy-feely spiritualism.—EDS.

feeboard Road. Once there, I walked through a grove of eucalyptus trees and alongside a bald pasture of starving cattle, past the guard napping in his gatehouse, and into the waiting arms of my monkey.

Journal Writing

When have you envied the life of a friend or relative? Write about what was attractive to you in that person's life—family relationships? educational or employment opportunities? travel experiences? something else? (To take your journal writing further, see "From Journal to Essay" on the next page.)

Questions on Meaning

1. What is the subject of Sedaris's comparison and contrast in this essay?
2. What do you think is the THESIS of this essay? Take into account both Sedaris's obvious envy of Hugh's childhood and Sedaris's awareness that Hugh's life was often lonely and insecure. Is the thesis stated or only implied?
3. There is a certain amount of IRONY in Sedaris's envy of Hugh's childhood. What is this irony? How does Sedaris make this irony explicit in paragraph 21?

Questions on Writing Strategy

1. Does Sedaris develop his comparison and contrast subject by subject or point by point? Briefly outline the essay to explain your answer.
2. Sedaris refers to Hugh's monkey in paragraphs 8, 20, and 21. In what sense does he use the monkey as a SYMBOL?
3. The first five paragraphs of the essay include a conversation between Sedaris and Hugh about Hugh's childhood. Why do you think the author opened the essay this way?
4. **OTHER METHODS.** How does Sedaris use NARRATION to develop his comparison and contrast?

Questions on Language

1. How does Sedaris use PARALLEL STRUCTURE in paragraph 8 to highlight the contrast between himself and Hugh? How does he then point up this parallelism?
2. Sedaris offers the image of himself as a "petty thief" in paragraph 21. What is the effect of this IMAGE?
3. Sedaris's language in this essay is notably SPECIFIC and CONCRETE. Point to examples of such language just in paragraph 6.
4. Consult a dictionary if necessary to learn the meanings of the following words: proximity, petty, autopsies, morgue (par. 2); hyenas (6); hawking, stocks (7);

leper (8); hangar (9); machetes (11); diplomatic (12); exoticism, coup, evacuate (13); ornamental, stein (16); fortitude (19); hobnobbing, symbiosis, report, canopy, eucalyptus (21).

Suggestions for Writing

1. **FROM JOURNAL TO ESSAY.** Starting from your journal entry (previous page), write an essay in which you compare and contrast your own experiences with those of someone whose life you've envied. Have your feelings changed over time? Why, or why not?
2. Hugh's experiences living with strangers gave him a "sense of fortitude" (par. 19), according to Sedaris. When have you ever gone through a difficult experience that left you somehow stronger? Write an essay about such an experience that shows how you were different before and after.
3. **CRITICAL WRITING.** How seriously does Sedaris want the readers of his essay to take him? Write an essay in which you analyze his TONE, citing specific passages from the text to support your conclusions.
4. **CONNECTIONS.** Sherman Alexie, in "Indian Education" (p. 103), writes about a childhood very different from either Sedaris's or Hugh's. In an essay, consider how Sedaris and Alexie might view each other's childhoods.

David Sedaris on Writing

Most of us are contented users of word processors, but not David Sedaris. In "Nutcracker.com," an essay in *Me Talk Pretty One Day*, Sedaris explains why he refuses to give up his typewriter.

I hate computers for any number of reasons, but I despise them most for what they've done to my friend the typewriter. In a democratic country you'd think there would be room for both of them, but computers won't rest until I'm making my ribbons from torn shirts and brewing Wite-Out in my bathtub. Their goal is to place the IBM Selectric II beside the feather quill and chisel in the museum of antiquated writing implements. They're power hungry, and someone needs to stop them.

When told I'm like the guy still pining for his eight-track tapes, I say, "You have eight-tracks? Where?" In reality I know nothing about them, yet I feel it's important to express some solidarity with others who have had the rug pulled out from beneath them. I don't care if it can count words or rearrange paragraphs at the push of a button, I don't want a computer. Unlike the faint scurry raised by fingers against a plastic computer keyboard, the smack and clatter of a typewriter suggests that you're actually building something. At the end of a miserable day, instead of grieving my virtual nothing, I can always look at my loaded wastepaper basket and tell myself that if I failed, at least I took a few trees down with me.

For Discussion

1. Why does Sedaris prefer writing with a typewriter instead of with a computer?
2. Defend the computerized word processor from Sedaris's attack. What are some advantages of the newer technology?

BRUCE CATTON

Bruce Catton (1899–1978) became America's best-known historian of the Civil War. As a boy in Benzonia, Michigan, Catton acted out historical battles on local playing fields. In his memoir *Waiting for the Morning Train* (1972), he recalls how he would listen by the hour to the memories of Union Army veterans. His studies at Oberlin College interrupted by service in World War I, Catton never finished his bachelor's degree. Instead, he worked as a reporter, columnist, and editorial writer for the *Cleveland Plain Dealer* and other newspapers, then became a speechwriter and information director for government agencies. Of Catton's eighteen books, seventeen were written after his fiftieth year. *A Stillness at Appomattox* (1953) won him both a Pulitzer Prize for history and a National Book Award; other notable works include *This Hallowed Ground* (1956) and *Gettysburg: The Final Fury* (1974). From 1954 until his death, Catton edited *American Heritage*, a magazine of history. President Gerald Ford awarded him a Medal of Freedom for his life's accomplishment.

Grant and Lee: A Study in Contrasts

"Grant and Lee: A Study in Contrasts" first appeared in *The American Story*, a book of essays written by eminent historians for interested general readers. Contrasting the two great Civil War generals allows Catton to portray not only two very different men but also the conflicting traditions they represented. Catton's essay builds toward the conclusion that, in one outstanding way, the two leaders were more than a little alike.

When Ulysses S. Grant and Robert E. Lee met in the parlor of a modest house at Appomattox Court House, Virginia, on April 9, 1865, to work out the terms for the surrender of Lee's Army of Northern Virginia, a great chapter in American life came to a close, and a great new chapter began. 1

These men were bringing the Civil War to its virtual finish. To be sure, other armies had yet to surrender, and for a few days the fugitive confederate government would struggle desperately and vainly, trying to find some way to go on living now that its chief support was gone. But in effect it was all over when Grant and Lee signed the papers. And the little room where they wrote out the terms was the scene of one of the poignant, dramatic contrasts in American history. 2

They were two strong men, these oddly different generals, and they represented the strengths of two conflicting currents that, through them, had come into final collision. 3

Back of Robert E. Lee was the notion that the old aristocratic concept   4
might somehow survive and be dominant in American life.

Lee was tidewater Virginia, and in his background were family, culture,   5
and tradition . . . the age of chivalry transplanted to a New World which was
making its own legends and its own myths. He embodied a way of life that had
come down through the age of knighthood and the English country squire.
America was a land that was beginning all over again, dedicated to nothing
much more complicated than the rather hazy belief that all men had equal
rights, and should have an equal chance in the world. In such a land Lee stood
for the feeling that it was somehow of advantage to human society to have a
pronounced inequality in the social structure. There should be a leisure class,
backed by ownership of land; in turn, society itself should be keyed to the land
as the chief source of wealth and influence. It would bring forth (according to
this ideal) a class of men with a strong sense of obligation to the community;
men who lived not to gain advantage for themselves, but to meet the solemn
obligations which had been laid on them by the very fact that they were privileged. From them the country would get its leadership; to them it could look
for the higher values—of thought, of conduct, of personal deportment—to
give it strength and virtue.

Lee embodied the noblest elements of this aristocratic ideal. Through   6
him, the landed nobility justified itself. For four years, the Southern states had
fought a desperate war to uphold the ideals for which Lee stood. In the end, it
almost seemed as if the Confederacy fought for Lee; as if he himself was the
Confederacy . . . the best thing that the way of life for which the Confederacy
stood could ever have to offer. He had passed into legend before Appomattox.
Thousands of tired, underfed, poorly clothed Confederate soldiers, long-since
past the simple enthusiasm of the early days of the struggle, somehow considered Lee the symbol of everything for which they had been willing to die. But
they could not quite put this feeling into words. If the Lost Cause, sanctified
by so much heroism and so many deaths, had a living justification, its justification was General Lee.

Grant, the son of a tanner on the Western frontier, was everything Lee   7
was not. He had come up the hard way, and embodied nothing in particular
except the eternal toughness and sinewy fiber of the men who grew up beyond
the mountains. He was one of a body of men who owed reverence and obeisance to no one, who were self-reliant to a fault, who cared hardly anything
for the past but who had a sharp eye for the future.

These frontier men were the precise opposites of the tidewater aristocrats.   8
Back of them, in the great surge that had taken people over the Alleghenies
and into the opening Western country, there was a deep, implicit dissatisfaction with a past that had settled into grooves. They stood for democracy, not

from any reasoned conclusion about the proper ordering of human society, but simply because they had grown up in the middle of democracy and knew how it worked. Their society might have privileges, but they would be privileges each man had won for himself. Forms and patterns meant nothing. No man was born to anything, except perhaps to a chance to show how far he could rise. Life was competition.

Yet along with this feeling had come a deep sense of belonging to a   9
national community. The Westerner who developed a farm, opened a shop, or set up in business as a trader could hope to prosper only as his own community prospered—and his community ran from the Atlantic to the Pacific and from Canada down to Mexico. If the land was settled, with towns and highways and accessible markets, he could better himself. He saw his fate in terms of the nation's own destiny. As its horizons expanded, so did his. He had, in other words, an acute dollars-and-cents stake in the continued growth and development of his country.

And that, perhaps, is where the contrast between Grant and Lee becomes   10
most striking. The Virginia aristocrat, inevitably, saw himself in relation to his own region. He lived in a static society which could endure almost anything except change. Instinctively, his first loyalty would go to the locality in which that society existed. He would fight to the limit of endurance to defend it, because in defending it he was defending everything that gave his own life its deepest meaning.

The Westerner, on the other hand, would fight with an equal tenacity for   11
the broader concept of society. He fought so because everything he lived by was tied to growth, expansion, and a constantly widening horizon. What he lived by would survive or fall with the nation itself. He could not possibly stand by unmoved in the face of an attempt to destroy the Union. He would combat it with everything he had, because he could only see it as an effort to cut the ground out from under his feet.

So Grant and Lee were in complete contrast, representing two dia-   12
metrically opposed elements in American life. Grant was the modern man emerging; beyond him, ready to come on the stage, was the great age of steel and machinery, of crowded cities and a restless, burgeoning vitality. Lee might have ridden down from the old age of chivalry, lance in hand, silken banner fluttering over his head. Each man was the perfect champion of his cause, drawing both his strengths and his weaknesses from the people he led.

Yet it was not all contrast, after all. Different as they were—in back-   13
ground, in personality, in underlying aspiration—these two great soldiers had much in common. Under everything else, they were marvelous fighters. Furthermore, their fighting qualities were really very much alike.

Each man had, to begin with, the great virtue of utter tenacity and fidel-   14
ity. Grant fought his way down the Mississippi Valley in spite of acute personal discouragement and profound military handicaps. Lee hung on in the
trenches at Petersburg after hope itself had died. In each man there was an
indomitable quality . . . the born fighter's refusal to give up as long as he can
still remain on his feet and lift his two fists.

Daring and resourcefulness they had, too; the ability to think faster and   15
move faster than the enemy. These were the qualities which gave Lee the daz-
zling campaigns of Second Manassas and Chancellorsville and won Vicksburg
for Grant.

Lastly, and perhaps greatest of all, there was the ability, at the end, to turn   16
quickly from war to peace once the fighting was over. Out of the way these two
men behaved at Appomattox came the possibility of a peace of reconciliation.
It was a possibility not wholly realized, in the years to come, but which did, in
the end, help the two sections to become one nation again . . . after a war
whose bitterness might have seemed to make such a reunion wholly impossible. No part of either man's life became him more than the part he played
in their brief meeting in the McLean house at Appomattox. Their behavior
there put all succeeding generations of Americans in their debt. Two great
Americans, Grant and Lee—very different, yet under everything very much
alike. Their encounter at Appomattox was one of the great moments of
American history.

Journal Writing

How do you respond to the opposing political beliefs represented by Grant and Lee?
During the American Civil War, nearly every citizen had an opinion and chose sides.
Do you think Americans today commit themselves as strongly to political and social
causes? In your journal, explain why, or why not. (To take your journal writing further,
see "From Journal to Essay" on p. 247.)

Questions on Meaning

1. What is Bruce Catton's PURPOSE in writing: to describe the meeting of two generals at a famous moment in history; to explain how the two men stood for opposing social forces in America; or to show how the two differed in personality?
2. SUMMARIZE the background and the way of life that produced Robert E. Lee; then
   do the same for Ulysses S. Grant. According to Catton, what ideals did each man
   represent?

3. In the historian's view, what essential traits did the two men have in common? Which trait does Catton think most important of all? For what reason?
4. How does this essay help you understand why Grant and Lee were such determined fighters?

Questions on Writing Strategy

1. From the content of this essay, and from knowing where it first appeared, what can you infer about Catton's original AUDIENCE? At what places in "Grant and Lee: A Study in Contrasts" does the writer expect his readers a familiarity with United States history?
2. What effect does the writer achieve by setting both his INTRODUCTION and his CONCLUSION in Appomattox?
3. For what reasons does Catton contrast the two generals *before* he compares them? Suppose he had reversed his outline, and had dealt first with Grant's and Lee's mutual resemblances. Why would his essay have been less effective?
4. Pencil in hand, draw a single line down the margin of every paragraph in which you find the method of contrast. Then draw a *double* line next to every paragraph in which you find the method of comparison. How much space does Catton devote to each method? Why didn't he give comparison and contrast equal time in his essay?
5. Closely read the first sentence of every paragraph and underline each word or phrase in it that serves as a TRANSITION. Then review your underlinings. How much COHERENCE has Catton given his essay?
6. What is the TONE of this essay—that is, what is the writer's attitude toward his two subjects? Is Catton poking fun at Lee by imagining the Confederate general as a knight of the Middle Ages, "lance in hand, silken banner fluttering over his head" (par. 12)?
7. **OTHER METHODS.** In identifying "two conflicting currents," Catton uses CLASSIFICATION to sort Civil War–era Americans into two groups represented by Lee and Grant. Catton then uses ANALYSIS to tease out the characteristics of each current, each type. How do classification and analysis serve Catton's comparison and contrast?

Questions on Language

1. In his opening paragraph, Catton uses a metaphor: American life is a book containing chapters. Find other FIGURES OF SPEECH in his essay (consulting Useful Terms if you need help). What do the figures of speech contribute?
2. Look up *poignant* in the dictionary. Why is it such a fitting word in paragraph 2? Why wouldn't *touching, sad,* or *teary* have been as good?
3. What information do you glean from the sentence "Lee was tidewater Virginia" (par. 5)?
4. Define *aristocratic* as Catton uses it in paragraphs 4 and 6.
5. Define *obeisance* (par. 7); *indomitable* (14).

Suggestions for Writing

1. **FROM JOURNAL TO ESSAY.** Using your journal entry (p. 245) as a starting point, write an essay that offers an explanation for public participation in or commitment to political and social causes today. What fires people up or turns them off? To help focus your essay, zero in on a specific issue, such as education, government spending, health insurance, or gun control.

2. In a brief essay full of specific examples, discuss: Do the "two diametrically opposed elements in American life" (as Catton calls them) still exist in the country today? Are there still any "landed nobility"?

3. In your thinking and your attitudes, whom do you more closely resemble—Grant or Lee? Compare and contrast your outlook with that of one famous American or the other. (A serious tone for this topic isn't required.)

4. **CRITICAL WRITING.** Although slavery, along with other issues, helped precipitate the Civil War, Catton in this particular essay does not deal with it. Perhaps he assumes that his readers will supply the missing context themselves. Is this a fair ASSUMPTION? If Catton had recalled the facts of slavery, would he have undermined any of his assertions about Lee? (Though the general of the pro-slavery Confederacy, Lee was personally opposed to slavery.) In a brief essay, judge whether or not the omission of slavery weakens the essay, and explain why.

5. **CONNECTIONS.** In "The Penalty of Death" (p. 516), H. L. Mencken maintains that capital punishment satisfies the need "to destroy the concrete scoundrels whose act has alarmed everyone, and thus made everyone unhappy." Mencken also says, "I do not argue that this yearning is noble; I simply argue that it is almost universal among human beings." How do Mencken's assertions illuminate Catton's final paragraph? In a brief essay, explain just what Grant and Lee accomplished at Appomattox.

Bruce Catton on Writing

Most of Bruce Catton's comments on writing, those that have been preserved, refer to the work of others. As editor of *American Heritage*, he was known for his blunt, succinct comments on unsuccessful manuscripts: "This article can't be repaired and wouldn't be much good if it were." Or: "The high-water mark of this piece comes at the bottom of page one, where the naked Indian nymph offers the hero strawberries. Unfortunately, this level is not maintained."

In a memoir published in *Bruce Catton's America* (1979), Catton's associate Oliver Jensen marvels that, besides editing *American Heritage* for twenty-four years (and contributing to nearly every issue), Catton managed to produce so many substantial books. "Concentration was no doubt the secret, that and getting an early start. For many years Catton was always the first person in the office, so early that most of the staff never knew when he did arrive. On his desk the little piles of yellow sheets grew slowly, with much larger piles in the wastebasket. A neat and orderly man, he preferred to type a new page than correct very much in pencil."

His whole purpose as a writer, Catton once said, was "to reexamine [our] debt to the past."

For Discussion

1. To which of Catton's traits does Oliver Jensen attribute the historian's impressive output?
2. Which characteristics of Catton the editor would you expect to have served him well as a writer?

NANCY MAIRS

A self-described "radical feminist, pacifist, and cripple," NANCY MAIRS aims to "speak the 'unspeakable.'" Her poetry, memoirs, and essays deal with many sensitive subjects, including her struggles with the debilitating disease of multiple sclerosis. Born in Long Beach, California, in 1943, Mairs grew up in New Hampshire and Massachusetts. She received a BA from Wheaton College in Massachusetts (1964) and an MFA in creative writing (1975) and a PhD in English literature (1984) from the University of Arizona. While working on her advanced degrees, Mairs taught high school and college writing courses and served as project director at the Southwest Institute for Research on Women. Her second book of poetry, *In All the Rooms of the Yellow House* (1984), received a Western States Arts Foundation book award. Her essays are published in *Plaintext* (1986), *Remembering the Bone-House* (1988), *Carnal Acts* (1990), *Ordinary Time* (1993), *Waist High in the World: A Life Among the Nondisabled* (1996), and *A Troubled Guest* (2001).

Disability

As a writer afflicted with multiple sclerosis, Nancy Mairs is in a unique position to examine how the culture responds to people with disabilities. In this essay from *Carnal Acts*, she draws two contrasts involving the media's depiction of disability and argues with her usual unsentimental candor that the media must treat disability as normal. The essay was first published in 1987 in the *New York Times*.

For months now I've been consciously searching for representation of 1 myself in the media, especially television. I know I'd recognize this self because of certain distinctive, though not unique, features: I am a forty-three-year-old woman crippled with multiple sclerosis; although I can still totter short distances with the aid of a brace and a cane, more and more of the time I ride in a wheelchair. Because of these appliances and my peculiar gait, I'm easy to spot even in a crowd. So when I tell you I haven't noticed any women like me on television, you can believe me.

Actually, last summer I did see a woman with multiple sclerosis portrayed 2 on one of those medical dramas that offer an illness-of-the-week like the daily special at your local diner. In fact, that was the whole point of the show: that this poor young woman had MS. She was terribly upset (understandably, I assure you) by the diagnosis, and her response was to plan a trip to Kenya while she was still physically capable of making it, against the advice of the young, fit, handsome doctor who had fallen in love with her. And she almost did it. At least, she got as far as a taxi to the airport, hotly pursued by the doctor. But at the last she succumbed to his blandishments and fled the taxi into his manly protective embrace. No escape to Kenya for this cripple.

Capitulation into the arms of a man who uses his medical powers to strip   3
one of even the urge toward independence is hardly the sort of representation I had in mind. But even if the situation had been sensitively handled, accord-ing to the woman her right to her own adventures, it wouldn't have been what I'm looking for. Such a television show, as well as films like *Duet for One* and *Children of a Lesser God,* in taking disability as its major premise, excludes the complexities that round out a character and make her whole. It's not about a woman who happens to be physically disabled; it's about physical disability and the determining factor of a woman's existence.

Take it from me, physical disability looms pretty large in one's life. But it   4
doesn't devour one wholly. I'm not, for instance, Ms. MS, a walking, talking embodiment of a chronic incurable degenerative disease. In most ways I'm just like every other woman of my age, nationality, and socioeconomic back-ground. I menstruate, so I have to buy tampons. I worry about smoker's breath, so I buy mouthwash. I smear my wrinkling skin with lotions. I put bleach in the washer so my family's undies won't be dingy. I drive a car, talk on the tele-phone, get runs in my pantyhose, eat pizza. In most ways, that is, I'm the advertisers' dream: Ms. Great American Consumer. And yet the advertisers, who determine nowadays who will get represented publicly and who will not, deny the existence of me and my kind absolutely.

I once asked a local advertiser why he didn't include disabled people in his   5
spots. His response seemed direct enough: "We don't want to give people the idea that our product is just for the handicapped." But tell me truly now: If you saw me pouring out puppy biscuits, would you think these kibbles were only for the puppies of the cripples? If you saw my blind niece ordering a Coke, would you switch to Pepsi lest you be struck sightless? No, I think the adver-tiser's excuse masked a deeper and more anxious rationale: To depict disabled people in the ordinary activities of daily life is to admit that there is something ordinary about disability itself, that it may enter anybody's life. If it is effaced completely, or at least isolated as a separate "problem," so that it remains at a safe distance from other human issues, then the viewer won't feel threatened by her or his own physical vulnerability.

This kind of effacement or isolation has painful, even dangerous conse-   6
quences, however. For the disabled person, these include self-degradation and a subtle kind of self-alienation not unlike that experienced by other minori-ties. Socialized human beings love to conform, to study others and then mold themselves to the contours of those whose images, for good reasons or bad, they come to love. Imagine a life in which feasible others—others you can

hope to be like—don't exist. At the least you might conclude that there is something queer about you, something ugly or foolish or shameful. In the extreme, you might feel as though you don't exist, in any meaningful social sense, at all. Everyone else is "there," sucking breath mints and splashing cologne and swigging wine coolers. You're "not there." And if not there, nowhere.

But this denial of disability imperils even you who are able-bodied, and not just by shrinking your insight into the physically and emotionally complex world you live in. Some disabled people call you TAPs, or Temporarily Abled Persons. The fact is that ours is the only minority you can join involuntarily, without warning, at any time. And if you live long enough, as you're increasingly likely to do, you may well join it. The transition will probably be difficult from a physical point of view no matter what. But it will be a good bit easier psychologically if you are accustomed to seeing disability as a normal characteristic, one that complicates but does not ruin human existence. Achieving this integration, for disabled and able-bodied people alike, requires that we insert disability daily into our field of vision: quietly, naturally, in the small and common scenes of our ordinary lives.

7

Journal Writing

Do you agree that many people respond with discomfort to those who are disabled? What do you feel when you see a stranger using a wheelchair: pity? sympathy? curiosity? uncertainty? admiration? fear? something else? In your journal, set down your answers to these questions as honestly as you can. What do you think causes these feelings? Consider how they are colored by your experiences with disability — whether you are disabled yourself, know someone who is disabled, or have no first-hand experience with disability. (To take your journal writing further, see "From Journal to Essay" on the next page.)

Questions on Meaning

1. Why does Mairs object to the TV movie about the woman with multiple sclerosis (pars. 2–3)?
2. What does Mairs mean by the phrase "Ms. Great American Consumer" (par. 4)?
3. Why, according to Mairs, should there be images of people with disabilities on television?
4. Restate Mairs's THESIS in your own words.
5. What is this essay's PURPOSE?

Questions on Writing Strategy

1. What does Mairs compare and contrast in this essay? How does the comparison help her achieve her purpose?
2. What key GENERALIZATIONS does Mairs make to support her thesis? Do you find them valid? Why, or why not?
3. How does Mairs use her INTRODUCTION to lay the groundwork for her essay? How does she make the TRANSITION from her introduction into the TV drama?
4. How would you characterize Mairs's TONE in this essay? Point out specific sentences and words that establish it. What is the EFFECT?
5. **OTHER METHODS.** Discuss how Mairs uses EXAMPLE to help build her case. What kinds of examples does she select? What are their effects?

Questions on Language

1. What is the function of IRONY in this essay (for example, "If you saw my blind niece ordering a Coke, would you switch to Pepsi lest you be struck sightless?")?
2. Look up *multiple sclerosis* in an encyclopedia or medical dictionary. What is the precise meaning of the term? How might advancing multiple sclerosis affect someone's ease of motion in a world designed for people who are not physically disabled?
3. Give definitions of the following words: gait (par. 1); blandishments (2); capitulation (3); degenerative (4); rationale, effaced (5); feasible (6).
4. What are the CONNOTATIONS of the words "crippled," "totter," "appliances," and "peculiar gait" (par. 1)? What is the effect of these words in the essay's introduction?
5. What do people with disabilities mean when they refer to "Temporarily Abled Persons" (par. 7)? Why might they use this phrase?

Suggestions for Writing

1. **FROM JOURNAL TO ESSAY.** Based on your journal reflections (previous page), write an essay that explains how your own responses to people with disabilities lead you to accept or dispute Mairs's call for depicting "disabled people in the ordinary activities of daily life."
2. Choose another group you think has been "effaced" in television advertising and programming—a racial, ethnic, or religious group, for instance. Write an essay detailing how and why that group is overlooked. How could representations of the group be incorporated into the media? What effects might such representation have?
3. Write an essay discussing how people with disabilities are treated in our society. You could NARRATE a day in the life of someone with a disability; you could compare and contrast the access and facilities your school provides physically average versus disabled students; you could CLASSIFY social attitudes toward disabilities, with examples of each type.
4. **CRITICAL WRITING.** Reread this essay carefully. Mairs tells us about herself through details and through tone (for example, through irony, intensity, and

humor). Write an essay on how Mairs's self-revelations do or do not help further her thesis.

5. **CONNECTIONS.** In "On Compassion" (p. 183), Barbara Lazear Ascher writes about the way people who are comfortable tend to respond to homeless people on the street, and she suggests that compassion must be "learned by having adversity at our window." Does what Ascher asks in relation to homeless people resemble what Mairs asks in relation to disabled people? In an essay, discuss the similarities and differences between these two writers' views of how people's attitudes could or should change.

Nancy Mairs on Writing

Nancy Mairs frequently writes about the calamities in her life, and she ponders why in an essay that appeared in the *New York Times Book Review* in February 1993. Why, for instance, did she record the details of her husband's grave illness? Perhaps because writing about one's misery is a way to overcome the isolation it creates. "There must have been millions keeping bedside vigils, whispering as I whispered over and over, 'Come back. Don't leave me. I need you,' each of us trapped in this profound and irrational solitude, as though walls of black glass had dropped on every side, shutting out the light, deadening all sound but the loved one's morphine-drugged breathing. I was not, in truth, alone."

In addition to this sense of kinship, Mairs also gains personal power from writing about illness. "The impulse, at least for someone of a writerly persuasion, is not to bemoan this condition but to remark on it in detail. Initially, one's motives for translating happenstance into acts of language may be quite private. Catastrophe tends to be composed not of a monolithic event but of a welter of little incidents, many of which bear no apparent relationship to one another, and language, in ordering these into recognizable patterns, counteracts disorientation and disintegration. This process of making sense of a flood of random data also produces the impression—generally quite groundless—of control, which may save one's sanity even though it can't save one's own or anyone else's life."

These therapeutic results, Mairs maintains, provide reason enough for keeping a private journal. However, going public "is an intrinsically social act, 'I' having no reason to speak aloud unless I posit 'you' there listening." The presence of the reader is especially important, Mairs says, "if I am seeking [. . .] to reconnect my self, now so utterly transformed by events unlike any I've experienced before as to seem a stranger even to myself, to the human community." The human community is no stranger to pain. "All of us who write out of calamity know this above all else: There is nothing exceptional about our lives, however they may differ in their particulars. What we can offer you, when the time comes, is companionship in a common venture. It's not a lot, I know, but it may come in handy. The narrator of personal disaster, I think, wants not to whine, not to boast, but to comfort."

But, Mairs finds, perhaps the most compelling reason of all to record personal affliction is to show "the spiritual maturation that suffering can force." "The writing about personal disaster that functions as literature tends not to be 'about' disaster at all," Mairs observes. Rather, it delineates a "progress toward sympathetic wisdom." The best writers "transcend their separate ordeals to speak generally, and generously, of the human condition." They write about "going on. All the way. To our common destination.

"To which none of us wants to go ignorant and alone," Mairs adds. "Hence, into the dark, we write."

For Discussion

1. Why does Mairs believe that writing about one's own misery is valuable, both for the writer and for readers?
2. How does Mairs distinguish between journal writing and writing with a reader in mind?

ALICE WALKER

ALICE WALKER is best known for her novel *The Color Purple* (1982), which won both a Pulitzer Prize and an American Book Award and was made into a movie by Steven Spielberg. Born into a sharecropping family in Eatonton, Georgia, in 1944, Walker is the youngest of eight children. She spent two years at Spelman College in Atlanta before transferring to Sarah Lawrence College. Upon graduation in 1965, Walker became active in the civil rights movement, helping to register voters in Georgia by day and pursuing her writing by night. She has won fellowships from the Radcliffe Institute, the Guggenheim Foundation, and the National Endowment for the Arts. In addition to *The Color Purple*, Walker's novels include *The Third Life of Grange Copeland* (1970), *The Temple of My Familiar* (1989), and *The Way Forward Is with a Broken Heart* (2000). She has also written several volumes of poetry; two short-story collections; a biography of Langston Hughes; an anthology of the work of Zora Neale Hurston; and the essays in the collections *In Search of Our Mothers' Gardens* (1983) and *Living by the Word* (1988). Walker has taught at numerous colleges and universities, including Jackson State College, Wellesley, Yale, and the University of California at Berkeley.

Everyday Use

In this short story about family, Walker reveals two sisters through the eyes of their mother. Published in 1973, the story appeared in *Harper's* magazine and then in Walker's collection *In Love and Trouble: Stories of Black Women*.

I will wait for her in the yard that Maggie and I made so clean and wavy yesterday afternoon. A yard like this is more comfortable than most people know. It is not just a yard. It is like an extended living room. When the hard clay is swept clean as a floor and the fine sand around the edges lined with tiny, irregular grooves, anyone can come and sit and look up into the elm tree and wait for the breezes that never come inside the house. 1

Maggie will be nervous until after her sister goes: She will stand hopelessly in corners, homely and ashamed of the burn scars down her arms and legs, eyeing her sister with a mixture of envy and awe. She thinks her sister has held life always in the palm of one hand, that "no" is a word the world never learned to say to her. 2

You've no doubt seen those TV shows where the child who has "made it" is confronted, as a surprise, by her own mother and father, tottering in weakly from backstage. (A pleasant surprise, of course: What would they do if parent 3 and child came on the show only to curse out and insult each other?) On TV mother and child embrace and smile into each other's faces. Sometimes the mother and father weep, the child wraps them in her arms and leans across the table to tell how she would not have made it without their help. I have seen these programs.

Sometimes I dream a dream in which Dee and I are suddenly brought together on a TV program of this sort. Out of a dark and soft-seated limousine I am ushered into a bright room filled with many people. There I meet a smiling, gray, sporty man like Johnny Carson who shakes my hand and tells me what a fine girl I have. Then we are on the stage and Dee is embracing me with tears in her eyes. She pins on my dress a large orchid, even though she has told me once that she thinks orchids are tacky flowers.

In real life I am a large, big-boned woman with rough, man-working hands. In the winter I wear flannel nightgowns to bed and overalls during the day. I can kill and clean a hog as mercilessly as a man. My fat keeps me hot in zero weather. I can work outside all day, breaking ice to get water for washing; I can eat pork liver cooked over the open fire minutes after it comes steaming from the hog. One winter I knocked a bull calf straight in the brain between the eyes with a sledge hammer and had the meat hung up to chill before nightfall. But of course all this does not show on television. I am the way my daughter would want me to be: a hundred pounds lighter, my skin like an uncooked barley pancake. My hair glistens in the hot bright lights. Johnny Carson has much to do to keep up with my quick and witty tongue.

But that is a mistake. I know even before I wake up. Who ever knew a Johnson with a quick tongue? Who can even imagine me looking a strange white man in the eye? It seems to me I have talked to them always with one foot raised in flight, with my head turned in whichever way is farthest from them. Dee, though. She would always look anyone in the eye. Hesitation was no part of her nature.

"How do I look, Mama?" Maggie says, showing just enough of her thin body enveloped in pink skirt and red blouse for me to know she's there, almost hidden by the door.

"Come out into the yard," I say.

Have you ever seen a lame animal, perhaps a dog run over by some careless person rich enough to own a car, sidle up to someone who is ignorant enough to be kind to him? That is the way my Maggie walks. She has been like this, chin on chest, eyes on ground, feet in shuffle, ever since the fire that burned the other house to the ground.

Dee is lighter than Maggie, with nicer hair and a fuller figure. She's a woman now, though sometimes I forget. How long ago was it that the other house burned? Ten, twelve years? Sometimes I can still hear the flames and feel Maggie's arms sticking to me, her hair smoking and her dress falling off her in little black papery flakes. Her eyes seemed stretched open, blazed open by the flames reflected in them. And Dee. I see her standing off under the sweet gum tree she used to dig gum out of; a look of concentration on her face as she watched the last dingy gray board of the house fall in toward the red-hot brick chimney. Why don't you do a dance around the ashes? I'd wanted to ask her. She had hated the house that much.

I used to think she hated Maggie, too. But that was before we raised the 11 money, the church and me, to send her to Augusta to school. She used to read to us without pity; forcing words, lies, other folks' habits, whole lives upon us two, sitting trapped and ignorant underneath her voice. She washed us in a river of make-believe, burned us with a lot of knowledge we didn't necessarily need to know. Pressed us to her with the serious way she read, to shove us away at just the moment, like dimwits, we seemed about to understand.

Dee wanted nice things. A yellow organdy dress to wear to her graduation 12 from high school; black pumps to match a green suit she'd made from an old suit somebody gave me. She was determined to stare down any disaster in her efforts. Her eyelids would not flicker for minutes at a time. Often I fought off the temptation to shake her. At sixteen she had a style of her own: and knew what style was.

I never had an education myself. After second grade the school was closed 13 down. Don't ask me why: In 1927 colored asked fewer questions than they do now. Sometimes Maggie reads to me. She stumbles along good-naturedly but can't see well. She knows she is not bright. Like good looks and money, quickness passed her by. She will marry John Thomas (who has mossy teeth in an earnest face) and then I'll be free to sit here and I guess just sing church songs to myself. Although I never was a good singer. Never could carry a tune. I was always better at a man's job. I used to love to milk till I was hooked in the side in '49. Cows are soothing and slow and don't bother you, unless you try to milk them the wrong way.

I have deliberately turned my back on the house. It is three rooms, just 14 like the one that burned, except the roof is tin; they don't make shingle roofs any more. There are no real windows, just some holes cut in the sides, like the portholes in a ship, but not round and not square, with rawhide holding the shutters up on the outside. This house is in a pasture, too, like the other one. No doubt when Dee sees it she will want to tear it down. She wrote me once that no matter where we "choose" to live, she will manage to come see us. But she will never bring her friends. Maggie and I thought about this and Maggie asked me, "Mama, when did Dee ever *have* any friends?"

She had a few. Furtive boys in pink shirts hanging about on washday after   15
school. Nervous girls who never laughed. Impressed with her they worshiped
the well-turned phrase, the cute shape, the scalding humor that erupted like
bubbles in lye. She read to them.

When she was courting Jimmy T she didn't have much time to pay to us,   16
but turned all her faultfinding power on him. He *flew* to marry a cheap city
gal from a family of ignorant flashy people. She hardly had time to recompose
herself.

When she comes I will meet — but there they are!   17

Maggie attempts to make a dash for the house, in her shuffling way, but I   18
stay her with my hand. "Come back here," I say. And she stops and tries to dig
a well in the sand with her toe.

It is hard to see them clearly through the strong sun. But even the first   19
glimpse of leg out of the car tells me it is Dee. Her feet were always neat-
looking, as if God himself had shaped them with a certain style. From the
other side of the car comes a short, stocky man. Hair is all over his head a foot
long and hanging from his chin like a kinky mule tail. I hear Maggie suck in
her breath. "Uhnnnh," is what it sounds like. Like when you see the wriggling
end of a snake just in front of your foot on the road. "Uhnnnh."

Dee next. A dress down to the ground, in this hot weather. A dress so loud   20
it hurts my eyes. There are yellows and oranges enough to throw back the light
of the sun. I feel my whole face warming from the heat waves it throws out.
Earrings gold, too, and hanging down to her shoulders. Bracelets dangling and
making noises when she moves her arm up to shake the folds of the dress out
of her armpits. The dress is loose and flows, and as she walks closer, I like it. I
hear Maggie go "Uhnnnh" again. It is her sister's hair. It stands straight up like
the wool on a sheep. It is black as night and around the edges are two long pig-
tails that rope about like small lizards disappearing behind her ears.

"Wa-su-zo-Tean-o!"[1] she says, coming on in that gliding way the dress   21
makes her move. The short stocky fellow with the hair to his navel is all
grinning and he follows up with "Asalamalakim, my mother and sister!" He
moves to hug Maggie but she falls back, right up against the back of my chair.
I feel her trembling there and when I look up I see the perspiration falling off
her chin.

"Don't get up," says Dee. Since I am stout it takes something of a push.   22
You can see me trying to move a second or two before I make it. She turns,
showing white heels through her sandals, and goes back to the car. Out she

---

[1] "Wa-su-zo-Tean-o" and "Asalamalakim" (next sentence) are greetings spelled as the
mother heard them. — EDS.

peeks next with a Polaroid. She stoops down quickly and lines up picture after picture of me sitting there in front of the house with Maggie cowering behind me. She never takes a shot without making sure the house is included. When a cow comes nibbling around the edge of the yard she snaps it and me *and* the house. Then she puts the Polaroid in the back seat of the car, and comes up and kisses me on the forehead.

Meanwhile Asalamalakim is going through the motions with Maggie's hand. Maggie's hand is as limp as a fish, and probably as cold, despite the sweat, and she keeps trying to pull it back. It looks like Asalamalakim wants to shake hands but wants to do it fancy. Or maybe he don't know how people shake hands. Anyhow, he soon gives up on Maggie. 23

"Well," I say. "Dee." 24

"No, Mama," she says. "Not 'Dee,' Wangero Leewanika Kemanjo!" 25

"What happened to 'Dee'?" I wanted to know. 26

"She's dead," Wangero said. "I couldn't bear it any longer being named after the people who oppress me." 27

"You know as well as me you was named after your aunt Dicie," I said. Dicie is my sister. She named Dee. We called her "Big Dee" after Dee was born. 28

"But who was *she* named after?" asked Wangero. 29

"I guess after Grandma Dee," I said. 30

"And who was she named after?" asked Wangero. 31

"Her mother," I said, and saw Wangero was getting tired. "That's about as far back as I can trace it," I said. Though, in fact, I probably could have carried it back beyond the Civil War through the branches. 32

"Well," said Asalamalakim, "there you are." 33

"Uhnnnh," I heard Maggie say. 34

"There I was not," I said, "before 'Dicie' cropped up in our family, so why should I try to trace it that far back?" 35

He just stood there grinning, looking down on me like somebody inspecting a Model A car. Every once in a while he and Wangero sent eye signals over my head. 36

"How do you pronounce this name?" I asked. 37

"You don't have to call me by it if you don't want to," said Wangero. 38

"Why shouldn't I?" I asked. "If that's what you want us to call you, we'll call you." 39

"I know it might sound awkward at first," said Wangero. 40

"I'll get used to it," I said. "Ream it out again." 41

Well, soon we got the name out of the way. Asalamalakim had a name twice as long and three times as hard. After I tripped over it two or three times he told me to just call him Hakim-a-barber. I wanted to ask him was he a barber, but I didn't really think he was, so I didn't ask. 42

"You must belong to those beef-cattle peoples down the road," I said.   43
They said "Asalamalakim" when they met you, too, but they didn't shake
hands. Always too busy: feeding the cattle, fixing the fences, putting up salt-
lick shelters, throwing down hay. When the white folks poisoned some of the
herd the men stayed up all night with rifles in their hands. I walked a mile and
a half just to see the sight.

Hakim-a-barber said, "I accept some of their doctrines, but farming and   44
raising cattle is not my style." (They didn't tell me, and I didn't ask, whether
Wangero [Dee] had really gone and married him.)

We sat down to eat and right away he said he didn't eat collards and pork   45
was unclean. Wangero, though, went on through the chitlins and corn bread,
the greens and everything else. She talked a blue streak over the sweet potatoes. Everything delighted her. Even the fact that we still used the benches her
daddy made for the table when we couldn't afford to buy chairs.

"Oh, Mama!" she cried. Then turned to Hakim-a-barber. "I never knew   46
how lovely these benches are. You can feel the rump prints," she said, running
her hands underneath her and along the bench. Then she gave a sigh and her
hand closed over Grandma Dee's butter dish. "That's it!" she said. "I knew
there was something I wanted to ask you if I could have." She jumped up from
the table and went over in the corner where the churn stood, the milk in it
clabber by now. She looked at the churn and looked at it.

"This churn top is what I need," she said. "Didn't Uncle Buddy whittle it   47
out of a tree you all used to have?"

"Yes," I said.   48

"Uh-huh," she said happily. "And I want the dasher,[2] too."   49

"Uncle Buddy whittle that, too?" asked the barber.   50

Dee (Wangero) looked up at me.   51

"Aunt Dee's first husband whittled the dash," said Maggie so low you   52
almost couldn't hear her. "His name was Henry, but they called him Stash."

"Maggie's brain is like an elephant's," Wangero said, laughing. "I can use   53
the churn top as a centerpiece for the alcove table," she said, sliding a plate
over the churn, "and I'll think of something artistic to do with the dasher."

When she finished wrapping the dasher the handle stuck out. I took it for   54
a moment in my hands. You didn't even have to look close to see where hands
pushing the dasher up and down to make butter had left a kind of sink in the
wood. In fact, there were a lot of small sinks; you could see where thumbs and
fingers had sunk into the wood. It was beautiful light yellow wood, from a tree
that grew in the yard where Big Dee and Stash had lived.

After dinner Dee (Wangero) went to the trunk at the foot of my bed and   55

[2] The plunger of the butter churn. — EDS.

started rifling through it. Maggie hung back in the kitchen over the dishpan. Out came Wangero with two quilts. They had been pieced by Grandma Dee and then Big Dee and me had hung them on the quilt frames on the front porch and quilted them. One was in the Lone Star pattern. The other was Walk Around the Mountain. In both of them were scraps of dresses Grandma Dee had worn fifty and more years ago. Bits and pieces of Grandpa Jarrell's Paisley shirts. And one teeny faded blue piece, about the size of a penny matchbox, that was from Great Grandpa Ezra's uniform that he wore in the Civil War.

"Mama," Wangero said sweet as a bird. "Can I have these old quilts?"   56

I heard something fall in the kitchen, and a minute later the kitchen door   57
slammed.

"Why don't you take one or two of the others?" I asked. "These old things   58
was just done by me and Big Dee from some tops your grandma pieced before
she died."

"No," said Wangero. "I don't want those. They are stitched around the   59
borders by machine."

"That'll make them last better," I said.   60

"That's not the point," said Wangero. "These are all pieces of dresses   61
Grandma used to wear. She did all this stitching by hand. Imagine!" She held
the quilts securely in her arms, stroking them.

"Some of the pieces, like those lavender ones, come from old clothes her   62
mother handed down to her," I said, moving up to touch the quilts. Dee
(Wangero) moved back just enough so that I couldn't reach the quilts. They
already belonged to her.

"Imagine!" she breathed again, clutching them closely to her bosom.   63

"The truth is," I said, "I promised to give them quilts to Maggie, for when   64
she marries John Thomas."

She gasped like a bee had stung her.   65

"Maggie can't appreciate these quilts!" she said. "She'd probably be back-   66
ward enough to put them to everyday use."

"I reckon she would," I said. "God knows I been saving 'em for long   67
enough with nobody using 'em. I hope she will!" I didn't want to bring up how
I had offered Dee (Wangero) a quilt when she went away to college. Then she
had told me they were old-fashioned, out of style.

"But they're *priceless*!" she was saying now, furiously; for she has a temper.   68
"Maggie would put them on the bed and in five years they'd be in rags. Less
than that!"

"She can always make some more," I said. "Maggie knows how to quilt."   69

Dee (Wangero) looked at me with hatred. "You just will not understand.   70
The point is these quilts, *these* quilts!"

"Well," I said, stumped. "What would *you* do with them?"   71

"Hang them," she said. As if that was the only thing you *could* do with 72
quilts.

Maggie by now was standing in the door. I could almost hear the sound   73
her feet made as they scraped over each other.

"She can have them, Mama," she said, like somebody used to never win-   74
ning anything, or having anything reserved for her. "I can 'member Grandma
Dee without the quilts."

I looked at her hard. She had filled her bottom lip with checkerberry snuff 75
and it gave her face a kind of dopey, hangdog look. It was Grandma Dee and
Big Dee who taught her how to quilt herself. She stood there with her scarred
hands hidden in the folds of her skirt. She looked at her sister with something
like fear but she wasn't mad at her. This was Maggie's portion. This was the
way she knew God to work.

When I looked at her like that something hit me in the top of my head   76
and ran down to the soles of my feet. Just like when I'm in church and the
spirit of God touches me and I get happy and shout. I did something I never
had done before: hugged Maggie to me, then dragged her on into the room,
snatched the quilts out of Miss Wangero's hands and dumped them into Maggie's lap. Maggie just sat there on my bed with her mouth open.

"Take one or two of the others," I said to Dee.   77

But she turned without a word and went out to Hakim-a-barber.   78

"You just don't understand," she said, as Maggie and I came out to the car. 79

"What don't I understand?" I wanted to know.   80

"Your heritage," she said. And then she turned to Maggie, kissed her, and 81
said, "You ought to try to make something of yourself, too, Maggie. It's really a
new day for us. But from the way you and Mama still live you'd never know it."

She put on some sunglasses that hid everything above the tip of her nose   82
and her chin.

Maggie smiled; maybe at the sunglasses. But a real smile, not scared. After 83
we watched the car dust settle I asked Maggie to bring me a dip of snuff. And
then the two of us sat there just enjoying, until it was time to go in the house
and go to bed.

Journal Writing

Do you think the quilts stitched by the narrator's mother should be put to "everyday
use," or should they be preserved as a reminder of family and cultural heritage? Write
about something owned by you or your family that has been passed down from earlier

generations. Is it still in everyday use? Why, or why not? (To take your journal writing further, see "From Journal to Essay" below.)

Questions on Meaning

1. Walker's short story is based on two sets of contrasts, one made directly between people, the other made more indirectly between attitudes. What are these contrasts?
2. Why has Dee taken on a new name? What is the point of the conversation in which she and her mother discuss the origin of her given name (pars. 24–35)?
3. Why do you think Dee makes sure to include the house when taking photographs of her mother and sister (par. 22)? Why does she want the quilts stitched by her grandmother? What IRONY can you find in her behavior?
4. Why do you think Walker titled this story "Everyday Use"?

Questions on Writing Strategy

1. What might Walker's PURPOSE have been in creating the contrasting sisters? What might the characters represent?
2. In what way does the conclusion of the story echo the beginning? What is the EFFECT of the story's opening and closing in this way?
3. **OTHER METHODS.** Walker's story is, of course, a NARRATIVE. Where does Walker use DESCRIPTION to enhance her narration?

Questions on Language

1. The mother states in paragraph 13 that she is uneducated and earlier makes the point that she doesn't have a "quick tongue" (par. 6). Does the mother's language seem consistent with and appropriate for her educational background? Why, or why not?
2. What effect does Walker achieve by using a dash and an exclamation point in the single sentence of paragraph 17?
3. What is the effect of the mother's referring to her daughter repeatedly as "Dee (Wangero)" and finally, in paragraph 76, as "Miss Wangero"?
4. Be sure you know the meanings of the following words, checking a dictionary if necessary: awe (par. 2); tottering (3); rawhide (14); scalding, lye (15); churn, clabber (46); snuff (75).

Suggestions for Writing

1. **FROM JOURNAL TO ESSAY.** Develop an essay about the family object or objects that you wrote about in your journal entry. Carefully describe the object, and explain its history, significance, and current use.
2. Think of siblings you know who are quite different from each other in looks, interests, behavior, or other attributes. (Your subjects could be you and your own sibling.) In an essay, compare and contrast the two people.

3. **CRITICAL WRITING.** ANALYZE the character of Dee/Wangero, in relation to her mother and sister as well as in her own right. How do you think Walker wants readers to respond to this character? How do you respond to her? Be sure to support your analysis with appropriate quotations from the text.

4. **CONNECTIONS.** "Everyday Use" was published ten years after Martin Luther King, Jr., delivered his famous "I Have a Dream" speech (p. 603). How does the story reflect the themes of "I Have a Dream"? How is Walker commenting on the civil rights movement and its aftermath?

Alice Walker on Writing

In an interview with David Bradley in the *New York Times Magazine*, Alice Walker described her method of writing as waiting for friendly spirits to visit her. Usually, she doesn't outline or devote much time to preliminary organization. She plunges in with a passion, and she sees a definite purpose in most of her work: to correct injustices. "I was brought up to try to see what was wrong, and right it. Since I am a writer, writing is how I right it. I was brought up to look at things that are out of joint, out of balance, and to try to bring them into balance. And as a writer that's what I do."

An articulate feminist, Walker has written in support of greater rights for women, including African American women. If most of her works are short — stories, essays, and poems — there is a reason: She sees thick, long-winded volumes as alien to a female sensibility. "The books women write can be more like us — much thinner, much leaner, much cleaner."

Much of Alice Walker's writing has emerged from painful experience: She has written of her impoverished early days on a Georgia sharecropper's farm, a childhood accident with a BB gun that cost her the sight of one eye, a traumatic abortion, years as a civil rights worker in Mississippi. "I think," she says, "writing really helps you heal yourself. I think if you write long enough, you will be a healthy person. That is, if you write what you need to write, as opposed to what will make money or what will make fame."

For Discussion

1. What does the author mean when she speaks of the importance of writing "what you need to write"?
2. What writers can you think of whose work has helped to right the world's wrongs?
3. Can you cite any exceptions to Walker's generalization that long books are alien to women's sensibilities?

ADDITIONAL WRITING TOPICS
Comparison and Contrast

1. In an essay replete with examples, compare and contrast the two subjects in any one of the following pairs:

   The main characters of two films, stories, or novels
   Women and men as consumers
   The styles of two runners
   Liberals and conservatives: their opposing views of the role of government
   How city dwellers and country dwellers spend their leisure time
   The presentation styles of two television news commentators

2. Approach a comparison and contrast essay on one of the following general subjects by explaining why you prefer one thing to the other:

   Computers: Macs and PCs
   Two buildings on campus or in town
   Two football teams
   German-made cars and Detroit-made cars
   Two horror movies
   Television when you were a child and television today
   City life and small-town or rural life
   Malls and main streets
   Two neighborhoods
   Two sports

3. Write an essay in which you compare a reality (what actually exists) with an ideal (what should exist). Some possible topics:

   The affordable car
   Available living quarters
   A job
   The college curriculum
   Public transportation
   Financial aid to college students

Process analysis in a series of photographs

The American Eadweard Muybridge (1830–1904) was the first person to make legible photographs of events occurring in small slivers of time. Well before the invention of the motion picture, Muybridge photographed moving people and animals to show through a lens what the naked eye could not see: the very process of locomotion, the precise way that body parts work together to propel a figure through space. In this series from 1884–86, Muybridge illuminates the mysterious flight of birds: Moment by moment, and from two different angles, we see how an eagle works its wings to move through the air. How does each step in the sequence seem to contribute to the eagle's flight?

8

PROCESS ANALYSIS
Explaining Step by Step

THE METHOD

A chemist working for a soft-drink firm is asked to improve on a competitor's product, Orange Quench. First, she chemically tests a sample to figure out what's in the drink. This is the method of DIVISION or ANALYSIS, the separation of something into its parts in order to understand it (see the following chapter). Then the chemist writes a report telling her boss how to make a drink like Orange Quench, but better. This recipe is a special kind of analysis, called PROCESS ANALYSIS: explaining step by step how to do something or how something is done.

Like any type of analysis, process analysis divides a subject into its components: It divides a continuous action into stages. Processes much larger and more involved than the making of an orange drink also may be analyzed. When geologists explain how a formation such as the Grand Canyon occurred—a process taking several hundred million years—they describe the successive layers of sediment deposited by oceans, floods, and wind; then the great uplift of the entire region by underground forces; and then the erosion, visible to us today, by the Colorado River and its tributaries, by little streams and flash floods, by crumbling and falling rock, and by wind. Exactly what are the geologists doing in this explanation? They are taking a complicated event (or process) and dividing it into parts. They are telling us what happened first, second, and third, and what is still happening today.

Because it is useful in explaining what is complicated, process analysis is a favorite method of scientists such as geologists. The method, however, may be useful to anybody. Two PURPOSES of process analysis are very familiar to you:

- A *directive process analysis* explains how to do something or make something. You meet it when you read a set of instructions for assembling newly purchased stereo components or follow the directions to an electronics store ("Turn right at the blinker and follow Patriot Boulevard for 2.4 miles . . .").
- An *informative process analysis* explains how something is done or how it takes place. This is the kind we often read out of curiosity. Such an essay may tell of events beyond our control: how atoms behave when split, how lions hunt, how a fertilized egg develops into a child.

In this chapter, you will find examples of both kinds of process analysis—both the "how to" and the "how." For instance, Lucinda Rosenfeld offers a directive for the sensitive work of dumping a friend, while Jessica Mitford spellbindingly informs us of how corpses are embalmed (but, clearly, she doesn't expect us to rush down to our basements and give her instructions a try).

Sometimes process analysis is used very imaginatively. Foreseeing that the sun eventually will cool, the earth shrink, the oceans freeze, and all life perish, an astronomer who cannot possibly behold the end of the world nevertheless can write a process analysis of it. An exercise in learned guesswork, such an essay divides a vast and almost inconceivable event into stages that, taken one at a time, become clearer and more readily imaginable.

Whether it is useful or useless (but fun to imagine), an effective process analysis can grip readers and even hold them fascinated. Say you were proposing a change in the procedures for course registration at your school. You could argue your point until you were out of words, but you would get nowhere if you failed to tell your readers exactly how the new process would work: That's what makes your proposal sing. Leaf through a current issue of a newsstand magazine, and you will find that process analysis abounds. You may meet, for instance, articles telling you how to tenderize cuts of meat, sew homemade designer jeans, lose fat, cut hair, arouse a bored mate, and score at Internet stock trading. Less practical, but not necessarily less interesting, are the informative articles: how brain surgeons work, how diamonds are formed, how cities fight crime. Readers, it seems, have an unslakable thirst for process analysis. In every issue of the *New York Times Book Review*, we find an entire best-seller list devoted to "Advice, How-to, and Miscellaneous," including books on how to make money in real estate, how to lose weight, how to find a good mate, and how to lose a bad one. Evidently, if anything will still make an American crack open a book, it is a step-by-step explanation of how he or she, too, can be a success at living.

THE PROCESS

Here are suggestions for writing an effective process analysis of your own. (In fact, what you are about to read is itself a process analysis.)

1. *Understand clearly the process you are about to analyze.* Think it through. This preliminary survey will make the task of writing far easier for you.
2. *Consider your thesis.* What is the point of your process analysis: Why are you bothering to tell readers about it? The THESIS SENTENCE for a process analysis need do no more than say what the subject is and maybe outline its essential stages. For instance:

The main stages in writing a process analysis are listing the steps in the process, drafting to explain the steps, and revising to clarify the steps.

But your readers will surely appreciate something livelier and more pointed, something that says "You can use this" or "This may surprise you" or "Listen up." Here are two examples of a thesis sentence from essays in this chapter:

[In a mortuary the body] is in short order sprayed, sliced, pierced, pickled, trussed, trimmed, creamed, waxed, painted, rouged, and neatly dressed — transformed from a common corpse into a Beautiful Memory Picture. (Jessica Mitford, "Behind the Formaldehyde Curtain")

Poisoning the earth can be difficult because the earth is always trying to cleanse and renew itself. (Linnea Saukko, "How to Poison the Earth")

3. *Think about preparatory steps.* If the reader should do something before beginning the process, list these steps. For instance, you might begin, "Remove the packing from around the components," or, "First, lay out three eggs, one pound of Sheboygan bratwurst, and a chopped jalapeño pepper."

4. *List the steps or stages in the process.* Try setting them down in chronological order, one at a time — if this is possible. Some processes, however, do not happen in an orderly sequence, but occur all at once. If, for instance, you are writing an account of a typical earthquake, what do you mention first? The shifting of underground rock strata? Cracks in the earth? Falling houses? Bursting water mains? Toppling trees? Mangled cars? Casualties? Here is a subject for which the method of CLASSIFICATION (Chap. 10) may come to your aid. You might sort out apparently simultaneous events into categories: injury to people; damage to homes, to land, to public property.

5. *Check the completeness and order of the steps.* Make sure your list includes *all* the steps in the right order. Sometimes a stage of a process may contain a number of smaller stages. Make sure none has been left out. If any seems particularly tricky or complicated, underline it on your list to remind yourself when you write your essay to slow down and detail it with extra care.

6. *Define your terms.* Ask yourself, "Do I need any specialized or technical terms?" If so, be sure to define them. You'll sympathize with your reader if you have ever tried to work a Malaysian-made VCR that comes with an instruction booklet written in translatorese, full of unexplained technical JARGON, or if you have ever tried to assemble a plastic tricycle according to a directive that begins, "Position sleeve casing on wheel center in fork with shaft in tong groove, and gently but forcibly tap in medium pal nut head."

7. *Use time-markers or TRANSITIONS.* These words or phrases indicate *when* one stage of a process stops and the next begins, and they greatly aid your

reader in following you. Here, for example, is a paragraph of plain medical prose that makes good use of the helpful time-markers printed in *italics*. (The paragraph is adapted from Alan Frank Guttmacher's *Pregnancy and Birth*.)

In the human, *thirty-six hours after* the egg is fertilized, a two-cell egg appears. A twelve-cell development takes place *in seventy-two hours*. The egg is *still* round and has increased little in diameter. In this respect it is like a real estate development. *At first* a road bisects the whole area, *then* a cross road divides it into quarters, and *later* other roads divide it into eighths and twelfths. This happens without the taking of any more land, simply by sub-division of the original tract. *On the third or fourth day*, the egg passes from the Fallopian tube into the uterus. *By the fifth day* the original single large cell has subdivided into sixty small cells and floats about the slitlike uterine cavity *a day or two longer*, *then* adheres to the cavity's inner lining. *By the twelfth day* the human egg is already firmly implanted. Impregnation is *now* completed, *as yet* unbeknown to the woman. *At present*, she has not even had time to miss her first menstrual period, and other symptoms of pregnancy are *still several days distant*.

Brief as these time-markers are, they define each stage of the human egg's journey. Note how the writer, after declaring in the second sentence that the egg forms twelve cells, backtracks for a moment and retraces the process by which the egg has subdivided, comparing it (by a brief ANALOGY) to a piece of real estate. When using time-markers, vary them so that they won't seem mechanical. If you can, avoid the monotonous repetition of a fixed phrase (*In the fourteenth stage . . .* , *In the fifteenth stage . . .*). Even boring time-markers, though, are better than none at all. As in any chronological narrative, words and phrases such as *in the beginning, first, second, next, then, after that, three seconds later, at the same time*, and *finally* can help a process to move smoothly in the telling and lodge firmly in the reader's mind.

8. *Be specific.* When you write a first draft, state your analysis in generous detail, even at the risk of being wordy. When you revise, it will be easier to delete than to amplify.

9. *Revise.* When your essay is finished, reread it carefully against the checklist on the next page. You might also enlist a friend's help. If your process analysis is a directive ("How to Eat an Ice-Cream Cone Without Dribbling"), see if the friend can follow your instructions without difficulty. If your process analysis is informative ("How a New Word Enters the Dictionary"), ask the friend whether the process unfolds as clearly in his or her mind as it does in yours.

CHECKLIST FOR REVISING A PROCESS ANALYSIS

✔ **THESIS.** Does your process analysis have a point? Have you made sure readers know what it is?

✔ **ORGANIZATION.** Have you arranged the steps of your process in a clear chronological order? If steps occur simultaneously, have you grouped them so that readers perceive some order?

✔ **COMPLETENESS.** Have you included all the necessary steps and explained each one fully? Is it clear how each one contributes to the result?

✔ **DEFINITIONS.** Have you explained the meanings of any terms your readers may not know?

✔ **TRANSITIONS.** Do time-markers distinguish the steps and clarify their sequence?

PROCESS ANALYSIS IN A PARAGRAPH: TWO ILLUSTRATIONS

Using Process Analysis to Write About Television

The following paragraph, written especially for *The Bedford Reader*, explains the process of setting the timer on a particular VCR. Though composed to be freestanding, the paragraph (ideally with an accompanying illustration) could easily be dropped into a complete set of instructions on how to operate the VCR.

The timer on your videocassette recorder permits you to record up to eight programs over a two-week period even when you are not at home. For each program you wish to record in your absence, locate an empty program number by pushing the *P* button until a flashing number appears on the TV screen. The next four steps set the information for the program. First, push the *Day* button until the day and date show on the screen. The screen will flash *On*. Next set the starting time (be sure the time is set correctly for AM or PM). Then push the *Off* button and set the ending time (again, watching AM or PM). When the times have been set, push the *Chan* button and set the channel using the unit's channel selector. You may review the program information by pushing the *Check* button. When you are satisfied that the settings are correct, push *Timer* to set the timer to operate. (The unit cannot be operated manually while the timer is on.)

Process to be explained with directive analysis

Step 1

Preview of steps 2–5
Step 2

Step 3
Step 4
Step 5
Step 6

Step 7

Transitions (underlined) clarify steps

Using Process Analysis in an Academic Discipline

This paragraph on our descent into sleep comes from a psychology text-book's section on "the most perplexing of our biological rhythms." Before this paragraph the authors review the history of sleep research; after it they continue to analyze the night-long process that follows this initial descent.

When you first climb into bed, close your eyes, and relax, your brain emits bursts of *alpha waves* in a regular, high-amplitude, low-frequency rhythm of 8–12 cycles per second. Alpha is associated with relaxing or not concentrating on anything in particular. Gradually these waves slow down even further and you drift into the Land of Nod, passing through four stages, each deeper than the previous one.

Steps preceding process

Process to be explained with informative analysis

1. *Stage 1.* Your brain waves become small and irregular, indicating activity with low voltage and mixed frequencies. You feel yourself drifting on the edge of consciousness, in a state of light sleep. If awakened, you may recall fantasies or a few visual images.

   Step 1

2. *Stage 2.* Your brain emits occasional short bursts of rapid, high-peaking waves called *sleep spindles*. Light sounds or minor noises probably won't disturb you.

   Step 2

3. *Stage 3.* In addition to the waves characteristic of stage 2, your brain occasionally emits very slow waves of about 1–3 cycles per second, with very high peaks. These *delta waves* are a sure sign that you will be hard to arouse. Your breathing and pulse have slowed down, your temperature has dropped, and your muscles are relaxed.

   Step 3

4. *Stage 4.* Delta waves have now largely taken over, and you are in deep sleep. It will take vigorous shaking or a loud noise to awaken you, and you won't be very happy about it. Oddly enough, though, if you talk or walk in your sleep, this is when you are likely to do so.

   Step 4

   —Carole Wade and Carol Tavris, *Psychology*

CASE STUDY
Using Process Analysis

As a sophomore at Mary Washington College in Virginia, Jennifer Meska was a resident assistant in a freshman dormitory, responsible for students' welfare and, when necessary, for establishing dormitory rules.

In the following memo to the dorm's residents, Meska explained what students must do in the three-times-yearly fire drills. Meska's aim in drafting the memo was to outline the drill procedure so that students could remember and follow it — in other words (though she didn't think of the task this way), to write a clear directive process analysis.

In her first draft, Meska ran the steps of the process together in a paragraph, and for some steps she omitted explanations that might motivate residents to follow them. The bulleted list in her revision and the added explanations make the steps more distinct and memorable.

TO: Residents of Russell Hall

FROM: Jennifer Meska

DATE: September 6, 2001

SUBJECT: Fire-drill procedure

To prepare for the possibility of a fire in our residence hall, we will run three unannounced fire drills throughout the year. These drills will familiarize you with the potentially lifesaving procedures to be used during a real fire.

A loud buzzing noise and flashing lights will signal the start of a fire drill. Each resident has three minutes to complete the following tasks and exit the building:

- Close all bedroom and bathroom windows to prevent additional oxygen from feeding the fire.

- Turn off all electrical appliances, including computers, televisions, fans, radios, and lights. Turning off appliances will prevent electrical surges from starting additional fires.

- Grab a towel to cover your mouth in case you come across any smoke-filled passages, and wear shoes to protect your feet from any dangerous debris.

- Don't take anything else with you. In a real fire, delay could cost you your life.

- Close your door behind you to retard the spread of the fire.

- Go immediately to the nearest exit.

The fire drills are mandated by the state, and all residence halls must pass them in the required three minutes. If you have any questions, please let me know.

LINNEA SAUKKO

LINNEA SAUKKO was born in Warren, Ohio, in 1956. After receiving a degree in environmental quality control from Muskingum Area Technical College, she spent three years as an environmental technician, developing hazardous waste programs and acting as adviser on chemical safety at a large corporation. Concerned about the lack of safe methods for disposing of hazardous waste, Saukko went back to school to earn a BA in geology (Ohio State University, 1985) so that she could help address this issue. She currently lives in Hilliard, Ohio, and works as a groundwater manager at the Ohio Environmental Protection Agency, evaluating various sites for possible contamination of the groundwater. She is also researching the long-range effects of declining populations of insect-eating birds due to pollution of their habitats.

How to Poison the Earth

"How to Poison the Earth" was written in response to an assignment given in a freshman composition class and was awarded a Bedford Prize in Student Writing. It was subsequently published in *Student Writers at Work: The Bedford Prizes* (1984). Saukko's essay is largely a directive process analysis, but it is also a SATIRE: By outwardly showing us one way to guarantee the fate of the earth, the author implicitly urges us not to do it.

Poisoning the earth can be difficult because the earth is always trying to cleanse and renew itself. Keeping this in mind, we should generate as much waste as possible from substances such as uranium-238, which has a half-life (the time it takes for half of the substance to decay) of one million years, or plutonium, which has a half-life of only 0.5 million years but is so toxic that if distributed evenly, ten pounds of it could kill every person on the earth. Because the United States generates about eighteen tons of plutonium per year, it is about the best substance for long-term poisoning of the earth. It would help if we would build more nuclear power plants because each one generates only 500 pounds of plutonium each year. Of course, we must include persistent toxic chemicals such as polychlorinated biphenyl (PCB) and dichlorodiphenyl trichloroethane (DDT) to make sure we have enough toxins to poison the earth from the core to the outer atmosphere. First, we must develop many different ways of putting the waste from these nuclear and chemical substances in, on, and around the earth.

Putting these substances in the earth is a most important step in the poisoning process. With deep-well injection we can ensure that the earth is poisoned all the way to the core. Deep-well injection involves drilling a hole that is a few thousand feet deep and injecting toxic substances at extremely high pressures so they will penetrate deep into the earth. According to the Environmental Protection Agency (EPA), there are about 360 such deep injection wells in the United States. We cannot forget the groundwater aquifers that are closer to the surface. These must also be contaminated. This is easily done by shallow-well injection, which operates on the same principle as deep-well injection, only closer to the surface. The groundwater that has been injected with toxins will spread contamination beneath the earth. The EPA estimates that there are approximately 500,000 shallow injection wells in the United States.

Burying the toxins in the earth is the next best method. The toxins from   3
landfills, dumps, and lagoons slowly seep into the earth, guaranteeing that contamination will last a long time. Because the EPA estimates there are only about 50,000 of these dumps in the United States, they should be located in areas where they will leak to the surrounding ground and surface water.

Applying pesticides and other poisons on the earth is another part of the   4
poisoning process. This is good for coating the earth's surface so that the poisons will be absorbed by plants, will seep into the ground, and will run off into surface water.

Surface water is very important to contaminate because it will transport   5
the poisons to places that cannot be contaminated directly. Lakes are good for long-term storage of pollutants while they release some of their contamination to rivers. The only trouble with rivers is that they act as a natural cleansing system for the earth. No matter how much poison is dumped into them, they will try to transport it away to reach the ocean eventually.

The ocean is very hard to contaminate because it has such a large volume   6
and a natural buffering capacity that tends to neutralize some of the contamination. So in addition to the pollution from rivers, we must use the ocean as a dumping place for as many toxins as possible. The ocean currents will help transport the pollution to places that cannot otherwise be reached.

Now make sure that the air around the earth is very polluted. Combustion   7
and evaporation are major mechanisms for doing this. We must continuously pollute because the wind will disperse the toxins while rain washes them from the air. But this is good because a few lakes are stripped of all living animals each year from acid rain. Because the lower atmosphere can cleanse itself fairly easily, we must explode nuclear tests bombs that shoot radioactive particles high into the upper atmosphere where they will circle the earth for years. Gravity must pull some of the particles to earth, so we must continue exploding these bombs.

So it is that easy. Just be sure to generate as many poisonous substances as   8
possible and be sure they are distributed in, on, and around the entire earth at
a greater rate than it can cleanse itself. By following these easy steps we can
guarantee the poisoning of the earth.

Journal Writing

Saukko's essay is SATIRE—that is, an indirect attack on human follies or flaws, using
IRONY to urge behavior exactly opposite what is really desired. In your journal, explore
when you have proposed satirical solutions to problems that seem ridiculous or overwhelming—for example, suggesting breaking all the dishes so that they don't have to
be washed again or barring pedestrians from city streets so that they don't interfere
with cars. What kinds of situations might lead you to make suggestions like these? (To
take your journal writing further, see "From Journal to Essay" on the facing page.)

Questions on Meaning

1. Is the author's main PURPOSE to amuse and entertain, to inform readers of ways
   they can make better use of natural resources, to warn readers about threats to the
   future of our planet, or to make fun of scientists? Support your answer with EVI-
   DENCE from the essay.
2. Describe at least three of the earth's mechanisms for cleansing its land, water, and
   atmosphere, as presented in this essay.
3. According to Saukko, many of our actions are detrimental, if not outright destructive, to our environment. Identify these practices and discuss them. If these
   activities are harmful to the earth, why are they permitted? Do they serve some
   other important goal or purpose? If so, what? Are there other ways that these
   goals might be reached?

Questions on Writing Strategy

1. How detailed and specific are Saukko's instructions for poisoning the earth?
   Which steps in this process would you be able to carry out, once you finished
   reading the essay? In what instances might an author choose not to provide concrete, comprehensive instructions for a procedure? Relate your answer to the
   TONE and purpose of this essay.
2. How is Saukko's essay organized? Follow the process carefully to determine
   whether it happens chronologically, with each step depending on the one before
   it, or whether it follows another order. How effective is this method of organization and presentation?

3. For what AUDIENCE is this essay intended? How can you tell?
4. What is the tone of this essay? Consider especially the title and the last paragraph as well as examples from the body of the essay. How does the tone contribute to Saukko's satire?
5. **OTHER METHODS.** Saukko doesn't mention every possible pollutant but instead focuses on certain EXAMPLES. Why do you think she chooses these particular examples? What serious pollutants can you think of that Saukko doesn't mention specifically?

Questions on Language

1. How do the phrases "next best method" (par. 3), "another part of the poisoning process" (4), and "[l]akes are good for long-term storage of pollutants" (5) signal the tone of this essay? Should they be read literally, IRONICALLY, metaphorically, or some other way?
2. Be sure you know how to define the following words: generate, nuclear, toxins (par. 1); lagoons, contamination (3); buffering, neutralize (6); combustion (7).

Suggestions for Writing

1. **FROM JOURNAL TO ESSAY.** Choose one of the solutions you wrote about in your journal (facing page), or propose a solution to a problem that your journal entry has suggested. Write an essay detailing this satirical solution, paying careful attention to explaining each step of the process and to maintaining your satiric tone throughout.
2. Write an essay defending and justifying the use of nuclear power plants, pesticides, or another pollutant Saukko mentions. This essay will require some research because you will need to argue that the benefits of these methods outweigh their hazardous and destructive effects. Be sure to support your claims with factual information and statistics. Or approach the issue from the same point of view that Saukko did, and argue against the use of nuclear power plants or pesticides. Substantiate your argument with data and facts, and be sure to propose alternative sources of power or alternative methods of insect control.
3. **CRITICAL WRITING.** What does Saukko gain or lose by using satire and irony to make her point? What would be the comparative strengths and weaknesses of an essay that approached the same pollution problems straightforwardly and sincerely, perhaps urging or pleading with readers to stop polluting?
4. **CONNECTIONS.** Saukko is not the only writer of irony in this book: Among other authors, Suzanne Britt (p. 223), Dave Barry (p. 229), Jessica Mitford (p. 290), Horace Miner (p. 301), Judy Brady (p. 320), Emily Prager (p. 334), H. L. Mencken (p. 516), and Jonathan Swift (p. 653) also employ it. Based on Saukko's essay and essays by at least two of these others, define *irony*. If you need a boost, supplement the definition in this book's Useful Terms with one in a dictionary of literary or rhetorical terms. But go beyond others' definitions to construct one of your own, using quotations from the essays as your support.

Linnea Saukko on Writing

"After I have chosen a topic," says Linnea Saukko, "the easiest thing for me to do is to write about how I really feel about it. The goal of 'How to Poison the Earth' was to inform people, or more specifically, to open their eyes.

"As soon as I decided on my topic, I made a list of all the types of pollution and I sat down and basically wrote the paper in less than two hours. The information seemed to pour from me onto the page. Of course I did a lot of editing afterward, but I never changed the idea and the tone that I started with."

For Discussion

When have you had the experience of writing on a subject that compelled your words to pour forth with little effort? What was the subject? What did you learn from this experience?

LUCINDA ROSENFELD

LUCINDA ROSENFELD, a journalist and novelist, was born in New York City in 1969 and grew up in New Jersey. She graduated from Cornell University in 1991 and since then has written for various publications, including the *New York Times Magazine, Harper's Bazaar, Elle, Word*, and *Talk*. From 1996 to 1998 she was the nightlife columnist for the *New York Post*. In 2000 Rosenfeld published her first novel, *What She Saw in Roger Mancuso, Gunter Hopstock, Jason Barry Gold, Spitty Clark, Jack Geezo, Humphrey Fung,* [. . .]—the list of the title and the book itself cover all the significant male relationships of the heroine's life between fifth grade and age twenty-five. Rosenfeld currently lives in Brooklyn, New York.

How to Dump a Friend

In this 2001 essay from the *New York Times on the Web*, Rosenfeld writes with her typical blend of perceptiveness and humor to advise readers about a difficult social problem.

1   The phone begins to ring—and ring and ring. "It was so great to see you," says Friend A. And "I hope you're not mad, but I loved your boots so much I went out and bought the same ones!" And "What are you doing Friday?" And "Do you have any lunch plans on Monday?" And "What about Tuesday?" And "I haven't seen you since Wednesday!" And "I know it's only Thursday but . . ." And "I just don't feel like you care about my life. I mean, *it's always about you, Lucinda.*"

2   We're all familiar with the benefits of friendship—blame James Taylor[1]—but what about when pals turn parasitic, sucking the very life out of us with their metastasizing demands for more time, attention and sympathy? In high school, blowing off a friend was as easy as sitting at a different table in the cafeteria. Or making a face and a snippy comment at the sight of her sloppy Joe. ("Are you really going to eat that?")

3   In the more passive-aggressive arena of adult life, the weeding process is typically accomplished via unreturned phone calls and the chronic cancellation of social engagements forty-five minutes before they're due to take place.

4   This is because, at heart, adults are huge wimps. I count myself among their ranks.

5   But is there a better way to cut bait?

6   In the case of acquaintances, the silent treatment is perfectly appropriate.

---

[1] Taylor's "You've Got a Friend" was a number-one hit in the early 1970s.—EDS.

Where time and emotion have been invested, however, an honest explanation is the least you can offer. Well, maybe not precisely. Where your friend's greatest crime is having an annoying personality, it's best to keep your objections general, as in, "There are times when I have really needed you to be there for me, Sally/Bob, and you haven't come through." After which you might want to list one or two of those times. For instance, "It really hurt my feelings when you blew off my blessing ceremony to attend a breathing workshop."

If something more serious has occurred, however, you need to spell it out, as in: "I will never forgive you for calling my mother and telling her I was addicted to horse tranquilizers. My mother and I have a difficult enough time getting along as it is."

Or, as Ruth Ehrenkranz, a psychoanalyst in New York, suggests relaying to your friend, "There has been irreparable damage here, and I just don't feel I could ever be close to you again."

I guess Ehrenkranz wouldn't have approved of the way I "broke up" with my best friend and roommate in college — namely by writing a string of expletives in the memo line of a check I owed her for back rent. In my own defense, things had already gotten pretty hairy by then, with my roommate padlocking her bedroom door with the telephone we shared behind it, and then moving to her boyfriend's for the week.

It's also important to know whom you're dumping before you dump. If you're saying so long to a vindictive psycho, put the blame on yourself. For example, instead of "Here's the thing, Sally/Bob, I look at you and start to feel sick," you might want to offer a more conciliatory "I have my own boundary issues right now, Sally/Bob, and I just don't have time for anyone else's."

Also be especially delicate when you and your dumpee have friends in common. This is the time to resort to euphemism, cliché and therapy-speak — for example, "I just feel as if we're at different points in our lives," as opposed to "Your presence casts a pall on every room you enter." Otherwise, prepare to burn bridges where traffic once flowed freely, as well as gain a reputation for unrestrained venality.

Your farewell address is likely to have the most impact if delivered in person, preferably in a neutral setting like a coffee shop, where quiet calm is the rule of the day, and food, therefore, is unlikely to fly. (Consider meeting at one of your homes only if you want to slug it out on the living-room floor and conclude the afternoon with a lachrymose journey down memory lane.)

If that's not possible, there's always the telephone. And if the thought of any verbal confrontation leaves you (the breaker-upper) dreading the dump so ferociously that you begin to fantasize about contracting a fatal disease in the interim, you have my permission to write a letter. In any case, e-mail is a no-no, not merely because your message is likely to be forwarded to every name in your friend's address book. It's also just impersonal enough to suggest that you don't care and never did.

Finally, whether you have any interest in having your mind changed, it's   14
only fair to allow your pal a rebuttal, if simply for the sake of seeming reasonable and kind.

Of course, the easiest way to dump a friend is not to dump him/her at all,   15
but rather to find a way to live together. Besides, your reasons for wanting to jump ship may have more to do with your own paranoia and narcissism than with your friend's. As Martin Devine, a psychologist, says: "When you're ending a friendship, first explore why somebody doesn't fit into your life anymore. For instance, if you're working in fashion or entertainment, and your classmate from Kentucky keeps calling, and she's someone who doesn't have a lot of black clothing, then you would want to question why you're holding onto a certain lifestyle at the exclusion of someone with whom you once had a good relationship."

On the other hand, you can always turn off the ringer.   16

Journal Writing

How do you respond to Rosenfeld's advice? Do you think the same kind of advice would apply to breaking up with a boyfriend or girlfriend in a long-term romantic relationship? In your journal, explore why, or why not. (To take your journal writing further, see "From Journal to Essay" on the next page.)

Questions on Meaning

1. Rosenfeld's process has three distinct stages. What are they?
2. Why does Rosenfeld believe that one shouldn't break off with friends (except mere acquaintances) without an explanation? Why does she advise against breaking off a friendship through an e-mail message? What does her advice suggest about how she feels about friendships?
3. Why does Rosenfeld believe that ending a friendship can be "especially delicate when you and your dumpee have friends in common" (par. 11)?
4. Why do you think Rosenfeld concludes by suggesting that, rather than dump a friend, one might instead "find a way to live together" (par. 15)?

Questions on Writing Strategy

1. What would you say is Rosenfeld's PURPOSE in this essay? Is it primarily to entertain readers, or is she offering serious advice? What makes you think so?

2. What ASSUMPTIONS does Rosenfeld seem to make about her AUDIENCE?
3. What EFFECT does Rosenfeld achieve by opening her essay as she does? How does she echo her opening in her concluding paragraph?
4. **OTHER METHODS.** Where in the essay does Rosenfeld use CLASSIFICATION? Why does she do so?

Questions on Language

1. What TONE does Rosenfeld establish in this essay? How does the language she uses contribute to this tone?
2. What is the effect of Rosenfeld's referring to a hypothetical friend as "Sally/Bob" (for example, par. 6) and "him/her" (15)?
3. In paragraphs 6, 7, 10, and 11, Rosenfeld includes examples of breaking off friendships that are fairly outrageous—for example, telling a friend, "Your presence casts a pall on every room you enter." Why do you suppose she includes such examples?
4. Consult a dictionary if you are not sure of the meanings of these words: parasitic, metastasizing (par. 2); passive-aggressive, via, chronic (3); expletives (9); vindictive (10); euphemism, cliché, pall, venality (11); lachrymose (12); ferociously, interim (13); paranoia, narcissism (15).

Suggestions for Writing

1. **FROM JOURNAL TO ESSAY.** Starting from your journal entry (previous page), write an essay offering concrete advice about how to break off a long-term romantic relationship. Like Rosenfeld, you may approach this process analysis humorously.
2. Write a process analysis about another aspect of friendship—the steps involved in becoming a good friend, for example, or in making friends when one finds oneself in a new environment such as school or a job.
3. **CRITICAL WRITING.** Write an EVALUATION of the advice Rosenfeld offers in "How to Dump a Friend." How appropriate and useful do you find it? Do some of her suggestions make more sense to you than others? What other sorts of advice, in your view, might she have added?
4. **CONNECTIONS.** In "The Ways We Lie" (p. 389), Stephanie Ericsson also offers advice about conducting human relationships, including examples of acceptable and unacceptable behavior. COMPARE AND CONTRAST Ericsson's approach with that of Rosenfeld, focusing particularly on each writer's tone and her apparent assumptions about her audience.

NIALA MAHARAJ
AND
DONOVAN HOHN

Niala Maharaj is a freelance journalist born in Trinidad who publishes in periodicals in Europe, Asia, the Caribbean, and the United States. Maharaj has also worked as an editor in Hong Kong, a television producer in Trinidad, and a publications coordinator in Rome. With Gaston Dorren she has written *The Game of the Rose: The Third World in the Global Flower Trade*, a book exploring how Third World workers and their environments are exploited by the cut-flower industry. Maharaj currently lives in Amsterdam, Holland.

Donovan Hohn was born in 1972 in San Francisco. After receiving a BA in English from Oberlin College in 1994, he moved to Lille, France, where, as a Fulbright teaching assistant, he helped French high schoolers learn English. Hohn then earned an MA in creative writing from Boston University. He has written for *The Boston Book Review* and for *Harper's* magazine, where he worked as a senior editor until 2001. He recently taught high-school English in Manhattan, where he now lives.

Thorny Truths About Flowers

Almost every month *Harper's* magazine publishes an "Annotation" consisting of a central illustration and marginal text about the illustration's meaning and implications. "Thorny Truths About Flowers," on the next two pages, is adapted from the February 2001 *Harper's*. Providing a process analysis, the piece surrounds an offering from an online catalog with an explanation of what it takes to get cut flowers into florists' shops and grocery stores.

"Flowers," wrote Goethe,[1] "are the beautiful words and hieroglyphs of nature, with which she shows how much she loves us"—a flourish of metaphor that is, alas, increasingly inapt. To survive the trip from flower-producing countries in Latin America to warehouses in Miami, to retail florists, to somebody's sweetheart, the cut flowers in this recent FTD.com catalog, like most of the more than 4 trillion sold in the US last year, were genetically engineered to stay preternaturally fresh up to two weeks after harvest. Designer-seed firms made them sturdy enough to be shipped in bulk, light enough to defray air-cargo costs, and uniform enough to be sorted and graded. Then there are the aesthetic concerns. Nearly every detail—the curl of a lily's petal, the fluffiness of a carnation, the confectionary pink of a rose—was selected for maximum desirability according to the specifications of fashion experts and marketing consultants. These blooms are hieroglyphs, in other words, not of nature but of global commerce.

As shown, this bouquet features some of the cheapest flowers money can buy. Ecuadoran farms sold 300 million roses to US importers in 1999 at an average price of 22¢ a stem; Colombian carnations fetched 11¢; Costa Rican lilies, a dime. Competition among poor countries to sell flowers to rich ones has pushed supply up, prices down. For this bouquet, growers would get about $4, more than $3 of which would go to overhead—US-made pesticides, Dutch seeds, Israeli greenhouses, Third World labor. After shipping fees (around 3¢ per stem by air, Bogotá to Miami, depending on fuel prices) and the importer's markup, a florist in the US could buy these flowers wholesale for less than $10.

[1] Johann Wolfgang von Goethe (1749–1832), a renowned German writer. — EDS.

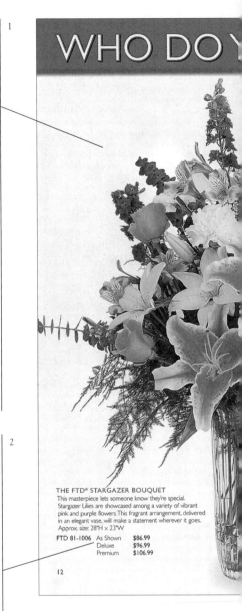

WHO DO Y

THE FTD® STARGAZER BOUQUET
This masterpiece lets someone know they're special. Stargazer Lilies are showcased among a variety of vibrant pink and purple flowers. This fragrant arrangement, delivered in an elegant vase, will make a statement wherever it goes.
Approx. size: 28"H x 23"W

FTD 81-1006 As Shown $86.99
            Deluxe $96.99
            Premium $106.99

OU LOVE?

Although a single bug discovered during USDA[2] inspections can get an entire plane-load of roses deported, flowers are subject to none of the pesticide controls that apply to edible crops. Third World producers thus grow them in sterilized soil in greenhouses fumigated as often as once a day with fungicides, insecticides, nemoticides, and herbicides. One fifth of these chemicals are carcinogens or toxins that have been restricted for health reasons in the US, and nearly two thirds of Colombia's 75,000 flower workers suffer from maladies — nausea, impaired vision, conjunctivitis, rashes, asthma, miscarriages, stillbirths, congenital malformations — associated with pesticide exposure. Workers spend up to eighteen hours a day, seven days a week, in poorly ventilated greenhouses producing the more than 100 million pesticide-laden roses that Americans buy every February.

Commercial floraculture consumes more water than many Third World flower-growing regions can sustain. On the Bogotá savanna, the water table has fallen so low that household taps run dry most of the week. What water remains is increasingly polluted: Many flower farms let pesticides leach into the groundwater or run off into the area's shriveling rivers. Flowers consume other resources too — electricity for greenhouses, gas for transport. To fill growing global demand, several 747s and DC-8s fly out of Bogotá every day, each one loaded with as many as 2,400,000 stems heated to keep them from freezing at high altitudes. Once on the ground, flowers are stored in refrigerated warehouses, then distributed by plane or refrigerated truck. The oil it took to produce and transport these flowers could fill this vase. The water it took could fill it many times over. Happy Valentine's Day!

[2] US Department of Agriculture. — EDS.

Journal Writing

Have Maharaj and Hohn made you think differently about the flowers carried by florists and other retailers? After reading this, will you be less likely to buy cut flowers or to enjoy receiving them as a gift? In your journal, explore why, or why not. (To take your journal writing further, see "From Journal to Essay" below.)

Questions on Meaning

1. What is the authors' implied THESIS?
2. Why are the authors critical of genetically engineered flowers (par. 1)?
3. What point are the authors making by connecting paragraph 2 with the price of the bouquet shown in the advertisement?

Questions on Writing Strategy

1. Why do you think the authors open with the quotation about flowers by the German poet Goethe?
2. What is the EFFECT of the sentence that concludes paragraph 4?
3. Why do the authors make the points that 4 trillion flowers are sold in the United States yearly (par. 1) and that more than 100 million roses are purchased each February (3)?
4. **OTHER METHODS.** The authors use process analysis to serve ARGUMENT AND PERSUASION. What elements of argument do you find in their text?

Questions on Language

1. The authors refer to "Third World" labor and producers. What do they mean by "Third World"?
2. What is the effect of this IMAGE in paragraph 4: "The oil it took to produce and transport these flowers could fill this vase"?
3. What is the play on words in the title?
4. Be sure you know the meaning of each of the following words, consulting a dictionary if necessary: hieroglyphs, inapt, preternaturally, defray, aesthetic, confectionary (par. 1); pesticides (2); fumigated, carcinogens, toxins, maladies, congenital, malformations (3); floraculture, savanna, leach, shriveling (4).

Suggestions for Writing

1. **FROM JOURNAL TO ESSAY.** As Maharaj and Hohn do in "Thorny Truths About Flowers," environmentalists and human rights activists often attempt to change people's behavior (driving gas-guzzling cars, eating fruit picked by exploited migrant laborers, buying clothing produced in foreign sweatshops) by showing

the negative consequences of such behavior on the environment or on workers. Based on your journal response about buying flowers (previous page) and on your responses to other environmental and human rights campaigns, how effective is such information in influencing your behavior? In an essay using EXAMPLES, explain why.

2. Find a magazine or television advertisement that you judge to be particularly manipulative—that is, using words and/or visual images in ways calculated to cause certain feelings and reactions, perhaps without the reader's or viewer's awareness. In an essay, describe the ad and ANALYZE how it goes about manipulating the attitudes of its target audience.

3. **CRITICAL WRITING.** In a brief essay, analyze each of the four charges Maharaj and Hohn bring against the global flower trade. What kinds of EVIDENCE do they use to support their claims? How do you EVALUATE the range and quality of evidence?

4. **CONNECTIONS.** COMPARE AND CONTRAST "Thorny Truths About Flowers" with Linnea Saukko's "How to Poison the Earth," which appears earlier in this chapter. Focus on the subject, PURPOSE, and writing strategy of each essay.

JESSICA MITFORD

Born in Batsford Mansion, England, in 1917, the daughter of Lord and Lady Redesdale, JESSICA MITFORD devoted much of her early life to defying her aristocratic upbringing. In her autobiography *Daughters and Rebels* (1960), she tells how she received a genteel schooling at home, then as a young woman moved to Loyalist Spain during the violent Spanish Civil War. Later, she emigrated to America, where for a time she worked in Miami as a bartender. She became one of her adopted country's most noted reporters: *Time* called her "Queen of the Muckrakers." Exposing with her typewriter what she regarded as corruption, abuse, and absurdity, Mitford wrote *The American Way of Death* (1963, revised as *The American Way of Death Revisited* in 1998), *Kind and Unusual Punishment: The Prison Business* (1973), and *The American Way of Birth* (1992). *Poison Penmanship* (1979) collects articles from *The Atlantic*, *Harper's*, and other magazines. *A Fine Old Conflict* (1976) is the second volume of Mitford's autobiography. And a novel, *Grace Had an English Heart* (1989), examines how the media transform ordinary people into celebrities. Jessica Mitford died in 1996.

Behind the Formaldehyde Curtain

The most famous (or infamous) thing Jessica Mitford wrote is *The American Way of Death*, a critique of the funeral industry. In this selection from the book, Mitford analyzes the twin processes of embalming and restoring a corpse, the practices she finds most objectionable. You may need a stable stomach to enjoy the selection, but in it you'll find a clear, painstaking process analysis, written with masterly style and outrageous wit. (For those who want to know, Mitford herself was cremated after her death.)

For a complementary view of cultural practices, read the essay following Mitford's, Horace Miner's "Body Ritual Among the Nacirema."

The drama begins to unfold with the arrival of the corpse at the mortuary. 1

Alas, poor Yorick! How surprised he would be to see how his counterpart 2 of today is whisked off to a funeral parlor and is in short order sprayed, sliced, pierced, pickled, trussed, trimmed, creamed, waxed, painted, rouged, and neatly dressed — transformed from a common corpse into a Beautiful Memory Picture. This process is known in the trade as embalming and restorative art, and is so universally employed in the United States and Canada that the funeral director does it routinely, without consulting corpse or kin. He regards as eccentric those few who are hardy enough to suggest that it might be dispensed with. Yet no law requires embalming, no religious doctrine commends it, nor is it dictated by considerations of health, sanitation, or even of personal daintiness. In no part of the world but in Northern America is it widely used. The purpose of embalming is to make the corpse presentable for viewing in a suitably costly container; and here too the funeral director routinely, without first consulting the family, prepares the body for public display.

Is all this legal? The processes to which a dead body may be subjected are   3
after all to some extent circumscribed by law. In most states, for instance, the signature of next of kin must be obtained before an autopsy may be performed, before the deceased may be cremated, before the body may be turned over to a medical school for research purposes; or such provision must be made in the decedent's will. In the case of embalming, no such permission is required nor is it ever sought.[1] A textbook, *The Principles and Practices of Embalming,* comments on this: "There is some question regarding the legality of much that is done within the preparation room." The author points out that it would be most unusual for a responsible member of a bereaved family to instruct the mortician, in so many words, to "embalm" the body of a deceased relative. The very term *embalming* is so seldom used that the mortician must rely upon custom in the matter. The author concludes that unless the family specifies otherwise, the act of entrusting the body to the care of a funeral establishment carries with it an implied permission to go ahead and embalm.

Embalming is indeed a most extraordinary procedure, and one must won-   4
der at the docility of Americans who each year pay hundreds of millions of dollars for its perpetuation, blissfully ignorant of what it is all about, what is done, how it is done. Not one in ten thousand has any idea of what actually takes place. Books on the subject are extremely hard to come by. They are not to be found in most libraries or bookshops.

In an era when huge television audiences watch surgical operations in the   5
comfort of their living rooms, when, thanks to the animated cartoon, the geography of the digestive system has become familiar territory even to the nursery school set, in a land where the satisfaction of curiosity about almost all matters is a national pastime, the secrecy surrounding embalming can, surely, hardly be attributed to the inherent gruesomeness of the subject. Custom in this regard has within this century suffered a complete reversal. In the early days of American embalming, when it was performed in the home of the deceased, it was almost mandatory for some relative to stay by the embalmer's

---

[1] Partly because of Mitford's attack, the Federal Trade Commission now requires the funeral industry to provide families with itemized price lists, including the price of embalming, to state that embalming is not required, and to obtain the family's consent to embalming before charging for it. Shortly before her death, however, Mitford observed that the FTC had "watered down" the regulations and "routinely ignored" consumer complaints about the funeral industry. —EDS.

side and witness the procedure. Today, family members who might wish to be in attendance would certainly be dissuaded by the funeral director. All others, except apprentices, are excluded by law from the preparation room.

A close look at what does actually take place may explain in large measure   6
the undertaker's intractable reticence concerning a procedure that has become his major *raison d'être*. Is it possible he fears that public information about embalming might lead patrons to wonder if they really want this ser-vice? If the funeral men are loath to discuss the subject outside the trade, the reader may, understandably, be equally loath to go on reading at this point. For those who have the stomach for it, let us part the formaldehyde curtain. [. . .]

The body is first laid out in the undertaker's morgue — or rather, Mr. Jones   7
is reposing in the preparation room — to be readied to bid the world farewell.

The preparation room in any of the better funeral establishments has the   8
tiled and sterile look of a surgery, and indeed the embalmer–restorative artist who does his chores there is beginning to adopt the term *dermasurgeon* (appro-priately corrupted by some mortician-writers as "demi-surgeon") to describe his calling. His equipment, consisting of scalpels, scissors, augers, forceps, clamps, needles, pumps, tubes, bowls, and basins, is crudely imitative of the surgeon's, as is his technique, acquired in a nine- or twelve-month post-high-school course in an embalming school. He is supplied by an advanced chemi-cal industry with a bewildering array of fluids, sprays, pastes, oils, powders, creams, to fix or soften tissue, shrink or distend it as needed, dry it here, restore the moisture there. There are cosmetics, waxes, and paints to fill and cover features, even plaster of Paris to replace entire limbs. There are ingenious aids to prop and stabilize the cadaver: a Vari-Pose Head Rest, the Edwards Arm and Hand Positioner, the Repose Block (to support the shoulders during the embalming), and the Throop Foot Positioner, which resembles an old-fashioned stocks.

Mr. John H. Eckels, president of the Eckels College of Mortuary Science,   9
thus describes the first part of the embalming procedure: "In the hands of a skilled practitioner, this work may be done in a comparatively short time and without mutilating the body other than by slight incision — so slight that it scarcely would cause serious inconvenience if made upon a living person. It is necessary to remove the blood, and doing this not only helps in the disinfect-ing, but removes the principal cause of disfigurements due to discoloration."

Another textbook discusses the all-important time element: "The earlier   10
this is done, the better, for every hour that elapses between death and em-balming will add to the problems and complications encountered [. . .]." Just how soon should one get going on the embalming? The author tells us, "On the basis of such scanty information made available to this profession through its rudimentary and haphazard system of technical research, we must conclude

that the best results are to be obtained if the subject is embalmed before life is completely extinct—that is, before cellular death has occurred. In the average case, this would mean within an hour after somatic death." For those who feel that there is something a little rudimentary, not to say haphazard, about this advice, a comforting thought is offered by another writer. Speaking of fears entertained in early days of premature burial, he points out, "One of the effects of embalming by chemical injection, however, has been to dispel fears of live burial." How true; once the blood is removed, chances of live burial are indeed remote.

To return to Mr. Jones, the blood is drained out through the veins and replaced by embalming fluid pumped in through the arteries. As noted in *The Principles and Practices of Embalming*, "every operator has a favorite injection and drainage point—a fact which becomes a handicap only if he fails or refuses to forsake his favorites when conditions demand it." Typical favorites are the carotid artery, femoral artery, jugular vein, subclavian vein. There are various choices of embalming fluid. If Flextone is used, it will produce a "mild, flexible rigidity. The skin retains a velvety softness, the tissues are rubbery and pliable. Ideal for women and children." It may be blended with B. and G. Products Company's Lyf-Lyk tint, which is guaranteed to reproduce "nature's own skin texture [. . .] the velvety appearance of living tissue." Suntone comes in three separate tints: Suntan; Special Cosmetic Tint, a pink shade "especially indicated for female subjects"; and Regular Cosmetic Tint, moderately pink.

About three to six gallons of a dyed and perfumed solution of formaldehyde, glycerin, borax, phenol, alcohol, and water is soon circulating through Mr. Jones, whose mouth has been sewn together with a "needle directed upward between the upper lip and gum and brought out through the left nostril," with the corners raised slightly "for a more pleasant expression." If he should be bucktoothed, his teeth are cleaned with Bon Ami and coated with colorless nail polish. His eyes, meanwhile, are closed with flesh-tinted eye caps and eye cement.

The next step is to have at Mr. Jones with a thing called a trocar. This is a long, hollow needle attached to a tube. It is jabbed into the abdomen, poked around the entrails and chest cavity, the contents of which are pumped out and replaced with "cavity fluid." This done, and the hole in the abdomen sewn up, Mr. Jones's face is heavily creamed (to protect the skin from burns which may be caused by leakage of the chemicals), and he is covered with a sheet and left unmolested for a while. But not for long—there is more, much more, in store for him. He has been embalmed, but not yet restored, and the best time to start the restorative work is eight to ten hours after embalming, when the tissues have become firm and dry.

The object of all this attention to the corpse, it must be remembered, is to   14
make it presentable for viewing in an attitude of healthy repose. "Our customs
require the presentation of our dead in the semblance of normality [. . .]
unmarred by the ravages of illness, disease, or mutilation," says Mr. J. Sheridan
Mayer in his *Restorative Art.* This is rather a large order since few people die
in the full bloom of health, unravaged by illness and unmarked by some dis-
figurement. The funeral industry is equal to the challenge: "In some cases the
gruesome appearance of a mutilated or disease-ridden subject may be quite
discouraging. The task of restoration may seem impossible and shake the confidence of the embalmer. This is the time for intestinal fortitude and determination. Once the formative work is begun and affected tissues are cleaned or
removed, all doubts of success vanish. It is surprising and gratifying to discover
the results which may be obtained."

The embalmer, having allowed an appropriate interval to elapse, returns   15
to the attack, but now he brings into play the skill and equipment of sculptor
and cosmetician. Is a hand missing? Casting one in plaster of Paris is a simple
matter. "For replacement purposes, only a cast of the back of the hand is necessary; this is within the ability of the average operator and is quite adequate."
If a lip or two, a nose, or an ear should be missing, the embalmer has at hand
a variety of restorative waxes with which to model replacements. Pores and
skin texture are simulated by stippling with a little brush, and over this cosmetics are laid on. Head off? Decapitation cases are rather routinely handled.
Ragged edges are trimmed, and head joined to torso with a series of splints,
wires, and sutures. It is a good idea to have a little something at the neck — a
scarf or a high collar — when time for viewing comes. Swollen mouth? Cut
out tissue as needed from inside the lips. If too much is removed, the surface
contour can easily be restored by padding with cotton. Swollen necks and
cheeks are reduced by removing tissue through vertical incisions made down
each side of the neck. "When the deceased is casketed, the pillow will hide
the suture incisions [. . .] as an extra precaution against leakage, the suture
may be painted with liquid sealer."

The opposite condition is more likely to present itself — that of emacia-   16
tion. His hypodermic syringe now loaded with massage cream, the embalmer
seeks out and fills the hollowed and sunken areas by injection. In this procedure the backs of the hands and fingers and the under-chin area should not be
neglected.

Positioning the lips is a problem that recurrently challenges the ingenuity   17
of the embalmer. Closed too tightly, they tend to give a stern, even disap-
proving expression. Ideally, embalmers feel, the lips should give the impression of being ever so slightly parted, the upper lip protruding slightly for a
more youthful appearance. This takes some engineering, however, as the lips

tend to drift apart. Lip drift can sometimes be remedied by pushing one or two straight pins through the inner margin of the lower lip and then inserting them between the two front upper teeth. If Mr. Jones happens to have no teeth, the pins can just as easily be anchored in his Armstrong Face Former and Denture Replacer. Another method to maintain lip closure is to dislocate the lower jaw, which is then held in its new position by a wire run through holes which have been drilled through the upper and lower jaws at the midline. As the French are fond of saying, *il faut souffrir pour être belle.*[2]

If Mr. Jones has died of jaundice, the embalming fluid will very likely turn him green. Does this deter the embalmer? Not if he has intestinal fortitude. Masking pastes and cosmetics are heavily laid on, burial garments and casket interiors are color-correlated with particular care, and Jones is displayed beneath rose-colored lights. Friends will say "How *well* he looks." Death by carbon monoxide, on the other hand, can be rather a good thing from the embalmer's viewpoint: "One advantage is the fact that this type of discoloration is an exaggerated form of a natural pink coloration." This is nice because the healthy glow is already present and needs but little attention. 18

The patching and filling completed, Mr. Jones is now shaved, washed, and dressed. Cream-based cosmetic, available in pink, flesh, suntan, brunette, and blond, is applied to his hands and face, his hair is shampooed and combed (and, in the case of Mrs. Jones, set), his hands manicured. For the horny-handed son of toil special care must be taken; cream should be applied to remove ingrained grime, and the nails cleaned. "If he were not in the habit of having them manicured in life, trimming and shaping is advised for better appearance — never questioned by kin." 19

Jones is now ready for casketing (this is the present participle of the verb "to casket"). In this operation his right shoulder should be depressed slightly "to turn the body a bit to the right and soften the appearance of lying flat on the back." Positioning the hands is a matter of importance, and special rubber positioning blocks may be used. The hands should be cupped slightly for a more lifelike, relaxed appearance. Proper placement of the body requires a delicate sense of balance. It should lie as high as possible in the casket, yet not so high that the lid, when lowered, will hit the nose. On the other hand, we are cautioned, placing the body too low "creates the impression that the body is in a box." 20

Jones is next wheeled into the appointed slumber room where a few last touches may be added — his favorite pipe placed in his hand or, if he was a great reader, a book propped into position. (In the case of little Master Jones 21

---

[2] You have to suffer to be beautiful. — EDS.

a Teddy bear may be clutched.) Here he will hold open house for a few days, visiting hours 10 AM to 9 PM.

All now being in readiness, the funeral director calls a staff conference to   22
make sure that each assistant knows his precise duties. Mr. Wilber Kriege writes: "This makes your staff feel that they are a part of the team, with a definite assignment that must be properly carried out if the whole plan is to succeed. You never heard of a football coach who failed to talk to his entire team before they go on the field. They have drilled on the plays they are to execute for hours and days, and yet the successful coach knows the importance of making even the benchwarming third-string substitute feel that he is important if the game is to be won." The winning of *this* game is predicated upon glass-smooth handling of the logistics. The funeral director has notified the pall-bearers whose names were furnished by the family, has arranged for the presence of clergyman, organist, and soloist, has provided transportation for everybody, has organized and listed the flowers sent by friends. In *Psychology of Funeral Service* Mr. Edward A. Martin points out, "He may not always do as much as the family thinks he is doing, but it is his helpful guidance that they appreciate in knowing they are proceeding as they should [. . .]. The important thing is how well his services can be used to make the family believe they are giving unlimited expression to their own sentiment."

The religious service may be held in a church or in the chapel of the   23
funeral home; the funeral director vastly prefers the latter arrangement, for not only is it more convenient for him but it affords him the opportunity to show off his beautiful facilities to the gathered mourners. After the clergyman has had his say, the mourners queue up to file past the casket for a last look at the deceased. The family is *never* asked whether they want an open-casket ceremony; in the absence of their instruction to the contrary, this is taken for granted. Consequently well over 90 per cent of all American funerals feature the open casket—a custom unknown in other parts of the world. Foreigners are astonished by it. An English woman living in San Francisco described her reaction in a letter to the writer:

> I myself have attended only one funeral here—that of an elderly fellow worker of mine. After the service I could not understand why everyone was walking towards the coffin (sorry, I mean casket), but thought I had better follow the crowd. It shook me rigid to get there and find the casket open and poor old Oscar lying there in his brown tweed suit, wearing a suntan makeup and just the wrong shade of lipstick. If I had not been extremely fond of the old boy, I have a horrible feeling that I might have giggled. Then and there I decided that I could never face another American funeral—even dead.

The casket (which has been resting throughout the service on a Clas-   24
sic Beauty Ultra Metal Casket Bier) is now transferred by a hydraulically

operated device called Porto-Lift to a balloon-tired, Glide Easy casket carriage which will wheel it to yet another conveyance, the Cadillac Funeral Coach. This may be lavender, cream, light green—anything but black. Interiors, of course, are color-correlated, "for the man who cannot stop short of perfection."

At graveside, the casket is lowered into the earth. This office, once the   25
prerogative of friends of the deceased, is now performed by a patented mechanical lowering device. A "Lifetime Green" artificial grass mat is at the ready to conceal the sere earth, and overhead, to conceal the sky, is a portable Steril Chapel Tent ("resists the intense heat and humidity of summer and the terrific storms of winter . . . available in Silver Gray, Rose, or Evergreen"). Now is the time for the ritual scattering of earth over the coffin, as the solemn words "earth to earth, ashes to ashes, dust to dust" are pronounced by the officiating cleric. This can today be accomplished "with a mere flick of the wrist with the Gordon Leak-Proof Earth Dispenser. No grasping of a handful of dirt, no soiled fingers. Simple, dignified, beautiful, reverent! The modern way!" The Gordon Earth Dispenser (at $5) is of nickel-plated brass construction. It is not only "attractive to the eye and long wearing"; it is also "one of the 'tools' for building better public relations" if presented as "an appropriate noncommercial gift" to the clergyman. It is shaped something like a saltshaker.

Untouched by human hand, the coffin and the earth are now united.   26

It is in the function of directing the participants through this maze of gad-   27
getry that the funeral director has assigned to himself his relatively new role of "grief therapist." He has relieved the family of every detail, he has revamped the corpse to look like a living doll, he has arranged for it to nap for a few days in a slumber room, he has put on a well-oiled performance in which the concept of *death* has played no part whatsoever—unless it was inconsiderately mentioned by the clergyman who conducted the religious service. He has done everything in his power to make the funeral a real pleasure for everybody concerned. He and his team have given their all to score an upset victory over death.

Journal Writing

Presumably, morticians embalm and restore corpses, and survivors support the work, because the practices are thought to ease the shock of death. Now that you know what goes on behind the scenes, how do you feel about a loved one's undergoing these procedures? (To take your journal writing further, see "From Journal to Essay" on p. 299.)

Questions on Meaning

1. What was your emotional response to this essay? Can you analyze your feelings?
2. To what does the author attribute the secrecy that surrounds the process of embalming?
3. What, according to Mitford, is the mortician's intent? What common obstacles to fulfilling it must be surmounted?
4. What do you understand from Mitford's remark in paragraph 10, on dispelling fears of live burial: "How true; once the blood is removed, chances of live burial are indeed remote"?
5. Do you find any implied PURPOSE in this essay? Does Mitford seem primarily out to rake muck, or does she offer any positive suggestions to Americans?

Questions on Writing Strategy

1. What is Mitford's TONE? In her opening two paragraphs, exactly what shows her attitude toward her subject?
2. Why do you think Mitford goes into so much grisly detail in analyzing the processes of embalming and restoration? How does the detail serve her purpose?
3. What is the EFFECT of calling the body Mr. Jones (or Master Jones)?
4. Paragraph by paragraph, what TRANSITIONS does the author employ? (If you need a refresher on this point, see the discussion of transitions on pp. 270–71.)
5. Into what stages has the author divided the embalming process?
6. To whom does Mitford address her process analysis? How do you know she isn't writing for an AUDIENCE of professional morticians?
7. Consider one of the quotations from the journals and textbooks of professionals and explain how it serves the author's general purpose.
8. **OTHER METHODS.** In paragraph 8, Mitford uses CLASSIFICATION in listing the embalmer's equipment and supplies. What groups does she identify, and why does she bother sorting the items at all?

Questions on Language

1. Explain the ALLUSION to Yorick in paragraph 2.
2. What IRONY do you find in this statement in paragraph 7: "The body is first laid out in the undertaker's morgue — or rather, Mr. Jones is reposing in the prepara-tion room"? Pick out any other words or phrases in the essay that seem ironic. Comment especially on those you find in the essay's last two sentences.
3. Why is it useful to Mitford's purpose that she cites the brand names of morticians' equipment and supplies (the Edwards Arm and Hand Positioner, Lyf-Lyk tint)? List all the brand names in the essay that are memorable.
4. Define the following words or terms: counterpart (par. 2); circumscribed, autopsy, cremated, decedent, bereaved (3); docility, perpetuation (4); inherent, manda-tory (5); intractable, reticence, *raison d'être*, formaldehyde (6); "dermasurgeon," augers, forceps, distend, stocks (8); somatic (10); carotid artery, femoral artery, jugular vein, subclavian vein, pliable (11); glycerin, borax, phenol, bucktoothed (12); trocar, entrails (13); stippling, sutures (15); emaciation (16); jaundice (18); predicated (22); queue (23); hydraulically (24); cleric, sere (25); therapist (27).

Suggestions for Writing

1. **FROM JOURNAL TO ESSAY.** Drawing on your personal response to Mitford's essay in your journal (p. 297), write a brief essay that ARGUES either for or against embalming and restoration. Consider the purposes served by these practices, both for the mortician and for the dead person's relatives and friends, as well as their costs and effects.

2. Search the Web or consult the *Readers' Guide to Periodical Literature* for information about the phenomenon of quick-freezing the dead. Set forth this process, including its hoped-for result of being able to revive the corpses in the far future.

3. ANALYZE some other process whose operations may not be familiar to everyone. (Have you ever held a job, or helped out in a family business, that has taken you behind the scenes? How is fast food prepared? How are cars serviced? How is a baby sat? How is a house constructed?) Detail it step by step, including transitions to clarify the steps.

4. **CRITICAL WRITING.** In attacking the funeral industry, Mitford also, implicitly, attacks the people who pay for and comply with the industry's attitudes and practices. What ASSUMPTIONS does Mitford seem to make about how we ought to deal with death and the dead? (Consider, for instance, her statements about the "docility of Americans, [. . .] blissfully ignorant" [par. 4] and the funeral director's making "the funeral a real pleasure for everybody concerned" [27].) Write an essay in which you interpret Mitford's assumptions and agree or disagree with them, based on your own reading and experience. If you like, defend the ritual of the funeral, or the mortician's profession, against Mitford's attack.

5. **CONNECTIONS.** Both Jessica Mitford and the author of the following essay, Horace Miner, use process analysis to reveal something about human behavior. How are the two authors' intentions the same or different? What does each want to accomplish with her or his analysis? Use EXAMPLES from both essays to support your claims.

Jessica Mitford on Writing

"Choice of subject is of cardinal importance," declared Jessica Mitford in *Poison Penmanship*. "One does by far one's best work when besotted by and absorbed in the matter at hand." After *The American Way of Death* was published, Mitford received hundreds of letters suggesting alleged rackets that ought to be exposed, and to her surprise, an overwhelming majority of these letters complained about defective and overpriced hearing aids. But Mitford never wrote a book blasting the hearing aid industry. "Somehow, although there may well be need for such an exposé, I could not warm up to hearing aids as a subject for the kind of thorough, intensive, long-range research that would be needed to do an effective job." She once taught a course at Yale on muckraking, with each student choosing a subject to investigate. "Those who

tackled hot issues on campus, such as violations of academic freedom or failure to implement affirmative-action hiring policies, turned in some excellent
work; but the lad who decided to investigate 'waste in the Yale dining halls'
was predictably unable to make much of this trivial topic." (The editors inter-
ject: We aren't sure that the topic is necessarily trivial, but obviously not
everyone would burn to write about it!)

The hardest problem Mitford faced in writing *The American Way of Death*,
she recalled, was doing her factual, step-by-step account of the embalming
process. She felt "determined to describe it in all its revolting details, but how
to make this subject palatable to the reader?" Her solution was to cast the
whole process analysis in the official JARGON of the mortuary industry, drawing on lists of taboo words and their EUPHEMISMS (or acceptable synonyms), as
published in the trade journal *Casket & Sunnyside:* "Mr., Mrs., Miss Blank, not
corpse or body; preparation room, not morgue; reposing room, not laying-out
room [. . .]." The story of Mr. Jones thus took shape, and Mitford's use of jargon, she found, added macabre humor to the proceedings.

For Discussion

1. What seem to be Mitford's criteria for an effective essay or book?
2. What is muckraking? Why do you suppose anyone would want to do it?

HORACE MINER

An anthropologist and teacher, HORACE MINER specialized in the cultures of Africa. He was born in 1912 in Saint Paul, Minnesota, and received degrees from the University of Kentucky (BA, 1933) and the University of Chicago (MA, 1935; PhD, 1937). Miner taught anthropology and sociology at Wayne State University and for many years at the University of Michigan, where he was also a researcher in the Museum of Anthropology. He retired from Michigan in 1980. Based on his field research, Miner wrote numerous journal articles and books, including *St. Denis: A French-Canadian Parish* (1939), *Culture and Agriculture* (1953), *Oasis and Casbah: Algerian Culture and Personality in Change* (1960), and *The City in Modern Africa* (1967). Miner died in 1993.

Body Ritual Among the Nacirema

As an anthropologist, Miner was adept at *ethnography*, studying and reporting on specific cultures. Miner's specialty was African cultures, but here he turned his ethnographer's eye on a North American culture that may seem familiar to you. Like Jessica Mitford in the previous selection, Miner uses process analysis to reveal and also to poke fun at customs. His essay first appeared in the journal *American Anthropologist* in June 1956 and has often been reprinted.

The anthropologist has become so familiar with the diversity of ways in   1
which different peoples behave in similar situations that he is not apt to be surprised by even the most exotic customs. In fact, if all of the logically possible combinations of behavior have not been found somewhere in the world, he is apt to suspect that they must be present in some yet undescribed tribe. This point has, in fact, been expressed with respect to clan organization by Murdock.[1] In this light, the magical beliefs and practices of the Nacirema present such unusual aspects that it seems desirable to describe them as an example of the extremes to which human behavior can go.

Professor Linton first brought the ritual of the Nacirema to the attention   2
of anthropologists twenty years ago, but the culture of this people is still very poorly understood. They are a North American group living in the territory between the Canadian Cree, the Yaqui and Tarahumare of Mexico, and the Carib and Arawak of the Antilles. Little is known of their origin, although tradition states that they came from the east. [. . .]

---

[1] George Peter Murdock (1897–1985) was an American anthropologist who attempted to identify and classify the cultures of the world. —EDS.

Nacirema culture is characterized by a highly developed market econ-   3
omy which has evolved in a rich natural habitat. While much of the people's
time is devoted to economic pursuits, a large part of the fruits of these labors
and a considerable portion of the day are spent in ritual activity. The focus
of this activity is the human body, the appearance and health of which
loom as a dominant concern in the ethos of the people. While such a concern
is certainly not unusual, its ceremonial aspects and associated philosophy are
unique.

The fundamental belief underlying the whole system appears to be that   4
the human body is ugly and that its natural tendency is to debility and disease.
Incarcerated in such a body, man's only hope is to avert these characteristics
through the use of the powerful influences of ritual and ceremony. Every
household has one or more shrines devoted to this purpose. The more powerful individuals in the society have several shrines in their houses and, in fact,
the opulence of a house is often referred to in terms of the number of such ritual centers it possesses. Most houses are of wattle and daub construction, but
the shrine rooms of the more wealthy are walled with stone. Poorer families
imitate the rich by applying pottery plaques to their shrine walls.

While each family has at least one such shrine, the rituals associated with   5
it are not family ceremonies but are private and secret. The rites are normally
only discussed with children, and then only during the period when they are
being initiated into these mysteries. I was able, however, to establish sufficient
rapport with the natives to examine these shrines and to have the rituals
described to me.

The focal point of the shrine is a box or chest which is built into the wall.   6
In this chest are kept the many charms and magical potions without which no
native believes he could live. These preparations are secured from a variety of
specialized practitioners. The most powerful of these are the medicine men,
whose assistance must be rewarded with substantial gifts. However, the medicine men do not provide the curative potions for their clients, but decide what
the ingredients should be and then write them down in an ancient and secret
language. This writing is understood only by the medicine men and by the
herbalists who, for another gift, provide the required charm.

The charm is not disposed of after it has served its purpose, but is placed   7
in the charm-box of the household shrine. As these magical materials are
specific for certain ills, and the real or imagined maladies of the people are
many, the charm-box is usually full to overflowing. The magical packets are so
numerous that people forget what their purposes were and fear to use them
again. While the natives are very vague on this point, we can only assume that
the idea in retaining all the old magical materials is that their presence in the

charm-box, before which the body rituals are conducted, will in some way protect the worshipper.

Beneath the charm-box is a small font. Each day every member of the family, in succession, enters the shrine room, bows his head before the charm-box, mingles different sorts of holy water in the font, and proceeds with a brief rite of ablution. The holy waters are secured from the Water Temple of the community, where the priests conduct elaborate ceremonies to make the liquid ritually pure. 8

In the hierarchy of magical practitioners, and below the medicine men in prestige, are specialists whose designation is best translated "holy-mouth-men." The Nacirema have an almost pathological horror of and fascination with the mouth, the condition of which is believed to have a supernatural influence on all social relationships. Were it not for the rituals of the mouth, they believe that their teeth would fall out, their gums bleed, their jaws shrink, their friends desert them, and their lovers reject them. They also believe that a strong relationship exists between oral and moral characteristics. For example, there is a ritual ablution of the mouth for children which is supposed to improve their moral fiber. 9

The daily body ritual performed by everyone includes a mouth-rite. Despite the fact that these people are so punctilious about care of the mouth, this rite involves a practice which strikes the uninitiated stranger as revolting. It was reported to me that the ritual consists of inserting a small bundle of hog hairs into the mouth, along with certain magical powders, and then moving the bundle in a highly formalized series of gestures. 10

In addition to the private mouth-rite, the people seek out a holy-mouth-man once or twice a year. These practitioners have an impressive set of paraphernalia, consisting of a variety of augers, awls, probes, and prods. The use of these objects in the exorcism of the evils of the mouth involves almost unbelievable ritual torture of the client. The holy-mouth-man opens the client's mouth and, using the above mentioned tools, enlarges any holes which decay may have created in the teeth. Magical materials are put into these holes. If there are not naturally occurring holes in the teeth, large sections of one or more teeth are gouged out so that the supernatural substance can be applied. In the client's view, the purpose of these ministrations is to arrest decay and to draw friends. The extremely sacred and traditional character of the rite is evident in the fact that the natives return to the holy-mouth-men year after year, despite the fact that their teeth continue to decay. 11

It is to be hoped that, when a thorough study of the Nacirema is made, there will be careful inquiry into the personality structure of these people. One has but to watch the gleam in the eye of a holy-mouth-man, as he jabs an 12 awl into an exposed nerve, to suspect that a certain amount of sadism is involved. If this can be established, a very interesting pattern emerges, for most of the population shows definite masochistic tendencies. It was to these that Professor Linton referred in discussing a distinctive part of the daily body ritual which is performed only by men. This part of the rite involves scraping and lacerating the surface of the face with a sharp instrument. Special women's rites are performed only four times during each lunar month, but what they lack in frequency is made up in barbarity. As part of this ceremony, women bake their heads in small ovens for about an hour. The theoretically interesting point is that what seems to be a preponderantly masochistic people have developed sadistic specialists.

The medicine men have an imposing temple, or *latipso*, in every community of any size. The more elaborate ceremonies required to treat very sick patients can only be performed at this temple. These ceremonies involve not only the thaumaturge but a permanent group of vestal maidens who move sedately about the temple chambers in distinctive costume and headdress.   13

The *latipso* ceremonies are so harsh that it is phenomenal that a fair proportion of the really sick natives who enter the temple ever recover. Small children whose indoctrination is still incomplete have been known to resist attempts to take them to the temple because "that is where you go to die." Despite this fact, sick adults are not only willing but eager to undergo the protracted ritual purification, if they can afford to do so. No matter how ill the supplicant or how grave the emergency, the guardians of many temples will not admit a client if he cannot give a rich gift to the custodian. Even after one has gained admission and survived the ceremonies, the guardians will not permit the neophyte to leave until he makes still another gift.   14

The supplicant entering the temple is first stripped of all his or her clothes. In everyday life the Nacirema avoids exposure of his body and its natural functions. Bathing and excretory acts are performed only in the secrecy of the household shrine, where they are ritualized as part of the body-rites. Psychological shock results from the fact that body secrecy is suddenly lost upon entry into the *latipso*. A man, whose own wife has never seen him in an excretory act, suddenly finds himself naked and assisted by a vestal maiden while he performs his natural functions into a sacred vessel. This sort of ceremonial treatment is necessitated by the fact that the excreta are used by a diviner to ascertain the course and nature of the client's sickness. Female clients, on the other hand, find their naked bodies are subjected to the scrutiny, manipulation and prodding of the medicine men.   15

Few supplicants in the temple are well enough to do anything but lie on their hard beds. The daily ceremonies, like the rites of the holy-mouth-men,   16 involve discomfort and torture. With ritual precision, the vestals awaken their miserable charges each dawn and roll them about on their beds of pain while performing ablutions, in the formal movements of which the maidens are highly trained. At other times they insert magic wands in the supplicant's mouth or force him to eat substances which are supposed to be healing. From time to time the medicine men come to their clients and jab magically treated needles into their flesh. The fact that these temple ceremonies may not cure, and may even kill the neophyte, in no way decreases the people's faith in the medicine men.

There remains one other kind of practitioner, known as a "listener." This witchdoctor has the power to exorcise the devils that lodge in the heads of people who have been bewitched. The Nacirema believe that parents bewitch their own children. Mothers are particularly suspected of putting a curse on children while teaching them the secret body rituals. The counter-magic of the witchdoctor is unusual in its lack of ritual. The patient simply tells the "listener" all his troubles and fears, beginning with the earliest difficulties he can remember. The memory displayed by the Nacirema in these exorcism sessions is truly remarkable. It is not uncommon for the patient to bemoan the rejection he felt upon being weaned as a babe, and a few individuals even see their troubles going back to the traumatic effects of their own birth. 17

In conclusion, mention must be made of certain practices which have their base in native esthetics but which depend upon the pervasive aversion to the natural body and its functions. There are ritual fasts to make fat people thin and ceremonial feasts to make thin people fat. Still other rites are used to make women's breasts larger if they are small, and smaller if they are large. General dissatisfaction with breast shape is symbolized in the fact that the ideal form is virtually outside the range of human variation. A few women afflicted with almost inhuman hyper-mammary development are so idolized that they make a handsome living by simply going from village to village and permitting the natives to stare at them for a fee. 18

Reference has already been made to the fact that excretory functions are ritualized, routinized, and relegated to secrecy. Natural reproductive functions are similarly distorted. Intercourse is taboo as a topic and scheduled as an act. Efforts are made to avoid pregnancy by the use of magical materials or by limiting intercourse to certain phases of the moon. Conception is actually very infrequent. When pregnant, women dress so as to hide their condition. Parturition takes place in secret, without friends or relatives to assist, and the majority of women do not nurse their infants. 19

Our review of the ritual life of the Nacirema has certainly shown them to be a magic-ridden people. It is hard to understand how they have managed to exist so long under the burdens which they have imposed upon themselves. 20

But even such exotic customs as these take on real meaning when they are viewed with the insight provided by Malinowski[2] when he wrote:

> Looking from far and above, from our high places of safety in the developed civilization, it is easy to see all the crudity and irrelevance of magic. But without its power and guidance early man could not have mastered his practical difficulties as he has done, nor could man have advanced to the higher stages of civilization.

Journal Writing

Think about the many little "rituals" you perform regularly: walking the dog, going to the movies or out to clubs with friends, washing dishes or your car. In your journal, write out all the steps of two or three of these routines, in chronological order and in as much detail as you can. (To take your journal writing further, see "From Journal to Essay" on the facing page.)

Questions on Meaning

1. At what point did you realize what Miner's true subject is? What tipped you off? Did you see the big hint in the spelling of *Nacirema*?
2. One of Miner's purposes is clearly to amuse readers through social SATIRE. But what other purposes does he seem to have?
3. What stereotype does Miner exploit for its humor at the end of paragraph 6?
4. At the beginning and end of the essay, Miner refers to the Nacirema as having "magical beliefs and practices" (par. 1) and as being "magic-ridden" (20). What kinds of cultures are usually described in this way? Why does Miner use such terms to describe the Nacirema?

Questions on Writing Strategy

1. Miner explains several processes under the umbrella of "body rituals." What are these processes in Americanese—that is, in the words we commonly use for them?
2. What is the EFFECT of Miner's opening paragraph? What do the academic TONE and mention of the anthropologist Murdock's work accomplish?
3. This essay originally appeared in *American Anthropologist*, a serious academic journal. In what ways are anthropologists the perfect AUDIENCE for Miner's humor? How do you respond differently to this essay than you think an anthropologist would?

---

[2] Bronislaw Malinowski (1884–1942) was a Polish-born British anthropologist who saw customs in terms of their functions in a culture. —EDS.

4. This essay was first published more than four decades ago. In what ways does it seem dated? What parts of it still seem fresh?
5. **OTHER METHODS.** Miner's humor involves DEFINITIONS of things that ordinarily need no defining: For instance, he refers to a toothbrush as a "small bundle of hog hairs" (par. 10). Find other examples of bizarre definitions of ordinary things. Other than humor, what is the effect of such definitions?

Questions on Language

1. Why do you think Miner chose the name "Nacirema" for his subjects? What associations does this name call up for you?
2. Explain the IRONY of the last paragraph.
3. Make sure you know the definitions of the following words, including some that are specific to the discipline of anthropology: ethos (par. 3); debility, incarcerated, opulence, wattle and daub (4); curative (6); font, ablution (8); hierarchy (9); punctilious (10); augers, awls, gouged, ministrations (11); sadism, masochistic, lacerating, preponderantly (12); thaumaturge (13); indoctrination, supplicant, neophyte (14); excretory, vestal, vessel, excreta, diviner (15); esthetics (18); parturition (19).

Suggestions for Writing

1. **FROM JOURNAL TO ESSAY.** Imagine that you are an observer from another planet reporting back to your authorities on Earth customs. Write them a letter describing the processes you have detailed in your journal (facing page). Remember, you don't understand the language of these earthlings and have no names for the processes you are writing about.
2. Miner satirizes our society's obsession with physical appearance, our hypochondria, our shame over our bodies, our overdependence on psychoanalysis—all in 1956. Evaluate the relevance of this essay today, considering where the concerns with our bodies have brought us. Do you think we are better or worse off, physically and mentally, than we were a hundred or even forty years ago? What's better? What's worse? Be specific.
3. **CRITICAL WRITING.** Anthropologists have sometimes been criticized for turning the people they study into weird and mysterious "others." How does Miner manage to criticize anthropology while working within it, on its own terms, and using its own language and methodology? Focus in particular on the implications of the last paragraph.
4. **CONNECTIONS.** Read or reread Jessica Mitford's "Behind the Formaldehyde Curtain" (p. 290). Taken together, what do Miner's and Mitford's essays say about the importance of the body in our culture? Write an essay either defending or criticizing Americans' obsession with the way they look.

ADDITIONAL WRITING TOPICS
Process Analysis

1. Write a *directive* process analysis (a "how-to" essay) in which, drawing on your own knowledge, you instruct someone in doing or making something. Divide the process into steps, and be sure to detail each step thoroughly. Some possible subjects (any of which may be modified or narrowed):

   How to find games (or another kind of software) on the Internet
   How to enlist people's confidence
   How to bake bread
   How to meditate
   How to teach a child to swim
   How to select a science fiction novel
   How to drive a car in snow or rain
   How to prepare yourself to take an intelligence test
   How to compose a photograph
   How to judge cattle
   How to buy a used motorcycle
   How to enjoy an opera
   How to organize your own rock group
   How to eat an artichoke
   How to groom a horse
   How to bellydance
   How to make a movie or videotape
   How to build (or fly) a kite
   How to start weight training
   How to aid a person who is choking
   How to behave on a first date
   How to get your own way
   How to kick a habit
   How to lose weight
   How to win at poker
   How to make an effective protest or complaint

   Or, if you don't like any of those topics, what else do you know that others might care to learn from you?

2. Step by step, working in chronological order, write a careful *informative* analysis of any one of the following processes. (This is not to be a "how-to" essay, but an essay that explains how something works or happens.) Make use of DESCRIPTION wherever necessary, and be sure to include frequent TRANSITIONS. If one of these topics gives you a better idea for a paper, go with your own subject.

   How a student is processed during orientation or registration
   How the student newspaper gets published
   How a particular Web search engine works

9

DIVISION OR ANALYSIS
Slicing into Parts

THE METHOD

A chemist working for a soft-drink company is asked to improve on a competitor's product, Orange Quench. (In Chap. 8, the same chemist was working on a different part of the same problem.) To do the job, the chemist first has to figure out what's in the drink. She smells the stuff and tastes it. Then she tests a sample chemically to discover the actual ingredients: water, corn syrup, citric acid, sodium benzoate, coloring. Methodically, the chemist has performed DIVISION or ANALYSIS: She has separated the beverage into its components. Orange Quench stands revealed, understood, ready to be bettered.

Division or analysis (the terms are interchangeable) is a key skill in learning and in life. It is an instrument allowing you to slice a large and complicated subject into smaller parts that you can grasp and relate to one another. With analysis you comprehend—and communicate—the structure of things. And when it works, you find in the parts an idea or conclusion about the subject that makes it clearer, truer, more comprehensive, or more vivid than before you started.

If you have worked with the previous two chapters, you have already used division or analysis in explaining a process (Chap. 8) and in comparing and contrasting (Chap. 7). To make a better Orange Quench (a process), the chemist might prepare a recipe that divides the process into separate steps or actions ("First, boil a gallon of water . . ."). When the batch was done, she might taste-test the two drinks, analyzing and then comparing their orange flavor, sweetness, and acidity. As you'll see in following chapters, too, division or analysis figures in all the other methods of developing ideas, for it is basic to any concerted thought, explanation, or evaluation.

Kinds of Division or Analysis

Although division or analysis always works the same way—separating a whole, singular subject into its elements, slicing it into parts—the method can be more or less difficult depending on how unfamiliar, complex, and abstract the subject is. Obviously, it's going to be much easier to analyze a chicken (wings, legs, thighs . . .) than a poem by T. S. Eliot (this image, that allusion . . .), easier to analyze the structure of a small business than that of a multinational conglomerate. Just about any subject *can* by analyzed and will be the clearer for it. In "I Want a Wife," an essay in this chapter, Judy Brady divides the role of a wife into its various functions or services. In an essay called "Teacher" from his book *Pot Shots at Poetry* (1980), Robert Francis divides the knowledge of poetry he imparted to his class into six pie sections. The first slice is what he told his students that they knew already.

The second slice is what I told them that they could have found out just as well or better from books. What, for instance, is a sestina?

The third slice is what I told them that they refused to accept. I could see it on their faces, and later I saw the evidence in their writing.

The fourth slice is what I told them that they were willing to accept and may have thought they accepted but couldn't accept since they couldn't fully understand. This also I saw in their faces and in their work. Here, no doubt, I was mostly to blame.

The fifth slice is what I told them that they discounted as whimsy or something simply to fill up time. After all, I was being paid to talk.

The sixth slice is what I didn't tell them, for I didn't try to tell them all I knew. Deliberately I kept back something—a few professional secrets, a magic formula or two.

There are always multiple ways to divide or analyze a subject, just as there are many ways to slice a pie. Francis could have divided his knowledge of poetry into knowledge of rhyme, knowledge of meter, knowledge of imagery, and so forth—basically following the components of a poem. In other words, the outcome of an analysis depends on the rule or principle used to do the slicing. This fact accounts for some of the differences among academic disciplines: A psychologist, say, may look at the individual person primarily as a bundle of drives and needs, whereas a sociologist may emphasize the individual's roles in society. Even within disciplines, different factions analyze differently, using different principles of division or analysis. Some psychologists are interested mainly in thought, others mainly in behavior; some psychologists focus mainly on emotional development, others mainly on moral development.

Analysis and Critical Thinking

Analysis plays a fundamental role in CRITICAL THINKING, READING, and WRITING, topics discussed in Chapter 1 (pp. 19–21 and 27–31). In fact, *analysis* and *criticism* are deeply related: The first comes from a Greek word meaning "to undo," the second from a Greek word meaning "to separate."

Critical thinking, reading, and writing go beneath the surface of the object, word, image, or whatever the subject is. When you work critically, you divide the subject into its elements, INFER the buried meanings and ASSUMPTIONS that define its essence, and SYNTHESIZE the parts into a new whole. Say a campaign brochure quotes a candidate as favoring "reasonable government expenditures on reasonable highway projects." The candidate will support new roads, right? Wrong. As a critical reader of the brochure, you quickly sense something fishy in the use (twice) of "reasonable." As an informed reader, you know (or find out) that the candidate has consistently opposed new roads, so the chances of her finding a highway project "reasonable" are slim. At the same time, her stand has been unpopular, so of course she wants to seem "reasonable" on the issue. Read critically, then, a campaign statement that seems to offer mild support for highways is actually a slippery evasion of any such commitment.

Analysis (a convenient term for the overlapping operations of analysis, inference, and synthesis) is very useful for exposing such evasiveness, but that isn't its only function. If you've read this far in this book, you've already done quite a bit of analytical/critical thinking as you read and analyzed the selections. The method will also help you understand a sculpture, perceive the importance of a case study in sociology, or form a response to an environmental impact report. And the method can be invaluable for straight thinking about popular culture, from TV to toys, as a number of the selections in this chapter demonstrate.

THE PROCESS

Subjects and Theses

Keep an eye out for writing assignments requiring division or analysis—in college and work, they won't be few or hard to find. They will probably include the word *analyze* or a word implying analysis such as *evaluate, examine, interpret, discuss,* or *criticize.* Any time you spot such a term, you know your job is to separate the subject into its elements, to infer their meanings, to explore the relations among them, and to draw a conclusion about the subject.

Almost any coherent entity—object, person, place, concept—is a fit subject for analysis *if* the analysis will add to the subject's meaning or significance. Little is deadlier than the rote analytical exercise that leaves the parts neatly dissected and the subject comatose on the page. As a writer, you have to animate the subject, and that means finding your interest. What about your subject seems curious? What's appealing? or mysterious? or awful? And what will be your PURPOSE in writing about the subject: Do you simply want to explain it, or do you want to argue for or against it?

Such questions can help you find the principle or framework you will use to divide the subject into parts. (As we mentioned before, there's more than one way to slice most subjects.) Say you're contemplating a hunk of bronze in the park. Why do you like the sculpture, or why don't you? What elements of its creation and physical form make it art? What is the point of such public art? What does this sculpture do to this park, or vice versa? Any of these questions could suggest a slant on the subject, a framework for analysis, and a purpose for writing, getting your analysis moving.

Finding your principle of analysis will lead you to your essay's THESIS as well—the main point you want to make about your subject. Expressed in a THESIS SENTENCE, this idea will help keep you focused and help your readers see your subject as a whole rather than a bundle of parts. Your essay on the bronze in the park, for instance, might have one of these thesis sentences:

> Though it may not be obvious at first, this bronze sculpture represents the city dweller's relationship with nature.

> Like much public art today, this bronze sculpture seems chiefly intended to make people ignore it.

> The huge bronze sculpture in the middle of McBean Park demonstrates that so-called public art does little for the public interest.

After any of these thesis sentences, you would go on to identify and explain the relevant elements of the sculpture: in the first case, maybe the sculpture's hints of plants and water and connection; in the second case, maybe the sculpture's blandness, lack of a clear message, and lack of artistic rigor; in the third case, maybe the sculpture's cost, uselessness, and ugliness. (Notice that each approach reveals something different in the sculpture, with very different results.)

In developing an essay by analysis, having an outline at your elbow can be a help. You don't want to overlook any parts or elements that should be included in your framework. (You needn't mention every feature in your final essay or give them all equal treatment, but any omissions or variations should be conscious.) And you want to use your framework consistently, not switching carelessly (and confusingly) from, say, the form of the sculpture to the cost of public art. In writing her brief essay "I Want a Wife," Judy Brady must have needed an outline to work out carefully the different activities of a wife, so that she covered them all and clearly distinguished them.

Evidence

Making a valid analysis is chiefly a matter of giving your subject thought, but for the result to seem useful and convincing to your readers, it will have to refer to the concrete world. The method requires not only cogitation, but open eyes and a willingness to provide EVIDENCE. The nature of the evidence will depend entirely on what you are analyzing—physical details for a sculpture, quotations for a poem, financial data for a business case study, statistics for a psychology case study, and so forth. The idea is to supply enough evidence to justify and support your particular slant on the subject.

A final caution: It's possible to get carried away with one's own analysis, to become so enamored of the details that the subject itself becomes dim or distorted. You can avoid this danger by keeping the subject literally in front of

you as you work (or at least imagining it vividly) and by maintaining an outline. It often helps to reassemble your subject at the end of the essay: That
gives you a chance to place your subject in a larger context, speculate on its
influence, or affirm its significance. By the end of the essay, your subject must
be a coherent whole truly represented by your analysis, not twisted, diminished, inflated, or obliterated. The reader should be intrigued by your subject,
yes, but also able to recognize it on the street.

CHECKLIST FOR REVISING A DIVISION OR ANALYSIS

✔ **PRINCIPLE OF ANALYSIS.** What is your particular slant on your subject, the
rule or principle you have used to divide your subject into its elements?
Where do you tell readers what it is?

✔ **COMPLETENESS.** Have you considered all the subject's elements required by
your principle of analysis?

✔ **CONSISTENCY.** Have you applied your principle of analysis consistently,
viewing your subject from a definite slant?

✔ **EVIDENCE.** Is your division or analysis well supported with concrete details,
quotations, data, or statistics, as appropriate?

✔ **SIGNIFICANCE.** Why should readers care about your analysis? Have you told
them something about your subject that wasn't obvious on its surface?

✔ **TRUTH TO SUBJECT.** Is your analysis faithful to the subject, not distorted,
exaggerated, deflated?

DIVISION OR ANALYSIS IN A PARAGRAPH:
TWO ILLUSTRATIONS

Using Division or Analysis
to Write About Television

The following paragraph analyzes the components of a television laugh
track, the recorded chorus that tells us when a comedy is funny. Though written
especially for *The Bedford Reader*, not as part of an essay, this brief analysis could itself be one component in an examination of TV comedy. Or, with
the related paragraph on page 362, illustrating CLASSIFICATION, it could contribute to an essay on, say, how the producers of TV comedies manipulate viewers.

Most television comedies, even some that boast live audiences,
rely on the laugh machine to fill too-quiet moments on the sound-
track. The effect of a canned laugh comes from its four overlapping

*Principle of analysis:
elements creating the
effect of a canned laugh*

elements. The first is style, from titter to belly laugh. The second is intensity, the volume, ranging from mild to medium to earsplitting. The third ingredient is duration, the length of the laugh, whether quick, medium, or extended. And finally, there's the number of laughers, from a lone giggler to a roaring throng. According to rumor (for its exact workings are a secret), the machine contains a bank of thirty-two tapes. Furiously working keys and tromping pedals, the operator plays the tapes singly or in combination to blend the four ingredients, as a maestro weaves a symphony out of brass, wood-winds, percussion, and strings.

1. Style
2. Intensity
3. Duration
4. Number

Details and examples clarify elements

Using Division or Analysis in an Academic Discipline

The next paragraph appeared first in a scholarly journal and then in a textbook on medical ethics. The author discusses four possible models for the doctor-patient relationship, ending with the one detailed below. The careful analysis supports his preference for this model over the others.

The model of social relationship which fits these conditions [of realistic equality between patient and doctor] is that of the con-tract or covenant. The notion of contract should not be loaded with legalistic implications, but taken in its more symbolic form as in the traditional religious or marriage "contract" or "covenant." Here two individuals or groups are interacting in a way where there are oblig-ations and expected benefits for both parties. The obligations and benefits are limited in scope, though, even if they are expressed in somewhat vague terms. The basic norms of freedom, dignity, truth-telling, promise-keeping, and justice are essential to a contractual relationship. The premise is trust and confidence even though it is recognized that there is not a full mutuality of interests. Social sanc-tions institutionalize and stand behind the relationship, in case there is a violation of the contract, but for the most part the assumption is that there will be a faithful fulfillment of the obligations.

— Robert M. Veatch,
"Models for Medicine in a Revolutionary Age"

Principle of analysis: elements of a contract between doctor and patient

1. Obligations and bene-fits for both parties

2. Obligations and benefits limited

3. Freedom, dignity, and other norms

4. Trust and confidence

5. Support of social sanctions (meaning that society upholds the relationship)

CASE STUDY
Using Division or Analysis

During her sophomore year at Boston University, Cortney Keim applied for transfer to Pomona College in California. As part of its application, Pomona requested a statement about Keim, her academic goals, and her reasons for wanting to transfer.

Keim tried several approaches to her statement, struggling to present herself as serious and unique. In one draft, she followed the cue of Pomona's request—providing a brief autobiography, a list of goals, and an explanation for choosing Pomona—but that version seemed obvious and dull. In the end, Keim settled on the fresher approach you see here. She first divides herself into parts and then details each one, showing its relevance to Pomona.

Application Statement of Cortney Keim

In applying for transfer to Pomona, I seek to develop the three main components of myself: actor, student, and explorer.

Pomona's strong theater curriculum will give me the background I need to embark on a career in acting. As unstable a career as it may prove to be, acting is my fire. I have always liked entertaining others (in high school, I was voted class clown), even if it involves making a display of myself. As I have had the chance to act in varied plays over the last few years, I have also found that interpreting an author's text allows me paradoxically to express myself and to lose myself. And, yes, I have loved the appreciation of an audience, the sighs or laughs in the right places, the applause at the end.

Yet acting is not all. In high school and for two years at Boston University, I have also relished the liberal arts courses I've taken and the writing I've done in those courses. The courses have introduced me to worlds of information and ideas I wouldn't have known otherwise, and the writing has let me make up my own text, my own version of reality. Liberal arts courses are hard work, harder in many ways than acting, but the work pays off. Pomona's respected liberal arts curriculum will help me become the rounded, thoughtful, disciplined student I hope to be for the rest of my life.

It's also significant to me that Pomona is a small school in California, so different from the huge university I attend now and so far from the East Coast city where I have lived all my life. The explorer in me needs a new horizon. At Pomona I anticipate the opportunity to be more involved in the activities of the college and to get to know a wider variety of people. In southern California, I expect to become familiar with a new climate, geography, and ecosystem.

Pomona promises to help me fulfill my needs to act, learn, and explore. In return, I promise to contribute whatever I can to the college and the larger community.

JUDY BRADY

JUDY BRADY, born in 1937 in San Francisco, where she now lives, earned a BFA in painting from the University of Iowa in 1962. Drawn into political action by her work in the feminist movement, she went to Cuba in 1973, where she studied class relationships as a way of understanding change in a society. "I am not a 'writer,'" Brady declares, "but really am a disenfranchised (and fired) housewife, now secretary." Despite her disclaimer, Brady has published articles occasionally—on union organizing and education in Cuba, among other topics—and she writes a regular column for the Women's Cancer Resource Center. In 1991 she published *1 in 3: Women with Cancer Confront an Epidemic*, an anthology of writings by women. Asked by an interviewer if she had won any awards lately, Brady responded, "People who do what I do don't get awards."

I Want a Wife

"I Want a Wife" first appeared in the Spring 1972 issue of Ms. magazine and has been reprinted often. The essay is one of the best-known manifestos in popular feminist writing. In it, Brady trenchantly divides the work of a wife into its multiple duties and functions, leading to an inescapable conclusion. If you find that Brady stereotypes men, read the essay after hers, Armin A. Brott's "Not All Men Are Sly Foxes," for a different view.

I belong to that classification of people known as wives. I am A Wife. 1 And, not altogether incidentally, I am a mother.

Not too long ago a male friend of mine appeared on the scene fresh from 2 a recent divorce. He had one child, who is, of course, with his ex-wife. He is looking for another wife. As I thought about him while I was ironing one evening, it suddenly occurred to me that I, too, would like to have a wife. Why do I want a wife?

I would like to go back to school so that I can become economically inde- 3 pendent, support myself, and, if need be, support those dependent upon me. I want a wife who will work and send me to school. And while I am going to school I want a wife to take care of my children. I want a wife to keep track of the children's doctor and dentist appointments. And to keep track of mine, too. I want a wife to make sure my children eat properly and are kept clean. I want a wife who will wash the children's clothes and keep them mended. I want a wife who is a good nurturant attendant to my children, who arranges for their schooling, makes sure that they have an adequate social life with their peers, takes them to the park, the zoo, etc. I want a wife who takes care of the children when they are sick, a wife who arranges to be around when the children need special care, because, of course, I cannot miss classes at school. My wife must arrange to lose time at work and not lose the job. It may mean a small cut in my wife's income from time to time, but I guess I can tolerate that. Needless to say, my wife will arrange and pay for the care of the children while my wife is working.

I want a wife who will take care of *my* physical needs. I want a wife who will keep my house clean. A wife who will pick up after my children, a wife who will pick up after me. I want a wife who will keep my clothes clean, ironed, mended, replaced when need be, and who will see to it that my personal things are kept in their proper place so that I can find what I need the minute I need it. I want a wife who cooks the meals, a wife who is a *good* cook. I want a wife who will plan the menus, do the necessary grocery shopping, prepare the meals, serve them pleasantly, and then do the cleaning up while I do my studying. I want a wife who will care for me when I am sick and sympathize with my pain and loss of time from school. I want a wife to go along when our family takes vacation so that someone can continue to care for me and my children when I need a rest and change of scene.

I want a wife who will not bother me with rambling complaints about a wife's duties. But I want a wife who will listen to me when I feel the need to explain a rather difficult point I have come across in my course of studies. And I want a wife who will type my papers for me when I have written them.

I want a wife who will take care of the details of my social life. When my wife and I are invited out by my friends, I want a wife who will take care of the babysitting arrangements. When I meet people at school that I like and want to entertain, I want a wife who will have the house clean, will prepare a special meal, serve it to me and my friends, and not interrupt when I talk about things that interest me and my friends. I want a wife who will have arranged that the children are fed and ready for bed before my guests arrive so that the children do not bother us. I want a wife who takes care of the needs of my guests so that they feel comfortable, who makes sure that they have an ashtray, that they are passed the hors d'oeuvres, that they are offered a second helping of the food, that their wine glasses are replenished when necessary, that their coffee is served to them as they like it. And I want a wife who knows that sometimes I need a night out by myself.

I want a wife who is sensitive to my sexual needs, a wife who makes love passionately and eagerly when I feel like it, a wife who makes sure that I am satisfied. And, of course, I want a wife who will not demand sexual attention when I am not in the mood for it. I want a wife who assumes the complete responsibility for birth control, because I do not want more children. I want a wife who will remain sexually faithful to me so that I do not have to clutter up my intellectual life with jealousies. And I want a wife who understands that *my* sexual needs may entail more than strict adherence to monogamy. I must, after all, be able to relate to people as fully as possible.

If, by chance, I find another person more suitable as a wife than the wife I   8
already have, I want the liberty to replace my present wife with another one. Naturally, I will expect a fresh, new life; my wife will take the children and be solely responsible for them so that I am left free.

When I am through with school and have a job, I want my wife to quit   9
working and remain at home so that my wife can more fully and completely take care of a wife's duties.

My God, who *wouldn't* want a wife?   10

———————

Journal Writing

Brady addresses the traditional obligations of a wife and mother. In your journal, jot down parallel obligations of a husband and father. (To take your journal writing further, see "From Journal to Essay" on the facing page.)

Questions on Meaning

1. Sum up the duties of a wife as Brady sees them.
2. To what inequities in the roles traditionally assigned to men and to women does "I Want a Wife" call attention?
3. What is the THESIS of this essay? Is it stated or implied?
4. Is Brady unfair to men?

Questions on Writing Strategy

1. What EFFECT does Brady obtain with the title "I Want a Wife"?
2. What do the first two paragraphs accomplish?
3. What is the TONE of this essay?
4. How do you explain the fact that Brady never uses the pronoun *she* to refer to a wife? Does this make her prose unnecessarily awkward?
5. What principle does Brady use to analyze the role of wife? Can you think of some other principle for analyzing the job?
6. Knowing that this essay was first published in Ms. magazine in 1972, what can you guess about its intended readers? Does "I Want a Wife" strike a college AUDI-ENCE today as revolutionary?
7. **OTHER METHODS.** Although she mainly divides or analyzes the role of wife, Brady also uses CLASSIFICATION to sort the many duties and responsibilities into manageable groups. What are the groups?

Questions on Language

1. What is achieved by the author's frequent repetition of the phrase "I want a wife"?
2. Be sure you know how to define the following words as Brady uses them: nurturant (par. 3); replenished (6); adherence, monogamy (7).
3. In general, how would you describe the DICTION of this essay? How well does it suit the essay's intended audience?

Suggestions for Writing

1. **FROM JOURNAL TO ESSAY.** Working from your journal entry (previous page), write an essay titled "I Want a Husband" in which, using examples as Brady does, you enumerate the roles traditionally assigned to men in our society.
2. Imagining that you want to employ someone to do a specific job, divide the task into its duties and functions. Then, guided by your analysis, write an accurate job description in essay form.
3. **CRITICAL WRITING.** In an essay, SUMMARIZE Brady's view as you understand it and then EVALUATE her essay. Consider: Is Brady fair? (If not, is unfairness justified?) Is the essay relevant today? (If not, what has changed?) Provide specific EVIDENCE from your experience, observation, and reading.
4. **CONNECTIONS.** Both "I Want a Wife" and Armin A. Brott's "Not All Men Are Sly Foxes" (next page) challenge traditional ideas about how men and women are supposed to divide the labor in a marriage. However, Brady's STYLE is fast paced and her tone is sarcastic, while Brott is more methodical and earnest. Which method of addressing these issues do you find more effective? Why? Write an essay that COMPARES AND CONTRASTS the essays' tones, styles, POINTS OF VIEW, and OBJECTIVE versus SUBJECTIVE language. What conclusions can you draw about the connection between the writers' strategies and their messages?

ARMIN A. BROTT

ARMIN A. BROTT is a freelance writer living in San Francisco. Born in 1958, he received a BA in Russian from San Francisco State University and an MBA that he calls "less useful than the degree in Russian" before embarking on a career in marketing. He turned to writing when his first child was born because he "wanted to be an active, involved father." Since that time he has contributed to the *New York Times Magazine*, the *Washington Post*, *Reader's Digest*, *Family Circle*, the *Saturday Evening Post*, *Playboy*, and other magazines. He treats issues that affect men: education, health, and especially fatherhood. His books include *The Expectant Father* (1995, with Jennifer Ash), *The New Father* (1997), *A Dad's Guide to the Toddler Years* (1998), *The Single Father* (1999), and *Throwaway Dads* (1999). Brott also hosts a weekly radio show in San Francisco, *Positive Parenting*.

Not All Men Are Sly Foxes

In this essay from a 1992 *Newsweek* magazine, Brott offers a different view of men from that taken by Judy Brady in the previous essay. While acknowledging that women and men are not yet equal in child care, Brott holds that children's books are hardly helping. He uses analysis to show that the Sly Fox remains much more common than the Caring Dad.

If you thought your child's bookshelves were finally free of openly (and 1 not so openly) discriminatory materials, you'd better check again. In recent years groups of concerned parents have persuaded textbook publishers to portray more accurately the roles that women and minorities play in shaping our country's history and culture. *Little Black Sambo* has all but disappeared from library and bookstore shelves; feminist fairy tales by such authors as Jack Zipes have, in many homes, replaced the more traditional (and obviously sexist) fairy tales. Richard Scarry, one of the most popular children's writers, has re-issued new versions of some of his classics; now female animals are pictured doing the same jobs as male animals. Even the terminology has changed: Males and females are referred to as mail "carriers" or "firefighters."

There is, however, one very large group whose portrayal continues to fol- 2 low the same stereotypical lines as always: fathers. The evolution of children's literature didn't end with *Goodnight Moon* and *Charlotte's Web*. My local public library, for example, previews 203 new children's picture books (for the under-five set) each *month*. Many of these books make a very conscious effort to take women characters out of the kitchen and the nursery and give them professional jobs and responsibilities.

Despite this shift, mothers are by and large still shown as the primary care-   3
givers and, more important, as the primary nurturers of their children. Men in
these books—if they're shown at all—still come home late after work and
participate in the child rearing by bouncing baby around for five minutes
before putting the child to bed.

In one of my two-year-old daughter's favorite books, *Mother Goose and the*   4
Sly Fox, "retold" by Chris Conover, a single mother (Mother Goose) of seven
tiny goslings is pitted against (and naturally outwits) the sly Fox. Fox, a
neglectful and presumably unemployed single father, lives with his filthy, hungry pups in a grimy hovel littered with the bones of their previous meals.
Mother Goose, a successful entrepreneur with a thriving lace business, still
finds time to serve her goslings homemade soup in pretty porcelain cups. The
story is funny and the illustrations marvelous, but the unwritten message is
that women take better care of their kids and men have nothing else to do but
hunt down and kill innocent, law-abiding geese.

The majority of other children's classics perpetuate the same negative   5
stereotypes of fathers. Once in a great while, people complain about *Babar*'s
colonialist slant (little jungle-dweller finds happiness in the big city and
brings civilization—and fine clothes—to his backward village). But I've
never heard anyone ask why, after his mother is killed by the evil hunter,
Babar is automatically an "orphan." Why can he find comfort only in the arms
of another female? Why do Arthur's and Celeste's mothers come alone to the
city to fetch their children? Don't the fathers care? Do they even have fathers?
I need my answers ready for when my daughter asks.

I recently spent an entire day on the children's floor of the local library   6
trying to find out whether these same negative stereotypes are found in the
more recent classics-to-be. The librarian gave me a list of the twenty most
popular contemporary picture books and I read every one of them. Of the
twenty, seven don't mention a parent at all. Of the remaining thirteen, four
portray fathers as much less loving and caring than mothers. In *Little Gorilla*,
we are told that the little gorilla's "mother loves him" and we see Mama gorilla
giving her little one a warm hug. On the next page we're also told that his
"father loves him," but in the illustration, father and son aren't even touching. Six of the remaining nine books mention or portray mothers as the only
parent, and only three of the twenty have what could be considered "equal"
treatment of mothers and fathers.

The same negative stereotypes also show up in literature aimed at the *par-*   7
ents of small children. In *What to Expect the First Year*, the authors answer
almost every question the parents of a newborn or toddler could have in the
first year of their child's life. They are meticulous in alternating between references to boys and girls. At the same time, they refer almost exclusively to

"mother" or "mommy." Men, and their feelings about parenting, are relegated to a nine-page chapter just before the recipe section.

Unfortunately, it's still true that, in our society, women do the bulk of the child care, and that thanks to men abandoning their families, there are too many single mothers out there. Nevertheless, to say that portraying fathers as unnurturing or completely absent is simply "a reflection of reality" is unacceptable. If children's literature only reflected reality, it would be like prime-time TV and we'd have books filled with child abusers, wife beaters and criminals.

Young children believe what they hear—especially from a parent figure. And since, for the first few years of a child's life, adults select the reading material, children's literature should be held to a high standard. Ignoring men who share equally in raising their children and continuing to show nothing but part-time or no-time fathers is only going to create yet another generation of men who have been told since boyhood—albeit subtly—that mothers are the truer parents and that fathers play, at best, a secondary role in the home. We've taken major steps to root out discrimination in what our children read. Let's finish the job.

———————————

Journal Writing

Do you agree with Brott that young children are strongly influenced by the books parents or teachers read to them? In your journal, list particular books from your childhood that stand out in your memory. What made these books come alive so that you still remember them today—the story, the illustrations, the language? (To take your journal writing further, see "From Journal to Essay" on the facing page.)

Questions on Meaning

1. What is the THESIS of Brott's essay? Where is it stated succinctly?
2. What does Brott ASSUME about his AUDIENCE in this essay? To what extent do you fit his assumptions?
3. Brott points out a difference between the illustration of the little gorilla with his mother and the one of him with his father (par. 6). Why is this difference significant?
4. What is the EFFECT of Brott's concluding sentences: "We've taken major steps to root out discrimination in what our children read. Let's finish the job"?

Questions on Writing Strategy

1. What principle of analysis does Brott use in examining the children's books? What elements does he perceive in these books?

2. What purpose does paragraph 7, with its reference to books for parents, serve in this essay about children's books?
3. **OTHER METHODS.** In paragraph 4, Brott provides vivid DESCRIPTION of Mother Goose's and Sly Fox's homes to show the differences between the two parents. What CONCRETE details help explain these differences?

Questions on Language

1. What is the difference between "caregivers" and "nurturers" as Brott uses the words in paragraph 3?
2. How would you analyze Brott's TONE? Give specific words and sentences that you think contribute to the tone.
3. If some of the following words are unfamiliar, look them up in a dictionary: discriminatory (par. 1); stereotypical, evolution (2); goslings, neglectful, hovel, entrepreneur, porcelain (4); perpetuate, colonialist (5); meticulous, exclusively, relegated (7); albeit, subtly (9).

Suggestions for Writing

1. **FROM JOURNAL TO ESSAY.** Working from your journal entry (previous page), write a brief essay that explores the messages sent by one of your childhood books. Did the book contain positive role models? negative ones? moral messages? values that you now embrace or reject? Did you learn anything in particular from this book? Based on your recollections, come to your own conclusions about what's appropriate or not in children's books.
2. Write an essay that analyzes another type of writing by examining its elements. You may choose any kind of writing that's familiar to you: news article, sports article, mystery, romance, science fiction, biography, and so on. Be sure to make your principle of analysis clear to your readers.
3. **CRITICAL WRITING.** "If children's literature only reflected reality," Brott claims, "it would be like prime-time TV and we'd have books filled with child abusers, wife beaters and criminals" (par. 8). However, Brott also suggests that "reality" contains a significant number of responsible, loving fathers. Does the claim about "reality" being "like prime-time TV" detract from Brott's argument on behalf of good fathers? Write an essay in which you explain how (or whether) Brott resolves this contradiction in his essay. It will probably be helpful to provide a clear DEFINITION of *reality* in this context.
4. **CONNECTIONS.** Look over Judy Brady's "I Want a Wife" (p. 320) and make a list of her implied complaints about the traditional roles of a wife. Now make a list of the responsibilities that Brott implies a good father is happy to take on. How could Brott's essay be viewed as a sort of response or solution to some of the problems Brady raises? Write an essay explaining the changes in traditional gender roles suggested by "I Want a Wife" and "Not All Men Are Sly Foxes" together.

SHELBY STEELE

Born in Chicago in 1946, SHELBY STEELE is a teacher and a writer whose work focuses on race relations in the United States. Steele became active in the civil rights movement during his undergraduate studies at Coe College in Iowa. After graduating in 1968, he taught African American literature at a school in East St. Louis, Illinois, while also obtaining an MA in sociology from Southern Illinois University. He then earned a PhD in English from the University of Utah. Steele possesses, in the words of the journalist Clarence Page, "an uncommonly sharp bulljive detector." His stress on the achievement of the individual and his opposition to social programs such as affirmative action have attracted protest, not least from his fellow African Americans. But, Steele insists, "The promised land guarantees nothing. It is only an opportunity, not a deliverance." Steele won the National Book Critics Circle Award for a collection of essays, *The Content of Our Character: A New Vision of Race in America* (1990). He also received an Emmy Award for his work on *Seven Days in Bensonhurst,* a 1991 PBS documentary that explored racial tension in New York City. His most recent book is *A Dream Deferred: The Second Betrayal of Black Freedom in America* (1998). Steele has taught English at San Jose State University since 1974 and has been a research fellow at the Hoover Institution since 1994.

Notes from the Hip-Hop Underground

In this editorial from the *Wall Street Journal* in March 2001, Steele analyzes hip-hop, the popular music whose often violent and vulgar themes have made it hugely controversial. What, Steele asks, are the elements in the music that touch the lives of both blacks and whites?

Think about it. If you were a slave, what sort of legend or myth would most warm your soul? One of the great legends in black American culture has always been that of the Bad Nigger. This figure flaunts the constraints, laws and taboos that bind a person in slavery. The BN is unbound and contemptuous, and takes his vengeance on the master's women simply to assert the broadest possible freedom. His very indifference to human feeling makes him a revolution incarnate. Nat Turner, a slave who in 1831 led an insurrection in which some sixty whites were massacred, was the BN come to life.

But for the most part, the BN is the imagination's compensation for the all-too-real impotence and confinement that slaves and segregated blacks actually endured. He lives out a compensatory grandiosity—a self-preening superiority combined with a trickster's cunning and a hyperbolic masculinity in which sexual potency is a vengeful and revolutionary force.

This cultural archetype, I believe, is at the center of rap or hip-hop cul-   3
ture. From "cop killer" Ice-T, Tupac Shakur and, today most noticeably, Sean
"Puffy" Combs and Eminem (who is white), we get versions of the BN in all
his sneering and inflated masculinity.

Having beaten gun and bribery charges in a high-profile New York trial,   4
Mr. Combs—who has just announced that he wishes to be known, hence-
forth, as "P. Diddy"—is the baddest BN for the moment. A man with both the
entrepreneurial genius and the fortune (estimated in the hundreds of millions
of dollars) to live far above the fray, he has nevertheless tried to live out the
BN archetype in a series of ego feuds, thuggish assaults, and late-night escapades that ought to bore a man of his talent and wealth.

Mr. Combs is caught in a contradiction. At the very least, he must pos-   5
ture, if not act out, BN themes, even as the actual condition of his life
becomes conspicuously bourgeois. Rap culture essentially markets BN themes
to American youth as an ideal form of adolescent rebellion. And this meeting
of a black cultural archetype with the universal impulse of youth to find themselves by thumbing their nose at adults is extremely profitable. But the rappers
and promoters themselves are pressured toward a thug life, simply to stay credible, by the very BN themes they sell. A rap promoter without an arrest record
can start to look a lot like Dick Clark.

But the Puffys of the world cannot market to an indifferent youth. The   6
important question is how the BN archetype—the slave's projection of law-
less power and revenge—has become the MTV generation's metaphor for
rebellion. And are conservatives right to see all this as yet more evidence of
America's decline?

I think the answer to these questions begins in one fact: that what many   7
of today's youth ironically share with yesterday's slave is a need for myths and
images that compensate for a sense of alienation and ineffectuality.

Of course, today's youth do not remotely live the lives of slaves and know   8
nothing of the alienation and importance out of which slaves conjured the
BN myth. Still, the injury to family life in America over the past thirty years
(from high divorce and illegitimacy rates, a sweeping sexual revolution, dual-
career households, etc.) may well have given us the most interpersonally
alienated generation in our history.

Too many of today's youth experienced a faithlessness and tenuousness   9
even in that all-important relationship with their parents. And outside the
home, institutions rarely offer the constancy, structure, high expectations,
and personal values they once did. So here is another kind of alienation that
also diminishes and generates a sense of helplessness, that sets up the need for

compensation—for an imagined self that is bigger than life, unbound, and powerful. Here the suburban white kid, gawky and materially privileged, is oddly simpatico with the black American experience.

The success of people like Mr. Combs is built on this sense of the sim-   10
patico. By some estimates, 80 percent of rap music is bought by white youth. And this makes for another irony. The blooming of white alienation has brought us the first generation of black entrepreneurs with wide-open access to the American mainstream. Russell Simmons, known as the "Godfather" of rap entrepreneurs, as well as Mr. Combs, Master P and others, have launched clothing lines, restaurant chains, record labels, and production companies—possibilities seeded, in a sense, by this strong new sympathy between black and white alienation.

Rap's adaptation, or update, of the BN archetype began in the post-'60s   11
black underclass. As is now well established, this was essentially a matriarchal world in which welfare-supported women became the center of households and men became satellite fathers only sporadically supporting or visiting their children by different women. The children of this world were not primed to support a music of teen romance—of "Stop in the Name of Love." The alienation was too withering. Not even the blues would do.

I think the appeal of the BN, on the deepest level, was his existential   12
indifference to feeling—what might be called his immunity to feeling. The slave wanted not to feel the loves and fears that bound him to other people and thus weakened him into an accommodation with slavery. Better not to love at all if it meant such an accommodation. So the BN felt nothing for anyone and had no fear even of death. He could slap a white man around with no regard for the consequences.

Rappers, too, gain freedom through immunity to feeling. Women are   13
"bitches" and "ho's," objects of lust but not of feeling. In many inner cities, where the illegitimacy rate is over 80 percent, where welfare has outbid the male as head of the household, where marriage is all but nonexistent and where the decimation of drugs is everywhere—in such places, a young person of tender feelings is certain to be devastated. Everything about rap—the misogynistic lyrics, the heaving swagger, the violent sexuality, the cynical hipness—screams "I'm bad because I don't feel." Nonfeeling is freedom. And it is important to note that this has nothing to do with race. In rap, the BN nurtures indifference toward those he is most likely to love.

Conservatives have rightly attacked rap for its misogyny, violence and   14
over-the-top vulgarity. But it is important to remember that this music is a fairly accurate message from a part of society where human connections are fractured and impossible, so fraught with disappointments and pain that only

an assault on human feeling itself can assuage. Rap makes the conservative argument about what happens when family life is eroded either by welfare and drugs, or by the stresses and indulgences of middle-class life.

I listened carefully to Eminem's recent Grammy performance, expecting,   15 I guess, to be disgusted. Instead I was drawn into a compelling rap about a boy who becomes a figure of terrible pathos. He is a male groupie who selfishly longs for the autograph of a rap star while he has his girlfriend tied up in the trunk of his car. Easy to be aghast at this until I remembered that Dosto-yevsky's[1] *Notes from the Underground*—the first modern novel, written more than 150 years ago—was also about a pathetic antihero whose alienation from modernity made him spiteful and finally cruel toward an innocent female.

Both works protest what we all protest—societies that lose people to   16 alienation. This does not excuse the vulgarity of rap. But the real problem is not as much rap's cartoonish bravado as what it compensates for.

Journal Writing

Steele refers to today's young people as perhaps "the most interpersonally alienated generation in our history" (par. 8). In your journal, respond to this GENERALIZATION. In your experience, do many teenagers and young adults suffer from an "injury to fam-ily life"? (To take your journal writing further, see "From Journal to Essay" on the next page.)

Questions on Meaning

1. How does Steele describe the historic image of the "Bad Nigger," or "BN"? What does he say is the source of this cultural archetype?
2. How, in Steele's view, is the BN related to hip-hop and its artists? In what sense does this relationship imply a contradiction?
3. Where does Steele state his THESIS in this essay? How does he go on to explain his thesis?
4. How, according to Steele, did the characteristics of "the post-'60s black under-class" (par. 11) influence rap's update of the "BN archetype"?

Questions on Writing Strategy

1. What principle of analysis does Steele use to examine hip-hop music—that is, what framework does he use to identify the music's elements? How does the prin-ciple of analysis relate to his thesis?

---

[1] Feodor Dostoyevsky (1821–81), a Russian novelist. —EDS.

2. In paragraphs 6 and 14 Steele refers to conservative critics of rap and hip-hop. What does this suggest about his intended AUDIENCE and PURPOSE?
3. In paragraph 15 what does Steele mean to achieve by mentioning the Russian novelist Dostoyevsky?
4. Why do you think Steele opens his essay with the sentence "Think about it," followed by a question?
5. **OTHER METHODS.** Steele's essay illustrates division or analysis but also CAUSE AND EFFECT. What principal causes and effects does Steele identify?

Questions on Language

1. In his opening paragraph, Steele suggests that the legend that would "most warm [the] soul" of someone in slavery was that of the BN. What is IRONIC about this image?
2. Steele writes that a "rap promoter without an arrest record can start to look a lot like Dick Clark" (par. 5). What does he mean?
3. Why do you think Steele uses the abbreviation "BN" for every reference to "Bad Nigger" except the first one?
4. Consult a dictionary if you are unsure of the meanings of any of the following words: flaunts, taboos, contemptuous, incarnate (par. 1); impotence, grandiosity, self-preening, hyperbolic (2); archetype (3); entrepreneurial, escapades (4); bourgeois (5); projection, metaphor (6); ineffectuality (7); interpersonally (8); tenuousness, simpatico (9); matriarchal, satellite, sporadically, withering (11); existential, immunity, accommodation (12); decimation, misogynistic, cynical (13); fraught, assuage, indulgences (14); pathos, aghast (15); bravado (16).

Suggestions for Writing

1. **FROM JOURNAL TO ESSAY.** Starting with your journal entry (previous page) and drawing on your own experiences and observations and information you've gained from the news media, write an essay in response to Steele's claim that today's youth may be "the most interpersonally alienated generation in our history" (par. 8). You may wish to support the claim, refute it, or take the middle ground.
2. Write an essay analyzing another aspect of popular culture—another type of popular music, perhaps, or violent computer games or "reality" television programs or teen horror movies. Your subject may appeal to you personally, but be sure to expand your discussion to explain your subject's broader appeal as well.
3. **CRITICAL WRITING.** The organization of this essay is rather complex. Try SUMMARIZING and outlining the essay to grasp how and why Steele moves from topic to topic and between general and specific assertions. (For example, why might he have delayed stating his thesis until par. 7?) Write a brief essay explaining what you understand to be Steele's reasoning for the organization.
4. **CONNECTIONS.** In "The Meanings of a Word" (p. 468), Gloria Naylor analyzes the use of the word *nigger* within and outside of African American culture. Obviously, considerable controversy surrounds this word, controversy recorded in the recent book *Nigger: The Strange Career of a Troublesome Word*, by African Amer-

ican scholar Randall Kennedy. Considering both Naylor's and Steele's uses of the word along with other uses you are aware of, write an essay in which you examine this "troublesome word" and whether you believe its use is ever acceptable or always offensive. Be sure to explain why you think as you do.

Shelby Steele on Writing

In the introduction to his book *The Content of Our Character*, Shelby Steele explains what prompted him to begin writing about race relations. Listening to a radio dialogue between a white interviewer and a local African American leader, Steele realized he was hearing "the standard media formula, the ideal public choreography of black and white [. . .] more a meeting of two postures than of two people." The interview was a bore because "each man had left his full self at home and brought only the 'received' part of himself to the studio." When it comes to race, Steele reflects, "Publicly, we usually adhere to the received wisdom that gives us the most advantageous 'racial face'; privately we are harassed by the uncensored thoughts and feelings that occur to us spontaneously."

Steele began writing to bridge the gap between his own public and private selves: "I was tired of my own public/private racial split, the absence of my own being from what I said to people about race. [. . .] It was both scary and exhilarating to write because it portended a new looseness with the going racial propriety and a good deal of personal vulnerability. But I felt that if I could only stay with myself, I might get somewhere. I had no interest in writing autobiography or even in being autobiographical, only in following the road from the private self to the public reality. [. . .] Though all the agonies of writing have been with me in abundance throughout the slow creation of this book, it has also been a joy to learn what I think."

For Discussion

1. Why was writing both "scary and exhilarating" for Steele?
2. Despite the "agonies of writing," Steele says, "it has also been a joy to learn what I think." Discuss a time when your own writing helped you explore your thoughts or feelings.

EMILY PRAGER

EMILY PRAGER was first published at age five when the *Houston Post* released her novel *Cinderella Goes to the Ball and Breaks Her Leg*. Born in 1952, she grew up in Houston, Asia, and New York City and graduated from Barnard College with a degree in anthropology. She wrote for *The National Lampoon Magazine*, cowrote and acted in the films *Mr. Mike's Mondo* and *Arena Brains*, and starred for four years in the soap opera *The Edge of Night*. Prager has written humor and social satire for numerous periodicals, collected in *In the Missionary Position* (1999), and she has published four books of fiction: *A Visit from the Footbinder and Other Stories* (1982), *Clea and Zeus Divorce* (1987), *Eve's Tattoo* (1991), and *Roger Fishbite: A Novel* (1999). Her most recent book, nonfiction, is *Wuhu Diary: On Taking My Adopted Daughter to Her Hometown in China* (2001).

Our Barbies, Ourselves

The Barbie doll is just a harmless plaything for little girls, right? Prager suspected not, even when she was a child, and some recent information confirmed her hunch. Using division or analysis, she shows here how Barbie represents a twisted ideal of women. The essay first appeared in *Interview* magazine in 1991.

I read an astounding obituary in the *New York Times* not too long ago. It concerned the death of one Jack Ryan. A former husband of Zsa Zsa Gabor, it said, Mr. Ryan had been an inventor and designer during his lifetime. A man of eclectic creativity, he designed Sparrow and Hawk missiles when he worked for the Raytheon Company, and, the notice said, when he consulted for Mattel he designed Barbie.[1]

If Barbie was designed by a man, suddenly a lot of things made sense to me, things I'd wondered about for years. I used to look at Barbie and wonder, What's wrong with this picture? What kind of woman designed this doll? Let's be honest: Barbie looks like someone who got her start at the Playboy Mansion. She could be a regular guest on *The Howard Stern Show*. It is a fact of Barbie's design that her breasts are so out of proportion to the rest of her body that if she were a human woman, she'd fall flat on her face.

If it's true that a woman didn't design Barbie, you don't know how much saner that makes me feel. Of course, that doesn't ameliorate the damage.

---

[1] After Prager wrote this essay, Barbie's thirty-fifth birthday was the occasion for a "biography" asserting that Ryan did not design the doll from scratch but supervised its evolution from a sophisticated adult doll made in Germany. —EDS.

There are millions of women who are subliminally sure that a thirty-nine-inch bust and a twenty-three-inch waist are the epitome of lovability. Could this account for the popularity of breast implant surgery?

I don't mean to step on anyone's toes here. I loved my Barbie. Secretly, I still believe that neon pink and turquoise blue are the only colors in which to decorate a duplex condo. And like many others of my generation, I've never married, simply because I cannot find a man who looks as good in clam diggers as Ken.

The question that comes to mind is, of course, Did Mr. Ryan design Barbie as a weapon? Because it *is* odd that Barbie appeared about the same time in my consciousness as the feminist movement—a time when women sought equality and small breasts were king. Or is Barbie the dream date of weapons designers? Or perhaps it's simpler than that: Perhaps Barbie is Zsa Zsa if she were eleven inches tall. No matter what, my discovery of Jack Ryan confirms what I have always felt: There is something indescribably masculine about Barbie—dare I say it, phallic. For all her giant breasts and high-heeled feet, she lacks a certain softness. If you asked a little girl what kind of doll she wanted for Christmas, I just don't think she'd reply, "Please, Santa, I want a hard-body."

On the other hand, you could say that Barbie, in feminist terms, is definitely her own person. With her condos and fashion plazas and pools and beauty salons, she is definitely a liberated woman, a gal on the move. And she has always been sexual, even totemic. Before Barbie, American dolls were flat-footed and breastless, and ineffably dignified. They were created in the image of little girls or babies. Madame Alexander was the queen of doll makers in the '50s, and her dollies looked like Elizabeth Taylor in *National Velvet*. They represented the kind of girls who looked perfect in jodhpurs, whose hair was never out of place, who grew up to be Jackie Kennedy—before she married Onassis. Her dolls' boyfriends were figments of the imagination, figments with large portfolios and three-piece suits and presidential aspirations, figments who could keep dolly in the style to which little girls of the '50s were programmed to become accustomed, a style that spasmed with the '60s and the appearance of Barbie. And perhaps what accounts for Barbie's vast popularity is that she was also a '60s woman: into free love and fun colors, anti-class, and possessed of a real, molded boyfriend, Ken, with whom she could chant a mantra.

But there were problems with Ken. I always felt weird about him. He had no genitals, and, even at age ten, I found that ominous. I mean, here was Barbie with these humongous breasts, and that was OK with the toy company. And then, there was Ken with that truncated, unidentifiable lump at his groin. I sensed injustice at work. Why, I wondered, was Barbie designed with such obvious sexual equipment and Ken not? Why was his treated as if it were more mysterious than hers? Did the fact that it was treated as such indicate that somehow his equipment, his essential maleness, was considered more powerful than hers, more worthy of the dignity of concealment? And if the issue in the mind of the toy company was obscenity and its possible damage to children, I still object. How do they think I felt, knowing that no matter how many water beds they slept in, or hot tubs they romped in, or swimming pools they lounged by under the stars, Barbie and Ken could never make love? No matter how much sexuality Barbie possessed, she would never turn Ken on. He would be forever withholding, forever detached. There was a loneliness about Barbie's situation that was always disturbing. And twenty-five years later, movies and videos are still filled with topless women and covered men. As if we're all trapped in Barbie's world and can never escape.

Journal Writing

While growing up, did you play with Barbie or another kind of doll—for instance, baby dolls, action figures like GI Joe, figures based on cartoon or movie characters? In your journal, describe your relationship with such toys, or explain why you never played with them. (To take your journal writing further, see "From Journal to Essay" on the facing page.)

Questions on Meaning

1. Why does Prager say that "suddenly a lot of things made sense" when she discovered that Barbie was designed by a man? Is she referring here only to Barbie's looks?
2. Are we supposed to believe the claims that Prager makes in paragraph 4? What is the point she is trying to make?
3. What is Prager's DEFINITION of a *feminist* in this essay? Where do you find this definition?
4. What is Prager's THESIS?

Questions on Writing Strategy

1. What elements of Barbie does Prager's analysis identify? What new picture of the doll does Prager arrive at as a result?
2. Prager refers to four famous women by name. What does each reference suggest? What is the EFFECT of her using these famous names?
3. Prager poses several RHETORICAL QUESTIONS, such as "Could this account for the popularity of breast implant surgery?" (par. 3), "Or is Barbie the dream date of

weapons designers?" (5), and "Why [. . .] was Barbie designed with such obvious sexual equipment and Ken not?" (7). What is the PURPOSE of these rhetorical questions?

4. **OTHER METHODS.** In her last paragraph Prager COMPARES AND CONTRASTS the ways the toy company depicted the sexuality of Barbie and Ken. What are the differences? What ideas of CAUSE AND EFFECT emerge from this comparison?

Questions on Language

1. Prager notes that Barbie is a product of a time when "small breasts were king" (par. 5). What is the significance of the word *king* in this context?
2. Why does Prager call Barbie "masculine" in paragraph 5? Does this description contradict Prager's view of Barbie as an unattainable and inappropriate feminine ideal?
3. Prager describes dolls' boyfriends before Barbie's Ken as "figments with large portfolios and three-piece suits and presidential aspirations" (par. 6). What are the CONNOTATIONS of this description?
4. Consult your dictionary if any of the following words are unfamiliar: eclectic (par. 1); ameliorate, subliminally, epitome (3); phallic (5); totemic, ineffably, jodhpurs (6); humongous, truncated (7).

Suggestions for Writing

1. **FROM JOURNAL TO ESSAY.** Drawing on your journal entry (facing page) and using your own experiences as EVIDENCE, write an essay that explains the influence of a particular doll or of dolls in general. Your essay may be serious or humorous, but it should include plenty of description and focus on cause and effect.
2. Prager asserts that knowing a man designed Barbie *explains* a lot of problems she always had with Barbie, but it does not *excuse* or *solve* the problems. What new knowledge can you think of that provided a reasonable explanation for a personal problem, while doing nothing to repair the situation? For instance, did you come to understand why your taxes or your rent increased, why you received a disappointing grade in a course, why someone dislikes you, or why a friend is depressed? In an essay, explain the situation, what you now understand about it, and finally, what it would take, in addition to the new information, to solve the problem.
3. **CRITICAL WRITING.** In paragraph 6 Prager suggests, with a tinge of IRONY, several ways to think of Barbie as contributing to the liberation rather than the oppression of women. What do *you* think of Barbie as a role model for girls? Write an essay supporting or refuting Prager's thesis. (If you haven't seen a Barbie doll in a while, you might visit a toy store or borrow a child's.) Is Barbie damaging, as Prager maintains, or liberating, or neither?
4. **CONNECTIONS.** Both Prager and Armin A. Brott, in "Not All Men Are Sly Foxes" (p. 324), examine cultural artifacts that could influence children's ideas of their own and the opposite sex. Consider a cultural artifact that affected you as a child, such as a television show, book, movie, toy, sport, or kind of music. (It may have influenced your views of sex roles but could also have influenced you in

other ways—for instance, by contributing to your values, your interests, your ideas about friendship or adult life.) Write an essay that analyzes your subject, identifying the elements that made it influential.

Emily Prager on Writing

Actually, this section should be titled "Emily Prager on *Reading and* Writing." In the Toronto, Canada, *Globe and Mail,* Prager made a passionate case for both:

As a writer, I worry a lot about literacy in the United States. In part, it's purely selfish. If most US high-school graduates can't read above a Grade 5 level, then I'm out of a job in ten years. Without a young, new audience to keep you on your toes, a writer can go stale. Your arteries can harden. You start writing only for your own generation and then you're like a snake eating its own tail: self-involved to the point of stasis. [. . .]

Americans, given the problems of drugs and dysfunctional school systems, have been left thoroughly, classically illiterate. This, in my estimation, is a form of spiritual bankruptcy—because the ultimate aim of classical literacy (the ability to read and write) is to be able to think, to form ideas, to fantasize goals, to hope, to imagine, to invent and reinvent, to believe in life.

Drugs in school have, of course, contributed mightily to classical illiteracy. By and large, when kids take drugs they do not read. Reading was itself the drug of my generation's childhood. Before we baby boomers found drugs, we read voraciously, addictively. I always say, only half-joking, that if teachers taught reading as the great drug it truly is, kids would want to do it.

But teachers don't. Reading is taught as some dry, dull, meaningless, academic pursuit. No mention is ever made of the high, the physical euphoria and bliss, the fantastic turn-on of intellectual understanding. It seems amazing now that mothers used to fear our reading. Go outside, they'd shout, threatened by our focus and solitude. Little did they know. [. . .]

It is interesting that the United States, with its national emphasis on freedom, should have come to this strange pass, but it has. The average American is, at this point, dubious both about the quality of his life and his sense of personal freedom. He is also desperate to rediscover these things, to find his depth, to relocate some magic and meaning in his existence.

This, television, computers and drug addiction cannot do. Only access to the great thought and history and art of the planet through reading, and the formulation of ideas and the sparking of imagination through writing, can feed the emptiness that we feel. Man cannot live by money and real estate alone.

Fortunately, Americans are easily bored. I somehow feel they might take up reading and writing again just because they're bored with everything else and need a new thrill.

Fine by me. Whatever makes them do it. Readers in their teens never read my books now and that saddens me. But I can live with it if, when I'm sixty, there's a whole crop of literate twenty-year-olds to keep my writing young.

For Discussion

1. What, according to Prager, has caused today's "classical illiteracy"? What can reading and writing provide that "television, computers and drug addiction" cannot?
2. Prager makes some negative GENERALIZATIONS about the teaching of reading today. On the basis of your own experience as a student, do you agree or disagree with these generalizations? Why?
3. How serious do you think Prager is in hoping for improved literacy because it would benefit her own writing (first and last paragraphs)?

JEAN KILBOURNE

JEAN KILBOURNE is a writer, lecturer, and filmmaker who focuses on what she sees as "the dangerous, often enormously dangerous, side effects of advertising"—ads that demean women, for instance, or that encourage addiction to alcohol or cigarettes. Born in Kansas in 1942, Kilbourne received a bachelor's degree from Wellesley College and master's and doctorate degrees in education from Boston University. She spent a few years teaching at a Massachusetts high school and at Emerson College, but her life changed course in 1976 when she ended a nearly twenty-year battle with alcoholism and began addressing her three perpetual concerns: advertising, addiction, and feminism. Kilbourne is a popular speaker who has lectured at more than a third of the colleges and universities in the United States, and she is well known for her documentaries *Killing Us Softly: Advertising's Image of Women* (1979; revised 1999), *A Pack of Lies: The Advertising of Tobacco* (1992), and *Sexual Harassment: Building Awareness on Campus* (1995). She has also written the 1999 book *Can't Buy My Love: How Advertising Changes the Way We Think and Feel* (formerly titled *Deadly Persuasion*). Kilbourne has been a visiting scholar at Wellesley since 1984.

"Can an Engine Pump the Valves in Your Heart?"

In this analysis of the messages in car advertising, Kilbourne finds much that is strange, objectionable, and even laughable. The essay is shortened for *The Bedford Reader* from its original form in *Can't Buy My Love*.

Nowhere is it clearer that advertising encourages us to feel we are in a relationship with our products than in car advertising. "Rekindle the romance," says a newspaper ad for a Jaguar. "Young, breathtaking beauty seeks sophisticated, self-assured individual who likes long drives and lasting relationships." Romance and rebellion are, broadly speaking, the two main themes. The romantic ads tell us the car will make us feel sexy and safe and loved, that it will give us passion and security in a world that is both humdrum and dangerous, and sometimes that it will substitute for human relationships. The rebellious ads emphasize how the car will make us feel tough, in control, free. "Goats understand your need to climb mountains," says an ad for a Toyota truck. "At least, male goats do."

In ad after ad, we are told that buying a car is like falling in love and getting married. "We don't sell cars," a Lexus ad tells us. "We merely facilitate love connections." And an ad for Mercedes-Benz begins, "Buying a car is like

340

getting married. It's a good idea to get to know the family first," while an ad for Acura promises "communication between road and driver that would make even a marriage counselor happy."

A Toyota Paseo ad pictures the car with the headline "Makes a better first 3 impression than your last date." The copy continues, "Finding the 'right' one isn't always easy. You want to be comfortable, have similar tastes and at the same time find it easy to be yourself. Choosing the right car isn't much different." Another ad in the same campaign features a woman standing very happily next to her car, with the copy "Stylish. Responsive. Fun. If it were a man you'd marry it." (Let's not even touch the idea of marrying someone because he's stylish and fun.) The ad continues, "Let's face it, there are a lot of similarities when it comes to choosing a car and a mate. While this may seem surprising to some, even more surprising is that in today's society the chances for a lasting relationship just may be greater with a car. [. . .] Drive the new Paseo. Fall in love." And a 1999 Toyota commercial begins with the camera caressing a car while a woman's sexy voice says, "If a car has its own personality, you'd want it to be soft but strong, frugal, and worthy of your respect." As we see closeups of headlights and cup-holders, the woman continues, "It should remember the little things that are important to you and be reasonable always. Like a best friend, it should be there for you every day."

"Hannah fell in love yesterday," says an ad for Ford Mustang. "Which 4 came as a big surprise to her boyfriend, Rick. But that's the way it's been since '64. Mustang = Love. It's hard to explain. Hannah says it's the spirit. Whatever it is, she loves her new Mustang. Oh, and whatshisname too." It is probably true that our chances for a lasting relationship are greater with our cars than our partners—but surely the solution can't be to fall in love with our cars, to depend on them rather than on each other.

Indeed, the ads tell us our cars are more likely to be true-blue and loyal 5 than our mates. A Honda ad pictures a snazzy red car with the following sentences above it: "It's not you, it's me. I need more space. I'm just going through a stage. I can't go out with one person now. I need a break. I'm not ready for a commitment. Can we just be friends?" The copy below the car says, "Lots of significant others. One car." And a Mazda ad with the tagline "A change from your high maintenance relationships" says, "European good looks. Athletic. Stable. Strong, silent type. Sounds like a good personals ad. Difference is, it's true."

Given the nature of the product, it makes sense that car advertisers mostly 6 sell long-term commitment. Sometimes, however, they offer the automotive equivalent of a one-night stand. Since the beginning, cars have been advertised as a way to impress and seduce women. (As one ad says, "It's not a car. It's an aphrodisiac.") For several years, the car itself has been featured as the

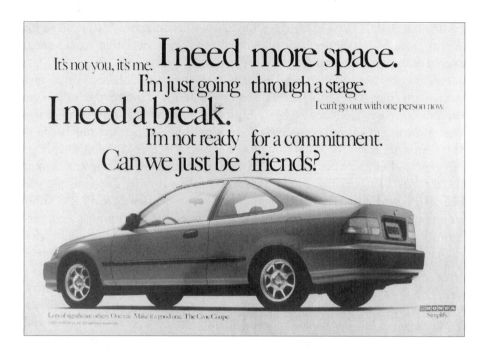

It's not you, it's me. **I need more space.**
I'm just going through a stage.
I need a break. I can't go out with one person now.
I'm not ready for a commitment.
Can we just be friends?

Lots of significant others. One car. Make it a good one. The Civic Coupe.

HONDA Simplify.

driver's passionate lover (in the words of one ad, "What happens when you cross sheet metal and desire"). "Deny yourself an obvious love affair?" asks an Audi ad, featuring a picture of the car. "Didn't you read *Romeo & Juliet?*"

Until recently the car was always symbolized as a woman. A Toyota Celica is described as having "vivacious curves, a shimmering body and [. . .] striking good looks." And Mercedes-Benz ran an ad featuring a photo of Marilyn Monroe's face, with the Mercedes-Benz symbol replacing her famous mole. No words were necessary. It was clear from the image that the car and the sex goddess were somehow one and the same. Sales increased by 35 percent. Vespa, the Italian motorcycle, also exploited Monroe in an ad entitled "Marilyn Vespoe," which features the motorcycle on pink satin sheets.

These days there's more equal opportunity for objectification, so while Mercury suggests we "think of it as a steel bikini," a BMW is advertised with the headline "Imagine Hercules in a steel tuxedo." And a tire ad tells us that "the most potent versions come equipped with Pirelli tires." Robyn Meredith suggests that Detroit's metal has had a sex change operation and describes the Dodge Durango as follows: "Muscles seem to ripple under its shiny sheet metal, causing its fenders to bulge. Its hood is lifted above the brawn, like the short neck of a wrestler rising from beefy trapezius muscles." Nissan's Pathfinder was nicknamed the "hardbody," and designers described the "triceps" around each wheel. Some think the change is due to more women buying cars, others that people have come to think of their cars as bodyguards in a dangerous world.

Countless ads today offer the car not only as a sex symbol, for women as well as for men, but as a substitute for sex. Chevrolet promises that "after Lumina satisfies what you need, it quickly responds to what you want." And an Infiniti ad asks, "What makes you happy? [. . .] Is it the sparkle in a lover's smile? [. . .] Or the warmth of a kiss goodnight? [. . .] But could it be a car?" "Is it wrong to be in love with a car?" asks an ad for the Honda Accord. It continues, "There's no reason to hide your true feelings. The deep, consuming passion you may now be experiencing for the 1999 Accord Coupe is perfectly normal. After all, who could blame you for giving in to the seductive powers of this sleek, sexy automobile?"

"Dim the lights, put on some music, and it's just you and 280 horses," says a Lincoln ad, promising "the perfect setting for an intimate meeting between you, your favorite road and the 280 horses of the Lincoln Mark VIII luxury coupe." And a BMW ad says, "If you do shiver, it'll be from excitement." Exactly what are these ads promising? What is the nature of the intimate meeting? Are we supposed literally to be turned on by the experience of driving these cars (or simply being inside them)? Is it progress that both men and women can now experience the thrill of having sex with their cars? Will people go parking by themselves before long? I can picture cars lined up by a beach on a moonlit night, the drivers in ecstasy, each one alone.

Sometimes people are no longer necessary at all. The passionate relationship is between the car and the sky or the car and the road. "Hugs the road. Kisses the sky," says a Mitsubishi ad, while an Oldsmobile ad tells us, "While some cars can hug the road, very few can actually seduce it." One of the most erotic ads I've ever seen is a 1999 television commercial for BMW. It begins with a sensuous closeup of a car driving along a road. There is no sound but music, and the ad is shot in black and white with a split screen. We see that the car is a convertible and that a man is driving. As the car goes around a curve, the word "Hug" appears on the screen. Next there is a closeup of the wheel against the road and the word "Kiss" appears. And then "Caress." In the climax of the commercial, so to speak, the car whooshes through a dark tunnel, while "The driver loves the car" appears on the screen. Next we see "The car loves the road." And then "The car loves the driver." The message continues to change—"The driver loves the car," and so forth. The commercial is so sexy, I longed for a cigarette ad afterward.

A Lexus campaign, similarly but less breathtakingly, describes sexy encounters between the car and asphalt, the car and a bridge, and so forth. In the print version, the road curves beautifully into the hills and the headline says, "Hug me." The copy continues, "The road is calling. It's a siren song from a sliver of asphalt that crosses the Mississippi. [. . .] The road is stretched before you. How will you embrace it?"

This Lexus campaign also epitomizes the theme of control and compe-   13
tition. One commercial begins with the road breathing, heaving, while a German-accented creepy voice says, "Hi, I'm Autobahn, lord of the highways. Do you think you have what it takes to tame me? Hmm? Do you? Try me. I dare you." The camera caresses the curves of the road and approaches a dark tunnel with a light at the end. A Lexus roars into view. The announcer says, "The all-new ES300. The road is calling. Answer it." As the car zooms away, the road says with an eerie laugh, "Come back. I let you win that time." In a world in which we so often feel powerless, how seductive is this promise of overpowering, not just other drivers but the road itself. We may be locked into our dull jobs, our mortgage payments, our disappointing spouses and needy children, but we become rulers of the world when we get into our cars.

People sometimes feel exempt from the laws of civilized behavior in their cars and thus wield them in a way they would wield no other "weapon." Ads   14
that encourage drivers to break the rules certainly contribute to this attitude. "The engineers of the Pontiac Grand Am see no shame in gutsy driving. Only in timid cars," declares one such ad. The copy continues, "If you're not exactly the shy type on the road, you belong in a Pontiac Grand Am. Because [. . .] it suits your driving style to a 'T.' As in 'tough.' Not as in 'tame.'" And an Audi ad says, "Why push the envelope when you can shred it?"

A 1997 Lexus campaign, introduced just before Halloween, looks like an   15
ad for a slasher film. In one version, the car emerges, as if from flames, from a forest of bare, blackened trees against an orange sky. The copy, in the script of witchcraft and alluding to Shakespeare's *Macbeth*, says:

> Distant thunder, cold as stone,
> a V8 screams down from its throne.
> One by one, each car succumbs.
> Something wicked
> This way comes.

Additional copy describes the car as "a fixture of intimidation" that "seethes within [. . .] the fiercest, fastest automatic sedan in the world." The slogan for this car from hell? "Faster, sleeker, meaner." Of course, this is overkill, so to speak, intended to be funny, ironic, at least on one level. But do we need advertising like this when people are literally killing each other with their cars?

Ad critic Bob Garfield apparently thinks so. He gave the campaign a rave   16
in his column, saying that "the listless, vanilla Lexus is finally imbued with a

fearsome character with which to battle the brawny German competition." Garfield presumably is personifying German cars such as BMW and Mercedes-Benz as the enemy, the competition. It may be precisely this personification of cars that leads to the extreme sensitivity to insult that some drivers feel.

Car ads often encourage this overidentification of owners with their auto-   17
mobiles. "Infiniti. Own one and you'll understand," says an ad featuring a woman asleep outdoors in a sleeping bag, while her car resides inside a spacious tent. Many ads encourage us to feel that the car has a soul as well as a personality. "Born again," says a Toyota ad for used cars. And Chrysler tells us, in an ad picturing a car, "They say the soul lives on. And it does."

"If they made a movie about your life, who would you want to star as your   18
car?" asks an ad for BMW. "You and your M3 are locked in an embrace with the road. Cut to a close-up of your gaping jaw as you feel the power of its engine. [. . .] The two of you ride off into the sunset." Who among us would want a movie about our life to end with us going off into the sunset, alone in our car?

Some ads go even further. The car is no longer a close companion or   19
a lover. It becomes the self. "Can an engine pump the valves in your heart?" asks an ad for Lexus, which features a man's body superimposed on the front of a car. "When was the last time you felt this connected to a car?" the ad

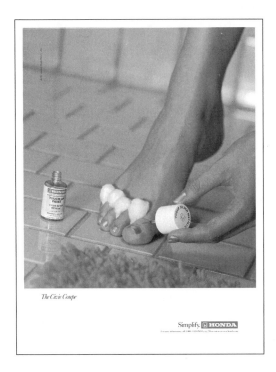

The Civic Coupe

Simplify. HONDA

concludes. Another ad in the campaign features the interior of the car, with a man's hand and arm becoming the gearshift. The copy says, "The symmetry is uncanny. It has a heart. . . . You have a heart. It has a conscience. . . . You have a conscience. [. . .] It's not simply a car you drive, it's one that gets under your skin."

A woman paints her toenails—with silver metallic touch-up paint for a   20
Honda. A British ad for Pirelli tires features Olympic athlete Carl Lewis running over mountains and leaping over rooftops. Toward the end, we see a closeup of his feet and his soles are treaded rubber, like tires. "Power is nothing without control," the announcer tells us.

Do we want the line that separates man from machine to disappear? If a   21
man feels that the car engine is his heart, that the tires are his feet, and that "power is nothing without control," no wonder he overreacts to "disrespectful" or "threatening" moves from another driver.

As always, taken individually, the car ads are funny, silly, exciting, some-   22
times breathtakingly clever, and seemingly insignificant. However, they have a cumulative direction and a cumulative impact. As is the case with many other products, the car in commercials has gone from being a symbol of power to the actual source of power (the engine that pumps the valves in our hearts), from a symbol of sex to an actual lover, from a conduit to relationships to the

important relationship itself, and from a prized possession to the very emblem of oneself. The car ads are an important part of a world in which things are becoming ever more, and people ever less, important.

Journal Writing

In your journal, respond to Kilbourne's analysis of car advertising based on your own experiences with cars. Has driving a car ever been a romantic or a rebellious experience for you? Do you think car ads have influenced your feelings about your own car or other cars? (To take your journal writing further, see "From Journal to Essay" on the next page.)

Questions on Meaning

1. How do assertions in paragraphs 1 and 22 work together as Kilbourne's THESIS? How would you state the thesis?
2. What two main appeals does Kilbourne claim car ads make to drivers? What specific appeals does she identify for each main type?
3. Do you think Kilbourne supports her thesis effectively? Why, or why not?

Questions on Writing Strategy

1. What is the overall framework (or principle of analysis) that Kilbourne uses to analyze car ads?
2. In what different ways does Kilbourne signal the TRANSITIONS among types of car ads?
3. In paragraphs 3, 6, 10, and 22 Kilbourne includes material in parentheses. What different functions do parentheses serve in this essay?
4. In paragraph 10 Kilbourne poses a series of RHETORICAL QUESTIONS. Does she mean for her readers to answer these questions mentally? What is their PURPOSE?
5. **OTHER METHODS.** What other main methods, besides division and analysis, does Kilbourne use to develop her thesis? Why are these other methods essential?

Questions on Language

1. What can you INFER about Kilbourne's attitude toward the language used in the car ads she quotes? What in the essay supports your inference?
2. Although Kilbourne's TONE is generally serious, she does include occasional jokes, such as the one at the end of paragraph 11. What is this joke, and how does it emphasize the point Kilbourne is making?
3. Why does Kilbourne use the phrase "so to speak" in the next to last sentence of paragraph 15?

4. Be sure to consult a dictionary if you are unsure of the meanings of any of these words: humdrum (par. 1); facilitate (2); frugal (3); equivalent, aphrodisiac (6); vivacious (7); objectification, potent (8); siren song (12); epitomizes (13); alluding, intimidation, seethes (15); imbued, personifying (16); superimposed, symmetry (19); cumulative, conduit, emblem (22).

Suggestions for Writing

1. **FROM JOURNAL TO ESSAY.** Take off from your journal entry (previous page) to explore whether and how car advertising has affected your feelings about cars and driving. The messages you've taken from car ads could resemble or differ from the romance and rebellion Kilbourne emphasizes. Or perhaps you believe yourself unaffected by advertising. If so, what makes you immune?
2. In an essay, consider ads for another consumer product—computers, for example, or hair shampoos, skin creams, soft drinks, fast-food restaurants, cellular phone services, or something else. ANALYZE a selection of ads for different brands, using as your principle of analysis the kind of relationships they encourage between their target audience and the product.
3. In paragraphs 14, 15, and 21 Kilbourne mentions that, increasingly, angry drivers use their cars as weapons against other drivers or pedestrians. Do some research about the phenomenon of "road rage," and write an essay explaining the apparent reasons for its increase over the last decade.
4. **CRITICAL WRITING.** EVALUATE the effectiveness of Kilbourne's essay. What do you think of her use of examples? Does she convince you that car ads have a "cumulative impact" that is essentially negative? Why, or why not?
5. **CONNECTIONS.** In "Pornoviolence" (p. 689), Tom Wolfe writes about another aspect of media culture that may influence an audience's self-image as well as social attitudes and behaviors. What ASSUMPTIONS do Wolfe and Kilbourne seem to share or not to share? What is similar and what is different in the main points of these two writers?

JAMAICA KINCAID

JAMAICA KINCAID was born Elaine Potter Richardson in 1949 on the Caribbean island of Antigua. She attended school in Antigua and struggled to become independent of her mother and her place. "I was supposed to be full of good manners and good speech," she has recalled. "Where the hell I was going to go with it I don't know." Kincaid took it to New York, where she went at age seventeen to work as a family helper. She briefly attended Franconia College on a photography scholarship and did odd jobs in New York. In the early 1970s, she became friends with George Trow, a writer for *The New Yorker*. Soon she was contributing to the magazine, and in 1976 she became a staff writer. Soon after, she began writing fiction, producing a collection of stories, *At the Bottom of the River* (1983), and three novels, *Annie John* (1985), *Lucy* (1990), and *The Autobiography of My Mother* (1996) — all based on her own life on Antigua and as an immigrant. Her nonfiction books include *A Small Place* (1988), also about Antigua; *My Brother* (1997), a National Book Award finalist; and *Talk Stories* (2000), a collection of her "Talk of the Town" pieces from *The New Yorker*. An avid gardener, Kincaid has also written *My Garden (Book)* (1999) and edited *My Favorite Plants: Writers and Gardeners on the Plants They Love* (1998). She lives in Vermont.

Girl

This very short story was collected in *At the Bottom of the River*. Much as Judy Brady does in "I Want a Wife" (p. 320), Kincaid analyzes the domain of the title female, both the roles she is expected to fill and the condition of being in her relationship. The writer Stephanie Vaughn has said that Kincaid's story "spills out in a single breath. [. . .] Its exhilarating motion gives me the sense of a writer carried over the precipice by the energy of her own vision."

Wash the white clothes on Monday and put them on the stone heap; wash the color clothes on Tuesday and put them on the clothesline to dry; don't walk barehead in the hot sun; cook pumpkin fritters in very hot sweet oil; soak your little cloths right after you take them off; when buying cotton to make yourself a nice blouse, be sure that it doesn't have gum on it, because that way it won't hold up well after a wash; soak salt fish overnight before you cook it; is it true that you sing benna[1] in Sunday school?; always eat your food in such a way that it won't turn someone else's stomach; on Sundays try to walk like a lady and not like the slut you are so bent on becoming; don't sing benna in Sunday school; you mustn't speak to wharf-rat boys, not even to give directions; don't eat fruits on the street — flies will follow you; *but I don't sing benna*

---

[1] Calypso music. — EDS.

on Sundays at all and never in Sunday school; this is how to sew on a button; this is how to make a buttonhole for the button you have just sewed on; this is how to hem a dress when you see the hem coming down and so to prevent yourself from looking like the slut I know you are so bent on becoming; this is how you iron your father's khaki shirt so that it doesn't have a crease; this is how you iron your father's khaki pants so that they don't have a crease; this is how you grow okra—far from the house, because okra tree harbors red ants; when you are growing dasheen,[2] make sure it gets plenty of water or else it makes your throat itch when you are eating it; this is how you sweep a corner; this is how you sweep a whole house; this is how you sweep a yard; this is how you smile to someone you don't like too much; this is how you smile to someone you don't like at all; this is how you smile to someone you like completely; this is how you set a table for tea; this is how you set a table for dinner; this is how you set a table for dinner with an important guest; this is how you set a table for lunch; this is how you set a table for breakfast; this is how to behave in the presence of men who don't know you very well, and this way they won't recognize immediately the slut I have warned you against becoming; be sure to wash every day, even if it is with your own spit; don't squat down to play marbles—you are not a boy, you know; don't pick people's flowers—you might catch something; don't throw stones at blackbirds, because it might not be a blackbird at all; this is how to make a bread pudding; this is how to make doukona;[3] this is how to make pepper pot; this is how to make a good medicine for a cold; this is how to make a good medicine to throw away a child before it even becomes a child; this is how to catch a fish; this is how to throw back a fish you don't like, and that way something bad won't fall on you; this is how to bully a man; this is how a man bullies you; this is how to love a man, and if this doesn't work there are other ways, and if they don't work don't feel too bad about giving up; this is how to spit up in the air if you feel like it, and this is how to move quick so that it doesn't fall on you; this is how to make ends meet; always squeeze bread to make sure it's fresh; *but what if the baker won't let me feel the bread?;* you mean to say that after all you are really going to be the kind of woman who the baker won't let near the bread?

---

[2] Taro, a tropical plant with an edible tuber.—EDS.
[3] A pudding made of plantains, fruit similar to bananas.—EDS.

Journal Writing

Are the motherly warnings received by the girl of this story anything like the warnings or instructions that were drilled into you when you were a young adolescent? In your journal, explore the advice you remember receiving while growing up. Who took responsibility for instructing you in "proper" behavior? (To take your journal writing further, see "From Journal to Essay" on the next page.)

Questions on Meaning

1. What are the CONNOTATIONS of the phrase "wharf-rat boys"? Why is the girl of the title supposed to avoid them?
2. What does it mean to "be the kind of woman who the baker won't let near the bread" (last line)?
3. What do the elements of the mother's advice add up to: What kind of life does she depict for her daughter?

Questions on Writing Strategy

1. Why do you think Kincaid wrote her story as one long sentence? What does she achieve?
2. What does Kincaid convey through the one comment and one question in italics?
3. Toward the end of this story, the mother says, "this is how to spit up in the air if you feel like it, and this is how to move quick so that it doesn't fall on you." What is the EFFECT of this particular piece of advice? What effect would it have if it were the last line of the story?
4. **OTHER METHODS.** The many obligations of a girl/woman can be CLASSIFIED into groups of skills and behaviors. What categories do you see? How do they help organize the story?

Questions on Language

1. What do the repeated directions about how to "sweep," "smile," and "set a table" suggest?
2. What can you conclude about the girl from the mother's scolding, "don't squat down to play marbles—you are not a boy, you know"?
3. Make sure you know the meanings of the following words: fritters, khaki, okra.
4. The fiction writer Stephanie Vaughn advises reading "Girl" aloud. She says, "I find that it is best to stand up when you read this story aloud, and to take a breath from the deepest region of your belly. When your lungs are full, when your shoulders are back, you begin to speak the story, and then you find that you are singing." Try it yourself. How is reading the story aloud different from reading it to yourself?

Suggestions for Writing

1. **FROM JOURNAL TO ESSAY.** "Adolescents' heads are stuffed with advice intended to make them conform to rigid cultural roles and values." Based on your own experience, do you agree or disagree with this statement? Write an essay explaining your position, using EXAMPLES from your journal entry as support.

2. It's fair to assume that "Girl" is at least partly autobiographical because Kincaid has often written or spoken about the influence of her mother. In "Jamaica Kincaid on Writing" (following), the author mentions rebelling against her mother's "magic." Elsewhere, she has said that her mother's close attention made Kincaid's past "a kind of museum. [. . .] Clearly, the way I became a writer is that my mother wrote my life for me and told it to me." What adult has had a large influence on you? How are you different today because of him or her? Write an essay identifying the parts of yourself that you can attribute to this person—in other words, analyzing yourself as the product of this person's interest (or lack of interest) in you.

3. **CRITICAL WRITING.** The story's speaker repeatedly and gloomily connects her daughter and a "slut." Write an essay analyzing Kincaid's use of *slut*. How does the mother seem to be defining this word? Why does she repeat it so often? Should we ASSUME that the daughter actually is a "slut"? What might be the effect of this repetition on the daughter? What is the effect on you, the reader?

4. **CONNECTIONS.** Judy Brady, in "I Want a Wife" (p. 320), and Kincaid both analyze women's traditional roles, although they have different perspectives on those roles. How are the roles they describe similar? What do the speakers' TONES convey about their attitudes toward their roles? Write an essay explaining how Brady and Kincaid use word choice, sentence structures, repetition, and other elements of tone to clarify their speakers' values and feelings.

Jamaica Kincaid on Writing

In a 1990 interview with Louise Kennedy in the *Boston Globe*, Jamaica Kincaid says that making sense of life is what motivates her writing. "I started out feeling alone," she remarks. "I grew up in a place where I was very alone. I didn't know then that I wanted to write; I didn't have that thought. But even if I had, I would have had no one to tell it to. They would have laughed before they threw me in a pond or something." With this beginning, Kincaid came to believe that the point of writing is not to please the reader. "Sometimes I feel—'I've pushed too far, I don't care, I don't care if you don't like this. I know it and it makes sense to me.'" The point, then, is to understand the world through the self. "I'm trying to discover the secret of myself. [. . .] For me everything passes through the self."

Kincaid's writing helps her come to terms with the conflicts in her life. "I could be dead or in jail. If you don't know how to make sense of what's

happened to you, if you see things but can't express them—it's so painful."
Part of Kincaid's pain growing up was the "magic" her mother held over her, a
power that fueled Kincaid's rebellion. "That feeling of rebellion is doomed,"
she says. "You can't succeed. But it's worth trying because you find out that you
can't. You have to try, or you die."

Although her native Antigua figures strongly in her writing, Kincaid cannot write there. "When I'm in the place where I'm from, I can't really think. I
just absorb it; I take it all in. Then I come back and take it out and unpack it
and walk through it." Her need for distance has led her to live in Vermont,
"the opposite of where I come from. It changes. It's mountainous. It has seasons." As for Antigua, Kincaid says, "I don't know how to live there, but I
don't know how to live without there."

For Discussion

1. How can not caring about the reader's response liberate a writer?
2. What does Kincaid mean by "everything passes through the self"? Do you experience this process from time to time?
3. How does the author view her place of birth? Do you find her last statement
   contradictory?

ADDITIONAL WRITING TOPICS

Division or Analysis

Write an essay by the method of division or analysis using one of the following subjects (or choose your own subject). In your essay, make sure your purpose and your principle of division or analysis are clear to your readers. Explain the parts of your subject so that readers know how each relates to the others and contributes to the whole.

1. The slang or technical terminology of a group such as stand-up comedians or computer hackers
2. An especially bad movie, television show, or book
3. A doll, game, or other toy from childhood
4. A typical TV commercial for a product such as laundry soap, deodorant, beer, or a luxury or economy car
5. An appliance or machine, such as a stereo speaker, a motorcycle, a microwave oven, or a camera
6. An organization or association, such as a social club, a sports league, or a support group
7. The characteristic appearance of a rock singer or a classical violinist
8. A year in the life of a student
9. Your favorite poem
10. A short story, an essay, or another work that made you think
11. The government of your community
12. The most popular video store (or other place of business) in town
13. The Bible
14. A band or an orchestra
15. A painting or statue

Classification in a poster

The anonymous Guerrilla Girls produce posters and other artifacts to "expose sexism and racism in politics, the art world, and the culture at large." In this poster from 1995, the Guerrilla Girls use the method of classification, or sorting into groups, to show the kinds of artists represented at three successive biennial exhibits at the Whitney Museum of American Art in New York City. The 1993 exhibit, the first ever featuring a minority of white male artists, was not a critical success. What does the poster show to have happened at the next exhibit? What do you take to be the Guerrilla Girls' point? (Hint: The misspelling of *Whitney* in the poster's title is deliberate.) What other ways can you think of to classify artists?

10

CLASSIFICATION
Sorting into Kinds

THE METHOD

To CLASSIFY is to make sense of the world by arranging many units—trucks, chemical elements, wasps, students—into more manageable groups. Zoologists classify animals, botanists classify plants—and their classifications help us to understand a vast and complex subject: life on earth. To help us find books in a library, librarians classify books into categories: fiction, biography, history, psychology, and so forth. For the convenience of readers, newspapers run classified advertising, grouping many small ads into categories such as Help Wanted and Cars for Sale.

Subjects and Reasons for Classification

The subject of a classification is always a number of things, such as peaches or political systems. (In contrast, DIVISION or ANALYSIS, the topic of the preceding chapter, usually deals with a solitary subject, a coherent whole, such as *a* peach or *a* political system.) The job of classification is to sort the things into groups or classes based on their similarities and differences. Say, for instance, you're going to write an essay about how people write. After interviewing a lot of writers, you determine that writers' processes differ widely, mainly in the amount of planning and rewriting they entail. (Notice that this determination involves analyzing the process of writing, separating it into steps. See Chap. 8.) On the basis of your findings, you create groups for planners, one-drafters, and rewriters. Once your groups are defined (and assuming they are valid), your subjects (the writers) almost sort themselves out.

Classification is done for a PURPOSE. In a New York City guidebook, Joan Hamburg and Norma Ketay discuss low-priced hotels. (Notice that already they are examining the members of a group: low-priced as opposed to medium- and high-priced hotels.) They cast the low-priced hotels into categories: Rooms for Singles and Students, Rooms for Families, Rooms for Servicepeople, and Rooms for General Occupancy. Always their purpose is evident: to match up the visitor with a suitable kind of room. When a classification has no purpose, it seems a silly and hollow exercise.

Just as you can ANALYZE a subject (or divide a pie) in many ways, you can classify a subject according to many principles. A different New York guidebook might classify all hotels according to price: grand luxury, luxury, commercial, low-priced (Hamburg and Ketay's category), fleabag, and flophouse. The purpose of this classification would be to match visitors to hotels fitting their pocketbooks. The principle you use in classifying things depends on your purpose. A linguist might explain the languages of the world by classifying them according to their origins (Romance languages, Germanic languages, Coptic languages . . .), but a student battling with a college language requirement might try to entertain fellow students by classifying languages into three groups: hard to learn, harder to learn, and unlearnable.

Kinds of Classification

The simplest classification is binary (or two-part), in which you sort things out into (1) those with a certain distinguishing feature and (2) those without it. You might classify a number of persons, let's say, into smokers and nonsmokers, heavy metal fans and nonfans, runners and nonrunners, believers and nonbelievers. Binary classification is most useful when your subject is easily divisible into positive and negative categories.

Classification can be complex as well. As Jonathan Swift reminds us,

> So, naturalists observe, a flea
> Hath smaller fleas that on him prey,
> And these have smaller yet to bite 'em.
> And so proceed *ad infinitum*.

In being faithful to reality, you will sometimes find that you have to sort out the members of categories into subcategories. Hamburg and Ketay did something of the kind when they subclassified the class of low-priced New York hotels. Writing about the varieties of one Germanic language, such as English, a writer could identify the subclasses of British English, North American English, Australian English, and so on.

As readers, we all enjoy watching a clever writer sort things into categories. We like to meet classifications that strike us as true and familiar. This pleasure may account for the appeal of magazine articles that classify things ("The Seven Common Garden Varieties of Moocher," "Five Embarrassing Types of Social Blunder"). Usefulness as well as pleasure may explain the popularity of classifications that EVALUATE things. In a survey of current movies, a newspaper critic might classify the films into categories: "Don't Miss," "Worth Seeing," "So-So," and "Never Mind." The magazine *Consumer Reports* uses this method of classifying in its comments on different brands of stereo speakers or canned tuna. Products are sorted into groups (excellent, good, fair, poor, and not acceptable), and the merits of each are discussed by the method of description. (Of a frozen pot pie: "Bottom crust gummy, meat spongy when chewed, with nondescript old-poultry and stale-flour flavor.")

THE PROCESS

Purposes and Theses

Classification will usually come into play when you want to impose order on a complex subject that includes many items. In one essay in this chapter, for instance, Stephanie Ericsson tackles the lies people tell one another. Sometimes you may use classification humorously, as Russell Baker does in another essay in this chapter, to give a charge to familiar experiences. Whichever use you make of classification, though, do it for a reason. The files of composition instructors are littered with student essays in which nothing was ventured and nothing gained by classification.

Things can be classified into categories that reveal truth, or into categories that don't tell us a thing. To sort out ten US cities according to their relative freedom from air pollution or their cost of living or the degree of progress they have made in civil rights might prove highly informative and useful. Such a classification might even tell us where we'd want to live. But to sort out the cities according to a superficial feature such as the relative size of their cat and dog populations wouldn't interest anyone, probably, except a veterinarian looking for a job.

Your purpose, your THESIS, and your principle of classification will all overlap at the point where you find your interest in your subject. Say you're curious about how other students write. Is your interest primarily in the materials they use (word processor, felt-tip pen, pencil), in where and when they write, or in how much planning and rewriting they do? Any of these could lead to a principle for sorting the students into groups. And that principle should be revealed in your THESIS SENTENCE (or sentences), letting readers know why you are classifying. Here, from the essays in this chapter, are two examples of classification thesis sentences:

> Inanimate objects are classified into three major categories—those that don't work, those that break down and those that get lost. (Russell Baker, "The Plot Against People")

> The primary function of writers, it seems, is to answer readers' questions. These fall into three categories. The third is the one that fascinates me most, but I'll identify the other two first. (Stephen King, "'Ever Et Raw Meat?'")

Categories

For a workable classification, make sure that the categories you choose don't overlap. If you were writing a survey of popular magazines for adults and you were sorting your subject into categories that included women's magazines and sports magazines, you might soon run into trouble. Into which category would you place *Women's Sports*? The trouble is that both categories take in the same item. To avoid this problem, you'll need to reorganize your classification on a different principle. You might sort out the magazines by their audiences: magazines mainly for women, magazines mainly for men, magazines for both women and men. Or you might group them according to subject matter: sports magazines, literary magazines, astrology magazines, fashion magazines, celebrity magazines, trade journals, and so on. *Women's Sports* would fit into either of those classification schemes, but into only *one* category in each scheme.

When you draw up a scheme of classification, be sure also that you include all essential categories. Omitting an important category can weaken the effect of your essay, no matter how well written it is. It would be a major oversight, for example, if you were to classify the residents of a dormitory according to their religious affiliations and not include a category for the numerous nonaffiliated. Your reader might wonder if your sloppiness in forgetting a category extended to your thinking about the topic as well.

Some form of outline can be helpful to keep the classes and their members straight as you develop and draft ideas. You might experiment with a diagram in which you jot down headings for the groups, with plenty of space around them, and then let each heading accumulate members as you think of them, the way a magnet attracts paper clips. This kind of diagram offers more flexibility than a vertical list or outline, and it may be a better aid for keeping categories from overlapping or disappearing.

CHECKLIST FOR REVISING A CLASSIFICATION

✔ **PURPOSE.** Have you classified for a reason? Will readers see why you bothered?

✔ **PRINCIPLE OF CLASSIFICATION.** Will readers also see what rule or principle you have used for sorting individuals into groups? Is this principle apparent in your thesis sentence?

✔ **CONSISTENCY.** Does each representative of your subject fall into one category only, so that categories don't overlap?

✔ **COMPLETENESS.** Have you mentioned all the essential categories suggested by your principle of classification?

✔ **EVIDENCE.** Have you provided enough examples for each category so that readers can clearly distinguish one from another?

CLASSIFICATION IN A PARAGRAPH: TWO ILLUSTRATIONS

Using Classification to Write About Television

Written for *The Bedford Reader*, the following paragraph uses classification to explain how a TV comedy's taped laugh track combines various laughs to sound like an actual rib-tickled audience. With the related paragraph on pages 316–17, which ANALYZES the elements of any particular kind of laugh, this paragraph could be part of a full behind-the-scenes essay on how TV comedies make us laugh, even despite ourselves.

Most canned laughs produced by laugh machines fall into one of five reliable sounds. There are *titters*, light vocal laughs with which an imaginary audience responds to a comedian's least wriggle or grimace. Some producers rely heavily on *chuckles*, deeper, more chesty responses. Most profound of all, *belly laughs* are summoned to acclaim broader jokes and sexual innuendos. When provided at full level of sound and in longest duration, the belly laugh becomes the Big Boffola. There are also *wild howls* or *screamers*, extreme responses used not more than three times per show, lest they seem fake. These are crowd laughs, and yet the machine also offers *freaky laughs*, the piercing, eccentric screeches of solitary kooks. With them, a producer affirms that even a canned audience may include one thorny individualist.

Thesis sentence names principle of classification

Categories:
1. *Titters*
2. *Chuckles*
3. *Belly laughs*

4. *Wild howls or screamers*
5. *Freaky laughs*

Examples clearly distinguish categories

Using Classification in an Academic Discipline

This paragraph comes from a textbook on human physical and cultural evolution. The author offers a standard classification of hand grips in order to explain one of several important differences between human beings and their nearest relatives, apes and monkeys.

There are two distinct ways of holding and using tools: the *power grip* and the *precision grip*, as John Napier termed them. Human infants and children begin with the power grip and progress to the precision grip. Think of how a child holds a spoon: first in the power grip, in its fist or between its fingers and palm, and later between the tips of the thumb and first two fingers, in the precision grip. Many primates have the power grip also. It is the way they get firm hold of a tree branch. But neither a monkey nor an ape has a thumb long enough or flexible enough to be completely *opposable* through rotation at the wrist, able to reach comfortably to the tips of all the other fingers, as is required for our delicate yet strong pre-

Thesis sentence names principle of classification

Two categories explained side by side

Second category explained in greater detail

cision grip. It is the opposability of our thumb and the independent control of our fingers that make possible nearly all the movements necessary to handle tools, to make clothing, to write with a pencil, to play a flute.

— Bernard Campbell, *Humankind Emerging*

CASE STUDY
Using Classification

The summer between his sophomore and junior years of college, Kharron Reid was seeking an internship in computer networking. After seeing several likely openings posted at his school's placement office, he began compiling a résumé that would make him appealing to potential employers.

Part of Reid's challenge in drafting his résumé was to bring order to what seemed a complex and unwieldy subject, his life. The main solution was to classify his activities and interests into clearly defined groups, such as work experience, education, and special skills. Classification wasn't a conscious choice for Reid: He didn't think, "I must classify." Instead, he recognized from advice he'd seen on résumé writing that some sorting was required.

In his first draft, Reid worked to emphasize his qualifications for the internship he sought. The group that gave him the most trouble was work experience: Should he list his jobs with the specifics of each one? Or should he further sort his work experience into skills (such as computer skills, administrative skills, and communication skills) and then list the specifics of his jobs under each subcategory? He tried the résumé both ways and finally opted for the former arrangement, which seemed more straightforward, potentially less confusing to readers.

Before he could prepare his final draft, Reid also needed to decide which to put first, the category of education or the category of work experience. Here, he decided on work experience first because it was directly related to the internships he now sought; his education was more broad based.

Reid's final résumé appears on the facing page. For the cover letter he wrote to go with the résumé, see page 181.

Kharron Reid
137 Chester Street, Apt. E
Allston, MA 02134
(617) 555-4009
kreid@bu.edu

OBJECTIVE
An internship that offers experience in information systems

EXPERIENCE

Pioneer Networking, Damani, MI, May–September 1998

As an intern, worked as a LAN specialist using a Unix-based server
- Connected eight workstations onto a LAN by laying physical platform and configuring software
- Assisted Network Engineer in monitoring operations of LAN

NBS Systems Corp., Denniston, MI, June–September 1997

As an intern, helped install seven WANs using Windows NT Workstation
- Planned layout for WANs
- Installed physical platform and configured servers

SPECIAL SKILLS

Computer proficiency:

Windows 98/XP, Windows NT/2000	QuarkXPress	HTML
Unix	Adobe Photoshop and Pagemaker	XML
Linux	CorelDRAW	JavaScript

Internet research

INTERESTS

Building computers, designing Web sites, wrestling

EDUCATION

Boston University, School of Management, 1997 to present

Current standing: sophomore
Double major: business administration and information systems
Courses: introductory and advanced programming, information systems 1 and 2, basic business courses

Lahser High School, Bloomfield Hills, MI, 1993–1997

Graduated with academic, college-preparatory degree

REFERENCES

Available on request from Office of Career Services, Boston University, 19 Deerfield Street, Boston, MA 02215

RUSSELL BAKER

Russell Baker is one of America's notable humorists and political satirists. Born in 1925 in Virginia, Baker was raised in New Jersey and Maryland by his widowed mother. After serving in the navy during World War II, he earned a BA from Johns Hopkins University in 1947. He became a reporter for the *Baltimore Sun* that year and then joined the *New York Times* in 1954, covering the State Department, the White House, and Congress. From 1962 until his retirement from the *Times* in 1998, he wrote a popular column that ranged over the merely bothersome (unreadable menus) and the serious (the Cold War). Baker has twice received the Pulitzer Prize, once for distinguished commentary and again for the first volume of his autobiography, *Growing Up* (1982). The most recent addition to the autobiography is *Looking Back* (2002). Many of Baker's columns have been collected in books, most recently *There's a Country in My Cellar* (1990). Baker has also written fiction and children's books and edited *Russell Baker's Book of American Humor* (1993). In 1993 he began his television career as host of PBS's *Masterpiece Theatre*.

The Plot Against People

The critic R. Z. Sheppard has commented that Baker can "best be appreciated for doing what a good humorist has always done: writing to preserve his sanity for at least one more day." In this piece from the *New York Times* in 1968, Baker uses classification for that purpose, taking aim, as he has often done, at things.

Inanimate objects are classified into three major categories—those that don't work, those that break down and those that get lost. 1

The goal of all inanimate objects is to resist man and ultimately to defeat him, and the three major classifications are based on the method each object uses to achieve its purpose. As a general rule, any object capable of breaking down at the moment when it is most needed will do so. The automobile is typical of the category. 2

With the cunning typical of its breed, the automobile never breaks down while entering a filling station with a large staff of idle mechanics. It waits until it reaches a downtown intersection in the middle of the rush hour, or until it is fully loaded with family and luggage on the Ohio Turnpike. 3

Thus it creates maximum misery, inconvenience, frustration and irritability among its human cargo, thereby reducing its owner's life span. 4

Washing machines, garbage disposals, lawn mowers, light bulbs, automatic laundry dryers, water pipes, furnaces, electrical fuses, television tubes, hose nozzles, tape recorders, slide projectors—all are in league with the auto- 5 mobile to take their turn at breaking down whenever life threatens to flow smoothly for their human enemies.

Many inanimate objects, of course, find it extremely difficult to break down. Pliers, for example, and gloves and keys are almost totally incapable of breaking down. Therefore, they have had to evolve a different technique for resisting man.   6

They get lost. Science has still not solved the mystery of how they do it, and no man has ever caught one of them in the act of getting lost. The most plausible theory is that they have developed a secret method of locomotion which they are able to conceal the instant a human eye falls upon them.   7

It is not uncommon for a pair of pliers to climb all the way from the cellar to the attic in its single-minded determination to raise its owner's blood pressure. Keys have been known to burrow three feet under mattresses. Women's purses, despite their great weight, frequently travel through six or seven rooms to find hiding space under a couch.   8

Scientists have been struck by the fact that things that break down virtually never get lost, while things that get lost hardly ever break down.   9

A furnace, for example, will invariably break down at the depth of the first winter cold wave, but it will never get lost. A woman's purse, which after all does have some inherent capacity for breaking down, hardly ever does; it almost invariably chooses to get lost.   10

Some persons believe this constitutes evidence that inanimate objects are not entirely hostile to man, and that a negotiated peace is possible. After all, they point out, a furnace could infuriate a man even more thoroughly by getting lost than by breaking down, just as a glove could upset him far more by breaking down than by getting lost.   11

Not everyone agrees, however, that this indicates a conciliatory attitude among inanimate objects. Many say it merely proves that furnaces, gloves and pliers are incredibly stupid.   12

The third class of objects—those that don't work—is the most curious of all. These include such objects as barometers, car clocks, cigarette lighters, flashlights and toy-train locomotives. It is inaccurate, of course, to say that they never work. They work once, usually for the first few hours after being brought home, and then quit. Thereafter, they never work again.   13

In fact, it is widely assumed that they are built for the purpose of not working. Some people have reached advanced ages without ever seeing some of these objects—barometers, for example—in working order.   14

Science is utterly baffled by the entire category. There are many theories about it. The most interesting holds that the things that don't work have attained the highest state possible for an inanimate object, the state to which things that break down and things that get lost can still only aspire.   15

They have truly defeated man by conditioning him never to expect any-   16
thing of them, and in return they have given man the only peace he receives
from inanimate society. He does not expect his barometer to work, his electric
locomotive to run, his cigarette lighter to light or his flashlight to illuminate,
and when they don't it does not raise his blood pressure.

He cannot attain that peace with furnaces and keys and cars and women's   17
purses as long as he demands that they work for their keep.

Journal Writing

What other ways can you think of to classify inanimate objects? In your journal, try
expanding on Baker's categories, or create new categories of your own based on a different principle—for example, objects no student can live without or objects no student would want to be caught dead with. (To take your journal writing further, see
"From Journal to Essay" on the facing page.)

Questions on Meaning

1. What is Baker's THESIS?
2. Why don't things that break down get lost, and vice versa?
3. Does Baker have any PURPOSE other than to make his readers smile?
4. How have inanimate objects "defeated man"?

Questions on Writing Strategy

1. What is the EFFECT of Baker's principle of classification? What categories are
   omitted here, and why?
2. Find three places where Baker uses hyperbole. (See *Figures of speech* in Useful
   Terms if you need a definition.) What is the EFFECT of the hyperbole?
3. How does the essay's INTRODUCTION help set its TONE? How does the CONCLUSION
   reinforce the tone?
4. **OTHER METHODS.** How does Baker use NARRATION to portray inanimate objects
   in the act of "resisting" people? Discuss how these mini-narratives make his classification more persuasive.

Questions on Language

1. Look up any of these words that are unfamiliar: plausible, locomotion (par. 7);
   invariably, inherent (10); conciliatory (12).
2. What are the CONNOTATIONS of the word "cunning" (par. 3)? What is its effect in
   this context?

3. Why does Baker use such expressions as "man," "some people," and "their human enemies" rather than *I* to describe those who come into conflict with inanimate objects? How might the essay have been different if Baker had relied on *I*?

Suggestions for Writing

1. **FROM JOURNAL TO ESSAY.** Write a brief, humorous essay based on one classification system from your journal entry (facing page). It may be helpful to use narration or DESCRIPTION in your classification. FIGURES OF SPEECH, especially hyperbole and understatement, can help you to establish a comic tone.
2. Think of a topic that would not generally be considered appropriate for a serious classification (some examples: game-show winners, body odors, stupid pet tricks, knock-knock jokes). Select a principle of classification and write a brief essay sorting the subject into categories. You may want to use a humorous tone; then again, you may want to approach the topic "seriously," counting on the contrast between subject and treatment to make your IRONY clear.
3. **CRITICAL WRITING.** In a short essay, discuss the likely AUDIENCE for "The Plot Against People." (Recall that it was first published in the *New York Times*.) What can you INFER from his EXAMPLES about Baker's own age and economic status? Does he ASSUME his audience is similar? How do the connections between author and audience help establish the essay's humor? Could this humor be seen as excluding some readers?
4. **CONNECTIONS.** Baker adopts a mock-serious tone here, one that pretends to almost scientific precision. How does Baker's tone COMPARE with the tone Horace Miner adopts in "Body Ritual Among the Nacirema" (p. 301)? What similarities and differences can you detect in each writer's STYLE of presentation? How do you think each writer's sense of his intended audience affected this style?

Russell Baker on Writing

In "Computer Fallout," an essay from the October 11, 1987, *New York Times Magazine*, Baker sets out to prove that computers make a writer's life easier, but he ends up somewhere else entirely. The skillful way he takes us along with him is what makes the journey enjoyable—and perhaps familiar.

The wonderful thing about writing with a computer instead of a typewriter or a lead pencil is that it's so easy to rewrite that you can make each sentence almost perfect before moving on to the next sentence.

An impressive aspect of using a computer to write with

One of the plusses about a computer on which to write

Happily, the computer is a marked improvement over both the typewriter and the lead pencil for purposes of literary composition, due to the ease with which rewriting can be effectuated, thus enabling

What a marked improvement the computer is for the writer over the typewriter and lead pencil

The typewriter and lead pencil were good enough in their day, but if Shakespeare had been able to access a computer with a good writing program

If writing friends scoff when you sit down at the computer and say, "The lead pencil was good enough for Shakespeare

One of the drawbacks of having a computer on which to write is the ease and rapidity with which the writing can be done, thus leading to the inclusion of many superfluous terms like "lead pencil," when the single word "pencil" would be completely, entirely and utterly adequate.

The ease with which one can rewrite on a computer gives it an advantage over such writing instruments as the pencil and typewriter by enabling the writer to turn an awkward and graceless sentence into one that is practically perfect, although it

The writer's eternal quest for the practically perfect sentence may be ending at last, thanks to the computer's gift of editing ease and swiftness to those confronting awkward, formless, nasty, illiterate sentences such as

Man's quest is eternal, but what specifically is it that he quests, and why does he

Mankind's quest is

Man's and woman's quest

Mankind's and womankind's quest

Humanity's quest for the perfect writing device

Eternal has been humanity's quest

Eternal have been many of humanity's quests

From the earliest cave writing, eternal has been the quest for a device that will forever prevent writers from using the word "quest," particularly when modified by such adjectives as "eternal," "endless," "tireless" and

Many people are amazed at the ease

Many persons are amazed by the ease

Lots of people are astounded when they see the nearly perfect sentences I write since upgrading my writing instrumentation from pencil and typewriter to

Listen, folks, there's nothing to writing almost perfect sentences with ease and rapidity provided you've given up the old horse-and-buggy writing mentality that says Shakespeare couldn't have written those great plays if he had enjoyed the convenience of electronic compositional instrumentation.

Folks, have you ever realized that there's nothing to writing almost

Have you ever stopped to think, folks, that maybe Shakespeare could have written even better if

To be or not to be, that is the central focus of the inquiry.

In the intrapersonal relationships played out within the mind as to the relative merits of continuing to exist as opposed to not continuing to exist

Live or die, a choice as ancient as humanities' eternal quest, is a tough choice which has confounded mankind as well as womankind ever since the option of dreaming was first perceived as a potentially negating effect of the quiescence assumed to be obtainable through the latter course of action.

I'm sick and tired of Luddites saying pencils and typewriters are just as good as computers for writing nearly perfect sentences when they—the Luddites, that is—have never experienced the swiftness and ease of computer writing which makes it possible to compose almost perfect sentences in practically no time at

Folks, are you sick and tired of

Are you, dear reader

Good reader, are you

A lot of you nice folks out there are probably just as sick and tired as I am of hearing people say they are sick and tired of this and that and

Listen, people, I'm just as sick and tired as you are of having writers and TV commercial performers who oil me in cornpone politician prose addressed to "you nice folks out

A curious feature of computers, as opposed to pencils and typewriters, is that when you ought to be writing something more interesting than a nearly perfect sentence

Since it is easier to revise and edit with a computer than with a typewriter or pencil, this amazing machine makes it very hard to stop editing and revising long enough to write a readable sentence, much less an entire newspaper column.

For Discussion

1. What is Baker's unstated THESIS? Does he convince you?
2. Do you find yourself ever having the problem Baker finally admits to in the last paragraph?

DEBORAH TANNEN

DEBORAH TANNEN is a linguist who is best known for her popular studies of communication between men and women. Born and raised in New York City, Tannen earned a BA from Harpur College (now the State University of New York at Binghamton); MAs from Wayne State University and the University of California at Berkeley; and a PhD in linguistics from Berkeley. She is University Professor at Georgetown University, has published many scholarly articles and books, and has lectured on linguistics all over the world. But her renown is more than academic: With television talk-show appearances, speeches to businesspeople and senators, and best-selling books like *You Just Don't Understand* (1990) and *Talking from 9 to 5* (1994), Tannen has become, in the words of one reviewer, "America's conversational therapist." Her latest books are *The Argument Culture* (1998) and *I Only Say This Because I Love You* (2001).

But What Do You Mean?

Why do men and women so often communicate badly, if at all? This question motivates much of Tannen's research and writing, including the essay here. Excerpted in *Redbook* magazine from Tannen's book *Talking from 9 to 5*, "But What Do You Mean?" classifies the conversational areas where men and women have the most difficulty.

Conversation is a ritual. We say things that seem obviously the thing to say, without thinking of the literal meaning of our words, any more than we expect the question "How are you?" to call forth a detailed account of aches and pains.

Unfortunately, women and men often have different ideas about what's appropriate, different ways of speaking. Many of the conversational rituals common among women are designed to take the other person's feelings into account, while many of the conversational rituals common among men are designed to maintain the one-up position, or at least avoid appearing one-down. As a result, when men and women interact—especially at work—it's often women who are at the disadvantage. Because women are not trying to avoid the one-down position, that is unfortunately where they may end up.

Here, the biggest areas of miscommunication.

1. Apologies

Women are often told they apologize too much. The reason they're told to stop doing it is that, to many men, apologizing seems synonymous with

372

putting oneself down. But there are many times when "I'm sorry" isn't self-deprecating, or even an apology; it's an automatic way of keeping both speakers on an equal footing. For example, a well-known columnist once interviewed me and gave me her phone number in case I needed to call her back. I misplaced the number and had to go through the newspaper's main switchboard. When our conversation was winding down and we'd both made ending-type remarks, I added, "Oh, I almost forgot—I lost your direct number, can I get it again?" "Oh, I'm sorry," she came back instantly, even though she had done nothing wrong and *I* was the one who'd lost the number. But I understood she wasn't really apologizing; she was just automatically reassuring me she had no intention of denying me her number.

Even when "I'm sorry" *is* an apology, women often assume it will be the   5
first step in a two-step ritual: I say "I'm sorry" and take half the blame, then you take the other half. At work, it might go something like this:

> A: When you typed this letter, you missed this phrase I inserted.
>
> B: Oh, I'm sorry. I'll fix it.
>
> A: Well, I wrote it so small it was easy to miss.

When both parties share blame, it's a mutual face-saving device. But   6
if one person, usually the woman, utters frequent apologies and the other doesn't, she ends up looking as if she's taking the blame for mishaps that aren't her fault. When she's only partially to blame, she looks entirely in the wrong.

I recently sat in on a meeting at an insurance company where the sole   7
woman, Helen, said "I'm sorry" or "I apologize" repeatedly. At one point she said, "I'm thinking out loud. I apologize." Yet the meeting was intended to be an informal brainstorming session, and *everyone* was thinking out loud.

The reason Helen's apologies stood out was that she was the only person   8
in the room making so many. And the reason I was concerned was that Helen felt the annual bonus she had received was unfair. When I interviewed her colleagues, they said that Helen was one of the best and most productive workers—yet she got one of the smallest bonuses. Although the problem might have been outright sexism, I suspect her speech style, which differs from that of her male colleagues, masks her competence.

Unfortunately, not apologizing can have its price too. Since so many   9
women use ritual apologies, those who don't may be seen as hard-edged. What's important is to be aware of how often you say you're sorry (and why), and to monitor your speech based on the reaction you get.

2. Criticism

A woman who cowrote a report with a male colleague was hurt when she   10
read a rough draft to him and he leapt into a critical response — "Oh, that's
too dry! You have to make it snappier!" She herself would have been more
likely to say, "That's a really good start. Of course, you'll want to make it a little
snappier when you revise."

Whether criticism is given straight or softened is often a matter of con-   11
vention. In general, women use more softeners. I noticed this difference when
talking to an editor about an essay I'd written. While going over changes she
wanted to make, she said, "There's one more thing. I know you may not agree
with me. The reason I noticed the problem is that your other points are so
lucid and elegant." She went on hedging for several more sentences until I put
her out of her misery: "Do you want to cut that part?" I asked — and of course
she did. But I appreciated her tentativeness. In contrast, another editor (a
man) I once called summarily rejected my idea for an article by barking, "Call
me when you have something new to say."

Those who are used to ways of talking that soften the impact of criticism   12
may find it hard to deal with the right-between-the-eyes style. It has its own
logic, however, and neither style is intrinsically better. People who prefer criticism given straight are operating on an assumption that feelings aren't
involved: "Here's the dope. I know you're good; you can take it."

3. Thank-Yous

A woman manager I know starts meetings by thanking everyone for com-   13
ing, even though it's clearly their job to do so. Her "thank-you" is simply a
ritual.

A novelist received a fax from an assistant in her publisher's office; it con-   14
tained suggested catalog copy for her book. She immediately faxed him her
suggested changes and said, "Thanks for running this by me," even though her
contract gave her the right to approve all copy. When she thanked the assistant, she fully expected him to reciprocate: "Thanks for giving me such a
quick response." Instead, he said, "You're welcome." Suddenly, rather than an
equal exchange of pleasantries, she found herself positioned as the recipient of
a favor. This made her feel like responding, "Thanks for nothing!"

Many women use "thanks" as an automatic conversation starter and   15
closer; there's nothing literally to say thank you for. Like many rituals typical
of women's conversation, it depends on the goodwill of the other to restore
the balance. When the other speaker doesn't reciprocate, a woman may feel
like someone on a seesaw whose partner abandoned his end. Instead of balancing in the air, she has plopped to the ground, wondering how she got there.

4. Fighting

Many men expect the discussion of ideas to be a ritual fight — explored   16
through verbal opposition. They state their ideas in the strongest possible
terms, thinking that if there are weaknesses someone will point them out, and
by trying to argue against those objections, they will see how well their ideas
hold up.

Those who expect their own ideas to be challenged will respond to   17
another's ideas by trying to poke holes and find weak links — as a way of *help-*
ing. The logic is that when you are challenged you will rise to the occasion:
Adrenaline makes your mind sharper; you get ideas and insights you would
not have thought of without the spur of battle.

But many women take this approach as a personal attack. Worse, they find   18
it impossible to do their best work in such a contentious environment. If
you're not used to ritual fighting, you begin to hear criticism of your ideas as
soon as they are formed. Rather than making you think more clearly, it makes
you doubt what you know. When you state your ideas, you hedge in order to
fend off potential attacks. Ironically, this is more likely to *invite* attack because
it makes you look weak.

Although you may never enjoy verbal sparring, some women find it help-   19
ful to learn how to do it. An engineer who was the only woman among four
men in a small company found that as soon as she learned to argue she was
accepted and taken seriously. A doctor attending a hospital staff meeting
made a similar discovery. She was becoming more and more angry with a male
colleague who'd loudly disagreed with a point she'd made. Her better judgment told her to hold her tongue, to avoid making an enemy of this powerful
senior colleague. But finally she couldn't hold it in any longer, and she rose to
her feet and delivered an impassioned attack on his position. She sat down in
a panic, certain she had permanently damaged her relationship with him. To
her amazement, he came up to her afterward and said, "That was a great rebuttal. I'm really impressed. Let's go out for a beer after work and hash out our
approaches to this problem."

5. Praise

A manager I'll call Lester had been on his new job six months when he   20
heard that the women reporting to him were deeply dissatisfied. When he
talked to them about it, their feelings erupted; two said they were on the verge
of quitting because he didn't appreciate their work, and they didn't want to
wait to be fired. Lester was dumbfounded: He believed they were doing a fine
job. Surely, he thought, he had said nothing to give them the impression he
didn't like their work. And indeed he hadn't. That was the problem. He had

said *nothing*—and the women assumed he was following the adage "If you can't say something nice, don't say anything." He thought he was showing confidence in them by leaving them alone.

Men and women have different habits in regard to giving praise. For ex-   21
ample, Deirdre and her colleague William both gave presentations at a conference. Afterward, Deirdre told William, "That was a great talk!" He thanked
her. Then she asked, "What did you think of mine?" and he gave her a lengthy
and detailed critique. She found it uncomfortable to listen to his comments.
But she assured herself that he meant well, and that his honesty was a signal
that she, too, should be honest when he asked for a critique of his performance.
As a matter of fact, she had noticed quite a few ways in which he could have
improved his presentation. But she never got a chance to tell him because he
never asked—and she felt put down. The worst part was that it seemed she had
only herself to blame, since she *had* asked what he thought of her talk.

But had she really asked for his critique? The truth is, when she asked for   22
his opinion, she was expecting a compliment, which she felt was more or less
required following anyone's talk. When he responded with criticism, she figured, "Oh, he's playing 'Let's critique each other'"—not a game she'd initiated, but one which she was willing to play. Had she realized he was going to
criticize her and not ask her to reciprocate, she would never have asked in the
first place.

It would be easy to assume that Deirdre was insecure, whether she was   23
fishing for a compliment or soliciting a critique. But she was simply talking
automatically, performing one of the many conversational rituals that allow us
to get through the day. William may have sincerely misunderstood Deirdre's
intention—or may have been unable to pass up a chance to one-up her when
given the opportunity.

6. Complaints

"Troubles talk" can be a way to establish rapport with a colleague. You   24
complain about a problem (which shows that you are just folks) and the other
person responds with a similar problem (which puts you on equal footing). But
while such commiserating is common among women, men are likely to hear it
as a request to *solve* the problem.

One woman told me she would frequently initiate what she thought   25
would be pleasant complaint-airing sessions at work. She'd talk about situations that bothered her just to talk about them, maybe to understand them
better. But her male office mate would quickly tell her how she could improve
the situation. This left her feeling condescended to and frustrated. She was
delighted to see this very impasse in a section in my book *You Just Don't*

Understand, and showed it to him. "Oh," he said, "I see the problem. How can we solve it?" Then they both laughed, because it had happened again: He short-circuited the detailed discussion she'd hoped for and cut to the chase of finding a solution.

Sometimes the consequences of complaining are more serious: A man   26
might take a woman's lighthearted griping literally, and she can get a reputation as a chronic malcontent. Furthermore, she may be seen as not up to solving the problems that arise on the job.

7. Jokes

I heard a man call in to a talk show and say, "I've worked for two women   27
and neither one had a sense of humor. You know, when you work with men, there's a lot of joking and teasing." The show's host and the guest (both women) took his comment at face value and assumed the women this man worked for were humorless. The guest said, "Isn't it sad that women don't feel comfortable enough with authority to see the humor?" The host said, "Maybe when more women are in authority roles, they'll be more comfortable with power." But although the women this man worked for *may* have taken themselves too seriously, it's just as likely that they each had a terrific sense of humor, but maybe the humor wasn't the type he was used to. They may have been like the woman who wrote to me: "When I'm with men, my wit or cleverness seems inappropriate (or lost!) so I don't bother. When I'm with my women friends, however, there's no hold on puns or cracks and my humor is fully appreciated."

The types of humor women and men tend to prefer differ. Research has   28
shown that the most common form of humor among men is razzing, teasing, and mock-hostile attacks, while among women it's self-mocking. Women often mistake men's teasing as genuinely hostile. Men often mistake women's mock self-deprecation as truly putting themselves down.

Women have told me they were taken more seriously when they learned   29
to joke the way the guys did. For example, a teacher who went to a national conference with seven other teachers (mostly women) and a group of administrators (mostly men) was annoyed that the administrators always found reasons to leave boring seminars, while the teachers felt they had to stay and take notes. One evening, when the group met at a bar in the hotel, the principal asked her how one such seminar had turned out. She retorted, "As soon as you left, it got much better." He laughed out loud at her response. The playful insult appealed to the men—but there was a trade-off. The women seemed to back off from her after this. (Perhaps they were put off by her using joking to align herself with the bosses.)

There is no "right" way to talk. When problems arise, the culprit may be   30
style differences—and *all* styles will at times fail with others who don't share
or understand them, just as English won't do you much good if you try to speak
to someone who knows only French. If you want to get your message across,
it's not a question of being "right"; it's a question of using language that's
shared—or at least understood.

Journal Writing

Tannen's ANECDOTE about the newspaper columnist (par. 4) illustrates that much of
what we say is purely automatic. Do you excuse yourself when you bump into inanimate objects? When someone says, "Have a good trip," do you answer, "You too," even
if the other person isn't going anywhere? Do you find yourself overusing certain words
or phrases such as "like" or "you know"? Pay close attention to these kinds of verbal
tics in your own and others' speech. Over the course of a few days, note as many of
them as you can in your journal. (To take your journal writing further, see "From Journal to Essay" on the facing page.)

Questions on Meaning

1. What is Tannen's PURPOSE in writing this essay? What does she hope it will
   accomplish?
2. What does Tannen mean when she writes, "Conversation is a ritual" (par. 1)?
3. What does Tannen see as the fundamental difference between men's and
   women's conversational strategies?
4. Why is "You're welcome" not always an appropriate response to "Thank you"?

Questions on Writing Strategy

1. This essay has a large cast of characters: twenty-three to be exact. What function
   do these characters serve? How does Tannen introduce them to the reader? Does
   she describe them in sufficient detail?
2. How does Tannen's DESCRIPTION of a columnist as "well-known" (par. 4) contribute to the effectiveness of her EXAMPLE?
3. Whom does Tannen see as her primary AUDIENCE? ANALYZE her use of the pronoun *you* in paragraphs 9 and 19. Whom does she seem to be addressing here?
   Why?
4. **OTHER METHODS.** For each of her seven areas of miscommunication, Tannen
   COMPARES AND CONTRASTS male and female communication styles and strategies.
   SUMMARIZE the main source of misunderstanding in each area.

Questions on Language

1. What is the EFFECT of "I put her out of her misery" (par. 11)? What does this phrase usually mean?
2. What does Tannen mean by a "right-between-the-eyes style" (par. 12)? What is the FIGURE OF SPEECH involved here?
3. What is the effect of Tannen's use of figurative verbs, such as "barking" (par. 11) and "erupted" (20)? Find at least one other example of the use of a verb in a non-literal sense.
4. Look up any of the following words whose meanings you are unsure of: synonymous, self-deprecating (par. 4); lucid, tentativeness (11); intrinsically (12); reciprocate (14); adrenaline, spur (17); contentious, hedge (18); sparring, rebuttal (19); adage (20); soliciting (23); commiserating (24); initiate, condescended, impasse (25); chronic, malcontent (26); razzing (28); retorted (29).

Suggestions for Writing

1. **FROM JOURNAL TO ESSAY.** Write an essay classifying the examples from your journal entry (previous page) into categories of your own devising. You might sort out the examples by context ("phone blunders," "faulty farewells"), by purpose ("nervous tics," "space fillers"), or by some other principle of classification. Given your subject matter, you might want to adopt a humorous TONE.
2. How well does your style of communication conform to that of your gender as described by Tannen? Write a short essay about a specific communication problem or misunderstanding you have had with someone of the opposite sex (sibling, friend, parent, significant other). How well does Tannen's differentiation of male and female communication styles account for your particular problem?
3. How true do you find Tannen's assessment of miscommunication between the sexes? Consider the conflicts you have observed between your parents, among fellow students or coworkers, in fictional portrayals in books and movies. Are Tannen's conclusions confirmed or called into question by your own observations and experiences? Write an essay confirming or questioning Tannen's GENERALIZATIONS, using your own examples.
4. **CRITICAL WRITING.** Tannen insists that "neither [communication] style is intrinsically better" (par. 12), that "There is no 'right' way to talk" (30). What do you make of this refusal to take sides in the battle of the sexes? Is Tannen always successful? Is absolute neutrality possible, or even desirable, when it comes to such divisive issues?
5. **CONNECTIONS.** What pictures of men and women emerge from Tannen's essay and from Dave Barry's "Batting Clean-Up and Striking Out" (p. 229)? In an essay, DEFINE each sex as portrayed by these two authors, and then agree or disagree with the definitions. Support your opinions with examples from your own observations and experience.

Deborah Tannen on Writing

Though Deborah Tannen's "But What Do You Mean?" is written for a general audience, Tannen is a linguistics scholar who does considerable academic writing. One debate among scholarly writers is whether it is appropriate to incorporate one's experiences and biases into academic writing, especially given the goal of objectivity in conducting and reporting research. The October 1996 *PMLA* (*Publications of the Modern Language Association of America*) printed a discussion of the academic uses of the personal, with contributions from more than two dozen scholars. Tannen's comments, excerpted here, focused on the first-person *I*.

When I write academic prose, I use the first person, and I instruct my students to do the same. The principle that researchers should acknowledge their participation in their work is an outgrowth of a humanistic approach to linguistic analysis. [. . .] Understanding discourse is not a passive act of decoding but a creative act of imagining a scene (composed of people engaged in culturally recognizable activities) within which the ideas being talked about have meaning. The listener's active participation in sense making both results from and creates interpersonal involvement. For researchers to deny their involvement in their interpreting of discourse would be a logical and ethical violation of this framework. [. . .]

[O]bjectivity in the analysis of interactions is impossible anyway. Whether they took part in the interaction or not, researchers identify with one or another speaker, are put off or charmed by the styles of participants. This one reminds you of a cousin you adore; that one sounds like a neighbor you despise. Researchers are human beings, not atomic particles or chemical elements. [. . .]

Another danger of claiming objectivity rather than acknowledging and correcting for subjectivity is that scholars who don't reveal their participation in interactions they analyze risk the appearance of hiding it. "Following is an exchange that occurred between a professor and a student," I have read in articles in my field. The speakers are identified as "A" and "B." The reader is not told that the professor, A (of course the professor is A and the student B), is the author. Yet that knowledge is crucial to contextualizing the author's interpretation. Furthermore, the impersonal designations A and B are another means of constructing a false objectivity. They obscure the fact that human interaction is being analyzed, and they interfere with the reader's understanding. The letters replace what in the author's mind are names and voices and personas that are the basis for understanding the discourse. Readers, given only initials, are left to scramble for understanding by imagining people in place of letters.

Avoiding self-reference by using the third person also results in the depersonalization of knowledge. Knowledge and understanding do not occur in abstract isolation. They always and only occur among people. [. . .] Denying that scholarship is a personal endeavor entails a failure to understand and correct for the inevitable bias that human beings bring to all their enterprises.

For Discussion

1. In arguing for the use of the first-person *I* in academic prose, Tannen is speaking primarily about its use in her own field, linguistics. From your experience with academic writing, is Tannen's argument applicable to other disciplines as well, such as history, biology, psychology, or government? Why, or why not? What have your teachers in various courses advised you about writing in the first person?

2. Try this experiment on the effects of the first person and third person (*he, she, they*): Write a passage of academic prose in one person or the other. (Tannen's example of professor A and student B can perhaps suggest a direction for your passage, or you may have one already written in a paper you've submitted.) Rewrite the passage in the other person, and ANALYZE the two versions. Does one sound more academic than the other? What are the advantages and disadvantages of each one?

STEPHEN KING

A prolific and hugely popular master of horror and dread, STEPHEN KING has written more than thirty books in the twenty-plus years he has been publishing. He was born in Portland, Maine, in 1947 and grew up in Indiana, Connecticut, and Maine, where he has lived for most of his adult life. He graduated in 1970 from the University of Maine at Orono, worked in an industrial laundry, and taught high-school English before the sales of his books allowed him to write full-time. Among King's best-known novels are *Carrie* (1974), *The Shining* (1977), *The Dead Zone* (1979), *Misery* (1987), and *Dolores Claiborne* (1992)—all of them also made into movies. His own screenplays include *Creepshow* (1982) and *Pet Sematary* (1987, from the 1985 novel). King has also published several books under the pen name Richard Bachman, most recently *The Regulators* (1996). His latest projects under his own name are the novels *Dreamcatcher* and *Black House* (both 2001), the story collection *Everything's Eventual* (2002), and the nonfiction book *On Writing: A Memoir of the Craft* (2000).

"Ever Et Raw Meat?"

King's books have sold nearly 100 million copies, and his readers are naturally curious about him. In this essay published in the *New York Times Book Review* in 1987, King reveals that he finds the public's interest sometimes gratifying, sometimes annoying, and sometimes very funny.

It seems to me that, in the minds of readers, writers actually exist to serve two purposes, and the more important may not be the writing of books and stories. The primary function of writers, it seems, is to answer readers' questions. These fall into three categories. The third is the one that fascinates me most, but I'll identify the other two first.

The One-of-a-Kind Questions

Each day's mail brings a few of these. Often they reflect the writer's field of interest—history, horror, romance, the American West, outer space, big business. The only thing they have in common is their uniqueness. Novelists are frequently asked where they get their ideas (see category No. 2), but writers must wonder where this relentless curiosity, these really strange questions, come from.

There was, for instance, the young woman who wrote to me from a penal institution in Minnesota. She informed me she was a kleptomaniac. She further informed me that I was her favorite writer, and she had stolen every one

382

of my books she could get her hands on. "But after I stole *Different Seasons* from the library and read it, I felt moved to send it back," she wrote. "Do you think this means you wrote this one the best?" After due consideration, I decided that reform on the part of the reader has nothing to do with artistic merit. I came close to writing back to find out if she had stolen *Misery* yet but decided I ought to just keep my mouth shut.

From Bill V. in North Carolina: "I see you have a beard. Are you morbid   4
of razors?"

From Carol K. in Hawaii: "Will you soon write of pimples or some other   5
facial blemish?"

From Don G., no address (and a blurry postmark): "Why do you keep up   6
this disgusting mother worship when anyone with any sense knows a MAN has no use to his mother once he is weaned?"

From Raymond R. in Mississippi: "Ever et raw meat?" (It's the laconic   7
ones like this that really get me.)

I have been asked if I beat my children and/or my wife. I have been asked   8
to parties in places I have never been and hope never to go. I was once asked to give away the bride at a wedding, and one young woman sent me an ounce of pot, with the attached question: "This is where I get my inspiration — where do you get yours?" Actually, mine usually comes in envelopes — the kind through which you can view your name and address printed by a computer — that arrive at the end of every month.

My favorite question of this type, from Anchorage, asked simply: "How   9
could you write such a why?" Unsigned. If E. E. Cummings[1] were still alive, I'd try to find out if he'd moved to the Big North.

The Old Standards

These are the questions writers dream of answering when they are col-   10
lecting rejection slips, and the ones they tire of quickest once they start to publish. In other words, they are the questions that come up without fail in every dull interview the writer has ever given or will ever give. I'll enumerate a few of them:

Where do you get your ideas? (I get mine in Utica.)   11

How do you get an agent? (Sell your soul to the Devil.)   12

Do you have to know somebody to get published? (Yes; in fact, it helps to   13
grovel, toady, and be willing to perform twisted acts of sexual depravity at a moment's notice, and in public if necessary.)

---

[1] E. E. Cummings (1894–1962) was an American poet noted for wordplay like that in the question King quotes. — EDS.

How do you start a novel? (I usually start by writing the number 1 in the   14
upper right-hand corner of a clean sheet of paper.)

How do you write best sellers? (Same way you get an agent.)   15

How do you sell your book to the movies? (Tell them they don't want it.)   16

What time of day do you write? (It doesn't matter; if I don't keep busy   17
enough, the time inevitably comes.)

Do you ever run out of ideas? (Does a bear defecate in the woods?)   18

Who is your favorite writer? (Anyone who writes stories I would have   19
written had I thought of them first.)

There are others, but they're pretty boring, so let us march on.   20

The Real Weirdies

Here I am, bopping down the street, on my morning walk, when some guy   21
pulls over in his pickup truck or just happens to walk by and says, "Hi, Steve!
Writing any good books lately?" I have an answer for this; I've developed it
over the years out of pure necessity. I say, "I'm taking some time off." I say that
even if I'm working like mad, thundering down homestretch on a book. The
reason *why* I say this is because no other answer seems to fit. Believe me, I
know. In the course of the trial and error that has finally resulted in "I'm taking some time off," I have discarded about 500 other answers.

Having an answer for "You writing any good books lately?" is a good thing,   22
but I'd be lying if I said it solves the problem of *what the question means*. It is
this inability on my part to make sense of this odd query, which reminds me of
that Zen riddle—"Why is a mouse when it runs?"—that leaves me feeling
mentally shaken and impotent. You see, it isn't just *one* question; it is a *bundle*
of questions, cunningly wrapped up in one package. It's like that old favorite,
"Are you still beating your wife?"

If I answer in the affirmative, it means I may have written—how many   23
books? two? four?—(all of them good) in the last—how long? Well, how long
is "lately"? It could mean I wrote maybe three good books just last week, or
maybe two *on this very walk up to Bangor International Airport and back!* On the
other hand, if I say no, what does *that* mean? I wrote three or four *bad* books in
the last "lately" (surely "lately" can be no longer than a month, six weeks at
the outside)?

Or here I am, signing books at the Betts' Bookstore or B. Dalton's in the   24
local consumer factory (nicknamed "the mall"). This is something I do twice
a year, and it serves much the same purpose as those little bundles of twigs
religious people in the Middle Ages used to braid into whips and flagellate
themselves with. During the course of this exercise in madness and self-
abnegation, at least a dozen people will approach the little coffee table where

I sit behind a barrier of books and ask brightly, "Don't you wish you had a rubber stamp?"

I have an answer to this one, too, an answer that has been developed over   25
the years in a trial-and-error method similar to "I'm taking some time off."
The answer to the rubber stamp question is: "No, I don't mind."

Never mind if I really do or don't (this time it's my own motivations I   26
want to skip over, you'll notice); the question is, Why does such an illogical
query occur to so many people? My signature is actually stamped on the covers of several of my books, but people seem just as eager to get these signed as
those that aren't so stamped. Would these questioners stand in line for the
privilege of watching me slam a rubber stamp down on the title page of *The
Shining* or *Pet Sematary*? I don't think they would.

If you still don't sense something peculiar in these questions, this one   27
might help convince you. I'm sitting in the cafe around the corner from my
house, grabbing a little lunch by myself and reading a book (reading at the
table is one of the few bad habits acquired in my youth that I have nobly
resisted giving up) until a customer or maybe even a waitress sidles up and
asks, "How come you're not reading one of your own books?"

This hasn't happened just once, or even occasionally; it happens *a lot*.   28
The computer-generated answer to this question usually gains a chuckle,
although it is nothing but the pure, logical and apparent truth. "I know how
they all come out," I say. End of exchange. Back to lunch, with only a pause to
wonder why people assume you want to read what you wrote, rewrote, read
again following the obligatory editorial conference and yet again during the
process of correcting the mistakes that a good copyeditor always prods,
screaming, from their hiding places (I once heard a crime writer suggest that
God could have used a copyeditor, and while I find the notion slightly blasphemous, I tend to agree).

And then people sometimes ask in that chatty, let's-strike-up-a-conversation   29
way people have, "How long does it take you to write a book?" Perfectly reasonable question—at least until you try to answer it and discover there *is*
no answer. This time the computer-generated answer is a total falsehood, but
it at least serves the purpose of advancing the conversation to some more discussable topic. "Usually about nine months," I say, "the same length of time
it takes to make a baby." This satisfies everyone but me. I know that nine
months is just an average, and probably a completely fictional one at that.
It ignores *The Running Man* (published under the name Richard Bachman),
which was written in four days during a snowy February vacation when I was
teaching high school. It also ignores *It* and my latest, *The Tommyknockers*. *It* is
over 1,000 pages long and took four years to write. *The Tommyknockers* is 400
pages shorter but took five years to write.

Do I mind these questions? Yes . . . and no. Anyone minds questions that   30
have no real answers and thus expose the fellow being questioned to be not a
real doctor but a sort of witch doctor. But no one—at least no one with a
modicum of simple human kindness—resents questions from people who
honestly want answers. And now and then someone will ask a really interesting question, like, Do you write in the nude? The answer—not generated by
computer—is: I don't think I ever have, but if it works, I'm willing to try it.

Journal Writing

Do you sympathize with King's attitude toward the questions he is asked by fans?
What are some questions you have been asked that you found either unanswerable or
unbearably tedious? Were they asked when you were in school or on a job? by younger
or older relatives? by an acquaintance who drove you crazy? by people you were meeting for the first time? Write down as many such questions as you can think of. (To take
your journal writing further, see "From Journal to Essay" on the facing page.)

Questions on Meaning

1. What is the THESIS of this essay? Why do you think King wrote it: to entertain
   readers? to gain sympathy for himself? to discourage readers from writing to him?
   some other reason? Explain your answer.
2. What is so "peculiar" about the questions King calls the "real weirdies" (pars.
   21–29)?
3. In paragraph 24 King draws a comparison between his signing of books and the
   self-flagellation (self-whipping) by people in the Middle Ages. What does he
   mean by this ANALOGY?

Questions on Writing Strategy

1. How does King distinguish the types of questions in the three categories of his
   classification? What, specifically, sets the questions in each category apart from
   those in the other two?
2. What is King's relationship with his AUDIENCE in this essay? How do you know?
   Recall that he wrote the essay for the *New York Times Book Review* and so could
   expect a well-educated and well-read audience.
3. How does King's concluding paragraph modify his response to readers' questions?
4. **OTHER METHODS.** How do King's many EXAMPLES work to illustrate his GENERAL-
   IZATION that the "primary function of writers, it seems, is to answer readers' questions" (par. 1)? What do all the examples have in common?

Questions on Language

1. Make sure you know the meanings of the following words: kleptomaniac (par. 3); morbid (4); weaned (6); laconic (7); enumerate (10); grovel, depravity (13); defecate (18); impotent (22); affirmative (23); self-abnegation (24); sidles (27); obligatory, blasphemous (28); modicum (30).
2. King directly addresses his readers at certain points—for instance, "Believe me" (par. 21), "You see" (22), "you'll notice" (26), and "If you still don't sense something peculiar" (27). Why do you think he addresses readers? What is the EFFECT?
3. In paragraphs 28–30 King mentions the "computer-generated answer" to some of the questions he has been asked. What does he mean by this metaphor? (See *Figures of speech* in Useful Terms for a definition of *metaphor*.)

Suggestions for Writing

1. **FROM JOURNAL TO ESSAY.** Develop your journal entry (previous page) into an essay in which you classify the questions you've been asked according to some clear principle—for instance, whether the questions are obvious, obscure, or off-the-wall; whether they are more often asked by men, women, or children; or whether they are innocent, prying, or simply rude. Like King, try to give each category an identifying label.
2. Teachers often tell us that the only stupid question is the one we don't ask. But King seems to think there are lots of stupid questions that unfortunately *do* get asked. Is there such a thing as a stupid question? How do you identify one?
3. **CRITICAL WRITING.** One might reasonably claim that those who are famous owe something to the fans who made them popular. Write an essay on this claim, using King as an extended example. Does King have an obligation to his fans? If so, does he live up to it? Use his work as EVIDENCE for your answers, including his fiction as well as "'Ever Et Raw Meat?'"
4. **CONNECTIONS.** Stephanie Ericsson, in "The Ways We Lie" (p. 389), suggests that lies can help us maintain a sense of being connected to others in good ways. King implies that questions to famous writers may do the same. After reading Ericsson's essay, write an essay of your own that examines how lies and questions may work as social glue. Consider all possible positions—lying versus being lied to, asking questions versus answering them. Is the sense of connection one-sided? Why, or why not?

Stephen King on Writing

The impressive publishing record of Stephen King depends on his regular writing habits. In 1992 he told W. C. Stoby of *Writer's Digest* that he works "four, four-and-a-half hours a day, seven days a week." It may be surprising, then, that King faces the same demons of procrastination that most of us do.

"For me," King says, "a lot of times the real barrier to getting to work — to getting to the typewriter or the word processor — comes before I get there. I had one of those days today when I thought to myself, 'I'm not sure if I can do this.' I have lot of days like that. I think it's kind of funny, really, that people think, 'Well, you're Stephen King; that doesn't happen to you,' as if I wasn't really the same as everybody else."

On the day in question King avoided getting to work by reading the sports page twice and working out at the Y. Eventually, though, he sat down to work. "And then," he says, "there's always those first few things where you feel awkward and there's a feeling of being in a medium where you don't precisely belong. But then you acclimate. There's nothing really very magical about it. If you've done it day in and day out, the cylinders all sort of fire over. I think the best trick is experience. After you've done that a certain amount of time, you know that it's going to get better."

In a 1991 interview, this time with Bill Goldstein of *Publishers Weekly,* King talked of his audience in a way that helps explain some of the attitudes toward readers expressed in "'Ever Et Raw Meat?'" "If the stuff you're writing is not for yourself, it won't work. I feel a certain pressure about my writing, and I have an idea of who reads my books; I am concerned with my readership. But it's kind of a combination love letter/poison-pen relationship, a sweet-and-sour thing. [. . .] I feel I ought to write something because people want to read something. But I think, 'Don't give them what they want — give them what *you* want.'"

For Discussion

1. King writes fiction mostly. Do you think his ideas on overcoming procrastination and thinking about readers have any relevance to writing nonfiction such as college papers? Why, or why not?
2. If King writes for himself more than for his readers, how do you think he manages to appeal to so many readers?

STEPHANIE ERICSSON

STEPHANIE ERICSSON is an insightful and frank writer who composes out of her own life. Her book on loss, *Companion Through the Darkness: Inner Dialogues on Grief* (1993), grew out of journal entries and extensive research into the grieving process following the sudden death of her husband while she was pregnant. Ericsson was born in 1953, grew up in San Francisco, and began writing at the age of fifteen. After studying filmmaking in college, she became a screenwriter's assistant and later a writer of situation comedies and advertising. During these years she struggled with substance abuse; after her recovery in 1980 she published *Shamefaced* and *Women of AA: Recovering Together* (both 1985). *Companion into the Dawn: Inner Dialogues on Loving* (1994) is Ericsson's most recent book. She lives in Saint Paul, Minnesota, with her two children.

The Ways We Lie

Ericsson wrote this essay from notes for *Companion into the Dawn*, and it was published in the *Utne Reader* for November/December 1992. With classification, Ericsson identifies the kinds of lies we all tell at one time or another. Lying, she finds, may be unavoidable and even sometimes beneficial. But then how do we know when to stop?

William Lutz's "The World of Doublespeak," the essay following Ericsson's, also uses classification to examine types of lies, specifically the verbal substitutions that make "the bad seem good, the negative appear positive."

The bank called today and I told them my deposit was in the mail, even 1 though I hadn't written a check yet. It'd been a rough day. The baby I'm pregnant with decided to do aerobics on my lungs for two hours, our three-year-old daughter painted the living-room couch with lipstick, the IRS put me on hold for an hour, and I was late to a business meeting because I was tired.

I told my client that traffic had been bad. When my partner came home, 2 his haggard face told me his day hadn't gone any better than mine, so when he asked, "How was your day?" I said, "Oh, fine," knowing that one more straw might break his back. A friend called and wanted to take me to lunch. I said I was busy. Four lies in the course of a day, none of which I felt the least bit guilty about.

We lie. We all do. We exaggerate, we minimize, we avoid confrontation, 3 we spare people's feelings, we conveniently forget, we keep secrets, we justify lying to the big-guy institutions. Like most people, I indulge in small falsehoods and still think of myself as an honest person. Sure I lie, but it doesn't hurt anything. Or does it?

I once tried going a whole week without telling a lie, and it was paralyzing.   4
I discovered that telling the truth all the time is nearly impossible. It means
living with some serious consequences: The bank charges me $60 in overdraft
fees, my partner keels over when I tell him about my travails, my client fires
me for telling her I didn't feel like being on time, and my friend takes it personally when I say I'm not hungry. There must be some merit to lying.

But if I justify lying, what makes me any different from slick politicians or   5
the corporate robbers who raided the S&L industry? Saying it's okay to lie one
way and not another is hedging. I cannot seem to escape the voice deep inside
me that tells me: When someone lies, someone loses.

What far-reaching consequences will I, or others, pay as a result of my lie?   6
Will someone's trust be destroyed? Will someone else pay *my* penance because
I ducked out? We must consider the *meaning of our actions*. Deception, lies,
capital crimes, and misdemeanors all carry meanings. *Webster's* definition of *lie*
is specific:

> 1: a false statement or action especially made with the intent to deceive;
> 2: anything that gives or is meant to give a false impression.

A definition like this implies that there are many, many ways to tell a lie.   7
Here are just a few.

The White Lie

A man who won't lie to a woman has very little consideration for her feelings.
—Bergen Evans

The white lie assumes that the truth will cause more damage than a   8
simple, harmless untruth. Telling a friend he looks great when he looks like
hell can be based on a decision that the friend needs a compliment more than
a frank opinion. But, in effect, it is the liar deciding what is best for the lied
to. Ultimately, it is a vote of no confidence. It is an act of subtle arrogance for
anyone to decide what is best for someone else.

Yet not all circumstances are quite so cut-and-dried. Take, for instance,   9
the sergeant in Vietnam who knew one of his men was killed in action but
listed him as missing so that the man's family would receive indefinite compensation instead of the lump-sum pittance the military gives widows and
children. His intent was honorable. Yet for twenty years this family kept their
hopes alive, unable to move on to a new life.

Façades

Et tu, Brute?
—Caesar

We all put up façades to one degree or another. When I put on a suit to go   10
to see a client, I feel as though I am putting on another face, obeying the
expectation that serious businesspeople wear suits rather than sweatpants. But
I'm a writer. Normally, I get up, get the kid off to school, and sit at my computer in my pajamas until four in the afternoon. When I answer the phone,
the caller thinks I'm wearing a suit (though the UPS man knows better).

But façades can be destructive because they are used to seduce others into   11
an illusion. For instance, I recently realized that a former friend was a liar.
He presented himself with all the right looks and the right words and offered
lots of new consciousness theories, fabulous books to read, and fascinating
insights. Then I did some business with him, and the time came for him to pay
me. He turned out to be all talk and no walk. I heard a plethora of reasonable
excuses, including in-depth descriptions of the big break around the corner. In
six months of work, I saw less than a hundred bucks. When I confronted him,
he raised both eyebrows and tried to convince me that I'd heard him wrong,
that he'd made no commitment to me. A simple investigation into his past
revealed a crowded graveyard of disenchanted former friends.

Ignoring the Plain Facts

Well, you must understand that Father Porter is only human.
—A Massachusetts priest

In the '60s, the Catholic Church in Massachusetts began hearing com-   12
plaints that Father James Porter was sexually molesting children. Rather
than relieving him of his duties, the ecclesiastical authorities simply moved
him from one parish to another between 1960 and 1967, actually providing
him with a fresh supply of unsuspecting families and innocent children to
abuse. After treatment in 1967 for pedophilia, he went back to work, this
time in Minnesota. The new diocese was aware of Father Porter's obsession
with children, but they needed priests and recklessly believed treatment had
cured him. More children were abused until he was relieved of his duties a year
later. By his own admission, Porter may have abused as many as a hundred
children.

Ignoring the facts may not in and of itself be a form of lying, but con-   13
sider the context of this situation. If a lie is *a false action done with the intent
to deceive,* then the Catholic Church's conscious covering for Porter created
irreparable consequences. The church became a co-perpetrator with Porter.

Deflecting

When you have no basis for an argument, abuse the plaintiff.
—Cicero

I've discovered that I can keep anyone from seeing the true me by being 14 selectively blatant. I set a precedent of being up-front about intimate issues, but I never bring up the things I truly want to hide; I just let people assume I'm revealing everything. It's an effective way of hiding.

Any good liar knows that the way to perpetuate an untruth is to deflect 15 attention from it. When Clarence Thomas exploded with accusations that the Senate hearings were a "high-tech lynching," he simply switched the focus from a highly charged subject to a radioactive subject.[1] Rather than defending himself, he took the offensive and accused the country of racism. It was a brilliant maneuver. Racism is now politically incorrect in official circles—unlike sexual harassment, which still rewards those who can get away with it.

Some of the most skilled deflectors are passive-aggressive people who, 16 when accused of inappropriate behavior, refuse to respond to the accusations. This you-don't-exist stance infuriates the accuser, who, understandably, screams something obscene out of frustration. The trap is sprung and the act of deflection successful, because now the passive-aggressive person can indignantly say, "Who can talk to someone as unreasonable as you?" The real issue is forgotten and the sins of the original victim become the focus. Feeling guilty of name-calling, the victim is fully tamed and crawls into a hole, ashamed. I have watched this fighting technique work thousands of times in disputes between men and women, and what I've learned is that the real culprit is not necessarily the one who swears the loudest.

Omission

The cruelest lies are often told in silence.
—R. L. Stevenson

Omission involves telling most of the truth minus one or two key facts 17 whose absence changes the story completely. You break a pair of glasses that are guaranteed under normal use and get a new pair, without mentioning that the first pair broke during a rowdy game of basketball. Who hasn't tried something like that? But what about omission of information that could make a difference in how a person lives his or her life?

---

[1] Ericsson refers to the 1991 hearings to confirm Thomas for the Supreme Court, at which Thomas was accused by Anita Hill of sexual harassment.—EDS.

For instance, one day I found out that rabbinical legends tell of another   18
woman in the Garden of Eden before Eve. I was stunned. The omission of the
Sumerian goddess Lilith from Genesis—as well as her demonization by
ancient misogynists as an embodiment of female evil—felt like spiritual robbery. I felt like I'd just found out my mother was really my stepmother. To take
seriously the tradition that Adam was created out of the same mud as his equal
counterpart, Lilith, redefines all of Judeo-Christian history.

Some renegade Catholic feminists introduced me to a view of Lilith that   19
had been suppressed during the many centuries when this strong goddess was
seen only as a spirit of evil. Lilith was a proud goddess who defied Adam's need
to control her, attempted negotiations, and when this failed, said adios and
left the Garden of Eden.

This omission of Lilith from the Bible was a patriarchal strategy to keep   20
women weak. Omitting the strong-woman archetype of Lilith from Western religions and starting the story with Eve the Rib has helped keep Christian and Jewish women believing they were the lesser sex for thousands of
years.

Stereotypes and Clichés

Where opinion does not exist, the status quo becomes stereotyped and all
originality is discouraged.
                                                    —Bertrand Russell

Stereotype and cliché serve a purpose as a form of shorthand. Our need for   21
vast amounts of information in nanoseconds has made the stereotype vital to
modern communication. Unfortunately, it often shuts down original thinking, giving those hungry for the truth a candy bar of misinformation instead of
a balanced meal. The stereotype explains a situation with just enough truth to
seem unquestionable.

All the "isms"—racism, sexism, ageism, et al.—are founded on and   22
fueled by the stereotype and the cliché, which are lies of exaggeration, omission, and ignorance. They are always dangerous. They take a single tree and
make it a landscape. They destroy curiosity. They close minds and separate
people. The single mother on welfare is assumed to be cheating. Any black
male could tell you how much of his identity is obliterated daily by stereotypes. Fat people, ugly people, beautiful people, old people, large-breasted
women, short men, the mentally ill, and the homeless all could tell you
how much more they are like us than we want to think. I once admitted to a
group of people that I had a mouth like a truck driver. Much to my surprise, a
man stood up and said, "I'm a truck driver, and I never cuss." Needless to say,
I was humbled.

Groupthink

Who is more foolish, the child afraid of the dark, or the man afraid of the light?

—Maurice Freehill

Irving Janis, in *Victims of Group Think*, defines this sort of lie as a psycho-   23
logical phenomenon within decision-making groups in which loyalty to the
group has become more important than any other value, with the result that
dissent and the appraisal of alternatives are suppressed. If you've ever worked
on a committee or in a corporation, you've encountered groupthink. It
requires a combination of other forms of lying—ignoring facts, selective
memory, omission, and denial, to name a few.

The textbook example of groupthink came on December 7, 1941. From as   24
early as the fall of 1941, the warnings came in, one after another, that Japan
was preparing for a massive military operation. The navy command in Hawaii
assumed Pearl Harbor was invulnerable—the Japanese weren't stupid enough
to attack the United States' most important base. On the other hand, racist
stereotypes said the Japanese weren't smart enough to invent a torpedo effective in less than 60 feet of water (the fleet was docked in 30 feet); after all, US
technology hadn't been able to do it.

On Friday, December 5, normal weekend leave was granted to all the   25
commanders at Pearl Harbor, even though the Japanese consulate in Hawaii
was busy burning papers. Within the tight, good-ole-boy cohesiveness of the
US command in Hawaii, the myth of invulnerability stayed well entrenched.
No one in the group considered the alternatives. The rest is history.

Out-and-Out Lies

The only form of lying that is beyond reproach is lying for its own sake.

—Oscar Wilde

Of all the ways to lie, I like this one the best, probably because I get tired   26
of trying to figure out the real meanings behind things. At least I can trust the
bald-faced lie. I once asked my five-year-old nephew, "Who broke the fence?"
(I had seen him do it.) He answered, "The murderers." Who could argue?

At least when this sort of lie is told it can be easily confronted. As the per-   27
son who is lied to, I know where I stand. The bald-faced lie doesn't toy with
my perceptions—it argues with them. It doesn't try to refashion reality, it tries
to refute it. *Read my lips*. . . . No sleight of hand. No guessing. If this were the
only form of lying, there would be no such things as floating anxiety or the
adult-children-of-alcoholics movement.

Dismissal

Pay no attention to that man behind the curtain!
I am the Great Oz!
> —The Wizard of Oz

Dismissal is perhaps the slipperiest of all lies. Dismissing feelings, percep-   28
tions, or even the raw facts of a situation ranks as a kind of lie that can do as
much damage to a person as any other kind of lie.

The roots of many mental disorders can be traced back to the dismissal of   29
reality. Imagine that a person is told from the time she is a tot that her perceptions are inaccurate. *"Mommy, I'm scared."* "No you're not, darling." *"I
don't like that man next door, he makes me feel icky."* "Johnny, that's a terrible
thing to say, of course you like him. You go over there right now and be nice
to him."

I've often mused over the idea that madness is actually a sane reaction to   30
an insane world. Psychologist R. D. Laing supports this hypothesis in *Sanity,
Madness and the Family*, an account of his investigation into the families of
schizophrenics. The common thread that ran through all of the families he
studied was a deliberate, staunch dismissal of the patient's perceptions from a
very early age. Each of the patients started out with an accurate grasp of reality, which, through meticulous and methodical dismissal, was demolished
until the only reality the patient could trust was catatonia.

Dismissal runs the gamut. Mild dismissal can be quite handy for forgiving   31
the foibles of others in our day-to-day lives. Toddlers who have just learned to
manipulate their parents' attention sometimes are dismissed out of necessity.
Absolute attention from the parents would require so much energy that no
one would get to eat dinner. But we must be careful and attentive about how
far we take our "necessary" dismissals. Dismissal is a dangerous tool, because
it's nothing less than a lie.

Delusion

We lie loudest when we lie to ourselves.
> —Eric Hoffer

I could write the book on this one. Delusion, a cousin of dismissal, is the   32
tendency to see excuses as facts. It's a powerful lying tool because it filters out
information that contradicts what we want to believe. Alcoholics who believe
that the problems in their lives are legitimate reasons for drinking rather than
results of the drinking offer the classic example of deluded thinking. Delusion
uses the mind's ability to see things in myriad ways to support what it wants to
be the truth.

But delusion is also a survival mechanism we all use. If we were to fully 33
contemplate the consequences of our stockpiles of nuclear weapons or global
warming, we could hardly function on a day-to-day level. We don't want to
incorporate that much reality into our lives because to do so would be paralyzing.

Delusion acts as an adhesive to keep the status quo intact. It shamelessly 34
employs dismissal, omission, and amnesia, among other sorts of lies. Its most
cunning defense is that it cannot see itself.

•   •   •

The liar's punishment [. . .] is that he cannot believe anyone else.
—George Bernard Shaw

These are only a few of the ways we lie. Or are lied to. As I said earlier, it's 35
not easy to entirely eliminate lies from our lives. No matter how pious we may
try to be, we will still embellish, hedge, and omit to lubricate the daily
machinery of living. But there is a world of difference between telling functional lies and living a lie. Martin Buber once said, "The lie is the spirit com-
mitting treason against itself." Our acceptance of lies becomes a cultural
cancer that eventually shrouds and reorders reality until moral garbage
becomes as invisible to us as water is to a fish.

How much do we tolerate before we become sick and tired of being sick 36
and tired? When will we stand up and declare our *right* to trust? When do we
stop accepting that the real truth is in the fine print? Whose lips do we read
this year when we vote for president? When will we stop being so reticent
about making judgments? When do we stop turning over our personal power
and responsibility to liars?

Maybe if I don't tell the bank the check's in the mail I'll be less tolerant of 37
the lies told me every day. A country song I once heard said it all for me:
"You've got to stand for something or you'll fall for anything."

Journal Writing

Ericsson says, "We lie. We all do" (par. 3)—and that must mean you, too. In your
journal, write about lies you have told. When is the last time you remember lying?
What was the most significant lie you ever told? In what circumstances have you felt
it was appropriate to lie? Have you ever been ashamed of a lie or faced serious consequences for lying? (To take your journal writing further, see "From Journal to Essay"
on the facing page.)

Questions on Meaning

1. What is Ericsson's THESIS?
2. Does Ericsson think it's possible to eliminate lies from our lives? What EVIDENCE does she offer?
3. If it were possible to eliminate lies from our lives, why would that be desirable?
4. What is this essay's PURPOSE?

Questions on Writing Strategy

1. Ericsson starts out by recounting her own four-lie day (pars. 1–2). What is the EFFECT of this INTRODUCTION?
2. At the beginning of each kind of lie, Ericsson provides an epigraph, a short quotation that forecasts a theme. Which of these epigraphs work best, do you think? What are your criteria for judgment?
3. What is the message of Ericsson's CONCLUSION? Does the conclusion work well? Why, or why not?
4. **OTHER METHODS.** Examine the way Ericsson uses DEFINITION and EXAMPLE to support her classification. Which definitions are clearest? Which examples are the most effective? Why?

Questions on Language

1. In paragraph 35 Ericsson writes, "Our acceptance of lies becomes a cultural cancer that eventually shrouds and reorders reality until moral garbage becomes as invisible to us as water is to a fish." How do the two FIGURES OF SPEECH in this sentence—cancer and garbage—relate to each other?
2. Occasionally Ericsson's anger shows through, as in paragraphs 12–13 and 18–20. Is the TONE appropriate in these cases? Why, or why not?
3. Look up any of these words you do not know: haggard (par. 2); travails (4); façades (10); plethora (11); ecclesiastical, pedophilia (12); irreparable, co-perpetrator (13); patriarchal, archetype (20); gamut (31); myriad (32); reticent (36).
4. Ericsson uses several words and phrases from the fields of psychology and sociology. Define: passive-aggressive (par. 16); floating anxiety, adult-children-of-alcoholics movement (27); schizophrenics, catatonia (30).

Suggestions for Writing

1. **FROM JOURNAL TO ESSAY.** Develop one or more of the lies you recalled in your journal (previous page) into an essay. You may choose to elaborate on your lies by classifying according to some principle or by NARRATING the story of a particular lie and its outcome. Try to give your reader a sense of your motivation for lying in the first place.
2. Ericsson writes, "All the 'isms'—racism, sexism, ageism, et al.—are founded on and fueled by the stereotype and the cliché, which are lies of exaggeration, omission, and ignorance. They are always dangerous. They take a single tree and make

it a landscape" (par. 22). Write an essay discussing stereotypes and how they work to encourage prejudice. Use Ericsson's definition as a base, and expand it to include stereotypes you find particularly injurious. How do these stereotypes oversimplify? How are they "dangerous"?

3. **CRITICAL WRITING.** EVALUATE the success of Ericsson's essay, considering espe-cially how effectively her evidence supports her GENERALIZATIONS. Are there important categories she overlooks, exceptions she neglects to account for, gaps in definitions or examples? Offer specific evidence for your own view, whether positive or negative.

4. **CONNECTIONS.** Ericsson begins her essay by acknowledging her own lies, and she often uses the first-person *I* or *we* in explaining her categories. In contrast, the author of the following essay, William Lutz, takes a more distant approach in clas-sifying the dishonest language called *doublespeak*. Which of these two approaches, confessional or more distant, do you find more effective, and why? When, in your view, is it appropriate to inject yourself into your writing, and when is it not?

Stephanie Ericsson on Writing

In an interview on the Amazon.com Web site, Stephanie Ericsson discussed when and why she began writing. At first, she said, she did not write to com-municate but to find and express herself.

I was fifteen in the year 1968, in the heart of hippie-saturated San Fran-cisco, and like the world, I, too, underwent a major transformation. These spiritual awakenings tend to sound lofty, but the truth is that they are always messy. I began writing regularly then, when I lost my family. There was no one to tell my feelings to, so I turned to the blank white page. The page will never contradict you, never ignore you, and never judge you. I could put the chaos outside of me, and move on. It was a survival tool that I became attached to.

For Discussion

1. Do you agree with Ericsson's assessment of the "blank white page" as benevolent and nonjudgmental?

2. In the passage above, Ericsson is talking about writing for oneself. Is it merely the absence of an audience that makes such writing potentially therapeutic? Why does articulating her thoughts—if only for herself—help Ericsson "move on"?

WILLIAM LUTZ

WILLIAM LUTZ was born in 1940 in Racine, Wisconsin. He received a BA from Dominican College, an MA from Marquette University, a PhD from the University of Nevada at Reno, and a JD from Rutgers School of Law. Since 1971 Lutz has taught at Rutgers University in Camden, New Jersey. For much of his career, Lutz's interest in words and composition has made him an active campaigner against misleading and irresponsible language. He is the author of the best-seller *Doublespeak: From Revenue Enhancement to Terminal Living* (1989) and its sequel, *The New Doublespeak: Why No One Knows What Anyone's Saying Anymore* (1996). For fourteen years, he edited the *Quarterly Review of Doublespeak*. He has written, cowritten, or edited numerous other books, including *The Cambridge Thesaurus of American English* and *Webster's New World Thesaurus*. In 1996 he received the George Orwell Award for Distinguished Contribution to Honesty and Clarity in Public Language.

The World of Doublespeak

In the previous essay, Stephanie Ericsson examines the damage caused by the outright lies we tell each other every day. But what if our language doesn't lie, exactly, and instead just obscures meanings we'd rather not admit to? Such intentional fudging, or *doublespeak*, is the sort of language Lutz specializes in, and here he uses classification to expose its many guises. "The World of Doublespeak" abridges the first chapter in Lutz's book *Doublespeak*; the essay's title is the chapter's subtitle.

There are no potholes in the streets of Tucson, Arizona, just "pavement deficiencies." The Reagan Administration didn't propose any new taxes, just "revenue enhancement" through new "user's fees." Those aren't bums on the street, just "non-goal oriented members of society." There are no more poor people, just "fiscal underachievers." There was no robbery of an automatic teller machine, just an "unauthorized withdrawal." The patient didn't die because of medical malpractice, it was just a "diagnostic misadventure of a high magnitude." The US Army doesn't kill the enemy anymore, it just "services the target." And the doublespeak goes on.

Doublespeak is language that pretends to communicate but really doesn't. It is language that makes the bad seem good, the negative appear positive, the unpleasant appear attractive or at least tolerable. Doublespeak is language that avoids or shifts responsibility, language that is at variance with its real or purported meaning. It is language that conceals or prevents thought; rather than extending thought, doublespeak limits it.

Doublespeak is not a matter of subjects and verbs agreeing; it is a matter   3
of words and facts agreeing. Basic to doublespeak is incongruity, the incongruity between what is said or left unsaid, and what really is. It is the incongruity between the word and the referent, between seem and be, between the
essential function of language—communication—and what doublespeak
does—mislead, distort, deceive, inflate, circumvent, obfuscate.

How to Spot Doublespeak

How can you spot doublespeak? Most of the time you will recognize double-   4
speak when you see or hear it. But, if you have any doubts, you can identify
doublespeak just by answering these questions: Who is saying what to whom,
under what conditions and circumstances, with what intent, and with what
results? Answering these questions will usually help you identify as doublespeak language that appears to be legitimate or that at first glance doesn't even
appear to be doublespeak.

First Kind of Doublespeak

There are at least four kinds of doublespeak. The first is the euphemism,   5
an inoffensive or positive word or phrase used to avoid a harsh, unpleasant, or
distasteful reality. But a euphemism can also be a tactful word or phrase which
avoids directly mentioning a painful reality, or it can be an expression used
out of concern for the feelings of someone else, or to avoid directly discussing
a topic subject to a social or cultural taboo.

When you use a euphemism because of your sensitivity for someone's feel-   6
ings or out of concern for a recognized social or cultural taboo, it is not doublespeak. For example, you express your condolences that someone has
"passed away" because you do not want to say to a grieving person, "I'm sorry
your father is dead." When you use the euphemism "passed away," no one is
misled. Moreover, the euphemism functions here not just to protect the feelings of another person, but to communicate also your concern for that person's
feelings during a period of mourning. When you excuse yourself to go to the
"restroom," or you mention that someone is "sleeping with" or "involved
with" someone else, you do not mislead anyone about your meaning, but you
do respect the social taboos about discussing bodily functions and sex in direct
terms. You also indicate your sensitivity to the feelings of your audience,
which is usually considered a mark of courtesy and good manners.

However, when a euphemism is used to mislead or deceive, it becomes   7
doublespeak. For example, in 1984 the US State Department announced that
it would no longer use the word "killing" in its annual report on the status of

human rights in countries around the world. Instead, it would use the phrase "unlawful or arbitrary deprivation of life," which the department claimed was more accurate. Its real purpose for using this phrase was simply to avoid discussing the embarrassing situation of government-sanctioned killings in countries that are supported by the United States and have been certified by the United States as respecting the human rights of their citizens. This use of a euphemism constitutes doublespeak, since it is designed to mislead, to cover up the unpleasant. Its real intent is at variance with its apparent intent. It is language designed to alter our perception of reality.

The Pentagon, too, avoids discussing unpleasant realities when it refers to bombs and artillery shells that fall on civilian targets as "incontinent ordnance." And in 1977 the Pentagon tried to slip funding for the neutron bomb unnoticed into an appropriations bill by calling it a "radiation enhancement device."

Second Kind of Doublespeak

A second kind of doublespeak is jargon, the specialized language of a trade, profession, or similar group, such as that used by doctors, lawyers, engineers, educators, or car mechanics. Jargon can serve an important and useful function. Within a group, jargon functions as a kind of verbal shorthand that allows members of the group to communicate with each other clearly, efficiently, and quickly. Indeed, it is a mark of membership in the group to be able to use and understand the group's jargon.

But jargon, like the euphemism, can also be doublespeak. It can be—and often is—pretentious, obscure, and esoteric terminology used to give an air of profundity, authority, and prestige to speakers and their subject matter. Jargon as doublespeak often makes the simple appear complex, the ordinary profound, the obvious insightful. In this sense it is used not to express but impress. With such doublespeak, the act of smelling something becomes "organoleptic analysis," glass becomes "fused silicate," a crack in a metal support beam becomes a "discontinuity," conservative economic policies become "distributionally conservative notions."

Lawyers, for example, speak of an "involuntary conversion" of property when discussing the loss or destruction of property through theft, accident, or condemnation. If your house burns down or if your car is stolen, you have suffered an involuntary conversion of your property. When used by lawyers in a legal situation, such jargon is a legitimate use of language, since lawyers can be expected to understand the term.

However, when a member of a specialized group uses its jargon to communicate with a person outside the group, and uses it knowing that the nonmember does not understand such language, then there is doublespeak. For example, on May 9, 1978, a National Airlines 727 airplane crashed while attempting to land at the Pensacola, Florida, airport. Three of the fifty-two passengers aboard the airplane were killed. As a result of the crash, National made an after-tax insurance benefit of $1.7 million, or an extra 18¢ a share dividend for its stockholders. Now National Airlines had two problems: It did not want to talk about one of its airplanes crashing, and it had to account for the $1.7 million when it issued its annual report to its stockholders. National solved the problem by inserting a footnote in its annual report which explained that the $1.7 million income was due to "the involuntary conversion of a 727." National thus acknowledged the crash of its airplane and the subsequent profit it made from the crash, without once mentioning the accident or the deaths. However, because airline officials knew that most stockholders in the company, and indeed most of the general public, were not familiar with legal jargon, the use of such jargon constituted doublespeak.

Third Kind of Doublespeak

A third kind of doublespeak is gobbledygook or bureaucratese. Basically, such doublespeak is simply a matter of piling on words, of overwhelming the audience with words, the bigger the words and the longer the sentences the better. Alan Greenspan, then chair of President Nixon's Council of Economic Advisors, was quoted in *The Philadelphia Inquirer* in 1974 as having testified before a Senate committee that "It is a tricky problem to find the particular calibration in timing that would be appropriate to stem the acceleration in risk premiums created by falling incomes without prematurely aborting the decline in the inflation-generated risk premiums." 13

Nor has Mr. Greenspan's language changed since then. Speaking to the meeting of the Economic Club of New York in 1988, Mr. Greenspan, now Federal Reserve chair, said, "I guess I should warn you, if I turn out to be particularly clear, you've probably misunderstood what I've said." Mr. Greenspan's doublespeak doesn't seem to have held back his career. 14

Sometimes gobbledygook may sound impressive, but when the quote is later examined in print it doesn't even make sense. During the 1988 presidential campaign, vice-presidential candidate Senator Dan Quayle explained the need for a strategic-defense initiative by saying, "Why wouldn't an enhanced deterrent, a more stable peace, a better prospect to denying the ones who enter conflict in the first place to have a reduction of offensive systems and an introduction to defense capability? I believe this is the route the country will eventually go." 15

The investigation into the *Challenger* disaster in 1986 revealed the double- 16 speak of gobbledygook and bureaucratese used by too many involved in the shuttle program. When Jesse Moore, NASA's associate administrator, was asked if the performance of the shuttle program had improved with each launch or if it had remained the same, he answered, "I think our performance in terms of the liftoff performance and in terms of the orbital performance, we knew more about the envelope we were operating under, and we have been pretty accurately staying in that. And so I would say the performance has not by design drastically improved. I think we have been able to characterize the performance more as a function of our launch experience as opposed to it improving as a function of time." While this language may appear to be jargon, a close look will reveal that it is really just gobbledygook laced with jargon. But you really have to wonder if Mr. Moore had any idea what he was saying.

Fourth Kind of Doublespeak

The fourth kind of doublespeak is inflated language that is designed to make   17
the ordinary seem extraordinary; to make everyday things seem impressive; to give an air of importance to people, situations, or things that would not normally be considered important; to make the simple seem complex. Often this kind of doublespeak isn't hard to spot, and it is usually pretty funny. While car mechanics may be called "automotive internists," elevator operators members of the "vertical transportation corps," used cars "pre-owned" or "experienced cars," and black-and-white television sets described as having "non-multicolor capability," you really aren't misled all that much by such language.

However, you may have trouble figuring out that, when Chrysler "initiates   18
a career alternative enhancement program," it is really laying off five thousand workers; or that "negative patient-care outcome" means the patient died; or that "rapid oxidation" means a fire in a nuclear power plant.

The doublespeak of inflated language can have serious consequences. In   19
Pentagon doublespeak, "pre-emptive counterattack" means that American forces attacked first; "engaged the enemy on all sides" means American troops were ambushed; "backloading of augmentation personnel" means a retreat by American troops. In the doublespeak of the military, the 1983 invasion of Grenada was conducted not by the US Army, Navy, Air Force, and Marines, but by the "Caribbean Peace Keeping Forces." But then, according to the Pentagon, it wasn't an invasion, it was a "predawn vertical insertion." [. . .]

The Dangers of Doublespeak

Doublespeak is not the product of carelessness or sloppy thinking. Indeed,   20
most doublespeak is the product of clear thinking and is carefully designed

and constructed to appear to communicate when in fact it doesn't. It is language designed not to lead but mislead. It is language designed to distort reality and corrupt thought. [. . .] In the world created by doublespeak, if it's not a tax increase, but rather "revenue enhancement" or "tax base broadening," how can you complain about higher taxes? If it's not acid rain, but rather "poorly buffered precipitation," how can you worry about all those dead trees? If that isn't the Mafia in Atlantic City, but just "members of a career-offender cartel," why worry about the influence of organized crime in the city? If Supreme Court Justice William Rehnquist wasn't addicted to the pain-killing drug his doctor prescribed, but instead it was just that the drug had "established an interrelationship with the body, such that if the drug is removed precipitously, there is a reaction," you needn't question that his decisions might have been influenced by his drug addiction. If it's not a Titan II nuclear-armed intercontinental ballistic missile with a warhead 630 times more powerful than the atomic bomb dropped on Hiroshima, but instead, according to air force colonel Frank Horton, it's just a "very large, potentially disruptive re-entry system," why be concerned about the threat of nuclear destruction? Why worry about the neutron bomb escalating the arms race if it's just a "radiation enhancement weapon"? If it's not an invasion, but a "rescue mission" or a "predawn vertical insertion," you won't need to think about any violations of US or international law.

Doublespeak has become so common in everyday living that many people   21
fail to notice it. Even worse, when they do notice doublespeak being used on them, they don't react, they don't protest. Do you protest when you are asked to check your packages at the desk "for your convenience," when it's not for your convenience at all but for someone else's? You see advertisements for "genuine imitation leather," "virgin vinyl," or "real counterfeit diamonds," but do you question the language or the supposed quality of the product? Do you question politicians who don't speak of slums or ghettos but of the "inner city" or "substandard housing" where the "disadvantaged" live and thus avoid talking about the poor who have to live in filthy, poorly heated, ramshackle apartments or houses? Aren't you amazed that patients don't die in the hospital anymore, it's just "negative patient-care outcome"?

Doublespeak such as that noted earlier that defines cab drivers as "urban   22
transportation specialists," elevator operators as members of the "vertical transportation corps," and automobile mechanics as "automotive internists" can be considered humorous and relatively harmless. However, when a fire in a nuclear reactor building is called "rapid oxidation," an explosion in a nuclear power plant is called an "energetic disassembly," the illegal overthrow of a legitimate government is termed "destabilizing a government," and lies are seen as "inoperative statements," we are hearing doublespeak that attempts to

avoid responsibility and make the bad seem good, the negative appear positive, something unpleasant appear attractive; and which seems to communicate but doesn't. It is language designed to alter our perception of reality and corrupt our thinking. Such language does not provide us with the tools we need to develop, advance, and preserve our culture and our civilization. Such language breeds suspicion, cynicism, distrust, and, ultimately, hostility.

Doublespeak is insidious because it can infect and eventually destroy the   23 function of language, which is communication between people and social groups. This corruption of the function of language can have serious and far-reaching consequences. We live in a country that depends upon an informed electorate to make decisions in selecting candidates for office and deciding issues of public policy. The use of doublespeak can become so pervasive that it becomes the coin of the political realm, with speakers and listeners convinced that they really understand such language. After a while we may really believe that politicians don't lie but only "misspeak," that illegal acts are merely "inappropriate actions," that fraud and criminal conspiracy are just "miscertification." President Jimmy Carter in April of 1980 could call the aborted raid to free the American hostages in Teheran an "incomplete success" and really believe that he had made a statement that clearly communicated with the American public. So, too, could President Ronald Reagan say in 1985 that "ultimately our security and our hopes for success at the arms reduction talks hinge on the determination that we show here to continue our program to rebuild and refortify our defenses" and really believe that greatly increasing the amount of money spent building new weapons would lead to a reduction in the number of weapons in the world. If we really believe that we understand such language and that such language communicates and promotes clear thought, then the world of *1984*,[1] with its control of reality through language, is upon us.

Journal Writing

Now that you know the name for it, when have you read or heard examples of doublespeak? Over the next few days, jot down examples of doublespeak that you recall or that you read and hear—from politicians or news commentators; in the lease

---

[1] In a section omitted from this abridgement of his chapter, Lutz discusses *1984*, the 1949 novel by George Orwell in which a frightening totalitarian state devises a language, called *newspeak,* to shape and control thought in politically acceptable forms. (For an example of Orwell's writing, see p. 629).—EDS.

for your dwelling or your car; in advertising and catalogs; from bosses, teachers, or other figures of authority; in overheard conversations. (To take your journal writing further, see "From Journal to Essay" below.)

Questions on Meaning

1. What is Lutz's THESIS? Where does he state it?
2. According to Lutz, four questions can help us identify doublespeak. What are they? How can they help us distinguish between truthful language and doublespeak?
3. What, according to Lutz, are "the dangers of doublespeak"?
4. What ASSUMPTIONS does the author make about his readers' educational backgrounds and familiarity with his subject?

Questions on Writing Strategy

1. What principle does Lutz use for creating his four kinds of doublespeak — that is, what mainly distinguishes the groups?
2. Lutz quotes Alan Greenspan twice in paragraphs 13–14. What is surprising about the comment in paragraph 14? Why does Lutz include this second quotation?
3. Lutz uses many quotations that were quite current when he first published this piece in 1989 but that now may seem dated — for instance, references to Presidents Carter and Reagan or to the nuclear arms race. Do these EXAMPLES undermine Lutz's essay in any way? Is his discussion of doublespeak still valid today? Explain your answers.
4. **OTHER METHODS.** Lutz's essay is not only a classification but also a DEFINITION of *doublespeak* and an examination of CAUSE AND EFFECT. Where are these other methods used most prominently? What do they contribute to the essay?

Questions on Language

1. How does Lutz's own language compare with the language he quotes as doublespeak? Do you find his language clear and easy to understand?
2. ANALYZE Lutz's language in paragraphs 22 and 23. How do the CONNOTATIONS of words such as "corrupt," "hostility," "insidious," and "control" strengthen the author's message?
3. The following list of possibly unfamiliar words includes only those found in Lutz's own sentences, not those in the doublespeak he quotes. Be sure you can define variance (par. 2); incongruity, referent (3); taboo (5); condolences (6); esoteric, profundity (10); condemnation (11); ramshackle (21); cynicism (22); insidious (23).

Suggestions for Writing

1. **FROM JOURNAL TO ESSAY.** Choose at least one of the examples of doublespeak noted in your journal (above), and write an essay explaining why it qualifies as

doublespeak. Which of Lutz's categories does it fit under? How did you recognize it? Can you understand what it means?

2. Just about all of us have resorted to doublespeak at one time or another—when making an excuse, when trying to conceal the fact that we're unprepared for an exam, when trying to impress a supervisor or potential employer. Write a NARRA- TIVE about a time you used deliberately unclear language, perhaps language that you yourself didn't understand. What were the circumstances? Did you con- sciously decide to use unclear language, or did it just leak out? How did others react to your use of this language?

3. **CRITICAL WRITING.** Can you determine from his essay who Lutz believes is responsible for the proliferation of doublespeak? Whose responsibility is it to cur- tail the use of doublespeak: just those who use it? the schools? the government? the media? we who hear it? Write an essay that considers these questions, citing specific passages from the essay and incorporating your own ideas.

4. **CONNECTIONS.** Read Stephanie Ericsson's "The Ways We Lie" (p. 389), which classifies the lies we tell in our daily lives. In what way, if any, do doublespeakers also lie? How, if at all, do the intentions of Ericsson's liars and Lutz's double- speakers differ? How, if at all, are their intentions the same? Are the results of lying and doublespeak, according to each author, different or the same? Write an essay that answers these questions and that points out any other similarities or differences you notice between liars and doublespeakers. Use EVIDENCE from the two essays or from your own experience to support your thesis.

William Lutz on Writing

In 1989 C-SPAN aired an interview between Brian Lamb and William Lutz. Lamb asked Lutz about his writing process. "I have a rule about writing," Lutz answered, "which I discovered when I wrote my dissertation: You never write a book, you write three pages, or you write five pages. I put off writing my dissertation for a year, because I could not think of writing this whole thing. [. . .] I had put off doing this book [*Doublespeak*] for quite a while, and my wife said, 'You've got to do the book.' And I said, 'Yes, I am going to, just as soon as I . . . ,' and, of course, I did every other thing I could possibly think of before that, and then I realized one day that she was right, I had to start writing. [. . .] So one day, I sit down and say, 'I am going to write five pages—that's all— and when I am done with five pages, I'll reward myself.' So I do the five pages, or the next time I will do ten pages or whatever number of pages, but I set a number of pages."

Perhaps wondering just how high Lutz's daily page count might go, Lamb asked Lutz how much he wrote at one time. "It depends," Lutz admitted. "I always begin a writing session by sitting down and rewriting what I wrote the previous day—and that is the first thing, and it does two things. First of all, it makes your writing a little bit better, because rewriting is the essential part of writing. And the second thing is to get you flowing again, get back into the mainstream. Truman Capote[1] once gave the best piece of advice for writers ever given. He said, 'Never pump the well dry; always leave a bucket there.' So, I never stop writing when I run out of ideas. I always stop when I have something more to write about, and write a note to myself, 'This is what I am going to do next,' and then I stop. The worst feeling in the world is to have written yourself dry and have to come back the next day, knowing that you are dry and not knowing where you are going to pick up at this point."

For Discussion

1. Though his work is devoted to words and writing, William Lutz once spent a great deal of time avoiding writing. What finally got him to stop procrastinating? When you are avoiding a writing assignment, is it the length of the project or something else that prevents you from getting to work?
2. Lutz always rewrites before he starts producing new material on the idea that he didn't develop on the previous day. How come? Do you think Lutz's strategy is a good one?

---

[1] Truman Capote (1924–84) was an American journalist and fiction writer. —EDS.

ADDITIONAL WRITING TOPICS

Classification

Write an essay by the method of classification, in which you sort one of the following subjects into categories of your own. Make clear your PURPOSE in classifying and the basis of your classification. Explain each class with DEFINITIONS and EXAMPLES (you may find it helpful to make up a name for each group). Check your classes to be sure they neither gap nor overlap.

1. Commuters, or people who use public transportation
2. Environmental problems or environmental solutions
3. Web sites
4. Vegetarians
5. Talk shows
6. The ills or benefits of city life
7. The recordings you own
8. Families
9. Stand-up comedians
10. Present-day styles of marriage
11. Vacations
12. College students today
13. Movies for teenagers or men or women
14. Waiters you'd never tip
15. Comic strips
16. Movie monsters
17. Sports announcers
18. Inconsiderate people
19. Radio stations
20. Mall millers (people who mill around malls)

Cause and effect in a cartoon

With simple drawings and perhaps a few words, editorial cartoonists often make striking comments on events. This cartoon by Mike Thompson, published in the *Detroit Free Press,* proposes a cause to explain a disturbing effect. What is the effect? What, according to Thompson, is the cause? How does the caption "Garbage in . . ." reinforce Thompson's explanation? What other causes might explain the effect depicted here? Do you agree or disagree with Thompson's view? Why?

11

CAUSE AND EFFECT
Asking Why

THE METHOD

Press the button of a doorbell and, inside the house or apartment, chimes sound. Why? Because the touch of your finger on the button closed an electrical circuit. But why did you ring the doorbell? Because you were sent by your dispatcher: You are a bill collector calling on a customer whose payments are three months overdue.

The touch of your finger on the button is the *immediate cause* of the chimes: the event that precipitates another. That you were ordered by your dispatcher to go ring the doorbell is a *remote cause*: an underlying, more basic reason for the event, not apparent to an observer. Probably, ringing the doorbell will lead to some results: The door will open, and you may be given a check—or a kick in the teeth.

To figure out reasons and results is to use the method of CAUSE AND EFFECT. Either to explain events or to argue for one version of them, you try to answer the question "Why did something happen?" or "What were the consequences?" or "What might be the consequences?" As part of answering such a question, you use DIVISION or ANALYSIS (Chap. 9) to separate the flow of events into causes.

Seeking causes, you can ask, for example, "Why do birds migrate?" "What has caused sales of Detroit-made cars to pick up (or decline) lately?" Looking for effects, you can ask "What have been the effects of the birth-control pill on the typical American family?" "What impact has the personal computer had on the nursing profession?" You can look to a possible future and ask "Of what use might a course in psychology be to me if I become an office manager?" "Suppose an asteroid the size of a sofa were to strike Philadelphia— what would be the probable consequences?" Essay exams in history and economics courses tend often to ask for either causes or effects: "What were the principal causes of America's involvement in the war in Vietnam?" "What were the immediate effects on the world monetary system of Franklin D. Roosevelt's removing the United States from the gold standard?"

Don't, by the way, confuse cause and effect with the method of PROCESS ANALYSIS (Chap. 8). Some process analysis essays, too, deal with happenings; but they focus more on repeatable events (rather than unique ones) and they explain *how* (rather than why) something happened. If you were explaining the process by which the doorbell rings, you might break the happening into stages—(1) the finger presses the button; (2) the circuit closes; (3) the current travels the wire; (4) the chimes make music—and you'd set forth the process in detail. But why did the finger press the button? What happened because the doorbell rang? To answer those questions, you need cause and effect.

In trying to explain why things happen, you can expect to find a whole array of causes—interconnected, perhaps, like the strands of a spiderweb. You'll want to do an honest job of unraveling, and this may take time. For a jury to acquit or convict an accused slayer, weeks of testimony from witnesses, detectives, and psychiatrists may be required, then days of deliberation. It took a great historian, Jakob Burckhardt, most of his lifetime to set forth a few reasons for the dawn of the Italian Renaissance. To be sure, juries must take great care when a life hangs in the balance; and Burckhardt, after all, was writing an immense book. To produce a college essay, you don't have forty years; but before you start to write, you will need to devote extra time and thought to seeing which facts are the causes, and which matter most.

To answer the questions "Why?" and "What followed as a result?" may sometimes be hard, but it can be satisfying—even illuminating. Indeed, to seek causes and effects is one way for the mind to discover order in a reality that otherwise might seem (as life came to seem to Macbeth) "a tale told by an idiot, full of sound and fury, signifying nothing."

THE PROCESS

Subjects and Purposes

The method of cause and effect tends to suggest itself: If you have a subject and soon start thinking "Why?" or "What results?" or "What if?" then you are on the way to analyzing causation. Your subject may be impersonal—like a political victory or a sports defeat—or it may be quite personal. Indeed, an excellent cause-and-effect paper may be written on a subject very near to you. You can ask yourself why you behaved in a certain way at a certain moment. You can examine the reasons for your current beliefs and attitudes. Writing such a paper, you might happen upon a truth you hadn't realized before.

Whether your subject is personal or impersonal, make sure it is manageable: You should be able to get to the bottom of it, given the time and information available. For a 500-word essay due Thursday, the causes of teenage rebellion would be a less feasible topic than why a certain thirteen-year-old you know ran away from home.

Before rushing to list causes or effects, stop a moment to consider what your PURPOSE might be in writing. Much of the time you'll seek simply to explain what did or might occur, discovering and laying out the connections as clearly and accurately as you can. But when reasonable people could disagree over causes or effects, you may want to go further, arguing for one interpretation over others. You'll still need to be clear and accurate in presenting your interpretation, but you'll also need to treat the others fairly. (See Chap. 13 on argument and persuasion.)

Causal Relations

Your toughest job in writing a cause-and-effect essay may be figuring out what caused what. Sometimes one event will appear to trigger another, and it in turn will trigger yet another, and another still, in an order we call a *causal chain*. A classic example of such a chain is set forth in a Mother Goose rhyme:

> For want of a nail the shoe was lost,
> For want of a shoe the horse was lost,
> For want of a horse the rider was lost,
> For want of a rider the battle was lost,
> For want of a battle the kingdom was lost—
> And all for the want of a nail.

In reality, causes are seldom so easy to find as that missing nail: They tend to be many and complicated. A battle may be lost for more than one reason. Perhaps the losing general had fewer soldiers and had a blinding hangover the morning he mapped out his battle strategy. Perhaps winter set in, expected reinforcements failed to arrive, and a Joan of Arc inspired the winning army. The downfall of a kingdom is not to be explained as though it were the toppling of the last domino in a file. Still, one event precedes another in time, and in discerning causes you don't ignore chronological order; you pay attention to it.

When you can see a number of apparent causes, weigh them and assign each a relative importance. Which do you find matter most? Often, you will see that causes are more important or less so: *major* or *minor*. If Judd acquires a heavy drug habit and also takes up residence in a video arcade, and as a result finds himself penniless, it is probably safe to assume that the drug habit is the major cause of his going broke and his addiction to video games a minor one. If you were writing about his sad case, you'd probably emphasize the drug habit by giving it most of your space, perhaps touching on video games briefly.

When seeking remote causes, look only as far back as necessary. Explaining why a small town has fallen on hard times, you might confine yourself to the immediate cause of the hardship: the closing of a factory. You might explain what caused the shutdown: a dispute between union and management. You might even go back to the cause of the dispute (announced firings) and the cause of the firings (loss of sales to a competitor). For a short essay, that might be far enough back in time to go; but if you were writing a whole book (*Pottsville: Its Glorious Past and Its Present Agony*), you might look to causes still more remote. You could trace the beginning of the decline of Pottsville back to the invention, in 1845, of a better carrot grater. A manageable short paper showing effects might work in the other direction, moving from the factory closing to its impact on the town: unemployment, the closing of stores and the only movie house, people packing up and moving away.

Two cautions about causal relations are in order here. One is to beware of confusing coincidence with cause. In the logical FALLACY called *post hoc* (short for the Latin *post hoc, ergo propter hoc,* "after this, therefore because of this"), one assumes, erroneously, that because A happened before B, A must have caused B. This is the error of the superstitious man who decides that he lost his job because a black cat walked in front of him. Another error is to oversimplify causes by failing to recognize their full number and complexity — claiming, say, that violent crime is simply a result of "all those gangster shows on TV." Avoid such wrong turns in reasoning by patiently looking for evidence before you write, and by giving it careful thought. (For a fuller list of such fallacies, or errors in reasoning, see pp. 508–09.)

Discovery of Causes

To help find causes of actions and events, you can ask yourself a few searching questions. These have been suggested by the work of the literary critic Kenneth Burke:

1. *What act am I trying to explain?*
2. *What is the character, personality, or mental state of whoever acted?*
3. *In what scene or location did the act take place, and in what circumstances?*
4. *What instruments or means did the person use?*
5. *For what purpose did the person act?*

Burke calls these elements a *pentad* (or set of five): the *act,* the *actor,* the *scene,* the *agency,* and the *purpose.* If you are trying to explain, for instance, why a person burned down a liquor shop, it will be revealing to ask about his character and mental state. Was the act committed by the shop's worried, debt-ridden owner? a mentally disturbed anti-alcohol crusader? a drunk who had been denied a purchase? The scene of the burning, too, might tell you something. Was the shop near a church, a mental hospital, or a fireworks factory? And what was the agency (or means of the act): a flaming torch or a flipped-away cigarette butt? To learn the purpose might be illuminating, whether it was to collect insurance on the shop, to get revenge, or to work what the actor believed to be the will of the Lord. You can further deepen your inquiry by seeing relationships between the terms of the pentad. Ask, for instance, what does the actor have to do with this scene? (Is he or she the neighbor across the street, who has been staring at the liquor shop resentfully for years?)[1]

You can use Burke's pentad to help explain the acts of groups as well as those of individuals. Why, for instance, did the sophomore class revel degenerate into a brawl? Here are some possible answers:

1. *Act:* the brawl
2. *Actors:* the sophs were letting off steam after exams, and a mean, tense spirit prevailed
3. *Scene:* a keg-beer party outdoors in the quad at midnight on a sticky and hot May night
4. *Agencies:* fists and sticks
5. *Purpose:* the brawlers were seeking to punish whoever kicked over the keg

Don't worry if not all the questions apply, if not all the answers are immediately forthcoming. Bring the pentad to bear on the sad case of Judd, the drug addict, and probably only the question about his character and mental state would help you much. Even a single hint, though, can help you write. Burke's pentad isn't meant to be a grim rigmarole; it is a means of discovery, to generate a lot of possible material for you—insights, observations, hunches to pursue. It won't solve each and every human mystery, but sometimes it will helpfully deepen your thought.

Purpose and Thesis

Your cause-and-effect writing may have started with a question, but you don't want your essay to leave your readers asking their own question: "Why did this writer bother to analyze causes and effects?" Forestall such a question by *telling* why: Assert your main idea in a THESIS SENTENCE or sentences.

The essays in this chapter provide good examples of thesis sentences that put across, concisely, what the subject is and why the author is bothering to analyze causes or effects. Here are a few examples:

> It is possible to stop most drug addiction in the United States within a very short time. Simply make all drugs available and sell them at cost. (Gore Vidal, "Drugs")

---

[1] If you are interested and care to explore the possibilities of Burke's pentad, you can pair up its five terms in ten different ways: act to actor, actor to scene, actor to agency, actor to purpose, act to scene, act to agency, act to purpose, scene to agency, scene to purpose, agency to purpose. This approach can go profoundly deep. We suggest you try writing ten questions (one for each pair) in the form "What does act have to do with actor?" Ask them of some act you'd like to explain.

Every time a disease cluster turns up, communities worry, scientists scramble for a cause and [. . .] lawyers start suing. Yet over and over again, despite years—sometimes decades—of efforts to link the disease with a cause, scientists usually come up empty handed. (Gina Kolata, "Probing Disease Clusters")

My suspicion is, in fact, that very few of us [. . .] have really responded to the AIDS crisis the way the federal government and educators would like us to believe. My guess is that we're all but ignoring it and that almost anyone who claims otherwise is lying. (Meghan Daum, "Safe-Sex Lies")

Final Word

In stating what you believe to be causes and effects, don't be afraid to voice a well-considered hunch. Your instructor doesn't expect you to write, in a short time, a definitive account of the causes of an event or a belief or a phenomenon—only to write a coherent and reasonable one. To discern all causes—including remote ones—and all effects is beyond the power of any one human mind. Still, admirable and well-informed writers on matters such as politics, economics, and world and national affairs are often canny guessers and brave drawers of inferences. At times, even the most cautious and responsible writer has to leap boldly over a void to strike firm ground on the far side. Consider your evidence. Focus your thinking. Look well before leaping. Then take off.

CHECKLIST FOR REVISING A CAUSE-AND-EFFECT ESSAY

✔ **SUBJECT.** Have you been able to cover your subject adequately in the time and space available? Should you perhaps narrow the subject so that you can fairly address the important causes and/or effects?

✔ **COMPLETENESS.** Have you included all relevant causes or effects? Does your analysis reach back to locate remote causes or forward to locate remote effects?

✔ **CAUSAL RELATIONS.** Have you presented a clear pattern of causes or effects? Have you distinguished the remote from the immediate, the major from the minor?

✔ **ACCURACY AND FAIRNESS.** Have you avoided the *post hoc* fallacy, assuming that A caused B just because it preceded B? Have you also avoided oversimplifying and instead covered causes or effects in all their complexity?

✔ **FOCUS.** For your readers' benefit, have you focused your analysis by stating your main idea succinctly in a thesis sentence or sentences?

CAUSE AND EFFECT IN A PARAGRAPH: TWO ILLUSTRATIONS

Using Cause and Effect to Write About Television

In the following paragraph, the writer poses and concisely answers a question about soccer's near-absence from American TV. The paragraph was written especially for *The Bedford Reader,* but it could serve as a component of a full essay, perhaps one analyzing how television affects sports in general.

Why is it that, despite a growing interest in soccer among American athletes, and despite its ranking as the most popular sport in the world, commercial television all but ignores it? Granted, soccer sometimes makes it to cable, as during the World Cup, but mostly it's shut out. The reason stems partly from the basic nature of commercial television, which exists not to inform and entertain but to sell. During most major sporting events on television—football, baseball, basketball, boxing—producers can take advantage of natural interruptions in the action to broadcast sales pitches; or, if the natural breaks occur too infrequently, the producers can contrive time-outs for the sole purpose of airing lucrative commercials. But soccer is played in two solid halves of forty-five minutes each; not even injury to a player is cause for a time-out. How, then, to insert the requisite number of commercial breaks without resorting to false fouls or other questionable tactics? After CBS aired a soccer match, on May 27, 1967, players reported, according to Stanley Frank, that before the game the referee had instructed them "to stay down every nine minutes." The resulting hue and cry rose all the way to the House Communications Subcommittee. From that day to this, no one has been able to figure out how to screen advertising jingles during a televised soccer game. The result is that commercial television has treated soccer almost as if it didn't exist.

Topic sentence: question to be answered

Analysis of causes

Commercial TV requires commercial breaks

Soccer is played with only one break

Example of failed attempt to adapt soccer to TV

Result: little soccer on TV

Using Cause and Effect in an Academic Discipline

This paragraph from a textbook on American history explains the causes of a "fateful decision" in the 1960s—fateful because, as the authors' text goes on to explain, the decision had grave and far-reaching consequences for the United States.

Many factors played a role in [President Lyndon] Johnson's fateful decision [to escalate the Vietnam War]. But the most obvious explanation is that the new president faced many pressures to expand the American involvement and only a very few to limit it.

Topic sentence: summary of causes to be discussed

As the untested successor to a revered and martyred president, he felt obliged to prove his worthiness for the office by continuing the policies of his predecessor. Aid to South Vietnam had been one of the most prominent of those policies. Johnson also felt it necessary to retain in his administration many of the important figures of the Kennedy years. In doing so, he surrounded himself with a group of foreign-policy advisers—Secretary of State Dean Rusk, Secretary of Defense Robert McNamara, National Security Adviser McGeorge Bundy—who strongly believed not only that the United States had an important obligation to resist communism in Vietnam, but that it possessed the ability and resources to make that resistance successful. As a result, Johnson seldom had access to information making clear how difficult the new commitment might become. A compliant Congress raised little protest to, and indeed at one point openly endorsed, Johnson's use of executive powers to lead the nation into war. And for several years at least, public opinion remained firmly behind him—in part because Barry Goldwater's bellicose remarks about the war during the 1964 campaign made Johnson seem by comparison to be a moderate on the issue. Above all, intervention in South Vietnam was fully consistent with nearly twenty years of American foreign policy. An anticommunist ally was appealing to the United States for assistance; all the assumptions of the containment doctrine seemed to require the nation to oblige. Johnson seemed unconcerned that the government of South Vietnam existed only because the United States had put it there, and that the regime had never succeeded in acquiring the loyalty of its people. Vietnam, he believed, provided a test of American willingness to fight communist aggression, a test he was determined not to fail.

—Richard N. Current et al., *American History: A Survey*

Causes:

Need to prove worthiness

Advisers urging involvement and shutting off alternative views

Congressional cooperation

Support of public opinion

Consistency with American foreign policy against communism

CASE STUDY
Using Cause and Effect

An ardent supporter of her school's track team, Kate Krueger was a sophomore during the team's first winning season in many years. At the end of the season, the student newspaper published a letter to the editor saying that the successes were due to a new coach. Krueger found this explanation inadequate and decided to say so in her own letter. The cause-and-effect analysis below appeared in the newspaper the following week.

Between the first draft and the final version of her letter, Krueger made one significant addition. At first, she ignored any contributions of the new coach, thinking that the original letter writer had more than covered them. But since Krueger actually agreed that the coach had helped the team, her first draft did what she accused the letter of doing: It oversimplified. In her revision, Krueger acknowledged the coach's contributions while also detailing the other causes she saw at work.

May 2, 2001

TO THE EDITOR:

I take issue with Tom Boatz's letter that was printed in the April 30 *Weekly*. Boatz attributes the success of this year's track team solely to the new coach, John Barak. I have several close friends who are athletes on the track team, so as an interested observer and fan I believe that Boatz oversimplified the causes of the team's recent success.

To be sure, Coach Barak did improve the training regimen and overall morale, and these have certainly contributed to the winning season. Both Coach Barak and the team members themselves can share credit for an impressive work ethic and a sense of camaraderie unequaled in previous years. However, several factors outside Coach Barak's control may have been even more influential.

This year's team gained several phenomenal freshman athletes, such as Kristin Hall, who anchored the 4x400 and 4x800 relays and played an integral part in setting several school records, and Eric Asper, who was undefeated in the shot put.

Even more important, and also unmentioned by Tom Boatz, is the college's increased funding for the track program. Last year the school allotted 50 percent more for equipment, and the results have been dramatic. For example, the new vaulting poles are now the correct length and correspond to the weights of the individual athletes, giving them more power and height. Some vaulters have been able to vault as much as a foot higher than their previous records. Similarly, new starting blocks have allowed the team's sprinters to drop valuable seconds off their times.

I agree with Tom Boatz that Coach Barak deserves much credit for the track team's successes. But the athletes do, too, and so does the college for at last supporting its track program.

— KATE KRUEGER '03

GINA KOLATA

A *New York Times* science reporter, GINA KOLATA conveys complicated scientific information in an engaging, understandable manner. She was born in 1948 in Baltimore and at the University of Maryland studied microbiology (BA, 1969) and mathematics (MA, 1973). While continuing her graduate work at the Massachusetts Institute of Technology, Kolata discovered that she was "impatient with the slow pace of research" and decided instead to pursue science journalism. She began as a copyeditor at *Science* magazine and soon became a staff writer. In 1987 she moved to the *New York Times*, where her writing focuses on medicine, biology, math, computers, and ethics. Kolata has written several books about issues in science: *The Baby Doctors: Probing the Limits of Fetal Medicine* (1990), *Sex in America: A Definitive Study* (1995), *Clone: The Road to Dolly and the Path Ahead* (1998), and, most recently, *Flu: The Story of the Great Influenza Pandemic of 1918 and the Search for the Virus That Caused It* (1999).

Probing Disease Clusters

In this article from the *New York Times* in January 1999, Kolata explores the facts about so-called disease clusters, cases of an illness that seem unusually prevalent in a given area and that are often linked to environmental causes. Kolata lays out the cause-and-effect debate without taking a position. In the next essay Atul Gawande examines the debate over cancer clusters in particular and does take a position.

The trouble began when Bobbie Gallagher noticed that her two-year-old daughter was behaving strangely, obsessively spinning and scrupulously setting her toys in rows. Alanna Gallagher turned out to have autism, a rare neurological disorder of unknown cause.

So did Alanna's little brother. So did about forty other children who lived in the Gallaghers' town of Brick, New Jersey, near the seashore.

The parents in Brick were alarmed. On average, one child in five hundred is autistic; in the town, the figure is about three times that.

But what does it mean? Does Brick have toxic chemicals in the water, pollutants in the air?

The problem, scientists say, may be impossible to resolve. It was yet another instance of a phenomenon that makes many statisticians shudder. It was a disease cluster—the Boy Who Cried Wolf of epidemiology.[1]

Every time a disease cluster turns up, communities worry, scientists scramble

[1] The branch of medicine focused on the causes, spread, and control of disease. —EDS.

for a cause and, as in the new movie based on Jonathan Harr's 1995 book, *A Civil Action*, about a leukemia cluster in Woburn, Massachusetts, lawyers start suing. Yet over and over again, despite years—sometimes decades—of efforts to link the disease with a cause, scientists usually come up empty handed.

It can sound paradoxical. Here are unusual numbers of people with a dis- 7
ease. Toxic chemicals are everywhere, and many of them cause cancers and other diseases in laboratory animals. Why should it be so hard to find a cause?

Some disease clusters have been successfully linked to toxins: Coal min- 8
ers got black lung disease; asbestos workers got mesothelioma. Workers clean-ing containers where polyvinyl chloride was synthesized, breathing in fumes, got cancer of the blood vessels of the liver until machines replaced them.

But these examples of proven cause and effect are the rare exceptions, 9
statisticians say. And they have two things in common: The chemical expo-sure was enormous, and the disease was extraordinarily rare.

Most disease clusters are very different. Autism, breast cancer and leu- 10
kemia are fairly common. And even when there does seem to be an unusually high incidence of a disease, the search for a chemical basis usually turns up minute amounts of toxic substances that also are found in other places where there are no clusters. In other words, linking the suspect chemicals to the dis-ease can be very hard. It can also be difficult to know if a cluster is anything more than a chance occurrence. And chance is hard to ignore.

Clusters will naturally appear even when events occur at random, said Dr. 11
Persi Diaconis, a statistician at Stanford University. "There was a famous example of this when bombs were hitting London during World War II," he said. "People were sure they were targeting individual places and they made up the most elaborate scenarios" to explain how the bomb targets were selected. But in the end, when the pattern was analyzed, the bombing turned out to be random.

Another problem is how to draw the boundaries of a cluster. 12

Dr. James Robins, a statistician at Harvard University's School of Public 13
Health, said it is a natural tendency to draw boundaries around groups of events to make clusters happen. If there are three children with cancer on a single block, you may draw your circle around the block—making that a clus-ter—rather than around the town as a whole, which may show no cluster.

Say you do find a cluster. Unless you identify, say, black lung or mesothe- 14
lioma, statisticians say, the next question is: How can you decide if the cluster was caused by blind random clumpings of cases, with no environmental cause, or by a toxin in the environment?

Why would only one town have a disease cluster, some experts ask, 15
while other places with the same pollutants in the air or water do not? One

possibility might be an unidentified chemical in a mix of pollutants that is unique to the town. But that, of course, raises questions of how to find it.

Finally, there is the indirect exposure problem. If there is no direct link   16
between chemicals and a disease, the tendency is to look for other exposures. Could the fathers, for example, have had their sperm affected when they were growing up? Or could the mothers have been exposed to chemicals during pregnancy? Some statisticians say that if people look hard enough and slice the data enough ways, an association will emerge. What it means is another question.

Others are optimistic. Suzanne Condon, the director of the bureau of   17
environmental health assessment at the Massachusetts Department of Public Health, said that in an unpublished study her department found that in the Woburn case, women who drank water from certain wells when they were pregnant were more likely to have children who developed leukemia. "We believe this sheds a lot of light on what happened in Woburn," she said. W. R. Grace, which was accused along with Beatrice Foods of dumping chemicals in a way that allowed them to reach the water supply, paid $8 million into a settlement fund. Both companies agreed to finance an expensive cleanup plan.

The Massachusetts health department, however, warned on its Web page,   18
"Findings should be interpreted with caution due to the limitations of conducting statistical analyses on small populations."

That may not be what people want to hear, statisticians concede.   19
"People—and I, too—find it hard to accept that it is just random chance that brought this horrible consequence," said Dr. David Freedman, a statistician at the University of California at Berkeley.

Some statisticians ask whether it is worthwhile to keep pouring money   20
and effort into searches for clusters and searches to explain them.

"The question is, at what point do you say we've seen too many like this?"   21
Dr. Robins asked. "Huge amounts of money" have gone to study disease clusters where the suspected cause was tiny amounts of chemicals, he added, and so far, "nothing has come of it."

––––––––––––

Journal Writing

Based on what you learned from "Probing Disease Clusters," write briefly in your journal about whether you think governments should devote resources to finding the causes of specific disease clusters, such as the autism cluster in Brick, New Jersey (pars. 1–4). (To take your journal writing further, see "From Journal to Essay" on the facing page.)

Questions on Meaning

1. What is a disease cluster? Why would a disease cluster concern people who live in the area where it occurs?
2. What reasons does Kolata give for the difficulty in clearly linking apparent disease clusters to environmental toxins?
3. Why would the subject of disease clusters especially interest the statisticians Kolata quotes? What is a statistician?

Questions on Writing Strategy

1. What is Kolata's PURPOSE here, and how does she fulfill that purpose for her intended AUDIENCE?
2. Kolata cites the opinions of experts in paragraphs 11, 13, 17–19, and 21. Why does she do so, particularly in her concluding paragraphs?
3. **OTHER METHODS.** What EXAMPLES of disease clusters does Kolata include? How do these examples help her develop her analysis of cause and effect?

Questions on Language

1. What does Kolata mean when she calls disease clusters "the Boy Who Cried Wolf of epidemiology" (par. 5)?
2. In paragraph 16 Kolata writes, "Some statisticians say that if people look hard enough and slice the data enough ways, an association will emerge." How does an "association" differ from a cause-and-effect relationship?
3. Consult a dictionary if you are unsure of the meanings of the following words: neurological (par. 1); leukemia (6); paradoxical (7); asbestos, mesothelioma, polyvinyl chloride, synthesized (8).

Suggestions for Writing

1. **FROM JOURNAL TO ESSAY.** Use your journal entry (facing page) to help you role-play for the following assignment. Imagine you are a New Jersey public health official whose agency has decided not to fund research into the causes of autism in the town of Brick (pars. 1–4). Write a letter to the parents there explaining your agency's decision. Alternatively, imagine you are the parent of an autistic child in that town, and write a letter to the state public health department explaining why such research should be funded. Be sure to keep your audience's potential objections in mind.
2. Consider a disease you've known firsthand or secondhand (because you or someone you know has had it). Do some research into current scientific thinking on the causes of this disease. In an essay, explain the disease and its causes, being sure to acknowledge any controversies about causes or effects.
3. **CRITICAL WRITING.** In an essay, ANALYZE the various causal relationships that Kolata discusses in "Probing Disease Clusters." Do you think the author adequately explains the relationships? Why, or why not?

4. **CONNECTIONS.** The following essay by Atul Gawande also focuses on disease clusters, specifically cancer clusters. COMPARE AND CONTRAST how Kolata and Gawande approach their subject, what they emphasize and de-emphasize, and what conclusions they reach. Does one essay strike you as more effective than the other? Why?

Gina Kolata on Writing

On the *New York Times*'s "Ask a Reporter" Web page, Gina Kolata was asked by a fifth grader what a reporter's job is. Her response could be applied to other kinds of writing as well.

A reporter must be able to recognize a good story and to know who the appropriate people are to interview. You have to be willing to look through any and all relevant documents rather than just taking people's word for what may be in them. You have to be honest and trustworthy, so that people will want to talk to you.and so that even if they do not like what the article says, they at least think they were treated fairly.

It takes a combination of skill with people, dogged research, storytelling ability and, sometimes, courage to write a great story. But, in the end, outstanding newspaper stories have changed the world.

For Discussion

1. Why do you think Kolata says, "You have to be willing to look through any and all relevant documents rather than just taking people's word for what may be in them"?
2. Which of the journalism requirements Kolata mentions apply to research writing in college? Which don't? Why?

ATUL GAWANDE

A doctor and a prominent medical writer, ATUL GAWANDE was born in 1965.
He grew up in Athens, Ohio, a largely white city in which, as the child of
Indian immigrants, he had a "little extra thing, [. . .] a leg up." After earning
graduate degrees in philosophy and economics from Oxford University and
in public health from Harvard University, Gawande worked in the Clinton
administration as a speechwriter and a senior adviser on health policy. But,
he observes, "there was a limit to how much I could say without some real-
world expertise. And medicine was always what I wanted to do." Gawande
attended Harvard Medical School and is currently a surgical resident in
Boston. While a resident, he began writing regularly for the online magazine
Slate and then became a staff writer for *The New Yorker*, where he focuses
on medical ethics and surgical error. Gawande has published two books,
Good Medicine (2000) and *Complications: A Surgeon's Notes on an Imperfect
Science* (2002).

The Cancer-Cluster Myth

Like the previous selection, Gina Kolata's "Probing Disease Clusters," this
essay examines what we know about the causes of apparent clusters of disease, specifically cancer. Gawande's title reveals his findings, but he well recognizes the beliefs and feelings on the other side, too. The essay first
appeared in *The New Yorker* in 1999 and then in *Best American Science and
Nature Writing 2000*.

Is it something in the water? During the past two decades, reports of cancer clusters—communities in which there seems to be an unusual number of
cancers—have soared. The place-names and the suspects vary, but the basic
story is nearly always the same. The Central Valley farming town of McFarland, California, came to national attention in the eighties after a woman
whose child was found to have cancer learned of four other children with cancer in just a few blocks around her home. Soon doctors identified six more
cases in the town, which had a population of 6,400. The childhood-cancer
rate proved to be four times as high as expected. Suspicion fell on groundwater wells that had been contaminated by pesticides, and lawsuits were filed
against six chemical companies.

In 1990, in Los Alamos, New Mexico, a local artist learned of seven cases
of brain cancer among residents of a small section of the town's Western
Area. How could seven cases of brain cancer in one neighborhood be merely
a coincidence? "I think there is something seriously wrong with the Western
Area," the artist, Tyler Mercier, told the *Times*. "The neighborhood may be

contaminated." In fact, the Los Alamos National Laboratory, which was the birthplace of the atomic bomb, had once dumped millions of gallons of radioactive and toxic waste in the surrounding desert, without providing any solid documentation about precisely what was dumped or where. In San Ramon, California, a cluster of brain cancers was discovered at a high-school class reunion. On Long Island, federal, state, and local officials are currently spending $21 million to try to find out why towns like West Islip and Levittown have elevated rates of breast cancer.

I myself live in a cancer cluster. A resident in my town—Newton, Mass-   3
achusetts—became suspicious of a decades-old dump next to an elementary school after her son developed cancer. She went from door to door and turned up forty-two cases of cancer within a few blocks of her home. The cluster is being investigated by the state health department.

No doubt, one reason for the veritable cluster of cancer clusters in recent   4
years is the widespread attention that cases like those in McFarland and Los Alamos received and the ensuing increase in public awareness and concern. Another reason, though, is the way in which states have responded to that concern: They've made available to the public data on potential toxic sites, along with information from "cancer registries" about local cancer rates. The result has been to make it easier for people to find worrisome patterns, and, more and more, they've done so. In the late eighties, public-health departments were receiving between 1,300 and 1,600 reports of feared cancer clusters, or "cluster alarms," each year. Last year, in Massachusetts alone, the state health department responded to between 3,000 and 4,000 cluster alarms. Under public pressure, state and federal agencies throughout the country are engaging in "cancer mapping" to find clusters that nobody has yet reported.

A community that is afflicted with an unusual number of cancers quite   5
naturally looks for a cause in the environment—in the ground, the water, the air. And correlations are sometimes found: The cluster may arise after, say, contamination of the water supply by a possible carcinogen. The problem is that when scientists have tried to confirm such causes, they haven't been able to. Raymond Richard Neutra, California's chief environmental health investigator and an expert on cancer clusters, points out that among hundreds of exhaustive, published investigations of residential clusters in the United States, not one has convincingly identified an underlying environmental cause. Abroad, in only a handful of cases has a neighborhood cancer cluster been shown to arise from an environmental cause. And only one of these cases ended with the discovery of an unrecognized carcinogen. It was in a Turkish village called Karain, where twenty-five cases of mesothelioma, a rare form of lung cancer, cropped up among fewer than eight hundred villagers. (Scientists traced the cancer to a mineral called erionite, which is abundant

in the soil there.) Given the exceedingly poor success rate of such investigations, epidemiologists[1] tend to be skeptical about their worth.

When public-health investigators fail to turn up any explanation for the
appearance of a cancer cluster, communities can find it frustrating, even suspicious. After all, these investigators are highly efficient in tracking down the
causes of other kinds of disease clusters. "Outbreak" stories usually start the
same way: Someone has an intuition that there are just too many people coming down with some illness and asks the health department to investigate.
With outbreaks, though, such intuitions are vindicated in case after case.
Consider the cluster of American Legionnaires who came down with an
unusual lung disease in Philadelphia in 1976; the startling number of limb
deformities among children born to Japanese women in the sixties; and the
appearance of rare *Pneumocystis carinii* pneumonia in five young homosexual
men in Los Angeles in 1981. All these clusters prompted what are called "hot-
pursuit investigations" by public-health authorities, and all resulted in the
definitive identification of a cause: namely, *Legionella* pneumonitis, or Legionnaires' disease; mercury poisoning from contaminated fish; and HIV infection.
In fact, successful hot-pursuit investigations of disease clusters take place
almost every day. A typical recent issue of the Centers for Disease Control's
Morbidity and Mortality Weekly Report described a cluster of six patients who
developed muscle pain after eating fried fish. Investigation by health authorities identified the condition as Haff disease, which is caused by a toxin sometimes present in buffalo fish. Four of the cases were traced to a single Louisiana
wholesaler, whose suppliers fished the same tributaries of the Mississippi
River.

What's more, for centuries scientists have succeeded in tracking down the
causes of clusters of cancers that aren't residential. In 1775 the surgeon Perci-
vall Pott discovered a cluster of scrotal-cancer cases among London chimney
sweeps. It was common practice then for young boys to do their job naked, the
better to slither down chimneys, and so high concentrations of carcinogenic
coal dust would accumulate in the ridges of their scrota. Pott's chimney sweeps
proved to be a classic example of an "occupational" cluster. Scientists have
also been successful in investigating so-called medical clusters. In the late
1960s, for example, the pathologist Arthur Herbst was surprised to come
across eight women between the ages of fifteen and twenty-two who had
clear-cell adenocarcinoma, a type of cervical cancer that had never been
seen in women so young. In 1971 he published a study linking the cases to an

[1] Scientists who study the causes, spread, and control of disease. —EDS.

anti-miscarriage drug called diethylstilbestrol, or DES, which the mothers of these women had taken during pregnancy. Subsequent studies confirmed the link with DES, which was taken by some 5 million pregnant women between 1938 and 1971. The investigation of medical and occupational cancer clusters has led to the discovery of dozens of carcinogens, including asbestos, vinyl chloride, and certain artificial dyes.

So why don't hot-pursuit investigations of neighborhood cancer clusters   8
yield such successes? For one thing, many clusters fall apart simply because they violate basic rules of cancer behavior. Cancer develops when a cell starts multiplying out of control, and the process by which this happens isn't straightforward. A carcinogen doesn't just flip some cancer switch to "on." Cells have a variety of genes that keep them functioning normally, and it takes an almost chance combination of successive mutations in these genes — multiple "hits," as cancer biologists put it — to make a cell cancerous rather than simply killing it. A carcinogen provides one hit. Other hits may come from a genetic defect, a further environmental exposure, a spontaneous mutation. Even when people have been subjected to a heavy dose of a carcinogen and many cells have been damaged, they will not all get cancer. (For example, DES causes clear-cell adenocarcinoma in only one out of a thousand women exposed to it in utero.) As a rule, it takes a long time before a cell receives enough hits to produce the cancer, and so, unlike infections or acute toxic reactions, the effect of a carcinogen in a community won't be seen for years. Besides, in a mobile society like ours, cancer victims who seem to be clustered may not all have lived in an area long enough for their cancers to have a common cause.

To produce a cancer cluster, a carcinogen has to hit a great many cells in   9
a great many people. A brief, low-level exposure to a carcinogen is unlikely to do the job. Raymond Richard Neutra has calculated that for a carcinogen to produce a sevenfold increase in the occurrence of a cancer (a rate of increase not considered particularly high by epidemiologists) a population would have to be exposed to 70 percent of the maximum tolerated dose in the course of a full year, or the equivalent. "This kind of exposure is credible as part of chemotherapy or in some work settings," he wrote in a 1990 paper, "but it must be very rare for most neighborhood and school settings." For that reason, investigations of occupational cancer clusters have been vastly more successful than investigations of residential cancer clusters.

Matters are further complicated by the fact that cancer isn't one disease.   10
What turns a breast cell into breast cancer isn't what turns a white blood cell into leukemia: The precise combination of hits varies. Yet some clusters lump together people with tumors that have entirely different biologies and are unlikely to have the same cause. The cluster in McFarland, for example, in-

volved eleven children with nine kinds of cancer. Some of the brain-cancer cases in the Los Alamos cluster were really cancers of other organs that had metastasized to the brain.

If true neighborhood clusters—that is, local clusters arising from a common environmental cause—are so rare, why do we see so many? In a sense, we're programmed to: Nearly all of them are the result of almost irresistible errors in perception. In a pioneering article published in 1971, the cognitive psychologists Daniel Kahneman and Amos Tversky identified a systematic error in human judgment, which they called the Belief in the Law of Small Numbers. People assume that the pattern of a large population will be replicated in all its subsets. But clusters will occur simply through chance. After seeing a long sequence of red on the roulette wheel, people find it hard to resist the idea that black is "due"—or else they start to wonder whether the wheel is rigged. We assume that a sequence of R-R-R-R-R-R is somehow less random than, say, R-R-B-R-B-B. But the two sequences are equally likely. (Casinos make a lot of money from the Belief in the Law of Small Numbers.) Truly random patterns often don't appear random to us. The statistician William Feller studied one classic example. During the Germans' intensive bombing of South London in the Second World War, a few areas were hit several times and others were not hit at all. The places that were not hit seemed to have been deliberately spared, and, Kahneman says, people became convinced that those places were where the Germans had their spies. When Feller analyzed the statistics of the bomb hits, however, he found that the distribution matched a random pattern.

Daniel Kahneman himself was involved in a similar case. "During the Yom Kippur War, in 1973, I was approached by people in the Israeli Air Force," he told me. "They had two squads that had left base, and when the squads came back one had lost four planes and the other had lost none. They wanted to investigate for all kinds of differences between the squadrons, like whether pilots in one squadron had seen their wives more than in the other. I told them to stop wasting their time." A difference of four lost planes could easily have occurred by chance. Yet Kahneman knew that if air force officials investigated they would inevitably find some measurable differences between the squadrons and feel compelled to act on them.

Human beings evidently have a deep-seated tendency to see meaning in the ordinary variations that are bound to appear in small samples. For example, most basketball players and fans believe that players have hot and cold streaks in shooting. In a paper entitled "The Hot Hand in Basketball," Tversky and two colleagues painstakingly analyzed the shooting of individual players in more than eighty games played by the Philadelphia 76ers, the New

Jersey Nets, and the New York Knicks during the 1980–1981 season. It turned out that basketball players—even notorious "streak shooters"—have no more runs of hits or misses than would be expected by chance. Because of the human tendency to perceive clusters in random sequences, however, Tversky and his colleagues found that "no amount of exposure to such sequences will convince the player, the coach, or the fan that the sequences are in fact random. The more basketball one watches and plays, the more opportunities one has to observe what appears to be streak shooting."

In epidemiology, the tendency to isolate clusters from their context is known as the Texas sharpshooter fallacy. Like a Texas sharpshooter who shoots at the side of a barn and then draws a bull's-eye around the bullet holes, we tend to notice cases first—four cancer patients on one street—and then define the population base around them. With rare conditions, such as Haff disease or mercury poisoning, even a small clutch of cases really would represent a dramatic excess, no matter how much Texas sharpshooting we did. But most cancers are common enough that noticeable residential clusters are bound to occur. Raymond Richard Neutra points out that given a typical registry of eighty different cancers, you could expect 2,750 of California's 5,000 census tracts to have statistically significant but perfectly random elevations of cancer. So if you check to see whether your neighborhood has an elevated rate of a specific cancer, chances are better than even that it does—and it almost certainly won't mean a thing. Even when you've established a correlation between a specific cancer and a potential carcinogen, scientists have hardly any way to distinguish the "true" cancer cluster that's worth investigating from the crowd of cluster impostors. 14

One helpful tip-off is an extraordinarily high cancer rate. In Karain, Turkey, the incidence of mesothelioma was more than *seven thousand times* as high as expected. In even the most serious cluster alarms that public-health departments have received, however, the cancer rate has been nowhere near that high. (The lawyer Jan Schlichtmann, of *Civil Action* fame, is now representing victims of a cancer cluster in Dover Township, New Jersey, where the childhood cancer rate is 30 percent higher than expected.) 15

This isn't to say that carcinogens in the local environment can't raise cancer rates; it's just that such increases disappear in all the background variation that occurs in small populations. In larger populations, it's a different story. The 1986 Chernobyl disaster exposed hundreds of thousands of people to radiation; scientists were able to establish that it caused a more than one-hundredfold increase in thyroid cancer among children years later. By contrast, investigating an isolated neighborhood cancer cluster is almost always a futile exercise. Investigators knock on doors, track down former residents, and check medical records. They sample air, soil, and water. Thousands, some- 16

times millions, of dollars are spent. And with all those tests, correlations inevitably turn up. Yet, years later, in case after case, nothing definite is confirmed.

"The reality is that they're an absolute, total, and complete waste of   17
taxpayer dollars," says Alan Bender, an epidemiologist with the Minnesota
Department of Health, which investigated more than 1,000 cancer clusters in
the state between 1984 and 1995. The problem of perception and politics,
however, remains. If you're a public-health official, try explaining why a dozen
children with cancer in one neighborhood doesn't warrant investigation.
According to a national study, health departments have been able to reassure
people by education in more than 70 percent of cluster alarms. Somewhere
between 1 and 3 percent of alarms, however, result in expensive on-site investigations. And the cases that are investigated aren't even the best-grounded
ones: They are the cases pushed by the media, enraged citizens, or politicians.
"Look, you can't just kiss people off," Bender says. In fact, Minnesota has built
such an effective public-response apparatus that it has not needed to conduct
a formal cluster investigation in three years.

Public-health departments aren't lavishly funded, and scientists are reluc-   18
tant to see money spent on something that has proved to be as unproductive
as neighborhood cluster alarms or cancer mapping. Still, public confidence is
poorly served by officials who respond to inquiries with a scientific brushoff
and a layer of bureaucracy. To be part of a cancer cluster is a frightening thing,
and it magnifies our ordinary response when cancer strikes: We want to hold
something or someone responsible, even allocate blame. Health officials who
understand the fear and anger can have impressive success, as the ones in
Minnesota have shown. But there are times when you cannot maintain public trust without acting on public concerns. Science alone won't put to rest
questions like the one a McFarland mother posed to the *Los Angeles Times:*
"How many more of our children must die before something is done?"

Journal Writing

In paragraph 11 Gawande writes, "Truly random patterns often don't appear random
to us." In paragraphs 11–13 he gives as examples the distribution of reds in a roulette
game, bomb hits in World War II London, plane losses in the Israeli Air Force, and
successful shots by basketball players. Can you think of other examples where clusters
seem evident? In your journal, speculate on why people are "programmed," as
Gawande puts it, to find patterns in things that are actually random. (To take your
journal writing further, see "From Journal to Essay" on the next page.)

Questions on Meaning

1. Gawande says that over "the past two decades, reports of cancer clusters [. . .] have soared" (par. 1). How does he explain this increase?
2. Why, in Gawande's view, do communities become frustrated when health experts cannot discover the causes of a local disease cluster?
3. What is "the Texas sharpshooter fallacy" (par. 14), and how does it affect people's perception of cancer clusters?
4. In paragraphs 5 and 14 Gawande uses "correlation" to describe links between toxins and cancers that are not, in the end, confirmed causes and effects. What is the difference between a "correlation" and a cause-and-effect relationship?
5. What is Gawande's THESIS? Where is it stated? How does it relate to the last two paragraphs of the essay?

Questions on Writing Strategy

1. What is Gawande's PURPOSE in this essay? Is he writing merely to inform, or is he attempting to persuade readers of something? How can you tell?
2. Why does Gawande open by citing a number of suspected neighborhood cancer clusters?
3. In paragraph 3 Gawande writes that he himself lives in a cancer cluster. What does this fact contribute to the essay?
4. Why might Gawande have chosen to conclude by quoting the concerned mother's question to the Los Angeles Times?
5. **OTHER METHODS.** In paragraphs 6–8 Gawande CLASSIFIES disease clusters into four groups. What are these groups, and how do they help the author make his point?

Questions on Language

1. Gawande's explanation in paragraphs 8–10 is fairly technical. How does he succeed in communicating this complex medical information to his intended AUDIENCE?
2. What is the effect of the quotation that starts paragraph 17?
3. If you are not sure of the meanings of the following words, check your dictionary: contaminated (par. 1); radioactive, toxic (2); veritable (4); afflicted, carcinogen, exhaustive (5); vindicated, deformities, pneumonia (6); accumulate, scrota, pathologist (7); mutations, genetic, spontaneous, in utero, mobile (8); chemotherapy (9); leukemia, metastasized (10); cognitive, replicated, roulette (11); inevitably (12); impostors (14); mesothelioma (15); thyroid (16); bureaucracy, allocate (18).

Suggestions for Writing

1. **FROM JOURNAL TO ESSAY.** Working from your journal entry (previous page), write an essay in which you propose some probable causes for the human tendency to

perceive patterns in what are essentially random occurrences. Like Gawande, use EXAMPLES to clarify your cause-and-effect explanation. You may also wish to classify your examples into groups.

2. In paragraph 16 Gawande refers to the 1986 Chernobyl disaster, in which a Russian nuclear reactor exploded. After doing some research about this event, write an essay in which you discuss its causes as well as its short- and long-term effects.

3. **CRITICAL WRITING.** How convinced are you by Gawande's essay, and why? In your answer you might consider two elements of the essay in particular: Gawande's use of EVIDENCE, including facts, examples, and expert opinions; and the extent to which Gawande presents himself as a reasonable, fair person by acknowledgment of opposing views, use of a moderate TONE, and other means.

4. **CONNECTIONS.** Gawande's essay and Gina Kolata's "Probing Disease Clusters" (p. 422) cover much of the same ground, but Gawande focuses just on cancer clusters and he adds considerably to the information presented by Kolata. What additional information does Gawande include? How does each essay's amount of information affect your response to it?

Atul Gawande on Writing

In a 2001 interview for the online edition of *The New Yorker*, Atul Gawande explained how he became a medical writer after working in government and attending medical school. Gawande's parents are both doctors, so he grew up with magazines like *The Journal of Urology* and *The New England Journal of Medicine* on the coffee table. "No one in my family is in the writing business, though," Gawande says. "And I never thought I would be, either. About four years ago, Persian Gulf War syndrome was in the news. A friend at the Internet magazine *Slate* asked if I would write a short little thing explaining what the syndrome was. I did. Then I wrote another piece for *Slate*. And pretty soon I found that the writing was a great way to keep me thinking, now and then, about policy and people while my day-to-day thinking was about procedures and persons."

As a medical writer who is also a doctor, Gawande faces tough questions when writing about errors and other problems occurring within medical practice. "I do have colleagues who question whether discussing these issues accomplishes anything—or only provides fodder for doctor bashing. [. . .] I was especially nervous about the essay that took a close look at a terrible, nearly fatal mistake that I had made, but I wrote it as a way of understanding why all doctors make mistakes. I feared the worst—that people would come away only seeing me as an incompetent doctor. I must say, however, that the reception of these pieces—among both patients and doctors—has been far more positive and thoughtful than I ever could have hoped for. It surprised me that colleagues—both at my hospital and elsewhere—wrote to say these were issues that had been troubling them as much as they had troubled me. They were glad to see some concrete suggestions on how to do better, and they were glad that it was understood as something more complex than the villainous doctor of the day who gets written up in the newspapers."

For Discussion

1. What does Gawande mean when he says, "writing was a great way to keep me thinking, now and then, about policy and people while my day-to-day thinking [as a practicing doctor] was about procedures and persons"?
2. Why did Gawande choose to publish an essay about "a nearly fatal mistake" that he had made as a doctor? How do you think writing helped him deal with his mistake? How would you respond to his writing about medical mistakes if you were one of his medical colleagues or one of his patients?

GORE VIDAL

GORE VIDAL was born in 1925 at the US Military Academy at West Point, where his father was an instructor. At the age of nineteen, he wrote his first novel, *Williwaw* (1946), while serving as a warrant officer aboard an army supply ship. Twenty-one other novels followed, including *Burr* (1973), *Duluth* (1983), *Lincoln* (1984), *Empire* (1987), and *Hollywood* (1989). He has also written mysteries under the pen name Edgar Box. As a playwright, he is best known for *Visit to a Small Planet* (1957), which was made into a film. The grandson of Senator T. P. Gore, who represented Oklahoma for thirty years, Vidal twice ran unsuccessfully for Congress, and in 1992 he portrayed a senator in the movie *Bob Roberts*. A provocative and perceptive literary and social critic, Vidal is a frequent contributor to *The New York Review of Books* and other magazines, and he has published more than a dozen collections of essays, most recently *The Essential Gore Vidal* (1999) and *The Last Empire* (2001). His latest books also include a memoir, *Palimpsest* (1995); a history, *The American Presidency* (1998); and a novel, *The Golden Age* (2000). Vidal divides his time between Italy and America.

Drugs

Vidal first published "Drugs" in 1970 on the *New York Times*'s op-ed page and then included the essay in *Homage to Daniel Shays: Collected Essays 1952–1972*. In just twelve short paragraphs, Vidal analyzes several sets of cause and effect: why making drugs illegal does not work to stop drug addiction and trafficking, why legalizing drugs would work, and why nonetheless legalization is unlikely to occur. "Drugs" is dated in some ways, but the problem it addresses has only worsened. Lately, an increasing number of social scientists, medical professionals, and politicians have urged that we consider just such a radical solution as Vidal proposes.

It is possible to stop most drug addiction in the United States within a very short time. Simply make all drugs available and sell them at cost. Label each drug with a precise description of what effect — good and bad — the drug will have on the taker. This will require heroic honesty. Don't say that marijuana is addictive or dangerous when it is neither, as millions of people know — unlike "speed," which kills most unpleasantly, or heroin, which is addictive and difficult to kick.

For the record, I have tried — once — almost every drug and liked none, disproving the popular Fu Manchu theory that a single whiff of opium will enslave the mind. Nevertheless many drugs are bad for certain people to take and they should be told why in a sensible way.

Along with exhortation and warning, it might be good for our citizens to   3
recall (or learn for the first time) that the United States was the creation of
men who believed that each man has the right to do what he wants with his
own life as long as he does not interfere with his neighbor's pursuit of happiness. (That his neighbor's idea of happiness is persecuting others does confuse
matters a bit.)

This is a startling notion to the current generation of Americans. They   4
reflect a system of public education which has made the Bill of Rights, literally, unacceptable to a majority of high-school graduates (see the annual Pur-
due reports) who now form the "silent majority"—a phrase which that
underestimated wit Richard Nixon took from Homer, who used it to describe
the dead.

Now one can hear the warning rumble begin: If everyone is allowed to   5
take drugs everyone will and the GNP will decrease, the Commies will stop us
from making everyone free, and we shall end up a race of zombies, passively
murmuring "groovy" to one another. Alarming thought. Yet it seems most
unlikely that any reasonably sane person will become a drug addict if he
knows in advance what addiction is going to be like.

Is everyone reasonably sane? No. Some people will always become drug   6
addicts just as some people will always become alcoholics, and it is just too
bad. Every man, however, has the power (and should have the legal right) to
kill himself if he chooses. But since most men don't, they won't be mainliners
either. Nevertheless, forbidding people things they like or think they might
enjoy only makes them want those things all the more. This psychological
insight is, for some mysterious reason, perennially denied our governors.

It is a lucky thing for the American moralist that our country has always   7
existed in a kind of time-vacuum: We have no public memory of anything
that happened before last Tuesday. No one in Washington today recalls what
happened during the years alcohol was forbidden to the people by a Congress
that thought it had a divine mission to stamp out Demon Rum—launching,
in the process, the greatest crime wave in the country's history, causing thousands of deaths from bad alcohol, and creating a general (and persisting) contempt among the citizenry for the laws of the United States.

The same thing is happening today. But the government has learned   8
nothing from past attempts at prohibition, not to mention repression.

Last year when the supply of Mexican marijuana was slightly curtailed by   9
the Feds, the pushers got the kids hooked on heroin and deaths increased dramatically, particularly in New York. Whose fault? Evil men like the Mafiosi?
Permissive Dr. Spock? Wild-eyed Dr. Leary? No.

The government of the United States was responsible for those deaths.   10
The bureaucratic machine has a vested interest in playing cops and robbers.

Both the Bureau of Narcotics and the Mafia want strong laws against the sale and use of drugs because if drugs are sold at cost there would be no money in it for anyone.

If there was no money in it for the Mafia, there would be no friendly playground pushers, and addicts would not commit crimes to pay for the next fix. Finally, if there was no money in it, the Bureau of Narcotics would wither away, something they are not about to do without a struggle. 11

Will anything sensible be done? Of course not. The American people are as devoted to the idea of sin and its punishment as they are to making money—and fighting drugs is nearly as big a business as pushing them. Since the combination of sin and money is irresistible (particularly to the professional politician), the situation will only grow worse. 12

Journal Writing

Vidal is convinced that the best way to combat the drug problem in this country is to "make all drugs available and sell them at cost." Does this seem like a good idea to you? What do you think would be the practical effects—positive or negative—of legalizing drugs? (To take your journal writing further, see "From Journal to Essay" on the next page.)

Questions on Meaning

1. What do you take to be Vidal's main PURPOSE in writing this essay? How well does he accomplish it?
2. For what reasons, according to Vidal, is it unlikely that our drug laws will be eased? Can you suggest other possible reasons why the Bureau of Narcotics favors strict drug laws?
3. Vidal's essay was first published more than three decades ago. Do you find the views expressed in it still timely, or out of date?

Questions on Writing Strategy

1. How would you characterize Vidal's humor? Find some examples of it.
2. Where in the essay does Vidal appear to anticipate the response of his AUDIENCE? How can you tell?
3. What function do the essay's RHETORICAL QUESTIONS perform?
4. **OTHER METHODS.** Study Vidal's use of EXAMPLE in paragraphs 8–10. Does the example of the US government's role in heroin deaths effectively support Vidal's point that restricting drug use does not work? Is Vidal guilty here of oversimplification (p. 415)?

Questions on Language

1. Know the definitions of the following terms: exhortation (par. 3); GNP (5); mainliners, perennially (6); curtailed (9).
2. How do you interpret Vidal's use of the phrase "underestimated wit" to describe Richard Nixon?

Suggestions for Writing

1. **FROM JOURNAL TO ESSAY.** Look back at your journal entry on the effects of legalizing drugs and at Vidal's explanations for why they have *not* been legalized. In an essay, explain why you think the United States resists legalizing drugs. You may support Vidal's moral and economic arguments, you may oppose one or several of his claims, or you may propose new reasons of your own. In any case, be sure to make clear, as Vidal does, the connection between the foreseeable effects of legalization and the reasoning that keeps drugs illegal.
2. Research the situation reported by Vidal in paragraphs 9 and 10. (Begin with the *New York Times Index* for the years 1969 and 1970.) Write an essay that clearly and objectively analyzes the causes of the situation.
3. **CRITICAL WRITING.** How readily do you accept Vidal's statement that "each man has the right to do what he wants with his own life"—including, presumably, to be a drug addict—"as long as he does not interfere with his neighbor's pursuit of happiness" (par. 3)? Do you accept Vidal's implicit ASSUMPTION that people with easy access to drugs are not necessarily threats to their neighbors? Back up your answers with EVIDENCE from your experience and reading.
4. **CONNECTIONS.** Like Vidal, Meghan Daum, in "Safe-Sex Lies" (p. 442), takes a controversial view. Write an essay that COMPARES AND CONTRASTS the ways these two authors present their views. Consider in your essay how each author establishes his or her authority and credibility; uses evidence such as personal experience, facts, and examples; anticipates readers' responses; and addresses readers through TONE.

Gore Vidal on Writing

"Do you find writing easy?" Gerald Clark asked Gore Vidal for the *Paris Review*. "Do you enjoy it?"

Oh, yes, of course I enjoy it. I wouldn't do it if I didn't. Whenever I get up in the morning, I write for about three hours. I write novels in longhand on yellow pads, exactly like the First Criminal Nixon. For some reason I write plays and essays on the typewriter. The first draft usually comes rather fast. One oddity: I never reread a text until I have finished the first draft. Otherwise it's too discouraging. Also, when you have the whole thing in front of you for the first time, you've forgotten most of it and see it fresh. Rewriting, however, is a slow, grinding business.

When I first started writing, I used to plan everything in advance, not only chapter to chapter but page to page. Terribly constricting—like doing a film from someone else's meticulous treatment. About the time of *The Judgment of Paris* [a novel published in 1952] I started improvising. I began with a mood. A sentence. The first sentence is all-important. [My novel] *Washington, D.C.* began with a dream, a summer storm at night in a garden above the Potomac—that was Merrywood, where I grew up.

The most interesting thing about writing is the way that it obliterates time. Three hours seem like three minutes. Then there is the business of surprise. I never know what is coming next. The phrase that sounds in the head changes when it appears on the page. Then I start probing it with a pen, finding new meanings. Sometimes I burst out laughing at what is happening as I twist and turn sentences. Strange business, all in all. One never gets to the end of it. That's why I go on, I suppose. To see what the next sentences I write will be.

For Discussion

1. What is it that Vidal seems to enjoy most about writing?
2. What advantage does he find in not planning every page in advance?

MEGHAN DAUM

Born in 1970 in Palo Alto, California, MEGHAN DAUM is a writer known for provocative, witty essays on American life. Daum graduated from Vassar College with a BA in English (1992) and from Columbia University with an MA in writing (1996). She worked on the staffs of *Allure* magazine and Columbia University Press before turning to writing full-time. On public radio Daum is a contributor to *This American Life* and a commentator for *Morning Edition*. In print she is a contributing writer for *Harper's Bazaar* and has been published in *The New Yorker, GQ,* and other magazines. Her collection of essays, *Misspent Youth,* came out in 2001. Daum recently emigrated from New York City to rural Nebraska.

Safe-Sex Lies

This essay from the *New York Times Magazine* caused a stir when it was first published in January 1996. Daum deftly analyzes several damaging effects of the media's coverage of AIDS, especially the anxiety, shame, mistrust, and dishonesty that she and others of her generation experience.

I have been tested for HIV three times. I've gone to clinics and stuck my arm out for those disposable needles, each time forgetting the fear and nausea that descend upon me before the results come back, those minutes spent in a publicly financed waiting room staring at a video loop about "living with" this thing that kills you. These tests have taken place over five years, and the results have always been negative—not surprisingly in retrospect, since I am not a member of a "high-risk group," don't sleep around and don't take pity on heroin-addicted bass players by going to bed with them in the hopes of being thanked in the liner notes of their first major independent release. Still, getting tested always seemed like the thing to do. Despite my demographic profile, despite the fact that I grew up middle class, attended an elite college and do not personally know any women or straight men within that demographic profile who have the AIDS virus, I am terrified of this disease. I went to a college where condoms and dental dams lay in baskets in dormitory lobbies, where it seemed incumbent on health service counselors to give us the straight talk, to tell us never, ever to have sex without condoms unless we wanted to die; that's right, *die,* shrivel overnight, vomit up our futures, pose a threat to others. (And they'd seen it happen, oh, yes, they had.) They gave us pamphlets, didn't quite explain how to use dental dams, told us where we could get tested, threw us more fistfuls of condoms (even some glow-in-the-dark brands, just for variety). This can actually be fun, they said, if only we'd adopt a better attitude.

We're told we can get this disease and we believe it and vow to protect   2
ourselves, and intend (really, truly) to stick by this rule, until we don't because
we just can't, because it's just not fair, because our sense of entitlement
exceeds our sense of vulnerability. So we blow off precaution again and again,
and then we get scared and get tested, and when it comes out OK, we run out
of the clinic, pamphlets in hand, eyes cast upward, promising ourselves we'll
never be stupid again. But of course we are stupid, again and again. And the
testing is always for the same reasons and with the same results, and soon it
becomes more like fibbing about SAT scores ten years after the fact than lying
about whether we practice unsafe sex, a lie that sounds like such a breach of
contract with ourselves that we might as well be talking about putting a
loaded gun under our pillow every night.

Still, I've gone into more than a few relationships with the safest of inten-   3
tions and discarded them after the fourth or fifth encounter. Perhaps this is a
shocking admission, but my hunch is that I'm not the only one doing it. My
suspicion is, in fact, that very few of us—"us" being the demographic profile
frequently charged with thinking we're immortal, the population accused of
being cynical and lazy and weak—have really responded to the AIDS crisis
the way the federal government and educators would like us to believe. My
guess is that we're all but ignoring it and that almost anyone who claims
otherwise is lying.

It seems there is a lot of lying going around. One of the main tenets of the   4
safe-sex message is that ageless mantra "you don't know where he's been,"
meaning that everyone is a potential threat, that we're all either scoundrels or
ignoramuses. "He didn't tell me he was shooting drugs," says an HIV-positive
woman on a public-service advertisement. Safe-sex "documentaries" on MTV
and call-in radio shows on pop stations give us woman after woman whose boyfriend "claimed he loved me but was sleeping around." The message we receive
is that trusting anyone is itself an irresponsible act, that having faith in an intimate partner, particularly women in relation to men, is a symptom of such profound naïveté that we're obviously not mature enough to be having sex anyway.

I find this reasoning almost more troubling than the disease itself. It flies   5
in the face of the social order from which I, as someone born in 1970, was supposed to benefit. That this reasoning runs counter to almost any feminist
ideology—the ideology that proclaimed, at least back in the seventies, that
women should feel free to ask men on dates and wear jeans and have
orgasms—is an admission that no AIDS-concerned citizen is willing to make.
Two decades after *The Joy of Sex* made sexual pleasure permissible for both
sexes and three decades after the pill put a government-approved stamp on
premarital sex, we're still told not to trust each other. We've entered a period
where mistrust equals responsibility, where fear signifies health.

Since I spent all of the seventies under the age of ten, I've never known a   6
significantly different sexual and social climate. Supposedly this makes it easier to live with the AIDS crisis. Health educators and AIDS activists like to
think that people of my generation can be made to unlearn what we never
knew, to break the reckless habits we didn't actually form. But what we have
learned thoroughly is how not to enjoy ourselves. Just like our mothers, whose
adolescences were haunted by the abstract taboo against being "bad" girls, my
contemporaries and I are discouraged from doing what feels good. As it did
with our mothers, the onus falls largely on the women. We know that it's
much easier for women to contract HIV from a man than the other way
around. We know that an "unsafe" man generally means someone who has
shot drugs or slept with other men, or possibly slept with prostitutes. We find
ourselves wondering about these things over dinner dates. We look for any
hints of homosexual tendencies, any references to a hypodermic moment. We
try to catch him in the lie we've been told he'll tell.

What could be sadder? We're not allowed to believe anyone anymore.   7
And the reason we're not isn't so much because of AIDS but because of the
anxiety that ripples around the disease. The information about AIDS that is
supposed to produce "awareness" has been subsumed into the aura of style.
AIDS awareness has become so much a part of the pop culture that not only
is it barely noticeable, it is largely ineffectual. MTV runs programs about safe
sex that are barely distinguishable from documentaries about Madonna. A
print advertisement for Benetton features a collage of hundreds of tiny photographs of young people, some of whom are shaded with the word AIDS written across their faces. Many are white and blond and have the tousled,
moneyed look common to more traditional fashion spreads or even yearbooks
from colleges like the one I attended. There is no text other than the company's slogan. There is no explanation of how these faces were chosen, no
public statement of whether these people actually have the disease or not. I
called Benetton for clarification and was told that the photographs were supposed to represent people from all over the world and that no one was known
to be HIV-positive—just as I suspected. The advertisement was a work of art,
which meant I could interpret the image any way I liked. This is how the
deliverers of the safe-sex message shoot themselves in the foot. Confronted
with arty effects instead of actual information, people like me are going to
believe what we want to believe, which, of course, is whatever isn't too scary.
So we turn the page.

Since I am pretty sure I do not sleep with bisexual men or IV drug users,   8
my main personal concern about AIDS is that men can get the virus from
women and subsequently pass it on to other women. According to the Cen-

ters for Disease Control's National AIDS Clearinghouse surveillance report, less than three-quarters of 1 percent of white non-Hispanic men with HIV infection contracted the virus through heterosexual sex with a non–IV drug-using woman. (Interestingly, the CDC labels this category as "risk not specified.") But this statistic seems too dry for MTV and campus health brochures, whose eye-catching "sex kills" rhetoric tells us nothing other than to ignore what we don't feel like thinking about. Obviously, there are still too many cases of HIV; there is a deadly risk in certain kinds of sexual behavior and therefore reason to take precautions. But until more people appear on television, look into the camera and tell me that they contracted HIV through heterosexual sex with someone who had no risk factors, I will continue to disregard the message.

Besides, the very sophistication that allows people like me to filter out   9
much of the hype behind music videos, fashion magazines and television talk shows is what we use to block out the safe-sex message. We are not a population that makes personal decisions based on the public service work of a rock star. We're not going to sacrifice the thing we believe we deserve, the experiences we waited for, because Levi Strauss is a major sponsor of MTV's coverage of World AIDS Day.

So the inconsistent behavior continues, as do the confessions among   10
friends and the lies to health-care providers during routine exams, because we just can't bear the terrifying lectures that ensue when we confess to not always protecting ourselves. Life in your twenties is fraught not only with financial and professional uncertainty, but also with a specter of death that floats above the pursuit of a sex life. And there is no solution, only the conclusion that invariably finishes the hushed conversations: The whole thing simply "sucks." It's a bummer on a grand scale.

Heterosexuals are receiving vague signals. We're told that if we are suffi-   11
ciently vigilant, we will probably be all right. We're being told to assume the worst and to not invite disaster by hoping for the best. We're being encouraged to keep our fantasies on a tight rein, otherwise we'll lose control of the whole buggy, and no one can say we weren't warned. So for us AIDS remains a private hell, smoldering beneath intimate conversations among friends and surfacing on those occasional sleepless nights when it occurs to us to wonder about it, upon which that dark hysteria sets in, and those catalogues of whom we've done it with and whom they might have done it with and oh-my-God-I'll-surely-die seem to project themselves onto the ceiling, the way fanged monsters did when we were children. But we fall asleep and then we wake up. And nothing has changed except our willingness to forget about it, which has become the ultimate survival mechanism. What my peers and I are left with

is a generalized anxiety, a low-grade fear and anger that resides at the core of everything we do. Our attitudes have been affected by the disease by leaving us scared, but our behavior has stayed largely the same. One result is a corrosion of the soul, a chronic dishonesty and fear that will most likely damage us more than the disease itself. In this world, peace of mind is a utopian concept.

Journal Writing

Writing in her midtwenties, Daum calls herself part of the "demographic profile frequently charged with thinking we're immortal, the population accused of being cynical and lazy and weak" (par. 3). Do you agree that many people in their late teens and twenties fit this description? In your journal, write your own characterization of this age group. (To take your journal writing further, see "From Journal to Essay" on the facing page.)

Questions on Meaning

1. What is Daum's PURPOSE in writing this essay? On whom, or what, is she placing blame? Does she offer any solutions in the essay, or is she merely outlining a problem previously unacknowledged?
2. What is Daum's THESIS? Where is it stated?
3. What does Daum mean by "our sense of entitlement exceeds our sense of vulnerability" (par. 2)?
4. Explain how AIDS awareness has become "part of the pop culture" (par. 7).
5. Explain the title's double meaning: What are the two kinds of "Safe-Sex Lies" discussed in the essay?

Questions on Writing Strategy

1. Daum asserts that the media exaggerate the prevalence of AIDS among heterosexuals who are not IV drug users. Explain the chain of causes and effects that she sees as leading from this exaggeration.
2. What is the TONE of the essay?
3. What is the EFFECT of Daum's confession in the second paragraph?
4. What AUDIENCE do you think Daum had in mind when she was writing this essay? Is she targeting all readers of the *New York Times* or a more specific subset of them?
5. **OTHER METHODS.** In paragraph 7 Daum uses an extended EXAMPLE of a Benetton ad to support her assertion that "[t]he information about AIDS that is supposed to produce 'awareness' has been subsumed into the aura of style." Why does it make a difference to Daum that the people represented in the Benetton ad are not known to be HIV-positive?

Questions on Language

1. Look up any of the following words you don't already know: retrospect, demographic, incumbent (par. 1); entitlement, breach (2); cynical (3); mantra, scoundrels, ignoramuses, naïveté (4); ideology (5); abstract, contemporaries, onus (6); subsumed, aura, tousled (7); surveillance (8); fraught, specter (10); vigilant, smoldering (11).
2. What is the effect of the word *those* in "those disposable needles" and "those minutes spent in a publicly financed waiting room" (par. 1)?
3. Daum's language is often quite informal, as in conversation—for instance, "unless we wanted to die; that's right, *die*" and "they'd seen it happen, oh, yes, they had" (par. 1); "It seems there is a lot of lying going around" (4); or "It's a bummer on a grand scale" (10). What is the effect of this language? Is it appropriate to Daum's subject and purpose? Why, or why not?

Suggestions for Writing

1. **FROM JOURNAL TO ESSAY.** Write an essay DEFINING the age group roughly from eighteen to thirty, drawing on your journal entry (facing page), Daum's essay, and any other sources that offer ideas. Keep in mind that characterization of such a large and diverse group will require GENERALIZATION on your part. How does your definition compare with other definitions you have heard in the media? Does any attempt to characterize an age group necessarily oversimplify? Do you find some value or interest in the exercise?
2. Write an essay about how AIDS has (or hasn't) changed your life, considering the following questions: Is AIDS something you think about often, or is it something "out there" that happens to other people? How do the media influence your attitudes toward the disease? If a cure for AIDS were discovered tomorrow, would your approach to sexuality and relationships change, or has AIDS permanently affected your attitudes?
3. **CRITICAL WRITING.** Analyze how Daum's "demographic profile" (par. 1) determines her perspective on AIDS. Do you find this limited perspective appropriate, or do you think Daum should have mentioned other views as well—perhaps of those who urge sexual abstinence or who care for AIDS patients or who have AIDS themselves? To what extent does Daum's limited perspective weaken or strengthen her essay?
4. **CONNECTIONS.** Daum and Armin A. Brott, in "Not All Men Are Sly Foxes" (p. 324), are both concerned about the subtle effects of words and pictures on an audience: Daum is interested in the way safe sex is marketed, the face advertising puts on AIDS; Brott is troubled by the negative stereotyping of fathers in books for children. Write an essay criticizing what you consider to be inaccurate or inappropriate media representation of a given group (for example, single mothers, gays and lesbians, lawyers, football players, fashion models). What message do these portrayals send to members of that group and to those outside the group? How might the portrayals be improved?

DON DeLILLO

DON DeLILLO, one of America's preeminent fiction writers, produces dark and often comic works exploring celebrity, consumerism, and other facets of American culture. The son of Italian immigrants, DeLillo was born in 1936 in New York City and grew up in the Bronx. He graduated from Fordham University in 1958 with a degree in communications and then, after searching unsuccessfully for a publishing job, reluctantly accepted work in an advertising agency. Five years later, DeLillo quit copywriting and began working on his first novel, *Americana* (1971). Halfway through the four years it took to write the book, DeLillo says, "it occurred to me almost in a flash that I was a writer. Whatever tentativeness I'd felt about the book dropped away." Since then, DeLillo has published eleven more novels, including *The Names* (1982), *White Noise* (1985), *Libra* (1988), *Mao II* (1991), *Underworld* (1997), and most recently *The Body Artist* (2001). DeLillo was awarded the National Book Award for fiction for *White Noise* and a PEN/Faulkner award for *Mao II*.

Videotape

As compelling as fictional TV and movies can be, showing heart-rending tragedy or sickening violence, they can't compare with documentary evidence of the real thing. In this short story from 1994, first published in *Antaeus* magazine, DeLillo's character explores his compulsive fascination with a video slice of life and death.

It shows a man driving a car. It is the simplest sort of family video. You see a man at the wheel of a medium Dodge. 1

It is just a kid aiming her camera through the rear window of the family car at the windshield of the car behind her. 2

You know about families and their video cameras. You know how kids get involved, how the camera shows them that every subject is potentially charged, a million things they never see with the unaided eye. They investigate the meaning of inert objects and dumb pets and they poke at family privacy. They learn to see things twice. 3

It is the kid's own privacy that is being protected here. She is twelve years old and her name is being withheld even though she is neither the victim nor the perpetrator of the crime but only the means of recording it. 4

It shows a man in a sport shirt at the wheel of his car. There is nothing else to see. The car approaches briefly, then falls back. 5

You know how children with cameras learn to work the exposed moments that define the family cluster. They break every trust, spy out the undefended 6 space, catching Mom coming out of the bathroom in her cumbrous robe and turbaned towel, looking bloodless and plucked. It is not a joke. They will shoot you sitting on the pot if they can manage a suitable vantage.

The tape has the jostled sort of noneventness that marks the family 7 product. Of course the man in this case is not a member of the family but a stranger in a car, a random figure, someone who has happened along in the slow lane.

It shows a man in his forties wearing a pale shirt open at the throat, the 8 image washed by reflections and sunglint, with many jostled moments.

It is not just another video homicide. It is a homicide recorded by a child 9 who thought she was doing something simple and maybe halfway clever, shooting some tape of a man in a car.

He sees the girl and waves briefly, wagging a hand without taking it off the 10 wheel — an underplayed reaction that makes you like him.

It is unrelenting footage that rolls on and on. It has an aimless determina- 11 tion, a persistence that lives outside the subject matter. You are looking into the mind of home video. It is innocent, it is aimless, it is determined, it is real.

He is bald up the middle of his head, a nice guy in his forties whose whole 12 life seems open to the hand-held camera.

But there is also an element of suspense. You keep on looking not because 13 you know something is going to happen — of course you do know something is going to happen and you do look for that reason but you might also keep on looking if you came across this footage for the first time without knowing the outcome. There is a crude power operating here. You keep on looking because things combine to hold you fast — a sense of the random, the amateurish, the accidental, the impending. You don't think of the tape as boring or interest- ing. It is crude, it is blunt, it is relentless. It is the jostled part of your mind, the film that runs through your hotel brain under all the thoughts you know you're thinking.

The world is lurking in the camera, already framed, waiting for the boy or 14 girl who will come along and take up the device, learn the instrument, shoot- ing old Granddad at breakfast, all stroked out so his nostrils gape, the cereal spoon baby-gripped in his pale fist.

It shows a man alone in a medium Dodge. It seems to go on forever. 15

There's something about the nature of the tape, the grain of the image, 16 the sputtering black-and-white tones, the starkness — you think this is more real, truer-to-life, than anything around you. The things around you have a rehearsed and layered and cosmetic look. The tape is superreal, or maybe underreal is the way you want to put it. It is what lies at the scraped bottom of all the layers you have added. And this is another reason why you keep on looking. The tape has a searing realness.

It shows him giving an abbreviated wave, stiff-palmed, like a signal flag at a siding. 17

You know how families make up games. This is just another game in which the child invents the rules as she goes along. She likes the idea of videotaping a man in his car. She has probably never done it before and she sees no reason to vary the format or terminate early or pan to another car. This is her game and she is learning it and playing it at the same time. She feels halfway clever and inventive and maybe slightly intrusive as well, a little bit of brazenness that spices any game. 18

And you keep on looking. You look because this is the nature of the footage, to make a channeled path through time, to give things a shape and a destiny. 19

Of course if she had panned to another car, the right car at the precise time, she would have caught the gunman as he fired. 20

The chance quality of the encounter. The victim, the killer, and the child with a camera. Random energies that approach a common point. There's something here that speaks to you directly, saying terrible things about forces beyond your control, lines of intersection that cut through history and logic and every reasonable layer of human expectation. 21

She wandered into it. The girl got lost and wandered clear-eyed into horror. This is a children's story about straying too far from home. But it isn't the family car that serves as the instrument of the child's curiosity, her inclination to explore. It is the camera that puts her in the tale. 22

You know about holidays and family celebrations and how somebody shows up with a camcorder and the relatives stand around and barely react because they're numbingly accustomed to the process of being taped and decked and shown on the VCR with the coffee and cake. 23

He is hit soon after. If you've seen the tape many times you know from the handwave exactly when he will be hit. It is something, naturally, that you wait for. You say to your wife, if you're at home and she is there, Now here is where he gets it. You say, Janet, hurry up, this is where it happens. 24

Now here is where he gets it. You see him jolted, sort of wire-shocked — then he seizes up and falls toward the door or maybe leans or slides into the door is the proper way to put it. It is awful and unremarkable at the same time. The car stays in the slow lane. It approaches briefly, then falls back. 25

You don't usually call your wife over to the TV set. She has her programs, you have yours. But there's a certain urgency here. You want her to see how it looks. The tape has been running forever and now the thing is finally going to happen and you want her to be here when he's shot. 26

Here it comes, all right. He is shot, head-shot, and the camera reacts, the child reacts — there is a jolting movement but she keeps on taping, there is a 27 sympathetic response, a nerve response, her heart is beating faster but she keeps the camera trained on the subject as he slides into the door and even as you see him die you're thinking of the girl. At some level the girl has to be present here, watching what you're watching, unprepared—the girl is seeing this cold and you have to marvel at the fact that she keeps the tape rolling.

It shows something awful and unaccompanied. You want your wife to see   28 it because it is real this time, not fancy movie violence—the realness beneath the layers of cosmetic perception. Hurry up, Janet, here it comes. He dies so fast. There is no accompaniment of any kind. It is very stripped. You want to tell her it is realer than real but then she will ask what that means.

The way the camera reacts to the gunshot—a startled reaction that   29 brings pity and terror into the frame, the girl's own shock, the girl's identification with the victim.

You don't see the blood, which is probably trickling behind his ear and   30 down the back of his neck. The way his head is twisted away from the door, the twist of the head gives you only a partial profile and it's the wrong side, it's not the side where he was hit.

And maybe you're being a little aggressive here, practically forcing your   31 wife to watch. Why? What are you telling her? Are you making a little statement? Like I'm going to ruin your day out of ordinary spite. Or a big statement? Like this is the risk of existing. Either way you're rubbing her face in this tape and you don't know why.

It shows the car drifting toward the guardrail and then there's a jostling   32 sense of two other lanes and part of another car, a split-second blur, and the tape ends here, either because the girl stopped shooting or because some central authority, the police or the district attorney or the TV station, decided there was nothing else you had to see.

This is either the tenth or eleventh homicide committed by the Texas   33 Highway Killer. The number is uncertain because the police believe that one of the shootings may have been a copycat crime.

And there is something about videotape, isn't there, and this particular   34 kind of serial crime? This is a crime designed for random taping and immediate playing. You sit there and wonder if this kind of crime became more possible when the means of taping and playing an event—playing it immediately after the taping—became part of the culture. The principal doesn't necessarily commit the sequence of crimes in order to see them taped and played. He commits the crimes as if they were a form of taped-and-played event. The crimes are inseparable from the idea of taping and playing. You sit there thinking that this is a crime that has found its medium, or vice versa—cheap mass production, the sequence of repeated images and victims, stark and glary and more or less unremarkable.

It shows very little in the end. It is a famous murder because it is on tape   35
and because the murderer has done it many times and because the crime was
recorded by a child. So the child is involved, the Video Kid as she is sometimes called because they have to call her something. The tape is famous and
so is she. She is famous in the modern manner of people whose names are
strategically withheld. They are famous without names or faces, spirits living
apart from their bodies, the victims and witnesses, the underage criminals, out
there somewhere at the edges of perception.

Seeing someone at the moment he dies, dying unexpectedly. This is rea-   36
son alone to stay fixed to the screen. It is instructional, watching a man shot
dead as he drives along on a sunny day. It demonstrates an elemental truth,
that every breath you take has two possible endings. And that's another thing.
There's a joke locked away here, a note of cruel slapstick that you are completely willing to appreciate. Maybe the victim's a chump, a dope, classically
unlucky. He had it coming, in a way, like an innocent fool in a silent movie.

You don't want Janet to give you any crap about it's on all the time, they   37
show it a thousand times a day. They show it because it exists, because they
have to show it, because this is why they're out there. The horror freezes your
soul but this doesn't mean that you want them to stop.

Journal Writing

Do you identify with the NARRATOR's obsession with the videotape of the man being
shot? When have you seen documentary footage of a crime or disaster, either once or
repeatedly? In your journal, reflect on how the footage affected you. (To take your
journal writing further, see "From Journal to Essay" on the facing page.)

Questions on Meaning

1. How does the fact that a twelve-year-old girl accidentally recorded the murder
   affect the narrator's response?
2. Why does the narrator want his wife to watch the death of the man on the tape?
3. In paragraph 34 the narrator makes a causal connection between certain kinds of
   serial crimes and the fact that videotaping and instant replay have become "part
   of the culture." What is this connection? Does it seem reasonable to you?

Questions on Writing Strategy

1. What reasons does the narrator give for his fascination with the replaying
   videotape?

2. Note how DeLillo's narrator doles out crucial pieces of information. When is it first clear that the video involves a victim? that it records a murder? that a gunshot caused the murder? that the driver was shot? that the video is being run on television? that the crime was committed by a serial killer? What effect does this slow release of details have on your reading of the story?

3. The narrator consistently uses the pronoun "you" rather than "I." Why do you suppose DeLillo chose this approach? (To see its effect, try rewriting pars. 23–26 with "I" or "me" instead of "you.")

4. The narrator uses verbs in the present tense—for instance, "It shows" or "Now here is where he gets it." Why is this tense appropriate for the story DeLillo is telling?

5. **OTHER METHODS.** In what way is DESCRIPTION an important part of DeLillo's story?

Questions on Language

1. In paragraph 7 the narrator refers to the victim as "a random figure." Find other references to randomness and words with similar meanings. What do these contribute to the narrator's vision of the event's greater significance?

2. The narrator says the tape has a "sort of noneventness" (par. 7) and that the crime is, in the end, "more or less unremarkable" (34). What do you think he means?

3. The narrator describes the tape as "superreal, or maybe underreal" and having "a searing realness" (par. 16) and being "realer than real" (28). How do you interpret this language?

4. Consult a dictionary if you are unsure of the meanings of any of the following words: inert (par. 3); perpetrator (4); cumbrous, vantage (6); starkness, searing (16); brazenness (18); principal (34); strategically (35); elemental, slapstick (36).

Suggestions for Writing

1. **FROM JOURNAL TO ESSAY.** Expand your journal entry (facing page) into an essay in which you identify and reflect on your responses to documentary footage of a crime or disaster. Were your responses anything like those of the narrator in DeLillo's story, or were they different? Were your responses affected by how often you saw the footage, whether once, twice, or more often? Why do you think you responded as you did?

2. Think of some important experience you have had—either positive, such as winning an award or having a child, or negative, such as being robbed or being in a car wreck. Write a story about the episode, either true-to-life or fictionalized. Follow DeLillo's example in using the second-person "you" and the present tense of verbs.

3. **CRITICAL WRITING.** ANALYZE DeLillo's use of repetition in "Videotape." What effects does it achieve? In what ways does such repetition echo his theme?

4. **CONNECTIONS.** COMPARE AND CONTRAST the narrator of "Videotape" with the narrator of Edgar Allan Poe's "The Tell-Tale Heart" (p. 117) or Alice Walker's

"Everyday Use" (p. 255). How is the narrative voice in each case suitable for the story being told?

Don DeLillo on Writing

In a 1993 interview published in *The Paris Review,* DeLillo defined writing as "a concentrated form of thinking." He explained, "I don't know what I think about certain subjects, even today, until I sit down and try to write about them."

When he sits down to work, his discarded draft pages sit nearby. "I want those pages nearby because there's always a chance I'll have to refer to something that's scrawled at the bottom of a sheet of paper somewhere. Discarded pages mark the physical dimensions of a writer's labor—you know, how many shots it took to get a certain paragraph right. [. . .] I find I'm more ready to discard pages than I used to be. I used to look for things to keep. I used to find ways to save a paragraph or sentence, maybe by relocating it. Now I look for ways to discard things. If I discard a sentence I like, it's almost as satisfying as keeping a sentence I like. I don't think I've become ruthless or perverse—just a bit more willing to believe that nature will restore itself. The instinct to discard is finally a kind of faith. It tells me there's a better way to do this page even though the evidence is not accessible at the present time."

While drafting, DeLillo types each paragraph on a separate page. When he finishes a paragraph, "even a three-line paragraph," he automatically starts the next one on a fresh page. When he first tried this technique, he said, "[it] enabled me to see a given set of sentences more clearly. It made rewriting easier and more effective. The white space on the page helped me concentrate more deeply on what I'd written."

Uncrowded pages help DeLillo concentrate on sentences. "The words [. . .] have a sculptural quality. They form odd correspondences. They match up not just through meaning but through sound and look. The rhythm of a sentence will accommodate a certain number of syllables. One syllable too many, I look for another word. There's always another word that means nearly the same thing, and if it doesn't then I'll consider altering the meaning of a sentence to keep the rhythm, the syllable beat. I'm completely willing to let language press meaning upon me. Watching the way in which words match up, keeping the balance in a sentence—these are sensuous pleasures. I might want *very* and *only* in the same sentence, spaced in a particular way, exactly so far apart. I might want *rapture* matched with *danger*—I like to match word endings. I type rather than write longhand because I like the way words and letters look [. . .]—finished, printed, beautifully formed."

For Discussion

1. Explain DeLillo's definition of *writing* in your own words.
2. Why does DeLillo find satisfaction in his "instinct to discard" parts of his writing that he likes?
3. What does DeLillo mean when he says that writing is filled with "sensuous pleasures"?

ADDITIONAL WRITING TOPICS

Cause and Effect

1. In a short essay, explain *either* the causes *or* the effects of a situation that concerns you. Narrow your topic enough to treat it in some detail, and provide more than a mere list of causes or effects. If seeking causes, you will have to decide carefully how far back to go in your search for remote causes. If stating effects, fill your essay with examples. Here are some topics to consider:

Labor strikes in professional sports
Children searching for pornography on the Internet
State laws mandating the use of seat belts in cars (or the wearing of helmets on motorcycles)
Friction between two roommates, or two friends
The pressure on students to get good grades
Some quirk in your personality, or a friend's
The increasing need for more than one breadwinner per family
The temptation to do something dishonest to get ahead
The popularity of a particular television program, comic strip, rock group, or pop singer
The steady increase in college costs
The scarcity of people in training for employment as skilled workers: plumbers, tool and die makers, electricians, masons, carpenters, to name a few
A decision to enter the ministry or a religious order
The fact that cigarette advertising is banned from television
The absence of a military draft
The fact that more couples are choosing to have only one child, or none
The growing popularity of private elementary and high schools
The fact that most Americans can communicate in no language other than English
Being "born again"
The fact that women increasingly get jobs formerly regarded as being for men only
The pressure on young people to conform to the standards of their peers
The emphasis on competitive sports in high school and college

2. In *Blue Highways* (1982), an account of his rambles around America, William Least Heat Moon explains why Americans, and not the British, settled the vast tract of northern land that lies between the Mississippi and the Rockies. He traces what he believes to be the major cause in this paragraph:

> Were it not for a web-footed rodent and a haberdashery fad in eighteenth-century Europe, Minnesota might be a Canadian province today. The beaver, almost as much as the horse, helped shape the course of early American history. Some *Mayflower* colonists paid their passage with beaver pelts; and a good fur could bring an Indian three steel knives or a five-foot stack could bring a musket. But even more influential were

the trappers and fur traders penetrating the great Northern wilderness between the Mississippi River and the Rocky Mountains, since it was their presence that helped hold the Near West against British expansion from the north; and it was their explorations that opened the heart of the nation to white settlement. These men, by making pelts the currency of the wilds, laid the base for a new economy that quickly overwhelmed the old. And all because European men of mode simply had to wear a beaver hat.

In a Least Heat Moon–like paragraph of your own, explain how a small cause produced a large effect. You might generate ideas by browsing in a history book—where you might find, for instance, that a cow belonging to Mrs. Patrick O'Leary is believed to have started the Great Chicago Fire of 1871 by kicking over a lighted lantern—or in a collection of *Ripley's Believe It or Not*. If some small event in your life has had large consequences, you might care to write instead from personal experience.

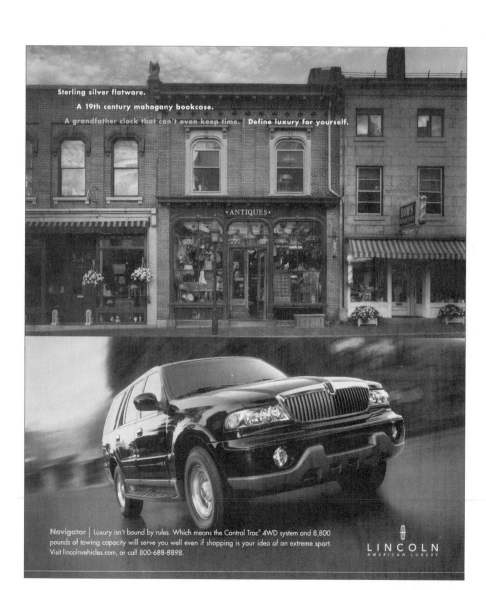

12

DEFINITION
Tracing a Boundary

Definition in an advertisement

Lincoln has long built and marketed its cars as luxury vehicles, so this advertisement for the Navigator fits right in. This time, though, the ad focuses on the very meaning of *luxury,* defining the word so as to fix it in the minds of potential customers—in this case, readers of *The New Yorker* magazine in November 2000. What examples of luxury does the ad offer, not only in the text at the top and bottom but also in the top photograph? What overall sense of the word *luxury* do the examples add up to? How does the definition relate to the Navigator in the bottom photograph? Why do you think Lincoln chose to advertise its sport-utility vehicle in this way?

THE METHOD

As a rule, when we hear the word DEFINITION, we immediately think of a dictionary. In that helpful storehouse—a writer's best friend—we find the literal and specific meaning (or meanings) of a word. The dictionary supplies this information concisely: in a sentence, in a phrase, or even in a *synonym*—a single word that means the same thing ("**narrative** [năr-e-tĭv] *n.* 1: story . . .").

Stating such a definition is often a good way to begin an essay when basic terms may be in doubt. A short definition can clarify your subject to your reader, and perhaps help you to limit what you have to say. If, for instance, you are going to discuss a demolition derby, explaining such a spectacle to readers who may never have seen one, you might offer at the outset a short definition of *demolition derby*, your subject and your key term.

In constructing a short definition, the usual procedure is to state the general class to which the subject belongs and then add any particular features that distinguish it. You could say: "A demolition derby is a contest"—that is its general class—"in which drivers ram old cars into one another until only one car is left running." Short definitions may be useful at *any* moment in an essay, whenever you introduce a technical term that readers may not know.

When a term is really central to your essay and likely to be misunderstood, a *stipulative definition* may be helpful. This fuller explanation stipulates, or specifies, the particular way you are using a term. The paragraph on page 465, defining *TV addiction*, could be a stipulative definition in an essay on the causes and cures of the addiction.

In this chapter, we are mainly concerned with *extended definition*, a kind of expository writing that relies on a variety of other methods. Suppose you wanted to write an essay to make clear what *poetry* means. You would specify its elements—rhythm, IMAGES, and so on—by using DIVISION or ANALYSIS. You'd probably provide EXAMPLES of each element. You might COMPARE AND CONTRAST poetry with prose. You might discuss the EFFECT of poetry on the reader. (Emily Dickinson, a poet herself, once stated the effect that reading a poem had on her: "I feel as if the top of my head were taken off.") In fact, extended definition, unlike other methods of writing discussed in this book, is perhaps less a method in itself than the application of a variety of methods to clarify a purpose. Like DESCRIPTION, extended definition tries to *show* a reader its subject. It does so by establishing boundaries, for its writer tries to differentiate a subject from anything that might be confused with it.

When Gloria Naylor, in her essay in this chapter, seeks to define the freighted word *nigger*, she recalls her experiences of the word as an African

American, recounting exactly what she heard in varying situations. Extended definition examines the nature of the subject, carefully summing up its chief characteristics and drawing boundaries around it, striving to answer the question "What makes this what it is, not something else?"

An extended definition can define a word (like *nigger*), a thing (a laser beam), a concept (TV addiction), or a general phenomenon (the popularity of the demolition derby). Unlike a sentence definition, or any you would find in a standard dictionary, an extended definition takes room: at least a paragraph, often an entire essay. In having many methods of writing at your disposal, you have ample freedom and wide latitude.

Outside an English course, how is this method of writing used? In a newspaper feature, a sportswriter defines what makes a *great team* great. In a journal article, a physician defines the nature of a previously unknown syndrome or disease. In a written opinion, a judge defines not only a word but a concept, *obscenity*. In a book review, a critic defines a newly prevalent kind of poem. In a letter to a younger brother or sister contemplating college, a student might define a *gut course* and how to recognize one.

Unlike a definition in a dictionary that sets forth the literal meaning of a word in an unimpassioned manner, some definitions imply biases. In defining *patron* to the earl of Chesterfield, who had tried to befriend him after ignoring his petitions for aid during his years of grinding poverty, Samuel Johnson wrote scornfully: "Is not a Patron, my Lord, one who looks with unconcern on a man struggling for life in the water, and, when he has reached the ground, encumbers him with help?" IRONY, a FIGURE OF SPEECH (metaphor), and a short definition have rarely been wielded with such crushing power. (*Encumbers*, by the way, is a wonderfully physical word in its context: It means "to burden with dead weight.")

THE PROCESS

Discovery of Meanings

The purpose of almost any extended definition is to explore a topic in its full complexity, to explain its meaning or sometimes to argue for (or against) a particular meaning. To discover this complexity, you may find it useful to ask yourself a series of questions. These questions may be applied both to individual subjects, such as a basketball superstar or a comet, and to collective subjects: institutions (like the American family, a typical savings bank, a university, the Church of Jesus Christ of Latter-Day Saints) and organizations (IBM, the Mafia, a rock band, a Little League baseball team). To illustrate how the questions might work, at least in one instance, let's say you plan to write a paper defining *sexism*.[1]

1. *Is this subject unique, or are there others of its kind? If it resembles others, in what ways? How is it different?* As you can see, these last two questions invite you to compare and contrast. Applied to the concept of sexism, these questions might prompt you to compare sexism with one or two other -isms, such as racism or ageism. Or the questions might remind you that sexists can be both women and men, leading you to note the differences.

2. *In what different forms does it occur, while keeping its own identity?* Specific examples might occur to you: your Uncle George, who won't hire any "damned females" in his auto repair shop, or a girlfriend who is nastily suspicious of all men. Each form — Uncle George and the girlfriend — might rate a description.

3. *When and where do we find it? Under what circumstances and in what situations?* Well, where have you been lately? At any parties where sexism reared its ugly head? In any classroom discussions? Consider other areas of your experience: Did you encounter any sexists while holding a part-time summer job?

4. *What is it at the present moment?* Perhaps you might make the point that sexism was once considered an exclusively male preserve but is now an attribute of women as well. Or you could observe that many men have gone underground with their sexism, refraining from expressing it blatantly while still harboring negative attitudes about women. In either case, you might care to draw examples from life.

5. *What does it do? What are its functions and activities?* Sexists stereotype and sometimes act to exclude or oppress people of the opposite sex. These questions might also invite you to reply with a PROCESS ANALYSIS: You might show, for instance, how a sexist man you know, a personnel director who determines pay scales, systematically eliminates women from better-paying jobs.

6. *How is it put together? What parts make it up? What holds these parts together?* You could apply analysis to the various beliefs and assumptions that, all together, make up sexism. This question might work well in writing about

---

[1] The six questions that follow are freely adapted from those first stated by Richard E. Young, Alton L. Becker, and Kenneth L. Pike, who have applied insights from psychology and linguistics to the writing process. Their procedure for generating ideas and discovering information is called *tagmemics*. To investigate subjects in greater depth, their own six questions may be used in nine possible combinations, as they explain in detail in *Rhetoric: Discovery and Change* (New York: Harcourt, 1970).

an organization: the personnel director's company, for instance, with its unfair hiring and promotion policies.

Not all these questions will fit every subject under the sun, and some may lead nowhere, but you will usually find them well worth asking. They can make you aware of points to notice, remind you of facts you already know. They can also suggest interesting points you need to find out more about.

Methods of Development

The preceding questions will give you a good start on using whatever method or methods of writing can best answer the overall question "What is the nature of this subject?" You will probably find yourself making use of much that you have learned earlier from this book. A short definition like the one for *demolition derby* on page 460 may be a good start for your essay, especially if you think your readers need a quick grounding in the subject or in your view of it. (But feel no duty to place a dictionaryish definition in the INTRODUCTION of every essay you write: The device is overused.) In explaining a demolition derby, if your readers already have at least a vague idea of the meaning of the term and need no short, formal definition of it, you could open your extended definition by NARRATING the events at a typical demolition derby, starting with a description of the lineup of old beat-up vehicles:

> One hundred worthless cars—everything from a 1960 Cadillac to a Dodge Dart to a recently wrecked Thunderbird, their glass removed, their radiators leaking—assemble on a racetrack or an open field. Their drivers, wearing crash helmets, buckle themselves into their seats, some pulling at beer cans to soften the blows to come.

You could proceed by example, listing demolition derbies you have known ("The great destruction of 184 vehicles took place at the Orleans County Fair in Barton, Vermont, in the summer of '00 . . ."). If you have enough examples, you could CLASSIFY them; or perhaps you could analyze a demolition derby, dividing it into its components of cars, drivers, judges, first-aid squad, and spectators, and discussing each. You could compare and contrast a demolition derby with that amusement park ride known as Bumper Cars or Dodge-'ems, in which small cars with rubber bumpers bash one another head-on, but (unlike cars in the derby) harmlessly. A process analysis of a demolition derby might help your readers understand the nature of the spectacle: how in round after round, cars are eliminated until one remains. You could ask "What causes the owners of old cars to want to smash them?" or "What causes people to watch the destruction?" or "What are the consequences?" To answer such questions in an essay, you would apply the method of CAUSE AND EFFECT.

Thesis

Opening up your subject with questions and developing it with various methods are good ways to see what your subject has to offer, but they can also leave you with a welter of ideas and a blurred focus. As in description, when all your details build to a DOMINANT IMPRESSION, so in definition you want to center all your thoughts and evidence about the subject on a single controlling idea, a THESIS. It's not essential to state this idea in a THESIS SENTENCE, although doing so can be a service to your readers. What is essential is that the idea govern.

Here, from the essays in this chapter, are three thesis sentences. Notice how each makes an assertion about the subject, and how we can detect the author's bias toward the subject.

> The word *chink* may have been created to harm, ridicule, and humiliate, but for us [Chinese Americans] it may have done the exact opposite. (Christine Leong, "Being a Chink")

> [I]ncreasingly unequal social rewards can conduce to a more truly egalitarian society, one that offers upward mobility equally to all who accept its rewarding disciplines. (George F. Will, "The Equity of Inequality")

> [W]e should give [the murder of the Jews] its true designation and not hide it behind polite, erudite terms [such as *holocaust*] created out of classical words. (Bruno Bettelheim, "The Holocaust")

Evidence

Writing an extended definition, you are like a mapmaker charting a territory, taking in some of what lies within the boundaries and ignoring what lies outside. The boundaries, of course, may be wide; and for this reason, the writing of an extended definition sometimes tempts a writer to sweep across a continent airily and to soar off into abstract clouds. Like any other method of expository writing, though, definition will work only for the writer who remembers the world of the senses and supports every generalization with concrete evidence.

There may be no finer illustration of the perils of definition than the scene, in Charles Dickens's novel *Hard Times*, of the grim schoolroom of a teacher named Gradgrind, who insists on facts but who completely ignores living realities. When a girl whose father is a horse trainer is unable to define a horse, Gradgrind blames her for not knowing what a horse is; and he praises the definition of a horse supplied by a pet pupil: "Quadruped. Graminivorous. Forty teeth, namely twenty-four grinders, four eye-teeth, and twelve incisive. Sheds coat in the spring; in marshy countries, sheds hoofs, too. Hoofs hard, but requiring to be shod with iron. Age known by marks in mouth." To anyone who didn't already know what a horse is, this list of facts would prove of little help. In writing an extended definition, never lose sight of the reality you are attempting to bound, even if its frontiers are as inclusive as those of *psychological burnout* or *human rights*. Give your reader examples, narrate an illustrative story, bring in specific description — in whatever method you use, keep coming down to earth. Without your eyes on the world, you will define no reality. You might define *animal husbandry* till the cows come home and never make clear what it means.

CHECKLIST FOR REVISING A DEFINITION

✔ **MEANINGS.** Have you explored your subject fully, turning up both its obvious and its not-so-obvious meanings?

✔ **METHODS OF DEVELOPMENT.** Have you used an appropriate range of other methods to develop your subject?

✔ **THESIS.** Have you focused your definition and kept within that focus, drawing clear boundaries around your subject?

✔ **EVIDENCE.** Is your definition specific? Do examples, anecdotes, and concrete details both pin the subject down and make it vivid for readers?

DEFINITION IN A PARAGRAPH: TWO ILLUSTRATIONS

Using Definition to Write About Television

The paragraph below SUMMARIZES the definition of *TV addiction* given in Marie Winn's essay on pages 486–88. The paragraph was written for *The Bedford Reader* as an example of definition, but its opening question suggests a broader use than just illustration: In a full essay on the causes and cures of the addiction, the paragraph could serve as a stipulative definition of the essay's key term.

Who is addicted to TV? According to Marie Winn, author of *The Plug-in Drug: Television, Children, and the Family*, TV addicts are similar to drug or alcohol addicts: They seek a more pleasurable experience than they can get from normal life; they depend on the source of this pleasure; and their lives are damaged by their dependency. TV addicts, says Winn, use TV to screen out the real world of feelings, worries, demands. They watch compulsively — four, five, even six hours on a work day. And they reject (usually passively, sometimes actively) interaction with family or friends, diverting or productive work at hobbies or chores, and chances for change and growth.

Definition of TV *addiction*

Comparison with drug or alcohol addiction

Analysis is of TV addicts' characteristics

Using Definition in an Academic Discipline

This paragraph from a biology textbook defines a term, *homology*, that is useful in explaining the evolution of different species from a common ancestor (the topic at this point in the textbook). The paragraph provides a brief definition, a more extensive one, and finally examples of the concept.

When the character traits found in any two species owe their resemblance to a common ancestry, taxonomists say the states are *homologous*, or are *homologues* of each other. *Homology* is defined as correspondence between two structures due to inheritance from a common ancestor. Homologous structures can be identical in appearance and can even be based on identical genes. However, such structures can diverge until they become very different in both appearance and function. Nevertheless, homologous structures usually retain certain basic features that betray a common ancestry. Consider the forelimbs of vertebrates. It is easy to make a detailed, bone-by-bone, muscle-by-muscle comparison of the forearm of a person and a monkey and to conclude that the forearms, as well as the various parts of the forearm, are homologous. The forelimb of a dog, however, shows marked differences from those of primates in both appearance and function. The forelimb is used for locomotion by dogs but for grasping and manipulation by people and monkeys. Even so, all of the bones can still be matched. The wing of a bird and the flipper of a seal are even more different from each other or from the human forearm, yet they too are constructed around bones that can be matched on a nearly perfect one-to-one basis.

—William K. Purves and Gordon H. Orians,
Life: The Science of Biology

Definition of homology *and related words*

Short definition

Refined definition

Examples:

Similar appearance, function, and structure

Dissimilar appearance and function, but similar structure

CASE STUDY
Using Definition

Susan Iessi was a freshman at the State University of New York at New Paltz when she volunteered to become a member of Hall Government, a dormitory association dedicated to student support. Discovering that many dorm residents, especially other freshmen, were unclear about the work of Hall Government, Iessi wrote the following statement.

Iessi's main goal of specifying Hall Government's purposes and responsibilities drew her into defining the mission of the association. After she drafted the statement, she showed it to other members. When one reader suggested that she explain the connections between Hall Government and other campus organizations, Iessi agreed: The change would clarify the boundaries of Hall Government. Iessi's final draft appears below.

The Mission of Hall Government

Hall Government consists of students who volunteer to provide the residents of their dormitory with social and emotional support. Hall Government creates opportunities for residents to meet other residents and build a network of friends through structured discussions, social events, and educational programs. It also mediates in situations such as conflicts between students and teachers or between roommates. The members of Hall Government believe that their support will encourage residents to provide support for each other as well, building a community in which students may learn and thrive during their college years.

Each dormitory's Hall Government functions independently. The groups have no formal relationship with the campus-wide elected student government but are sponsored and funded by the Residence Hall Student Association.

GLORIA NAYLOR

GLORIA NAYLOR describes herself as "just a girl from Queens who can turn a sentence," but she is well known for bringing African American women vividly within the fold of American literature. She was born in 1950 in New York City and served for some years as a missionary for the Jehovah's Witnesses, working "for better world conditions." While in college, she made her living as a telephone operator. She graduated from Brooklyn College in 1981 and received an MA in African American literature from Yale University in 1983. While teaching at several universities and publishing numerous stories and essays, Naylor has written five interconnected novels: *The Women of Brewster Place* (1982), *Linden Hills* (1985), *Mama Day* (1988), *Bailey's Cafe* (1992), and *The Men of Brewster Place* (1998). *The Women of Brewster Place* won the American Book Award for best first novel, and Naylor has also received fellowships from the National Endowment for the Arts and the Guggenheim Foundation. She lives in New York City.

The Meanings of a Word

When she was in third grade, Naylor was stung by a word that seemed new. Only later did she realize that she'd been hearing the word all her life, but in an entirely different context. In "The Meanings of a Word," she uses definition to explore the varying meanings that context creates. The essay first appeared in the *New York Times* in 1986.

The essay following this one, Christine Leong's "Being a Chink," responds directly to Naylor and extends her point about context and meaning.

Language is the subject. It is the written form with which I've managed to keep the wolf away from the door and, in diaries, to keep my sanity. In spite of this, I consider the written word inferior to the spoken, and much of the frustration experienced by novelists is the awareness that whatever we manage to capture in even the most transcendent passages falls far short of the richness of life. Dialogue achieves its power in the dynamics of a fleeting moment of sight, sound, smell, and touch.

I'm not going to enter the debate here about whether it is language that shapes reality or vice versa. That battle is doomed to be waged whenever we seek intermittent reprieve from the chicken and egg dispute. I will simply take the position that the spoken word, like the written word, amounts to a nonsensical arrangement of sounds or letters without a consensus that assigns "meaning." And building from the meanings of what we hear, we order reality. Words themselves are innocuous; it is the consensus that gives them true power.

I remember the first time I heard the word *nigger*. In my third-grade class, 3
our math tests were being passed down the rows, and as I handed the papers to
a little boy in back of me, I remarked that once again he had received a much
lower mark than I did. He snatched his test from me and spit out that word.
Had he called me a nymphomaniac or a necrophiliac, I couldn't have been
more puzzled. I didn't know what a nigger was, but I knew that whatever it
meant, it was something he shouldn't have called me. This was verified when
I raised my hand, and in a loud voice repeated what he had said and watched
the teacher scold him for using a "bad" word. I was later to go home and ask
the inevitable question that every black parent must face—"Mommy, what
does *nigger* mean?"

And what exactly did it mean? Thinking back, I realize that this could not 4
have been the first time the word was used in my presence. I was part of a large
extended family that had migrated from the rural South after World War II
and formed a close-knit network that gravitated around my maternal grandparents. Their ground-floor apartment in one of the buildings they owned in
Harlem was a weekend mecca for my immediate family, along with countless
aunts, uncles, and cousins who brought along assorted friends. It was a
bustling and open house with assorted neighbors and tenants popping in and
out to exchange bits of gossip, pick up an old quarrel, or referee the ongoing
checkers game in which my grandmother cheated shamelessly. They were all
there to let down their hair and put up their feet after a week of labor in the
factories, laundries, and shipyards of New York.

Amid the clamor, which could reach deafening proportions—two or 5
three conversations going on simultaneously, punctuated by the sound of a
baby's crying somewhere in the back rooms or out on the street—there was
still a rigid set of rules about what was said and how. Older children were sent
out of the living room when it was time to get into the juicy details about
"you-know-who" up on the third floor who had gone and gotten herself
"p-r-e-g-n-a-n-t!" But my parents, knowing that I could spell well beyond my
years, always demanded that I follow the others out to play. Beyond sexual
misconduct and death, everything else was considered harmless for our young
ears. And so among the anecdotes of the triumphs and disappointments in the
various workings of their lives, the word *nigger* was used in my presence, but it
was set within contexts and inflections that caused it to register in my mind as
something else.

In the singular, the word was always applied to a man who had distin- 6
guished himself in some situation that brought their approval for his strength,
intelligence, or drive:

"Did Johnny *really* do that?" 7

"I'm telling you, that nigger pulled in $6,000 of overtime last year. Said he [8] got enough for a down payment on a house."

When used with a possessive adjective by a woman—"my nigger"—it [9] became a term of endearment for her husband or boyfriend. But it could be more than just a term applied to a man. In their mouths it became the pure essence of manhood—a disembodied force that channeled their past history of struggle and present survival against the odds into a victorious statement of being: "Yeah, that old foreman found out quick enough—you don't mess with a nigger."

In the plural, it became a description of some group within the commu- [10] nity that had overstepped the bounds of decency as my family defined it. Parents who neglected their children, a drunken couple who fought in public, people who simply refused to look for work, those with excessively dirty mouths or unkempt households were all "trifling niggers." This particular circle could forgive hard times, unemployment, the occasional bout of depression— they had gone through all of that themselves—but the unforgivable sin was a lack of self-respect.

A woman could never be a "nigger" in the singular, with its connotation [11] of confirming worth. The noun *girl* was its closest equivalent in that sense, but only when used in direct address and regardless of the gender doing the addressing. *Girl* was a token of respect for a woman. The one-syllable word was drawn out to sound like three in recognition of the extra ounce of wit, nerve, or daring that the woman had shown in the situation under discussion.

"G-i-r-l, stop. You mean you said that to his face?" [12]

But if the word was used in a third-person reference or shortened so that [13] it almost snapped out of the mouth, it always involved some element of communal disapproval. And age became an important factor in these exchanges. It was only between individuals of the same generation, or from any older person to a younger (but never the other way around), that *girl* would be considered a compliment.

I don't agree with the argument that use of the word *nigger* at this social [14] stratum of the black community was an internalization of racism. The dynamics were the exact opposite: The people in my grandmother's living room took a word that whites used to signify worthlessness or degradation and rendered it impotent. Gathering there together, they transformed *nigger* to signify the varied and complex human beings they knew themselves to be. If the word was to disappear totally from the mouths of even the most liberal of white society, no one in that room was naive enough to believe it would disappear from white minds. Meeting the word head-on, they proved it had absolutely nothing to do with the way they were determined to live their lives.

So there must have been dozens of times that *nigger* was spoken in front 15 of me before I reached the third grade. But I didn't "hear" it until it was said by a small pair of lips that had already learned it could be a way to humiliate me. That was the word I went home and asked my mother about. And since she knew that I had to grow up in America, she took me in her lap and explained.

———————

Journal Writing

As Naylor shows, the language of stereotypes can be powerful and painful to encounter. In your journal, recall when you have experienced or witnessed this kind of labeling. What were your reactions? Keep in mind that race is but one object of stereotypes. Consider income, education, body type or other physical attributes, sexual preference, activities, or neighborhood, for just a few other characteristics. (To take your journal writing further, see "From Journal to Essay" on the next page.)

Questions on Meaning

1. Why does Naylor think that written language is inferior to spoken language (par. 1)?
2. In paragraph 15, Naylor says that although the word *nigger* had been used in her presence many times, she didn't really "hear" the word until a mean little boy said it. How do you explain this contradiction?
3. Naylor says that "the people in my grandmother's living room [. . .] transformed *nigger*" (par. 14). How?
4. What is Naylor's primary PURPOSE in this essay?

Questions on Writing Strategy

1. In her first two paragraphs, Naylor discusses language in the ABSTRACT. How are these paragraphs connected to her stories about the word *nigger*? Why do you think she begins the essay this way? Is this INTRODUCTION effective or not? Why?
2. Look back at the last two sentences of Naylor's essay. What is the EFFECT of ending on this idea?
3. Go through Naylor's essay and note which paragraphs discuss the racist uses of *nigger* and which discuss the nonracist uses. How do Naylor's organization and the space she devotes to each use help Naylor make her point?
4. **OTHER METHODS.** After each DEFINITION of the words *nigger* and *girl*, Naylor gives an EXAMPLE in the form of a quotation. These examples are in paragraphs 7–10 (for instance, "Yeah, that old foreman found out quick enough — you don't mess with a nigger" [9]) and paragraph 12 ("G-i-r-l, stop. You mean you said that to his face?"). What do such examples add to Naylor's definitions?

Questions on Language

1. What is "the chicken and egg dispute" (par. 2)? What does this dispute say about the relationship between language and reality?
2. What do the words *nymphomaniac* and *necrophiliac* CONNOTE in paragraph 3?
3. If you don't know the meanings of the following words, look them up in a dictionary: transcendent, dynamics (par. 1); intermittent, reprieve, consensus, innocuous (2); verified (3); gravitated, mecca (4); clamor, inflections (5); endearment, disembodied (9); unkempt, trifling (10); communal (13); stratum, internalization, degradation, rendered, impotent, naive (14).

Suggestions for Writing

1. **FROM JOURNAL TO ESSAY.** Using as examples the experiences you wrote about in your journal entry (previous page), write an essay modeled on Naylor's in which you define "the meanings of a word" (or words). Do you find, too, that meaning varies with context? If so, make the variations clear.
2. Can you think of other labels that may be defined in more than one way? (These might include *smart, childish, old-fashioned, artistic, proud, attractive, heroic,* and so on.) Choose one such label, and write one paragraph for each possible definition. Be sure to explain the contexts for each definition and to give enough examples so that the meanings are clear.
3. **CRITICAL WRITING.** Naylor claims that words are "nonsensical [. . .] without a consensus that assigns 'meaning'" (par. 2). If so, how do we understand the meaning of a word like *nigger,* when Naylor has shown us that there is more than one consensus about its meaning? Does Naylor contradict herself? Write an essay that either supports or refutes Naylor's claim about meaning and context. You will need to consider how she and you define *consensus.*
4. **CONNECTIONS.** The next essay, Christine Leong's "Being a Chink," identifies a moment when Leong was first struck by the negative power of racist language. Write an essay that COMPARES AND CONTRASTS Naylor's and Leong's reactions to a derogatory label. How did the context help shape their reactions?

Gloria Naylor on Writing

Studying literature in college was somewhat disappointing for Gloria Naylor. "What I wanted to see," she told William Goldstein of *Publishers Weekly,* "were reflections of me and my existence and experience." Then, reading African American literature in graduate school, she discovered that "blacks have been writing in this country since this country has been writing and have a literary heritage of their own. Unfortunately, they haven't had encouragement or recognition for their efforts. [. . .] What had happened was that when black people wrote, it wasn't quite [considered] serious work — it was race work or protest work."

For Naylor this discovery was a turning point. "I wanted to become a writer because I felt that my presence as a black woman and my perspective as a woman in general had been underrepresented." Her work tries to "articulate experiences that want articulating — for those readers who reflect the subject matter, black readers, and for those who don't, basically white middle-class readers."

For Discussion

1. What does Naylor mean when she says that she tries to "articulate experiences that want articulating"?
2. Naylor is motivated to write by a consciousness of herself as an African American and a woman. How do you see this motivation driving her essay "The Meanings of a Word"?

CHRISTINE LEONG

CHRISTINE LEONG was born in New York City in 1976 and attended Stuyvesant High School there, graduating in 1994. At the Stern School of Business at New York University, she majored in finance and information systems and interned at an investment firm. After graduating with a BS in 1998, she took a job as a consultant at J. P. Morgan in New York. In her free time, Leong writes, reads, takes pictures, and participates in outdoor activities. "The one thing I couldn't live without," she says, "is music."

Being a Chink

Leong wrote this essay for her freshman composition class at NYU, and it was published in Mercer Street, 1995–96, a collection of NYU students' essays. As you'll see, Leong was inspired by Gloria Naylor's "The Meanings of a Word" (p. 468) to report her own experiences and to define a word that can be either hurtful or warm, depending on the speaker.

The power of language is something that people often underestimate. It is   1
the one thing that allows people to communicate with each other, to be understood, to be heard. It gives us identity, personality, social status, and it also creates communities, defining both insiders and outsiders. Language has the ability to heal or to harm, to praise or belittle, to promote peace or even to glorify hate. But perhaps most important, language is the tool used to define us and differentiate us from the next person. Names and labels are what separate us from each other. Sometimes these things are innocuous, depending on the particular word and the context in which it is used. Often they serve to ridicule and humiliate.

I remember the first time I saw the word *chink*. I used to work over the   2
summers at my father's Chinese restaurant, the Oriental, to earn a few extra dollars of spending money. It was a warm, sunny Friday morning, and I was busy performing my weekly task of cleaning out the storage area under the cash register at the front of the store. Armed with a large can of Pledge furniture polish and an old cloth, I started attacking the old oak shelves, sorting through junk mail that had accumulated over the last week, separating the bills and other important things that had to be set aside for later, before wiping each wooden panel clean. It was a pretty uneventful chore, that is, until I got to the bottom shelf, the last of three. I always hated cleaning this particular shelf because it required me to get down on my hands and knees behind the counter and reach all the way back into the compartment to dig out all the stuff that managed to get wedged against the wall.

After bending to scoop all the papers out of that third cubicle, I began to   3
sort through them haphazardly. A few old menus, a gum wrapper (I always
wondered how little things like that got stuffed in there), some promotional
flyers, two capless pens, a dusty scratch pad, and something that appeared to
be a little white envelope. Nothing seemed unusual until I examined that last
item more closely. It was an old MidLantic envelope from the bank across the
street. I was just about to crumple it up and throw it into the trash can when
I decided to check if there was any money left in it. Too lazy to deal with the
actual "chore" of opening the envelope, I held it up to the light.

As the faint yellow glow from the antique light fixture above me shone   4
through the envelope, turning it transparent, my suspicion that it was empty
was confirmed. However, what I found was more shocking than anything I
could have imagined. There, outlined by the light, was the word *chink* written
backwards. I quickly lowered my arm onto the cool, smooth surface of the
counter and flipped the envelope onto its other side, refusing to believe what
I had just read. On the back, in dark blue ink with a large circle drawn around
it, was the word CHINK written in my father's handwriting.

Up until that moment, I hadn't known that my father knew such words,   5
and thinking again, perhaps he didn't know this one either. After all, it was a
habit of his to write down English words he did not know when he heard them
and look them up in the dictionary later that day, learning them and adding
them to his vocabulary. My mind began spinning with all the possible reasons
he had written this particular word down. I wondered if an angry patron who
had come in earlier had called him that.

I was shocked at that possibility, but I was not surprised. Being one of only   6
two Asian families living and running a business in a small suburban town pre-
dominately inhabited by old Caucasian people was bound to breed some kind
of discrimination, if not hatred. I know that my father might not have known
exactly what the word *chink* meant, but he must have had a good idea, because
he never came to ask me about it as he did with all the other slang words that
couldn't be found in the dictionary. It's funny, though, I do not remember the
first time I was called a *chink*. I only remember the pain and outrage I felt the
first time I saw it in writing, perhaps the first time I discovered that someone
had used that hateful word to degrade my father.

In her essay "The Meanings of a Word," Gloria Naylor examines the var-   7
ious meanings of the word *nigger*, definitions that have consensual meanings
throughout society and others that vary according to how and when the word
is used. In this piece, Naylor uses personal examples to describe how "the
people in [her] grandmother's living room took a word that whites used to signify worthlessness or degradation and rendered it impotent," by transforming
nigger into a word signifying "the varied and complex human beings that they

knew themselves to be." Naylor goes on to add that although none of these people were foolish enough to believe that the word *nigger* would magically be erased from the minds of all humankind, they were convinced that their "head-on" approach of dealing with the label that society had put on them "proved that it had absolutely nothing to do with the way they were determined to live their lives."

It has been nearly eight years since that day I stumbled across the bank   8
envelope. Since then we have moved from that suburb in New Jersey to New York City, where the Asian population is much larger, and the word *chink,* although still heard, is either heard less frequently or in a rather "harmless" manner between myself and fellow Chinese (Asian) teenage friends. I do not remember how it happened exactly. I just know that we have been calling each other *chink* for quite a long while now. The word has never been used to belittle or degrade, but rather as a term of endearment, a loving insult between friends, almost but not quite exactly the way *nigger* is sometimes used among black people. It is a practice that we still engage in today, and although we know that there are times when the use of the word *chink* is very inappropriate, it is an accepted term within our circle.

Do not misunderstand us, we are all intelligent Asian youths, all graduat-   9
ing from New York City's top high school, all college students, and we know what the word *chink* truly means. We know, because over the years we have heard it countless times, from strangers on the streets and in stores, from fellow students and peers, and in some instances even from teachers, although it might not have been meant for us to hear.

So you see, even though we may use the term *chink* rather casually, it is   10
only used that way amongst ourselves because we know that when we say it to each other it is truly without malice or harmful intent. I do not think that any of us knows exactly why we do it, but perhaps it is our own way, like the characters in Naylor's piece, of dealing with a label that can never be removed. It is not determined by who we are on the inside, or what we are capable of accomplishing, but instead by what we look like—the shape of our eyes, the color of our skin, the texture of our hair, and our delicate features. Perhaps we intentionally misuse the word as a symbol of our overcoming the stereotypes that American society has imposed upon us, a way of showing that although others have tried to make us feel small, weak, and insignificant, we are the opposite. We are strong, we are determined, we are the voices of the future, and we refuse to let a simple word paralyze us, belittle us, or control us.

The word *chink* may have been created to harm, ridicule, and humiliate,   11
but for us it may have done the exact opposite. In some ways it has helped us find a certain comfort in each other, each of us knowing what the other has gone through, a common thread of racism binding us all together, a strange

union born from the word *chink* that was used against us, and a shared goal of perseverance.

Journal Writing

Although children often assume they will be protected by their parents, Leong presents a situation in which she felt the need to protect her father. Can you identify with Leong's feelings? Have you ever felt particularly angry or defensive on behalf of a parent? In your journal, explore why and what happened as a result. (To take your journal writing further, see "From Journal to Essay" on the next page.)

Questions on Meaning

1. In paragraph 9 Leong says that she and her friends "know what the word *chink* truly means." Where in her essay does she explain this "true" meaning?
2. What has the word *chink* come to mean when Leong and her friends use it? Where in the essay does Leong explain this?
3. One might argue that the THESIS of Leong's essay is that language is not absolute. Is her PURPOSE, then, to propose a new DEFINITION for a word, to teach the reader something about how labels work, or to explain how adapting a racist term can be a form of gaining power? How do you know?

Questions on Writing Strategy

1. Look carefully at Gloria Naylor's essay "The Meanings of a Word" (p. 468). What structural similarities do you notice between it and Leong's? Why do you think Leong adapts these features of Naylor's essay?
2. In paragraph 3 Leong details all the forgotten items she finds under the counter. What is the EFFECT of ending with the "old MidLantic envelope from the bank across the street"?
3. What is the main purpose of the extended example from Naylor's essay in paragraph 7?
4. Why is Leong so careful to explain that she and her friends are all intelligent and educated (par. 9)?
5. **OTHER METHODS.** Leong suggests CAUSE AND EFFECT when she expresses shock and disbelief at seeing the word *chink* in writing (par. 4). Why does Leong react so strongly to the writing on the envelope?

Questions on Language

1. In paragraph 10 Leong explains that she and her friends are "dealing with a label that can never be removed." What other words does she use in this paragraph to suggest the potential helplessness of being permanently labeled?

2. What do the CONNOTATIONS of "term of endearment" (par. 8) indicate about the way Leong and her friends have redefined *chink*?
3. Make sure you know the meanings of the following words: status, belittle, innocuous (par. 1); cubicle, haphazardly (3); Caucasian, degrade (6); consensual (7); malice (10); perseverance (11).

Suggestions for Writing

1. **FROM JOURNAL TO ESSAY.** Write an essay that explores why and how children might feel compelled to act like parents toward their own parents. Is this a shift that comes with age? with specific circumstances? out of the blue? Make some GENERALIZATIONS about this process, using as EVIDENCE the personal recollections from your journal entry (previous page).
2. As Leong explains in her INTRODUCTION, not all labels are intended to be hurtful. Often they are shorthand ways for our families and friends to identify us, perhaps reflecting something about our appearance ("Red," "Slim") or our interests ("Sport," "Chef"). What do your family or friends call you? Write several paragraphs giving a careful definition of this label. Where did it come from? Why is it appropriate (or not)?
3. **CRITICAL WRITING.** In her opening paragraph Leong says that "language is the tool used to define us." But she goes on to explain how she and her friends *refuse* to be defined by racist language. Does this apparent contradiction weaken her essay? Why, or why not? (To answer this question, consider the purpose of Leong's essay; see "Meaning" question 3.)
4. **CONNECTIONS.** Both Leong and Gloria Naylor, in "The Meanings of a Word" (p. 468), show that racist language can be taken over by those against whom it is directed. They also show that for groups or communities to redefine, and thus to own, these racist slurs can be empowering. Do you find their ARGUMENTS convincing, or do these redefinitions reveal what Naylor denies—namely, "an internalization of racism" (par. 14)? In an essay, explain your opinion on this issue, using as evidence passages from Naylor's and Leong's essays as well as insights and EXAMPLES from your own observations and experience.

Christine Leong on Writing

For *The Bedford Reader,* Christine Leong commented on the difficulties of writing and the rewards that can ensue.

Writing is something that comes easily for many people, but unfortunately I am not one of them. For me the writing process is one of the hardest and quite possibly is *the* most nerve-wracking thing that I have ever experienced. I can't even begin to count all the hours I have spent throughout the course of my life staring at a blank computer screen, trying desperately to come up with the right combination of words to express my thoughts and feelings, and although after many hours of frustration I eventually end up with something, I am never happy with it because I am undoubtedly my own worst critic. Perhaps my mentality of "it's not good enough yet" stems from my belief that writing can never really be completed; to me it has no beginning and no end but is rather a small representation of who I am at a given moment in time, and I believe that the more things I experience in life, the more I am able to contribute to my writing. Thus, whatever I write always has the potential of being better; there's always room for improvement via more revisions, greater insight, and about a hundred more drafts.

I used to believe that writing always had to make sense, but since then I have learned that there are many things in this life that do not adhere to this "rule." I now realize that writing doesn't necessarily have to be grammatically correct or even sensible, and the only thing that really matters is that whatever is written is truly inspired. Passion comes through very clearly in a writer's words, and the more emotion that goes into a piece, the more impact it will ultimately have on the reader. In recent years I have learned that there are no real writing guidelines, and that writing is much like any other art form: It can be abstract or it can follow more traditional "themes." However, in order for a piece of writing to be effective, in the sense that it can differentiate itself from any other writing sample and hopefully have some significance to the reader, I believe that it has to come from within.

The majority of what I write about, and that which I feel is worth reading, is inspired by actual experiences that I have had. For example, "Being a Chink" began as an assignment in a freshman writing workshop class in college. When first presented with the task of writing it, I was at a complete loss for words and had absolutely no clue where to start. However, after reading Gloria Naylor's "The Meanings of a Word," I was reminded of one of the most traumatic and memorable events in my life. The piece triggered a very strong memory, and before long I found myself writing down anything that came into my head, letting my thoughts and emotions flow freely in the form of words without thinking about whether or not they made any kind of sense. Many hours later I discovered that I had written the basic structure of what would eventually be my final product. I must honestly say that I can't really recall the actual process of writing "Being a Chink"; it was just an essay that seemed to take on a life and form of its own. Perhaps that, along with its universal theme, is what makes it such a strong piece. It not only is a recollection from my adolescence but is something that defines the very essence of the person that I have become since then.

In retrospect, I now realize that writing "Being a Chink" was not only about completing an essay and fulfilling a writing requirement; it was also about the acknowledgment of my own growth as a person. In many ways, without my initially being aware of it, the piece has helped me come to terms with one of the most controversial issues that I have ever been faced with.

For Discussion

1. Does Leong's characterization of writing as "nerve-wracking" ring bells with you? How do you overcome writer's block?
2. What do you think about Leong's statement that "writing doesn't necessarily have to be grammatically correct or even sensible, and the only thing that really matters is that whatever is written is truly inspired"? In your experience with writing, what are the roles of correctness, sense, and inspiration? What matters most to you? What matters most to readers?

GEORGE F. WILL

The columnist, television commentator, and author GEORGE FREDERICK
WILL is widely known for his conservative thought about American politics
and society. He was born in 1941 in Champaign, Illinois, and attended Trin-
ity College (BA, 1962), Oxford University, and Princeton University (PhD,
1967). After working as a professor of politics, a staff member of the US Senate, and Washington editor of the *National Review,* Will began writing his
own political commentary for the *Washington Post* in 1974. His syndicated
column now appears twice a week in more than 450 newspapers. He has
been a contributing editor of *Newsweek* since 1976 and also appears regularly
on television news programs. Will's columns are collected in several books,
including *The Pursuit of Happiness and Other Sobering Thoughts* (1978), *The
Pursuit of Virtue and Other Tory Notions* (1982), *The Leveling Wind: Politics,
Culture, and Other News* (1994), and most recently *The Woven Figure: Conservatism and America's Fabric* (1997). In 1977 Will received a Pulitzer Prize
for distinguished commentary. Though best known for his political writing,
Will has also written *Men at Work* (1990) and *Bunts* (1998), both nonfiction
books about his other passion in life, baseball.

The Equity of Inequality

Is there a difference between *equal* and *equitable* and *egalitarian?* Definitely,
says Will, and the distinction is important to understanding the ideals and
values of the United States. This essay appeared first in 1995 in the *Washington Post* and then in Will's collection *The Woven Figure.*

A monk asks a superior if it is permissible to smoke while praying. The   1
superior says certainly not. Next day the monk asks the superior if it is permissible to pray while smoking. That, says the superior, is not merely permissible, it is admirable. The moral of the story is that much depends on how a
thing is presented.

Consider, for example, this lead paragraph from a *New York Times* news   2
story: "New studies on the growing concentration of American wealth and
income challenge a cherished part of the country's self-image: They show that
rather than being an egalitarian society, the United States has become the
most economically stratified of industrial nations." But the same data could be
reported as demonstrating that the United States, more than any other industrial nation, values equality, sensibly understood. And as demonstrating that
this nation's distribution of wealth is an incentive to rational behavior in contemporary economic conditions.

The studies purportedly show that the wealthiest 1 percent and wealthiest   3
20 percent of American households have a larger portion of the nation's
wealth than they used to have, and a larger portion than the wealthiest
households in other industrial nations have. Furthermore, the least wealthy
20 percent of Americans have a smaller portion of the nation's wealth than
the bottom 20 percent have in other industrial nations.

Now, let's assume the data are accurate, although income and wealth sta-   4
tistics involve judgments that can skew comparisons with other eras and
nations. However, the data, even if accurate, need not compel the essentially
political judgment expressed in the *Times* paragraph above.

In it, note the word "egalitarian." What the country's self-image actually   5
celebrates is broad if imperfect equal opportunity for striving—for the pursuit
of happiness. Americans have never been egalitarian in emphasizing equality
of outcomes. Concerning that, elsewhere in the *Times* story there occurs this
essentially political assessment: "Most economists believe that wealth and
income are more concentrated in the United States than in Japan. But while
data show that wealth is more equitably distributed in Japan, the government
there has not released enough detailed information to make statistical comparisons possible."

Note the use of the phrase "more equitably" as synonymous with "more   6
equally." That peculiar usage flows from an idea that Americans have generally considered peculiar—the idea that equality of condition is a key component of social justice.

A society that values individualism, enterprise, and a market economy is   7
neither surprised nor scandalized when the unequal distribution of marketable
skills produces large disparities in the distribution of wealth. This does not
mean that social justice must be defined as whatever distribution of wealth the
market produces. But it does mean that there is a presumption in favor of
respecting the market's version of distributive justice. Certainly there is today
no prima facie[1] case against the moral acceptability of increasingly large disparities of wealth.

[The twentieth] century's experience with government attempts to use   8
progressive taxation to influence the distribution of income suggests the
weakness of that instrument and the primacy of social and cultural forces in
determining the distribution of wealth. Consider three things that might conduce to a smaller gap between the most and least affluent households. Stopping immigration would reduce downward pressure on wages. A stock market
crash would devalue the portfolios of the wealthy. And curtailing access to

---

[1]Latin meaning "first face." In a prima facie law case, the evidence seems sufficient to
arrive at a judgment.—EDS.

college and postgraduate education would limit the disparities in the marketable skills that increasingly account for income disparities.

But to suggest such "solutions" is to understand that the problem of   9
increasing inequalities of wealth is not a problem we will pay just any price to remedy, and may not be a problem at all. In an increasingly knowledge-based economy, education disparities drive income disparities, which are incentives for the rising generation to take education seriously as a decisive shaper of individuals' destinies.

In today's deregulated global economy, with highly mobile capital and an   10
abundance of cheap labor, the long-term prosperity of an advanced nation is a function of a high rate of savings—the deferral of gratification that makes possible high rates of investment in capital, research and development, and education. All these forms of social capital are good for society as a whole and are encouraged by high rewards for those who accept the discipline.

That is why promoting more equal distribution of wealth might not be   11
essential to, or even compatible with, promoting a more equitable society. And why increasingly unequal social rewards can conduce to a more truly egalitarian society, one that offers upward mobility equally to all who accept its rewarding disciplines.

Journal Writing

Will holds that a "truly egalitarian society [. . .] offers upward mobility equally to all who accept its rewarding disciplines." In your journal, explore how you define *egalitarian*. Is the United States an egalitarian society? Why, or why not? (To take your journal writing further, see "From Journal to Essay" on the next page.)

Questions on Meaning

1. What is Will's THESIS? Where does he state it?
2. The *New York Times* article Will quotes in paragraph 2 suggests that differences in income distribution among the rich and the poor in the United States are leading to a society that is no longer "egalitarian." How does Will challenge the *Times* writer's implied definition of *egalitarian*?
3. What is Will's point in paragraphs 8–9?
4. Ultimately, what is Will's advice for Americans who aren't well-off?

Questions on Writing Strategy

1. What is the point of Will's opening ANECDOTE? How does it serve his PURPOSE?

2. True or false: Will assumes that his readers are more likely to be prosperous than to be poor. Explain your answer.
3. **OTHER METHODS.** What pattern of CAUSE AND EFFECT does Will identify? What is his point in doing so?

Questions on Language

1. How does Will distinguish between the concepts of "more equitably" and "more equally" (par. 6) in relation to the distribution of wealth in the United States? Why does he consider the first phrase a "peculiar usage" that is "essentially political"?
2. In reporting on new studies of income distribution in the United States, why does Will use the word "purportedly" (par. 3) and the sentence "let's assume the data are accurate" (4)?
3. What does Will mean by the phrase "rewarding disciplines" (par. 11)?
4. Consult a dictionary if you are unsure of the meanings of the following words: stratified, incentive, rational (par. 2); skew, compel (4); synonymous (6); disparities, presumption (7); progressive, primacy, conduce, portfolios, curtailing (8); deregulated, capital, deferral, gratification (10).

Suggestions for Writing

1. **FROM JOURNAL TO ESSAY.** Starting from your journal entry (previous page), write an essay in which you define *egalitarian* by your own lights. Consult a dictionary first to be sure of the word's basic meanings, but feel free to elaborate based on your own experiences, observations, and reading. You may, like Will, choose to define partly by COMPARISON AND CONTRAST of *egalitarian* and *equal*.
2. Think of a word whose meaning could vary depending on who's doing the defining—*sportsmanship*, for example, or *entertainment* or *courage*. Write an essay in which you present common definitions for the term and then set out your own definition in detail.
3. **CRITICAL WRITING.** One of Will's central assumptions is that the United States offers its citizens "broad if imperfect equal opportunity for striving" (par. 5). Do you agree with this assumption? Write an essay in which you either support or argue against this belief, based on EXAMPLES from your own experiences and observations.
4. **CONNECTIONS.** In "On Compassion" (p. 183), Barbara Lazear Ascher writes about a specific effect of income disparity in the United States: homeless people living on city streets. Write an essay in which you compare and contrast the ideas presented in "On Compassion" and in "The Equity of Inequality." How might Will respond to Ascher and Ascher to Will? You may, if you wish, compose your essay in the form of a dialogue between the two writers.

George F. Will on Writing

In 1992 Brian Lamb of the C-SPAN show *Booknotes* asked George F. Will how he writes. (A complete transcript of the interview can be found on the show's Web site at *http://www.booknotes.org.*)

WILL: I write [. . .] with a fountain pen.

LAMB: Big, huge Mont Blanc pen.

WILL: Everything with a fountain pen, and I write books with it.

LAMB: What do you write it on?

WILL: Yellow tablets.

LAMB: Richard Nixon used to do that.

WILL: Yes. I don't care. I still do it.

LAMB: Where do you write?

WILL: In my office in Georgetown, on airplanes, everywhere. I have an itch to write. I would explode if I couldn't write.

LAMB: How often do you write?

WILL: I write five columns every two weeks to begin with, and then I write book reviews and I write books.

For Discussion

1. What connections might there be between Will's use of a fountain pen and his "itch to write"?
2. Do you draft mainly on a computer or on paper with pencil or pen? What are the advantages and disadvantages of each method?

MARIE WINN

Marie Winn was born in Czechoslovakia in 1936. As a child she immigrated with her family to New York City, where she attended public school. She graduated from Radcliffe College and went on to Columbia University for further study. She has contributed articles to the *New York Times Magazine*, the *New York Times Book Review*, *Smithsonian*, and the *Wall Street Journal*, where she now writes a column on nature and bird watching. She is also the author of eleven books for both adults and children, including *The Fireside Book of Fun and Game Songs* (1974). Three of her books for adults raise difficult issues of child rearing and have attracted much attention: *The Plug-In Drug: Television, Children, and the Family* (1977, revised 1985), *Children Without Childhood* (1983), and *Unplugging the Plug-In Drug* (1987). Winn's most recent book, *Red-Tails in Love: A Wildlife Drama in Central Park* (1998), tells the story of a pair of red-tailed hawks that nested on a New York highrise and the community of people who observed them.

TV Addiction

Do you know someone who can't stop watching television? In this excerpt from *The Plug-In Drug*, Winn defines the troubling malady named in the title. The essay actually performs double duty as a definition, first explaining *addiction*, then *TV addiction*.

The word "addiction" is often used loosely and wryly in conversation. People will refer to themselves as "mystery book addicts" or "cookie addicts." E. B. White[1] writes of his annual surge of interest in gardening: "We are hooked and are making an attempt to kick the habit." Yet nobody really believes that reading mysteries or ordering seeds by catalogue is serious enough to be compared with addictions to heroin or alcohol. The word "addiction" is here used jokingly to denote a tendency to overindulge in some pleasurable activity.

People often refer to being "hooked on TV." Does this, too, fall into the lighthearted category of cookie eating and other pleasures that people pursue with unusual intensity, or is there a kind of television viewing that falls into the more serious category of destructive addiction?

When we think about addiction to drugs or alcohol, we frequently focus on negative aspects, ignoring the pleasures that accompany drinking or drug-taking. And yet the essence of any serious addiction is a pursuit of pleasure, a search for a "high" that normal life does not supply. It is only the inability to

[1] See page 670. —Eds.

486

function without the addictive substance that is dismaying, the dependence of the organism upon a certain experience and an increasing inability to function normally without it. Thus a person will take two or three drinks at the end of the day not merely for the pleasure drinking provides, but also because he "doesn't feel normal" without them.

An addict does not merely pursue a pleasurable experience and need to experience it in order to function normally. He needs to *repeat* it again and again. Something about that particular experience makes life without it less than complete. Other potentially pleasurable experiences are no longer possible, for under the spell of the addictive experience, his life is peculiarly distorted. The addict craves an experience and yet he is never really satisfied. The organism may be temporarily sated, but soon it begins to crave again.

Finally, a serious addiction is distinguished from a harmless pursuit of pleasure by its distinctly destructive elements. A heroin addict, for instance, leads a damaged life: His increasing need for heroin in increasing doses prevents him from working, from maintaining relationships, from developing in human ways. Similarly an alcoholic's life is narrowed and dehumanized by his dependence on alcohol.

Let us consider television viewing in the light of the conditions that define serious addictions.

Not unlike drugs or alcohol, the television experience allows the participant to blot out the real world and enter into a pleasurable and passive mental state. The worries and anxieties of reality are as effectively deferred by becoming absorbed in a television program as by going on a "trip" induced by drugs or alcohol. And just as alcoholics are only inchoately aware of their addiction, feeling that they control their drinking more than they really do ("I can cut it out any time I want—I just like to have three or four drinks before dinner"), people similarly overestimate their control over television watching. Even as they put off other activities to spend hour after hour watching television, they feel they could easily resume living in a different, less passive style. But somehow or other while the television set is present in their homes, the click doesn't sound. With television pleasures available, those other experiences seem less attractive, more difficult somehow.

A heavy viewer (a college English instructor) observes: "I find television almost irresistible. When the set is on, I cannot ignore it. I can't turn it off. I feel sapped, will-less, enervated. As I reach out to turn off the set, the strength goes out of my arms. So I sit there for hours and hours."

The self-confessed television addict often feels he "ought" to do other things—but the fact that he doesn't read and doesn't plant his garden or sew or crochet or play games or have conversations means that those activities are no longer as desirable as television viewing. In a way a heavy viewer's life is as imbalanced by his television "habit" as a drug addict's or an alcoholic's. He is living in a holding pattern, as it were, passing up the activities that lead to growth or development or a sense of accomplishment. This is one reason people talk about their television viewing so ruefully, so apologetically. They are aware that it is an unproductive experience, that almost any other endeavor is more worthwhile by any human measure.

Finally, it is the adverse effect of television viewing on the lives of so many people that defines it as a serious addiction. The television habit distorts the sense of time. It renders other experiences vague and curiously unreal while taking on a greater reality for itself. It weakens relationships by reducing and sometimes eliminating normal opportunities for talking, for communicating. 　10

And yet television does not satisfy, else why would the viewer continue to watch hour after hour, day after day? "The measure of health," writes Lawrence Kubie, "is flexibility . . . and especially the freedom to cease when sated." But the television viewer can never be sated with his television experiences — they do not provide the true nourishment that satiation requires — and thus he finds that he cannot stop watching. 　11

Journal Writing

If you like to watch television, Winn's essay may seem exaggerated. After all, isn't turning on the TV a great way to unwind or to be entertained? In your journal, write about your own relationship to television. How often do you watch? Does TV viewing interfere with your life, or do you have it under control? What does TV viewing do for (or to) your life? If you don't watch TV at all, write instead about why you don't. (To take your journal writing further, see "From Journal to Essay" on the facing page.)

Questions on Meaning

1. What distinction does Winn make between the "harmless pursuit of pleasure" and addiction?
2. In paragraph 2 Winn poses the question that leads to her THESIS. What is the answer to this question? Do you find it explicitly stated anywhere?
3. What does Winn think are the main problems caused by excessive TV viewing?
4. Does Winn think there can be anything good about watching television? How do you know?

Questions on Writing Strategy

1. Why does Winn take such care to define *addiction* (pars. 3–5)? What does this stipulative definition do for the essay?

2. Winn does not answer her thesis question immediately after she asks it (par. 2). Why, do you think? What is the EFFECT of this delay?
3. Throughout her essay, Winn puts a number of words and phrases in quotation marks—for example, "hooked on TV" (par. 2), "high" (3), "trip" (7), "ought" (9). What does this punctuation contribute to Winn's essay?
4. **OTHER METHODS.** Study Winn's COMPARISON between drug or alcohol addiction and TV addiction. How are the two similar? Are they different in any way?

Questions on Language

1. Especially in paragraphs 4 and 11, Winn uses several metaphors of eating to explain addiction. (See *Figures of speech* in Useful Terms if you need a definition of *metaphor*.) If you do not know the meanings of *craves, sated, nourishment,* and *satiated,* look them up in a dictionary. What is the effect of using such terms to define addiction?
2. What does Winn mean when she describes addiction as "living in a holding pattern" (par. 9)?
3. Consult a dictionary if you don't know the meanings of any of the following words: wryly, denote (par. 1); dismaying, organism (3); dehumanized (5); inchoately (7); sapped, enervated (8); ruefully, apologetically, endeavor (9); adverse, renders, vague (10).

Suggestions for Writing

1. **FROM JOURNAL TO ESSAY.** If you are a TV watcher, write an essay that compares and contrasts your relationship with TV and Winn's definition of *TV addiction*: Would Winn consider you a television addict? Do you consider yourself one? Is it possible to watch a lot of television without being an addict? If you are not a TV watcher (or not much of one), write an essay that compares and contrasts your life with that of a frequent watcher (not necessarily an addict): How do you benefit? What might you be missing?
2. As Winn's opening paragraph points out, people often claim to be "addicted" to all kinds of things. From your experience, you probably know that such addictions can include everything from spy novels to Snickers candy bars to driving dangerously. Write an essay defining an addiction (but not to cigarettes, drugs, alcohol, or television). Your essay's TONE may be serious or humorous, but you should give your readers a sense of the addiction's CAUSES AND EFFECTS as well as EXAMPLES of its sufferers.
3. **CRITICAL WRITING.** "Finally, it is the adverse effect of television viewing on the lives of so many people that defines it as a serious addiction" (par. 10). Do you agree with this statement? Does the number of people affected define an addiction as "serious"? If fewer people suffered the "adverse effect" of TV viewing, would it not be a serious addiction? Or, in contrast, do the huge numbers of TV viewers remove the behavior from addicted to normal? Write an essay that either confirms or refutes Winn's assertion, using examples to support your opinion.
4. **CONNECTIONS.** Gore Vidal's "Drugs" (p. 437) proposes legalizing drugs as a solution to the problem of drug addiction and its effects on our society. Following

Vidal's model (though not his precise recommendations, of course, since television is already legal), propose a solution to the problem of TV addiction. Your solution may be serious or humorous, and it may approach the problem at the level of the individual addict or at the level of society as a whole.

Marie Winn on Writing

For Marie Winn, the most enjoyable part of writing is making improvements. "I love spending an hour or two with a dictionary and a thesaurus looking for a more nearly perfect word," she declares in an account of her working habits written for *The Bedford Reader*. "Or taking my pen and ruthlessly pruning all the unnecessary adjectives (a practice I can wholeheartedly recommend to you), or fooling around with the rhythm of a sentence or a paragraph by changing a verb into a participle, or making any number of little changes that a magazine editor I work with ruefully calls 'mouse milking.'"

But the proportion of time Winn spends at this "delightful occupation" is small. "For me, the pleasure and pain of writing go on simultaneously. Once I have finally forced myself to bite the bullet and get to work, as soon as the flow of writing stops—after a few sentences or paragraphs or, if I am extraordinarily lucky, a few pages—then, as a little reward for having actually written something and also as a procrastinating measure to delay the painful necessity of having to write something again, I play with the words and sentences on the page.

"That's the trouble, of course: There have to be words and sentences on the page before I can enjoy the pleasure of playing with them. Somehow I have to transform the vague and confused tangle of ideas in my head into an orderly and logical sequence on a blank piece of paper. That's the real hell of writing: the inescapable need to think clearly. [. . .] You have to figure it out, make it all hang together, consider the implications, the alternatives, eliminate the contradictions, the extraneous thoughts, the illogical conclusions. I *hate* that part of writing and I have a feeling you know perfectly well what I'm talking about."

For Discussion

1. For Winn, what is the most difficult part of the writing process? What part does she most enjoy?
2. What does the author see as the role that thinking plays in writing?

BRUNO BETTELHEIM

Described in his *New York Times* obituary as "a psychoanalyst of great impact" and "a gifted writer [. . .] with a great literary and moral sensibility," BRUNO BETTELHEIM was born in Austria in 1903 and died in the United States in 1990. Growing up in the Vienna of Sigmund Freud, Bettelheim became interested in psychoanalysis as a young teenager and trained as a psychologist at the University of Vienna. He had already earned a wide reputation when he was imprisoned by the Nazis in the Buchenwald and Dachau concentration camps. When released because of American intervention in 1939, Bettelheim immigrated to Chicago. After several research and teaching positions, in 1944 he began teaching at the University of Chicago and continued there until his retirement in 1973. Bettelheim's work concentrated on children with severe emotional disorders such as autism and psychosis, and many of his theories were provocative and controversial. Some of his well-known books, all on children, are *Love Is Not Enough* (1950), *Truants from Life* (1955), *The Children of the Dream* (1969), and *The Uses of Enchantment* (1976).

The Holocaust

In two books, *The Informed Heart* (1960) and *Surviving, and Other Essays* (1979), Bettelheim probed his and others' experiences in the Nazis' concentration camps. What follows is a freestanding slice of a much longer essay, "The Holocaust—One Generation After," from *Surviving*. With cool passion, Bettelheim uses definition to set the record straight on a loaded word.

To begin with, it was not the hapless victims of the Nazis who named their incomprehensible and totally unmasterable fate the "holocaust." It was the Americans who applied this artificial and highly technical term to the Nazi extermination of the European Jews. But while the event when named as mass murder most foul evokes the most immediate, most powerful revulsion, when it is designated by a rare technical term, we must first in our minds translate it back into emotionally meaningful language. Using technical or specially created terms instead of words from our common vocabulary is one of the best-known and most widely used distancing devices, separating the intellectual from the emotional experience. Talking about "the holocaust" permits us to manage it intellectually where the raw facts, when given their ordinary names, would overwhelm us emotionally—because it was catastrophe beyond comprehension, beyond the limits of our imagination, unless we force ourselves against our desire to extend it to encompass these terrible events.

This linguistic circumlocution began while it all was only in the planning

stage. Even the Nazis—usually given to grossness in language and action—
shied away from facing openly what they were up to and called this vile mass
murder "the final solution of the Jewish problem." After all, solving a problem
can be made to appear like an honorable enterprise, as long as we are not
forced to recognize that the solution we are about to embark on consists of the
completely unprovoked, vicious murder of millions of helpless men, women,
and children. The Nuremberg judges of these Nazi criminals followed their
example of circumlocution by coining a neologism out of one Greek and one
Latin root: genocide. These artificially created technical terms fail to connect
with our strongest feelings. The horror of murder is part of our most common
human heritage. From earliest infancy on, it arouses violent abhorrence in us.
Therefore in whatever form it appears we should give such an act its true designation and not hide it behind polite, erudite terms created out of classical
words.

3   To call this vile mass murder "the holocaust" is not to give it a special
name emphasizing its uniqueness which would permit, over time, the word
becoming invested with feelings germane to the event it refers to. The correct
definition of *holocaust* is "burnt offering." As such, it is part of the language of
the psalmist, a meaningful word to all who have some acquaintance with the
Bible, full of the richest emotional connotations. By using the term "holocaust," entirely false associations are established through conscious and unconscious connotations between the most vicious of mass murders and ancient
rituals of a deeply religious nature.

4   Using a word with such strong unconscious religious connotations when
speaking of the murder of millions of Jews robs the victims of this abominable
mass murder of the only thing left to them: their uniqueness. Calling the most
callous, most brutal, most horrid, most heinous mass murder a burnt offering
is a sacrilege, a profanation of God and man.

5   Martyrdom is part of our religious heritage. A martyr, burned at the stake,
is a burnt offering to his god. And it is true that after the Jews were asphyxiated, the victims' corpses were burned. But I believe we fool ourselves if we
think we are honoring the victims of systematic murder by using this term,
which has the highest moral connotations. By doing so, we connect for our
own psychological reasons what happened in the extermination camps with
historical events we deeply regret, but also greatly admire. We do so because
this makes it easier for us to cope; only in doing so we cope with our distorted
image of what happened, not with the events the way they did happen.

6   By calling the victims of the Nazis martyrs, we falsify their fate. The true
meaning of *martyr* is: "One who voluntarily undergoes the penalty of death for
refusing to renounce his faith" (*Oxford English Dictionary*). The Nazis made
sure that nobody could mistakenly think that their victims were murdered for

their religious beliefs. Renouncing their faith would have saved none of them. Those who had converted to Christianity were gassed, as were those who were atheists, and those who were deeply religious Jews. They did not die for any conviction, and certainly not out of choice.

Millions of Jews were systematically slaughtered, as were untold other "undesirables," not for any convictions of theirs, but only because they stood in the way of the realization of an illusion. They neither died for their convictions, nor were they slaughtered because of their convictions, but only in consequence of the Nazis' delusional belief about what was required to protect the purity of their assumed superior racial endowment, and what they thought necessary to guarantee them the living space they believed they needed and were entitled to. Thus while these millions were slaughtered for an idea, they did not die for one.

Millions—men, women, and children—were processed after they had been utterly brutalized, their humanity destroyed, their clothes torn from their bodies. Naked, they were sorted into those who were destined to be murdered immediately, and those others who had a short-term usefulness as slave labor. But after a brief interval they, too, were to be herded into the same gas chambers into which the others were immediately piled, there to be asphyxiated so that, in their last moments, they could not prevent themselves from fighting each other in vain for a last breath of air.

To call these most wretched victims of a murderous delusion, of destructive drives run rampant, martyrs or a burnt offering is a distortion invented for our comfort, small as it may be. It pretends that this most vicious of mass murders had some deeper meaning; that in some fashion the victims either offered themselves or at least became sacrifices to a higher cause. It robs them of the last recognition which could be theirs, denies them the last dignity we could accord them: to face and accept what their death was all about, not embellishing it for the small psychological relief this may give us.

We could feel so much better if the victims had acted out of choice. For our emotional relief, therefore, we dwell on the tiny minority who did exercise some choice: the resistance fighters of the Warsaw ghetto, for example, and others like them. We are ready to overlook the fact that these people fought back only at a time when everything was lost, when the overwhelming majority of those who had been forced into the ghettos had already been exterminated without resisting. Certainly those few who finally fought for their survival and their convictions, risking and losing their lives in doing so, deserve our admiration; their deeds give us a moral lift. But the more we dwell on these few, the more unfair are we to the memory of the millions who were slaughtered—who gave in, did not fight back—because we deny them the only thing which up to the very end remained uniquely their own: their fate.

Journal Writing

In his first paragraph Bettelheim writes about the use of "technical or specially created terms" that are "distancing devices, separating the intellectual from the emotional experience." Within particular fields—sports, dance, music, business, medicine, cooking, auto mechanics—technical terms do often work like shorthand for insiders and sound like code to outsiders. In your journal, write about how you moved from outsider to insider in an activity or a field you know well. Where, when, and how did you learn the meanings of specialized terms? (To take your journal writing further, see "From Journal to Essay" on the facing page.)

Questions on Meaning

1. Why does Bettelheim believe that *holocaust* is an inappropriate term for the mass murder of Jews during World War II? Why does he say this sort of "linguistic circumlocution" is used? (What is a "linguistic circumlocution"?)
2. What is Bettelheim's PURPOSE here?
3. According to Bettelheim, what do we do besides using unemotional terms to distance ourselves from the murder of the Jews?
4. Does Bettelheim suggest an alternative term for *holocaust*?

Questions on Writing Strategy

1. Where does Bettelheim stress etymologies, or word histories, and dictionary definitions? What is their EFFECT?
2. What does Bettelheim accomplish with paragraph 8? Why is this paragraph essential?
3. How would you characterize Bettelheim's TONE? What creates it? Is it appropriate, do you think?
4. In several places Bettelheim repeats or restates passages—for instance, "By doing so [. . .] We do so [. . .] only in doing so" (par. 5), or "stood in the way of the realization of an illusion [. . .] in consequence of the Nazis' delusional belief [. . .] slaughtered for an idea" (7). Do you think such repetition and restatement is deliberate on Bettelheim's part? Why, or why not?
5. **OTHER METHODS.** Bettelheim's definition is an ARGUMENT. What is the THESIS of his argument? What EVIDENCE supports the thesis?

Questions on Language

1. ANALYZE the words Bettelheim uses to refer to the murder of the Jews. How do the words support his argument?
2. What is the effect of Bettelheim's use of *we*—for instance, in paragraphs 5 and 10?

3. Look up any unfamiliar words: hapless (par. 1); neologism, abhorrence, erudite (2); germane, psalmist (3); abominable, callous, heinous, sacrilege, profanation (4); asphyxiated (5); delusional, endowment (7); rampant, embellishing (9).

Suggestions for Writing

1. **FROM JOURNAL TO ESSAY.** Write an essay in which you define and discuss the specialized terms in the activity or field you wrote of in your journal (facing page). What are the most important and common terms? What do they mean? How did you learn their meanings? What purpose do these terms serve — or what problems do they cause?

2. Although Bettelheim does not use the term, he is objecting to the use of a EUPHEMISM, or inoffensive word, in place of a word that might wound or offend. Euphemisms abound in the speech of politicians: The economy undergoes a "slowdown" or a "downturn"; people who are laid off are "downsized"; lying is "misspeaking." Drawing on Bettelheim's arguments as you see fit, write an essay about one or more euphemisms appearing in a daily newspaper. What do the euphemisms accomplish, and for whom? What do they conceal, and who is hurt? (For further insight into this topic, see William Lutz's "The World of Doublespeak" on p. 399.)

3. **CRITICAL WRITING.** Research the word *holocaust* in a dictionary of word histories (an etymological dictionary) and an interpretation of the Bible. (A librarian can direct you to these sources.) On the basis of your research, do you agree or disagree with Bettelheim's rejection of the word? (In your answer, consider whether the word's wide use for the Nazi murders has provided it with new meanings.)

4. **CONNECTIONS.** Read "I Have a Dream," by Martin Luther King, Jr. (p. 603). COMPARE it with Bettelheim's essay for their purposeful use of repetition and restatement. How does each author use this device? For what aim? What is the EFFECT? If you like, you can narrow your comparison to one representative passage of each essay. Just be sure to use quotations to support your comparison.

ADDITIONAL WRITING TOPICS
Definition

1. Write an essay in which you define an institution, trend, phenomenon, or abstraction as specifically and concretely as possible. Following are some suggestions designed to stimulate ideas. Before you begin, limit your subject.

Responsibility
Fun
Sorrow
Unethical behavior
The environment
Education
Progress
Advertising
Happiness
Fads
Feminism
Marriage
Sportsmanship
Leadership
Leisure
Originality
Character
Imagination
Democracy
A smile
A classic (of music, literature, art, or film)
Dieting
Meditation
Friendship

2. In a brief essay, define one of the following. In each instance, you have a choice of something good or something bad to talk about.

A good or bad boss
A good or bad parent
A good or bad host
A good or bad TV newscaster
A good or bad physician
A good or bad nurse
A good or bad minister, priest, or rabbi
A good or bad roommate
A good or bad driver
A good or bad disk jockey

3. In a paragraph, define one of the following slang expressions for someone who has never heard the term: *dis, wigged out, dweeb, awesome, fool around, wimp, druggie, snob, freak, loser, loner, freeloader, burnout, soul, quack, "chill," pig-out, gross out, winging it, "bad," "sweet."*

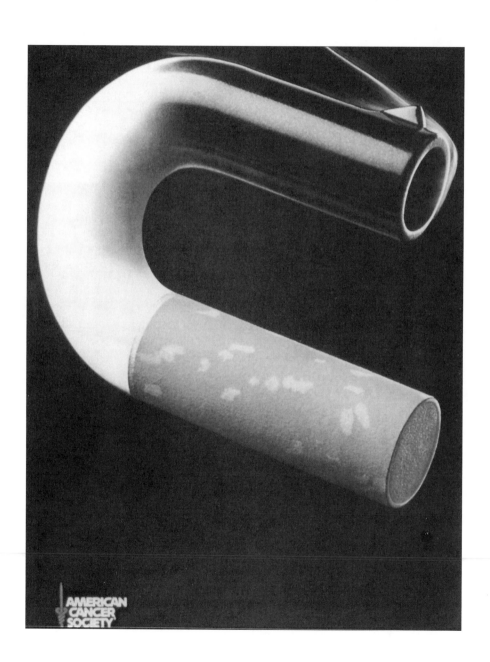

AMERICAN CANCER SOCIETY

13

ARGUMENT AND PERSUASION
Stating Opinions and Proposals

Argument and persuasion in an advertisement

The American Cancer Society has long sponsored public-service ads aimed at persuading people to avoid unhealthful behavior, especially smoking. In this ad the society uses a visual comparison to make a wordless argument. What is being compared? What similarities does the comparison rely on? At the same time, what differences does the ad ignore? Does neglecting these differences undermine the argument? How effective do you find the ad overall?

THE METHOD

Practically every day, we try to persuade ourselves or someone else. We usually attempt such persuasion without being aware that we follow any special method at all. Often, we'll state an *opinion:* We'll tell someone our own way of viewing things. We say to a friend, "I'm starting to like Senator Clark. Look at all she's done to help people with disabilities. Look at her voting record on toxic waste." And, having stated these opinions, we might go on to make a *proposal*, to recommend that some action be taken. Addressing our friend, we might suggest, "Hey, Senator Clark is talking on campus at four-thirty. Want to come with me and listen to her?"

Sometimes you try to convince yourself that a certain way of interpreting things is right. You even set forth an opinion in writing—as in a letter to a friend who has asked, "Now that you're at New Age College, how do you like the place?" You may write a letter of protest to a landlord who wants to raise your rent, pointing out that the bathroom hot water faucet doesn't work. As a concerned citizen, you may wish to speak your mind in an occasional letter to a newspaper or to your elected representatives.

In many professions, one is expected to persuade people in writing. Before arguing a case in court, a lawyer prepares briefs setting forth all the points in favor of his or her side. Businesspeople regularly put in writing their ideas for new products and ventures, for improvements in cost control and job efficiency. Researchers write proposals for grants to obtain money to support their work. Scientists write and publish papers to persuade the scientific community that their findings are valid, often stating hypotheses, or tentative opinions.

Even if you never produce a single persuasive work (which is very unlikely), you will certainly encounter such works directed at you. In truth, we live our lives under a steady rain of opinions and proposals. Organizations that work for causes campaign with posters and direct mail, all hoping that we will see things their way. Moreover, we are bombarded with proposals from people who wish us to act. Religious leaders urge us to lead more virtuous lives. Advertisers urge us to rush right out and buy the large economy size.

Small wonder, then, that argument and persuasion—and CRITICAL THINKING of argument and persuasion—may be among the most useful skills a college student can acquire. Time and again, your instructors will ask you to criticize or to state opinions, either in class or in writing. You may be asked to state your view of anything from the electoral college to animal rights. You may be asked to judge the desirability or undesirability of compulsory testing for AIDS or the revision of existing immigration laws. On an examination in, say, sociology, you may be asked, "Suggest three practical approaches to the most pressing needs of disadvantaged people in urban areas." Critically reading other people's arguments and composing your own, you will find, helps you discover what you think, refine it, and share what you believe.

Is there a difference between argument and persuasion? It is, admittedly, not always clear. Strictly speaking, PERSUASION aims to influence readers' actions, or their support for an action, by engaging their beliefs and feelings, while ARGUMENT aims to win readers' agreement with an assertion or claim by engaging their powers of reasoning. But most effective persuasion or argument contains elements of both methods; hence the confusion. In this book we tend to use the terms interchangeably.

One other point: We tend to talk here about *writing* argument and persuasion, but most of what we say has to do with *reading* them as well. When we discuss your need, as a writer, to support your assertions, we are also discussing your need, as a reader, to question the support other authors provide for their assertions. In reading arguments critically, you apply the critical thinking skills we discussed in Chapter 1 — ANALYSIS, INFERENCE, SYNTHESIS, EVALUATION — to a particular kind of writing.

Basic Considerations

Transaction Between Writer and Reader

Unlike some television advertisers, responsible writers of argument and persuasion do not try to storm people's minds. In writing a paper for a course, you persuade by gentler means: by sharing your view with readers willing to consider it. You'll want to learn how to express your view clearly and vigorously. But to be fair and persuasive, it is important to understand your readers' views as well.

In stating your opinion, you present the truth as you see it: "The immigration laws discourage employers from hiring nonnative workers" or "The immigration laws protect legal aliens." To persuade your readers that your view makes sense, you need not begin by proclaiming that, by Heaven, your view is absolutely right and should prevail. Instead, you might begin by trying to state what your readers probably think, as best you can infer it. You don't consider views that differ from your own merely to flatter your readers. You do so to correct your own view and make it more accurate. Regarded in this light, argument and persuasion aren't cynical ways to pull other people's strings. Writer and reader become two sensible people trying to find a common ground. This view will relieve you, whenever you have to state your opinions in writing, of the terrible obligation to be 100 percent right at all times.

Thesis Sentence

In an argument you champion or defend your opinion about something. This opinion is the THESIS, or *claim*, of your argument, and it will probably appear in your essay as your THESIS SENTENCE or sentences. Usually, but not always, you'll state your thesis sentence at the beginning of your essay, making a play for readers' attention and clueing them in to your purpose. But if you think readers may have difficulty accepting your thesis until they've heard some or all of your argument, then you might save the thesis sentence for the middle or end.

The essays in this chapter provide a variety of thesis sentences as models. Here are three examples:

> [F]or crimes involving the deliberate and inexcusable taking of human life, by men openly defiant of all civilized order—for such crimes [the death penalty] seems [. . .] a just and proper punishment. (H. L. Mencken, "The Penalty of Death")

> I think the observable reluctance of the majority of Americans to assert themselves in minor matters is related to our increased sense of helplessness in an age of technology and centralized political and economic power. (William F. Buckley, Jr., "Why Don't We Complain?")

> Today there is more pressure placed on students to do well [in school]. [. . .] This new pressure is what is causing the increase in cheating. (Colleen Wenke, "Too Much Pressure")

Evidence and Appeals

To support the thesis of your argument, you need EVIDENCE—anything that demonstrates what you're claiming. Evidence may include facts, statistics (facts expressed in numbers), expert opinions, examples, reported experience. It should be accurate, should fairly represent the available facts and opinions, should relate directly to your claims, and should be ample to convince readers of your claims. (For concise examples of using evidence effectively, see the paragraphs and case study on pp. 512–15.)

Even the best-supported argument also must appeal to readers' intelligence and to their feelings. In appealing to reason—a RATIONAL APPEAL—you'll want to rely on conventional methods of reasoning (see the facing page) and supply evidence according to the criteria stated above. In appealing to feelings—an EMOTIONAL APPEAL—you'll want to acknowledge what you know of readers' sympathies and beliefs and also show how your argument relates to them.

Emotional appeal requires vigilance, from both writers and readers, because it can be manipulative. "Do you really want to deprive your children of what's best for them?" asks a pitch for a certain learn-to-read program, appealing to pride or shame while neglecting to provide evidence that the program works. Another kind of writing, generally not cynical, relies heavily on emotional appeal for the purpose of inspiring readers who are already partial to the writer's message. (An impressive example is "I Have a Dream" by Martin Luther King, Jr., reprinted on pp. 603–07.) But even in an argument directed at a skeptical audience and based largely on reason and evidence, an emotional appeal can stir readers by fair means to constructive belief and action. Such an appeal recognizes that we are not intellectual robots but creatures with feelings. Indeed, in any effective argument, a writer had better engage the feelings of readers or they may reply, "True enough, but who cares?" Argument, to succeed in persuading, makes us feel that a writer's views are close to our own.

Yet another resource in argument is ETHICAL APPEAL: impressing your reader that you are a well-informed person of good will, good sense, and good moral character—and, therefore, to be believed. You make such an appeal by collecting ample evidence, reasoning carefully, using an appropriate emotional appeal, and writing well. You can also cite or quote respected authorities. If you don't know whether an authority is respected, you can ask a reference librarian for tips on finding out, or talk to an instructor who is a specialist in that field.

In arguing, you don't prove your assertion in the same irrefutable way in which a chemist demonstrates that hydrogen will burn. If you say, "Health coverage for the uninsured should be given top priority in Congress," that kind of claim isn't clearly either true or false. Argument takes place in areas that invite more than one opinion. In writing an argument, you help your reader see and understand just one open-eyed, open-minded view of reality.

Reasoning

When we argue rationally, we reason—that is, we make statements that lead to a conclusion. From the time of the ancient Greeks down to our own day, distinctly different methods of proceeding from statements to conclusions have been devised. This section will tell you of a recent, informal method of reasoning and also of two traditional methods. Understanding these methods, knowing how to use them, and being able to recognize when they are misused will make you a better writer *and* reader.

The Toulmin Method

Data, claim, and warrant. In recent decades, a simple, practical method of reasoning has been devised by the British philosopher Stephen Toulmin.[1] Helpfully, Toulmin has divided a typical argument into three parts:

1. The DATA: *the evidence to prove something*
2. The CLAIM: *what you are proving with the data*
3. The WARRANT: *the assumption or principle that connects the data to the claim*

Any clear, explicit argument has to have all three parts. Toulmin's own example of such an argument is this:

Of course, the data for a larger, more controversial claim will be more extensive. Here are some claims that would call for many more data, perhaps thousands of words.

> The war on drugs is not winnable.
>
> The United States must help to destroy drug production in South America.
>
> Drug addiction is a personal matter.

The warrant at the center. The warrant, that middle term, is often crucially important. It is usually an ASSUMPTION or a GENERALIZATION that explains *why* the claim follows from the data. Often a writer won't bother to state a warrant because it is obvious: "In his bid for reelection, Mayor Perkins failed miserably. Out of 5,000 votes cast for both candidates, he received only 200." The warrant might be stated, "To make what I would consider a strong showing, he would have had to receive 2,000 votes or more," but it is clear that 200 out of 5,000 is a small minority, and no further explanation seems necessary.

A flaw in many arguments, though, is that the warrant is not clear. A clear warrant is essential. To be persuaded, a reader needs to understand your assumptions and the thinking that follows from them. If you were to argue, "Drug abuse is a serious problem in the United States. Therefore, the United States must

---

[1] *The Uses of Argument* (1969) sets forth Toulmin's system in detail. His views are further explained and applied by Douglas Ehninger and Wayne Brockriede in *Decision by Debate* (2nd ed., 1978) and by Toulmin himself, with Richard Rieke and Allan Janik, in *An Introduction to Reasoning* (2nd ed., 1984).

help to destroy drug production in Latin America," then your reader might well be left wondering why the second statement follows from the first. But if you were to add, between the statements, "As long as drugs are manufactured in Latin America, they will be smuggled into the United States, and drug abuse will continue," then you supply a warrant. You show why your claim follows from your data—which, of course, you must also supply to make your case.

The unstated warrant can pitch an argument into trouble—whether your own or another writer's. Since warrants are usually assumptions or generalizations, rather than assertions of fact, they are valid only if readers accept or agree that they are valid. With stated warrants, any weaknesses are more likely to show. Suppose someone asserts that a certain woman should not be elected mayor because women cannot form ideas independently of their husbands and this woman's husband has bad ideas on how to run the city. At least the warrant—that women cannot form ideas independently of their husbands—is out there on the table, exposed for all to inspect. But unstated warrants can be just as absurd, or even just doubtful, and pass unnoticed because they are not exposed. Here's the same argument without its warrant: "She shouldn't be elected mayor because her husband has bad ideas on how to run the city."

Here's another argument with an unstated warrant, this one adapted from a magazine advertisement: "Scientists have no proof, just statistical correlations, linking smoking and heart disease, so you needn't worry about the connection." Now, the fact that this ad was placed by a cigarette manufacturer would tip off any reasonably alert reader to beware of bias in the claim. To discover the slant, we need to examine the unstated warrant, which runs something like this: "Since they are not proof, statistical correlations are worthless as guides to behavior." It is true that statistical correlations are not scientific proof, by which we generally mean repeated results obtained under controlled laboratory conditions—the kind of conditions to which human beings cannot ethically be subjected. But statistical correlations *can* establish connections and in fact inform much of our healthful behavior, such as getting physical exercise, avoiding fatty foods, brushing our teeth, and not driving while intoxicated. The advertiser's unstated warrant isn't valid, so neither is the argument.

Example of a Toulmin argument.   Let's look at how the data-claim-warrant scheme can work in constructing an argument. In an assignment for her course in English composition, Maire Flynn was asked to produce a condensed argument in three short paragraphs. The first paragraph was to set forth some data; the second, a claim; and the third, a warrant. The result became a kind of outline that the writer could then expand into a whole essay. Following is Flynn's argument.

DATA

Over the past five years, assistance in the form of food stamps has not had the effect of decreasing the number of people on welfare. Despite this help, 95 percent of long-term recipients remain below the poverty line today.

CLAIM

The present system of distributing food stamps is a dismal failure, a less effective way to help the needy than other possible ways.

WARRANT

No one is happy to receive charity. We need to encourage people to quit the welfare rolls; we need to make sure that government aid goes only to the deserving. More effective than giving out food stamps would be to help untrained young people learn job skills; to help single mothers with small children to obtain child care, freeing them for the job market; and to enlarge and improve our state employment counseling and job-placement services. The problem of poverty will be helped only if more people will find jobs and become self-sufficient.

In her warrant paragraph, Flynn spells out her reasons for holding her opinion—the one she states in her claim. "The warrant," she found, "was the hardest part to write," but hers turned out to be clear. Like any good warrant, hers expresses those thoughts that her data set in motion. Another way of looking at the warrant: It is the thinking that led the writer on to the opinion she holds. In this statement of her warrant, Flynn makes clear her assumptions: that people who can support themselves don't deserve food stamps and that a person is better off (and happier) holding a job than receiving charity. By generating more ideas and evidence, she was easily able to expand both the data paragraph and the warrant paragraph, and the result was a coherent essay of seven hundred words.

How, by the way, would someone who didn't accept Flynn's warrant argue with her? What about old, infirm, or disabled persons who cannot work? What quite different assumptions about poverty might be possible?

Deductive and Inductive Reasoning

Stephen Toulmin's method of argument is a fairly recent—and very helpful—way to analyze and construct arguments. Two other reliable methods date back to the Greek philosopher Aristotle, who identified the complementary processes of INDUCTIVE REASONING (induction) and DEDUCTIVE REASONING (deduction). In *Zen and the Art of Motorcycle Maintenance*, Robert M. Pirsig gives examples of deductive and inductive reasoning:

If the cycle goes over a bump and the engine misfires, and then goes over another bump and the engine misfires, and then goes over another bump and the engine misfires, and then goes over a long smooth stretch of road and there is no misfiring, and then goes over a fourth bump and the engine misfires again, one can logically conclude that the misfiring is caused by the bumps. That is induction: reasoning from particular experiences to general truths.

Deductive inferences do the reverse. They start with general knowledge and predict a specific observation. For example if, from reading the hierarchy of facts about the machine, the mechanic knows the horn of the cycle is powered exclusively by electricity from the battery, then he can logically infer that if the battery is dead the horn will not work. That is deduction.

In inductive reasoning, the method of the sciences, we collect bits of evidence on which to base generalizations. From interviews with a hundred self-identified conservative Republicans (the evidence), you might conclude that conservative Republicans favor less government regulation of business (the generalization). The more evidence you have, the more trustworthy your generalization is, but it would never be airtight unless you talked to every conservative Republican in the country. Since such thoroughness is impractical if not impossible, inductive reasoning involves making an *inductive leap* from the evidence to the conclusion. The smaller the leap—the more evidence you have—the better.

Deductive reasoning works the other way, from a general statement to particular cases. The basis of deduction is the SYLLOGISM, a three-step form of reasoning practiced by Aristotle:

All men are mortal.
Socrates is a man.
Therefore, Socrates is mortal.

The first statement (the major premise) is a generalization about a large group: It is the result of inductive reasoning. The second statement (the minor premise) says something about a particular member of that large group. The third statement (the conclusion) follows inevitably from the premises and applies the generalization to the particular: If the premises are true, then the conclusion must be true. Here is another syllogism:

MAJOR PREMISE: Conservative Republicans favor less government regulation of business.

MINOR PREMISE: William F. Buckley, Jr., is a conservative Republican.

CONCLUSION: Therefore, William F. Buckley, Jr., favors less government regulation of business.

Problems with deductive reasoning start in the premises. In 1633, Scipio Chiaramonti, professor of philosophy at the University of Pisa, came up with this untrustworthy syllogism: "Animals, which move, have limbs and muscles. The earth has no limbs and muscles. Hence, the earth does not move." This is bad deductive reasoning, and its flaw is to assume that all things need limbs and muscles to move—ignoring raindrops, rivers, and many other moving things. In the next pages, we'll look at some of the things that can go wrong with any kind of reasoning.

Logical Fallacies

In arguments we read and hear, we often meet logical FALLACIES: errors in reasoning that lead to wrong conclusions. From the time when you start thinking about your proposition or claim and planning your paper, you'll need to watch out for them. To help you recognize logical fallacies when you see them or hear them, and so guard against them when you write, here is a list of the most common.

- *Non sequitur* (from the Latin, "it does not follow"): stating a conclusion that doesn't follow from the first premise or premises. "I've lived in this town a long time—why, my grandfather was the first mayor—so I'm against putting fluoride in the drinking water."
- *Oversimplification:* supplying neat and easy explanations for large and complicated phenomena. "No wonder drug abuse is out of control. Look at how the courts have hobbled police officers." Oversimplified solutions are also popular: "All these teenage kids that get in trouble with the law—why, they ought to ship 'em over to China. That would straighten 'em out!" (See also p. 415.)
- *Hasty generalization:* leaping to a generalization from inadequate or faulty evidence. The most familiar hasty generalization is the stereotype: "Men aren't sensitive enough to be day-care providers." "Women are too emotional to fight in combat."
- *Either/or reasoning:* assuming that a reality may be divided into only two parts or extremes; assuming that a given problem has only one of two possible solutions. "What's to be done about the trade imbalance with Asia? Either we ban all Asian imports, or American industry will collapse." Obviously, either/or reasoning is a kind of extreme oversimplification.
- *Argument from doubtful or unidentified authority:* "We ought to castrate all sex offenders; Uncle Oswald says we should." Or: "According to reliable sources, my opponent is lying."
- *Argument ad hominem* (from the Latin, "to the man"): attacking a person's views by attacking his or her character. "Mayor Burns is divorced and

estranged from his family. How can we listen to his pleas for a city nursing home?"

- *Begging the question:* taking for granted from the start what you set out to demonstrate. When you reason in a *logical* way, you state that because something is true, then, as a result, some other truth follows. When you beg the question, however, you repeat that what is true is true. If you argue, for instance, that dogs are a menace to people because they are dangerous, you don't prove a thing, since the idea that dogs are dangerous is already assumed in the statement that they are a menace. Beggars of questions often just repeat what they already believe, only in different words. This fallacy sometimes takes the form of arguing in a circle, or demonstrating a premise by a conclusion and a conclusion by a premise: "I am in college because that is the right thing to do. Going to college is the right thing to do because it is expected of me."

- *Post hoc, ergo propter hoc* (from the Latin, "after this, therefore because of this"), or *post hoc* for short: assuming that because B follows A, B was caused by A. "Ever since the city suspended height restrictions on skyscrapers, the city budget has been balanced." (See also p. 415.)

- *False analogy:* the claim of persuasive likeness when no significant likeness exists. An ANALOGY asserts that because two things are comparable in some respects, they are comparable in other respects as well. Analogies cannot serve as evidence in a rational argument because the differences always outweigh the similarities; but analogies can reinforce such arguments *if* the subjects are indeed similar in some ways. If they aren't, the analogy is false. Many observers see the "war on drugs" as a false and damaging analogy because warfare aims for clear victory over a specific, organized enemy, whereas the complete eradication of illegal drugs is probably unrealistic and, in any event, the "enemy" isn't well defined: the drugs themselves? users? sellers? producers? the producing nations? (These critics urge approaching drugs as a social problem to be skillfully managed and reduced.)

THE PROCESS

In stating an opinion, you set forth and support a claim—a truth you believe. You may find such a truth by thinking and feeling, by reading, by talking to your instructors or fellow students, by listening to a discussion of some problem or controversy.

In stating a proposal, you already have an opinion in mind, and from there, you go on to urge an action or a solution to a problem. Usually, these two statements will take place within the same piece of writing: A writer will first set forth a view ("Compact discs are grossly overpriced") and then go right on to a proposal ("Compact discs should be discounted in the college store").

Whether your essay states an opinion, a proposal, or both, it is likely to contain similar ingredients. One essential is your THESIS—the proposition or claim you are going to defend. As we noted earlier (p. 502), the likeliest spot for your thesis statement is near the start of your essay, where you might also explain why you think the thesis worth upholding, perhaps showing how it concerns your readers. If you plan to include both an opinion and a proposal in your essay, you may wish to set forth your opinion first, saving your proposal for later, perhaps for your conclusion.

Your thesis stated, introduce your least important point first. Then build in a crescendo to the strongest point you have. This structure will lend emphasis to your essay and perhaps make your chain of ideas more persuasive as the reader continues to follow it.

For every point, give evidence: facts, figures, examples, expert opinions. If you introduce statistics, make sure that they are up to date and fairly represented. In an essay advocating a law against smoking, it would be unfair to declare that "in Pottsville, Illinois, last year, 50 percent of all deaths were caused by lung cancer" if only two people died in Pottsville last year—one of them struck by a car.

If you are arguing fairly, you should be able to face potential criticisms fairly, and give your critics due credit, by recognizing the objections you expect your assertion will meet. This is the strategy H. L. Mencken uses in "The Penalty of Death" in this chapter, and he introduces it in his essay right at the beginning. (You might also tackle the opposition at the end of your essay or at relevant points throughout.) Notice that Mencken takes pains to dispense with his opponents: He doesn't just dismiss them; he reasons with them.

In your CONCLUSION, briefly restate your claim, if possible in a fresh, pointed way. (For example, see the concluding sentence in the essay by William F. Buckley, Jr., in this chapter.) In an essay with a strong emotional component, you may want to end with an appeal to feelings.

Finally, don't forget the power of humor in argument. You don't have to crack gratuitous jokes, but there is often an advantage in having a reader or listener who laughs on your side. When Abraham Lincoln debated Stephen Douglas, he triumphed in his reply to Douglas's snide remark that Lincoln had once been a bartender. "I have long since quit my side of the bar," Lincoln declared, "while Mr. Douglas clings to his as tenaciously as ever."

In arguing—doing everything you can to bring your reader around to your view—you can draw on any method of writing discussed in this book. Arguing for or against further reductions in welfare funding, you might give

EXAMPLES of wasteful spending, or of neighborhoods where welfare funds are still needed. You might analyze the CAUSES of social problems that call for welfare funds, or foresee the likely EFFECTS of cutting welfare programs or of keeping them. You might COMPARE AND CONTRAST the idea of slashing welfare funds with the idea of increasing them. You could use NARRATION to tell a pointed story; you could use DESCRIPTION to portray certain welfare recipients and their neighborhoods. If it suited your purposes, you could employ several of these methods in writing a single argument.

You will rarely find, when you begin to write a persuasive paper, that you have too much evidence to support your claim. But unless you're writing a term paper and have months to spend on it, you're limited in how much evidence you can gather. Begin by stating your claim. Make it narrow enough to support in the time you have available. For a paper due a week from now, the opinion that "our city's downtown area has a serious litter problem" can probably be backed up in part by your own eyewitness reports. But to support the claim "Litter is one of the worst environmental problems of North American cities," you would surely need to spend time in a library.

In rewriting, you may find yourself tempted to keep all the evidence you have collected with such effort. Of course, some of it may not support your claim; some may seem likely to persuade the reader only to go to sleep. If so, throw it out. A stronger argument will remain.

CHECKLIST FOR REVISING ARGUMENT OR PERSUASION

✔ **AUDIENCE.** Have you taken account of your readers' probable views? Have you reasoned with readers, not attacked them? Are your emotional appeals appropriate to readers' likely feelings? Do you acknowledge opposing views?

✔ **THESIS.** Does your argument have a thesis, a claim about how your subject is or should be? Is the thesis narrow enough to argue convincingly in the space and time available? Is it stated clearly? Is it reasonable?

✔ **EVIDENCE.** Is your thesis well supported with facts, statistics, expert opinions, and examples? Is your evidence accurate, representative, relevant, and ample?

✔ **WARRANT.** Have you made sound connections between your evidence and your thesis or claim?

✔ **LOGICAL FALLACIES.** Have you avoided common errors in reasoning, such as oversimplifying or begging the question? (See pp. 508–09 for a list of fallacies.)

✔ **STRUCTURE.** Does your organization lead readers through your argument step by step, building to your strongest ideas and frequently connecting your evidence to your central claim?

ARGUMENT AND PERSUASION IN A PARAGRAPH: TWO ILLUSTRATIONS

Arguing About Television

This self-contained paragraph, written for *The Bedford Reader*, argues that TV news aims for entertainment at the expense of serious coverage of events and issues. The argument here could serve a number of different purposes in full essays: For instance, in a paper claiming that television is our least reliable source of news, the paragraph would give one cause of unreliability; or in an essay analyzing television news, the paragraph would examine one element.

Television news has a serious failing: It's show business. Unlike a newspaper, its every image has to entertain the average beer drinker. To score high ratings and win advertisers, the visual medium favors the spectacular: riots, tornados, air crashes. Now that satellite transmission invites live coverage, newscasters go for the fast-breaking story at the expense of thoughtful analysis. "The more you can get data out instantly," says media critic Jeff Greenfield, "the more you rely on instant data to define the news." TV zooms in on people who make news, but, to avoid boredom, won't let them argue or explain. (How can they, in speeches limited to fifteen seconds?) In 1996, as American missiles bombed military sites in Iraq, President Clinton held a press conference to explain the action. His lengthy remarks were clipped to twenty seconds on one news broadcast, and then an anchorwoman digested the opposition to a single line: "Republicans tonight were critical of the president's actions." During the 2000 presidential election, both candidates sometimes deliberately packaged bad news so that it could not be distilled to a sound bite on the evening news—and thus would not make the evening news at all. Americans who rely on television for their news (two-thirds, according to recent polls) exist on a starvation diet.

Topic sentence: the claim

Evidence:
Expert opinion

Facts and examples

Statistic

Arguing in an Academic Discipline

Taken from a textbook on public relations, the following paragraph argues that lobbyists (who work to persuade public officials in behalf of a cause) are not slick manipulators but something else. The paragraph falls in the textbook's section on lobbying as a form of public relations, and its purpose is to correct a mistaken definition.

Although the public stereotypes a lobbyist as a fast-talking person twisting an elected official's arm to get special concessions, the reality is quite different. Today's lobbyist, who may be fully employed by one industry or represent a variety of clients, is often a quiet-

Topic sentence: the claim

spoken, well-educated man or woman armed with statistics and research reports. Robert Gray, former head of Hill and Knowlton's Washington office and a public affairs expert for thirty years, adds, "Lobbying is no longer a booze and buddies business. It's presenting honest facts and convincing Congress that your side has more merit than the other." He rejects lobbying as being simply "influence peddling and button-holing" top administration officials. Although the public has the perception that lobbying is done only by big business, Gray correctly points out that a variety of special interests also do it. These may include such groups as the Sierra Club, Mothers Against Drunk Driving, the National Association of Social Workers, the American Civil Liberties Union, and the American Federation of Labor. Even the American Society of Plastic and Reconstructive Surgeons hired a Washington public relations firm in their battle against restrictions on breast implants. Lobbying, quite literally, is an activity in which widely diverse groups and organizations engage as an exercise of free speech and representation in the marketplace of ideas. Lobbyists often balance each other and work toward legislative compromises that not only benefit their self-interests but society as a whole.

Evidence:
Expert opinion

Facts and examples

—Dennis L. Wilcox, Phillip H. Ault, and Warren K. Agee,
Public Relations: Strategies and Tactics

CASE STUDY
Using Argument and Persuasion

As a college freshman, Kristen Corcoran commuted to school at night. In the following letter, she appealed to her college's president to have a parking ticket canceled because legal parking was unavailable.

Corcoran's letter is a model of argument for a specific purpose, but it didn't start out that way. In her much longer first draft, she let her anger push her into detailing every one of her five previous parking difficulties and criticizing the president personally for not solving the problem. She did not get to her request to have the ticket canceled until the very end.

Reviewing her draft, Corcoran realized that she was trying to negotiate with the president, not tell her off, and for that a more direct, conciliatory approach was needed. In the revision you see here, Corcoran focuses immediately on her purpose for writing, summarizes her problems with parking, and takes the tack of informing, rather than criticizing, the president.

1073 Dogwood Terrace
North Andover, MA 01845
May 2, 2001

President Delores Reed
North State College
755 Little Road
Danvers, MA 01923

Dear President Reed:

I write to ask you to rescind a ten-dollar citation I received on April 4 for parking in North State's Lot E. I know that this lot is reserved for faculty use, but flooding in three of the four commuter lots left me with no reasonable parking alternatives. The campus police have not been able to help me, so I turn to you.

As you know, flooding is a recurring problem at North State, but perhaps you don't know how it affects commuting students. April 4 was one of six evenings this semester when I arrived to find Lots A, C, and D overrun by nearby marshes. On the other nights, Lot B filled quickly with cars and I was forced on two occasions to hunt for parking in the crowded residential areas off-campus. On April 4, I chose not to spend a half-hour finding a space and parked in Lot E. Many of its spaces are vacant at night when there are fewer classes and most campus offices are closed.

I understand from the campus police that North State has no plan for solving this seasonal problem. I, like hundreds of other commuter students, paid fifty dollars for a parking permit in the beginning of the semester and should be able to expect convenient parking like that described in North State's brochures. The parking problem is a serious one that affects not only commuters, who make up more than half of the student body, but also North State's neighbors, who are inconvenienced by crowds of cars monopolizing their streets each spring.

Please rescind my ticket and try to create some solutions to this problem. As a first step, may I suggest amending the school's parking policy to allow commuter use of Lot E in emergencies?

Sincerely,

Kristen Corcoran

Kristen Corcoran

H. L. MENCKEN

HENRY LOUIS MENCKEN (1880–1956) was a native of Baltimore, where for four decades he worked as newspaper reporter, editor, and columnist. In the 1920s, his boisterous, cynical observations on American life, appearing regularly in *The Smart Set* and later in *The American Mercury* (which he founded and edited), made him probably the most widely quoted writer in the country. As an editor and literary critic, Mencken championed Sinclair Lewis, Theodore Dreiser, and other realistic writers. As a social critic, he leveled blasts at pomp, hypocrisy, and the middle classes (whom he labeled "the booboisie"). (The publication of *The Diary of H. L. Mencken* in 1989 revealed more of its author's outspoken opinions and touched off a controversy: Was Mencken a bigot? The debate goes on.) In 1933, when Mencken's attempts to laugh off the Depression began to ring hollow, his magazine died. He then devoted himself to revising and supplementing *The American Language* (4th ed., 1948), his learned and highly entertaining survey of a nation's speech habits and vocabulary. Two dozen of Mencken's books are now in print, including *A Mencken Chrestomathy* (1949), a representative selection of his best writings of various kinds; and *A Choice of Days* (1980), a selection from his memoirs.

The Penalty of Death

Above all, Mencken was a humorist whose thought had a serious core. He argues by first making the reader's jaw drop, then inducing a laugh, and finally causing the reader to ponder, "Hmmmm—what if he's right?" The following still-controversial essay, from *Prejudices, Fifth Series* (1926), shows Mencken the persuader in top form as he argues in favor of capital punishment. In the essay following Mencken's, Michael Kroll takes a very different approach to arguing about the same issue.

Of the arguments against capital punishment that issue from uplifters, two are commonly heard most often, to wit:

1. That hanging a man (or frying him or gassing him) is a dreadful business, degrading to those who have to do it and revolting to those who have to witness it.
2. That it is useless, for it does not deter others from the same crime.

The first of these arguments, it seems to me, is plainly too weak to need serious refutation. All it says, in brief, is that the work of the hangman is unpleasant. Granted. But suppose it is? It may be quite necessary to society for all that. There are, indeed, many other jobs that are unpleasant, and yet no one thinks of abolishing them—that of the plumber, that of the soldier, that of the garbageman, that of the priest hearing confessions, that of the sandhog, and so on. Moreover, what evidence is there that any actual hangman complains of his work? I have heard none. On the contrary, I have known many who delighted in their ancient art, and practiced it proudly.

In the second argument of the abolitionists there is rather more force, but 3 even here, I believe, the ground under them is shaky. Their fundamental error consists in assuming that the whole aim of punishing criminals is to deter other (potential) criminals—that we hang or electrocute A simply in order to so alarm B that he will not kill C. This, I believe, is an assumption which confuses a part with the whole. Deterrence, obviously, is *one* of the aims of punishment, but it is surely not the only one. On the contrary, there are at least a half dozen, and some are probably quite as important. At least one of them, practically considered, is *more* important. Commonly, it is described as revenge, but revenge is really not the word for it. I borrow a better term from the late Aristotle: *katharsis*. *Katharsis*, so used, means a salubrious discharge of emotions, a healthy letting off of steam. A schoolboy, disliking his teacher, deposits a tack upon the pedagogical chair; the teacher jumps and the boy laughs. This is *katharsis*. What I contend is that one of the prime objects of all judicial punishments is to afford the same grateful relief (*a*) to the immediate victims of the criminal punished, and (*b*) to the general body of moral and timorous men.

These persons, and particularly the first group, are concerned only indi- 4 rectly with deterring other criminals. The thing they crave primarily is the satisfaction of seeing the criminal actually before them suffer as he made them suffer. What they want is the peace of mind that goes with the feeling that accounts are squared. Until they get that satisfaction they are in a state of emotional tension, and hence unhappy. The instant they get it they are comfortable. I do not argue that this yearning is noble; I simply argue that it is almost universal among human beings. In the face of injuries that are unimportant and can be borne without damage it may yield to higher impulses; that is to say, it may yield to what is called Christian charity. But when the injury is serious Christianity is adjourned, and even saints reach for their sidearms. It is plainly asking too much of human nature to expect it to conquer so natural an impulse. A keeps a store and has a bookkeeper, B. B steals $700, employs it in playing at dice or bingo, and is cleaned out. What is A to do? Let B go? If he does so he will be unable to sleep at night. The sense of injury, of injustice, of frustration will haunt him like pruritus. So he turns B over to the police, and they hustle B to prison. Thereafter A can sleep. More, he has pleasant dreams. He pictures B chained to the wall of a dungeon a hundred feet underground, devoured by rats and scorpions. It is so agreeable that it makes him forget his $700. He has got his *katharsis*.

The same thing precisely takes place on a larger scale when there is a   5
crime which destroys a whole community's sense of security. Every law-abiding
citizen feels menaced and frustrated until the criminals have been struck
down—until the communal capacity to get even with them, and more than
even, has been dramatically demonstrated. Here, manifestly, the business of
deterring others is no more than an afterthought. The main thing is to destroy
the concrete scoundrels whose act has alarmed everyone, and thus made
everyone unhappy. Until they are brought to book that unhappiness continues; when the law has been executed upon them there is a sigh of relief. In
other words, there is *katharsis*.

I know of no public demand for the death penalty for ordinary crimes,   6
even for ordinary homicides. Its infliction would shock all men of normal
decency of feeling. But for crimes involving the deliberate and inexcusable
taking of human life, by men openly defiant of all civilized order—for such
crimes it seems, to nine men out of ten, a just and proper punishment. Any
lesser penalty leaves them feeling that the criminal has got the better of society—that he is free to add insult to injury by laughing. That feeling can be
dissipated only by a recourse to *katharsis*, the invention of the aforesaid Aristotle. It is more effectively and economically achieved, as human nature now
is, by wafting the criminal to realms of bliss.

The real objection to capital punishment doesn't lie against the actual   7
extermination of the condemned, but against our brutal American habit of
putting it off so long. After all, every one of us must die soon or late, and a
murderer, it must be assumed, is one who makes that sad fact the cornerstone
of his metaphysic. But it is one thing to die, and quite another thing to lie for
long months and even years under the shadow of death. No sane man would
choose such a finish. All of us, despite the Prayer Book, long for a swift and
unexpected end. Unhappily, a murderer, under the irrational American system, is tortured for what, to him, must seem a whole series of eternities. For
months on end he sits in prison while his lawyers carry on their idiotic buf-
foonery with writs, injunctions, mandamuses, and appeals. In order to get his
money (or that of his friends) they have to feed him with hope. Now and
then, by the imbecility of a judge or some trick of juridic science, they actually justify it. But let us say that, his money all gone, they finally throw up
their hands. Their client is now ready for the rope or the chair. But he must
still wait for months before it fetches him.

That wait, I believe, is horribly cruel. I have seen more than one man sit-   8
ting in the death-house, and I don't want to see any more. Worse, it is wholly
useless. Why should he wait at all? Why not hang him the day after the last
court dissipates his last hope? Why torture him as not even cannibals would
torture their victims? The common answer is that he must have time to make

his peace with God. But how long does that take? It may be accomplished, I believe, in two hours quite as comfortably as in two years. There are, indeed, no temporal limitations upon God. He could forgive a whole herd of murderers in a millionth of a second. More, it has been done.

Journal Writing

Mencken condemns "our brutal American habit" of delaying executions for court appeals (par. 7). Do you agree with his opinion? In your journal, write down your own opinions of American methods of trying the accused, sentencing the convicted, or appealing the sentences of convicted criminals in the United States. Does the system seem just to you? (To take your journal writing further, see "From Journal to Essay" on the next page.)

Questions on Meaning

1. Identify Mencken's main reasons for his support of capital punishment. What is his THESIS?
2. In paragraph 3 Mencken asserts that there are at least half a dozen reasons for punishing offenders. In his essay, he mentions two, deterrence and revenge. What others can you supply?
3. For which class of offenders does Mencken advocate the death penalty?
4. What is Mencken's "real objection" to capital punishment?

Questions on Writing Strategy

1. How would you characterize Mencken's humor? Point to examples of it. In light of the grim subject, do you find the humor funny?
2. In his first paragraph, Mencken pares his subject down to manageable size. What techniques does he employ for this purpose?
3. At the start of paragraph 7, Mencken shifts his stance from concern for the victims of crime to concern for prisoners awaiting execution. Does the shift help or weaken the effectiveness of his earlier justification for capital punishment?
4. Do you think the author expects his AUDIENCE to agree with him? At what points does he seem to recognize the fact that some readers may see things differently?
5. In paragraphs 2 and 3, Mencken uses ANALOGIES in an apparent attempt to strengthen his argument. What are the analogies? Do they seem false to you? (See p. 509 for a discussion of false analogy.) Do you think Mencken would agree with your judgment?
6. **OTHER METHODS.** To explain what he sees as the most important aim of capital punishment, Mencken uses DEFINITION. What does he define, and what techniques does he use to make the definition clear?

Questions on Language

1. Mencken opens his argument by referring to those who reject capital punishment as "uplifters." What CONNOTATIONS does this word have for you? Does the use of this "loaded" word strengthen or weaken Mencken's position? Explain.
2. Be sure you know the meanings of the following words: refutation, sandhog (par. 2); salubrious, pedagogical, timorous (3); pruritus (4); wafting (6); mandamuses, juridic (7).
3. What emotional overtones can you detect in Mencken's reference to the hangman's job as an "ancient art" (par. 2)?
4. Writing at a time when there was no debate over the usage, Mencken often uses "man" and "he" for examples that could be either a man or a woman (such as A in par. 4) and uses "men" to mean people in general ("all men of normal decency of feeling," par. 6). Does this usage weaken the essay? Why, or why not?

Suggestions for Writing

1. **FROM JOURNAL TO ESSAY.** Develop a focused and persuasive thesis from the opinions you expressed in your journal entry (previous page), and support it with EVIDENCE from your reading and observations. (You may also wish to do research among the many books and articles written on the criminal justice system.) Rather than take on the entire administration of justice, follow Mencken's model and narrow your thesis to one aspect of the system.
2. In a brief essay, argue for or against humor as a technique of argument or persuasion. Use EXAMPLES from Mencken's essay as evidence.
3. **CRITICAL WRITING.** Write an essay refuting Mencken's argument; or take Mencken's side but supply any additional reasons you can think of. In either case, begin your argument with an ANALYSIS of Mencken's argument, and use examples (real or hypothetical) to support your view.
4. **CONNECTIONS.** Compare this essay with the following one by Michael Kroll, "The Unquiet Death of Robert Harris." Imagine a debate between the two writers. How would Kroll respond to Mencken's argument that fallible human beings can't do without *katharsis*? How would Mencken answer Kroll's charge that turning death into a public spectacle is barbarous? On what point do they agree?

H. L. Mencken on Writing

"All my work hangs together," wrote H. L. Mencken in a piece called "Addendum on Aims," "once the main ideas under it are discerned. Those ideas are chiefly of a skeptical character. I believe that nothing is unconditionally true, and hence I am opposed to every statement of positive truth and to every man who states it. Such men seem to me to be either idiots or scoundrels. To one category or the other belong all theologians, professors, editorial writers, right-thinkers, etc. [. . .] Whether [my work] appears to be burlesque, or serious criticism, or mere casual controversy, it is always directed against one thing: unwarranted pretension."

Mencken cheerfully acknowledged his debts to his teachers: mostly writers he read as a young man and newspaper editors he worked under. "My style of writing is chiefly grounded upon an early enthusiasm for Huxley,[1] the greatest of all masters of orderly exposition. He taught me the importance of giving to every argument a simple structure. As for the fancy work on the surface, it comes chiefly from an anonymous editorial writer in the *New York Sun*, circa 1900. He taught me the value of apt phrases. My vocabulary is pretty large; it probably runs to 25,000 words. It represents much labor. I am constantly expanding it. I believe that a good phrase is better than a Great Truth—which is usually buncombe. I delight in argument, not because I want to convince, but because argument itself is an end."

In another essay, "The Fringes of Lovely Letters," Mencken wrote that "what is in the head infallibly oozes out of the nub of the pen. If it is sparkling Burgundy the writing is full of life and charm. If it is mush the writing is mush too." He recalls the example of President Warren G. Harding, who once sent a message to Congress that was quite incomprehensible. "Why? Simply because Dr. Harding's thoughts, on the high and grave subjects he discussed, were so muddled that he couldn't understand them himself. But on matters within his range of customary meditation he was clear and even charming, as all of us are. [. . .] Style cannot go beyond the ideas which lie at the heart of it. If they are clear, it too will be clear. If they are held passionately, it will be eloquent."

For Discussion

1. According to Mencken, what PURPOSE animates his writing?
2. What relationship does Mencken see between a writer's thought and his or her STYLE?
3. Where in his views on writing does Mencken use FIGURES OF SPEECH to advantage?

---

[1] Thomas Henry Huxley (1825–95), an English biologist and educator, wrote many essays popularizing science. In Victorian England, Huxley was the leading exponent and defender of Charles Darwin's theory of evolution. — EDS.

MICHAEL KROLL

MICHAEL KROLL is a writer and investigator specializing in the criminal justice system. Born in 1943 and raised in rural California, Kroll graduated in
1965 from the University of California at Berkeley with a BA in political science. For more than two decades he has been a journalist and editor with the
Pacific News Service, writing about juvenile justice, capital punishment, and
prisons. His articles have appeared in periodicals such as the *Los Angeles
Times*, the *New York Times*, *California Lawyer*, and *The Progressive*, and he
has been a guest on talk shows. With a special interest in capital punishment, Kroll also founded the Death Penalty Information Center in Washington, DC, and he conducts investigations on behalf of prisoners who are
condemned to death.

The Unquiet Death of Robert Harris

Kroll met Robert Alton Harris in 1984, when Harris was awaiting execution
for the 1978 murders of two teenagers. The two men became friends, giving
Kroll a uniquely personal view of Harris's long journey to the gas chamber
and to death on April 21, 1992. In this narrative of the journey's end, published in *The Nation* a few months afterward, Kroll makes an argument
against what he witnessed. Contrast this essay with the previous one, H. L.
Mencken's "The Penalty of Death."

1   "Ladies and gentlemen. Please stay in your places until your escort comes
for you. Follow your escort, as instructed. Thank you."

2   The words were spoken in the manner of the operator of the Jungle Cruise
at Disneyland: well-rehearsed and "professional." They were spoken by the
public information officer of California's San Quentin penitentiary, Vernell
Crittendon, as we waited to be ushered out of the gas chamber where my
friend Robert Harris was slumped over, dead, in Chair B.

3   When not conveying us to and from the gas chamber, our "escorts"
guarded us in a small, tidy office with barred windows facing the east gate,
where a circus of media lights lit up the night sky, letting us see silhouettes in
the darkness. There were two desks, the exact number of straight-backed
chairs needed to accommodate us, some nineteen-cent bags of potato chips, a
couple of apples and bananas, and bad coffee.

4   We—a psychologist and lawyer who knew Robert Harris professionally,
his brother Randy, whom he had designated to witness the gassing, and I, a
close friend for nearly a decade—had entered at the west gate at 10 PM as instructed to present our credentials (a written invitation from Warden Daniel
Vasquez himself) and submit to a thorough pat-down search and a metal

detector. Our escorts took us in a prison van to the front of the old fortress and escorted us up a few steps into the office of one G. Mosqueda, program administrator. Then we began what we thought at the time would be a short vigil. It turned out to be eight hours.

We'd been there only a few minutes when another staff person arrived   5
wearing a civilian suit and a name tag that identified him as Martinez. He walked up to Randy, pointed his finger, and said, "Randall Harris. Come with me!" Randy smiled, got up, and followed him out. (Randy thought they were taking him for counseling. It was a fair assumption; counselors had been provided to advise members of the victims' families who had come to witness the execution. This was to insure, Warden Vasquez told them, that "there is only one casualty in that room.")

When they brought him back, he told his own horror story. He had been   6
ordered to submit to a full body-cavity search. "We have learned from a reliable source that you are planning something," Martinez had said. Randy was ordered to open his mouth for inspection, take his clothes off, bend over, lift his testicles, pull back his foreskin. "If you try anything," Martinez had threatened, "you'll be sorry, and so will your brother."

His brother was waiting just a few feet from the gas chamber.   7

After Randy rejoined us, shaken and humiliated, our escort gave us our   8
marching orders. "When the phone rings and I get the order to go, stand and follow me quickly." The phone, which had the kind of clanging ring that scares you to death even when you are not already scared to death, rang many times that night, and each time our hearts stopped. But *the* call did not come at midnight. It did not come for a long time. With no television to inform us, we waited, hour after hour, wondering what was happening, drinking bad coffee and asking to be escorted to the bathroom.

Later, we learned that in those hours the US Court of Appeals for the   9
Ninth Circuit had granted three stays of execution. One concerned newly discovered evidence that Robert's brother Danny, who had participated in the crime but served fewer than four years in exchange for his testimony against Robert, had actually fired the first shot. The two other stays — including one signed by ten judges — were based on the pending suit challenging the constitutionality of cyanide gas as a method of execution. Each of the three stays was dissolved by the US Supreme Court.

Finally, a little after three o'clock, the call came and Mendez said, "Now."   10

We followed him into the freezing, brilliant night, but Mendez stopped us   11
just short of the entrance to the gas chamber. Shivering, we watched the other witnesses being led out of the cold — the media into one building opposite the gas chamber and the victims' family members into the East Block visiting room just beyond it. After a while, responding to words coming over his

walkie-talkie that I could not hear, Mendez led us into the main visiting room to our immediate right. I had been in this room many times, but never at night, and never, as now, was it deserted of staff and inmates.

Finally the wait was over. Mendez spoke into his walkie-talkie. "Okay," he said, and then turned his attention to us. "Let's go."   12

We, the family and friends of the condemned, were led to risers along a wall behind and to the left of the chamber. Three burly guards brought Robert in and strapped him quickly to Chair B. His back was to us. He could see us only by craning his neck and peering over his left shoulder. From behind him, I looked over his right shoulder into the unblinking red eye of the video camera that was trained on his face in order to assist US District Judge Marilyn Patel in determining whether death by lethal gas is cruel and unusual punishment. He peered around the room, making eye contact, smiling and nodding at people he knew. I held my breath. A guard's digital watch started beeping. She smiled sheepishly and covered it with her sleeve.   13

Minutes passed. Some people whispered. Some smiled. And then the phone rang. The phone to the gas chamber rings for only one reason: A stay of execution has been granted. But nothing happened. Nobody moved — nobody except Robert, that is, who twisted and turned trying to figure out what was happening. He peered down between his legs to see if he could see the vat of acid beneath him. He sniffed the air and mouthed the words, "Pull it." More minutes passed. He peered over his left shoulder where I was just out his line of vision. "Where's Mike?" he mouthed.   14

I jumped down to the lower riser and walked over to the window. A female guard ordered me back to my place, but not before Robert saw me, smiled, and settled down.   15

Ten minutes after the phone rang, the gas chamber door was opened and the three guards unfastened Robert and took him from the chamber. Nothing like that had ever happened in the history of the gas chamber. (I later learned that during that eternity, California's attorney general, Dan Lungren, had been on the phone to the clerk of the US Supreme Court informing him that Robert was in the chamber. Lungren begged the justices to overturn the stay. But the court wanted to read what circuit court Judge Harry Pregerson had written in the fourth and last stay of execution, so Lungren was told to take Robert from the chamber.)   16

We were escorted back to Mosqueda's office to continue waiting. I shook uncontrollably for a long time, and cried openly. My escort suggested I needed medical attention, hinting I might have to leave. I forced back my tears and pulled myself together, although I could not stop trembling.   17

We resumed the grim vigil, cut off from the outside world. Just after six in the morning, I saw the witnesses from the victims' families being led past our   18 window toward the chamber. Some were laughing. As honored guests, they had been playing video games, napping in the warden's home, and eating specially prepared food. My heart stopped. Something was happening. Karen, the lawyer with us, called the office where lawyers who supported Harris had gathered, and was told the stay of execution was still in place. But, as with the aborted execution attempt, they were the last to know.

Within fifteen seconds, the phone clattered to life, and Mendez told us   19
the stay had been dissolved. (He did not tell us the Supreme Court had ordered all federal courts to enter no more stays of execution regardless of the issues.) We were going again.

Quickly we moved through the chill dawn air toward the chamber. Randy   20
whispered in my ear, "Slow down." Near the entrance, Vernell Crittendon stood watching the procession move smoothly into the chamber. He pumped his upturned fist three times, the way football players do when their team has scored.

When they brought Robert in, he was grim-faced, tired and ashen.   21
Beyond the horror of having stood at the brink of the abyss just two and a half hours before, he had been up for several days and nights. He was under horrific pressure. Again, he nodded to acquaintances. He did not smile. He faced to his right and said "I'm sorry" to the father of murder victim Michael Baker. He craned his neck left once more and nodded quickly toward us. "It's all right," he reassured us. After about two minutes, he sniffed the air, then breathed deeply several times.

His head began to roll and his eyes closed, then opened again. His head   22
dropped, then came up with an abrupt jerk, and rolled some more. It was grotesque and hideous, and I looked away. When I looked back, his head came up again, and I covered my mouth. Randy was whimpering in pain next to me, and we clutched each other. The lawyer, sobbing audibly, put her arms around us and tried to comfort us. I could not stop shivering. Reverend Harris, Robert's second cousin and spiritual adviser, who had been with Robert in the holding cell almost until the moment they took him away, whispered, "He's ready. He was tired. It's all right. His punishment is over."

He writhed for seven minutes, his head falling on his chest, saliva drool-   23
ing from his open mouth. He lifted his head again and again. Seven minutes. A lifetime. Nine more minutes passed with his head slumped on his chest. His heart, a survivor's heart, had kept pumping for nine more minutes, while we held each other. Some of the witnesses laughed. I thought of the label "Laughing Killer," affixed to Robert by the media, and knew these good people would never be described as laughing killers.

We were in the middle of something indescribably ugly. Not just the cold-   24
blooded killing of a human being, and not even the fact that we happened to

love him—but the ritual of it, the participation of us, the witnesses, the witnessing itself of this most private and personal act. It was nakedly barbaric. Nobody could say this had anything to do with justice, I thought. Yet this medieval torture chamber is what a large majority of my fellow Californians, including most in the room with me, believe in. The implications of this filled me with fear—fear for myself and for all of us, a fear I am ashamed to confess—while my friend was being strangled slowly to death in front of me.

Some witnesses began shuffling nervously. People looked at their watches.   25
Then a guard stepped forward and announced that Robert Alton Harris, CDC Prisoner B-66883, had expired in the gas chamber at 6:21 AM, sixteen minutes after the cyanide had been gently lowered into the sulfuric acid.

It was the moment Crittendon had been waiting for. He stepped into the   26
middle of the quiet room, his Jheri-Kurls reflecting the eerie green light from the gas chamber where my friend lay dead, slumped forward against the straps in Chair B.

"Ladies and gentlemen. Please stay in your places until your escort comes   27
for you. Follow your escort, as instructed. Thank you."

Our guard came and we followed him out. The eighteen media witnesses,   28
who had stood against the wall opposite us scribbling on paper provided by the prison, preceded us out of the room. As they had been for weeks, they were desperate for a Harris family member to say something to them. "Is this a Harris? Is this a Harris?" a reporter standing just outside the door shouted, pointing at each of us as we emerged into the first light of morning over San Francisco Bay.

My god, it was a beautiful day.   29

Journal Writing

Kroll calls the execution of Harris "indescribably ugly" and "nakedly barbaric" (par. 24). How do you respond to this characterization of capital punishment? In your journal, write down as many reasons both for and against capital punishment as you can think of. The reasons may be moral, emotional, or purely pragmatic. Write down whatever comes to mind. (To take your journal writing further, see "From Journal to Essay" on the facing page.)

Questions on Meaning

1. Is Kroll's PURPOSE merely to serve as a witness to his friend's execution, or is there an unstated proposal in the essay? If so, what is it?

2. Why did the execution take so long? What was taking place behind the scenes?
3. What can you INFER about Kroll's opinion of the Supreme Court's decision to dissolve all three of the Court of Appeals' stays of execution (par. 9)? How does he indirectly make this opinion known?
4. How do you read the last sentence of the essay? Is it merely IRONIC?
5. Do you think Kroll is against the death penalty, or merely against the way it was carried out in this case?

Questions on Writing Strategy

1. At what three points does Kroll pause in the story of the execution? What does he accomplish each time?
2. What is the TONE of the essay? How does it contribute to Kroll's ETHICAL APPEAL (see p. 503)?
3. Is Kroll's approach generally based on a RATIONAL or an EMOTIONAL APPEAL (see pp. 502–03)?
4. What is the EFFECT of Kroll's DESCRIPTION of the victims' families in paragraphs 18 and 23? How does Kroll's POINT OF VIEW shape this description?
5. Why does Kroll describe Harris's death in such detail (pars. 22–23)?
6. **OTHER METHODS.** This essay is an example of NARRATION being used in the service of an argument. What advantage does Kroll gain by presenting his argument in the form of a personal account?

Questions on Language

1. Make sure you know the meanings of the following words: silhouettes (par. 3); vigil (4); stays (9); burly (13); ashen, abyss (21); grotesque (22); barbaric (24).
2. What is Kroll's objection to Vernell Crittendon's tone (pars. 1–2)? What do you make of his job title: "public information officer"?
3. What is the tone of the phrase "a written invitation from Warden Daniel Vasquez himself" (par. 4)?
4. How does Kroll's use of reported speech contribute to his portrait of the prison officials?

Suggestions for Writing

1. **FROM JOURNAL TO ESSAY.** Write an essay in which you argue either for or against the death penalty. Support your argument with the EVIDENCE in favor of your position that you developed in your journal writing (facing page). As for the evidence that contradicts your opinion, use it to try to anticipate, and respond to, readers' likely objections to your view.
2. What is your opinion on televising public executions? How would a televised account of an execution differ from the kind of written narrative Kroll provides? What are the advantages of each method of narration, visual and written?
3. **CRITICAL WRITING.** Kroll's THESIS about the barbarity of staging executions as public spectacle comes nearly at the end of the essay (par. 24), yet he hints

throughout the essay that this is the aspect of his friend's execution that disturbs him the most. How does Kroll prepare the reader for his statement of thesis? What details emphasize the packaging of the execution as public entertainment?

4. **CONNECTIONS.** In "The Penalty of Death" (p. 516), H. L. Mencken approaches the death penalty quite differently from Kroll. Not only do their opinions differ fundamentally, but Mencken's view is broad and ABSTRACT, while Kroll's is intensely personal; and Mencken's appeal is largely rational, while Kroll's is largely emotional. In an essay, discuss the effectiveness of these two essays apart from the opinions they support—that is, focus on the authors' strategies of argument rather than on the arguments themselves. What are the advantages and disadvantages of each strategy?

CHITRA DIVAKARUNI

Born in 1956 in Calcutta, India, CHITRA BANERJEE DIVAKARUNI spent nineteen years in her homeland before immigrating to the United States. She holds an MA from Wright State University and a PhD from the University of California at Berkeley. Her books, often addressing the immigrant experience in America, include the novels *The Mistress of Spice* (1997), *Sister of My Heart* (1999), and *The Vine of Desire* (2002); the collections of stories *Arranged Marriage* (1995) and *The Unknown Errors of Our Lives* (2001); and the collections of poems *Leaving Yuba City* (1997) and *Black Candle* (2000). Divakaruni has received a number of awards for her work, including the Before Columbus Foundation's 1996 American Book Award. Since 1991, Divakaruni has been the president of MAITRI, a San Francisco–based, non-profit organization that helps South Asian victims of domestic abuse.

Live Free and Starve

Some of the consumer goods sold in the United States—shoes, clothing, toys, rugs—are made in countries whose labor practices do not meet US standards for safety and fairness. As these practices have gained wide publicity in recent years, Americans have been horrified at tales of children put to work by force or under contracts (called *indentures*) with the children's parents. Shouldn't the United States use its power to stop such practices? In this essay, Divakaruni argues that efforts to do so, though certainly well intentioned, are nonetheless misguided. The essay first appeared in the online magazine *Salon* in October 1997.

For a different and broader view of how those in wealthy countries can help the less fortunate, see the next essay, Peter Singer's "The Singer Solution to World Poverty."

Some days back, the House passed a bill that stated that the United States would no longer permit the import of goods from factories where forced or indentured child labor was used.[1] My liberal friends applauded the bill. It was a triumphant advance in the field of human rights. Now children in Third World countries wouldn't have to spend their days chained to their posts in factories manufacturing goods for other people to enjoy while their childhoods slipped by them. They could be free and happy, like American children.

---

[1] The bill Divakaruni writes of has not been enacted, nor have similar bills that are under consideration by Congress. However, partial measures are in effect. For instance, amendments attached to other laws mandate toughened eligibility requirements for countries desiring trade benefits and require research by the Department of Labor into the costs and benefits of actively reducing child labor. —EDS.

I am not so sure.   2

It is true that child labor is a terrible thing, especially for those children   3
who are sold to employers by their parents at the age of five or six and have
no way to protect themselves from abuse. In many cases it will be decades —
perhaps a lifetime, due to the fines heaped upon them whenever they make
mistakes — before they can buy back their freedom. Meanwhile these children,
mostly employed by rug-makers, spend their days in dark, ill-ventilated rooms
doing work that damages their eyes and lungs. They aren't even allowed to
stand up and stretch. Each time they go to the bathroom, they suffer a pay cut.

But is this bill, which, if it passes the Senate and is signed by President   4
Clinton, will lead to the unemployment of almost a million children, the
answer? If the children themselves were asked whether they would rather
work under such harsh conditions or enjoy a leisure that comes without the
benefit of food or clothing or shelter, I wonder what their response would be.

It is easy for us in America to make the error of evaluating situations in   5
the rest of the world as though they were happening in this country and propose solutions that make excellent sense — in the context of our society. Even
we immigrants, who should know better, have wiped from our minds the
memory of what it is to live under the kind of desperate conditions that force
a parent to sell his or her child. Looking down from the heights of Maslow's
pyramid,[2] it seems inconceivable to us that someone could actually prefer
bread to freedom.

When I was growing up in Calcutta, there was a boy who used to work in   6
our house. His name was Nimai, and when he came to us, he must have been
about ten or so, just a little older than my brother and I. He'd been brought to
our home by his uncle, who lived in our ancestral village and was a field
laborer for my grandfather. The uncle explained to my mother that Nimai's
parents were too poor to feed their several children, and while his older brothers were already working in the fields and earning their keep, Nimai was too
frail to do so. My mother was reluctant to take on a sickly child who might
prove more of a burden than a help, but finally she agreed, and Nimai lived
and worked in our home for six or seven years. My mother was a good
employer — Nimai ate the same food that we children did and was given new
clothes during Indian New Year, just as we were. In the time between his
chores — dusting and sweeping and pumping water from the tube-well and
running to the market — my mother encouraged him to learn to read and

---

[2] The psychologist Abraham Maslow (1908–70) proposed a "hierarchy of needs" in the
shape of a five-level pyramid with survival needs at the bottom and "self-actualization" and
"self-transcendence" at the top. According to Maslow, one must satisfy the needs at each level
before moving up to the next. — EDS.

write. Still, I would not disagree with anyone who says that it was hardly a desirable existence for a child.

But what would life have been like for Nimai if an anti–child-labor law   7 had prohibited my mother from hiring him? Every year, when we went to visit our grandfather in the village, we were struck by the many children we saw by the mud roads, their ribs sticking out through the rags they wore. They trailed after us, begging for a few paise.[3] When the hunger was too much to bear, they stole into the neighbors' fields and ate whatever they could find—raw potatoes, cauliflower, green sugar cane and corn torn from the stalk—even though they knew they'd be beaten for it. Whenever Nimai passed these children, he always walked a little taller. And when he handed the bulk of his earnings over to his father, there was a certain pride in his eye. Exploitation, you might be thinking. But he thought he was a responsible member of his family.

A bill like the one we've just passed is of no use unless it goes hand in   8 hand with programs that will offer a new life to these newly released children. But where are the schools in which they are to be educated? Where is the money to buy them food and clothing and medication, so that they don't return home to become the extra weight that capsizes the already shaky raft of their family's finances? Their own governments, mired in countless other problems, seem incapable of bringing these services to them. Are we in America who, with one blithe stroke of our congressional pen, rendered these children jobless, willing to shoulder that burden? And when many of these children turn to the streets, to survival through thievery and violence and begging and prostitution—as surely in the absence of other options they must—are we willing to shoulder that responsibility?

Journal Writing

Write a journal response to Divakaruni's argument against legislation that would ban goods produced by forced or indentured child laborers. Do you basically agree or disagree with the author? Why? (To take your journal writing further, see "From Journal to Essay" on the next page.)

Questions on Meaning

1. What do you take to be Divakaruni's PURPOSE in this essay? At what point did it become clear?

[3] *Paise* are the smallest unit of Indian currency, worth a fraction of an American penny.— EDS.

2. What are "Third World countries" (par. 1)?
3. From the further information given in the footnote on page 530, what does it mean to be "[l]ooking down from the heights of Maslow's pyramid" (par. 5)? What point is Divakaruni making here?
4. In paragraph 8 Divakaruni suggests some of the reasons that children in other countries may be forced or sold into labor. What are they?

Questions on Writing Strategy

1. Where in her argument does Divakaruni specifically acknowledge her audience's likely views?
2. What is the EFFECT of Divakaruni's final paragraph? Does it strengthen her argument? Why, or why not?
3. **OTHER METHODS.** What does the extended EXAMPLE of Nimai (pars. 6–7) contribute to Divakaruni's argument? What, if anything, does it add to Divakaruni's authority? What does it tell us about child labor abroad?

Questions on Language

1. Divakaruni says that laboring children could otherwise be "the extra weight that capsizes the already shaky raft of their family's finances" (par. 8). How does this metaphor capture the problem of children in poor families? (See *Figures of speech* in Useful Terms for a definition of *metaphor*.)
2. What do the words in paragraph 7 tell you about Divakaruni's attitude toward the village children? Is it disdain? pity? compassion? horror?
3. Consult a dictionary if you need help in defining the following: indentured (par. 1); inconceivable (5); exploitation (7); mired, blithe (8).

Suggestions for Writing

1. **FROM JOURNAL TO ESSAY.** The kind of legislation Divakaruni takes issue with is still pending in the US Congress. Starting from your journal entry (previous page), write a letter to your representative or one of your senators taking a position for or against such legislation. You can use quotations from Divakaruni's essay if they serve your purpose, but the letter should center on your own views of the issue. When you've finished your letter, send it. (You can find your representative's and your senators' names and addresses on the Web at *http://www .fedgate.org.*)
2. When, if ever, do you think child labor can be justified? Like most people, you probably believe that forced or indentured child labor is unacceptable for any reason, but what about other situations—for instance, children working in their family's business? What kind of paid work, for how many hours a week, is appropriate for, say, a ten- or twelve-year-old child? Where do you draw the line between occasional babysitting or lawn mowing and full-time factory work?
3. **CRITICAL WRITING.** Divakaruni's argument depends significantly on appeals to readers' emotions (see pp. 502–03). Locate one emotional appeal that either helps

to convince you of the author's point or, in your mind, weakens the argument. What does the appeal ASSUME about the reader's (your) feelings or values? Why are the assumptions correct or incorrect in your case? How, specifically, does the appeal strengthen or undermine Divakaruni's argument?

4. **CONNECTIONS.** COMPARE AND CONTRAST Divakaruni's argument in "Live Free and Starve" with the argument made by Peter Singer in the next essay, "The Singer Solution to World Poverty." Which of the two arguments do you find more persuasive? Why?

Chitra Divakaruni on Writing

Chitra Divakaruni is both a writer and a community worker, reaching out to refugees and other disadvantaged people through organizations such as MAITRI, which she helped found. In a 1998 interview in *Atlantic Unbound* (the online version of *The Atlantic Monthly*), Katie Bolick asked Divakaruni how her activism and writing affected one another. Here is Divakaruni's response.

Being helpful where I can has always been an important value for me. I did community work in India, and I continue to do it in America, because being involved in my community is something I feel I need to do. Activism has given me enormous satisfaction — not just as a person, but also as a writer. The lives of people I would have only known from the outside, or had stereotyped notions of, have been opened up to me. My hotline work with MAITRI has certainly influenced both my life and my writing immensely. Overall, I have a great deal of sensitivity that I did not have before, and a lot of my preconceptions have changed. I hope that translates into my writing and reaches my readers.

For Discussion

1. What evidence does "Live Free and Starve" give to support Divakaruni's statement about how her activist work has affected her writing?

2. What does Divakaruni mean when she speaks of lives that she "would have only known from the outside"? Of what use is "insider's" knowledge to an activist? to a writer?

3. Do you have a project or activity — comparable to Divakaruni's activism — that you believe positively affects your writing? What is it? How does it help you as you write?

PETER SINGER

The philosopher PETER SINGER is both greatly influential and hotly controversial. He was born in 1946 in Melbourne, Australia, and received degrees from the University of Melbourne (BA, 1967; MA, 1969) and Oxford University (B.Phil., 1971). He has taught philosophy at a number of schools, and in 1999 he became a professor of bioethics at Princeton University. Singer's philosophy "is shaped," he says, "by an abhorrence of suffering and cruelty." His book *Animal Liberation* (1975) helped found the modern animal-rights movement and gained Singer international attention. In the book Singer argues against human cruelty to other animals and even against humans having any better claim to life than other animals. As Singer has put it elsewhere, "A human being doesn't have value just by virtue of being a human." Singer has written many other controversial books and essays in which he applies severe reason—some say inhumane coldness—to euthanasia, test-tube babies, cloning, genetic engineering, and other ethical dilemmas. His works include *Practical Ethics* (1979), *Should the Baby Live? The Problem of Handicapped Infants* (1985), *How Are We to Live?* (1994), *Rethinking Life and Death* (1995), and, most recently, *Writings on an Ethical Life* (2000).

The Singer Solution to World Poverty

In a typical provocation, Singer here issues a dare: Prove your moral decency by sacrificing to ease poverty around the globe. This essay first appeared on September 5, 1999, in the *New York Times Magazine*, whose readers responded with a huge outpouring of letters, both pro and con. The essay was also included in *Best American Essays 2000*.

Relieving poverty is also the concern of Chitra Divakaruni in the previous essay, "Live Free and Starve."

In the Brazilian film *Central Station,* Dora is a retired schoolteacher who makes ends meet by sitting at the station writing letters for illiterate people. Suddenly she has an opportunity to pocket a thousand dollars. All she has to do is persuade a homeless nine-year-old boy to follow her to an address she has been given. (She is told he will be adopted by wealthy foreigners.) She delivers the boy, gets the money, spends some of it on a television set, and settles down to enjoy her new acquisition. Her neighbor spoils the fun, however, by telling her that the boy was too old to be adopted—he will be killed and his organs sold for transplantation. Perhaps Dora knew this all along, but after her neighbor's plain speaking, she spends a troubled night. In the morning Dora resolves to take the boy back.

Suppose Dora had told her neighbor that it is a tough world, other people have nice new TVs too, and if selling the kid is the only way she can get one, well, he was only a street kid. She would then have become, in the eyes of the audience, a monster. She redeems herself only by being prepared to bear considerable risks to save the boy.

At the end of the movie, in cinemas in the affluent nations of the world, people who would have been quick to condemn Dora if she had not rescued the boy go home to places far more comfortable than her apartment. In fact, the average family in the United States spends almost one third of its income on things that are no more necessary to them than Dora's new TV was to her. Going out to nice restaurants, buying new clothes because the old ones are no longer stylish, vacationing at beach resorts — so much of our income is spent on things not essential to the preservation of our lives and health. Donated to one of a number of charitable agencies, that money could mean the difference between life and death for children in need.

All of which raises a question: In the end, what is the ethical distinction between a Brazilian who sells a homeless child to organ peddlers and an American who already has a TV and upgrades to a better one, knowing that the money could be donated to an organization that would use it to save the lives of kids in need?

Of course, there are several differences between the two situations that could support different moral judgments about them. For one thing, to be able to consign a child to death when he is standing right in front of you takes a chilling kind of heartlessness; it is much easier to ignore an appeal for money to help children you will never meet. Yet for a utilitarian philosopher like myself — that is, one who judges whether acts are right or wrong by their consequences — if the upshot of the American's failure to donate the money is that one more kid dies on the streets of a Brazilian city, then it is in some sense just as bad as selling the kid to the organ peddlers. But one doesn't need to embrace my utilitarian ethic to see that at the very least, there is a troubling incongruity in being so quick to condemn Dora for taking the child to the organ peddlers while at the same time not regarding the American consumer's behavior as raising a serious moral issue.

In his 1996 book, *Living High and Letting Die*, the New York University philosopher Peter Unger presented an ingenious series of imaginary examples designed to probe our intuitions about whether it is wrong to live well without giving substantial amounts of money to help people who are hungry, malnourished, or dying from easily treatable illnesses like diarrhea. Here's my paraphrase of one of these examples:

Bob is close to retirement. He has invested most of his savings in a very rare and valuable old car, a Bugatti, which he has not been able to insure. The

Bugatti is his pride and joy. In addition to the pleasure he gets from driving and caring for his car, Bob knows that its rising market value means that he will always be able to sell it and live comfortably after retirement. One day when Bob is out for a drive, he parks the Bugatti near the end of a railway siding and goes for a walk up the track. As he does so, he sees that a runaway train, with no one aboard, is running down the railway track. Looking farther down the track, he sees the small figure of a child very likely to be killed by the runaway train. He can't stop the train and the child is too far away to warn of the danger, but he can throw a switch that will divert the train down the siding where his Bugatti is parked. Then nobody will be killed—but the train will destroy his Bugatti. Thinking of his joy in owning the car and the financial security it represents, Bob decides not to throw the switch. The child is killed. For many years to come, Bob enjoys owning his Bugatti and the financial security it represents.

Bob's conduct, most of us will immediately respond, was gravely wrong.   8
Unger agrees. But then he reminds us that we too have opportunities to save the lives of children. We can give to organizations like UNICEF or Oxfam America. How much would we have to give one of these organizations to have a high probability of saving the life of a child threatened by easily preventable diseases? (I do not believe that children are more worth saving than adults, but since no one can argue that children have brought their poverty on themselves, focusing on them simplifies the issues.) Unger called up some experts and used the information they provided to offer some plausible estimates that include the cost of raising money, administrative expenses, and the cost of delivering aid where it is most needed. By his calculation, $200 in donations would help a sickly two-year-old transform into a healthy six-year-old—offering safe passage through childhood's most dangerous years. To show how practical philosophical argument can be, Unger even tells his readers that they can easily donate funds by using their credit card and calling one of these toll-free numbers: (800) 367-5437 for UNICEF; (800) 693-2687 for Oxfam America.

Now you too have the information you need to save a child's life. How   9
should you judge yourself if you don't do it? Think again about Bob and his Bugatti. Unlike Dora, Bob did not have to look into the eyes of the child he was sacrificing for his own material comfort. The child was a complete stranger to him and too far away to relate to in an intimate, personal way. Unlike Dora too, he did not mislead the child or initiate the chain of events imperiling him. In all these respects, Bob's situation resembles that of people able but unwilling to donate to overseas aid and differs from Dora's situation.

If you still think that it was very wrong of Bob not to throw the switch   10
that would have diverted the train and saved the child's life, then it is hard to

see how you could deny that it is also very wrong not to send money to one of the organizations listed above. Unless, that is, there is some morally important difference between the two situations that I have overlooked.

Is it the practical uncertainties about whether aid will really reach the 11 people who need it? Nobody who knows the world of overseas aid can doubt that such uncertainties exist. But Unger's figure of $200 to save a child's life was reached after he had made conservative assumptions about the proportion of the money donated that will actually reach its target.

One genuine difference between Bob and those who can afford to donate 12 to overseas aid organizations but don't is that only Bob can save the child on the tracks, whereas there are hundreds of millions of people who can give $200 to overseas aid organizations. The problem is that most of them aren't doing it. Does this mean that it is all right for you not to do it?

Suppose that there were more owners of priceless vintage cars — Carol, 13 Dave, Emma, Fred, and so on, down to Ziggy — all in exactly the same situation as Bob, with their own siding and their own switch, all sacrificing the child in order to preserve their own cherished car. Would that make it all right for Bob to do the same? To answer this question affirmatively is to endorse follow-the-crowd ethics — the kind of ethics that led many Germans to look away when the Nazi atrocities were being committed. We do not excuse them because others were behaving no better.

We seem to lack a sound basis for drawing a clear moral line between 14 Bob's situation and that of any reader of this article with $200 to spare who does not donate it to an overseas aid agency. These readers seem to be acting at least as badly as Bob was acting when he chose to let the runaway train hurtle toward the unsuspecting child. In the light of this conclusion, I trust that many readers will reach for the phone and donate that $200. Perhaps you should do it before reading further.

•   •   •

Now that you have distinguished yourself morally from people who put 15 their vintage cars ahead of a child's life, how about treating yourself and your partner to dinner at your favorite restaurant? But wait. The money you will spend at the restaurant could also help save the lives of children overseas! True, you weren't planning to blow $200 tonight, but if you were to give up dining out just for one month, you would easily save that amount. And what is one month's dining out compared to a child's life? There's the rub. Since there are a lot of desperately needy children in the world, there will always be another child whose life you could save for another $200. Are you therefore obliged to keep giving until you have nothing left? At what point can you stop?

Hypothetical examples can easily become farcical. Consider Bob. How far   16
past losing the Bugatti should he go? Imagine that Bob had got his foot stuck
in the track of the siding, and if he diverted the train, then before it rammed
the car it would also amputate his big toe. Should he still throw the switch?
What if it would amputate his foot? His entire leg?

As absurd as the Bugatti scenario gets when pushed to extremes, the point   17
it raises is a serious one: Only when the sacrifices become very significant
indeed would most people be prepared to say that Bob does nothing wrong
when he decides not to throw the switch. Of course, most people could be
wrong; we can't decide moral issues by taking opinion polls. But consider for
yourself the level of sacrifice that you would demand of Bob, and then think
about how much money you would have to give away in order to make a
sacrifice that is roughly equal to that. It's almost certainly much, much more
than $200. For most middle-class Americans, it could easily be more like
$200,000.

Isn't it counterproductive to ask people to do so much? Don't we run the   18
risk that many will shrug their shoulders and say that morality, so conceived,
is fine for saints but not for them? I accept that we are unlikely to see, in the
near or even medium-term future, a world in which it is normal for wealthy
Americans to give the bulk of their wealth to strangers. When it comes to
praising or blaming people for what they do, we tend to use a standard that is
relative to some conception of normal behavior. Comfortably off Americans
who give, say, 10 percent of their income to overseas aid organizations are so
far ahead of most of their equally comfortable fellow citizens that I wouldn't
go out of my way to chastise them for not doing more. Nevertheless, they
should be doing much more, and they are in no position to criticize Bob for
failing to make the much greater sacrifice of his Bugatti.

At this point various objections may crop up. Someone may say, "If every   19
citizen living in the affluent nations contributed his or her share, I wouldn't
have to make such a drastic sacrifice, because long before such levels were
reached the resources would have been there to save the lives of all those children dying from lack of food or medical care. So why should I give more than
my fair share? Another, related objection is that the government ought to
increase its overseas aid allocations, since that would spread the burden more
equitably across all taxpayers.

Yet the question of how much we ought to give is a matter to be decided   20
in the real world—and that, sadly, is a world in which we know that most
people do not, and in the immediate future will not, give substantial amounts
to overseas aid agencies. We know too that at least in the next year, the
United States government is not going to meet even the very modest United

Nations–recommended target of 0.7 percent of gross national product; at the moment it lags far below that, at 0.09 percent, not even half of Japan's 0.22 percent or a tenth of Denmark's 0.97 percent. Thus, we know that the money we can give beyond that theoretical "fair share" is still going to save lives that would otherwise be lost. While the idea that no one need do more than his or her fair share is a powerful one, should it prevail if we know that others are not doing their fair share and that children will die preventable deaths unless we do more than our fair share? That would be taking fairness too far.

Thus, this ground for limiting how much we ought to give also fails. In the world as it is now, I can see no escape from the conclusion that each one of us with wealth surplus to his or her essential needs should be giving most of it to help people suffering from poverty so dire as to be life-threatening. That's right: I'm saying that you shouldn't buy that new car, take that cruise, redecorate the house, or get that pricy new suit. After all, a thousand-dollar suit could save five children's lives.   21

So how does my philosophy break down in dollars and cents? An American household with an income of $50,000 spends around $30,000 annually on necessities, according to the Conference Board, a nonprofit economic research organization. Therefore, for a household bringing in $50,000 a year, donations to help the world's poor should be as close as possible to $20,000. The $30,000 required for necessities holds for higher incomes as well. So a household making $100,000 could cut a yearly check for $70,000. Again, the formula is simple: Whatever money you're spending on luxuries, not necessities, should be given away.   22

Now, evolutionary psychologists tell us that human nature just isn't sufficiently altruistic to make it plausible that many people will sacrifice so much for strangers. On the facts of human nature, they might be right, but they would be wrong to draw a moral conclusion from those facts. If it is the case that we ought to do things that, predictably, most of us won't do, then let's face that fact head-on. Then, if we value the life of a child more than going to fancy restaurants, the next time we dine out we will know that we could have done something better with our money. If that makes living a morally decent life extremely arduous, well, then that is the way things are. If we don't do it, then we should at least know that we are failing to live a morally decent life — not because it is good to wallow in guilt but because knowing where we should be going is the first step toward heading in that direction.   23

When Bob first grasped the dilemma that faced him as he stood by that railway switch, he must have thought how extraordinarily unlucky he was to be placed in a situation in which he must choose between the life of an innocent child and the sacrifice of most of his savings. But he was not unlucky at all. We are all in that situation.   24

Journal Writing

In your journal, write your immediate response to Singer's essay. How does the essay apply to you? Is Singer's solution valid, or not? Why? (To take your journal writing further, see "From Journal to Essay" on the facing page.)

Questions on Meaning

1. Where does Singer state his THESIS outright? What is it?
2. How does Singer's thesis relate to his PURPOSE as suggested by his final two paragraphs?
3. What distinctions does Singer draw between those who spend on themselves rather than send money to help poor children overseas and those who would sell homeless children to be killed for their organs? Why does Bob, the Bugatti owner, belong more in the former than in the latter group?
4. What is Singer's point in taking the example of Bob to extremes (pars. 16–17)?

Questions on Writing Strategy

1. Singer makes a basic ASSUMPTION about the affluence of his AUDIENCE. Is the assumption justified, given where the essay was first published? If the assumption is not true of you, does the argument then not apply to you?
2. How do you think Singer expects his audience to respond to the break that occurs between paragraphs 14 and 15? How did you respond?
3. What do paragraphs 18–21 contribute to Singer's argument?
4. Does Singer's argument rely primarily on INDUCTIVE reasoning or on DEDUCTIVE reasoning? Explain.
5. Singer frequently poses questions in his essay. For instance, in paragraph 9 he asks, "How should you judge yourself if you don't [donate money to save a child's life]?" What do these questions accomplish?
6. **OTHER METHODS.** Where in the essay does Singer use COMPARISON AND CONTRAST? Why does he use it?

Questions on Language

1. What does Singer mean by "utilitarian ethic" (par. 5)? To answer this question, you may want to look up *utilitarian* in a dictionary.
2. Why does Singer make such a point of the phrase "fair share" in paragraphs 19–20?
3. Consult a dictionary if you are unsure of the meanings of any of the following words: illiterate, acquisition, transplantation (par. 1); ethical, peddlers (4); consign, incongruity (5); ingenious, diarrhea (6); plausible (8); imperiling (9); affirmatively, atrocities (13); farcical (16); counterproductive, chastise (18); equitably (19); theoretical, preventable (20); dire (21); evolutionary, altruistic, arduous, wallow (23); dilemma (24).

Suggestions for Writing

1. **FROM JOURNAL TO ESSAY.** Using your journal writing (facing page) as a starting point, EVALUATE Singer's proposal from your own perspective. How do you respond to the "utilitarian ethic" (par. 5) that underlies Singer's argument? How do you respond to the charge that by spending money on what we don't require instead of donating it for poverty relief, we are allowing children to die? Singer states the modest hope that "the next time we dine out we will know that we could have done something better [helped to save a child] with our money" (23). Will his hope be achieved with you? Why, or why not?

2. Think of another problem—social, ethical, or practical—that holds particular meaning for you. Write an essay in which you propose your own solution to the problem. You may also, like Singer, offer a solution that will get readers thinking about their own relationship to the problem.

3. In paragraph 23 Singer suggests that he does not mean for his readers to "wallow in guilt." To what extent do you think that a sense of guilt—or avoiding a sense of guilt—motivates people to perform charitable acts or otherwise to behave in ways that are not in their own immediate self-interest? Are there other factors that are equally, or more, important? Answer these questions in an essay, being sure to support your thesis with examples and other specifics.

4. **CRITICAL WRITING.** ANALYZE Singer's argument as an argument, considering the effectiveness of his evidence and his reasoning, the kinds of appeals he makes and their appropriateness, and whether and how he considers possible opposing arguments. Is his a strong argument? Why, or why not?

5. **CONNECTIONS.** How might Singer's utilitarian ethic apply to the argument Chitra Divakaruni makes in "Live Free and Starve" (p. 529) and to the broader issue of forced child labor in the Third World?

Peter Singer on Writing

Unlike most modern philosophers, Peter Singer has a large general audience outside the academic world, an audience he carefully considers when writing. "We philosophers often forget that the ordinary reader is not so used to abstract thinking," Singer told Richard Atcheson in an interview for the *Princeton Weekly*. "I always strive to be clear and to eliminate unnecessary jargon." Singer also makes his writing more accessible by using concrete examples from real-life situations: "Putting real people and real examples into the work helps the reader to follow what you're doing."

In his clear, concrete writing, Singer approaches delicate issues with a cold precision that feeds the rage of some critics. For example, Singer believes that parents should have the right to end the life of a severely disabled newborn: "Killing a disabled infant is not morally equivalent to killing a person.

Very often it is not wrong at all." Asked about the angry attacks on such state-ments, Singer told Bob Abernathy of *Religion and Ethics Newsweekly,* "What I'm saying is controversial. Clearly, it goes against an ethic that has been around for a long time. I think that ethic is in the process of change, anyway; but I have, perhaps, brought out a little more clearly and bluntly than some people the way in which that ethic needs to change. And I've refused to try to disguise or camouflage what I'm saying behind a veil which says, for example, 'We're not killing; we're merely letting die.' [. . .] I think it's my refusal to draw that nice veil over things that makes them look better that has led to some of this opposition."

For Discussion

1. How is Singer's awareness of his audience reflected in his writing? Do you find what he says true of "The Singer Solution to World Poverty"? Why, or why not?
2. Leaving aside his opinions on the issues themselves, what do you think of Singer's aim to write bluntly about difficult ethical issues? Judging from "The Singer Solution to World Poverty," is his an effective approach? How did this aspect of Singer's essay affect you?

WILLIAM F. BUCKLEY, JR.

Born in New York in 1925, WILLIAM FRANK BUCKLEY, JR., is one of the most articulate proponents of American conservatism. Shortly after his graduation from Yale, he published *God and Man at Yale* (1951), a memoir espousing conservative political values and traditional Christian principles. Since then, he has written more than twenty works on politics and government, published a syndicated newspaper column, and founded and edited *The National Review*, a magazine of conservative opinion. His most recent nonfiction books are *Nearer My God: An Autobiography of Faith* (1997) and *Let Us Talk of Many Things* (2000), a collection of his speeches. He has also written several books on sailing and more than a dozen novels. In 1991 Buckley was awarded the Presidential Medal of Freedom. With all his publications and honors, however, Buckley is probably best known for *Firing Line*, his weekly television debate program that ran from 1966 to 1999. As the program's several million viewers learned, he is a man of wry charm. When he was half-seriously running for mayor of New York City in 1965, someone asked him what he would do if elected. "Demand a recount," he replied.

Why Don't We Complain?

Most people riding in an overheated commuter train would perspire quietly. For Buckley, this excess of warmth sparks an indignant essay, first published in *Esquire* in 1961, in which he takes to task both himself and his fellow Americans. Does the essay appeal mainly to reason or to emotion? And what would happen if everyone were to do as Buckley urges?

It was the very last coach and the only empty seat on the entire train, so there was no turning back. The problem was to breathe. Outside, the temperature was below freezing. Inside the railroad car the temperature must have been about 85 degrees. I took off my overcoat, and a few minutes later my jacket, and noticed that the car was flecked with the white shirts of the passengers. I soon found my hand moving to loosen my tie. From one end of the car to the other, as we rattled through Westchester County, we sweated; but we did not moan.

I watched the train conductor appear at the head of the car. "Tickets, all tickets, please!" In a more virile age, I thought, the passengers would seize the conductor and strap him down on a seat over the radiator to share the fate of his patrons. He shuffled down the aisle, picking up tickets, punching commutation cards. *No one addressed a word to him.* He approached my seat, and I drew a deep breath of resolution. "Conductor," I began with a considerable edge to my voice. Instantly the doleful eyes of my seatmate turned tiredly from his newspaper to fix me with a resentful stare: What question could be so important as to justify my sibilant intrusion into his stupor? I was shaken by those eyes. I am incapable of making a discreet fuss, so I mumbled a question about what time we were due in Stamford (I didn't even ask whether it would be before or after dehydration could be expected to set in), got my reply, and went back to my newspaper and to wiping my brow.

The conductor had nonchalantly walked down the gauntlet of eighty   3 sweating American freemen, and not one of them had asked him to explain why the passengers in that car had been consigned to suffer. There is nothing to be done when the temperature *outdoors* is 85 degrees, and indoors the air conditioner has broken down; obviously when that happens there is nothing to do, except perhaps curse the day that one was born. But when the temperature outdoors is below freezing, it takes a positive act of will on somebody's part to set the temperature *indoors* at 85. Somewhere a valve was turned too far, a furnace overstocked, a thermostat maladjusted: something that could easily be remedied by turning off the heat and allowing the great outdoors to come indoors. All this is so obvious. What is not obvious is what has happened to the American people.

It isn't just the commuters, whom we have come to visualize as a supine   4 breed who have got on to the trick of suspending their sensory faculties twice a day while they submit to the creeping dissolution of the railroad industry. It isn't just they who have given up trying to rectify irrational vexations. It is the American people everywhere.

A few weeks ago at a large movie theater I turned to my wife and said,   5 "The picture is out of focus." "Be quiet," she answered. I obeyed. But a few minutes later I raised the point again, with mounting impatience. "It will be all right in a minute," she said apprehensively. (She would rather lose her eyesight than be around when I make one of my infrequent scenes.) I waited. It was *just* out of focus—not glaringly out, but out. My vision is 20-20, and I assume that is the vision, adjusted, for most people in the movie house. So, after hectoring my wife throughout the first reel, I finally prevailed upon her to admit that it *was* off, and very annoying. We then settled down, coming to rest on the presumption that: a) someone connected with the management of the theater must soon notice the blur and make the correction; or b) that someone seated near the rear of the house would make the complaint in behalf of those of us up front; or c) that—any minute now—the entire house would explode into catcalls and foot stamping, calling dramatic attention to the irksome distortion.

What happened was nothing. The movie ended, as it had begun, *just* out   6 of focus, and as we trooped out, we stretched our faces in a variety of contortions to accustom the eye to the shock of normal focus.

I think it is safe to say that everybody suffered on that occasion. And I 7 think it is safe to assume that everyone was expecting someone else to take the initiative in going back to speak to the manager. And it is probably true even that if we had supposed the movie would run right through the blurred image, someone surely would have summoned up the purposive indignation to get up out of his seat and file his complaint.

But notice that no one did. And the reason no one did is because we are 8 all increasingly anxious in America to be unobtrusive, we are reluctant to make our voices heard, hesitant about claiming our rights; we are afraid that our cause is unjust, or that if it is not unjust, that it is ambiguous; or if not even that, that it is too trivial to justify the horrors of a confrontation with Author-ity; we will sit in an oven or endure a racking headache before undertaking a head-on, I'm-here-to-tell-you complaint. That tendency to passive compliance, to a heedless endurance, is something to keep one's eyes on—in sharp focus.

I myself can occasionally summon the courage to complain, but I cannot, 9 as I have intimated, complain softly. My own instinct is so strong to let the thing ride, to forget about it—to expect that someone will take the matter up, when the grievance is collective, in my behalf—that it is only when the provocation is at a very special key, whose vibrations touch simultaneously a complexus of nerves, allergies, and passions, that I catch fire and find the reserves of courage and assertiveness to speak up. When that happens, I get quite carried away. My blood gets hot, my brow wet, I become unbearably and unconscionably sarcastic and bellicose; I am girded for a total showdown.

Why should that be? Why could not I (or anyone else) on that railroad 10 coach have said simply to the conductor, "Sir"—I take that back: that sounds sarcastic—"Conductor, would you be good enough to turn down the heat? I am extremely hot. In fact, I tend to get hot every time the temperature reaches 85 degr—." Strike that last sentence. Just end it with the simple statement that you are extremely hot, and let the conductor infer the cause.

Every New Year's Eve I resolve to do something about the Milquetoast in 11 me and vow to speak up, calmly, for my rights, and for the betterment of our society, on every appropriate occasion. Entering last New Year's Eve I was for-tified in my resolve because that morning at breakfast I had had to ask the waitress three times for a glass of milk. She finally brought it—after I had fin-ished my eggs, which is when I don't want it anymore. I did not have the man-liness to order her to take the milk back, but settled instead for a cowardly sulk, and ostentatiously refused to drink the milk—though I later paid for it—rather than state plainly to the hostess, as I should have, why I had not drunk it, and would not pay for it.

So by the time the New Year ushered out the Old, riding in on my morn- 12 ing's indignation and stimulated by the gastric juices of resolution that flow so faithfully on New Year's Eve, I rendered my vow. Henceforward I would conquer my shyness, my despicable disposition to supineness. I would speak out like a man against the unnecessary annoyances of our time.

Forty-eight hours later, I was standing in line at the ski repair store in Pico   13
Peak, Vermont. All I needed, to get on with my skiing, was the loan, for one minute, of a small screwdriver, to tighten a loose binding. Behind the counter in the workshop were two men. One was industriously engaged in servicing the complicated requirements of a young lady at the head of the line, and obviously he would be tied up for quite a while. The other—"Jiggs," his workmate called him—was a middle-aged man, who sat in a chair puffing a pipe, exchanging small talk with his working partner. My pulse began its telltale acceleration. The minutes ticked on. I stared at the idle shopkeeper, hoping to shame him into action, but he was impervious to my telepathic reproof and continued his small talk with his friend, brazenly insensitive to the nervous demands of six good men who were raring to ski.

Suddenly my New Year's Eve resolution struck me. It was now or never.   14
I broke from my place in line and marched to the counter. I was going to control myself. I dug my nails into my palms. My effort was only partially successful.

"If you are not too busy," I said icily, "would you mind handing me a screw-   15
driver?"

Work stopped and everyone turned his eyes on me, and I experienced that   16
mortification I always feel when I am the center of centripetal shafts of curiosity, resentment, perplexity.

But the worst was yet to come. "I am sorry, sir," said Jiggs deferentially,   17
moving the pipe from his mouth. "I am not supposed to move. I have just had a heart attack." That was the signal for a great whirring noise that descended from heaven. We looked, stricken, out the window, and it appeared as though a cyclone had suddenly focused on the snowy courtyard between the shop and the ski lift. Suddenly a gigantic army helicopter materialized, and hovered down to a landing. Two men jumped out of the plane carrying a stretcher, tore into the ski shop, and lifted the shopkeeper onto the stretcher. Jiggs bade his companion good-bye and was whisked out the door, into the plane, up to the heavens, down—we learned—to a nearby army hospital. I looked up manfully—into a score of man-eating eyes. I put the experience down as a reversal.

As I write this, on an airplane, I have run out of paper and need to reach   18
into my briefcase under my legs for more. I cannot do this until my empty lunch tray is removed from my lap. I arrested the stewardess as she passed empty-handed down the aisle on the way to the kitchen to fetch the lunch trays for the passengers up forward who haven't been served yet. "Would you

please take my tray?" "Just a *moment*, sir!" she said, and marched on sternly. Shall I tell her that since she is headed for the kitchen *anyway*, it could not delay the feeding of the other passengers by more than two seconds necessary to stash away my empty tray? Or remind her that not fifteen minutes ago she spoke unctuously into the loudspeaker the words undoubtedly devised by the airline's highly paid public relations counselor: "If there is anything I or Miss French can do for you to make your trip more enjoyable, *please* let us—" I have run out of paper.

I think the observable reluctance of the majority of Americans to assert   19
themselves in minor matters is related to our increased sense of helplessness in an age of technology and centralized political and economic power. For generations, Americans who were too hot, or too cold, got up and did something about it. Now we call the plumber, or the electrician, or the furnace man. The habit of looking after our own needs obviously had something to do with the assertiveness that characterized the American family familiar to readers of American literature. With the technification of life goes our direct responsibility for our material environment, and we are conditioned to adopt a position of helplessness not only as regards the broken air conditioner, but as regards the overheated train. It takes an expert to fix the former, but not the latter; yet these distinctions, as we withdraw into helplessness, tend to fade away.

Our notorious political apathy is a related phenomenon. Every year,   20
whether the Republican or the Democratic Party is in office, more and more power drains away from the individual to feed vast reservoirs in far-off places; and we have less and less say about the shape of events which shape our future. From this alienation of personal power comes the sense of resignation with which we accept the political dispensations of a powerful government whose hold upon us continues to increase.

An editor of a national weekly news magazine told me a few years ago that   21
as few as a dozen letters of protest against an editorial stance of his magazine was enough to convene a plenipotentiary meeting of the board of editors to review policy. "So few people complain, or make their voices heard," he explained to me, "that we assume a dozen letters represent the inarticulated views of thousands of readers." In the past ten years, he said, the volume of mail has noticeably decreased, even though the circulation of his magazine has risen.

When our voices are finally mute, when we have finally suppressed the   22
natural instinct to complain, whether the vexation is trivial or grave, we shall have become automatons, incapable of feeling. When Premier Khrushchev[1]

---

[1]Nikita Khrushchev (1894–1971) was premier of the former Soviet Union from 1958 to 1964. —EDS.

first came to this country late in 1959 he was primed, we are informed, to experience the bitter resentment of the American people against his tyranny, against his persecutions, against the movement which is responsible for the great number of American deaths in Korea, for billions in taxes every year, and for life everlasting on the brink of disaster; but Khrushchev was pleasantly surprised, and reported back to the Russian people that he had been met with overwhelming cordiality (read: apathy), except, to be sure, for "a few fascists who followed me around with their wretched posters, and should be horse-whipped."

I may be crazy, but I say there would have been lots more posters in a soci-   23
ety where train temperatures in the dead of winter are not allowed to climb to 85 degrees without complaint.

━━━━━━━━━━━━

Journal Writing

One reason we don't complain, according to Buckley, is that we expect someone else to do so for us. Do you agree? Do you ever "take the initiative" (par. 7) to complain about big or little hassles, or do you too sit in silent annoyance? Answer in your journal, explaining why. (To take your journal writing further, see "From Journal to Essay" on the facing page.)

Questions on Meaning

1. How does Buckley account for his failure to complain to the train conductor? What reasons does he give for not taking action when he notices that the movie he is watching is out of focus?
2. Where does Buckley finally place the blame for the average American's reluctance to try to "rectify irrational vexations"?
3. By what means does the author bring his argument around to the subject of political apathy?
4. What THESIS does Buckley attempt to support? What is his PURPOSE?

Questions on Writing Strategy

1. In taking to task not only his fellow Americans but also himself, does Buckley strengthen or weaken his charge that, as a people, Americans do not complain enough?
2. Judging from the vocabulary displayed in this essay, would you say that Buckley is writing for a highly specialized AUDIENCE or an educated but nonspecialized general audience?

3. As a whole, is Buckley's essay an example of appeal to emotion or reasoned argument or both? Give EVIDENCE for your answer.
4. **OTHER METHODS.** Buckley includes as evidence four NARRATIVES of his personal experiences. What is the point of the narrative about Jiggs (pars. 13–17)?

Questions on Language

1. Define the following words: virile, doleful, sibilant (par. 2); supine (4); hectoring (5); unobtrusive, ambiguous (8); intimated, unconscionably, bellicose (9); ostentatiously (11); despicable (12); impervious (13); mortification, centripetal (16); deferentially (17); unctuously (18); notorious, dispensations (20); plenipotentiary, inarticulated (21); automatons (22).
2. What does Buckley's use of the capital A in *Authority* (par. 8) contribute to the sentence in which he uses it?
3. What is Buckley talking about when he alludes to "the Milquetoast in me" (par. 11)? (Notice how well the ALLUSION fits into the paragraph, with its emphasis on breakfast and a glass of milk.)

Suggestions for Writing

1. **FROM JOURNAL TO ESSAY.** Write an essay about one moment when you either spoke up against an annoyance or didn't complain when you should have. Narrate this incident, also using the information from your journal entry (facing page) to help explain why you did or did not act.
2. Think of some disturbing incident you have witnessed, or some annoying treatment you have received in a store or other public place, and write a letter of complaint to whomever you believe responsible. Be specific in your evidence, be temperate in your language, make clear what you would like to come of your complaint (your proposal), and be sure to put your letter in the mail.
3. **CRITICAL WRITING.** Write a paper in which you ANALYZE and EVALUATE any one of Buckley's ideas. For instance: Do we feel as helpless as Buckley says (par. 19)? Are we politically apathetic, and if so should the government be blamed (par. 20)? For that matter, do we not complain? Support your view with evidence from your experience, observation, or reading.
4. **CONNECTIONS.** Both Buckley and Barbara Huttmann, in "A Crime of Compassion" (p. 112), make a strong ETHICAL APPEAL (see p. 503), going out of their way to convince readers of their goodwill, reasonableness, and authority. Write an essay in which you analyze the ethical appeal of both authors, using quotations and PARAPHRASES from both essays to support your analysis.

William F. Buckley, Jr., on Writing

In the autobiographical *Overdrive*, Buckley recalls a conversation with a friend and fellow columnist: "George Will[1] once told me how deeply he loves to write. 'I wake in the morning,' he explained to me, 'and I ask myself: Is this one of the days I have to write a column? And if the answer is yes, I rise a happy man.' I, on the other hand, wake neither particularly happy nor unhappy, but to the extent that my mood is affected by the question whether I need to write a column that morning, the impact of Monday-Wednesday-Friday"—the days when he must write a newspaper column—"is definitely negative. Because I do not like to write, for the simple reason that writing is extremely hard work, and I do not 'like' extremely hard work."

Still, in the course of a "typical year," Buckley estimates that he produces not only 150 newspaper columns, but also a dozen longer articles, eight or ten speeches, fifty introductions for his television program, various editorial pieces for the magazine he edits, *The National Review*, and a book or two. "Why do I do so much? [. . .] It is easier to stay up late working for hours than to take one tenth the time to inquire into the question whether the work is worth performing."

In the introduction to another book, *A Hymnal: The Controversial Arts*, Buckley states an attitude toward writing that most other writers would not share. "I have discovered, in sixteen years of writing columns," he declares, "that there is no observable difference in the quality of that which is written at very great speed (twenty minutes, say), and that which takes three or four times as long. [. . .] Pieces that take longer to write sometimes, on revisiting them, move along grumpily."

For Discussion

1. Given that he so dislikes writing, why does Buckley do it?
2. Buckley's attitude toward giving time to writing is unusual. What is the more usual view of writing?

[1] See page 481. —EDS.

LAURA FRASER

LAURA FRASER was born in 1961 in Denver, Colorado. Since graduating from Wesleyan University (BA, 1982), she has been a freelance writer whose work has appeared in numerous publications, including *Glamour, Vogue,* and *Mother Jones.* A recovered bulimic, Fraser was motivated to write her first book after struggling for many years with her weight. In that book, *Losing It: False Hopes and Fat Profits in the Diet Industry* (1997), Fraser investigates America's obsession with thinness and the businesses that cater to it. Fraser's latest book is *An Italian Affair* (2001), a travelogue and memoir of an intermittent two-year romance. She has taught magazine writing at the University of California at Berkeley and currently lives in San Francisco.

Why I Stopped Being a Vegetarian

As its title indicates, Fraser's essay is part explanation—a funny and self-revealing one at that—but it also offers an argument both for and ultimately against vegetarianism. The essay was published in the January 7, 2000, issue of the online magazine *Salon.*

Until a few months ago, I had been a vegetarian for fifteen years. Like most people who call themselves vegetarians (somewhere between 4 and 10 percent of us, depending on the definition; only 1 percent of Americans are vegans, eating no animal products at all), I wasn't strict about it. I ate dairy products and eggs, as well as fish. That made me a pesco-ovo-lacto-vegetarian, which isn't a category you can choose for special meals on airlines.

About a year ago, in Italy, it dawned on me that a little pancetta was really good in pasta, too. After failing to convince myself that pancetta was a vegetable, I became a pesco-ovo-lacto-pancetta-vegetarian, with a "Don't Ask, Don't Tell" policy about chicken broth. It was a slippery slope from there.

Nevertheless, for most of those fifteen years, hardly a piece of animal flesh crossed my lips. Over the course of that time, many people asked me why I became a vegetarian. I came up with vague answers: my health, the environment, the impracticality and heartlessness of killing animals for food when we can survive perfectly well on soy burgers. It was political, it was emotional and it made me special, not to mention slightly morally superior to all those blood-thirsty carnivores out there.

The truth is, I became a vegetarian in college for two reasons. One was that meat was more expensive than lentils, and I was broke, or broke enough to choose to spend my limited budget on other classes of ingestibles. The other was that I was not a lesbian.

This is not to say that all lesbians are carnivores; in fact, there's probably a higher percentage of vegetarians among lesbians than most other groups. But there was a fair amount of political pressure to be something in those days. Since, as a privileged white girl from suburban Denver, I couldn't really identify with any oppressed minority group, I was faced with becoming a lesbian in order to prove my political mettle. I had to decide between meat and men, and for better or worse, I became a vegetarian.

The identity stuck, even though the political imperative for my label   6
faded. It wasn't an identity that ever really fit: My friends thought it odd that such an otherwise hedonistic woman should have that one ascetic streak. It was against my nature, they said. But by then, I'd started to believe the other arguments about vegetarianism.

First was health. There's a lot of evidence that vegetarians live longer,   7
have lower cholesterol levels and are thinner than meat eaters. This is somewhat hard to believe, since for the first few years of not eating meat, I was basically a cheesetarian. Try leafing through some of those vegetarian recipe books from the early '80s: You added three cups of grated cheddar to everything but the granola. Then vegetarianism went through that mathematical phase where you had to figure out which proteins you had to combine with which in order to get a complete protein. Since many nutritionists will tell you people don't need that much protein anyway, I gave up, going for days and days without so much as contemplating beans or tofu.

For whatever haphazard combination of proteins I ate, being a vegetarian   8
did seem to have a stunning effect on my cholesterol level. This, of course, could be genetic. But when I had a very involved physical exam once at the Cooper Institute for Aerobic Fitness in Dallas, my total cholesterol level was a super-low 135, and my ratio of HDL (good) cholesterol to LDL (evil) was so impressive that the doctor drawled, "Even if you had heart disease, you would be reversing it." This good news, far from reassuring me that I could well afford a few barbecued ribs now and then, spurred me on in my vegetarianism, mainly because my cholesterol numbers effectively inoculated me against the doctor's advice that I also needed to lose fifteen pounds.

"Why?" I asked. "Don't you lose weight to lower your cholesterol?"   9

He couldn't argue with that. Whether or not most vegetarians are leaner   10
than carnivores, in my case I was happy to more than make up the calories with carbohydrates, which, perhaps not coincidentally, I always craved.

After the health rationale came the animal rights one. Like most vegetar-   11
ians, I cracked Peter Singer's[1] philosophical treatise on animal rights, and

---

[1] Utilitarianism, as Singer defines it in "The Singer Solution to World Poverty" (p. 534), is a standard that "judges whether acts are right or wrong by their consequences." Singer's book on animal rights is *Animal Liberation* (1975). —EDS.

bought his utilitarian line that if you don't have to kill animals, and it potentially causes suffering, you shouldn't do it. (Singer, now at Princeton, has recently come under attack for saying that if a human being's incapacitated life causes more suffering than good, it is OK to kill him.)

It's hard to know where to stop with utilitarianism. Do I need a cashmere   12
sweater more than those little shorn goats need to be warm themselves? Do animals really suffer if they have happy, frolicking lives before a quick and painless end? Won't free-range[2] do?

My animal rights philosophy had a lot of holes from the start. First of all,   13
I excluded fish from the animal kingdom—not only because fish taste delicious grilled with a little butter and garlic, but also because they make it a lot easier to be a vegetarian when you go out to restaurants. Now that's utilitarian. Besides, as soon as you start spending your time fretting about the arguments that crowd the inner pens of animal rights philosophy—do fish think?—then you know you're experiencing a real protein deficiency.

I rationalized the fish thing by telling myself I would eat anything I would   14
kill myself. I had been fly-fishing with my dad and figured a few seconds of flopping around was outweighed by the merits of trout almondine. (Notice that I, not the fish, was doing the figuring.) But who was I kidding? If I were hungry enough, I'd kill a cow in a heartbeat. I'd practically kill a cow just for a great pair of shoes.

Which brings me to the leather exception. As long as other people are   15
eating cow, I decided, I might as well recycle the byproducts and diminish the harm by wearing leather jackets and shoes. When everyone stopped eating meat, I'd stop buying leather jackets and shoes. In the meantime, better stock up.

Then there's the environmental rationale. There is no doubt, as Frances   16
Moore Lappe first pointed out in her 1971 book *Food First,* that there is a huge loss of protein resources going from grain to meat, and that some animals, especially cattle and Americans, use up piggish amounts of water, grain and crop land.

But the problem really isn't meat, but too much meat—overgrazing, over-   17
fishing and overconsumption. If Americans just ate less meat—like driving cars less often—the problem could be alleviated without giving up meat entirely. That approach has worked for centuries, and continues to work in Europe.

All my deep vegetarian questioning was silenced one day when a friend   18
ordered roasted rosemary chicken for two. I thought I'd try "just a bite," and

---

[2] Free-range animals are not penned up in a small space but are allowed to move about freely in ample space. — EDS.

then I was ripping into it like a starving hyena. Roasted chicken, I realized, is wonderful. Meat is good.

From a culinary point of view, that's obvious. Consider that most vegetarians live in America and England, places tourists do not visit for the food. You don't find vegetarians in France, and rarely in Italy. Enough said.   19

As for health, if nutritionists are always telling you to "listen to your body," mine was definitely shouting for more meat. One roasted bird unleashed fifteen years' worth of cravings. All of a sudden I felt like I had a bass note playing in my body to balance out all those soprano carbohydrates. Forget about winning the low-cholesterol Olympics. For the first time in a long time, I felt satisfied.   20

As a vegetarian, not only had I denied myself something I truly enjoyed, I had been antisocial. How many times had I made a hostess uncomfortable by refusing the main course at a dinner party, lamely saying I'd "eat around it"? How often did my vegetarianism cause other people to go to extra trouble to make something special for me to eat, and why did it never occur to me that that was selfish? How about the time, in a small town in Italy, when the chef had presented me with a plate of very special local sausage, since I was the American guest—and I had refused it, to the mortification of my Italian friends? Or when a then-boyfriend, standing in the meat section of the grocery store, forlornly told a friend, "If only I had a girlfriend who ate meat"? If eating is a socially conscious act, you have to be conscious of the society of your fellow *Homo sapiens* along with the animals. And we humans, as it happens, are omnivores.   21

Journal Writing

In her conclusion Fraser says that her refusal to eat meat was sometimes rude and even selfish. Do you agree? In your journal, write about a time when you may have behaved rudely or selfishly—or maybe just coolly—because you were upholding a personal principle such as never lying or never cheating or, for that matter, never eating meat. (To take your journal writing further, see "From Journal to Essay" on the facing page.)

Questions on Meaning

1. Fraser offers three general arguments for not eating meat. What are they? How does she question the validity of these arguments?
2. What, for Fraser, are the strongest arguments in favor of eating meat, at least occasionally? How do they relate to her THESIS?
3. What is Fraser's apparent PURPOSE here? What makes you think so?

Questions on Writing Strategy

1. Fraser focuses almost exclusively on herself in this essay. How does she expand on her own experiences to apply her argument to vegetarians more generally? Does her largely personal approach damage her argument? Why, or why not?
2. How would you describe Fraser's TONE in this essay? What is its EFFECT on you as a reader?
3. **OTHER METHODS.** In what sense is Fraser's essay an argument based on EXAMPLE?

Questions on Language

1. In paragraph 2 Fraser writes that she "became a pesco-ovo-lacto-pancetta-vegetarian, with a 'Don't Ask, Don't Tell' policy about chicken broth." What points is she making in this sentence?
2. What is the effect of Fraser calling herself a "cheesetarian" in paragraph 7?
3. How does Fraser use the word "inoculated" in paragraph 8 for comic effect? How about the word "recycle" in paragraph 15?
4. Be sure that you know the meaning of the following words, checking a dictionary if necessary: pancetta (par. 2); carnivores (3); ingestibles (4); mettle (5); imperative, hedonistic, ascetic (6); cholesterol, tofu (7); carbohydrates (10); incapacitated (11); frolicking (12); deficiency (13); rationalized, almondine (14); alleviated (17); culinary (19); mortification, forlornly, *Homo sapiens*, omnivores (21).

Suggestions for Writing

1. **FROM JOURNAL TO ESSAY.** Picking up from your journal writing (facing page), explain when, if ever, your principles should be compromised in order to accommodate the feelings of others. For example, if you believe in always telling the truth, are there still times when it is better to lie? Or does the principle of telling the truth always outweigh other concerns? Use specific examples to develop your thesis.
2. Fraser refers to the argument based on animal rights as a rationale for not eating meat. Do you think animals have rights that are abused for the sake of human self-interest? Or do you believe that human self-interest generally takes precedence? In an essay, argue for or against the idea of animal rights. You might consider issues such as experimenting on animals to test potentially life-saving medical procedures, protecting endangered species to the detriment of economic interests, and capturing and confining wild animals for people to observe in zoos.
3. **CRITICAL WRITING.** ANALYZE Fraser's use of humor in this essay. Do you think the humor contributes positively to her argument, or does it undercut the points she is trying to make? Cite specific passages to support your view.
4. **CONNECTIONS.** In paragraphs 11–12 Fraser refers to the utilitarianism of Peter Singer, whose "The Singer Solution to World Poverty" (p. 534) explains the philosophy in a bit more detail. From Singer's and Fraser's essays and from research in an encyclopedia, write a one-paragraph DEFINITION of *utilitarianism* in your own words. Add examples of your own (that is, don't use poverty or animal rights).

Laura Fraser on Writing

Since publishing *An Italian Affair* about a romantic relationship she was involved in, Laura Fraser has often been asked, "How could you write something so personal?" She answers in "On Writing a Book About One's Personal Life," an essay appearing in the online magazine *Bold Type*. "*An Italian Affair* began simply as something I wrote for myself, for my journal," Fraser writes. "I've always kept a journal, to blow off steam, tell my secrets, sort through personal conundrums, and to try to get to the heart of matters I'm muddling through in my ever-vexing romantic life. I've always thought it was a little strange, and even sad, that for the most part, I've considered the writing I've done for myself to be better than the writing I've done for magazines, where often you can't use your true voice—or heart. In my journal, I write with a stripped-down emotionalism that isn't very useful in the world of investigative journalism."

When she wrote of her Italian experience in her journal, Fraser realized that she had "what writers are always looking for, and rarely stumble across—a story." She started publishing short pieces about the experience in *Salon* and eventually turned the pieces into a full-length book. She was nervous about publishing such personal work, but, she says, "I was having fun—for the first time, publishing stories in my real, formerly secret journal voice."

For Discussion

1. How would you define VOICE in writing? (If you need help, see the definition in Useful Terms.)
2. How has Fraser's journal writing differed from her writing as an investigative journalist?
3. How is your writing for yourself different from your writing for others, such as in papers for your courses? How does knowing that you will have an AUDIENCE affect your voice?

COLLEEN WENKE

COLLEEN WENKE was born in 1979 and grew up in Queens, New York. After graduating from Boston College in 2001 with a degree in psychology, she moved back to New York City and took a job as a project coordinator at a real estate investment and development firm. She plans eventually to pursue a career in medicine. An avid traveler, Wenke spent a semester at the University of New South Wales in Sydney, Australia, and she has recently taken trips to Europe and Southeast Asia. She is also an enthusiast of extreme sports, such as skydiving, rappelling, white-water rafting, and scuba diving.

Too Much Pressure

Why are more students cheating in school? In this essay written when she was a college freshman, Wenke explores several reasons, finding one especially compelling. "Too Much Pressure" was published in the 1998 edition of *Fresh Ink*, a collection of work by students in Boston College's first-year writing course.

You hear the clock ticking in your head, and your teacher keeps erasing, in ten-minute decrements, the time you have left to complete the test. You do not remember anything from the last month of class. You probably should have studied more, watched less television, and spent less time on the phone. All the "should haves" are not important now. You need to finish the test and get out of here. The thought of a big fat F and a "See me" on the top of your midterm scares you. You remember the small piece of paper you have hidden in your pocket just in case. For a fleeting moment you think about what will happen if you are caught; then you slip the paper from your pocket onto the desktop. You transfer all the required information onto the test in time. You smile in anticipation of the A you are going to get. You think of how easy it was to cheat. All that matters is getting the grade.

Cheating is taking work done by somebody else, be it a friend or someone you do not know, and writing your name on it and saying it is your work. Any time I walked through my high school cafeteria or the hallways, I saw people cheating. It came in many forms, from copying homework to giving out copies of the exam. Students even wrote the answers to a Scantron exam down the sides of number-2 pencils and gave the pencils to their friends. My history teacher freshman year had a name for these students: "cafeteria scholars." These were the students who pulled 90s by knowing what the test questions were before they got to the classroom. Their friends who had taken the exam earlier in the day would tell them the questions and answers during lunch.

557

The teachers knew that these things went on, yet nobody seemed to do anything about them. I thought this was the way school went. The people who were cheating were doing the best in all of my classes. I would study for hours and still pull Bs. They would pull As.

I remember conversations over the dinner table with my parents on the   3
subject of cheating. My parents were disgusted at the apathetic views my brothers and I held. We really didn't think it was a big deal to copy homework. I thought everyone cheated, probably even my parents and teachers when they were my age. But my parents swore that they had never cheated. Did I believe them? Not really. I thought that they were giving us the "it was so much better when we were growing up" speech.

I soon learned differently. In the article "When the Ends Justify the   4
Means," written by Robin Stansbury, a reporter for the Connecticut newspaper *The Courant*, I found that my parents were telling the truth. Stansbury reports that "cheating in school has probably been around since the first exam was given." But he goes on to say, "State and national statistics show cheating among high-school students has risen dramatically during the past fifty years."[1] Reading this upset me and made me think about what had caused this increase. I hoped this was not a reflection of moral decline in the people who would soon be running my country. I blamed our school system for not instilling the proper values in its students. I figured that the dramatic change in the role of the family over the past generation, from two-parent homes with a working father and a mother who stayed at home and watched her children to families which have only a single parent or in which both parents work outside the home, meant schools needed to include moral standards in the curriculum. I believed schools were not fulfilling their role and therefore were producing students who do not know the difference between right and wrong.

An article written by Robert L. Maginnis, a policy analyst in the Cultural   5
Studies Project at the Family Research Council, indicates my hypothesis had some truth to it. Maginnis states that "the erosion of values is traceable largely to changes in institutions which have traditionally been responsible for imparting them to our youth." He defines "these key institutions [to] include family, school, church, media and government." I agree with Maginnis, but I can't accept these factors as the only sources in the increase of cheating in the classroom. The facts seem contradictory. If my parents' generation had such high morals and wouldn't cheat, wouldn't they teach their children the same? My parents had taught me that cheating was wrong, yet I seemed to accept it.

---

[1] Wenke uses the MLA style of source citation, discussed on pages 55–66. Here and later, she does not provide parenthetical text citations because she names the authors in the text and because her sources — two Web documents and a television program — did not have numbered pages she could cite. — EDS.

There is a new "class" of cheaters today. In the past, as one would expect, the students who cheated were the ones who could not pass or did not do the work. They were the lazy students. But today the majority of the students who admit to cheating are college-bound overachievers. The students who are trying to juggle too many activities are resorting to compromising their integrity for a good grade. There is too much competition between students, which leads to increased pressure to do well. Cheating becomes a way to get the edge over the other students in the class. In addition, penalties for getting caught are mild. If you were caught cheating at my high school, you received a zero for the test. Your parents were not called, and you were not suspended. True, a zero would hurt your grade severely if all grades for each quarter counted. But there was a loophole in the system: Each quarter the lowest grade was dropped. If the zero grade was dropped, it made no difference; the average was not affected. Students who cheated on all the tests but only got caught once still received good grades.

A main difference between school today and school when my parents were enrolled is that we are now very goal-oriented and will compromise our values to achieve these goals. Stansbury sees this compromise of values and reports in his article that "cheating is a daily occurrence in high school. [. . .] What this says is that many of our students today do not have much internal integrity." Stansbury argues that students "want a goal, and how to get the goal is somewhat irrelevant." Today there is more pressure placed on students to do well. They are expected to receive good grades, play a sport, and volunteer if they are to be looked at by a good college. With a B tainting your transcript, a college might not look at you. This new pressure is what is causing the increase in cheating. Maginnis agrees with Stansbury and goes further, reporting, "A national survey found a shift in motivation away from altruism and toward concern with making money and getting power and status." Like Stansbury, Maginnis says that "students are finding it easier to rationalize lying or cheating in pursuit of their goals." And what goals are these students pursuing? They want the best grades so that they can get into the best schools and get the highest-paying jobs. Starting in the classroom, we are sending the message that it is acceptable to cheat as long as you do not get caught and you do the best.

Dean Morton, a broadcaster for *Good Morning America*, reported that according to a national survey conducted in 1997 by *Who's Who in American High School Students*, as many as 98 percent of students who participated in the survey admitted to cheating. The segment of the show was even entitled "Guess What? Cheaters Do Prosper." Like Stansbury and Maginnis, this survey also concluded that it is now the common belief among students that cheaters are getting ahead in life. Stansbury interviewed several high-school students in his article and discovered that many of them feel cheaters do get ahead in the classroom: "In high school, the cheaters always win. They don't get caught and they are the ones getting 100 on the exams when the noncheaters are getting 80s and 90s. Cheaters do win." We are sending a message to our youth that it is acceptable to cheat as long as you don't get caught and you are getting As. In this kind of society, morals take a back seat to how much you earn and how prosperous you are.

Students who would not usually cheat get sucked into believing it is the 9
only way to get ahead in school: If the cheaters are doing better than they are and not getting caught, then they had better try it. Stansbury proposes that there is such an enormous increase in cheating because more students are joining in: "They see others cheating and they think they are being unfairly disadvantaged." He adds that the "only way many of them feel they can keep in the game, to get into the right schools, is to cheat." In high school I always felt at a disadvantage, because everybody else was cheating and doing better than I was, even if only by a few points. My friends felt the same way, that copying work or cheating was the only way to keep up with the rest of the class. It frustrated me, because the cheaters were not earning their grades. But there were plenty of times when I was in a jam and copied homework from friends. Thinking about this now, I wonder what allowed me to push aside my conviction that cheating was wrong. I wasn't bringing in cheat sheets and didn't know the questions to tests before I got there, but I was cheating nonetheless.

How should we respond to the huge increase in cheating over the past 10
generation? We need to step back and look at the broader picture. We are creating a society in which people feel it is acceptable to cheat. This attitude will not stop in the classroom, but will carry on into the business world. Those who are cheating are the ones getting the grades and getting into the best schools. They are the "smart" ones. They in turn are the ones who will be running our country. They will become the heads of businesses and presidents of big corporations. Are these the people we want to have the power? In all likelihood they will not stop cheating once they get to the top. They become the people we idolize and aspire to be like. Because they are powerful, we consider them clever, highly respectable people. I do not hold any respect for a dishonest cheater. The phrase "honest businessman" will truly be an oxymoron. I am scared to think of the consequences of having cheaters rule our country. Is our society teaching that this is the only way to get ahead in life? Does obtaining status and power make you good? Schools are drifting away from emphasizing learning and are emphasizing the grade instead. When the thirst for knowledge is replenished in a student's mind, the desire for the grade without the work will dissolve. Only then will cheating decline.

Works Cited

Maginnis, Robert L. "Cheating Scandal Points to Moral Decline." Washington: Family Research Council, 1994. 3 May 1997 <http://www.frc.org/perspeceivelpv94dled.html>.

Morton, Dean. "Guess What? Cheaters Do Prosper." *Good Morning America.* ABC. WCVB, Boston. 16 Apr. 1997.

Stansbury, Robin. "Cheating in Connecticut's Classrooms: When the Ends Justify the Means." *Hartford Courant* 2 Mar. 1997. 2 May 1997 <http://www.ctnow.com/news/hc-specialUcheating/daY1.html>.

Journal Writing

Do you agree with Wenke that most students think cheating is acceptable? In your journal, write down your views of how common cheating is in your school and what students' attitudes are toward it. (To take your journal writing further, see "From Journal to Essay" on the next page.)

Questions on Meaning

1. What reasons does Wenke suggest for the increase in cheating among students?
2. What does Wenke see as a possible negative consequence of cheating among students today?
3. What solution does Wenke offer for the problem of student cheating?

Questions on Writing Strategy

1. How effective do you find Wenke's opening paragraph? What does it suggest to you about her intended AUDIENCE?
2. Wenke cites several outside sources in the course of her essay. What do these sources contribute to her argument?
3. What is the EFFECT of Wenke's admission that she herself copied homework from friends in high school (par. 9)? Does this admission add to or detract from Wenke's ethical appeal? Why?
4. **OTHER METHODS.** Wenke's argument is based largely on CAUSE AND EFFECT ANALYSIS. Does her analysis seem sound to you? Do you think she overemphasizes some causes or overlooks others? Explain.

Questions on Language

1. Find examples of COLLOQUIAL EXPRESSIONS in Wenke's essay. What is the effect of such language? Does it strike you as appropriate?

2. What does Wenke mean when she says, "The phrase 'honest businessman' will truly be an oxymoron" (par. 10)? What is an *oxymoron*?
3. Use a dictionary if necessary to help you define any of the following words: decrements (par. 1); apathetic (3); hypothesis (5); integrity (6); altruism, rationalize (7); replenished (10).

Suggestions for Writing

1. **FROM JOURNAL TO ESSAY.** Based on your journal entry (previous page), write an essay in which you analyze the problem of student cheating at your school. Who does it? Why? What do others think about it? What does the school do about it? If cheating is uncommon at your school, analyze why.
2. Wenke refers to the intense pressure students are under today to get good grades as well as to participate in sports and other extracurricular activities. Besides cheating, what are some other consequences of the pressure faced by contemporary students—including positive consequences, if you think there are any? Drawing on your own experiences as well as the experiences of people you know, write an essay about what happens to students when they feel they are under pressure to excel.
3. **CRITICAL WRITING.** In an essay, EVALUATE Wenke's argument. How well does she convince you of the extent of the problem of student cheating and of its causes? How well do you think she develops her proposed solutions?
4. **CONNECTIONS.** In "The Ways We Lie" (p. 389), Stephanie Ericsson categorizes the kinds of lies people tell in everyday life. In what sense is cheating a form of lying? Which of Ericsson's categories might it belong to? On the scale of lying, how bad is cheating? Are cheaters likely to lie in other ways as well?

ADDITIONAL WRITING TOPICS

Argument and Persuasion

1. Write a persuasive essay in which you express a deeply felt opinion. In it, address a particular person or audience. For instance, you might direct your essay

   To a friend unwilling to attend a ballet performance (or a wrestling match) with you on the grounds that such an event is a waste of time

   To a teacher who asserts that more term papers, and longer ones, are necessary for students to master academic writing

   To a state trooper who intends to give you a ticket for speeding

   To a male employer skeptical of hiring women

   To a developer who plans to tear down a historic house

   To someone who sees no purpose in studying a foreign language

   To a high-school class whose members don't want to go to college

   To an older generation skeptical of the value of "all that noise" (meaning current popular music)

   To an atheist who asserts that religion just distracts us from the here and now

   To the members of a library board who want to ban a certain book

2. Write a letter to your campus newspaper, or to a city newspaper, in which you argue for or against a certain cause or view. You may wish to object to a particular feature, column, or editorial in the paper. Send your letter and see if it is published.

3. Write a short letter to your congressional or state representative, arguing in favor of (or against) the passage of some pending legislation. See a news magazine or a newspaper for a worthwhile bill to write about. Or else write in favor of some continuing cause: for instance, requiring (or not requiring) cars to reduce exhaust emissions, reducing (or increasing) military spending, providing (or reducing) aid to the arts, expanding (or reducing) government loans to college students.

4. Write an essay arguing that something you feel strongly about should be changed, removed, abolished, enforced, repeated, revised, reinstated, or reconsidered. Be sure to propose some plan for carrying out whatever suggestions you make. Possible topics, listed to start you thinking, are these:

   Gun laws
   Low-income housing
   Graduation requirements
   The mandatory retirement age
   ROTC programs in schools and colleges
   Movie ratings (G, PG, PG-13, R, NC-17, X)
   School prayer
   Fraternities and sororities
   Dress codes in primary and secondary schools
   TV advertising

5. On the model of Maire Flynn's three-part condensed argument on pages 505–06, write a condensed argument in three paragraphs demonstrating data, claim, and warrant. For a topic, consider any of the preceding ideas or any problem or controversy in this morning's newspaper.

PART THREE

MIXING THE METHODS

Everywhere in this book, we have tried to prove how flexible the methods of development are. All the preceding essays offer superb examples of DESCRIPTION or CLASSIFICATION or DEFINITION or ARGUMENT, but every one also illustrates other methods, too—description in PROCESS ANALYSIS, ANALYSIS and NARRATION in COMPARISON, EXAMPLES and CAUSE AND EFFECT in argument.

In this part of the book, we take this point even further by abandoning the individual methods. Instead, we offer a collection of fourteen essays and one poem, many of them considered classics, all of them by well-known writers. The selections range widely in their subjects and approaches, but they share a significant feature: All the authors draw on whatever methods of development, at whatever length, will help them achieve their PURPOSES with readers. (To show how the writers combine methods, we have highlighted the most significant ones in the note preceding each essay.)

You have already begun to command the methods by focusing on them individually, making each a part of your kit of writing tools. Now, when you face a writing assignment, you can consider whether and how each method may help you sharpen your focus, develop your ideas, and achieve your aim. Indeed, as we noted in Chapter 2, one way to approach a subject is to apply each method to it, one by one. The following list distills the discussion on pages 37–38 to a set of questions that you can ask about any subject:

1. *Narration:* Can you tell a story about the subject?
2. *Description:* Can you use your senses to illuminate the subject?
3. *Example:* Can you point to instances that will make the subject concrete and specific?
4. *Comparison and contrast:* Will setting the subject alongside another generate useful information?
5. *Process analysis:* Will a step-by-step explanation of how the subject works add to the reader's understanding?
6. *Division or analysis:* Can slicing the subject into its parts produce a clearer vision of it?
7. *Classification:* Is it worthwhile to sort the subject into kinds or groups?
8. *Cause and effect:* Does it add to the subject to ask why it happened or what its results are?
9. *Definition:* Can you trace a boundary that will clarify the meaning of the subject?
10. *Argument and persuasion:* Can you state an opinion or make a proposal about the subject?

Rarely will every one of these questions produce fruit for a given essay, but inevitably two or three or four will. Try the whole list when you're stuck at the beginning of an assignment or when you're snagged in the middle of a draft. You'll find the questions are as good at removing obstacles as they are at generating ideas.

SANDRA CISNEROS

Born in 1954 in Chicago, SANDRA CISNEROS attended Loyola University, where she received a BA in 1976. Two years later, she earned an MFA from the University of Iowa Writers' Workshop. While at Iowa, she embraced her Chicano heritage in her writing, turning to her childhood for inspiration. Most of her published work deals explicitly with issues of ethnic heritage, poverty, and personal identity. She is the author of two short-story collections—*The House on Mango Street* (1984) and *Woman Hollering Creek* (1991)—and several books of poems, including *My Wicked, Wicked Ways* (1987). Cisneros has received numerous awards, including two from the National Endowment for the Arts and the Lannan Foundation Literary Award. In 1995 she was named a MacArthur fellow.

Only Daughter

How could a man who had little interest in reading, whose only ambition for his daughter was marriage, prove to be the main reason that daughter became a writer? In this essay from a 1990 *Glamour* magazine, Cisneros explains.

"Only Daughter" mixes several methods of development to show the difficult yet fruitful bond between daughter and father:

Narration (Chap. 4): paragraphs 9–12, 15–22
Description (Chap. 5): paragraphs 7, 13, 16–21
Cause and effect (Chap. 11): paragraphs 3, 5, 7, 8
Definition (Chap. 12): paragraphs 1–2

Once, several years ago, when I was just starting out my writing career, 1
I was asked to write my own contributor's note for an anthology I was part of. I wrote: "I am the only daughter in a family of six sons. *That* explains everything."

Well, I've thought about that ever since, and yes, it explains a lot to me, 2
but for the reader's sake I should have written: "I am the only daughter in a *Mexican* family of six sons." Or even: "I am the only daughter of a Mexican father and a Mexican-American mother." Or: "I am the only daughter of a working-class family of nine." All of these had everything to do with who I am today.

I was/am the only daughter and *only* a daughter. Being an only daughter in 3
a family of six sons forced me by circumstance to spend a lot of time by myself because my brothers felt it beneath them to play with a *girl* in public. But that aloneness, that loneliness, was good for a would-be writer—it allowed me time to think and think, to imagine, to read and prepare myself.

Being only a daughter for my father meant my destiny would lead me to become someone's wife. That's what he believed. But when I was in fifth grade and shared my plans for college with him, I was sure he understood. I remember my father saying, *"Que bueno, mi'ja,* that's good." That meant a lot to me, especially since my brothers thought the idea hilarious. What I didn't realize was that my father thought college was good for girls—for finding a husband. After four years in college and two more in graduate school, and still no husband, my father shakes his head even now and says I wasted all that education. 4

In retrospect, I'm lucky my father believed daughters were meant for husbands. It meant it didn't matter if I majored in something silly like English. After all, I'd find a nice professional eventually, right? This allowed me the liberty to putter about embroidering my little poems and stories without my father interrupting with so much as a "What's that you're writing?" 5

But the truth is, I wanted him to interrupt. I wanted my father to understand what it was I was scribbling, to introduce me as "My only daughter, the writer." Not as "This is my only daughter. She teaches." *El maestra*—teacher. Not even *profesora.* 6

In a sense, everything I have ever written has been for him, to win his approval even though I know my father can't read English words, even though my father's only reading includes the brown-ink *Esto* sports magazines from Mexico City and the bloody *¡Alarma!* magazines that feature yet another sighting of *La Virgen de Guadalupe* on a tortilla or a wife's revenge on her philandering husband by bashing his skull in with a *molcajete* (a kitchen mortar made of volcanic rock). Or the *fotonovelas,* the little picture paperbacks with tragedy and trauma erupting from the characters' mouths in bubbles. 7

My father represents, then, the public majority. A public who is uninterested in reading, and yet one whom I am writing about and for, and privately trying to woo. 8

When we were growing up in Chicago, we moved a lot because of my father. He suffered periodic bouts of nostalgia. Then we'd have to let go our flat, store the furniture with mother's relatives, load the station wagon with baggage and bologna sandwiches, and head south. To Mexico City. 9

We came back, of course. To yet another Chicago flat, another Chicago neighborhood, another Catholic school. Each time, my father would seek out the parish priest in order to get a tuition break, and complain or boast: "I have seven sons." 10

He meant *siete hijos,* seven children, but he translated it as "sons." "I have seven sons." To anyone who would listen. The Sears Roebuck employee who sold us the washing machine. The short-order cook where my father ate his ham-and-eggs breakfasts. "I have seven sons." As if he deserved a medal from the state. 11

My papa. He didn't mean anything by that mistranslation, I'm sure. But   12
somehow I could feel myself being erased. I'd tug my father's sleeve and whisper: "Not seven sons. Six! and *one daughter*."

When my oldest brother graduated from medical school, he fulfilled my   13
father's dream that we study hard and use this—our heads, instead of this—
our hands. Even now my father's hands are thick and yellow, stubbed by a history of hammer and nails and twine and coils and springs. "Use this," my
father said, tapping his head, "and not this," showing us those hands. He
always looked tired when he said it.

Wasn't college an investment? And hadn't I spent all those years in col-   14
lege? And if I didn't marry, what was it all for? Why would anyone go to college
and then choose to be poor? Especially someone who had always been poor.

Last year, after ten years of writing professionally, the financial rewards   15
started to trickle in. My second National Endowment for the Arts Fellowship.
A guest professorship at the University of California, Berkeley. My book,
which sold to a major New York publishing house.

At Christmas, I flew home to Chicago. The house was throbbing, same as   16
always; hot *tamales* and sweet *tamales* hissing in my mother's pressure cooker,
and everybody—mother, six brothers, wives, babies, aunts, cousins—talking
too loud and at the same time, like in a Fellini[1] film, because that's just how
we are.

I went upstairs to my father's room. One of my stories had just been trans-   17
lated into Spanish and published in an anthology of Chicano writing, and I
wanted to show it to him. Ever since he recovered from a stroke two years ago,
my father likes to spend his leisure hours horizontally. And that's how I found
him, watching a Pedro Infante movie on Galavision and eating rice pudding.

There was a glass filmed with milk on the bedside table. There were sev-   18
eral vials of pills and balled Kleenex. And on the floor, one black sock and a
plastic urinal that I didn't want to look at but looked at anyway. Pedro Infante
was about to burst into song, and my father was laughing.

I'm not sure if it was because my story was translated into Spanish, or   19
because it was published in Mexico, or perhaps because the story dealt with
Tepeyac, the *colonia* my father was raised in, but at any rate, my father
punched the mute button on his remote control and read my story.

I sat on the bed next to my father and waited. He read it very slowly. As if   20
he were reading each line over and over. He laughed at all the right places and
read lines he liked out loud. He pointed and asked questions: "Is this So-and-
so?" "Yes," I said. He kept reading.

[1] Federico Fellini (1920–93), an Italian, directed *La Strada*, *La Dolce Vita*, *Satyricon*, and
other movies. —EDS.

When he was finally finished, after what seemed like hours, my father   21
looked up and asked: "Where can we get more copies of this for the relatives?"

Of all the wonderful things that happened to me last year, that was the   22
most wonderful.

Journal Writing

Cisneros's father thinks of success primarily in terms of financial rewards. Do you
agree? In your journal, consider the meaning of *success*, focusing on these questions:
Whom in your own life do you consider to be successful, and why? Where do your
ideas of success come from—your parents? your friends? your schooling? the media?
(To take your journal writing further, see "From Journal to Essay" on the next page.)

Questions on Meaning

1. What do you take to be Cisneros's main PURPOSE in this essay?
2. Cisneros writes, "I am the only daughter in a family of six sons. *That* explains
   everything" (par. 1). What does it explain in this essay?
3. What are some of the parallels Cisneros draws between her father and "the public majority" (par. 8)?
4. Why do you think her father's appreciation of her story was, for Cisneros, "the
   most wonderful" thing that happened to her in a year that was already good?

Questions on Writing Strategy

1. Does Cisneros seem to be writing mainly for other Mexican Americans or for a
   wider AUDIENCE? Cite passages from the essay to support your answer.
2. What can you INFER about Cisneros's stories and poems from the information
   about her education (par. 4), the details about her father's reading (7–8), and the
   list of her successes (15)?
3. **MIXED METHODS.** Cisneros's INTRODUCTION (pars. 1–2) gives a DEFINITION of the
   author. How effective is this introduction for setting up the essay that follows?
4. **MIXED METHODS.** Perhaps a third of Cisneros's essay is devoted to a NARRATIVE
   and DESCRIPTION of a Christmas visit home (pars. 16–22). Why do you think Cisneros relates this incident in so much detail? What do we gain from knowing
   what was cooking, what her father was watching on TV, or what questions he
   asked as he read Cisneros's story?

Questions on Language

1. What are the contrasting ideas in Cisneros's paired phrases "the only daughter
   and *only* a daughter" (par. 3)?

2. How do Cisneros's words convey her feeling about her father's translation of *siete hijos* as "seven sons" (pars. 11–12)?
3. Consult a dictionary if you need help in defining the following: retrospect, putter (par. 5); philandering, mortar (7); woo (8).

Suggestions for Writing

1. **FROM JOURNAL TO ESSAY.** Write an extended definition of *success* that also examines the sources of your definition, as you explored them in your journal (previous page). (The sources could be negative as well as positive — that is, your own ideas may have formed in reaction *against* others' ideas as well as in agreement *with* them.) Be sure your essay has a clear THESIS and plenty of EXAMPLES to make your definition precise.
2. Cisneros writes of differences from her father that frustrated her but that also motivated her to achieve. In a narrative and descriptive essay, relate some aspect of a relationship with a parent or other figure of authority that you found troubling or even maddening at the time but that now seems to have shaped you in positive ways. Did a parent (or someone else) push you to study when you wanted to play sports or hang out with your friends? make you attend religious services when they seemed unimportant? refuse to acknowledge accomplishments you were proud of? try to direct you onto a path you didn't care to take?
3. **CRITICAL WRITING.** Cisneros attributes many of her father's attitudes to his Mexican heritage. As an extension of the previous assignment, consider whether Cisneros's experiences are particular to Mexican American families or are common in all families, whatever their ethnicity. Are conflicts between children and their parents inevitable, do you think? Why, or why not?
4. **CONNECTIONS.** Both Cisneros's "Only Daughter" and John McPhee's "Silk Parachute" (p. 623) examine a relationship with a parent. How are the two authors' parents different? How are the authors' feelings about their parents similar and different? Write an essay of COMPARISON AND CONTRAST that quotes or PARAPHRASES passages from both essays as EVIDENCE.
5. **CONNECTIONS.** Several authors in this book recall interaction with a parent and use dialogue to make the interaction vivid. Examples include M. F. K. Fisher's "The Broken Chain" (p. 13), Amy Tan's "Fish Cheeks" (p. 92), Brad Manning's "Arm Wrestling with My Father" (p. 136), Sarah Vowell's "Shooting Dad" (p. 144), and John McPhee's "Silk Parachute" (p. 623). Try your hand at using dialogue in a brief narrative that recalls a significant incident between yourself and a parent. Then write briefly about your experience using dialogue: How easy or difficult was it to remember who said what? How easy or difficult was it to make the speakers sound like themselves?

Sandra Cisneros on Writing

A bilingual author, Sandra Cisneros writes primarily in English. Yet Spanish influences her English sentences, and she frequently uses Spanish words in her prose. She spoke with Feroza Jussawalla and Reed Way Dasenbrock about how Spanish affects her writing:

"What it does is change the rhythm of my writing. I think that incorporating the Spanish, for me, allows me to create new expressions in English— to say things that have never been said before. And I get to do that by translating literally. I love calling stories by Spanish expressions. I have this story called 'Salvador, Late or Early.' It's a nice title. It means 'sooner or later,' *tarde o temprano,* which literally translates as 'late or early.' All of a sudden something happens to the English, something really new is happening, a new spice is added to the English language."

In some of her work, Cisneros uses Spanish and then offers a translation for English readers. At other times, she thinks complete translation is unnecessary: "See, sometimes, you don't have to say the whole thing. Now I'm learning how you can say something in English so that you know the person is saying it in Spanish. I like that. You can say a phrase in Spanish, and you can choose not to translate it, but you can make it understood through the context. 'And then my *abuelita* called me a *sin verguenza* and cried because I am without shame,' you see? Just in the sentence you can weave it in. To me it's really fun to be doing that; to me it's like I've uncovered this whole motherlode that I haven't tapped into. All the *expresiones* in Spanish when translated make English wonderful."

That said, Cisneros believes that "[t]he readers who are going to like my stories the best and catch all the subtexts and all the subtleties, that even my editor can't catch, are Chicanas. When there are Chicanas in the audience, and they laugh, they are laughing at stuff that we talk about among ourselves. And there's no way that my editor at Random House is ever going to get those jokes." This seems particularly true, she finds, when she's making use of Mexican and Southwestern myths and legends about which the general public might not be aware. "That's why I say the real ones who are going to get it are the Latinos, the Chicanos. They're going to get it in that they're going to understand the myth and how I've revised it. When I talked to someone at *Interview* magazine, I had to explain to him what I was doing with *la llorona,* *La Malinche,* and the Virgin of Guadalupe in the story ['Woman Hollering Creek']. But he said, 'Hey, I didn't know that, but I still got the story.' You can get it at some other level. He reminded me, 'Sandra, if you're from Ireland, you're going to get a lot more out of Joyce than if you're not, but just because you're not Irish doesn't mean you're not going to get it at another level.'"

For Discussion

1. In the passages quoted here, Sandra Cisneros is talking about her fiction writing. Do her thoughts about Spanish apply to the kind of English she uses when she writes a nonfiction piece like "Only Daughter"?
2. In "Only Daughter," Sandra Cisneros writes of her father: "In a sense, everything I have ever written has been for him, to win his approval, even though I know my father can't read English words [. . .]." How does this square with her claim that Chicana readers are her best readers?
3. Who is the reader who would best understand your essays?

JUDITH ORTIZ COFER

A native of Puerto Rico who has lived most of her life in the United States, JUDITH ORTIZ COFER writes poetry, fiction, and essays about her heritage and the balancing of two cultures. Born in Hormigueros, Puerto Rico, in 1952, she earned a BA from Augusta College in 1974 and an MA from Florida Atlantic University in 1977. Cofer started out as a bilingual teacher in the schools of Palm Beach County, Florida, and she is now a professor of English and creative writing at the University of Georgia. Her publications include collections of poetry, among them *Peregrina* (1986) and *Terms of Survival* (1987); a novel, *The Line of the Sun* (1989); two books of essays, *Silent Dancing* (1990) and *Woman in Front of the Sun* (2000); a book of stories for young people, *An Island Like You: Stories of the Barrio* (1995); and a collection of stories and poems, *The Year of Our Revolution* (1998). As a native Spanish speaker who challenged herself to learn English, she is always experimenting, she says, with "the 'infinite variety' and power of language."

Silent Dancing

Cofer immigrated to New Jersey from Puerto Rico when she was three years old. In this much-reprinted essay, she links views of old home movies and bits of dreams with her adult recollections to describe her family's and her own immigrant experience. The essay first appeared in *The Georgia Review* and then as the title essay in Cofer's collection *Silent Dancing*.

As a reminiscence, "Silent Dancing" relies much on narration and description and on other methods as well.

Narration (Chap. 4): paragraphs 2–4, 14–15, 18, 20, 27–29
Description (Chap. 5): paragraphs 1, 3–4, 10–13, 16–17, 20–24, 30, 32
Example (Chap. 6): paragraphs 4, 6–8, 13–15, 18, 21–23
Comparison and contrast (Chap. 7): paragraphs 4, 12–13, 19, 25–26, 31
Cause and effect (Chap. 11): paragraphs 5, 29
Definition (Chap. 12): paragraphs 25, 26

We have a home movie of this party. Several times my mother and I have watched 1
it together, and I have asked questions about the silent revelers coming in and out of focus. It is grainy and of short duration, but it's a great visual aid to my memory of life at that time. And it is in color—the only complete scene in color I can recall from those years.

We lived in Puerto Rico until my brother was born in 1954. Soon after, 2 because of economic pressures on our growing family, my father joined the United States Navy. He was assigned to duty on a ship in Brooklyn Yard—

a place of cement and steel that was to be his home base in the States until his retirement more than twenty years later. He left the Island first, alone, going to New York City and tracking down his uncle who lived with his family across the Hudson River in Paterson, New Jersey. There my father found a tiny apartment in a huge tenement that had once housed Jewish families but was just being taken over and transformed by Puerto Ricans, overflowing from New York City. In 1955 he sent for us. My mother was only twenty years old, I was not quite three, and my brother was a toddler when we arrived at El Building, as the place had been christened by its newest residents.

My memories of life in Paterson during those first few years are all in   3
shades of gray. Maybe I was too young to absorb vivid colors and details, or to discriminate between the slate blue of the winter sky and the darker hues of the snow-bearing clouds, but that single color washes over the whole period. The building we lived in was gray, as were the streets, filled with slush the first few months of my life there. The coat my father had bought for me was similar in color and too big; it sat heavily on my thin frame.

I do remember the way the heater pipes banged and rattled, startling all of   4
us out of sleep until we got so used to the sound that we automatically shut it out or raised our voices above the racket. The hiss from the valve punctuated my sleep (which has always been fitful) like a nonhuman presence in the room — a dragon sleeping at the entrance of my childhood. But the pipes were also a connection to all the other lives being lived around us. Having come from a house designed for a single family back in Puerto Rico — my mother's extended-family home — it was curious to know that strangers lived under our floor and above our heads, and that the heater pipe went through everyone's apartment. (My first spanking in Paterson came as a result of playing tunes on the pipes in my room to see if there would be an answer.) My mother was as new to this concept of beehive life as I was, but she had been given strict orders by my father to keep the doors locked, the noise down, ourselves to ourselves.

It seems that Father had learned some painful lessons about prejudice   5
while searching for an apartment in Paterson. Not until years later did I hear how much resistance he had encountered with landlords who were panicking at the influx of Latinos into a neighborhood that had been Jewish for a couple of generations. It made no difference that it was the American phenomenon of ethnic turnover which was changing the urban core of Paterson, and that the human flood could not be held back with an accusing finger.

"You Cuban?" one man had asked my father, pointing at his name tag on   6
the navy uniform — even though my father had the fair skin and light brown hair of his northern Spanish background, and the name Ortiz is as common in Puerto Rico as Johnson is in the United States.

"No," my father had answered, looking past the finger into his adversary's   7
angry eyes. "I'm Puerto Rican."

"Same shit." And the door closed.   8

My father could have passed as European, but we couldn't. My brother and I   9
both have our mother's black hair and olive skin, and so we lived in El Building
and visited our great-uncle and his fair children on the next block. It was their
private joke that they were the German branch of the family. Not many years
later that area too would be mainly Puerto Rican. It was as if the heart of the
city map were being gradually colored brown—*café con leche*[1] brown. Our color.

The movie opens with a sweep of the living room. It is "typical" immigrant   10
Puerto Rican decor for the time: The sofa and chairs are square and hard-looking,
upholstered in bright colors (blue and yellow in this instance) and covered with the
transparent plastic that furniture salesmen then were so adept at convincing women
to buy. The linoleum on the floor is light blue; where it had been subjected to spike
heels, as it was in most places, there were dime-size indentations all over it that can-
not be seen in this movie. The room is full of people dressed up: dark suits for the
men, red dresses for the women. When I have asked my mother why most of the
women are in red that night, she has shrugged and said, "I don't remember. Just a
coincidence." She doesn't have my obsession for assigning symbolism to everything.

The three women in red sitting on the couch are my mother, my eighteen-year-   11
old cousin, and her brother's girlfriend. The novia[2] *is just up from the Island, which*
is apparent in her body language. She sits up formally, her dress pulled over her
knees. She is a pretty girl, but her posture makes her look insecure, lost in her full-
skirted dress, which she has carefully tucked around her to make room for my gor-
geous cousin, her future sister-in-law. My cousin has grown up in Paterson and is in
her last year of high school. She doesn't have a trace of what Puerto Ricans call la
mancha (literally, the stain: the mark of the new immigrant—something about the
posture, the voice, or the humble demeanor that makes it obvious to everyone the
person has just arrived on the mainland). My cousin is wearing a tight, sequined,
cocktail dress. Her brown hair has been lightened with peroxide around the bangs,
and she is holding a cigarette expertly between her fingers, bringing it up to her mouth
in a sensuous arc of her arm as she talks animatedly. My mother, who has come up
to sit between the two women, both only a few years younger than herself, is some-
where between the poles they represent in our culture.

It became my father's obsession to get out of the barrio, and thus we were   12
never permitted to form bonds with the place or with the people who lived

---

[1] Spanish for "coffee with milk."—EDS.

[2] Fiancée, or a girl just arrived from Puerto Rico.—EDS.

there. Yet El Building was a comfort to my mother, who never got over yearning for *la isla*.[3] She felt surrounded by her language: The walls were thin, and voices speaking and arguing in Spanish could be heard all day. *Salsas* blasted out of radios, turned on early in the morning and left on for company. Women seemed to cook rice and beans perpetually—the strong aroma of boiling red kidney beans permeated the hallways.

Though Father preferred that we do our grocery shopping at the super-   13
market when he came home on weekend leaves, my mother insisted that she could cook only with products whose labels she could read. Consequently, during the week I accompanied her and my little brother to La Bodega—a hole-in-the-wall grocery store across the street from El Building. There we squeezed down three narrow aisles jammed with various products. Goya and Libby's—those were the trademarks that were trusted by her *mamá*, so my mother bought many cans of Goya beans, soups, and condiments, as well as little cans of Libby's fruit juices for us. And she also bought Colgate toothpaste and Palmolive soap. (The final *e* is pronounced in both these products in Spanish, so for many years I believed that they were manufactured on the Island. I remember my surprise at first hearing a commercial on television in which "Colgate" rhymed with "ate.") We always lingered at La Bodega, for it was there that Mother breathed best, taking in the familiar aromas of the foods she knew from Mamá's kitchen. It was also there that she got to speak to the other women of El Building without violating outright Father's dictates against fraternizing with our neighbors.

Yet Father did his best to make our "assimilation" painless. I can still see   14
him carrying a real Christmas tree up several flights of stairs to our apartment, leaving a trail of aromatic pine. He carried it formally, as if it were a flag in a parade. We were the only ones in El Building that I knew of who got presents on both Christmas and *día de Reyes*, the day when the Three Kings brought gifts to Christ and to Hispanic children.

Our supreme luxury in El Building was having our own television set. It   15
must have been a result of Father's guilt feelings over the isolation he had imposed on us, but we were among the first in the barrio to have one. My brother quickly became an avid watcher of Captain Kangaroo and Jungle Jim, while I loved all the series showing families. By the time I started first grade, I could have drawn a map of Middle America as exemplified by the lives of characters in *Father Knows Best*, *The Donna Reed Show*, *Leave It to Beaver*, *My Three Sons*, and (my favorite) *Bachelor Father*, where John Forsythe treated his adopted teenage daughter like a princess because he was rich and had a Chinese houseboy to do everything for him. In truth, compared to our neighbors

---

[3] The island. —EDS.

in El Building, *we* were rich. My father's navy check provided us with financial security and a standard of living that the factory workers envied. The only thing his money could not buy us was a place to live away from the barrio—his greatest wish, Mother's greatest fear.

In the home movie the men are shown next, sitting around a card table set up in 16
one corner of the living room, playing dominoes. The clack of the ivory pieces was a familiar sound. I heard it in many houses on the Island and in many apartments in Paterson. In Leave It to Beaver, *the Cleavers played bridge in every other episode; in my childhood, the men started every social occasion with a hotly debated round of dominoes. The women would sit around and watch, but they never participated in the games.*

Here and there you can see a small child. Children were always brought to par- 17
ties and, whenever they got sleepy, were put to bed in the host's bedroom. Babysitting was a concept unrecognized by the Puerto Rican women I knew: A responsible mother did not leave her children with any stranger. And in a culture where children are not considered intrusive, there was no need to leave the children at home. We went where our mother went.

Of my preschool years I have only impressions: the sharp bite of the wind 18
in December as we walked with our parents toward the brightly lit stores downtown; how I felt like a stuffed doll in my heavy coat, boots, and mittens; how good it was to walk into the five-and-dime and sit at the counter drinking hot chocolate. On Saturdays our whole family would walk downtown to shop at the big department stores on Broadway. Mother bought all our clothes at Penney's and Sears, and she liked to buy her dresses at the women's specialty shops like Lerner's and Diana's. At some point we'd go into Woolworth's and sit at the soda fountain to eat.

We never ran into other Latinos at these stores or when eating out, and it 19
became clear to me only years later that the women from El Building shopped mainly in other places—stores owned by other Puerto Ricans or by Jewish merchants who had philosophically accepted our presence in the city and decided to make us their good customers, if not real neighbors and friends. These establishments were located not downtown but in the blocks around our street, and they were referred to generically as La Tienda, El Bazar, La Bodega, La Botánica. Everyone knew what was meant. These were the stores where your face did not turn a clerk to stone, where your money was as green as anyone else's.

One New Year's Eve we were dressed up like child models in the Sears cat- 20
alogue: my brother in a miniature man's suit and bow tie, and I in black

patent-leather shoes and a frilly dress with several layers of crinoline under-neath. My mother wore a bright red dress that night, I remember, and spike heels; her long black hair hung to her waist. Father, who usually wore his navy uniform during his short visits home, had put on a dark civilian suit for the occasion: We had been invited to his uncle's house for a big celebration. Everyone was excited because my mother's brother—Hernan—a bachelor who could indulge himself with luxuries—had bought a home movie camera, which he would be trying out that night.

Even the home movie cannot fill in the sensory details such a gathering   21
left imprinted in a child's brain. The thick sweetness of women's perfumes mixing with the ever-present smells of food cooking in the kitchen: meat and plantain *pasteles,* as well as the ubiquitous rice dish made special with pigeon peas—*gandules*—and seasoned with precious *sofrito* sent up from the Island by somebody's mother or smuggled in by a recent traveler. *Sofrito* was one of the items that women hoarded, since it was hardly ever in stock at La Bodega. It was the flavor of Puerto Rico.

The men drank Palo Viejo rum, and some of the younger ones got weepy.   22
The first time I saw a grown man cry was at a New Year's Eve party: He had been reminded of his mother by the smells in the kitchen. But what I remem-ber most were the boiled *pasteles,* plantain or yucca rectangles stuffed with corned beef or other meats, olives, and many other savory ingredients, all wrapped in banana leaves. Everybody had to fish one out with a fork. There was always a "trick" *pastel*—one without stuffing—and whoever got that one was the "New Year's Fool."

There was also the music. Long-playing albums were treated like precious   23
china in these homes. Mexican recordings were popular, but the songs that brought tears to my mother's eyes were sung by the melancholy Daniel Santos, whose life as a drug addict was the stuff of legend. Felipe Rodríguez was a par-ticular favorite of couples, since he sang about faithless women and broken-hearted men. There is a snatch of one lyric that has stuck in my mind like a needle on a worn groove: *De piedra ha de ser mi cama, de piedra la cabezera . . . la mujer que a mi me quiera . . . ha de quererme de veras. Ay, Ay, Ay, corazón, porque no amas . . .* I must have heard it a thousand times since the idea of a bed made of stone, and its connection to love, first troubled me with its dis-turbing images.

The five-minute home movie ends with people dancing in a circle—the   24
creative filmmaker must have set it up, so that all of them could file past him. It is both comical and sad to watch silent dancing. Since there is no justifica-tion for the absurd movements that music provides for some of us, people appear frantic, their faces embarrassingly intense. It's as if you were watching

sex. Yet for years, I've had dreams in the form of this home movie. In a recurring scene, familiar faces push themselves forward into my mind's eye, plastering their features into distorted close-ups. And I'm asking them: "Who is *she*? Who is the old woman I don't recognize? Is she an aunt? Somebody's wife? Tell me who she is."

"See the beauty mark on her cheek as big as a hill on the lunar landscape of her face—well, that runs in the family. The women on your father's side of the family wrinkle early; it's the price they pay for that fair skin. The young girl with the green stain on her wedding dress is *la novia*—just up from the Island. See, she lowers her eyes when she approaches the camera, as she's supposed to. Decent girls never look at you directly in the face. *Humilde*, humble, a girl should express humility in all her actions. She will make a good wife for your cousin. He should consider himself lucky to have met her only weeks after she arrived here. If he marries her quickly, she will make him a good Puerto Rican–style wife; but if he waits too long, she will be corrupted by the city, just like your cousin there." 25

"She means me. I do what I want. This is not some primitive island I live on. Do they expect me to wear a black mantilla on my head and go to mass every day? Not me. I'm an American woman, and I will do as I please. I can type faster than anyone in my senior class at Central High, and I'm going to be a secretary to a lawyer when I graduate. I can pass for an American girl anywhere—I've tried it. At least for Italian, anyway—I never speak Spanish in public. I hate these parties, but I wanted the dress. I look better than any of these *humildes* here. My life is going to be different. I have an American boyfriend. He is older and has a car. My parents don't know it, but I sneak out of the house late at night sometimes to be with him. If I marry him, even my name will be American. I hate rice and beans—that's what makes these women fat." 26

"Your *prima*[4] is pregnant by that man she's been sneaking around with. Would I lie to you? I'm your *tía política*,[5] your great-uncle's common-law wife—the one he abandoned on the Island to go marry your cousin's mother. I was not invited to this party, of course, but I came anyway. I came to tell you that story about your cousin that you've always wanted to hear. Do you remember the comment your mother made to a neighbor that has always haunted you? The only thing you heard was your cousin's name, and then you saw your mother pick up your doll from the couch and say: 'It was as big as this doll when they flushed it down the toilet.' This image has bothered you for years, hasn't it? You had nightmares about babies being flushed down the toilet, and you wondered why anyone would do such a horrible thing. You didn't dare ask your mother about it. She would only tell you that you 27

[4] Cousin.—EDS.
[5] Aunt-in-law.—EDS.

had not heard her right, and yell at you for listening to adult conversations. But later, when you were old enough to know about abortions, you suspected.

"I am here to tell you that you were right. Your cousin was growing an *americanito* in her belly when this movie was made. Soon after, she put something long and pointy into her pretty self, thinking maybe she could get rid of the problem before breakfast and still make it to her first class at the high school. Well, *niña*,[6] her screams could be heard downtown. Your aunt, her *mamá*, who had been a midwife on the Island, managed to pull the little thing out. Yes, they probably flushed it down the toilet. What else could they do with it—give it a Christian burial in a little white casket with blue bows and ribbons? Nobody wanted that baby—least of all the father, a teacher at her school with a house in West Paterson that he was filling with real children, and a wife who was a natural blonde.   28

"Girl, the scandal sent your uncle back to the bottle. And guess where your cousin ended up? Irony of ironies. She was sent to a village in Puerto Rico to live with a relative on her mother's side: a place so far away from civilization that you have to ride a mule to reach it. A real change in scenery. She found a man there—women like that cannot live without male company—but believe me, the men in Puerto Rico know how to put a saddle on a woman like her. *La gringa*,[7] they call her. Ha, ha, ha. *La gringa* is what she always wanted to be . . ."   29

The old woman's mouth becomes a cavernous black hole I fall into. And as I fall, I can feel the reverberations of her laughter. I hear the echoes of her last mocking words: *la gringa, la gringa!* And the conga line keeps moving silently past me. There is no music in my dream for the dancers.   30

When Odysseus visits Hades to see the spirit of his mother,[8] he makes an offering of sacrificial blood, but since all the souls crave an audience with the living, he has to listen to many of them before he can ask questions. I, too, have to hear the dead and the forgotten speak in my dream. Those who are still part of my life remain silent, going around and around in their dance. The others keep pressing their faces forward to say things about the past.   31

My father's uncle is last in line. He is dying of alcoholism, shrunken and shriveled like a monkey, his face a mass of wrinkles and broken arteries. As he comes closer I realize that in his features I can see my whole family. If you were to stretch that rubbery flesh, you could find my father's face, and deep within *that* face—my own. I don't want to look into those eyes ringed in purple. In a few years he will retreat into silence, and take a long, long time to die. *Move*   32

[6] Child. —EDS.
[7] Foreigner or outsider, especially a North American or Briton. —EDS.
[8] An episode in the *Odyssey*, usually attributed to Homer, who flourished in the ninth or eighth century BC. In Greek mythology, Hades rules the underworld. —EDS.

back, Tío, I tell him. I don't want to hear what you have to say. Give the dancers room to move. Soon it will be midnight. Who is the New Year's Fool this time?

Journal Writing

In paragraphs 24–33 Cofer describes a recurring dream she has had for years. Think of a dream you've had that stays with you for some reason. Write down as many details of the dream as you can. (To take your journal writing further, see "From Journal to Essay" on the next page.)

Questions on Meaning

1. What do you think is Cofer's PURPOSE in this essay? Does she have something specific she wants the reader to understand?
2. Of her father, Cofer writes, "The only thing his money could not buy us was a place to live away from the barrio—his greatest wish, Mother's greatest fear" (par. 15). Why was moving her father's greatest wish? Why did her mother fear it? What passages from the essay support your answer?
3. Are the quoted speeches in paragraphs 25–29 real or imagined? Use EVIDENCE from the essay to support your answer.

Questions on Writing Strategy

1. What are the contents of the passages in italics (pars. 1, 10–11, 16–17) and the ones in smaller type (25–29)? How do these passages work with those in regular type? What is their EFFECT?
2. How well does the observation in paragraph 24, "It is both comical and sad to watch silent dancing," convey the dominant impression of Cofer's essay? What, if anything, would you add to "comical and sad"?
3. What does the dialogue contribute to Cofer's TONE?
4. **MIXED METHODS.** What does Cofer's DESCRIPTION of Paterson and her childhood apartment (pars. 3–4) tell us about Cofer herself as a child?
5. **MIXED METHODS.** Paragraph 11 offers three EXAMPLES of Puerto Rican women: Cofer's mother, her assimilated cousin, and the cousin's brother's girlfriend. How do these three examples illustrate a cultural shift Puerto Rican immigrants were experiencing at the time the home movie was made?

Questions on Language

1. How might "silent dancing" serve as a metaphor for memory? (See *Figures of speech* in Useful Terms for a definition of *metaphor*.)
2. What larger meaning can we INFER from this sentence in paragraph 23: "Long-playing albums were treated like precious china in these homes"?

3. Consult a dictionary if you need help in defining the following words: influx (par. 5); adept (10); animatedly (11); barrio (12); assimilation (14); avid (15); plantain (22); mantilla (26).

Suggestions for Writing

1. **FROM JOURNAL TO ESSAY.** In an essay, describe the dream you wrote about in your journal (previous page), but also do more: Try to interpret the dream in the context of your life when you had it. What do you think it meant? Why did you have it when you did? What did it tell you?
2. Have you had the experience of being isolated from your surroundings, whether because of language or culture or because of some other barrier—being new in town, feeling friendless, or even just having to study when everyone else was having fun? Describe the experience in an essay, using plenty of details to help your readers understand your feelings.
3. **CRITICAL WRITING.** ANALYZE the different tones of Cofer herself, her cousin (par. 26), and her *tía política* (25, 27–29). How do their tones convey the different experiences and expectations of these three women?
4. **CONNECTIONS.** In "No Name Woman" (p. 609), Maxine Hong Kingston writes about an aunt who was disgraced after she became pregnant outside of marriage. COMPARE AND CONTRAST the family story in Kingston's essay with the one Cofer tells about her cousin in "Silent Dancing" (pars. 27–29). How are the two women and their fates similar, and how are they different? What do their stories suggest about their respective cultures?
5. **CONNECTIONS.** Several other writers in this book focus on the struggle to assimilate into mainstream American culture while maintaining one's ethnic ties: for example, Amy Tan in "Fish Cheeks" (p. 92), Sherman Alexie in "Indian Education" (p. 103), Jhumpa Lahiri in "Indian Takeout" (p. 153), and Richard Rodriguez in "Aria: A Memoir of a Bilingual Childhood" (p. 639). Based on "Silent Dancing" and one or more of these other essays, consider this aspect of the immigrant experience in the United States—the challenges of assimilation, the effects of prejudice, and the role of family ties and cultural loyalty.

Judith Ortiz Cofer on Writing

In the 1980s Cofer told *Contemporary Authors* why she so often chooses her family as her writing subject. She was speaking of her poetry, but the same could be said of her stories and essays as well. "My family is one of the main topics of my poetry," Cofer explained, "the ones left behind on the island of Puerto Rico, and the ones who came to the United States. In tracing their lives, I discover more about mine. The place of birth itself becomes a metaphor for the things we all must leave behind; the assimilation of a new culture is the coming into maturity by accepting the terms necessary for survival. My poetry is the study of this process of change, assimilation, and transformation."

For Discussion

1. What does Cofer mean when she says that "the assimilation of a new culture is the coming into maturity by accepting the terms necessary for survival"? Does this statement apply only to immigrants or to nonimmigrants as well? Why?
2. If you have ever written about your family or a relative, what did the experience tell you about your kin? What did it tell you about yourself?

C. DAY LEWIS

The poet laureate of Great Britain from 1968 until his death in 1972, CECIL DAY LEWIS was born in Ballintubber, Ireland, in 1904. After graduating from Oxford University, Day Lewis spent several years teaching before becoming an editor for the British Ministry of Information. He later returned to Oxford, where he was a professor of poetry from 1951 to 1956. Among Day Lewis's many volumes of poetry are *A Time to Dance* (1935), *Overtures to Death, and Other Poems* (1938), and *Poems in Wartime* (1940). Though best known as a poet, Day Lewis was a writer of diverse talents who published novels, children's books, collections of criticism, and translations of the Roman poet Virgil. Under the pseudonym Nicholas Blake, Day Lewis also wrote more than twenty detective novels.

The Expulsion: Masaccio

This poem, which appears in *The Complete Poems of C. Day Lewis,* examines *The Expulsion from the Garden of Eden* by the Italian painter Masaccio (1401–28?). Considered one of the greatest works of the Italian Renaissance, *The Expulsion* is a seven-foot-high fresco—that is, a painting made on damp plaster—in the Brancacci Chapel of Santa Maria del Carmine in Florence. The fresco was recently restored to remove centuries of grime and the leaves encircling the figures' bodies, which were not Masaccio's work but a much later addition. We reproduce the unrestored version here because it is the one Day Lewis wrote of. The restoration may be seen on the Web at *http:// gallery.euroweb.hu/tours/brancacc/expuls.html.*

Day Lewis's brief poem draws mainly on two methods: description (Chap. 5) in lines 1–11 and 20 and division or analysis (Chap. 9) throughout.

They stumble in naked grief, as refugees
From a flood or pogrom, dispossessed of all
But a spray of leaf like barbed wire round the loins.
For sight, she has mere sockets gouged and charred
By nightmare, and her mouth is a bottomless pit   5
Of desolation. Her lord, accomplice, dupe,
Ashamed of his failure, as if he cannot face it
Covers his eyes.
           We know they left behind
A place where fruits and animals were kind   10
And time no enemy. But did they know their loss
As more than a child's when its habitual toys

Are confiscated for some innocent fault,
Or take the accusing cosmic voice that called
To be the same as their dear old garden god's?   15
The sword that pickets paradise also goads
Towards self-knowledge. More they shall come to wish
Than brutal comfort of committed flesh.
Masaccio paints us both
A childish tragedy — hunched back, bawling mouth,   20
And the hour when the animal knew that it must die
And with that stroke put on humanity.

Journal Writing

Ignoring Day Lewis's poem for the moment, give Masaccio's fresco a close look and, in your journal, write down what you see. (To take your journal writing further, see "From Journal to Essay" on the facing page.)

Questions on Meaning

1. What do you take to be the main idea of Day Lewis's poem?
2. How does Day Lewis's likening of Adam and Eve to "refugees / From a flood or pogrom" (lines 1–2) affect your reading of the poem? (Be sure you know the meaning of *pogrom*.) What does this image — along with the idea of Adam and Eve mistaking "the accusing cosmic voice that called" with that of "their dear old garden god's" (lines 14–15) — suggest about how Day Lewis imagines a supreme being?
3. When Day Lewis writes "More they shall come to wish / Than brutal comfort of committed flesh" (lines 17–18), what do you think he means by "more"?

Questions on Writing Strategy

1. If you are familiar with the biblical story of the expulsion of Adam and Eve from the Garden of Eden, what important element of the story does Day Lewis omit? Why might he have done so?
2. **MIXED METHODS.** Why is DESCRIPTION important to this poem?
3. **MIXED METHODS.** What elements of *The Expulsion* does Day Lewis's ANALYSIS focus on especially? How do these elements contribute to the conclusion in lines 19–22?

Questions on Language

1. What is the EFFECT of Day Lewis's referring to Adam as Eve's "lord, accomplice, dupe" (line 6)?
2. In what sense does the word "us" in line 19 have a double meaning?
3. What is the meaning of "put on humanity" in the last line?
4. Consult a dictionary if you are unsure of the meanings of the following words: dispossessed (line 2); loins (3); gouged, charred (4); desolation (6); habitual (12); confiscated (13); pickets, goads (16).

Suggestions for Writing

1. **FROM JOURNAL TO ESSAY.** Working from your journal entry (facing page), write an essay in which you describe and interpret Masaccio's *Expulsion from the Garden of Eden*. You may but need not mention elements of the painting that Day Lewis covers in his poem.
2. Over the centuries many artists have depicted the expulsion from the Garden of Eden. Find examples of several such images through your library or via the Internet (for example, *http://cedar.evansville.edu/~ecoleweb/imagesA.html* provides links to such paintings and sculptures under the entry "Adam"). Choose one of these works, and write an essay in which you COMPARE AND CONTRAST it with Masaccio's fresco.
3. **CRITICAL WRITING.** Review your answers to the questions on meaning, writing strategy, and language. Then write an essay analyzing Day Lewis's poem. Be sure to express and support a clear THESIS.
4. **CONNECTIONS.** Read Joyce Carol Oates's "Edward Hopper's *Nighthawks*, 1942" (p. 165), another poem about a painting. In an essay, compare and contrast how Oates and Day Lewis use works of visual art as the basis for their poems. Focus particularly on each poet's use of description to support the poem's theme.
5. **CONNECTIONS.** How does the idea of death in Day Lewis's poem relate to the idea of death as Virginia Woolf presents it in the essay "The Death of the Moth" (p. 699)? In a brief essay, explore any connections you find between the two works.

C. Day Lewis on Writing

In "The Pattern of Images," an essay from his collection *The Poetic Image*, C. Day Lewis takes readers through the process of writing a poem. In these excerpts from the essay, he begins by comparing the task of a poet to that of a fisherman.

Let us imagine a fisherman sitting on an island, brooding in the fisherman's trance-like pose over his lines and the sea into which they disappear:

The lines are baited with something that has already come out of the sea, the *donnée*[1] of the poem, its initial mood or thought or image: from time to time the poet feels a thrill on one of his lines; something has taken the bait; delicately he plays it, hauling carefully in, for the fish in this sea are terribly elusive creatures; and when he gets it out, it may not be the one he wants, so — unless he is the kind of angler who is satisfied with anything that has fins — he throws it back again. Now there are certain points to be noticed about this picture. Clearly, the fisherman will not get a bite if there are no fish in the vicinity; and nothing he can do will compel the fish to take his bait. He must just wait patiently, hoping that he has the right sort of bait on his hooks. He cannot intervene until the thrill on the line tells him that something is ready to be brought up from the unconscious. And a thrill, of course, may only mean that he has hooked up some seaweed, tin-can or old boot lying, barely covered by the tide, on the shallow foreshore of consciousness. [. . .]

When the *donnée* of a poem comes, as more often than not it does, in the form of an image, the poet will interrogate this image, trying to discover what it means and whither it would lead him. It may be his first clue to the theme and shape of the as yet unwritten poem. During this process of interrogation, other images begin to associate themselves with the key one. It is at this stage that the poet's trickiest problem arises: On the one hand, he must keep an open mind for the inflowing images, because, if the flow stopped, the poem would run dry of material; on the other hand, as the poem begins to take shape, he must move gradually from the receptive to the critical attitude, in order that the image-pattern may come more and more under the control of his technique. [. . .]

How does one know which fish to keep and which to throw back? Sometimes the thrill of recognition is as unmistakable for the poet as it will be, later, for the reader. More commonly, an image is chosen without excitement, after much conscious deliberation, because it is seen to fit best a certain place in the pattern and lead on most energetically to the next development. Yet it cannot be said too often that a poet does not fully know what is the poem he is writing until he has written it. [. . .]

At any moment during the actual composition of a poem, a new image may come into the poet's mind, either spontaneously and as it might seem irrelevantly thrown up out of his memory, or having been deliberately sought after to serve the poem's meaning at this point and to extend the image-pattern: Meditating on this new image, the poet sees that it has in fact supplied him with something "even better than he knew how to desire," that through it there is revealed to him at last the meaning, not fully apprehended

[1] French, "fundamental idea" or "theme." — EDS.

before, of the poem he is writing. In the light of this discovery, the whole image-pattern must be reviewed and revised, and when this is done, it is as if the poem has given itself a shake and darted off in an altered direction knowing clearly now what it is aiming at.

For Discussion

1. How are writing and fishing similar, according to Day Lewis? Do you think this comparison holds true for other types of writing as well?
2. Explain Day Lewis's statement that "a poet does not fully know what is the poem he is writing until he has written it." Have you had the experience—writing for yourself, to a friend, or for school—of discovering from the act of writing what you want to write or what it means? Do you agree with Day Lewis, or do you think it's important to have a clear idea of what you're trying to express before you begin writing?
3. In your own writing, have you ever suddenly had an idea that, if implemented, would force you to change much of what you had already written? What did you do?

STEPHEN JAY GOULD

A paleontologist and collector of snails, STEPHEN JAY GOULD was born in New York City in 1941, went to Antioch College, and took a doctorate from Columbia University. From the age of twenty-five, Gould taught biology, geology, and the history of science at Harvard, where his courses were among the most popular. Although he often wrote for specialists (*Ontogeny and Phylogeny*, 1977), Gould is best known for essays that explore science in prose a layperson can enjoy. For twenty-seven years, until 2000, he wrote a monthly column for *Natural History* magazine. These and other essays have been collected in many books, including *The Panda's Thumb* (1980), *Hens' Teeth and Horses' Toes* (1983), *Eight Little Piggies* (1993), *Dinosaur in a Haystack* (1995), and *Leonardo's Mountain of Clams and the Diet of Worms* (1998). His most recent books are *Rocks of Ages* (1999), which attempts to heal the rift between science and religion; *The Structure of Evolutionary Theory* (2002), in which he proposes a new framework for thinking about Darwinism; and *I Have Landed: Splashes and Reflections from a Life in Natural History* (2002), a collection of essays. In 1981 Gould received a grant from the MacArthur Foundation. In 1999 he became president of the American Association for the Advancement of Science. He died in 2002 at the age of 60.

Sex, Drugs, Disasters, and the Extinction of Dinosaurs

In this essay, Stephen Jay Gould tackles one of the greatest mysteries in the evolution of life on this planet: the extinction of dinosaurs. Employing both scholarship and wit, Gould works backward from a specific effect (the fact that dinosaurs are extinct) to ask "Why?" The essay originally appeared in a 1984 *Discover* magazine and then in Gould's fourth essay collection, *The Flamingo's Smile*.

Though Gould relies most notably on cause and effect (examining several possible causes), he also makes extensive use of several other methods to answer his central question:

Comparison and contrast (Chap. 7): paragraphs 4–5, 18–24
Process analysis (Chap. 8): paragraphs 4–5, 9–12, 14, 16
Division or analysis (Chap. 9): paragraphs 18–22
Cause and effect (Chap. 11): throughout
Argument and persuasion (Chap. 13): paragraphs 18–25

Science, in its most fundamental definition, is a fruitful mode of inquiry,   1
not a list of enticing conclusions. The conclusions are the consequence, not the essence.

My greatest unhappiness with most popular presentations of science concerns their failure to separate fascinating claims from the methods that scientists use to establish the facts of nature. Journalists, and the public, thrive on controversial and stunning statements. But science is, basically, a way of knowing—in P. B. Medawar's apt words, "the art of the soluble." If the growing corps of popular science writers would focus on *how* scientists develop and defend those fascinating claims, they would make their greatest possible contribution to public understanding.

Consider three ideas, proposed in perfect seriousness to explain that greatest of all titillating puzzles—the extinction of dinosaurs. Since these three notions invoke the primally fascinating themes of our culture—sex, drugs, and violence—they surely reside in the category of fascinating claims. I want to show why two of them rank as silly speculation, while the other represents science at its grandest and most useful.

Science works with testable proposals. If, after much compilation and scrutiny of data, new information continues to affirm a hypothesis, we may accept it provisionally and gain confidence as further evidence mounts. We can never be completely sure that a hypothesis is right, though we may be able to show with confidence that it is wrong. The best scientific hypotheses are also generous and expansive: They suggest extensions and implications that enlighten related, and even far distant, subjects. Simply consider how the idea of evolution has influenced virtually every intellectual field.

Useless speculation, on the other hand, is restrictive. It generates no testable hypothesis, and offers no way to obtain potentially refuting evidence. Please note that I am not speaking of truth or falsity. The speculation may well be true; still, if it provides, in principle, no material for affirmation or rejection, we can make nothing of it. It must simply stand forever as an intriguing idea. Useless speculation turns in on itself and leads nowhere; good science, containing both seeds for its potential refutation and implications for more and different testable knowledge, reaches out. But, enough preaching. Let's move on to dinosaurs, and the three proposals for their extinction.

1. *Sex.*   Testes function only in a narrow range of temperature (those of mammals hang externally in a scrotal sac because internal body temperatures are too high for their proper function). A worldwide rise in temperature at the close of the Cretaceous period caused the testes of dinosaurs to stop functioning and led to their extinction by sterilization of males.
2. *Drugs.*   Angiosperms (flowering plants) first evolved toward the end of the dinosaurs' reign. Many of these plants contain psychoactive agents, avoided by mammals today as a result of their bitter taste. Dinosaurs had

neither means to taste the bitterness nor livers effective enough to detoxify the substances. They died of massive overdoses.

3. *Disasters.*   A large comet or asteroid struck the earth some 65 million
years ago, lofting a cloud of dust into the sky and blocking sunlight, thereby
suppressing photosynthesis and so drastically lowering world temperatures
that dinosaurs and hosts of other creatures became extinct.

Before analyzing these three tantalizing statements, we must establish a basic
ground rule often violated in proposals for the dinosaurs' demise. *There is no
separate problem of the extinction of dinosaurs.* Too often we divorce specific
events from their wider contexts and systems of cause and effect. The fundamental fact of dinosaur extinction is its synchrony with the demise of so many
other groups across a wide range of habitats, from terrestrial to marine.

The history of life has been punctuated by brief episodes of mass extinc-   6
tion. A recent analysis by University of Chicago paleontologists Jack Sep-
koski and Dave Raup, based on the best and most exhaustive tabulation of
data ever assembled, shows clearly that five episodes of mass dying stand well
above the "background" extinctions of normal times (when we consider all
mass extinctions, large and small, they seem to fall in a regular 26-million-
year cycle). The Cretaceous debacle, occurring 65 million years ago and separating the Mesozoic and Cenozoic eras of our geological time scale, ranks
prominently among the five. Nearly all the marine plankton (single-celled
floating creatures) died with geological suddenness; among marine inverte-
brates, nearly 15 percent of all families perished, including many previously
dominant groups, especially the ammonites (relatives of squids in coiled
shells). On land, the dinosaurs disappeared after more than 100 million years
of unchallenged domination.

In this context, speculations limited to dinosaurs alone ignore the larger   7
phenomenon. We need a coordinated explanation for a system of events that
includes the extinction of dinosaurs as one component. Thus it makes little
sense, though it may fuel our desire to view mammals as inevitable inheritors
of the earth, to guess that dinosaurs died because small mammals ate their eggs
(a perennial favorite among untestable speculations). It seems most unlikely
that some disaster peculiar to dinosaurs befell these massive beasts—and that
the debacle happened to strike just when one of history's five great dyings had
enveloped the earth for completely different reasons.

The testicular theory, an old favorite from the 1940s, had its root in an   8
interesting and thoroughly respectable study of temperature tolerances in
the American alligator, published in the staid *Bulletin of the American Museum*

of Natural History in 1946 by three experts on living and fossil reptiles—E. H. Colbert, my own first teacher in paleontology; R. B. Cowles; and C. M. Bogert.

The first sentence of their summary reveals a purpose beyond alligators: 9 "This report describes an attempt to infer the reactions of extinct reptiles, especially the dinosaurs, to high temperatures as based upon reactions observed in the modern alligator." They studied, by rectal thermometry, the body temperatures of alligators under changing conditions of heating and cooling. (Well, let's face it, you wouldn't want to try sticking a thermometer under a 'gator's tongue.) The predictions under test go way back to an old theory first stated by Galileo in the 1630s—the unequal scaling of surfaces and volumes. As an animal, or any object, grows (provided its shape doesn't change), surface areas must increase more slowly than volumes—since surfaces get larger as length squared, while volumes increase much more rapidly, as length cubed. Therefore, small animals have high ratios of surface to volume, while large animals cover themselves with relatively little surface.

Among cold-blooded animals lacking any physiological mechanism for   10 keeping their temperatures constant, small creatures have a hell of a time keeping warm—because they lose so much heat through their relatively large surfaces. On the other hand, large animals, with their relatively small surfaces, may lose heat so slowly that, once warm, they may maintain effectively constant temperatures against ordinary fluctuations of climate. (In fact, the resolution of the "hot-blooded dinosaur" controversy that burned so brightly a few years back may simply be that, while large dinosaurs possessed no physiological mechanism for constant temperature, and were not therefore warm-blooded in the technical sense, their large size and relatively small surface area kept them warm.)

Colbert, Cowles, and Bogert compared the warming rates of small and   11 large alligators. As predicted, the small fellows heated up (and cooled down) more quickly. When exposed to a warm sun, a tiny 50-gram (1.76-ounce) alligator heated up one degree Celsius every minute and a half, while a large alligator, 260 times bigger at 13,000 grams (28.7 pounds), took seven and a half minutes to gain a degree. Extrapolating up to an adult 10-ton dinosaur, they concluded that a one-degree rise in body temperature would take eighty-six hours. If large animals absorb heat so slowly (through their relatively small surfaces), they will also be unable to shed any excess heat gained when temperatures rise above a favorable level.

The authors then guessed that large dinosaurs lived at or near their opti-   12 mum temperatures; Cowles suggested that a rise in global temperatures just before the Cretaceous extinction caused the dinosaurs to heat up beyond their optimal tolerance—and, being so large, they couldn't shed the unwanted heat. (In a most unusual statement within a scientific paper, Colbert and Bogert then explicitly disavowed this speculative extension of their empirical work on alligators.) Cowles conceded that this excess heat probably wasn't enough to kill or even to enervate the great beasts, but since testes often function only within a narrow range of temperature, he proposed that this global rise might have sterilized all the males, causing extinction by natural contraception.

The overdose theory has recently been supported by UCLA psychiatrist [13] Ronald K. Siegel. Siegel has gathered, he claims, more than 2,000 records of animals who, when given access, administer various drugs to themselves—from a mere swig of alcohol to massive doses of the big H. Elephants will swill the equivalent of twenty beers at a time, but do not like alcohol in concentrations greater than 7 percent. In a silly bit of anthropocentric speculation, Siegel states that "elephants drink, perhaps, to forget [. . .] the anxiety produced by shrinking rangeland and the competition for food."

Since fertile imaginations can apply almost any hot idea to the extinction [14] of dinosaurs, Siegel found a way. Flowering plants did not evolve until late in the dinosaurs' reign. These plants also produced an array of aromatic, amino-acid-based alkaloids—the major group of psychoactive agents. Most mammals are "smart" enough to avoid these potential poisons. The alkaloids simply don't taste good (they are bitter); in any case, we mammals have livers happily supplied with the capacity to detoxify them. But, Siegel speculates, perhaps dinosaurs could neither taste the bitterness nor detoxify the substances once ingested. He recently told members of the American Psychological Association: "I'm not suggesting that all dinosaurs OD'd on plant drugs, but it certainly was a factor." He also argued that death by overdose may help explain why so many dinosaur fossils are found in contorted positions. (Do not go gently into that good night.)

Extraterrestrial catastrophes have long pedigrees in the popular literature [15] of extinction, but the subject exploded again in 1979, after a long lull, when the father-son, physicist-geologist team of Luis and Walter Alvarez proposed that an asteroid, some 10 km in diameter, struck the earth 65 million years ago. (Comets, rather than asteroids, have since gained favor. Good science is self-corrective.)

The force of such a collision would be immense, greater by far than the [16] megatonnage of all the world's nuclear weapons. In trying to reconstruct a scenario that would explain the simultaneous dying of dinosaurs on land and so many creatures in the sea, the Alvarezes proposed that a gigantic dust cloud, generated by particles blown aloft in the impact, would so darken the earth that photosynthesis would cease and temperatures drop precipitously. (Rage, rage against the dying of the light.) The single-celled photosynthetic oceanic plankton, with life cycles measured in weeks, would perish outright, but land plants might survive through the dormancy of their seeds (land plants were not much affected by the Cretaceous extinction, and any adequate theory must account for the curious pattern of differential survival). Dinosaurs would die by starvation and freezing; small, warm-blooded mammals, with more modest requirements for food and better regulation of body temperature, would squeak through. "Let the bastards freeze in the dark," as bumper stickers of our chauvinistic neighbors in sunbelt states proclaimed several years ago during the Northeast's winter oil crisis.

All three theories, testicular malfunction, psychoactive overdosing, and asteroidal zapping, grab our attention mightily. As pure phenomenology, they rank about equally high on any hit parade of primal fascination. Yet one represents expansive science, the others restrictive and untestable speculation. The proper criterion lies in evidence and methodology; we must probe behind the superficial fascination of particular claims.   17

How could we possibly decide whether the hypothesis of testicular frying is right or wrong? We would have to know things that the fossil record cannot provide. What temperatures were optimal for dinosaurs? Could they avoid the absorption of excess heat by staying in the shade, or in caves? At what temperatures did their testicles cease to function? Were late Cretaceous climates ever warm enough to drive the internal temperatures of dinosaurs close to this ceiling? Testicles simply don't fossilize, and how could we infer their temperature tolerances even if they did? In short, Cowles's hypothesis is only an intriguing speculation leading nowhere. The most damning statement against it appeared right in the conclusion of Colbert, Cowles, and Bogert's paper, when they admitted: "It is difficult to advance any definite arguments against this hypothesis." My statement may seem paradoxical—isn't a hypothesis really good if you can't devise any arguments against it? Quite the contrary. It is simply untestable and unusable.   18

Siegel's overdosing has even less going for it. At least Cowles extrapolated his conclusion from some good data on alligators. And he didn't completely violate the primary guideline of siting dinosaur extinction in the context of a general mass dying—for rise in temperature could be the root cause of a general catastrophe, zapping dinosaurs by testicular malfunction and different groups for other reasons. But Siegel's speculation cannot touch the extinction of ammonites or oceanic plankton (diatoms make their own food with good sweet sunlight; they don't OD on the chemicals of terrestrial plants). It is simply a gratuitous, attention-grabbing guess. It cannot be tested, for how can we   19 know what dinosaurs tasted and what their livers could do? Livers don't fossilize any better than testicles.

The hypothesis doesn't even make any sense in its own context. Angiosperms were in full flower ten million years before dinosaurs went the way of all flesh. Why did it take so long? As for the pains of a chemical death recorded in contortions of fossils, I regret to say (or rather I'm pleased to note for the dinosaurs' sake) that Siegel's knowledge of geology must be a bit deficient: Muscles contract after death and geological strata rise and fall with motions of the earth's crust after burial—more than enough reason to distort a fossil's pristine appearance. [20]

The impact story, on the other hand, has a sound basis in evidence. It can be tested, extended, refined, and, if wrong, disproved. The Alvarezes did not just construct an arresting guess for public consumption. They proposed their hypothesis after laborious geochemical studies with Frank Asaro and Helen Michael had revealed a massive increase of iridium in rocks deposited right at the time of extinction. Iridium, a rare metal of the platinum group, is virtually absent from indigenous rocks of the earth's crust; most of our iridium arrives on extraterrestrial objects that strike the earth. [21]

The Alvarez hypothesis bore immediate fruit. Based originally on evidence from two European localities, it led geochemists throughout the world to examine other sediments of the same age. They found abnormally high amounts of iridium everywhere—from continental rocks of the western United States to deep sea cores from the South Atlantic. [22]

Cowles proposed his testicular hypothesis in the mid-1940s. Where has it gone since then? Absolutely nowhere, because scientists can do nothing with it. The hypothesis must stand as a curious appendage to a solid study of alligators. Siegel's overdose scenario will also win a few press notices and fade into oblivion. The Alvarezes' asteroid falls into a different category altogether, and much of the popular commentary has missed this essential distinction by focusing on the impact and its attendant results, and forgetting what really matters to a scientist—the iridium. If you talk just about asteroids, dust, and darkness, you tell stories no better and no more entertaining than fried testicles or terminal trips. It is the iridium—the source of testable evidence—that counts and forges the crucial distinction between speculation and science. [23]

The proof, to twist a phrase, lies in the doing. Cowles's hypothesis has generated nothing in thirty-five years. Since its proposal in 1979, the Alvarez hypothesis has spawned hundreds of studies, a major conference, and attendant publications. Geologists are fired up. They are looking for iridium at all other extinction boundaries. Every week exposes a new wrinkle in the scientific press. Further evidence that the Cretaceous iridium represents extrater- [24]

restrial impact and not indigenous volcanism continues to accumulate. As I revise this essay in November 1984 (this paragraph will be out of date when [it] is published), new data include chemical "signatures" of other isotopes indicating unearthly provenance, glass spherules of a size and sort produced by impact and not by volcanic eruptions, and high-pressure varieties of silica formed (so far as we know) only under the tremendous shock of impact.

My point is simply this: Whatever the eventual outcome (I suspect it will   25 be positive), the Alvarez hypothesis is exciting, fruitful science because it generates tests, provides us with things to do, and expands outward. We are having fun, battling back and forth, moving toward a resolution, and extending the hypothesis beyond its original scope.

As just one example of the unexpected, distant cross-fertilization that   26 good science engenders, the Alvarez hypothesis made a major contribution to a theme that has riveted public attention in the past few months—so-called nuclear winter. In a speech delivered in April 1982, Luis Alvarez calculated the energy that a ten-kilometer asteroid would release on impact. He compared such an explosion with a full nuclear exchange and implied that all-out atomic war might unleash similar consequences.

This theme of impact leading to massive dust clouds and falling tempera-   27 tures formed an important input to the decision of Carl Sagan and a group of colleagues to model the climatic consequences of nuclear holocaust. Full nuclear exchange would probably generate the same kind of dust cloud and darkening that may have wiped out the dinosaurs. Temperatures would drop precipitously and agriculture might become impossible. Avoidance of nuclear war is fundamentally an ethical and political imperative, but we must know the factual consequences to make firm judgments. I am heartened by a final link across disciplines and deep concerns—another criterion, by the way, of science at its best: A recognition of the very phenomenon that made our evolution possible by exterminating the previously dominant dinosaurs and clearing a way for the evolution of large mammals, including us, might actually help to save us from joining those magnificent beasts in contorted poses among the strata of the earth.

Journal Writing

Gould proposes several possible CAUSES for the same EFFECT. Why do you think considering various possible causes for a particular effect is important in scientific inquiry? How does the same thing apply in everyday life? Think of a situation that affects you directly—your breakup with a close friend, a course you are having particular difficulties with, a problem you face at work, something you have recently become interested in (or lost interest in), or the like. Then, in your journal, write down all the causes you can think of for this situation. (To take your journal writing further, see "From Journal to Essay" below.)

Questions on Meaning

1. According to Gould, what constitutes a scientific hypothesis? What constitutes useless speculation? Where in the essay do you find his DEFINITIONS of these terms?
2. State, in your own words, the THESIS of this essay.
3. What does Gould perceive to be the major flaws in the testicular malfunction and drug overdose theories about the extinction of dinosaurs? Cite his specific reasons for discrediting each theory.
4. What is the connection between nuclear holocaust and the extinction of dinosaurs? (See the essay's last paragraph.)

Questions on Writing Strategy

1. How do you understand the phrases "hit parade of primal fascination" (par. 17) and "the hypothesis of testicular frying" (18)? Is the TONE here somber, silly, whimsical, ironic, or what?
2. Paragraphs 14 and 16 both contain references to Dylan Thomas's poem "Do Not Go Gentle into That Good Night." (The poem's title is used in par. 14; "Rage, rage against the dying of the light," one of the poem's refrains, appears in par. 16.) If you are not familiar with the poem, look it up. Is it necessary to know the poem to understand Gould's use of these lines? What is the effect of these ALLUSIONS?
3. **MIXED METHODS.** In explaining the Alvarezes' hypothesis about the causes of the dinosaurs' extinction, Gould outlines a causal chain. Draw a diagram to illustrate this chain.
4. **MIXED METHODS.** How does the PROCESS ANALYSIS in paragraphs 4–5, 9–12, 14, and 16 help Gould analyze the possible causes of dinosaur extinction? What would the essay lack without these paragraphs?

Questions on Language

1. What do you take the following sentence to mean: "There is no separate problem of the extinction of dinosaurs" (par. 5)? Separate from what? According to Gould, then, what *is* the problem being discussed?
2. Be sure you can define the following words: enticing (par. 1); hypothesis (4); psychoactive, photosynthesis, synchrony (5); paleontology (8); extrapolating (11); empirical (12); gratuitous (19).

Suggestions for Writing

1. **FROM JOURNAL TO ESSAY.** Expand and refine your journal entry (above) into a formal essay that explains the causes of the situation that affects you. Make sure

to give your AUDIENCE a clear sense of the situation. You may want to rely on NAR-RATION, telling the story of the circumstances.

2. As Gould himself predicts (par. 24), his summary of the research into the Alvarez hypothesis is now dated: More data have accumulated; the hypothesis has been challenged, tested, revised. Do research in the library or on the Web to find articles written over the past several years about the extinction of the dinosaurs. Write an essay updating Gould's in which you summarize the significant EVIDENCE for and against the Alvarez hypothesis.

3. **CRITICAL WRITING.** Apply Gould's distinction between hypothesis and speculation (pars. 4–5) in an area you know well—for instance, Civil War battles, dance, basketball, waste recycling, carpentry, nursing. What, in your area, is the equivalent of the useful hypothesis? What is the equivalent of the useless speculation? Be as specific as possible so that a reader outside the field can understand you.

4. **CONNECTIONS.** Gould's is one of several essays in this book written by specialists for an audience of nonspecialists; others include Bruce Catton's "Grant and Lee" (p. 242), Linnea Saukko's "How to Poison the Earth" (p. 276), Deborah Tannen's "But What Do You Mean?" (p. 372), William Lutz's "The World of Doublespeak" (p. 399), and Atul Gawande's "The Cancer-Cluster Myth" (p. 427). In an essay, compare Gould's essay with one of these others in terms of complexity of material, use and explanation of specialized vocabulary, and clarity of explanation. Overall, which essay do you find more effective in explaining a specialized subject for nonspecialists?

5. **CONNECTIONS.** COMPARE AND CONTRAST Gould's essay with Atul Gawande's "The Cancer-Cluster Myth" (p. 427), taking as your main point of comparison each author's attitudes toward the science he discusses and toward its implications. To gauge attitudes, look not only at what the authors say but also at their tones.

Stephen Jay Gould on Writing

In his prologue to *The Flamingo's Smile*, Stephen Jay Gould positions himself in a long and respectable tradition of writers who communicate scientific ideas to a general audience. To popularize, he says, does not mean to trivialize, cheapen, or adulterate. "I follow one cardinal rule in writing these essays," he insists. "No compromises. I will make language accessible by defining or eliminating jargon; I will not simplify concepts. I can state all sorts of highfalutin, moral justifications for this approach (and I do believe in them), but the basic reason is simple and personal. I write these essays primarily to aid my own quest to learn and understand as much as possible about nature in the short time allotted."

In his own view, Gould was lucky: He was a writer carried along by a single, fascinating theme. "If my volumes work at all, they owe their reputation to coherence supplied by the common theme of evolutionary theory. I have a wonderful advantage among essayists because no other theme so beautifully encompasses both the particulars that fascinate and the generalities that instruct. [. . .] Each essay is both a single long argument and a welding together of particulars."

For Discussion

1. What differences would occur naturally between the work of a scientist writing for other scientists and the work of Gould, who wrote about science for a general AUDIENCE?
2. How does the author defend himself against the possible charge that, as a popularizer of science, he trivializes his subject?

MARTIN LUTHER KING, JR.

MARTIN LUTHER KING, JR. (1929–68), was born in Atlanta, the son of a Baptist minister, and was himself ordained in the same denomination. Stepping to the forefront of the civil rights movement in 1955, King led African Americans in a boycott of segregated city buses in Montgomery, Alabama; became the first president of the Southern Christian Leadership Conference; and staged sit-ins and mass marches that helped bring about the Civil Rights Act passed by Congress in 1964 and the Voting Rights Act of 1965. He received the Nobel Peace Prize in 1964. While King preached "nonviolent resistance," he was himself the target of violence. He was stabbed in New York, pelted with stones in Chicago; his home in Montgomery was bombed; and ultimately he was assassinated in Memphis by a sniper. On his tombstone near Atlanta's Ebenezer Baptist Church are these words from the spiritual he quotes at the conclusion of "I Have a Dream": "Free at last, free at last, thank God almighty, I'm free at last." Martin Luther King's birthday, January 15, is now a national holiday.

I Have a Dream

In Washington, DC, on August 28, 1963, King's campaign of nonviolent resistance reached its historic climax. On that date, commemorating the centennial of Lincoln's Emancipation Proclamation freeing the slaves, King led a march of 200,000 persons, black and white, from the Washington Monument to the Lincoln Memorial. Before this throng, and to millions who watched on television, he delivered this unforgettable speech.

Intended to inspire and motivate its audience, King's speech is a model of a certain kind of persuasion. To make his point, King draws on a number of methods:

Narration (Chap. 4): paragraphs 1–2
Description (Chap. 5): paragraphs 2, 4
Example (Chap. 6): paragraphs 6–9, 12–16, 21–22
Comparison and contrast (Chap. 7): paragraphs 3–4, 6
Cause and effect (Chap. 11): paragraphs 5, 7, 19
Argument and persuasion (Chap. 13): throughout

Five score years ago, a great American, in whose symbolic shadow we   1
stand, signed the Emancipation Proclamation. This momentous decree came as a great beacon light of hope to millions of Negro slaves who had been seared in the flames of withering injustice. It came as a joyous daybreak to end the long night of captivity.

But one hundred years later, we must face the tragic fact that the Negro   2
is still not free. One hundred years later, the life of the Negro is still sadly

crippled by the manacles of segregation and the chains of discrimination. One hundred years later, the Negro lives on a lonely island of poverty in the midst of a vast ocean of material prosperity. One hundred years later, the Negro is still languishing in the corners of American society and finds himself in exile in his own land. So we have come here today to dramatize an appalling condition.

In a sense we have come to our nation's capital to cash a check. When the architects of our republic wrote the magnificent words of the Constitution and the Declaration of Independence, they were signing a promissory note to which every American was to fall heir. This note was a promise that all men would be guaranteed the unalienable rights of life, liberty, and the pursuit of happiness. 3

It is obvious today that America has defaulted on this promissory note insofar as her citizens of color are concerned. Instead of honoring this sacred obligation, America has given the Negro people a bad check; a check which has come back marked "insufficient funds." But we refuse to believe that the bank of justice is bankrupt. We refuse to believe that there are insufficient funds in the great vaults of opportunity of this nation. So we have come to cash this check—a check that will give us upon demand the riches of freedom and the security of justice. We have also come to this hallowed spot to remind America of the fierce urgency of *now*. This is no time to engage in the luxury of cooling off or to take the tranquilizing drugs of gradualism. *Now* is the time to make real the promises of Democracy. *Now* is the time to rise from the dark and desolate valley of segregation to the sunlit path of racial justice. *Now* is the time to open the doors of opportunity to all of God's children. *Now* is the time to lift our nation from the quicksands of racial injustice to the solid rock of brotherhood. 4

It would be fatal for the nation to overlook the urgency of the moment and to underestimate the determination of the Negro. This sweltering summer of the Negro's legitimate discontent will not pass until there is an invigorating autumn of freedom and equality; 1963 is not an end, but a beginning. Those who hope that the Negro needed to blow off steam and will now be content will have a rude awakening if the nation returns to business as usual. There will be neither rest nor tranquillity in America until the Negro is granted his citizenship rights. The whirlwinds of revolt will continue to shake the foundations of our nation until the bright day of justice emerges. 5

But there is something that I must say to my people who stand on the warm threshold which leads into the palace of justice. In the process of gaining our rightful place we must not be guilty of wrongful deeds. Let us not seek to satisfy our thirst for freedom by drinking from the cup of bitterness and hatred. We must forever conduct our struggle on the high plane of dig- 6 nity and discipline. We must not allow our creative protest to degenerate into physical violence. Again and again we must rise to the majestic heights of meeting physical force with soul force. The marvelous new militancy which has engulfed the Negro community must not lead us to a distrust of all white people, for many of our white brothers, as evidenced by their presence here today, have come to realize that their destiny is tied up with our destiny and their freedom is inextricably bound to our freedom. We cannot walk alone.

And as we walk, we must make the pledge that we shall march ahead. We cannot turn back. There are those who are asking the devotees of civil rights, "When will you be satisfied?" We can never be satisfied as long as the Negro is the victim of the unspeakable horrors of police brutality. We can never be satisfied as long as our bodies, heavy with the fatigue of travel, cannot gain lodging in the motels of the highways and the hotels of the cities. We cannot be satisfied as long as the Negro's basic mobility is from a smaller ghetto to a larger one. We can never be satisfied as long as a Negro in Mississippi cannot vote and a Negro in New York believes he has nothing for which to vote. No, no, we are not satisfied, and we will not be satisfied until justice rolls down like waters and righteousness like a mighty stream.

I am not unmindful that some of you have come here out of great trials and tribulations. Some of you have come fresh from narrow jail cells. Some of you have come from areas where your quest for freedom left you battered by the storms of persecution and staggered by the winds of police brutality. You have been the veterans of creative suffering. Continue to work with the faith that unearned suffering is redemptive.

Go back to Mississippi, go back to Alabama, go back to South Carolina, go back to Georgia, go back to Louisiana, go back to the slums and ghettos of our northern cities, knowing that somehow this situation can and will be changed. Let us not wallow in the valley of despair.

I say to you today, my friends, that in spite of the difficulties and frustrations of the moment I still have a dream. It is a dream deeply rooted in the American dream.

I have a dream that one day this nation will rise up and live out the true meaning of its creed: "We hold these truths to be self-evident; that all men are created equal."

I have a dream that one day on the red hills of Georgia the sons of former slaves and the sons of former slaveowners will be able to sit down together at the table of brotherhood.

I have a dream that one day even the state of Mississippi, a desert state sweltering with the heat of injustice and oppression, will be transformed into an oasis of freedom and justice.

I have a dream that my four little children will one day live in a nation   14
where they will not be judged by the color of their skin but by the content of
their character.

I have a dream today.   15

I have a dream that one day the state of Alabama, whose governor's lips   16
are presently dripping with the words of interposition and nullification, will
be transformed into a situation where little black boys and black girls will be
able to join hands with little white boys and white girls and walk together as
sisters and brothers.

I have a dream today.   17

I have a dream that one day every valley shall be exalted, every hill and   18
mountain shall be made low, the rough places will be made plain, and the
crooked places will be made straight, and the glory of the Lord shall be
revealed, and all flesh shall see it together.

This is our hope. This is the faith with which I return to the South. With   19
this faith we will be able to hew out of the mountain of despair a stone of
hope. With this faith we will be able to transform the jangling discords of
our nation into a beautiful symphony of brotherhood. With this faith we
will be able to work together, to pray together, to struggle together, to go to
jail together, to stand up for freedom together, knowing that we will be free
one day.

This will be the day when all of God's children will be able to sing with   20
new meaning

> My country, 'tis of thee,
> Sweet land of liberty,
>   Of thee I sing:
> Land where my fathers died,
> Land of the pilgrims' pride,
> From every mountainside
>   Let freedom ring.

And if America is to be a great nation this must become true. So let free-   21
dom ring from the prodigious hilltops of New Hampshire. Let freedom ring
from the mighty mountains of New York. Let freedom ring from the height-
ening Alleghenies of Pennsylvania!

Let freedom ring from the snowcapped Rockies of Colorado!   22

Let freedom ring from the curvaceous peaks of California!   23

But not only that; let freedom ring from Stone Mountain of Georgia!   24

Let freedom ring from Lookout Mountain of Tennessee!   25

Let freedom ring from every hill and molehill of Mississippi. From every   26
mountainside, let freedom ring.

When we let freedom ring, when we let it ring from every village and 27
every hamlet, from every state and every city, we will be able to speed up that
day when all of God's children, black men and white men, Jews and Gentiles,
Protestants and Catholics, will be able to join hands and sing in the words of
the old Negro spiritual, "Free at last! free at last! thank God almighty, we are
free at last!"

Journal Writing

Do you think we have moved closer to fulfilling King's dream in the decades since he
gave this famous speech? In your journal, explore why or why not. (To take your journal writing further, see "From Journal to Essay" on the next page.)

Questions on Meaning

1. What is the apparent PURPOSE of this speech?
2. What THESIS does King develop in his first four paragraphs?
3. What does King mean by the "marvelous new militancy which has engulfed the
   Negro community" (par. 6)? Does this contradict King's nonviolent philosophy?
4. In what passages of his speech does King notice events of history? Where does he
   acknowledge the historic occasion on which he is speaking?

Questions on Writing Strategy

1. What indicates that King's words were meant primarily for an AUDIENCE of listeners, and only secondarily for a reading audience? To hear these indications, try
   reading the speech aloud. What uses of PARALLELISM do you notice?
2. Where in the speech does King acknowledge that not all of his listeners are
   African American?
3. How much EMPHASIS does King place on the past? How much does he place on
   the future?
4. **MIXED METHODS.** Analyze the ETHICAL APPEAL of King's ARGUMENT (see p. 503).
   Where in the speech, for instance, does he present himself as reasonable despite
   his passion? To what extent does his personal authority lend power to his words?
5. **MIXED METHODS.** The DESCRIPTION in paragraphs 2 and 4 depends on metaphor,
   a FIGURE OF SPEECH in which one thing is said to be another thing. How do the
   metaphors in these paragraphs work for King's purpose?

Questions on Language

1. In general, is the language of King's speech ABSTRACT or CONCRETE? How is this
   level appropriate to his message and to the span of history with which he deals?

2. Point to memorable figures of speech besides those examined in the "Mixed Methods" question on the preceding page.
3. Define *momentous* (par. 1); *manacles, languishing* (2); *promissory note, unalienable* (3); *defaulted, hallowed, gradualism* (4); *inextricably* (6); *mobility, ghetto* (7); *tribulations, redemptive* (8); *interposition, nullification* (16); *prodigious* (21); *curvaceous* (23); *hamlet* (27).

Suggestions for Writing

1. **FROM JOURNAL TO ESSAY.** Use your journal entry (previous page) to write an essay that explains your sense of how well the United States has progressed toward realizing King's dream. You may choose to focus on America as a whole or on your particular community, but you should use specific EVIDENCE to support your opinion.
2. Propose some course of action in a situation that you consider an injustice. Racial injustice is one possible area, or unfairness to any minority, or to women, children, the elderly, ex-convicts, the disabled, the poor. If possible, narrow your subject to a particular incident or a local situation on which you can write knowledgeably.
3. **CRITICAL WRITING.** What can you INFER from this speech about King's own attitudes toward oppression and injustice? Does he follow his own injunction not "to satisfy our thirst for freedom by drinking from the cup of bitterness and hatred" (par. 6)? Explain your answer, using evidence from the speech.
4. **CONNECTIONS.** King's "I Have a Dream" and H. L. Mencken's "The Penalty of Death" (p. 516) both seek to influence readers, either to cause them to act or to change their views. Yet the two authors take very different approaches to achieve their purposes. COMPARE AND CONTRAST the authors' persuasive strategies, considering especially their effectiveness for the situation each writes about and the audience each addresses.
5. **CONNECTIONS.** King's speech was delivered in 1963. Brent Staples's essay "Black Men and Public Space" (p. 205) was first published in 1986. In an essay, explore the changes, if any, that are evident in the ASSUMPTIONS the authors make about their audiences' attitudes, about race in general, and about racism.

MAXINE HONG KINGSTON

MAXINE HONG KINGSTON grew up caught between two complex and very different cultures: the China of her parents and the America of her surroundings. In her first two books, *The Woman Warrior: Memoirs of a Girlhood Among Ghosts* (1976) and *China Men* (1980), Kingston combines Chinese myth and history with family tales to create a dreamlike world that shifts between reality and fantasy. Born in 1940 in Stockton, California, Kingston was the first American-born child of a scholar and a medical practitioner who became laundry workers in this country. After graduating from the University of California at Berkeley (BA, 1962), Kingston taught English at California and Hawaii high schools and at the University of Hawaii. She now teaches at UC Berkeley, where she is Chancellor's Distinguished Professor. Kingston has contributed essays, poems, and stories to *The New Yorker,* the *New York Times Magazine, Ms.,* and other periodicals. Her most recent books are the novel *Tripmaster Monkey: His Fake Book* (1989) and a collection of essays, *Hawai'i One Summer* (1998). In 1997 she was awarded the National Humanities Medal.

No Name Woman

"No Name Woman" is part of *The Woman Warrior.* Like much of Kingston's writing, it blends the "talk-stories" of Kingston's elders, her own vivid imaginings, and the reality of her experience—this time to discover why her Chinese aunt drowned herself in the family well.

Kingston develops "No Name Woman" with four main methods, all intertwined: In the context of narrating her own experiences, she seeks the causes of her aunt's suicide by comparing various narratives of it, and she employs description to make the narratives concrete and vivid. The main uses of these methods appear below:

Narration (Chap. 4): paragraphs 1–8, 14, 16–20, 23, 28–30, 34–35, 37–46
Description (Chap. 5): paragraphs 4–8, 21, 23–27, 31, 37, 40–46
Comparison and contrast (Chap. 7): paragraphs 15–18, 20–24, 27–28, 31
Cause and effect (Chap. 11): paragraphs 10–11, 15–18, 21–25, 29–31, 33–39, 44–48

"You must not tell anyone," my mother said, "what I am about to tell you. In China your father had a sister who killed herself. She jumped into the family well. We say that your father has all brothers because it is as if she had never been born.

"In 1924 just a few days after our village celebrated seventeen hurry-up weddings—to make sure that every young man who went 'out on the road' would responsibly come home—your father and his brothers and your grandfather and his brothers and your aunt's new husband sailed for America, the Gold Mountain. It was your grandfather's last trip. Those lucky enough to get contracts waved good-bye from the decks. They fed and guarded the stowaways and helped them off in Cuba, New York, Bali, Hawaii. 'We'll meet in California next year,' they said. All of them sent money home.

"I remember looking at your aunt one day when she and I were dressing; I had not noticed before that she had such a protruding melon of a stomach. But I did not think, 'She's pregnant,' until she began to look like other pregnant women, her shirt pulling and the white tops of her black pants showing. She could not have been pregnant, you see, because her husband had been gone for years. No one said anything. We did not discuss it. In early summer she was ready to have the child, long after the time when it could have been possible.

"The village had also been counting. On the night the baby was to be born the villagers raided our house. Some were crying. Like a great saw, teeth strung with lights, files of people walked zigzag across our land, tearing the rice. Their lanterns doubled in the disturbed black water, which drained away through the broken bunds. As the villagers closed in, we could see that some of them, probably men and women we knew well, wore white masks. The people with long hair hung it over their faces. Women with short hair made it stand up on end. Some had tied white bands around their foreheads, arms, and legs.

"At first they threw mud and rocks at the house. Then they threw eggs and began slaughtering our stock. We could hear the animals scream their deaths—the roosters, the pigs, a last great roar from the ox. Familiar wild heads flared in our night windows; the villagers encircled us. Some of the faces stopped to peer at us, their eyes rushing like searchlights. The hands flattened against the panes, framed heads, and left red prints.

"The villagers broke in the front and the back doors at the same time, even though we had not locked the doors against them. Their knives dripped with the blood of our animals. They smeared blood on the doors and walls. One woman swung a chicken, whose throat she had slit, splattering blood in red arcs about her. We stood together in the middle of our house, in the family hall with the pictures and tables of the ancestors around us, and looked straight ahead.

"At that time the house had only two wings. When the men came back, we would build two more to enclose our courtyard and a third one to begin a second courtyard. The villagers pushed through both wings, even your grandparents' rooms, to find your aunt's, which was also mine until the men returned. From this room a new wing for one of the younger families would grow. They ripped up her clothes and shoes and broke her combs, grinding them underfoot. They tore her work from the loom. They scattered the cooking fire and rolled the new weaving in it. We could hear them in the kitchen breaking our bowls and banging the pots. They overturned the great waist-high earthenware jugs; duck eggs, pickled fruits, vegetables burst out and mixed in acrid torrents. The old woman from the next field swept a broom through the air and loosed the spirits-of-the-broom over our heads. 'Pig.' 'Ghost.' 'Pig,' they sobbed and scolded while they ruined our house.

"When they left, they took sugar and oranges to bless themselves. They   8
cut pieces from the dead animals. Some of them took bowls that were not broken and clothes that were not torn. Afterward we swept up the rice and sewed it back up into sacks. But the smells from the spilled preserves lasted. Your aunt gave birth in the pigsty that night. The next morning when I went up for the water, I found her and the baby plugging up the family well.

"Don't let your father know that I told you. He denies her. Now that you   9
have started to menstruate, what happened to her could happen to you. Don't humiliate us. You wouldn't like to be forgotten as if you had never been born. The villagers are watchful."

Whenever she had to warn us about life, my mother told stories that ran   10
like this one, a story to grow up on. She tested our strength to establish realities. Those in the emigrant generations who could not reassert brute survival died young and far from home. Those of us in the first American generations have had to figure out how the invisible world the emigrants built around our childhoods fit in solid America.

The emigrants confused the gods by diverting their curses, misleading   11
them with crooked streets and false names. They must try to confuse their offspring as well, who, I suppose, threaten them in similar ways—always trying to get things straight, always trying to name the unspeakable. The Chinese I know hide their names; sojourners take new names when their lives change and guard their real names with silence.

Chinese-Americans, when you try to understand what things in you are   12
Chinese, how do you separate what is peculiar to childhood, to poverty, insanities, one family, your mother who marked your growing with stories, from what is Chinese? What is Chinese tradition and what is the movies?

If I want to learn what clothes my aunt wore, whether flashy or ordinary,   13
I would have to begin, "Remember Father's drowned-in-the-well sister?" I cannot ask that. My mother has told me once and for all the useful parts. She will add nothing unless powered by Necessity, a riverbank that guides her life. She plants vegetable gardens rather than lawns; she carries the odd-shaped tomatoes home from the fields and eats food left for the gods.

Whenever we did frivolous things, we used up energy; we flew high kites.   14

We children came up off the ground over the melting cones our parents brought home from work and the American movie on New Year's Day—*Oh, You Beautiful Doll* with Betty Grable one year, and *She Wore a Yellow Ribbon* with John Wayne another year. After the one carnival ride each, we paid in guilt; our tired father counted his change on the dark walk home.

Adultery is extravagance. Could people who hatch their own chicks and   15
eat the embryos and the heads for delicacies and boil the feet in vinegar for party food, leaving only the gravel, eating even the gizzard lining—could such people engender a prodigal aunt? To be a woman, to have a daughter in starvation time was a waste enough. My aunt could not have been the lone romantic who gave up everything for sex. Women in the old China did not choose. Some man had commanded her to lie with him and be his secret evil. I wonder whether he masked himself when he joined the raid on her family.

Perhaps she encountered him in the fields or on the mountain where the   16
daughters-in-law collected fuel. Or perhaps he first noticed her in the market-place. He was not a stranger because the village housed no strangers. She had to have dealings with him other than sex. Perhaps he worked an adjoining field, or he sold her the cloth for the dress she sewed and wore. His demand must have surprised, then terrified her. She obeyed him; she always did as she was told.

When the family found a young man in the next village to be her hus-   17
band, she stood tractably beside the best rooster, his proxy, and promised before they met that she would be his forever. She was lucky that he was her age and she would be the first wife, an advantage secure now. The night she first saw him, he had sex with her. Then he left for America. She had almost forgotten what he looked like. When she tried to envision him, she only saw the black and white face in the group photograph the men had had taken before leaving.

The other man was not, after all, much different from her husband. They   18
both gave orders: she followed. "If you tell your family, I'll beat you. I'll kill you. Be here again next week." No one talked sex, ever. And she might have separated the rapes from the rest of living if only she did not have to buy her oil from him or gather wood in the same forest. I want her fear to have lasted just as long as rape lasted so that the fear could have been contained. No drawn-out fear. But women at sex hazarded birth and hence lifetimes. The fear did not stop but permeated everywhere. She told the man, "I think I'm preg-nant." He organized the raid against her.

On nights when my mother and father talked about their life back home,   19
sometimes they mentioned an "outcast table" whose business they still seemed to be settling, their voices tight. In a commensal tradition, where food is pre-cious, the powerful older people made wrongdoers eat alone. Instead of letting

them start separate new lives like the Japanese, who could become samurais and geishas, the Chinese family, faces averted but eyes glowering sideways, hung on to the offenders and fed them leftovers. My aunt must have lived in the same house as my parents and eaten at an outcast table. My mother spoke about the raid as if she had seen it, when she and my aunt, a daughter-in-law to a different household, should not have been living together at all. Daughters-in-law lived with their husbands' parents, not their own; a synonym for marriage in Chinese is "taking a daughter-in-law." Her husband's parents could have sold her, mortgaged her, stoned her. But they had sent her back to her own mother and father, a mysterious act hinting at disgraces not told me. Perhaps they had thrown her out to deflect the avengers.

She was the only daughter; her four brothers went with her father, hus- 20 band, and uncles "out on the road" and for some years became western men. When the goods were divided among the family, three of the brothers took land, and the youngest, my father, chose an education. After my grandparents gave their daughter away to her husband's family, they had dispensed all the adventure and all the property. They expected her alone to keep the traditional ways, which her brothers, now among the barbarians, could fumble without detection. The heavy, deep-rooted women were to maintain the past against the flood, safe for returning. But the rare urge west had fixed upon our family, and so my aunt crossed boundaries not delineated in space.

The work of preservation demands that the feelings playing about in one's 21 guts not be turned into action. Just watch their passing like cherry blossoms. But perhaps my aunt, my forerunner, caught in a slow life, let dreams grow and fade and after some months or years went toward what persisted. Fear at the enormities of the forbidden kept her desires delicate, wire and bone. She looked at a man because she liked the way the hair was tucked behind his ears, or she liked the question-mark line of a long torso curving at the shoulder and straight at the hip. For warm eyes or a soft voice or a slow walk — that's all — a few hairs, a line, a brightness, a sound, a pace, she gave up family. She offered us up for a charm that vanished with tiredness, a pigtail that didn't toss when the wind died. Why, the wrong lighting could erase the dearest thing about him.

It could very well have been, however, that my aunt did not take subtle 22 enjoyment of her friend, but, a wild woman, kept rollicking company. Imagining her free with sex doesn't fit, though. I don't know any women like that, or men either. Unless I see her life branching into mine, she gives me no ancestral help.

To sustain her being in love, she often worked at herself in the mirror, 23 guessing at the colors and shapes that would interest him, changing them frequently in order to hit on the right combination. She wanted him to look back.

On a farm near the sea, a woman who tended her appearance reaped a   24
reputation for eccentricity. All the married women blunt-cut their hair in
flaps about their ears or pulled it back in tight buns. No nonsense. Neither
style blew easily into heart-catching tangles. And at their weddings they displayed themselves in their long hair for the last time. "It brushed the backs of
my knees," my mother tells me. "It was braided, and even so, it brushed the
backs of my knees."

At the mirror my aunt combed individuality into her bob. A bun could   25
have been contrived to escape into black streamers blowing in the wind or in
quiet wisps about her face, but only the older women in our picture album wear
buns. She brushed her hair back from her forehead, tucking the flaps behind her
ears. She looped a piece of thread, knotted into a circle between her index fingers and thumbs, and ran the double strand across her forehead. When she
closed her fingers as if she were making a pair of shadow geese bite, the string
twisted together catching the little hairs. Then she pulled the thread away from
her skin, ripping the hairs out neatly, her eyes watering from the needles of pain.
Opening her fingers, she cleaned the thread, then rolled it along her hairline
and the tops of her eyebrows. My mother did the same to me and my sisters and
herself. I used to believe that the expression "caught by the short hairs" meant a
captive held with a depilatory string. It especially hurt at the temples, but my
mother said we were lucky we didn't have to have our feet bound when we were
seven. Sisters used to sit on their beds and cry together, she said, as their mothers or their slave removed the bandages for a few minutes each night and let the
blood gush back into their veins. I hope that the man my aunt loved appreciated
a smooth brow, that he wasn't just a tits-and-ass man.

Once my aunt found a freckle on her chin, at a spot that the almanac said   26
predestined her for unhappiness. She dug it out with a hot needle and washed
the wound with peroxide.

More attention to her looks than these pullings of hairs and pickings at   27
spots would have caused gossip among the villagers. They owned work clothes
and good clothes, and they wore good clothes for feasting the new seasons.
But since a woman combing her hair hexes beginnings, my aunt rarely found
an occasion to look her best. Women looked like great sea snails — the corded
wood, babies, and laundry they carried were the whorls on their backs. The
Chinese did not admire a bent back; goddesses and warriors stood straight.
Still there must have been a marvelous freeing of beauty when a worker laid
down her burden and stretched and arched.

Such commonplace loveliness, however, was not enough for my aunt. She   28
dreamed of a lover for the fifteen days of New Year's, the time for families to
exchange visits, money, and food. She plied her secret comb. And sure
enough she cursed the year, the family, the village, and herself.

Even as her hair lured her imminent lover, many other men looked at her. 29
Uncles, cousins, nephews, brothers would have looked, too, had they been
home between journeys. Perhaps they had already been restraining their
curiosity, and they left, fearful that their glances, like a field of nesting birds,
might be startled and caught. Poverty hurt, and that was their first reason for
leaving. But another, final reason for leaving the crowded house was the
never-said.

She may have been unusually beloved, the precious only daughter, spoiled 30
and mirror gazing because of the affection the family lavished on her. When
her husband left, they welcomed the chance to take her back from the in-laws;
she could live like the little daughter for just a while longer. There are stories
that my grandfather was different from other people, "crazy ever since the little
Jap bayoneted him in the head." He used to put his naked penis on the dinner
table, laughing. And one day he brought home a baby girl, wrapped up inside
his brown western-style greatcoat. He had traded one of his sons, probably my
father, the youngest, for her. My grandmother made him trade back. When he
finally got a daughter of his own, he doted on her. They must have all loved
her, except perhaps my father, the only brother who never went back to
China, having once been traded for a girl.

Brothers and sisters, newly men and women, had to efface their sexual 31
color and present plain miens. Disturbing hair and eyes, a smile like no other,
threatened the ideal of five generations living under one roof. To focus blurs,
people shouted face to face and yelled from room to room. The immigrants I
know have loud voices, unmodulated to American tones even after years away
from the village where they called their friendships out across the fields. I have
not been able to stop my mother's screams in public libraries or over tele-
phones. Walking erect (knees straight, toes pointed forward, not pigeon-toed,
which is Chinese-feminine) and speaking in an inaudible voice, I have tried
to turn myself American-feminine. Chinese communication was loud, public.
Only sick people had to whisper. But at the dinner table, where the family
members came nearest one another, no one could talk, not the outcasts nor
any eaters. Every word that falls from the mouth is a coin lost. Silently they
gave and accepted food with both hands. A preoccupied child who took his
bowl with one hand got a sideways glare. A complete moment of total attention is due everyone alike. Children and lovers have no singularity here, but
my aunt used a secret voice, a separate attentiveness.

She kept the man's name to herself throughout her labor and dying; she 32
did not accuse him that he be punished with her. To save her inseminator's
name she gave silent birth.

He may have been somebody in her own household, but intercourse with 33
a man outside the family would have been no less abhorrent. All the village

were kinsmen, and the titles shouted in loud country voices never let kinship be forgotten. Any man within visiting distance would have been neutralized as a lover—"brother," "younger brother," "older brother"—one hundred and fifteen relationship titles. Parents researched birth charts probably not so much to assure good fortune as to circumvent incest in a population that has but one hundred surnames. Everybody has eight million relatives. How useless then sexual mannerisms, how dangerous.

As if it came from an atavism deeper than fear, I used to add "brother" 34 silently to boys' names. It hexed the boys, who would or would not ask me to dance, and made them less scary and as familiar and deserving of benevolence as girls.

But, of course, I hexed myself also—no dates. I should have stood up, 35 both arms waving, and shouted out across libraries, "Hey, you! Love me back." I had no idea, though, how to make attraction selective, how to control its direction and magnitude. If I made myself American-pretty so that the five or six Chinese boys in the class fell in love with me, everyone else—the Caucasian, Negro, and Japanese boys—would too. Sisterliness, dignified and honorable, made much more sense.

Attraction eludes control so stubbornly that whole societies designed to 36 organize relationships among people cannot keep order, not even when they bind people to one another from childhood and raise them together. Among the very poor and the wealthy, brothers married their adopted sisters, like doves. Our family allowed some romance, paying adult brides' prices and providing dowries so that their sons and daughters could marry strangers. Marriage promises to turn strangers into friendly relatives—a nation of siblings.

In the village structure, spirits shimmered among the live creatures, bal- 37 anced and held in equilibrium by time and land. But one human being flaring up into violence could open up a black hole, a maelstrom that pulled in the sky. The frightened villagers, who depended on one another to maintain the real, went to my aunt to show her a personal, physical representation of the break she made in the "roundness." Misallying couples snapped off the future, which was to be embodied in true offspring. The villagers punished her for acting as if she could have a private life, secret and apart from them.

If my aunt had betrayed the family at a time of large grain yields and 38 peace, when many boys were born, and wings were being built on many houses, perhaps she might have escaped such severe punishment. But the men—hungry, greedy, tired of planting in dry soil, cuckolded—had been forced to leave the village in order to send food-money home. There were ghost plagues, bandit plagues, wars with the Japanese, floods. My Chinese brother and sister had died of an unknown sickness. Adultery, perhaps only a mistake during good times, became a crime when the village needed food.

The round moon cakes and round doorways, the round tables of graduated 39
size that fit one roundness inside another, round windows and rice bowls —
these talismans had lost their power to warn this family of the law: A family
must be whole, faithfully keeping the descent line by having sons to feed the
old and the dead who in turn look after the family. The villagers came to show
my aunt and lover-in-hiding a broken house. The villagers were speeding up
the circling of events because she was too shortsighted to see that her infi-
delity had already harmed the village, that waves of consequences would
return unpredictably, sometimes in disguise, as now, to hurt her. This roundness had to be made coin-sized so that she would see its circumference: punish
her at the birth of her baby. Awaken her to the inexorable. People who refused
fatalism because they could invent small resources insisted on culpability.
Deny accidents and wrest fault from the stars.

After the villagers left, their lanterns now scattering in various directions 40
toward home, the family broke their silence and cursed her. "Aiaa, we're going
to die. Death is coming. Death is coming. Look what you've done. You've
killed us. Ghost! Dead Ghost! Ghost! You've never been born." She ran out
into the fields, far enough from the house so that she could no longer hear
their voices, and pressed herself against the earth, her own land no more.
When she felt the birth coming, she thought that she had been hurt. Her body
seized together. "They've hurt me too much," she thought. "This is gall, and it
will kill me." With forehead and knees against the earth, her body convulsed
and then relaxed. She turned on her back, lay on the ground. The black well
of sky and stars went out and out and out forever; her body and her complexity seemed to disappear. She was one of the stars, a bright dot in blackness,
without home, without a companion, in eternal cold and silence. An agoraphobia rose in her, speeding higher and higher, bigger and bigger; she would
not be able to contain it; there would be no end to fear.

Flayed, unprotected against space, she felt pain return, focusing her body. 41
This pain chilled her — a cold, steady kind of surface pain. Inside, spasmodically, the other pain, the pain of the child, heated her. For hours she lay
on the ground, alternately body and space. Sometimes a vision of normal
comfort obliterated reality: She saw the family in the evening gambling at
the dinner table, the young people massaging their elders' backs. She saw
them congratulating one another, high joy on the mornings the rice shoots
came up. When these pictures burst, the stars drew out further apart. Black
space opened.

She got to her feet to fight better and remembered that old-fashioned 42
women gave birth in their pigsties to fool the jealous, pain-dealing gods, who
do not snatch piglets. Before the next spasms could stop her, she ran to the
pigsty, each step a rushing out into emptiness. She climbed over the fence and

knelt in the dirt. It was good to have a fence enclosing her, a tribal person alone.

Laboring, this woman who had carried her child as a foreign growth that 43
sickened her every day, expelled it at last. She reached down to touch the hot, wet, moving mass, surely smaller than anything human, and could feel that it was human after all—fingers, toes, nails, nose. She pulled it up on to her belly, and it lay curled there, butt in the air, feet precisely tucked one under the other. She opened her loose shirt and buttoned the child inside. After resting, it squirmed and thrashed and she pushed it up to her breast. It turned its head this way and that until it found her nipple. There, it made little snuf-fling noises. She clenched her teeth at its preciousness, lovely as a young calf, a piglet, a little dog.

She may have gone to the pigsty as a last act of responsibility: She would 44
protect this child as she had protected its father. It would look after her soul, leaving supplies on her grave. But how would this tiny child without family find her grave when there would be no marker for her anywhere, nei-ther in the earth nor the family hall? No one would give her a family hall name. She had taken the child with her into the wastes. At its birth the two of them had felt the same raw pain of separation, a wound that only the fam-ily pressing tight could close. A child with no descent line would not soften her life but only trail after her, ghostlike, begging her to give it purpose. At dawn the villagers on their way to the fields would stand around the fence and look.

Full of milk, the little ghost slept. When it awoke, she hardened her 45
breasts against the milk that crying loosens. Toward morning she picked up the baby and walked to the well.

Carrying the baby to the well shows loving. Otherwise abandon it. Turn 46
its face into the mud. Mothers who love their children take them along. It was probably a girl; there is some hope of forgiveness for boys.

"Don't tell anyone you had an aunt. Your father does not want to hear her 47
name. She has never been born." I have believed that sex was unspeakable and words so strong and fathers so frail that "aunt" would do my father myste-rious harm. I have thought that my family, having settled among immigrants who had also been their neighbors in the ancestral land, needed to clean their name, and a wrong word would incite the kinspeople even here. But there is more to this silence: They want me to participate in her punishment. And I have.

In the twenty years since I heard this story I have not asked for details nor 48
said my aunt's name; I do not know it. People who comfort the dead can also chase after them to hurt them further—a reverse ancestor worship. The real

punishment was not the raid swiftly inflicted by the villagers, but the family's deliberately forgetting her. Her betrayal so maddened them, they saw to it that she would suffer forever, even after death. Always hungry, always needing, she would have to beg food from other ghosts, snatch and steal it from those whose living descendants give them gifts. She would have to fight the ghosts massed at crossroads for the buns a few thoughtful citizens leave to decoy her away from village and home so that the ancestral spirits could feast unharassed. At peace, they could act like gods, not ghosts, their descent lines providing them with paper suits and dresses, spirit money, paper houses, paper automobiles, chicken, meat, and rice into eternity—essences delivered up in smoke and flames, steam and incense rising from each rice bowl. In an attempt to make the Chinese care for people outside the family, Chairman Mao encourages us now to give our paper replicas to the spirits of outstanding soldiers and workers, no matter whose ancestors they may be. My aunt remains forever hungry. Goods are not distributed evenly among the dead.

My aunt haunts me—her ghost drawn to me because now, after fifty years 49
of neglect, I alone devote pages of paper to her, though not origamied into houses and clothes. I do not think she always means me well. I am telling on her, and she was a spite suicide, drowning herself in the drinking water. The Chinese are always very frightened of the drowned one, whose weeping ghost, wet hair hanging and skin bloated, waits silently by the water to pull down a substitute.

Journal Writing

Most of us have heard family stories that left lasting impressions—ghost stories like Kingston's, biographies of ancestors, explanations for traditions, family superstitions, and so on. Write in your journal about a family story you remember vividly from your childhood. (To take your journal writing further, see "From Journal to Essay" on the next page.)

Questions on Meaning

1. What PURPOSE does Kingston have in telling her aunt's story? How does this differ from her mother's purpose in relating the tale?
2. According to Kingston, who could have been the father of her aunt's child? Who could not?
3. Kingston says that her mother told stories "to warn us about life." What warning does this story provide?
4. Why is Kingston so fascinated by her aunt's life and death?

Questions on Writing Strategy

1. Whom does Kingston seem to include in her AUDIENCE: her family and other older Chinese? second-generation Chinese Americans like herself? other Americans? How might she expect each of these groups to respond to her essay?
2. Why is Kingston's opening line—her mother's "You must not tell anyone"— especially fitting for this essay? What secrets are being told? Why does Kingston divulge them?
3. As Kingston tells her tale of her aunt, some events are based on her mother's story or her knowledge of Chinese customs, and some are wholly imaginary. What is the EFFECT of blending these several threads of reality, perception, and imagination?
4. **MIXED METHODS.** Examine the details in the two contrasting NARRATIVES of how Kingston's aunt became pregnant: one in paragraphs 15–18 and the other in paragraphs 21–28. How do the details create different realities? Which version does Kingston seem more committed to? Why?
5. **MIXED METHODS.** Kingston COMPARES AND CONTRASTS various versions of her aunt's story, trying to find the CAUSES that led her aunt to drown in the well. In the end, what causes does Kingston seem to accept?

Questions on Language

1. How does Kingston's language—lyrical, poetic, full of FIGURES OF SPEECH and other IMAGES—reveal her relationship to her Chinese heritage? Find phrases that are especially striking.
2. Look up any of these words you do not know: bunds (par. 4); acrid (7); frivolous (14); tractably, proxy (17); hazarded (18); commensal (19); delineated (20); depilatory (25); plied (28); miens (31); abhorrent, circumvent (33); atavism (34); maelstrom (37); talismans, inexorable, fatalism, culpability (39); gall, agoraphobia (40); spasmodically (41).
3. Sometimes Kingston indicates that she is reconstructing or imagining events through verbs like "would have" and words like "maybe" and "perhaps" ("Perhaps she encountered him in the fields," par. 16). Other times she presents obviously imaginary events as if they actually happened ("Once my aunt found a freckle on her chin," 26). What effect does Kingston achieve with these apparent inconsistencies?

Suggestions for Writing

1. **FROM JOURNAL TO ESSAY.** Develop the family story from your journal (previous page) into a narrative essay. Build in the context of the story as well: Who told it to you? What purpose did he or she have in telling it to you? How does it illustrate your family's beliefs and values?
2. Write an essay explaining the role of ancestors in Chinese family and religious life, supplementing what Kingston says with research in the library or on the Web or (if you are Chinese American) drawing on your own experiences.

3. **CRITICAL WRITING.** ANALYZE the ideas about gender roles revealed in "No Name Woman," both in China and in the Chinese American culture Kingston grew up in. How have these ideas affected Kingston? Do you perceive any semblance of them in contemporary American culture?

4. **CONNECTIONS.** Both Kingston and Gloria Naylor, in "The Meanings of a Word" (p. 468), examine communication within their families. Relate an incident or incidents from your own childhood that portray something about the communication within your family. You might want to focus on the language of communication, such as the words used to discuss (or not discuss) a taboo topic, the special family meanings for familiar words, a misunderstanding between you and an adult about something the adult said. Use dialogue and as much concrete detail as you can to clarify your experience and its significance.

5. **CONNECTIONS.** Amy Tan in "Fish Cheeks" (p. 92) and Christine Leong in "Being a Chink" (p. 474) also write about relationships between parents and children in Chinese American families. In an essay, ANALYZE what these two essays along with Kingston's suggest about the experiences of the children of Chinese immigrants to the United States.

Maxine Hong Kingston on Writing

In an interview with Jean W. Ross published in *Contemporary Authors* in 1984, Maxine Hong Kingston discusses the writing and revising of *The Woman Warrior*. Ross asks Kingston to clarify an earlier statement that she had "no idea how people who don't write endure their lives." Kingston replies: "When I said that, I was thinking about how words and stories create order. Some of the things that happen to us in life seem to have no meaning, but when you write them down you find the meanings for them; or, as you translate life into words, you force a meaning. Meaning is intrinsic in words and stories."

Ross then asks if Kingston used an outline and planned to blend fact with legend in *The Woman Warrior*. "Oh no, no," Kingston answers. "What I have at the beginning of a book is not an outline. I have no idea of how stories will end or where the beginning will lead. Sometimes I draw pictures. I draw a blob and then I have a little arrow and it goes to this other blob, if you want to call that an outline. It's hardly even words; it's like a doodle. Then when it turns into words, I find the words lead me to various scenes and stories which I don't know about until I get there. I don't see the order until very late in the writing and sometimes the ending just comes. I just run up against it. All of a sudden the book's over and I didn't know it would be over."

A question from Ross about whether her emotions enter her writing leads Kingston to talk about revision. "Well, when I first set something down I feel the emotions I write about. But when I do a second draft, third draft, ninth draft, then I don't feel very emotional. The rewriting is very intellectual; all my education and reading and intellect are involved. The mechanics of sentences, how one phrase or word goes with another one—all that happens in later drafts. There's a very emotional first draft and a very technical last draft."

For Discussion

1. Do you agree with Kingston that when you write things down you find their meaning? Give examples of when the writing process has or hasn't clarified an experience for you.
2. Kingston doodles as a way to discover her material. How do you discover what you have to say?
3. What does Kingston mean by "the mechanics of sentences"? Do you consider this element as you revise?

JOHN McPHEE

The acclaimed nonfiction writer JOHN MCPHEE creates an elegantly detailed bridge between specialists and nonspecialists on subjects as diverse as basketball, orange growing, the Alaskan frontier, and the environmental problem of discarded tires. McPhee was born in 1931 in Princeton, New Jersey, and graduated from Princeton University in 1953. He has been a staff writer for *The New Yorker* since 1964 and Ferris Professor of Journalism at Princeton since 1975. In more than two dozen books, McPhee has provided readers, in the words of the critic T. H. Watkins, with "swift, lucid, authoritative stuff produced with a reporter's sure eye and a writer's love of language." His best-known books include *Coming into the Country* (1977), *The Control of Nature* (1989), and *Annals of the Former World* (1998), the last two exploring a favorite subject of McPhee's, the ever-changing earth. Described by McPhee as "three pounds of literary geology," *Annals of the Former World* won the Pulitzer Prize in 1999.

Silk Parachute

In this uncharacteristic piece of autobiography, McPhee portrays his mother through a series of scenes. The essay originally appeared in *The New Yorker* in 1997.

"Silk Parachute" is significantly an essay of example and definition: McPhee provides views of his mother as a way of defining her. Other methods come into play as well.

Narration (Chap. 4): paragraphs 7–15, 17–19
Description (Chap. 5): paragraphs 14, 18–19
Example (Chap. 6): throughout
Comparison and contrast (Chap. 7): paragraphs 1–16 versus 17–19
Process analysis (Chap. 8): paragraph 19
Definition (Chap. 12): throughout

When your mother is ninety-nine years old, you have so many memories 1
of her that they tend to overlap, intermingle, and blur. It is extremely difficult to single out one or two, impossible to remember any that exemplify the whole.

It has been alleged that when I was in college she heard that I had stayed 2
up all night playing poker and wrote me a letter that used the word "shame" forty-two times. I do not recall this.

I do not recall being pulled out of my college room and into the church 3
next door.

It has been alleged that on December 24, 1936, when I was five years old, 4
she sent me to my room at or close to 7 PM for using four-letter words while trimming the Christmas tree. I do not recall that.

The assertion is absolutely false that when I came home from high school with an A-minus she demanded an explanation for the minus. [5]

It has been alleged that she spoiled me with protectionism, because I was the youngest child and therefore the most vulnerable to attack from overhead—an assertion that I cannot confirm or confute, except to say that facts don't lie. [6]

We lived only a few blocks from the elementary school and routinely ate lunch at home. It is reported that the following dialogue and ensuing action occurred on January 22, 1941: [7]

"Eat your sandwich." [8]

"I don't want to eat my sandwich." [9]

"I made that sandwich, and you are going to eat it, Mister Man. You filled yourself up on penny candy on the way home, and now you're not hungry." [10]

"I'm late. I have to go. I'll eat the sandwich on the way back to school." [11]

"Promise?" [12]

"Promise." [13]

Allegedly, I went up the street with the sandwich in my hand and buried it in a snowbank in front of Dr. Wright's house. My mother, holding back the curtain in the window of the side door, was watching. She came out in the bitter cold, wearing only a light dress, ran to the snowbank, dug out the sandwich, chased me up Nassau Street, and rammed the sandwich down my throat, snow and all. I do not recall any detail of that story. I believe it to be a total fabrication. [14]

There was the case of the missing Cracker Jack at Lindel's corner store. Flimsy evidence pointed to Mrs. McPhee's smallest child. It has been averred that she laid the guilt on with the following words: "'Like mother like son' is a saying so true, the world will judge largely of mother by you." It has been asserted that she immediately repeated that proverb three times, and also recited it on other occasions too numerous to count. I have absolutely no recollection of her saying that about the Cracker Jack or any other controlled substance. [15]

We have now covered everything even faintly unsavory that has been reported about this person in ninety-nine years, and even those items are a collection of rumors, half-truths, prevarications, false allegations, inaccuracies, innuendos, and canards. [16]

This is the mother who—when Alfred Knopf[1] wrote her twenty-two-year-old son a letter saying, "The readers' reports in the case of your manuscript would not be very helpful, and I think might discourage you completely"— [17]

---

[1] Alfred A. Knopf (pronounced "K-nopf") published distinguished fiction and nonfiction under the imprint bearing his name. He lived from 1892 to 1984.—EDS.

said, "Don't listen to Alfred Knopf. Who does Alfred Knopf think he is, any-way? Someone should go in there and k-nock his block off." To the best of my recollection, that is what she said.

I also recall her taking me, on or about March 8th, my birthday, to the 18 theatre in New York every year, beginning in childhood. I remember those journeys as if they were today. I remember *A Connecticut Yankee*. Wednesday, March 8, 1944. Evidently, my father had written for the tickets, because she and I sat in the last row of the second balcony. Mother knew what to do about that. She gave me for my birthday an elegant spyglass, sufficient in power to bring the Connecticut Yankee back from Vermont. I sat there watching the play through my telescope, drawing as many guffaws from the surrounding audience as the comedy on the stage.

On one of those theatre days—when I was eleven or twelve—I asked her 19 if we could start for the city early and go out to LaGuardia Field to see the comings and goings of airplanes. The temperature was well below the freeze point and the March winds were so blustery that the wind-chill factor was forty below zero. Or seemed to be. My mother figured out how to take the sub-way to a stop in Jackson Heights and a bus from there—a feat I am unable to duplicate to this day. At LaGuardia, she accompanied me to the observation deck and stood there in the icy wind for at least an hour, maybe two, while I, spellbound, watched the DC-3s coming in on final, their wings flapping in the gusts. When we at last left the observation deck, we went downstairs into the terminal, where she bought me what appeared to be a black rubber ball but on closer inspection was a pair of hollow hemispheres hinged on one side and folded together. They contained a silk parachute. Opposite the hinge, each hemisphere had a small nib. A piece of string wrapped round and round the two nibs kept the ball closed. If you threw it high into the air, the string unwound and the parachute blossomed. If you sent it up with a tennis racquet, you could put it into the clouds. Not until the development of the ten-megabyte hard disk would the world ever know such a fabulous toy. Folded just so, the parachute never failed. Always, it floated back to you—silkily, beautifully—to start over and float back again. Even if you abused it, whacked it really hard—gracefully, lightly, it floated back to you.

Journal Writing

McPhee portrays his mother by providing numerous EXAMPLES of her behavior toward him. Think of someone important to you, whether a parent, another relative, a friend, a teacher, a boss. Then write down as many examples as you can of interactions that typify your relationship with that person. (To take your journal writing further, see "From Journal to Essay" on the facing page.)

Questions on Meaning

1. Why did the proverb that McPhee's mother recites in paragraph 15 induce guilt in her son?
2. What qualities are we meant to understand about McPhee's mother from her statement, "Don't listen to Alfred Knopf. Who does Alfred Knopf think he is, anyway? Someone should go in there and k-nock his block off" (par. 17)?
3. What does McPhee's response to the parachute (par. 19) — especially the final sentence — tell about his feelings for his mother?

Questions on Writing Strategy

1. McPhee's impression of his mother accumulates through incidents, but he does not explicitly GENERALIZE about what the incidents add up to. In a sentence or two, provide your own generalization about McPhee's mother. What is the EFFECT of McPhee's leaving this work to the reader?
2. In the first half of the essay, McPhee uses a kind of legal language — for instance, "It has been alleged" (pars. 2, 4, 6); "I do not recall" (2, 3, 4); "The assertion is absolutely false" (5); "I believe it to be a total fabrication" (14). What does he convey with this language?
3. McPhee presents his recollections of the "dialogue and ensuing action [. . .] on January 22, 1941" with meticulous detail, including specifics such as "Dr. Wright's house" and "Nassau Street" (pars. 8–14). How do these details and his reporting of later events contradict his assertion that "I believe [the story] to be a total fabrication"?
4. **MIXED METHODS.** McPhee's essay CONTRASTS two kinds of memories of his mother — the ones reported before paragraph 16 and the ones reported after that point. How does McPhee's TONE shift at paragraph 17 to support this contrast?
5. **MIXED METHODS.** Where in the essay does McPhee combine NARRATION and DESCRIPTION, and with what PURPOSE?

Questions on Language

1. What does a phrase like "Mister Man" in paragraph 10 evoke?
2. Study these words McPhee uses to describe the silk parachute (par. 19): "silkily," "gracefully," "lightly." How do the words have different CONNOTATIONS when applied to the parachute and to McPhee's mother?
3. Consult a dictionary if you need help defining the following: alleged (par. 2); protectionism, confute (6); averred (15); prevarications, innuendos, canards (16); guffaws (18).

Suggestions for Writing

1. **FROM JOURNAL TO ESSAY.** Develop the best examples from your journal entry (facing page) into a detailed portrait of the person. You may, like McPhee, opt to leave your generalization about the person—your THESIS—unstated, but make sure readers will be able to form the generalization themselves.

2. As an alternative to the assignment above, NARRATE a single extended event that illustrates the character of a significant person in your life and your relationship with that person. Use dialogue and plenty of DESCRIPTION to make your narrative vivid and to make it clear what your extended example illustrates.

3. **CRITICAL WRITING.** Write an essay that ANALYZES McPhee's use of legal language in the first half of "Silk Parachute" (question 2 on writing strategy can give you a start). What does this language convey about McPhee's relationship with his mother and about the writer as an adult? How would the essay be different if McPhee had not used the language? To support your analysis, use specific examples, including quotations, from the essay.

4. **CONNECTIONS.** Read "Silk Parachute" along with Sarah Vowell's "Shooting Dad" (p. 144). Both essays describe a parent through examples from memory. Write an essay COMPARING AND CONTRASTING the language each author uses to characterize his or her parent. Narrow your discussion to, say, three to five words in each essay that seem most central to the author's portrait, and use examples from the essays to show why these words are central.

5. **CONNECTIONS.** Memory and its uncertainties also play a role in David Sedaris's "Remembering My Childhood on the Continent of Africa" (p. 234) and E. B. White's "Once More to the Lake" (p. 670). In an essay, analyze how either or both of these writers and McPhee deal with the subject of memory.

John McPhee on Writing

A teacher of writing himself, John McPhee has often shared his ideas and experiences with interviewers. In a 1991 article published in the journal *College Composition and Communication*, Douglas Vipond and Russell A. Hunt quote McPhee on his conception of audience:

"As I am sitting composing a sentence, my primary thought is not imagining a reader, and whether the reader is grasping this. I think that what I'm doing is trying to put it in the way that seems most effective to *me*. Not that I'm 'writing for myself,' in that old cliché, but since I have nothing to go on but what's in my own head—in terms of selection of things that I'm going to set on the paper, and all the choices that go with that—I listen to the sentence until I both hear it and see it as something that I want. And it would be a given that a person reading it would *share* the effect that the sentence has earlier had on me."

McPhee has often been classed as a "literary journalist" because of his skill at sifting and conveying factual information with a distinctive grace and flow. (At Princeton he teaches a course called "The Literature of Fact.") Speaking to Vipond and Hunt, McPhee explained something of his technique with details:

"If you can find a specific, firm, and correct image, it's always going to be better than a generality, and hence I tend, for example, to put in trade names and company names. [. . .] You'd say 'Sony' instead of 'tape recorder' if the context made it clear you meant to say tape recorder. It's not because you're on the take from Sony, it's because the image, at least to this writer or reader, strikes a clearer note."

For Discussion

1. How does McPhee's practice of writing "something that I want" differ from "writing for [him]self"? What role does CRITICAL READING seem to play in his writing process?
2. Visualize a tape recorder. Then visualize a Sony tape recorder. What does the second image conjure up that the first one doesn't? How does this contrast illuminate McPhee's point that a "specific, firm, and correct image" is "better than a generality"?

GEORGE ORWELL

GEORGE ORWELL was the pen name of Eric Blair (1903–50), born in Bengal, India, the son of an English civil servant. After attending Eton on a scholarship, he joined the British police in Burma, where he acquired a distrust for the methods of the empire. Then followed years of tramping, odd jobs, and near-starvation—recalled in *Down and Out in Paris and London* (1933). From living on the fringe of society and from his reportorial writing about English miners and factory workers, Orwell deepened his sympathy with underdogs. Severely wounded while fighting in the Spanish Civil War, he wrote a memoir, *Homage to Catalonia* (1938), voicing disillusionment with Loyalists who, he claimed, sought not to free Spain but to exterminate their political enemies. A socialist by conviction, Orwell kept pointing to the dangers of a collective state run by totalitarians. In *Animal Farm* (1945), he satirized Soviet bureaucracy; and in his famous novel *1984* (1949), he foresaw a regimented England whose government perverts truth and spies on citizens by two-way television. (The motto of the state and its leader: Big Brother Is Watching You.)

Shooting an Elephant

Orwell wrote compellingly of his experiences as a police officer in Burma. In this selection from *Shooting an Elephant and Other Essays* (1950), he combines personal experience and piercing insight to expose both an oppressive government and himself as the government's hireling.

"Shooting an Elephant" is foremost a narrative, but Orwell uses description, example, and cause and effect as well to develop and give significance to his tale.

Narration (Chap. 4): throughout
Description (Chap. 5): paragraphs 2, 4–12
Example (Chap. 6): paragraphs 1–2, 4, 14
Cause and effect (Chap. 11): paragraphs 1–2, 6–7

In Moulmein, in Lower Burma, I was hated by large numbers of people— 1 the only time in my life that I have been important enough for this to happen to me. I was subdivisional police officer of the town, and in an aimless, petty kind of way anti-European feeling was very bitter. No one had the guts to raise a riot, but if a European woman went through the bazaars alone somebody would probably spit betel juice over her dress. As a police officer I was an obvious target and was baited whenever it seemed safe to do so. When a nimble Burman tripped me up on the football field and the referee (another Burman) looked the other way, the crowd yelled with hideous laughter. This happened more than once. In the end the sneering yellow faces of young men that met me everywhere, the insults hooted after me when I was at a safe distance, got badly on my nerves. The young Buddhist priests were the worst of all. There were several thousands of them in the town and none of them seemed to have anything to do except stand on street corners and jeer at Europeans.

All this was perplexing and upsetting. For at that time I had already made up my mind that imperialism was an evil thing and the sooner I chucked up my job and got out of it the better. Theoretically—and secretly, of course—I was all for the Burmese and all against the oppressors, the British. As for the job I was doing, I hated it more bitterly than I can perhaps make clear. In a job like that you see the dirty work of Empire at close quarters. The wretched prisoners huddling in the stinking cages of the lockups, the grey, cowed faces of the long-term convicts, the scarred buttocks of the men who had been flogged with bamboos—all these oppressed me with an intolerable sense of guilt. But I could get nothing into perspective. I was young and ill-educated and I had had to think out my problems in the utter silence that is imposed on every Englishman in the East. I did not even know that the British Empire is dying, still less did I know that it is a great deal better than the younger empires that are going to supplant it. All I knew was that I was stuck between my hatred of the empire I served and my rage against the evil-spirited little beasts who tried to make my job impossible. With one part of my mind I thought of the British Raj[1] as an unbreakable tyranny, as something clamped down, in *saecula saeculorum*,[2] upon the will of prostrate peoples; with another part I thought that the greatest joy in the world would be to drive a bayonet into a Buddhist priest's guts. Feelings like these are the normal by-products of imperialism; ask any Anglo-Indian official, if you can catch him off duty.

One day something happened which in a roundabout way was enlightening. It was a tiny incident in itself, but it gave me a better glimpse than I had had before of the real nature of imperialism—the real motives for which despotic governments act. Early one morning the subinspector at a police station the other end of town rang me up on the phone and said that an elephant was ravaging the bazaar. Would I please come and do something about it? I did not know what I could do, but I wanted to see what was happening and I got on to a pony and started out. I took my rifle, an old .44 Winchester and much too small to kill an elephant, but I thought the noise might be useful *in terrorem*.[3] Various Burmans stopped me on the way and told me about the elephant's doings. It was not, of course, a wild elephant, but a tame one which

---

[1] British imperial government. *Raj* in Hindi means "reign," a word similar to *rajah*, "ruler."—EDS.

[2] Latin, "world without end."—EDS.

[3] Latin, "to give warning."—EDS.

had gone "must." It had been chained up, as tame elephants always are when their attack of "must" is due, but on the previous night it had broken its chain and escaped. Its mahout,[4] the only person who could manage it when it was in that state, had set out in pursuit, but had taken the wrong direction and was now twelve hours' journey away, and in the morning the elephant had suddenly reappeared in the town. The Burmese population had no weapons and were quite helpless against it. It had already destroyed somebody's bamboo hut, killed a cow and raided some fruit stalls and devoured the stock; also it had met the municipal rubbish van and, when the driver jumped out and took to his heels, had turned the van over and inflicted violences upon it.

The Burmese subinspector and some Indian constables were waiting for   4
me in the quarter where the elephant had been seen. It was a very poor quarter, a labyrinth of squalid bamboo huts, thatched with palmleaf, winding all over a steep hillside. I remember that it was a cloudy, stuffy morning at the beginning of the rains. We began questioning the people as to where the elephant had gone and, as usual, failed to get any definite information. That is invariably the case in the East; a story always sounds clear enough at a distance, but the nearer you get to the scene of events the vaguer it becomes. Some of the people said that the elephant had gone in one direction, some said that he had gone in another, some professed not even to have heard of any elephant. I had almost made up my mind that the whole story was a pack of lies, when we heard yells a little distance away. There was a loud, scandalized cry of "Go away, child! Go away this instant!" and an old woman with a switch in her hand came round the corner of a hut, violently shooing away a crowd of naked children. Some more women followed, clicking their tongues and exclaiming; evidently there was something that the children ought not to have seen. I rounded the hut and saw a man's dead body sprawling in the mud. He was an Indian, a black Dravidian coolie, almost naked, and he could not have been dead many minutes. The people said that the elephant had come suddenly upon him round the corner of the hut, caught him with its trunk, put its foot on his back and ground him into the earth. This was the rainy season and the ground was soft, and his face had scored a trench a foot deep and a couple of yards long. He was lying on his belly with arms crucified and head sharply twisted to one side. His face was coated with mud, the eyes wide open, the teeth bared and grinning with an expression of unendurable agony. (Never tell me, by the way, that the dead look peaceful. Most of the corpses I have seen looked devilish.) The friction of the great beast's foot had stripped the skin from his back as neatly as one skins a rabbit. As soon as I saw the dead man I sent an orderly to a friend's house nearby to borrow an elephant rifle. I

[4]Keeper or groom, a servant of the elephant's owner. — EDS.

had already sent back the pony, not wanting it to go mad with fright and throw me if it smelled the elephant.

The orderly came back in a few minutes with a rifle and five cartridges, and meanwhile some Burmans had arrived and told us that the elephant was in the paddy fields below, only a few hundred yards away. As I started forward practically the whole population of the quarter flocked out of the houses and followed me. They had seen the rifle and were all shouting excitedly that I was going to shoot the elephant. They had not shown much interest in the elephant when he was merely ravaging their homes, but it was different now that he was going to be shot. It was a bit of fun to them, as it would be to an English crowd; besides they wanted the meat. It made me vaguely uneasy. I had no intention of shooting the elephant—I had merely sent for the rifle to defend myself if necessary—and it is always unnerving to have a crowd following you. I marched down the hill, looking and feeling a fool, with the rifle over my shoulder and an ever-growing army of people jostling at my heels. At the bottom, when you got away from the huts, there was a metalled road and beyond that a miry waste of paddy fields a thousand yards across, not yet ploughed but soggy from the first rains and dotted with coarse grass. The elephant was standing eight yards from the road, his left side towards us. He took not the slightest notice of the crowd's approach. He was tearing up bunches of grass, beating them against his knees to clean them and stuffing them into his mouth.

I had halted on the road. As soon as I saw the elephant I knew with perfect certainty that I ought not to shoot him. It is a serious matter to shoot a working elephant—it is comparable to destroying a huge and costly piece of machinery—and obviously one ought not to do it if it can possibly be avoided. And at that distance, peacefully eating, the elephant looked no more dangerous than a cow. I thought then and I think now that his attack of "must" was already passing off; in which case he would merely wander harmlessly about until the mahout came back and caught him. Moreover, I did not in the least want to shoot him. I decided that I would watch him for a little while to make sure that he did not turn savage again, and then go home.

But at that moment, I glanced round at the crowd that had followed me. It was an immense crowd, two thousand at the least and growing every minute. It blocked the road for a long distance on either side. I looked at the sea of yellow faces above the garish clothes—faces all happy and excited over this bit of fun, all certain that the elephant was going to be shot. They were watching me as they would watch a conjuror about to perform a trick. They did not like me, but with the magical rifle in my hands I was momentarily worth watching. And suddenly I realized that I should have to shoot the elephant after all. The people expected it of me and I had got to do it; I could feel their two thousand wills pressing me forward, irresistibly. And it was at this moment, as I stood there with the rifle in my hands, that I first grasped the hollowness, the futility of the white man's dominion in the East. Here was I, the white man with his gun, standing in front of the unarmed native crowd — seemingly the leading actor of the piece; but in reality I was only an absurd puppet pushed to and fro by the will of those yellow faces behind. I perceived in this moment that when the white man turns tyrant it is his own freedom that he destroys. He becomes a sort of hollow, posing dummy, the conventionalized figure of a sahib. For it is the condition of his rule that he shall spend his life in trying to impress the "natives," and so in every crisis he has got to do what the "natives" expect of him. He wears a mask, and his face grows to fit it. I had got to shoot the elephant. I had committed myself to doing it when I sent for the rifle. A sahib has got to act like a sahib; he has got to appear resolute, to know his own mind and do definite things. To come all that way, rifle in hand, with two thousand people marching at my heels, and then to trail feebly away, having done nothing — no, that was impossible. The crowd would laugh at me. And my whole life, every white man's life in the East, was one long struggle not to be laughed at.

But I did not want to shoot the elephant. I watched him beating his   8 bunch of grass against his knees, with that preoccupied grandmotherly air that elephants have. It seemed to me that it would be murder to shoot him. At that age I was not squeamish about killing animals, but I had never shot an elephant and never wanted to. (Somehow it always seems worse to kill a *large* animal.) Besides, there was the beast's owner to be considered. Alive, the elephant was worth at least a hundred pounds; dead, he would only be worth the value of his tusks, five pounds, possibly. But I had got to act quickly. I turned to some experienced-looking Burmans who had been there when we arrived, and asked them how the elephant had been behaving. They all said the same thing: He took no notice of you if you left him alone, but he might charge if you went too close to him.

It was perfectly clear to me what I ought to do. I ought to walk up to   9 within, say, twenty-five yards of the elephant and test his behavior. If he charged, I could shoot; if he took no notice of me, it would be safe to leave him until the mahout came back. But also I knew that I was going to do no such thing. I was a poor shot with a rifle and the ground was soft mud into which one would sink at every step. If the elephant charged and I missed him, I should have about as much chance as a toad under a steamroller. But even then I was not thinking particularly of my own skin, only of the watchful yellow faces behind. For at that moment, with the crowd watching me, I was not afraid in the ordinary sense, as I would have been if I had been alone. A white man mustn't be frightened in front of "natives"; and so, in general, he isn't frightened. The sole thought in my mind was that if anything went wrong those two thousand Burmans would see me pursued, caught, trampled on, and reduced to a grinning corpse like that Indian up the hill. And if that happened it was quite probable that some of them would laugh. That would never do. There was only one alternative. I shoved the cartridges into the magazine and lay down on the road to get a better aim.

The crowd grew very still, and a deep, low, happy sigh, as of people who see the theater curtain go up at last, breathed from innumerable throats. They were going to have their bit of fun after all. The rifle was a beautiful German thing with cross-hair sights. I did not then know that in shooting an elephant one would shoot to cut an imaginary bar running from ear-hole to ear-hole. I ought, therefore, as the elephant was sideways on, to have aimed straight at his ear-hole; actually I aimed several inches in front of this, thinking the brain would be further forward.   10

When I pulled the trigger I did not hear the bang or feel the kick — one never does when a shot goes home — but I heard the devilish roar of glee that went up from the crowd. In that instant, in too short a time, one would have thought, even for the bullet to get there, a mysterious, terrible change had come over the elephant. He neither stirred nor fell, but every line of his body had altered. He looked suddenly stricken, shrunken, immensely old, as though the frightful impact of the bullet had paralyzed him without knocking him down. At last, after what seemed a long time — it might have been five seconds, I dare say — he sagged flabbily to his knees. His mouth slobbered. An enormous senility seemed to have settled upon him. One could have imagined him thousands of years old. I fired again into the same spot. At the second shot he did not collapse but climbed with desperate slowness to his feet and stood weakly upright, with legs sagging and head drooping. I fired a third time. That was the shot that did for him. You could see the agony of it jolt his whole body and knock the last remnant of strength from his legs. But in falling he seemed for a moment to rise, for as his hind legs collapsed beneath him he seemed to tower upward like a huge rock toppling, his trunk reaching skywards like a tree. He trumpeted, for the first and only time. And then down he came, his belly towards me, with a crash that seemed to shake the ground even where I lay.   11

I got up. The Burmans were already racing past me across the mud. It was obvious that the elephant would never rise again, but he was not dead. He was breathing very rhythmically with long rattling gasps, his great mound of a side painfully rising and falling. His mouth was wide open. I could see far down into caverns of pale pink throat. I waited a long time for him to die, but his breathing did not weaken. Finally I fired my two remaining shots into the spot where I thought his heart must be. The thick blood welled out of him like red   12 velvet, but still he did not die. His body did not even jerk when the shots hit him, the tortured breathing continued without a pause. He was dying, very slowly and in great agony, but in some world remote from me where not even a bullet could damage him further. I felt I had got to put an end to that dreadful noise. It seemed dreadful to see the great beast lying there, powerless to move and yet powerless to die, and not even to be able to finish him. I sent back for my small rifle and poured shot after shot into his heart and down his throat. They seemed to make no impression. The tortured gasps continued as steadily as the ticking of a clock.

In the end I could not stand it any longer and went away. I heard later that it took him half an hour to die. Burmans were bringing dahs and baskets even before I left, and I was told they had stripped his body almost to the bones by the afternoon. 13

Afterwards, of course, there were endless discussions about the shooting of the elephant. The owner was furious, but he was only an Indian and could do nothing. Besides, legally I had done the right thing, for a mad elephant has to be killed, like a mad dog, if its owner fails to control it. Among the Europeans opinion was divided. The older men said I was right, the younger men said it was a damn shame to shoot an elephant for killing a coolie, because the elephant was worth more than any damn Coringhee coolie. And afterwards I was very glad that the coolie had been killed; it put me legally in the right and it gave me sufficient pretext for shooting the elephant. I often wondered whether any of the others grasped that I had done it solely to avoid looking a fool. 14

Journal Writing

How do you respond to Orwell's decision to shoot the elephant even though he believed it unnecessary to do so? Do you have any sympathy for his action? Recall a time when you acted against your better judgment in order to save face in front of others. Write as honestly as you can about what motivated you and what mistakes you made. (To take your journal writing further, see "From Journal to Essay" on the next page.)

Questions on Meaning

1. How would you answer the exasperated student who, after reading this essay, exploded, "Why didn't Orwell just leave his gun at home?"
2. Why did Orwell shoot the elephant?
3. Describe the epiphany that Orwell experiences in the course of the event he writes about. (An *epiphany* is a sudden realization of a truth.)

4. In the last paragraph of his essay, Orwell says he was "glad that the coolie had been killed." How do you account for this remark?
5. What is the PURPOSE of this essay?

Questions on Writing Strategy

1. In addition to serving as an INTRODUCTION to Orwell's essay, what function is performed by paragraphs 1 and 2?
2. From what circumstances does the IRONY of Orwell's essay spring?
3. What does "Shooting an Elephant" gain from having been written years after the events it recounts?
4. **MIXED METHODS.** Look at paragraphs 11–12. What does the blend of NARRATION and DESCRIPTION here contribute to the story? How does it further Orwell's purpose?
5. **MIXED METHODS.** How do the EXAMPLES in paragraphs 1 and 2 illustrate Orwell's conflict about his work as a police officer in Burma?

Questions on Language

1. What do you understand by Orwell's statement that the elephant had "gone 'must'" (par. 3)? Look up *must* or its variant *musth* in your dictionary.
2. What examples of English (as opposed to American) usage do you find in Orwell's essay?
3. Define, if necessary, bazaars, betel (par. 1); intolerable, supplant, prostrate (2); despotic (3); labyrinth, squalid, invariably (4); dominion, sahib (7); magazine (9); innumerable (10); senility (11).

Suggestions for Writing

1. **FROM JOURNAL TO ESSAY.** Write a narrative essay from your journal entry (previous page). Tell the story of your action, and consider what the results were, what you might have done differently, and what you learned from the experience.
2. With what examples of governmental face saving are you familiar? If none leaps to mind, read a newspaper or watch the news on television to catch public officials in the act of covering themselves. (Not only national government but local or student government may provide examples.) In an essay, ANALYZE two or three examples: What do you think was really going on that needed covering? Did the officials succeed in saving face, or did their efforts fail? Were the efforts harmful in any way?
3. **CRITICAL WRITING.** Orwell is honest with himself and his readers in acknowledging his mistakes as a government official. Write an essay that examines the degree to which confession may, or may not, erase blameworthiness for misdeeds. Does Orwell remain just as guilty as he would have been if he had not taken responsibility for his actions? Why, or why not? Feel free to supplement your analysis of Orwell's case with examples from your own life or from the news.

4. **CONNECTIONS.** Read William Lutz's "The World of Doublespeak" (p. 399), which CLASSIFIES language that deliberately conceals or misleads. In an essay, examine which of Lutz's categories of doublespeak seem to arise from the motives Orwell describes in paragraph 7: the need "to impress," to do what is expected of one, "to appear resolute," "not to be laughed at." Use specific examples from Lutz's essay — or from your own experience — to support your ideas.
5. **CONNECTIONS.** Like "Shooting an Elephant," Virginia Woolf's "The Death of the Moth" (p. 699) also blends narration and description. COMPARE AND CONTRAST the two essays, not on their purposes, which are vastly different, but on this blending. What senses do the authors rely on? How do they keep their narratives moving? How much of themselves do they inject into their essays?

George Orwell on Writing

George Orwell explains the motives for his own writing in the essay "Why I Write" (1946), from which we reprint the following excerpts.

What I have most wanted to do throughout the past ten years is to make political writing into an art. My starting point is always a feeling of partisanship, a sense of injustice. When I sit down to write a book, I do not say to myself, "I am going to produce a work of art." I write it because there is some lie that I want to expose, some fact to which I want to draw attention, and my initial concern is to get a hearing. But I could not do the work of writing a book, or even a long magazine article, if it were not also an esthetic experience. Anyone who cares to examine my work will see that even when it is downright propaganda it contains much that a full-time politician would consider irrelevant. I am not able, and I do not want, completely to abandon the worldview that I acquired in childhood. So long as I remain alive and well I shall continue to feel strongly about prose style, to love the surface of the earth, and to take a pleasure in solid objects and scraps of useless information. It is no use trying to suppress that side of myself. The job is to reconcile my ingrained likes and dislikes with the essentially public, nonindividual activities that this age forces on all of us.

It is not easy. It raises problems of construction and of language, and it raises in a new way the problem of truthfulness. Let me give just one example of the cruder kind of difficulty that arises. My book about the Spanish civil war, *Homage to Catalonia,* is, of course, a frankly political book, but in the main it is written with a certain detachment and regard for form. I did try very hard in it to tell the whole truth without violating my literary instincts. But among other things it contains a long chapter, full of newspaper quotations and the like, defending the Trotskyists who were accused of plotting with Franco. Clearly such a chapter, which after a year or two would lose its interest for any ordinary reader, must ruin the book. A critic whom I respect read me a lecture about it. "Why did you put in all that stuff?" he said. "You've turned what might have been a good book into journalism." What he said was true, but I could not have done otherwise. I happened to know, what very few people in England had been allowed to know, that innocent men were being falsely accused. If I had not been angry about that I should never have written the book.

In one form or another this problem comes up again. The problem of language is subtler and would take too long to discuss. I will only say that of late years I have tried to write less picturesquely and more exactly. In any case I find that by the time you have perfected any style of writing, you have always outgrown it. *Animal Farm* was the first book in which I tried, with full consciousness of what I was doing, to fuse political purpose and artistic purpose into the whole. [. . .]

Looking back through the last page or two, I see that I have made it appear as though my motives in writing were wholly public-spirited. I don't want to leave that as the final impression. All writers are vain, selfish, and lazy, and at the very bottom of their motives there lies a mystery. Writing a book is a horrible, exhausting struggle, like a long bout of some painful illness. One would never undertake such a thing if one were not driven on by some demon whom one can neither resist nor understand. For all one knows that demon is simply the same instinct that makes a baby squall for attention. And yet it is also true that one can write nothing readable unless one constantly struggles to efface one's own personality. Good prose is like a windowpane. I cannot say with certainty which of my motives are the strongest, but I know which of them deserve to be followed. And looking back through my work, I see that it is invariably where I lacked a *political* purpose that I wrote lifeless books and was betrayed into purple passages, sentences without meaning, decorative adjectives, and humbug generally.

For Discussion

1. What does Orwell mean by his "political purpose" in writing? by his "artistic purpose"? How did he sometimes find it hard to fulfill both purposes?
2. Think about Orwell's remark that "one can write nothing readable unless one constantly struggles to efface one's own personality." From your own experience, have you found any truth in this observation, or any reason to think otherwise?

RICHARD RODRIGUEZ

The son of Spanish-speaking Mexican Americans, RICHARD RODRIGUEZ was born in 1944 in San Francisco. After graduation from Stanford in 1967, he earned an MA from Columbia, studied at the Warburg Institute in London, and received a PhD in English literature from the University of California at Berkeley. He once taught but now devotes himself to writing and lecturing. Rodriguez's essays have appeared in *The American Scholar, Change,* and many other magazines. He is an editor at Pacific News Service and a contributing editor for *US News & World Report, Harper's,* and the *Los Angeles Times.* His on-air essays for PBS's *Newshour with Jim Lehrer* won him the George Foster Peabody Award in 1997. In 1982 he published *Hunger of Memory,* a widely discussed book of autobiographical essays. *Mexico's Children* (1991) is a study of Mexicans in America, and *Days of Obligation: An Argument with My Mexican Father* (1992) is also a memoir. Rodriguez's latest book is *Brown* (2002), in which he explores color and race in American society.

Aria: A Memoir of a Bilingual Childhood

"Aria: A Memoir of a Bilingual Childhood" is taken from *Hunger of Memory.* First published in *The American Scholar* in 1981, this poignant memoir sets forth the author's views of bilingual education. To the child Rodriguez, Spanish was a private language, English a public one. Would the boy have learned faster and better if his teachers had allowed him the use of his native language in school?

In this essay, four main methods of development serve a fifth, argument. The argument is pervasive but most explicit in the paragraphs listed below.

Narration (Chap. 4): paragraphs 1–3, 5–9, 13, 16–18, 21, 23–37
Description (Chap. 5): paragraphs 7–11, 13, 16–18, 21, 23–29
Comparison and contrast (Chap. 7): paragraphs 10–11, 14, 22, 29–30, 33–35, 38–40
Cause and effect (Chap. 11): paragraphs 12, 15, 18–20, 28–32, 36, 38–40
Argument and persuasion (Chap. 13): paragraphs 4, 19–20, 38–39

I remember, to start with, that day in Sacramento, in a California now 1 nearly thirty years past, when I first entered a classroom—able to understand about fifty stray English words. The third of four children, I had been preceded by my older brother and sister to a neighborhood Roman Catholic school. But neither of them had revealed very much about their classroom experiences. They left each morning and returned each afternoon, always together, speaking Spanish as they climbed the five steps to the porch. And their mysterious books, wrapped in brown shopping-bag paper, remained on the table next to the door, closed firmly behind them.

An accident of geography sent me to a school where all my classmates   2
were white and many were the children of doctors and lawyers and business
executives. On that first day of school, my classmates must certainly have
been uneasy to find themselves apart from their families, in the first institution
of their lives. But I was astonished. I was fated to be the "problem student"
in class.

The nun said, in a friendly but oddly impersonal voice: "Boys and girls,   3
this is Richard Rodriguez." (I heard her sound it out: *Rich-heard Road-ree-
guess*.) It was the first time I had heard anyone say my name in English.
"Richard," the nun repeated more slowly, writing my name down in her book.
Quickly I turned to see my mother's face dissolve in a watery blur behind the
pebbled-glass door.

Now, many years later, I hear of something called "bilingual education"—   4
a scheme proposed in the late 1960s by Hispanic-American social activists,
later endorsed by a congressional vote. It is a program that seeks to permit
non–English-speaking children (many from lower class homes) to use their
"family language" as the language of school. Such, at least, is the aim its supporters announce. I hear them, and am forced to say no: It is not possible for
a child, any child, ever to use his family's language in school. Not to understand this is to misunderstand the public uses of schooling and to trivialize the
nature of intimate life.

Memory teaches me what I know of these matters. The boy reminds the   5
adult. I was a bilingual child, but of a certain kind: "socially disadvantaged,"
the son of working-class parents, both Mexican immigrants.

In the early years of my boyhood, my parents coped very well in America.   6
My father had steady work. My mother managed at home. They were nobody's
victims. When we moved to a house many blocks from the Mexican-American
section of town, they were not intimidated by those two or three neighbors
who initially tried to make us unwelcome. ("Keep your brats away from my
sidewalk!") But despite all they achieved, or perhaps because they had so
much to achieve, they lacked any deep feeling of ease, of belonging in public.
They regarded the people at work or in crowds as being very distant from us.
Those were the others, *los gringos*. That term was interchangeable in their
speech with another, even more telling: *los americanos*.

I grew up in a house where the only regular guests were my relations. On   7
a certain day, enormous families of relatives would visit us, and there would be
so many people that the noise and the bodies would spill out to the backyard
and onto the front porch. Then for weeks no one would come. (If the doorbell
rang, it was usually a salesman.) Our house stood apart—gaudy yellow in a
row of white bungalows. We were the people with the noisy dog, the people

who raised chickens. We were the foreigners on the block. A few neighbors would smile and wave at us. We waved back. But until I was seven years old, I did not know the name of the old couple living next door or the names of the kids living across the street.

In public, my father and mother spoke a hesitant, accented, and not always grammatical English. And then they would have to strain, their bodies tense, to catch the sense of what was rapidly said by *los gringos*. At home, they returned to Spanish. The language of their Mexican past sounded in counterpoint to the English spoken in public. The words would come quickly, with ease. Conveyed through those sounds was the pleasing, soothing, consoling reminder that one was at home.

During those years when I was first learning to speak, my mother and father addressed me only in Spanish; in Spanish I learned to reply. By contrast, English (*inglés*) was the language I came to associate with gringos, rarely heard in the house. I learned my first words of English overhearing my parents speaking to strangers. At six years of age, I knew just enough words for my mother to trust me on errands to stores one block away—but no more.

I was then a listening child, careful to hear the very different sounds of Spanish and English. Wide-eyed with hearing, I'd listen to sounds more than to words. First, there were English (gringo) sounds. So many words still were unknown to me that when the butcher or the lady at the drugstore said something, exotic polysyllabic sounds would bloom in the midst of their sentences. Often the speech of people in public seemed to me very loud, booming with confidence. The man behind the counter would literally ask, "What can I do for you?" But by being so firm and clear, the sound of his voice said that he was a gringo; he belonged in public society. There were also the high, nasal notes of middle-class American speech—which I rarely am conscious of hearing today because I hear them so often, but could not stop hearing when I was a boy. Crowds at Safeway or at bus stops were noisy with the birdlike sounds of *los gringos*. I'd move away from them all—all the chirping chatter above me.

My own sounds I was unable to hear, but I knew that I spoke English poorly. My words could not extend to form complete thoughts. And the words I did speak I didn't know well enough to make distinct sounds. (Listeners would usually lower their heads to hear better what I was trying to say.) But it was one thing for *me* to speak English with difficulty; it was more troubling to hear my parents speaking in public: their high-whining vowels and guttural consonants; their sentences that got stuck with "eh" and "ah" sounds; the confused syntax; the hesitant rhythm of sounds so different from the way gringos spoke. I'd notice, moreover, that my parents' voices were softer than those of gringos we would meet.

I am tempted to say now that none of this mattered. (In adulthood I am embarrassed by childhood fears.) And, in a way, it didn't matter very much that my parents could not speak English with ease. Their linguistic difficulties had no serious consequences. My mother and father made themselves understood at the county hospital clinic and at government offices. And yet, in another way, it mattered very much. It was unsettling to hear my parents struggle with English. Hearing them, I'd grow nervous, and my clutching trust in their protection and power would be weakened.

There were many times like the night at a brightly lit gasoline station (a 13 blaring white memory) when I stood uneasily hearing my father talk to a teenage attendant. I do not recall what they were saying, but I cannot forget the sounds my father made as he spoke. At one point his words slid together to form one long word—sounds as confused as the threads of blue and green oil in the puddle next to my shoes. His voice rushed through what he had left to say. Toward the end, he reached falsetto notes, appealing to his listener's understanding. I looked away at the lights of passing automobiles. I tried not to hear any more. But I heard only too well the attendant's reply, his calm, easy tones. Shortly afterward, headed for home, I shivered when my father put his hand on my shoulder. The very first chance that I got, I evaded his grasp and ran on ahead into the dark, skipping with feigned boyish exuberance.

But then there was Spanish: *español*, the language rarely heard away from 14 the house; *español*, the language which seemed to me therefore a private language, my family's language. To hear its sounds was to feel myself specially recognized as one of the family, apart from *los otros*. A simple remark, an inconsequential comment could convey that assurance. My parents would say something to me and I would feel embraced by the sounds of their words. Those sounds said: *I am speaking with ease in Spanish. I am addressing you in words I never use with los gringos. I recognize you as someone special, close, like no one outside. You belong with us. In the family. Ricardo.*

At the age of six, well past the time when most middle-class children no 15 longer notice the difference between sounds uttered at home and words spoken in public, I had a different experience. I lived in a world compounded of sounds. I was a child longer than most. I lived in a magical world, surrounded by sounds both pleasing and fearful. I shared with my family a language enchantingly private—different from that used in the city around us.

Just opening or closing the screen door behind me was an important experience. I'd rarely leave home all alone or without feeling reluctance. Walking down the sidewalk, under the canopy of tall trees, I'd warily notice the (suddenly) silent neighborhood kids who stood warily watching me. Nervously, I'd arrive at the grocery store to hear there the sounds of the gringo, reminding me that in this so-big world I was a foreigner. But if leaving home was never routine, neither was coming back. Walking toward our house, climbing the steps from the sidewalk, in summer when the front door was open, I'd hear voices beyond the screen door talking in Spanish. For a second or two I'd stay, linger there listening. Smiling, I'd hear my mother call out, saying in Spanish, "Is that you, Richard?" Those were her words, but all the while her sounds would assure me: *You are home now. Come close inside. With us.* "*Sí,*" I'd reply.

Once more inside the house, I would resume my place in the family. The   17
sounds would grow harder to hear. Once more at home, I would grow less conscious of them. It required, however, no more than the blurt of the doorbell to alert me all over again to listen to sounds. The house would turn instantly quiet while my mother went to the door. I'd hear her hard English sounds. I'd wait to hear her voice turn to soft-sounding Spanish, which assured me, as surely as did the clicking tongue of the lock on the door, that the stranger was gone.

Plainly it is not healthy to hear such sounds so often. It is not healthy to   18
distinguish public from private sounds so easily. I remained cloistered by sounds, timid and shy in public, too dependent on the voices at home. I remember many nights when my father would come back from work, and I'd hear him call out to my mother in Spanish, sounding relieved. In Spanish, his voice would sound the light and free notes that he never could manage in English. Some nights I'd jump up just hearing his voice. My brother and I would come running into the room where he was with our mother. Our laughing (so deep was the pleasure!) became screaming. Like others who feel the pain of public alienation, we transformed the knowledge of our public separateness into a consoling reminder of our intimacy. Excited, our voices joined in a celebration of sounds. *We are speaking now the way we never speak out in public—we are together,* the sounds told me. Some nights no one seemed willing to loosen the hold that sounds had on us. At dinner we invented new words that sounded Spanish, but made sense only to us. We pieced together new words by taking, say, an English verb and giving it Spanish endings. My mother's instructions at bedtime would be lacquered with mock-urgent tones. Or a word like *sí,* sounded in several notes, would convey added measures of feeling. Tongues lingered around the edges of words, especially fat vowels, and we happily sounded that military drum roll, the twirling roar of the Spanish *r*. Family language, my family's sounds: the voices of my parents and sisters and brother. Their voices insisting: *You belong here. We are family members. Related. Special to one another. Listen!* Voices singing and sighing, rising and straining, then surging, teeming with pleasure which burst syllables into fragments of laughter. At times it seemed there was steady quiet only when, from another room, the rustling whispers of my parents faded and I edged closer to sleep.

Supporters of bilingual education imply today that students like me miss a   19
great deal by not being taught in their family's language. What they seem not
to recognize is that, as a socially disadvantaged child, I regarded Spanish as a
private language. It was a ghetto language that deepened and strengthened my
feeling of separateness. What I needed to learn in school was that I had the
right, and the obligation, to speak the public language. The odd truth is that
my first-grade classmates could have become bilingual, in the conventional
sense of the word, more easily than I. Had they been taught early (as upper-
middle-class children often are taught) a "second language" like Spanish or
French, they could have regarded it simply as another public language. In my
case, such bilingualism could not have been so quickly achieved. What I did
not believe was that I could speak a single public language.

Without question, it would have pleased me to have heard my teachers   20
address me in Spanish when I entered the classroom. I would have felt much
less afraid. I would have imagined that my instructors were somehow "related"
to me; I would indeed have heard their Spanish as my family's language.
I would have trusted them and responded with ease. But I would have
delayed—postponed for how long?—having to learn the language of public
society. I would have evaded—and for how long?—learning the great lesson
of school: that I had a public identity.

Fortunately, my teachers were unsentimental about their responsibility.   21
What they understood was that I needed to speak public English. So their voices
would search me out, asking me questions. Each time I heard them I'd look up
in surprise to see a nun's face frowning at me. I'd mumble, not really meaning
to answer. The nun would persist. "Richard, stand up. Don't look at the floor.
Speak up. Speak to the entire class, not just to me!" But I couldn't believe English could be my language to use. (In part, I did not want to believe it.) I continued to mumble. I resisted the teacher's demands. (Did I somehow suspect
that once I learned this public language my family life would be changed?)
Silent, waiting for the bell to sound, I remained dazed, diffident, afraid.

Because I wrongly imagined that English was intrinsically a public lan-   22
guage and Spanish was intrinsically private, I easily noted the difference
between classroom language and the language at home. At school, words were
directed to a general audience of listeners. ("Boys and girls . . .") Words were
meaningfully ordered. And the point was not self-expression alone, but to
make oneself understood by many others. The teacher quizzed: "Boys and
girls, why do we use that word in this sentence? Could we think of a better
word to use there? Would the sentence change its meaning if the words were
differently arranged? Isn't there a better way of saying much the same thing?"
(I couldn't say. I wouldn't try to say.)

Three months passed. Five. A half year. Unsmiling, ever watchful, my   23
teachers noted my silence. They began to connect my behavior with the slow
progress my brother and sisters were making. Until, one Saturday morning,
three nuns arrived at the house to talk to our parents. Stiffly they sat on the
blue living-room sofa. From the doorway of another room, spying on the visitors, I noted the incongruity, the clash of two worlds, the faces and voices of
school intruding upon the familiar setting of home. I overheard one voice
gently wondering, "Do your children speak only Spanish at home, Mrs.
Rodriguez?" While another voice added, "That Richard especially seems so
timid and shy."

That Rich-heard!   24

With great tact, the visitors continued, "Is it possible for you and your   25
husband to encourage your children to practice their English when they are
home?" Of course my parents complied. What would they not do for their
children's well-being? And how could they question the Church's authority
which those women represented? In an instant they agreed to give up the language (the sounds) which had revealed and accentuated our family's closeness. The moment after the visitors left, the change was observed. "*Ahora,*
speak to us only *en inglés,*" my father and mother told us.

At first, it seemed a kind of game. After dinner each night, the family   26
gathered together to practice "our" English. It was still then *inglés,* a language
foreign to us, so we felt drawn to it as strangers. Laughing, we would try to
define words we could not pronounce. We played with strange English sounds,
often overanglicizing our pronunciations. And we filled the smiling gaps of
our sentences with familiar Spanish sounds. But that was cheating, somebody
shouted, and everyone laughed.

In school, meanwhile, like my brother and sisters, I was required to attend   27
a daily tutoring session. I needed a full year of this special work. I also needed
my teachers to keep my attention from straying in class by calling out, "*Rich-
heard*"—their English voices slowly loosening the ties to my other name, with
its three notes, *Ri-car-do.* Most of all, I needed to hear my mother and father
speak to me in a moment of seriousness in "broken"—suddenly heartbreak-
ing—English. This scene was inevitable. One Saturday morning I entered the
kitchen where my parents were talking, but I did not realize that they were
talking in Spanish until, the moment they saw me, their voices changed and
they began speaking English. The gringo sounds they uttered startled me.
Pushed me away. In that moment of trivial misunderstanding and profound
insight, I felt my throat twisted by unsounded grief. I simply turned and left
the room. But I had no place to escape to where I could grieve in Spanish. My
brother and sisters were speaking English in another part of the house.

Again and again in the days following, as I grew increasingly angry, I was 28
obliged to hear my mother and father encouraging me: "Speak to us *en inglés*."
Only then did I determine to learn classroom English. Thus, sometime afterward it happened: One day in school, I raised my hand to volunteer an answer
to a question. I spoke out in a loud voice and I did not think it remarkable
when the entire class understood. That day I moved very far from being the
disadvantaged child I had been only days earlier. Taken hold at last was the
belief, the calming assurance, that I *belonged* in public.

Shortly after, I stopped hearing the high, troubling sounds of *los gringos*. A 29
more and more confident speaker of English, I didn't listen to how strangers
sounded when they talked to me. With so many English-speaking people
around me, I no longer heard American accents. Conversations quickened.
Listening to persons whose voices sounded eccentrically pitched, I might note
their sounds for a few seconds, but then I'd concentrate on what they were
saying. Now when I heard someone's tone of voice—angry or questioning or
sarcastic or happy or sad—I didn't distinguish it from the words it expressed.
Sound and word were thus tightly wedded. At the end of each day I was often
bemused, and always relieved, to realize how "soundless," though crowded
with words, my day in public had been. An eight-year-old boy, I finally came
to accept what had been technically true since my birth: I was an American
citizen.

But diminished by then was the special feeling of closeness at home. Gone 30
was the desperate, urgent, intense feeling of being at home among those with
whom I felt intimate. Our family remained a loving family, but one greatly
changed. We were no longer so close, no longer bound tightly together by the
knowledge of our separateness from *los gringos*. Neither my older brother nor
my sisters rushed home after school anymore. Nor did I. When I arrived home,
often there would be neighborhood kids in the house. Or the house would be
empty of sounds.

Following the dramatic Americanization of their children, even my par- 31
ents grew more publicly confident—especially my mother. First she learned
the names of all the people on the block. Then she decided we needed to have
a telephone in our house. My father, for his part, continued to use the word
gringo, but it was no longer charged with bitterness or distrust. Stripped of any
emotional content, the word simply became a name for those Americans not
of Hispanic descent. Hearing him, sometimes, I wasn't sure if he was pro-
nouncing the Spanish word *gringo*, or saying gringo in English.

There was a new silence at home. As we children learned more and more 32
English, we shared fewer and fewer words with our parents. Sentences needed
to be spoken slowly when one of us addressed our mother or father. Often the

parent wouldn't understand. The child would need to repeat himself. Still the parent misunderstood. The young voice, frustrated, would end up saying, "Never mind"—the subject was closed. Dinners would be noisy with the clinking of knives and forks against dishes. My mother would smile softly between her remarks; my father, at the other end of the table, would chew and chew his food while he stared over the heads of his children.

My mother! My father! After English became my primary language, I no   33
longer knew what words to use in addressing my parents. The old Spanish words (those tender accents of sound) I had earlier used—*mamá* and *papá*— I couldn't use anymore. They would have been all-too-painful reminders of how much had changed in my life. On the other hand, the words I heard neighborhood kids call their parents seemed equally unsatisfactory. "Mother" and "father," "ma," "pa," "dad," "pop" (how I hated the all-American sound of that last word)—all these I felt were unsuitable terms of address for *my* parents. As a result, I never used them at home. Whenever I'd speak to my parents, I would try to get their attention by looking at them. In public conversations, I'd refer to them as my "parents" or my "mother" and "father."

My mother and father, for their part, responded differently, as their chil-   34
dren spoke to them less. My mother grew restless, seemed troubled and anx-ious at the scarceness of words exchanged in the house. She would question me about my day when I came home from school. She smiled at my small talk. She pried at the edges of my sentences to get me to say something more. ("What . . . ?") She'd join conversations she overheard, but her intrusions often stopped her children's talking. By contrast, my father seemed to grow reconciled to the new quiet. Though his English somewhat improved, he tended more and more to retire into silence. At dinner he spoke very little. One night his children and even his wife helplessly giggled at his garbled English pronunciation of the Catholic "Grace Before Meals." Thereafter he made his wife recite the prayer at the start of each meal, even on formal occa-sions when there were guests in the house.

Hers became the public voice of the family. On official business it was she,   35
not my father, who would usually talk to strangers on the phone or in stores. We children grew so accustomed to his silence that years later we would rou-tinely refer to his "shyness." (My mother often tried to explain: Both of his parents died when he was eight. He was raised by an uncle who treated him as little more than a menial servant. He was never encouraged to speak. He grew up alone—a man of few words.) But I realized my father was not shy when-ever I'd watch him speaking Spanish with relatives. Using Spanish, he was quickly effusive. Especially when talking with other men, his voice would spark, flicker, flare alive with varied sounds. In Spanish he expressed ideas and

feelings he rarely revealed when speaking English. With firm Spanish sounds he conveyed a confidence and authority that English would never allow him.

The silence at home, however, was not simply the result of fewer words 36 passing between parents and children. More profound for me was the silence created by my inattention to sounds. At about the time I no longer bothered to listen with care to the sounds of English in public, I grew careless about listening to the sounds made by the family when they spoke. Most of the time I would hear someone speaking at home and didn't distinguish his sounds from the words people uttered in public. I didn't even pay much attention to my parents' accented and ungrammatical speech—at least not at home. Only when I was with them in public would I become alert to their accents. But even then their sounds caused me less and less concern. For I was growing increasingly confident of my own public identity.

I would have been happier about my public success had I not recalled, 37 sometimes, what it had been like earlier, when my family conveyed its intimacy through a set of conveniently private sounds. Sometimes in public, hearing a stranger, I'd hark back to my lost past. A Mexican farm worker approached me one day downtown. He wanted directions to some place. "*Hijito,* . . ." he said. And his voice stirred old longings. Another time I was standing beside my mother in the visiting room of a Carmelite convent, before the dense screen which rendered the nuns shadowy figures. I heard several of them speaking Spanish in their busy, singsong, overlapping voices, assuring my mother that, yes, yes, we were remembered, all our family was remembered, in their prayers. Those voices echoed faraway family sounds. Another day a dark-faced old woman touched my shoulder lightly to steady herself as she boarded a bus. She murmured something to me I couldn't quite comprehend. Her Spanish voice came near, like the face of a never-before-seen relative in the instant before I was kissed. That voice, like so many of the Spanish voices I'd hear in public, recalled the golden age of my childhood.

Bilingual educators say today that children lose a degree of "individuality" 38 by becoming assimilated into public society. (Bilingual schooling is a program popularized in the seventies, that decade when middle-class "ethnics" began to resist the process of assimilation—the "American melting pot.") But the bilingualists oversimplify when they scorn the value and necessity of assimilation. They do not seem to realize that a person is individualized in two ways. So they do not realize that, while one suffers a diminished sense of *private* individuality by being assimilated into public society, such assimilation makes possible the achievement of *public* individuality.

Simplistically again, the bilingualists insist that a student should be 39 reminded of his difference from others in mass society, of his "heritage." But they equate mere separateness with individuality. The fact is that only in private—with intimates—is separateness from the crowd a prerequisite for individuality; an intimate "tells" me that I am unique, unlike all others, apart from the crowd. In public, by contrast, full individuality is achieved, paradoxically, by those who are able to consider themselves members of the crowd. Thus it happened for me. Only when I was able to think of myself as an American, no longer an alien in gringo society, could I seek the rights and opportunities necessary for full public individuality. The social and political advantages I enjoy as a man began on the day I came to believe that my name is indeed *Rich-heard Road-ree-guess*. It is true that my public society today is often impersonal; in fact, my public society is usually mass society. But despite the anonymity of the crowd, and despite the fact that the individuality I achieve in public is often tenuous—because it depends on my being one in a crowd—I celebrate the day I acquired my new name. Those middle-class ethnics who scorn assimilation seem to me filled with decadent self-pity, obsessed by the burden of public life. Dangerously, they romanticize public separateness and trivialize the dilemma of those who are truly socially disadvantaged.

If I rehearse here the changes in my private life after my Americanization, 40 it is finally to emphasize a public gain. The loss implies the gain. The house I returned to each afternoon was quiet. Intimate sounds no longer greeted me at the door. Inside there were other noises. The telephone rang. Neighborhood kids ran past the door of the bedroom where I was reading my schoolbooks— covered with brown shopping-bag paper. Once I learned the public language, it would never again be easy for me to hear intimate family voices. More and more of my day was spent hearing words, not sounds. But that may only be a way of saying that on the day I raised my hand in class and spoke loudly to an entire roomful of faces, my childhood started to end.

Journal Writing

Rodriguez remembers thinking as a child, "We are speaking now the way we never speak out in public—we are together" (par. 18). In your journal, write about any aspect of language spoken by you and your family when you were a child—language different from what you heard in public. Perhaps, like Rodriguez's family, your family spoke a language other than the dominant one in the larger culture. Or perhaps your private language consisted of a special vocabulary, inside jokes, ALLUSIONS, particular tones of voice, or other differences. (To take your journal writing further, see "From Journal to Essay" on the next page.)

Questions on Meaning

1. Rodriguez's essay is both memoir and ARGUMENT. What is the thrust of the author's argument?
2. How did the child Rodriguez react when, in his presence, his parents had to struggle to make themselves understood by *"los gringos"*?
3. What does the author mean when he says, "I was a child longer than most" (par. 15)?
4. According to the author, what impact did the Rodriguez children's use of English have on relationships within the family?
5. Contrast the child Rodriguez's view of the nuns who insisted he speak English with his adult view.

Questions on Writing Strategy

1. How effective an INTRODUCTION is Rodriguez's first paragraph?
2. Several times in his essay Rodriguez shifts from memoir to argument and back again. What is the overall EFFECT of these shifts? Do they strengthen or weaken the author's stance against bilingual education?
3. Twice in his essay (in pars. 1 and 40) the author mentions schoolbooks wrapped in shopping-bag paper. How does the use of this detail enhance his argument?
4. What AUDIENCE probably would not like this essay? Why would they not like it?
5. **MIXED METHODS.** Examine how Rodriguez uses DESCRIPTION to COMPARE AND CONTRAST the sounds of Spanish and English (pars. 10, 11, 13, 14, 18, 33, 37). What sounds does he evoke? What are the differences among them?
6. **MIXED METHODS.** Rodriguez's essay is an argument supported mainly by personal NARRATIVE — Rodriguez's own experience. What kind of ETHICAL APPEAL (p. 503) does the narrative make? What can we INFER about Rodriguez's personality, intellect, fairness, and trustworthiness?

Questions on Language

1. Consult the dictionary if you need help defining these words: counterpoint (par. 8); polysyllabic (10); guttural, syntax (11); falsetto, exuberance (13); inconsequential (14); cloistered, lacquered (18); diffident (21); intrinsically (22); incongruity (23); bemused (29); effusive (35); assimilated (38); paradoxically, tenuous, decadent (39).
2. In Rodriguez's essay, how do the words *public* and *private* relate to the issue of bilingual education? What important distinction does the author make between *individuality* and *separateness* (par. 39)?
3. What exactly does the author mean when he says, "More and more of my day was spent hearing words, not sounds" (par. 40)?

Suggestions for Writing

1. **FROM JOURNAL TO ESSAY.** Expanding on your journal entry (previous page), write an essay DEFINING the distinctive quality of the language spoken in your home

when you were a child. What effect, if any, did this language have on you when you went out into public? Does it influence your memories of childhood? Do you revert to this private language when you are with your family?

2. Bilingual education is a controversial issue with EVIDENCE and strong feelings on both sides. In a page or so of preliminary writing, respond to Rodriguez's essay with your own gut feelings on the issue. Then do some library research to extend, support, or refute your views. (Consult the *Readers' Guide to Periodical Literature* or *InfoTrac* as a first step.) In a well-reasoned and well-supported essay, give your opinion on whether or not public schools should teach children in their "family language."

3. **CRITICAL WRITING.** In his argument against bilingual education, Rodriguez offers no data from studies, no testimony from education experts, indeed no evidence at all except his personal experience. In an essay, ANALYZE and EVALUATE this evidence: How convincing do you find it? Is it adequate to support the argument? (In your essay consider Rodriguez's ethical appeal, the topic of the sixth question on writing strategy, previous page.)

4. **CONNECTIONS.** Rodriguez's mother and father seem to have had a definite idea of their parental obligations to their children. Look at Jamaica Kincaid's story "Girl" (p. 349) and write a COMPARISON between that mother's sense of parental obligations and the Rodriguezes'. What, for example, is the connection between good parenting and teaching one's child to conform? In both cases, you will have to infer the parents' values from their actions and words. Use evidence from both works to support your inferences.

5. **CONNECTIONS.** In "Indian Education" (p. 103) Sherman Alexie also writes about the effect of schooling on his relationship to his family and his ethnic culture. In an essay, compare and contrast the experiences of Rodriguez and Alexie, focusing on how the two writers' views of education are similar and different.

Richard Rodriguez on Writing

For *The Bedford Reader*, Richard Rodriguez described the writing of "Aria."

From grammar school to college, my teachers offered perennial encouragement: "Write about what you know." Every year I would respond with the student's complaint: "I have nothing to write about . . . I haven't done anything." (Writers, real writers, I thought, lived in New York or Paris; they smoked on the back jackets of library books, their chores done.)

Stories die for not being told. My story got told because I had received an education; my teachers had given me the skill of stringing words together in a coherent line. But it was not until I was a man that I felt any need to write my story. A few years ago I left graduate school, quit teaching for political reasons (to protest affirmative action). But after leaving the classroom, as the months passed, I grew desperate to talk to serious people about serious things. In the great journals of the world, I noticed, there was conversation of a sort, glamorous company of a sort, and I determined to join it. I began writing to stay alive—not as a job, but to stay alive.

Even as you see my essay now, in cool printer's type, I look at some pages and cannot remember having written them. Or else I can remember earlier versions—unused incident, character, description (rooms, faces)—crumbled and discarded. Flung from possibility. They hit the wastebasket, those pages, and yet, defying gravity with a scratchy, starchy resilience, tried to reopen themselves. Then they fell silent. I read certain other sentences now and they recall the very day they were composed—the afternoon of rain or the telephone call that was to come a few moments after, the house, the room where these sentences were composed, the pattern of the rug, the wastebasket. (In all there were about thirty or forty versions that preceded this final "Aria.") I tried to describe my experiences exactly, at once to discover myself and to reveal myself. Always I had to write against the fear I felt that no one would be able to understand what I was saying.

As a reader, I have been struck by the way those novels and essays that are most particular, most particularly about one other life and time (Hannibal, Missouri; one summer; a slave; the loveliness of a muddy river) most fully achieve universality and call to be cherished. It is a paradox apparently: The more a writer unearths the detail that makes a life singular, the more a reader is led to feel a kind of sharing. Perhaps the reason we are able to respond to the life that is so different is because we all, each of us, think privately that we are different from one another. And the more closely we examine another life in its misery or wisdom or foolishness, the more it seems we take some version of ourselves.

It is, in any case, finally you that I end up having to trust not to laugh, not to snicker. Even as you regard me in these lines, I try to imagine your face as you read. You who read "Aria," especially those of you with your theme-divining yellow felt pen poised in your hand, you for whom this essay is yet another assignment, please do not forget that it is my life I am handing you in these pages—memories that are as personal for me as family photographs in an old cigar box.

For Discussion

1. What seems to be Rodriguez's attitude toward his AUDIENCE when he writes? Do you think he writes chiefly for his readers, or for himself? Defend your answer.
2. Rodriguez tells us what he said when, as a student, he was told, "Write about what you know." What do you think he would say now?

JONATHAN SWIFT

JONATHAN SWIFT (1667–1745), the son of English parents who had settled in Ireland, divided his energies among literature, politics, and the Church of England. Dissatisfied with the quiet life of an Anglican parish priest, Swift spent much of his time in London hobnobbing with writers and producing pamphlets in support of the Tory Party. In 1713 Queen Anne rewarded his political services with an assignment the London-loving Swift didn't want: to supervise St. Patrick's Cathedral in Dublin. There, as Dean Swift, he ended his days—beloved by the Irish, whose interests he defended against the English government. Although Swift's chief works include the remarkable satires *The Battle of the Books* and *A Tale of a Tub* (both 1704) and scores of fine poems, he is best remembered for *Gulliver's Travels* (1726), an account of four imaginary voyages. This classic is always abridged when it is given to children because of its frank descriptions of human filth and viciousness. In *Gulliver's Travels*, Swift pays tribute to the reasoning portion of "that animal called man," and delivers a stinging rebuke to the rest of him.

A Modest Proposal

Three consecutive years of drought and sparse crops had worked hardship upon the Irish when Swift wrote this ferocious essay in the summer of 1729. At the time, there were said to be thirty-five thousand wandering beggars in the country: Whole families had quit their farms and had taken to the roads. Large landowners, of English ancestry, preferred to ignore their tenants' sufferings and lived abroad to dodge taxes and payment of church duties. Swift had no special fondness for the Irish, but he hated the inhumanity he witnessed.

Although printed as a pamphlet in Dublin, Swift's essay is clearly meant for English readers as well as Irish ones. When circulated, the pamphlet caused a sensation in both Ireland and England and had to be reprinted seven times in the same year. Swift is an expert with plain, vigorous English prose, and "A Modest Proposal" is a masterpiece of SATIRE and IRONY. (If you are uncertain what Swift argues for, see the discussion of these devices in Useful Terms.)

"A Modest Proposal" is an argument developed chiefly by process analysis and cause and effect. These two methods mix with notable uses of description, example, and comparison and contrast.

Description (Chap. 5): paragraphs 1–2, 19
Example (Chap. 6): paragraphs 1–2, 6, 10, 14, 18, 32
Comparison and contrast (Chap. 7): paragraph 17
Process analysis (Chap. 8): paragraphs 4, 6–7, 10–17
Cause and effect (Chap. 11): paragraphs 4–5, 13, 21–29, 31, 33
Argument and persuasion (Chap. 13): throughout

For Preventing the Children of Poor People in Ireland
from Being a Burden to Their Parents or Country,
and for Making Them Beneficial to the Public

It is a melancholy object to those who walk through this great town[1] or travel in the country, when they see the streets, the roads, and cabin doors, crowded with beggars of the female sex, followed by three, four, or six children, all in rags and importuning every passenger for an alms. These mothers, instead of being able to work for their honest livelihood, are forced to employ all their time in strolling to beg sustenance for their helpless infants, who, as they grow up, either turn thieves for want of work, or leave their dear native country to fight for the Pretender in Spain, or sell themselves to the Barbados.[2]

I think it is agreed by all parties that this prodigious number of children in the arms, or on the backs, or at the heels of their mothers, and frequently of their fathers, is in the present deplorable state of the kingdom a very great additional grievance; and therefore whoever could find out a fair, cheap, and easy method of making these children sound, useful members of the commonwealth would deserve so well of the public as to have his statue set up for a preserver of the nation.

But my intention is very far from being confined to provide only for the children of professed beggars; it is of a much greater extent, and shall take in the whole number of infants at a certain age who are born of parents in effect as little able to support them as those who demand our charity in the streets.

As to my own part, having turned my thoughts for many years upon this important subject, and maturely weighed the several schemes of other projectors,[3] I have always found them grossly mistaken in their computation. It is true, a child just dropped from its dam may be supported by her milk for a solar year, with little other nourishment; at most not above the value of two shillings, which the mother may certainly get, or the value in scraps, by her lawful occupation of begging; and it is exactly at one year that I propose to provide for them in such a manner as instead of being a charge upon their parents or the parish, or wanting food and raiment for the rest of their lives, they shall on the contrary contribute to the feeding, and partly to the clothing, of many thousands.

---

[1] Dublin. — Eds.

[2] The Pretender was James Stuart, exiled in Spain; in 1718 many Irishmen had joined an army seeking to restore him to the English throne. Others wishing to emigrate had signed papers as indentured servants, agreeing to work for a number of years in the Barbados or other British colonies in exchange for their ocean passage. — Eds.

[3] Planners. — Eds.

There is likewise another great advantage in my scheme, that it will pre- 5
vent those voluntary abortions, and that horrid practice of women murdering
their bastard children, alas, too frequent among us, sacrificing the poor innocent babes, I doubt, more to avoid the expense than the shame, which would
move tears and pity in the most savage and inhuman breast.

The number of souls in this kingdom being usually reckoned one million 6
and a half, of these I calculate there may be about two hundred thousand
couples whose wives are breeders; from which number I subtract thirty thousand couples who are able to maintain their own children, although I apprehend there cannot be so many under the present distress of the kingdom; but
this being granted, there will remain an hundred and seventy thousand breeders. I again subtract fifty thousand for those women who miscarry, or whose
children die by accident or disease within the year. There only remain an hundred and twenty thousand children of poor parents annually born. The question therefore is, how this number shall be reared and provided for, which, as
I have already said, under the present situation of affairs, is utterly impossible
by all the methods hitherto proposed. For we can neither employ them in
handicraft or agriculture; we neither build houses (I mean in the country) nor
cultivate land. They can very seldom pick up a livelihood stealing till they
arrive at six years old, except where they are of towardly parts;[4] although I
confess they learn the rudiments much earlier, during which time they can
however be looked upon only as probationers, as I have been informed by a
principal gentleman in the country of Cavan, who protested to me that he
never knew above one or two instances under the age of six, even in a part of
the kingdom so renowned for the quickest proficiency in that art.

I am assured by our merchants that a boy or a girl before twelve years old 7
is no salable commodity; and even when they come to this age they will not
yield above three pounds, or three pounds and half a crown at most on the
Exchange; which cannot turn to account either to the parents or the kingdom, the charge of nutriment and rags having been at least four times that
value.

I shall now therefore humbly propose my own thoughts, which I hope will 8
not be liable to the least objection.

I have been assured by a very knowing American of my acquaintance in 9
London, that a young healthy child well nursed is at a year old a most delicious, nourishing, and wholesome food, whether stewed, roasted, baked, or
boiled; and I make no doubt that it will equally serve in a fricassee or a ragout.[5]

I do therefore humbly offer it to public consideration that of the hundred 10

[4] Teachable wits, innate abilities. — EDS.
[5] Stew. — EDS.

and twenty thousand children, already computed, twenty thousand may be reserved for breed, whereof only one fourth part to be males, which is more than we allow to sheep, black cattle, or swine; and my reason is that these children are seldom the fruits of marriage, a circumstance not much regarded by our savages, therefore one male will be sufficient to serve four females. That the remaining hundred thousand may at a year old be offered in sale to the persons of quality and fortune through the kingdom, always advising the mother to let them suck plentifully in the last month, so as to render them plump and fat for a good table. A child will make two dishes at an entertainment for friends; and when the family dines alone, the fore or hind quarter will make a reasonable dish, and seasoned with a little pepper or salt will be very good boiled on the fourth day, especially in winter.

I have reckoned upon a medium that a child just born will weigh twelve   11
pounds, and in a solar year it tolerably nursed increaseth to twenty-eight pounds.

I grant this food will be somewhat dear, and therefore very proper for   12
landlords, who, as they have already devoured most of the parents, seem to have the best title to the children.

Infant's flesh will be in season throughout the year, but more plentiful in   13
March, and a little before and after. For we are told by a grave author, an eminent French physician,[6] that fish being a prolific diet, there are more children born in Roman Catholic countries about nine months after Lent than at any other season; therefore, reckoning a year after Lent, the markets will be more glutted than usual, because the number of popish infants is at least three to one in this kingdom; and therefore it will have one other collateral advantage, by lessening the number of Papists among us.

I have already computed the charge of nursing a beggar's child (in which   14
list I reckon all cottagers, laborers, and four-fifths of the farmers) to be about two shillings per annum, rags included; and I believe no gentleman would repine to give ten shillings for the carcass of a good fat child, which, as I have said, will make four dishes of excellent nutritive meat, when he hath only some particular friend or his own family to dine with him. Thus the squire will learn to be a good landlord, and grow people among the tenants; the mother will have eight shillings net profit, and be fit for work till she produces another child.

Those who are more thrifty (as I must confess the times require) may flay   15
the carcass; the skin of which artificially[7] dressed will make admirable gloves for ladies, and summer boots for fine gentlemen.

---

[6] Swift's favorite French writer, François Rabelais, sixteenth-century author; not "grave" at all, but a broad humorist. —EDS.

[7] With art or craft. —EDS.

As to our city of Dublin, shambles[8] may be appointed for this purpose in   16
the most convenient parts of it, and butchers we may be assured will not be
wanting; although I rather recommend buying the children alive, and dressing
them hot from the knife as we do roasting pigs.

A very worthy person, a true lover of his country, and whose virtues I   17
highly esteem, was lately pleased in discoursing on this matter to offer a
refinement upon my scheme. He said that many gentlemen of his kingdom,
having of late destroyed their deer, he conceived that the want of venison
might be well supplied by the bodies of young lads and maidens, not exceed-
ing fourteen years of age nor under twelve, so great a number of both sexes in
every county being now ready to starve for want of work and service; and these
to be disposed of by their parents, if alive, or otherwise by their nearest relations. But with due deference to so excellent a friend and so deserving a
patriot, I cannot be altogether in his sentiments; for as to the males, my American acquaintance assured me from frequent experience that their flesh was
generally tough and lean, like that of our schoolboys, by continual exercise,
and their taste disagreeable; and to fatten them would not answer the charge.
Then as to the females, it would, I think with humble submission, be a loss to
the public, because they soon would become breeders themselves; and besides,
it is not improbable that some scrupulous people might be apt to censure such
a practice (although indeed very unjustly) as a little bordering upon cruelty;
which, I confess, hath always been with me the strongest objection against
any project, how well soever intended.

But in order to justify my friend, he confessed that this expedient was put   18
into his head by the famous Psalmanazar,[9] a native of the island Formosa, who
came from thence to London above twenty years ago, and in conversation
told my friend that in his country when any young person happened to be put
to death, the executioner sold the carcass to persons of quality as a prime
dainty; and that in his time the body of a plump girl of fifteen, who was crucified for an attempt to poison the emperor, was sold to his Imperial Majesty's
prime minister of state, and other great mandarins of the court, in joints from
the gibbet, at four hundred crowns. Neither indeed can I deny that if the same
use were made of several plump young girls in this town, who without one
single groat to their fortunes cannot stir abroad without a chair, and appear at
the playhouse and assemblies in foreign fineries which they never will pay for,
the kingdom would not be the worse.

---

[8] Butcher shops or slaughterhouses. —EDS.
[9] Georges Psalmanazar—a Frenchman who pretended to be Japanese, the author of a completely imaginary *Description of the Isle Formosa* (1705)—had become a well-known figure in
gullible London society. —EDS.

Some persons of a desponding spirit are in great concern about that vast 19
number of poor people who are aged, diseased, or maimed, and I have been
desired to employ my thoughts what course may be taken to ease the nation of
so grievous an encumbrance. But I am not in the least pain upon that matter,
because it is very well known that they are every day dying and rotting by cold
and famine, and filth and vermin, as fast as can be reasonably expected. And
as to the younger laborers, they are now in almost as hopeful a condition.
They cannot get work, and consequently pine away for want of nourishment
to a degree that if any time they are accidentally hired to common labor, they
have not strength to perform it; and thus the country and themselves are happily delivered from the evils to come.

I have too long digressed, and therefore shall return to my subject. I think 20
the advantages by the proposal which I have made are obvious and many, as
well as of the highest importance.

For first, as I have already observed, it would greatly lessen the number of 21
Papists, with whom we are yearly overrun, being the principal breeders of the
nation as well as our most dangerous enemies; and who stay at home on purpose to deliver the kingdom to the Pretender, hoping to take their advantage
by the absence of so many good Protestants, who have chosen rather to leave
their country than to stay at home and pay tithes against their conscience to
an Episcopal curate.

Secondly, the poorer tenants will have something valuable of their own, 22
which by law may be made liable to distress,[10] and help to pay their landlord's
rent, their corn and cattle being already seized and money a thing unknown.

Thirdly, whereas the maintenance of an hundred thousand children, from 23
two years old and upwards, cannot be computed at less than ten shillings a
piece per annum, the nation's stock will be thereby increased fifty thousand
pounds per annum, besides the profit of a new dish introduced to the tables of
all gentlemen of fortune in the kingdom who have any refinement in taste.
And the money will circulate among ourselves, the goods being entirely of our
own growth and manufacture.

Fourthly, the constant breeders, besides the gain of eight shillings sterling 24
per annum by the sale of their children, will be rid of the charge of maintaining them after the first year.

Fifthly, this food would likewise bring great custom to taverns, where the 25
vintners will certainly be so prudent as to procure the best receipts for dressing it to perfection, and consequently have their houses frequented by all the
fine gentlemen, who justly value themselves upon their knowledge in good

---

[10] Subject to seizure by creditors. — EDS.

eating; and a skillful cook, who understands how to oblige his guests, will contrive to make it as expensive as they please.

Sixthly, this would be a great inducement to marriage, which all wise   26
nations have either encouraged by rewards or enforced by laws and penalties.
It would increase the care and tenderness of mothers toward their children,
when they were sure of a settlement for life to the poor babes, provided in
some sort by the public, to their annual profit instead of expense. We should
see an honest emulation among the married women, which of them could
bring the fattest child to the market. Men would become as fond of their wives
during the time of their pregnancy as they are now of their mares in foal, their
cows in calf, or sows when they are ready to farrow; nor offer to beat or kick
them (as is too frequent a practice) for fear of a miscarriage.

Many other advantages might be enumerated. For instance, the addition   27
of some thousand carcasses in our exportation of barreled beef, the propagation of swine's flesh, and improvements in the art of making good bacon, so
much wanted among us by the great destruction of pigs, too frequent at our
tables, which are no way comparable in taste or magnificence to a well-grown,
fat, yearling child, which roasted whole will make a considerable figure at a
lord mayor's feast or any other public entertainment. But this and many others I omit, being studious of brevity.

Supposing that one thousand families in this city would be constant cus-   28
tomers for infants' flesh, besides others who might have it at merry meetings,
particularly weddings and christenings, I compute that Dublin would take off
annually about twenty thousand carcasses, and the rest of the kingdom (where
probably they will be sold somewhat cheaper) the remaining eighty thousand.

I can think of no one objection that will possibly be raised against this   29
proposal, unless it should be urged that the number of people will be thereby
much lessened in the kingdom. This I freely own, and it was indeed one principal design in offering it to the world. I desire the reader will observe, that I
calculate my remedy for this one individual kingdom of Ireland and for no
other that ever was, is, or I think ever can be upon earth. Therefore let no
man talk to me of other expedients: of taxing our absentees at five shillings a
pound: of using neither clothes nor household furniture except what is of our
own growth and manufacture: of utterly rejecting the materials and instruments that promote foreign luxury: of curing the expensiveness of pride, vanity, idleness, and gaming in our women: of introducing a vein of parsimony,
prudence, and temperance: of learning to love our country, in the want of
which we differ even from Laplanders and the inhabitants of Topinamboo:[11]

---

[11] A district of Brazil. — EDS.

of quitting our animosities and factions, nor acting any longer like the Jews, who were murdering one another at the very moment their city was taken:[12] of being a little cautious not to sell our country and conscience for nothing: of teaching landlords to have at least one degree of mercy toward their tenants: lastly, of putting a spirit of honesty, industry, and skill into our shopkeepers; who, if a resolution could now be taken to buy only our native goods, would immediately unite to cheat and exact upon us in the price, the measure, and the goodness, nor could ever yet be brought to make one fair proposal of just dealing, though often and earnestly invited to it.

Therefore I repeat, let no man talk to me of these and the like expedients, till he hath at least some glimpse of hope that there will ever be some hearty and sincere attempt to put them in practice.   30

But as to myself, having been wearied out for many years with offering vain, idle, visionary thoughts, and at length utterly despairing of success, I fortunately fell upon this proposal, which, as it is wholly new, so it hath something solid and real, of no expense and little trouble, full in our own power, and whereby we can incur no danger in disobliging England. For this kind of commodity will not bear exportation, the flesh being of too tender a consistence to admit a long continuance in salt, although perhaps I could name a country which would be glad to eat up our whole nation without it.   31

After all, I am not so violently bent upon my own opinion as to reject any offer proposed by wise men, which shall be found equally innocent, cheap, easy, and effectual. But before something of that kind shall be advanced in contradiction to my scheme, and offering a better, I desire the author or authors will be pleased maturely to consider two points. First, as things now stand, how they will be able to find food and raiment for an hundred thousand useless mouths and backs. And secondly, there being a round million of creatures in human figure throughout this kingdom, whose sole subsistence put into a common stock would leave them in debt two millions of pounds sterling, adding those who are beggars by profession to the bulk of farmers, cottagers, and laborers, with their wives and children who are beggars in effect; I desire those politicians who dislike my overture, and may perhaps be so bold to attempt an answer, that they will first ask the parents of these mortals whether they would not at this day think it a great happiness to have been sold for food at a year old in this manner I prescribe, and thereby have avoided such a perpetual scene of misfortunes as they have since gone through by the oppression of landlords, the impossibility of paying rent without money or trade, the want of common sustenance, with neither house nor clothes to   32

[12] During the Roman siege of Jerusalem (AD 70), prominent Jews were executed on the charge of being in league with the enemy. —EDS.

cover them from the inclemencies of the weather, and the most inevitable prospect of entailing the like or greater miseries upon their breed forever.

I profess, in the sincerity of my heart, that I have not the least personal interest in endeavoring to promote this necessary work, having no other motive than the public good of my country, by advancing our trade, providing for infants, relieving the poor, and giving some pleasure to the rich. I have no children by which I can propose to get a single penny; the youngest being nine years old, and my wife past childbearing. 33

Journal Writing

Swift's proposal is aimed at a serious social problem of his day. In your journal, consider a contemporary problem that—like the poverty and starvation Swift describes—seems to require drastic action. For instance, do you believe that a particular group of people is neglected, mistreated, or victimized? Turn to the news media for ideas if no problem comes immediately to mind. (To take your journal writing further, see "From Journal to Essay" on the next page.)

Questions on Meaning

1. On the surface, what is Swift proposing?
2. Beneath his IRONY, what is Swift's argument?
3. What do you take to be the PURPOSE of Swift's essay?
4. How does the introductory paragraph serve Swift's purpose?
5. Comment on the statement "I can think of no one objection that will possibly be raised against this proposal" (par. 29). What objections can you think of?

Questions on Writing Strategy

1. Describe the mask of the personage through whom Swift writes.
2. By what means does the writer attest to his reasonableness?
3. At what point in the essay did it become clear to you that the proposal isn't modest but horrible?
4. **MIXED METHODS.** As an essay of ARGUMENT, does "A Modest Proposal" appeal primarily to reason or to emotion? (See p. 502 for a discussion of the distinction.)
5. **MIXED METHODS.** What does Swift's argument gain by his careful attention to PROCESS ANALYSIS and to CAUSE AND EFFECT?

Questions on Language

1. How does Swift's choice of words enforce the monstrousness of his proposal? Note especially words from the vocabulary of breeding and butchery.

2. Consult your dictionary for the meanings of any of the following words not yet in your vocabulary: importuning, sustenance (par. 1); prodigious, commonwealth (2); computation, raiment (4); apprehend, rudiments, probationers (6); nutriment (7); fricassee (9); repine (14); flay (15); scrupulous, censure (17); mandarins (18); desponding, encumbrance (19); per annum (23); vintners (25); emulation, foal, farrow (26); expedients, parsimony, animosities (29); disobliging, consistence (31); overture, inclemencies (32).

Suggestions for Writing

1. **FROM JOURNAL TO ESSAY.** Write an essay in which you propose a solution to the problem raised in your journal (previous page). Your essay may be either of the following:
   a. A straight argument, giving EVIDENCE, in which you set forth possible solutions to the problem.
   b. An ironic proposal in the manner of Swift. If you do this one, find a device other than cannibalism to eliminate the victims or their problems. You don't want to imitate Swift too closely; he is probably inimitable.
2. In an encyclopedia, look into what has happened in Ireland since Swift wrote. Choose a specific contemporary aspect of Irish-English relations, research it in books and periodicals, and write a report on it.
3. **CRITICAL WRITING.** Choose several examples of irony in "A Modest Proposal" that you find particularly effective. In a brief essay, ANALYZE Swift's use of irony. Do your examples of irony depend on understating, overstating, or saying the opposite of what is meant? How do they improve on literal statements? What is the value of irony in argument?
4. **CONNECTIONS.** Read H. L. Mencken's "The Penalty of Death" (p. 516) alongside "A Modest Proposal," and analyze the use of irony and humor in these two essays. How heavily does each author depend on irony and humor to make his argument? Do these elements strengthen both authors' arguments? What evidence does each offer that would also work in a more straightforward argument?
5. **CONNECTIONS.** Analyze the ways Swift and Martin Luther King, Jr., in "I Have a Dream" (p. 603), create sympathy for the oppressed groups they are concerned about. Concentrate not only on what they say but on the words they use and their TONE. Then write a process analysis explaining techniques for portraying oppression so as to win the reader's sympathy. Use quotations or PARAPHRASES from Swift's and King's essays as examples. If you can think of other techniques that neither author uses, by all means include and illustrate them as well.

Jonathan Swift on Writing

Although surely one of the most inventive writers in English literature, Swift voiced his contempt for writers of his day who bragged of their newness and originality. In *The Battle of the Books,* he compares such a self-professed original to a spider who "spins and spits wholly from himself, and scorns to own any obligation or assistance from without." Swift has the fable-writer Aesop praise that writer who, like a bee gathering nectar, draws from many sources.

> Erect your schemes with as much method and skill as you please; yet if the materials be nothing but dirt, spun out of your own entrails (the guts of modern brains), the edifice will conclude at last in a cobweb. [. . .] As for us Ancients, we are content, with the bee, to pretend to nothing of our own beyond our wings and our voice, that is to say, our flights and our language. For the rest, whatever we have got has been by infinite labor and search and ranging through every corner of nature; the difference is, that, instead of dirt and poison, we have rather chosen to fill our hives with honey and wax, thus furnishing mankind with the two noblest of things, which are sweetness and light.

Swift's advice for a writer would seem to be: Don't just invent things out of thin air; read the best writers of the past. Observe and converse. Do legwork.

Interestingly, when in *Gulliver's Travels* Swift portrays his ideal beings, the Houyhnhnms, a race of noble and intelligent horses, he includes no writers at all in their society. "The Houyhnhnms have no letters," Gulliver observes, "and consequently their knowledge is all traditional." Still, "in poetry they must be allowed to excel all other mortals; wherein the justness of their description are indeed inimitable." (Those very traits — striking comparisons and detailed descriptions — make much of Swift's own writing memorable.)

In his great book, in "A Modest Proposal," and in virtually all he wrote, Swift's purpose was forthright and evident. He declared in "Verses on the Death of Dr. Swift,"

> As with a moral view designed
> To cure the vices of mankind:
> Yet malice never was his aim;
> He lashed the vice but spared the name.
> No individual could resent,
> Where thousands equally were meant.
> His satire points at no defect
> But what all mortals may correct.

For Discussion

1. Try applying Swift's parable of the spider and the bee to our own day. How much truth is left in it?
2. Reread thoughtfully the quotation from Swift's poem. According to the poet, what faults or abuses can a satiric writer fall into? How may these be avoided?
3. What do you take to be Swift's main PURPOSE as a writer? In your own words, SUMMARIZE it.

CORNEL WEST

Philosopher, educator, writer, and speaker, CORNEL WEST was born in 1953 in Tulsa, Oklahoma, and grew up in Sacramento, California. An articulate and persuasive orator even as a young boy, West once led his elementary-school classmates in a protest against unequal treatment of African Americans. West majored in Near Eastern languages and literature at Harvard University, graduating in 1973. He earned a PhD from Princeton University in 1980, taught religion and African American studies there from 1988 to 1994, and returned there in 2002 as professor of religion. His numerous publications include the essay collections *Prophetic Fragments* (1988), *Race Matters* (1993), and *The Cornel West Reader* (1999). He recently recorded *Sketches of My Culture*, an album combining rap, jazz, and rhythm and blues into what West calls a "danceable education" that traces the history of African Americans.

Race Matters

In this preface to the 2001 edition of his book *Race Matters*, West succinctly summarizes his vision of the condition of African Americans—and of the United States—at the opening of the twenty-first century.

"Race Matters" is a work of argument and persuasion using several other methods as well.

Example (Chap. 6): paragraphs 1, 4, 8, 10
Comparison and contrast (Chap. 7): paragraphs 3–4, 8
Division or analysis (Chap. 9): paragraphs 9–10
Cause and effect (Chap. 11): paragraphs 1, 5–11
Definition (Chap. 12): paragraph 2
Argument and persuasion (Chap. 13): throughout

Black people in the United States differ from all other modern people owing to the unprecedented levels of unregulated and unrestrained violence directed at them. No other people have been taught systematically to hate themselves—psychic violence—reinforced by the powers of state and civic coercion—physical violence—for the primary purpose of controlling their minds and exploiting their labor for nearly four hundred years. The unique combination of American terrorism—Jim Crow[1] and lynching—as well as American barbarism—slave trade and slave labor—bears witness to the distinctive American assault on black humanity. This vicious ideology and practice of white supremacy has left its indelible mark on all spheres of American

[1] The label given legalized discrimination against African Americans, derived from the title of a minstrel song. —EDS.

life—from the prevailing crimes of Amerindian reservations to the discriminatory realities against Spanish-speaking Latinos to racial stereotypes against
Asians. Yet the fundamental litmus test for American democracy—its economy, government, criminal justice system, education, mass media, and culture—remains: How broad and intense are the arbitrary powers used and
deployed against black people? In this sense, the problem of the twenty-first
century remains the problem of the color line.

The basic aim of a democratic regime is to curb the use of arbitrary   2
powers—especially of government and economic institutions—against its
citizens. Based on this uncontroversial criterion, the history of American
democracy in regard to black people from 1776 to 1965 was a colossal failure.
This also holds for red, brown, and yellow peoples. For one generation—
thirty-five years—we have embarked on a multiracial democracy with significant breakthroughs and glaring silences.

Racial progress is undeniable in America. Never before have we had such   3
a colorful menagerie of professionals in business, education, politics, sports,
and the labor movement. Glass ceilings have been pierced—not smashed—
by extraordinary persons of color. Overt forms of discrimination have been
attacked and forced to become more covert.

Yet the legacy of white supremacy lingers—often in the face of the very   4
denials of its realities. The most visible examples are racial profiling, drug convictions (black people consume 12 percent of illegal drugs in America yet suffer nearly 70 percent of its convictions!), and death-row executions. And the
less visible ones are unemployment levels, infant mortality rates, special education placements, and psychic depression treatments.

The most immediate consequence of the recent experience of multiracial   5
democracy is increasing class division and distance in American society and
black communities. This is so primarily because the advent of the multiracial
American regime coincided with escalating levels of wealth inequality. The
new inclusion of people of color within the professional slices of American
society occurred alongside the expansion of unaccountable corporate power
in the economy and government and the unleashing of arbitrary police power
in poor communities of color, especially black, brown, and red. The result
is black middle-class achievements that constitute black progress alongside
devastated black working and poor communities that yield unprecedented
increases in prison populations and overlooked victims of police abuse.
Decrepit schools, inadequate health care, unavailable childcare, and too few
jobs with a living wage set the stage for this social misery.

Democracy matters in race matters because class and gender matter in   6
American society and black life. Wealth inequality (the top 1 percent have
wealth equivalent to the bottom 95 percent, or 48 percent of the financial net

wealth in the country!) tips the balance against fair opportunity in education, employment, and other crucial life-chances. Corporate power—with its plutocratic, patriarchal, and pigmentocratic realities—lessens the abilities of citizens and workers to have a meaningful voice in shaping their destiny. Police power—disproportionately used against poor communities of color—requires just and fair regulation if it is not to be viewed as illegitimate and arbitrary.

The major culprit of democratic possibilities here and abroad is the ever- 7 expanding market culture that puts everything and everyone up for sale. The expansion of corporate power is driven by this pervasive commercialization and commodification for two basic reasons. First, market activities of buying and selling, advertising and promoting weaken nonmarket activities of caring and sharing, nurturing and connecting. Short-term stimulation and instant titillation edge out quality relations and substantive community. Second, private aims trump public aspirations. Individual success—sometimes at any cost by any means—downplays fair and just transactions so workers' and citizens' power is weakened. And no democracy can survive, no matter how strong its markets are, without a serious public life and commitment to fairness and justice. [. . .]

The impact of the market culture on black life has been devastating. As 8 Stanley Crouch rightly has noted, fifty years ago black communities were the most civilized and humane in America—highly nurturing, caring, loving, and self-respecting behind the walls of American apartheid. The market invasion, including the ugly drug invasion, has transformed too many black neighborhoods into hoods, black civic communities into black uncivil combat zones. This transformation results from the double impact of strong market forces and vicious white supremacist (and male supremacist, heterosexist) stereotypes that disproportionately shape black perceptions and practice. Needless to say, this holds for American society as a whole. But for a hated and hunted people whose prize possessions have been subversive memory, personal integrity, and self-respect, to become captive to historical amnesia, materialistic obsessions, and personal accommodation for acceptance at any costs yields black nihilism and collective suicide.

The major tragedy of black America in the past decade or so is the low 9 quality of black leadership and the relative inattention to the deep crisis of black youth. To put it bluntly, we simply do not have enough black leaders who love and respect black people enough to tell them the truth—and trust them with the truth. We have too many black leaders who give in too quickly and sell out too easily. And, like Wednesday night at the Apollo Theater, most black folk know who is for real, committed, and serious, and who is not. But too often, the choice for high-quality leadership is limited. And we find ourselves between a rock and a hard place.

This is especially so in regard to black youth. With roughly 40 percent of   10
black children living in poverty and almost 10 percent of all black young adult
men in prison, we face a crisis of enormous proportions. Yet this crisis is not
even a blip on the national radar screen of American politics. This is a shame
and disgrace—and black leaders must bear some of the responsibility. How
can black youth respect black leaders when their plight and predicament is so
flagrantly ignored by the mainstream—a mainstream black leaders speak to
and influence? With few exceptions—Al Sharpton, Marian Wright Edelman,
the Black Radical Congress, NAACP's ACT-SO programs for young people,
and a few others—black leadership tends to downplay the black youth realities at the expense of black professional advancement. Again, this priority is
an issue of class and gender in black America. And it is now coming back to
haunt black leaders.

As we enter the twenty-first century, we must connect the urgent black   11
domestic issues to pressing class and gender issues in the corporate globalization around the world. As Danny Glover constantly reminds us, environmental, consumers', and workers' protections in our increasingly interdependent
world of capitalist markets are crucial if race matters are to be enhanced. If
pro-democracy movements weaken—and citizens and workers become more
feeble—race matters will explode. And we know the ugly cycle this will yield.
We must do better—but only if we muster the vision, courage, and will to do so.

Journal Writing

One of West's key points is that obsession with individual achievement has greatly
lessened concern for the welfare of the community as a whole: "private aims trump
public aspirations" (par. 7). In your journal, explore your views of this assertion. Do
you think people are mostly concerned with their own well-being at the expense of
others? If so, is this necessarily a bad thing? (To take your journal writing further, see
"From Journal to Essay" on the next page.)

Questions on Meaning

1. What is West's THESIS? Where is it stated? How does it relate to his ultimate
   PURPOSE?
2. "Racial progress is undeniable in America," West acknowledges (par. 3), citing an
   increasing number of minority professionals; yet he claims that many serious
   problems still remain. What are these problems? To what does he attribute them?
3. How does West criticize the quality of black leadership in the United States?
4. How are "black domestic issues" (par. 11) related to global issues of class and gender, according to West?

Questions on Writing Strategy

1. Why do you suppose West's introduction focuses on the historical injustices done to African Americans? How does West relate this history to contemporary issues?
2. Does West seem to be writing primarily for an African American AUDIENCE, or does he see his readers more broadly? What makes you think so?
3. **MIXED METHODS.** Where does West rely on CAUSE AND EFFECT? Why is this method important to his overall strategy?
4. **MIXED METHODS.** In paragraph 8 West makes an important CONTRAST. What is it, and what is his point in doing so?

Questions on Language

1. Examine West's TONE, particularly the words he uses and the sentences he constructs. How would you characterize the tone? Is it effective? Why, or why not?
2. In what two senses does West use the word *matters* in the title of his book and this essay and at the beginning of paragraph 6?
3. What does West mean when he writes that "we [black people] find ourselves between a rock and a hard place" (par. 9)?
4. Be sure you can define the following words, consulting your dictionary if you need help: unprecedented, psychic, coercion, ideology, litmus test (par. 1); regime, criterion, colossal (2); menagerie (3); advent, unaccountable, decrepit (5); disproportionately (6); commodification, titillation, substantive, trump (7); apartheid, nihilism (8); plight, predicament, flagrantly (10); globalization, muster (11).

Suggestions for Writing

1. **FROM JOURNAL TO ESSAY.** Taking off from your journal entry (previous page), write an essay in which you explore your views about the contemporary focus on individual success and the extent to which such a focus may erode what West calls "a serious public life and commitment to fairness and justice" (par. 7). Do you see the problem West does? If not, why? If so, what solutions can you propose?
2. In paragraph 4 and elsewhere, West refers to racial profiling by law-enforcement agencies. In your library or online, research the prevalence of racial profiling today, whom it is most likely to affect, and the legal issues involved. In an essay, make a case for or against racial profiling, being sure to take into account the arguments of those who would disagree with you.
3. **CRITICAL WRITING.** Respond to West's central contention that "race matters," that Americans should be especially concerned about a legacy of racism that still affects the United States. Do you agree with West, or do you think his claims are exaggerated? In your essay, address West's specific points with your own ideas on the subject.
4. **CONNECTIONS.** In "Notes from the Hip-Hop Underground" (p. 328), Shelby Steele, like West an African American academic, also considers the legacy of racism in the United States, its current consequences, and the influences of consumer culture on those who feel alienated or downtrodden. Compare and con-

trast the ideas of Steele and West, focusing in part on each writer's purpose. Do you find yourself more in agreement with one or the other writer? Why?

5. **CONNECTIONS.** George F. Will, in "The Equity of Inequality" (p. 481), makes a very different argument from West's. ANALYZE the ASSUMPTIONS of these two writers. Then, in an essay, consider how Will would respond to West's ideas and how West would respond to Will's.

E. B. WHITE

ELWYN BROOKS WHITE (1899–1985) for half a century was a regular contributor to *The New Yorker*, and his essays, editorials, anonymous features for "The Talk of the Town," and fillers helped build the magazine a reputation for wit and good writing. If as a child you read *Charlotte's Web* (1952), you have met E. B. White before. The book reflects some of his own life on a farm in North Brooklin, Maine. His *Letters* were collected in 1976, his *Essays* in 1977, and his *Poems and Sketches* in 1981. On July 4, 1963, President Kennedy named White in the first group of Americans to receive the Presidential Medal of Freedom, with a citation that called him "an essayist whose concise comment [. . .] has revealed to yet another age the vigor of the English sentence."

Once More to the Lake

"Once More to the Lake" first appeared in *Harper's* magazine in 1941. Perhaps if a duller writer had written the essay, or an essay with the same title, we wouldn't much care about it, for at first its subject seems as personal and ordinary as a letter home. White's loving and exact portrayal, however, brings this lakeside camp to life for us. In the end, the writer arrives at an awareness that shocks him—shocks us, too, with a familiar sensory detail.

"Once More to the Lake" is a stunning mixture of description and narration, but it is also more. To make his observations and emotions clear and immediate, White relies extensively on several other methods of development as well.

Narration (Chap. 4): throughout
Description (Chap. 5): throughout
Example (Chap. 6): paragraphs 2, 7–8, 11, 12
Comparison and contrast (Chap. 7): paragraphs 4–7, 9–10, 11–12
Process analysis (Chap. 8): paragraphs 9, 10, 12

August 1941

One summer, along about 1904, my father rented a camp on a lake   1
in Maine and took us all there for the month of August. We all got ring-worm from some kittens and had to rub Pond's Extract on our arms and legs night and morning, and my father rolled over in a canoe with all his clothes on; but outside of that the vacation was a success and from then on none of us ever thought there was any place in the world like that lake in Maine. We returned summer after summer—always on August 1 for one month. I have since become a salt-water man, but sometimes in summer there are days when the restlessness of the tides and the fearful cold of the sea water and

the incessant wind that blows across the afternoon and into the evening make me wish for the placidity of a lake in the woods. A few weeks ago this feeling got so strong I bought myself a couple of bass hooks and a spinner and returned to the lake where we used to go, for a week's fishing and to revisit old haunts.

I took along my son, who had never had any fresh water up his nose and who had seen lily pads only from train windows. On the journey over to the lake I began to wonder what it would be like. I wondered how time would have marred this unique, this holy spot—the coves and streams, the hills that the sun set behind, the camps and the paths behind the camps. I was sure that the tarred road would have found it out, and I wondered in what other ways it would be desolated. It is strange how much you can remember about places like that once you allow your mind to return into the grooves that lead back. You remember one thing, and that suddenly reminds you of another thing. I guess I remembered clearest of all the early mornings, when the lake was cool and motionless, remembered how the bedroom smelled of the lumber it was made of and of the wet woods whose scent entered through the screen. The partitions in the camp were thin and did not extend clear to the top of the rooms, and as I was always the first up I would dress softly so as not to wake the others, and sneak out into the sweet outdoors and start out in the canoe, keeping close along the shore in the long shadows of the pines. I remembered being very careful never to rub my paddle against the gunwale for fear of disturbing the stillness of the cathedral.

The lake had never been what you would call a wild lake. There were cottages sprinkled around the shores, and it was in farming country although the shores of the lake were quite heavily wooded. Some of the cottages were owned by nearby farmers, and you would live at the shore and eat your meals at the farmhouse. That's what our family did. But although it wasn't wild, it was a fairly large and undisturbed lake and there were places in it that, to a child at least, seemed infinitely remote and primeval.

I was right about the tar: It led to within half a mile of the shore. But when I got back there, with my boy, and we settled into a camp near a farmhouse and into the kind of summertime I had known, I could tell that it was going to be pretty much the same as it had been before—I knew it, lying in bed the first morning smelling the bedroom and hearing the boy sneak quietly out and go off along the shore in a boat. I began to sustain the illusion that he was I, and therefore, by simple transposition, that I was my father. This sensation persisted, kept cropping up all the time we were there. It was not an entirely new feeling, but in this setting it grew much stronger. I seemed to be living a dual existence. I would be in the middle of some simple act, I would be picking up a bait box or laying down a table fork, or I would be saying something and suddenly it would be not I but my father who was saying the words or making the gesture. It gave me a creepy sensation.

We went fishing the first morning. I felt the same damp moss covering the worms in the bait can, and saw the dragonfly alight on the tip of my rod as it hovered a few inches from the surface of the water. It was the arrival of this fly that convinced me beyond any doubt that everything was as it always had been, that the years were a mirage and that there had been no years. The small waves were the same, chucking the rowboat under the chin as we fished at anchor, and the boat was the same boat, the same color green and the ribs broken in the same places, and under the floorboards the same fresh water leavings and debris—the dead hellgrammite, the wisps of moss, the rusty discarded fishhook, the dried blood from yesterday's catch. We stared silently at the tips of our rods, at the dragonflies that came and went. I lowered the tip of mine into the water, tentatively, pensively dislodging the fly, which darted two feet away, poised, darted two feet back, and came to rest again a little farther up the rod. There had been no years between the ducking of this dragonfly and the other one—the one that was part of memory. I looked at the boy, who was silently watching his fly, and it was my hands that held his rod, my eyes watching. I felt dizzy and didn't know which rod I was at the end of.

We caught two bass, hauling them in briskly as though they were mackerel, pulling them over the side of the boat in a businesslike manner without any landing net, and stunning them with a blow on the back of the head. When we got back for a swim before lunch, the lake was exactly where we had left it, the same number of inches from the dock, and there was only the merest suggestion of a breeze. This seemed an utterly enchanted sea, this lake you could leave to its own devices for a few hours and come back to, and find that it had not stirred, this constant and trustworthy body of water. In the shallows, the dark, water-soaked sticks and twigs, smooth and old, were undulating in clusters on the bottom against the clean ribbed sand, and the track of the mussel was plain. A school of minnows swam by, each minnow with its small individual shadow, doubling the attendance, so clear and sharp in the sunlight. Some of the other campers were in swimming, along the shore, one of them with a cake of soap, and the water felt thin and clear and unsubstantial. Over the years there had been this person with the cake of soap, this cultist, and here he was. There had been no years.

Up to the farmhouse to dinner through the teeming dusty field, the road under our sneakers was only a two-track road. The middle track was missing, the one with the marks of the hooves and the splotches of dried, flaky manure. There had always been three tracks to choose from in choosing which track to walk in; now the choice was narrowed down to two. For a moment I missed terribly the middle alternative. But the way led past the tennis court, and something about the way it lay there in the sun reassured me; the tape had loosened along the backline, the alleys were green with plantains and other weeds, and the net (installed in June and removed in September) sagged in the dry noon, and the whole place steamed with midday heat and hunger and emptiness. There was a choice of pie for dessert, and one was blueberry and one was apple, and the waitresses were the same country girls, there having been no passage of time, only the illusion of it as in a dropped curtain — the waitresses were still fifteen; their hair had been washed, that was the only difference — they had been to the movies and seen the pretty girls with the clean hair.

Summertime, oh, summertime, pattern of life indelible, the fade-proof lake, the woods unshatterable, the pasture with the sweetfern and the juniper forever and ever, summer without end; this was the background, and the life along the shore was the design, the cottages with their innocent and tranquil design, their tiny docks with the flagpole and the American flag floating against the white clouds in the blue sky, the little paths over the roots of the trees leading from camp to camp and the paths leading back to the outhouses and the can of lime for sprinkling, and at the souvenir counters at the store the miniature birchbark canoes and the postcards that showed things looking a little better than they looked. This was the American family at play, escaping the city heat, wondering whether the newcomers in the camp at the head of the cove were "common" or "nice," wondering whether it was true that the people who drove up for Sunday dinner at the farmhouse were turned away because there wasn't enough chicken.

It seemed to me, as I kept remembering all this, that those times and those summers had been infinitely precious and worth saving. There had been jollity and peace and goodness. The arriving (at the beginning of August) had been so big a business in itself, at the railway station the farm wagon drawn up, the first smell of the pine-laden air, the first glimpse of the smiling farmer, and the great importance of the trunks and your father's enormous authority in such matters, and the feel of the wagon under you for the long ten-mile haul, and at the top of the last long hill catching the first view of the lake after eleven months of not seeing this cherished body of water. The shouts and cries of the other campers when they saw you, and the trunks to be unpacked, to give up their rich burden. (Arriving was less exciting nowadays, when you sneaked up in your car and parked it under a tree near the camp and took out the bags and in five minutes it was all over, no fuss, no loud wonderful fuss about trunks.)

Peace and goodness and jollity. The only thing that was wrong now, really, was the sound of the place, an unfamiliar nervous sound of the outboard motors. This was the note that jarred, the one thing that would sometimes break the illusion and set the years moving. In those other summertimes all motors were inboard; and when they were at a little distance, the noise they made was a sedative, an ingredient of summer sleep. They were one-cylinder and two-cylinder engines, and some were make-and-break and some were jump-spark, but they all made a sleepy sound across the lake. The one-lungers throbbed and fluttered, and the twin-cylinder ones purred and purred, and that was a quiet sound, too. But now the campers all had outboards. In the daytime, in the hot mornings, these motors made a petulant irritable sound; at night in the still evening when the afterglow lit the water, they whined about one's ears like mosquitoes. My boy loved our rented outboard, and his great desire was to achieve single-handed mastery over it, and authority, and he soon learned the trick of choking it a little (but not too much), and the adjustment of the needle valve. Watching him I would remember the things you could do with the old one-cylinder engine with the heavy flywheel, how you could have it eating out of your hand if you got really close to it spiritually. Motorboats in those days didn't have clutches, and you would make a landing by shutting off the motor at the proper time and coasting in with a dead rudder. But there was a way of reversing them, if you learned the trick, by cutting the switch and putting it on again exactly on the final dying revolution of the flywheel, so that it would kick back against compression and begin reversing. Approaching a dock in a strong following breeze, it was difficult to slow up sufficiently by the ordinary coasting method, and if a boy felt he had complete mastery over his motor, he was tempted to keep it running beyond its time and then reverse it a few feet from the dock. It took a cool nerve, because if you threw the switch a twentieth of a second too soon you would catch the flywheel when it still had speed enough to go up past center, and the boat would leap ahead, charging bull-fashion at the dock.

We had a good week at the camp. The bass were biting well and the sun 11 shone endlessly, day after day. We would be tired at night and lie down in the accumulated heat of the little bedrooms after the long hot day and the breeze would stir almost imperceptibly outside and the smell of the swamp drift in through the rusty screens. Sleep would come easily and in the morning the red squirrel would be on the roof, tapping out his gay routine. I kept remembering everything, lying in bed in the mornings—the small steamboat that had a long rounded stern like the lip of a Ubangi, and how quietly she ran on the moonlight sails, when the older boys played their mandolins and the girls sang and we ate doughnuts dipped in sugar, and how sweet the music was on the water in the shining night, and what it had felt like to think about girls then. After breakfast we would go up to the store and the things were in the same place—the minnows in a bottle, the plugs and spinners disarranged and pawed over by the youngsters from the boys' camp, the Fig Newtons and the

Beeman's gum. Outside, the road was tarred and cars stood in front of the store. Inside, all was just as it had always been, except there was more Coca-Cola and not so much Moxie and root beer and birch beer and sarsaparilla. We would walk out with a bottle of pop apiece and sometimes the pop would backfire up our noses and hurt. We explored the streams, quietly, where the turtles slid off the sunny logs and dug their way into the soft bottom; and we lay on the town wharf and fed worms to the tame bass. Everywhere we went I had trouble making out which was I, the one walking at my side, the one walking in my pants.

One afternoon while we were at the lake a thunderstorm came up. It was   12 like the revival of an old melodrama that I had seen long ago with childish awe. The second-act climax of the drama of the electrical disturbance over a lake in America had not changed in any important respect. This was the big scene, still the big scene. The whole thing was so familiar, the first feeling of oppression and heat and a general air around camp of not wanting to go very far away. In midafternoon (it was all the same) a curious darkening of the sky, and a lull in everything that had made life tick; and then the way the boats suddenly swung the other way at their moorings with the coming of a breeze out of the new quarter, and the premonitory rumble. Then the kettle drum, then the snare, then the bass drum and cymbals, then crackling light against the dark, and the gods grinning and licking their chops in the hills. Afterward the calm, the rain steadily rustling in the calm lake, the return of light and hope and spirits, and the campers running out in joy and relief to go swimming in the rain, their bright cries perpetuating the deathless joke about how they were getting simply drenched, and the children screaming with delight at the new sensation of bathing in the rain, and the joke about getting drenched linking the generations in a strong indestructible chain. And the comedian who waded in carrying an umbrella.

When the others went swimming my son said he was going in, too. He   13 pulled his dripping trunks from the line where they had hung all through the shower and wrung them out. Languidly, and with no thought of going in, I watched him, his hard little body, skinny and bare, saw him wince slightly as he pulled up around his vitals the small, soggy, icy garment. As he buckled the swollen belt, suddenly my groin felt the chill of death.

Journal Writing

White strongly evokes the lake camp as a place that was important to him as a child. What place or places were most important to you as a child? In your journal, jot down some memories. (To take your journal writing further, see "From Journal to Essay" below.)

Questions on Meaning

1. How do you account for the distortions that creep into the author's sense of time?
2. What does the discussion of inboard and outboard motors (par. 10) have to do with the author's divided sense of time?
3. To what degree does White make us aware of his son's impression of this trip to the lake?
4. What do you take to be White's main PURPOSE in the essay? At what point do you become aware of it?

Questions on Writing Strategy

1. In paragraph 4 the author first introduces his confused feeling that he has gone back in time to his own childhood, an idea that he repeats and expands throughout his account. What is the function of these repetitions?
2. Try to describe the impact of the essay's final paragraph. By what means is it achieved?
3. To what extent is this essay written to appeal to any but middle-aged readers? Is it comprehensible to anyone whose vacations were never spent at a Maine summer cottage?
4. What is the TONE of White's essay?
5. **MIXED METHODS.** White's DESCRIPTION depends on many IMAGES that are not FIGURES OF SPEECH but literal translations of sensory impressions. Locate four such images.
6. **MIXED METHODS.** Within White's description and NARRATION of his visit to the lake, what purpose is served by the COMPARISON AND CONTRAST between the lake now and when he was a boy?

Questions on Language

1. Be sure you know the meanings of the following words: incessant, placidity (par. 1); gunwale (2); primeval (3); transposition (4); hellgrammite (5); undulating, cultist (6); indelible, tranquil (8); petulant (10); imperceptibly (11); premonitory (12); languidly (13).
2. Comment on White's DICTION in his reference to the lake as "this unique, this holy spot" (par. 2).
3. Explain what White is describing in the sentence that begins, "Then the kettle drum" (par. 12). Where else does the author use figures of speech?

Suggestions for Writing

1. **FROM JOURNAL TO ESSAY.** Choose one of the places suggested by your journal entry (above), and write an essay describing the place now, revisiting it as an

adult. (If you haven't visited the place since childhood, you can imagine what seeing it now would be like.) Your description should draw on your childhood memories, making them as vivid as possible for the reader, but you should also consider how your POINT OF VIEW toward the place differs now.

2. In a descriptive paragraph about a real or imagined place, try to appeal to each of your reader's five senses.

3. **CRITICAL WRITING.** While on the vacation he describes, White wrote to his wife, Katharine, "This place is as American as a drink of Coca Cola. The white collar family having its annual liberty." Obviously, not everyone has a chance at the lakeside summers White enjoyed. To what extent, if at all, does White's privileged point of view deprive his essay of universal meaning and significance? Write an essay answering this question. Back up your ideas with EVIDENCE from White's essay.

4. **CONNECTIONS.** In White's "Once More to the Lake" and Brad Manning's "Arm Wrestling with My Father" (p. 136), the writers reveal a changing sense of what it means to be a father. Write an essay that examines the similarities and differences in their definitions of fatherhood. How does a changing idea of what it means to be a son connect with this redefinition of fatherhood?

5. **CONNECTIONS.** White's essay is full of images that place his audience in a setting important to him in childhood. M. F. K. Fisher, in "The Broken Chain" (p. 13), also uses vivid images to evoke childhood. After reading these two essays, write an essay of your own ANALYZING four or five images from each that strike you as especially evocative. What sense impression does each image draw on? What does each one tell you about the author's feelings?

E. B. White on Writing

"You asked me about writing—how I did it," E. B. White replied to a seventeen-year-old who had written to him, wanting to become a professional writer but feeling discouraged. "There is no trick to it. If you like to write and want to write, you write, no matter where you are or what else you are doing or whether anyone pays any heed. I must have written half a million words (mostly in my journal) before I had anything published, save for a couple of short items in *St. Nicholas*.[1] If you want to write about feelings, about the end of the summer, about growing, write about it. A great deal of writing is not 'plotted'—most of my essays have no plot structure, they are a ramble in the woods, or a ramble in the basement of my mind. You ask, 'Who cares?' Everybody cares. You say, 'It's been written before.' Everything has been written before. [. . .] Henry Thoreau, who wrote *Walden*, said, 'I learned this at least by

---

[1] A magazine for children, popular early in the twentieth century. —EDS.

my experiment: that if one advances confidently in the direction of his dreams and endeavors to live the life which he has imagined, he will meet with a success unexpected in common hours.' The sentence, after more than a hundred years, is still alive. So, advance confidently."

In trying to characterize his own writing, White was modest in his claims. To his brother Stanley Hart White, he once remarked, "I discovered a long time ago that writing of the small things of the day, the trivial matters of the heart, the inconsequential but near things of this living, was the only kind of creative work which I could accomplish with any sincerity or grace. As a reporter, I was a flop, because I always came back laden not with facts about the case, but with a mind full of the little difficulties and amusements I had encountered in my travels. Not till *The New Yorker* came along did I ever find any means of expressing those impertinences and irrelevancies. Thus yesterday, setting out to get a story on how police horses are trained, I ended by writing a story entitled "How Police Horses Are Trained" which never even mentions a police horse, but has to do entirely with my own absurd adventures at police headquarters. The rewards of such endeavor are not that I have acquired an audience or a following, as you suggest (fame of any kind being a Pyrrhic victory), but that sometimes in writing of myself—which is the only subject anyone knows intimately—I have occasionally had the exquisite thrill of putting my finger on a little capsule of truth, and heard it give the faint squeak of mortality under my pressure, an antic sound."

For Discussion

1. Sometimes young writers are counseled to study the market and then try to write something that will sell. How would you expect E. B. White to have reacted to such advice?
2. What, exactly, does White mean when he says, "Everything has been written before"? How might an aspiring writer take this remark as encouragement?
3. What interesting distinction does White make between reporting and essay writing?

TERRY TEMPEST WILLIAMS

Born in 1955, TERRY TEMPEST WILLIAMS grew up in Salt Lake City, Utah. A writer, naturalist, and passionate advocate for the preservation of America's wilderness, Williams says she is "a woman whose ideas have been shaped by the Colorado Plateau and the Great Basin." Williams studied English and environmental education at the University of Utah, from which she received BA and MA degrees. She has taught at the Navajo reservation in Montezuma Creek and has served as naturalist-in-residence at the Utah Museum of Natural History. Williams is the author of many books about nature, including *Pieces of White Shell: A Journey to Navajo Land* (1984), *Coyote's Canyon* (1989), *Refuge: An Unnatural History of Family and Place* (1991), and *Red: Desert Passions* (2001). She lives near Salt Lake City.

The Clan of One-Breasted Women

In this powerful essay of grief and anger, Williams' explains how events changed her from an observer to an activist. The essay first appeared in the magazine *Northern Lights* in 1990 and then as the epilogue to Williams's book *Refuge*.

"The Clan of One-Breasted Women" develops by no dominant method but by at least six:

Narration (Chap. 4): paragraphs 6–19, 23–29, 39–48, 50–58
Description (Chap. 5): paragraphs 16, 32, 39, 41–46, 56
Example (Chap. 6): paragraphs 22, 23–29
Comparison and contrast (Chap. 7): paragraphs 30–32 versus 37
Cause and effect (Chap. 11): paragraphs 4–6, 19, 34–36
Argument and persuasion (Chap. 13): paragraphs 19–38

1   I belong to a Clan of One-Breasted Women. My mother, my grandmothers, and six aunts have all had mastectomies. Seven are dead. The two who survive have just completed rounds of chemotherapy and radiation.

2   I've had my own problems: two biopsies for breast cancer and a small tumor between my ribs diagnosed as a "borderline malignancy."

3   This is my family history.

4   Most statistics tell us breast cancer is genetic, hereditary, with rising percentages attached to fatty diets, childlessness, or becoming pregnant after thirty. What they don't say is living in Utah may be the greatest hazard of all.

5   We are a Mormon family with roots in Utah since 1847. The "word of wisdom" in my family aligned us with good foods—no coffee, no tea, tobacco, or alcohol. For the most part, our women were finished having their babies by

the time they were thirty. And only one faced breast cancer prior to 1960. Traditionally, as a group of people, Mormons have a low rate of cancer.

Is our family a cultural anomaly? The truth is, we didn't think about it. 6
Those who did, usually the men, simply said, "bad genes." The women's attitude was stoic. Cancer was part of life. On February 16, 1971, the eve of my mother's surgery, I accidently picked up the telephone and overheard her ask my grandmother what she could expect.

"Diane, it is one of the most spiritual experiences you will ever 7
encounter."

I quietly put down the receiver. 8

Two days later, my father took my brothers and me to the hospital to visit 9
her. She met us in the lobby in a wheelchair. No bandages were visible. I'll never forget her radiance, the way she held herself in a purple velvet robe, and how she gathered us around her.

"Children, I am fine. I want you to know I felt the arms of God 10
around me."

We believed her. My father cried. Our mother, his wife, was thirty-eight 11
years old.

A little over a year after Mother's death, Dad and I were having dinner 12
together. He had just returned from St. George, where the Tempest Company was completing the gas lines that would service southern Utah. He spoke of his love for the country, the sandstoned landscape, bare-boned and beautiful. He had just finished hiking the Kolob trail in Zion National Park. We got caught up in reminiscing, recalling with fondness our walk up Angel's Landing on his fiftieth birthday and the years our family had vacationed there.

Over dessert, I shared a recurring dream of mine. I told my father that for 13
years, as long as I could remember, I saw this flash of light in the night in the desert—that this image had so permeated my being that I could not venture south without seeing it again, on the horizon, illuminating buttes and mesas.

"You did see it," he said. 14

"Saw what?" 15

"The bomb. The cloud. We were driving home from Riverside, California. 16
You were sitting on Diane's lap. She was pregnant. In fact, I remember the day, September 7, 1957. We had just gotten out of the Service. We were driving north, past Las Vegas. It was an hour or so before dawn, when this explosion went off. We not only heard it, but felt it. I thought the oil tanker in front of us had blown up. We pulled over and suddenly, rising from the desert floor, we saw it, clearly, this golden-stemmed cloud, the mushroom. The sky seemed to vibrate with an eerie pink glow. Within a few minutes, a light ash was raining on the car.

I stared at my father. 17

"I thought you knew that," he said. "It was a common occurrence in the   18
fifties."

It was at this moment that I realized the deceit I had been living under.   19
Children growing up in the American Southwest, drinking contaminated
milk from contaminated cows, even from the contaminated breasts of their
mothers, my mother—members, years later, of the Clan of One-Breasted
Women.

It is a well-known story in the Desert West, "The Day We Bombed Utah,"   20
or more accurately, the years we bombed Utah: Above ground atomic testing
in Nevada took place from January 27, 1951, through July 11, 1962. Not only
were the winds blowing north covering "low-use segments of the population"
with fallout and leaving sheep dead in their tracks, but the climate was right.
The United States of the 1950s was red, white, and blue. The Korean War was
raging. McCarthyism was rampant. Ike was it, and the cold war was hot. If you
were against nuclear testing, you were for a communist regime.

Much has been written about this "American nuclear tragedy." Public   21
health was secondary to national security. The Atomic Energy Commissioner,
Thomas Murray, said, "Gentlemen, we must not let anything interfere with
this series of tests, nothing."

Again and again, the American public was told by its government, in   22
spite of burns, blisters, and nausea, "It has been found that the tests may be
conducted with adequate assurance of safety under conditions prevailing at
the bombing reservations." Assuaging public fears was simply a matter of public relations. "Your best action," an Atomic Energy Commission booklet read,
"is not to be worried about fallout." A news release typical of the times stated,
"We find no basis for concluding that harm to any individual has resulted from
radioactive fallout."

On August 30, 1979, during Jimmy Carter's presidency, a suit was filed,   23
Irene Allen v. The United States of America. Mrs. Allen's case was the first on an
alphabetical list of twenty-four test cases, representative of nearly twelve hundred plaintiffs seeking compensation from the United States government for
cancers caused by nuclear testing in Nevada.

Irene Allen lived in Hurricane, Utah. She was the mother of five children   24
and had been widowed twice. Her first husband, with their two oldest boys,
had watched the tests from the roof of the local high school. He died of
leukemia in 1956. Her second husband died of pancreatic cancer in 1978.

In a town meeting conducted by Utah Senator Orrin Hatch, shortly   25
before the suit was filed, Mrs. Allen said, "I am not blaming the government,
I want you to know that, Senator Hatch. But I thought if my testimony could
help in any way so this wouldn't happen again to any of the generations coming up after us . . . I am happy to be here this day to bear testimony of this."

God-fearing people. This is just one story in an anthology of thousands.   26

On May 10, 1984, Judge Bruce S. Jenkins handed down his opinion. Ten   27
of the plaintiffs were awarded damages. It was the first time a federal court had
determined that nuclear tests had been the cause of cancers. For the remaining
fourteen test cases, the proof of causation was not sufficient. In spite of the split
decision, it was considered a landmark ruling. It was not to remain so for long.

In April 1987, the Tenth Circuit Court of Appeals overturned Judge Jenk-   28
ins's ruling on the ground that the United States was protected from suit by
the legal doctrine of sovereign immunity, a centuries-old idea from England in
the days of absolute monarchs.

In January 1988, the Supreme Court refused to review the Appeals Court   29
decision. To our court system it does not matter whether the United States
government was irresponsible, whether it lied to its citizens, or even that citizens died from the fallout of nuclear testing. What matters is that our government is immune: "The King can do no wrong."

In Mormon culture, authority is respected, obedience is revered, and   30
independent thinking is not. I was taught as a young girl not to "make waves"
or "rock the boat."

"Just let it go," Mother would say. "You know how you feel, that's what   31
counts."

For many years, I have done just that—listened, observed, and quietly   32
formed my own opinions, in a culture that rarely asks questions because it has
all the answers. But one by one, I have watched the women in my family die
common, heroic deaths. We sat in waiting rooms hoping for good news, but
always receiving the bad. I cared for them, bathed their scarred bodies, and
kept their secrets. I watched beautiful women become bald as Cytoxan, cis-
platin, and Adriamycin[1] were injected into their veins. I held their foreheads
as they vomited green-black bile, and I shot them with morphine when the
pain became inhuman. In the end, I witnessed their last peaceful breaths,
becoming a midwife to the rebirth of their souls.

The price of obedience has become too high.   33

The fear and inability to question authority that ultimately killed rural   34
communities in Utah during atmospheric testing of atomic weapons is the
same fear I saw in my mother's body. Sheep. Dead sheep. The evidence is
buried.

I cannot prove that my mother, Diane Dixon Tempest, or my grandmoth-   35
ers, Lettie Romney Dixon and Kathryn Blackett Tempest, along with my
aunts developed cancer from nuclear fallout in Utah. But I can't prove they
didn't.

---

[1] Drugs used in chemotherapy. —EDS.

My father's memory was correct. The September blast we drove through   36
in 1957 was part of Operation Plumbbob, one of the most intensive series
of bomb tests to be initiated. The flash of light in the night in the desert,
which I had always thought was a dream, developed into a family nightmare.
It took fourteen years, from 1957 to 1971, for cancer to manifest in my
mother—the same time, Howard L. Andrews, an authority in radioactive
fallout at the National Institutes of Health, says radiation cancer requires to
become evident. The more I learn about what it means to be a "downwinder,"
the more questions I drown in.

What I do know, however, is that as a Mormon woman of the fifth gener-   37
ation of Latter-day Saints, I must question everything, even if it means losing
my faith, even if it means becoming a member of a border tribe among my own
people. Tolerating blind obedience in the name of patriotism or religion ultimately takes our lives.

When the Atomic Energy Commission described the country north of the   38
Nevada Test Site as "virtually uninhabited desert terrain," my family and the
birds at Great Salt Lake were some of the "virtual uninhabitants."

One night, I dreamed women from all over the world circled a blazing fire   39
in the desert. They spoke of change, how they hold the moon in their bellies
and wax and wane with its phases. They mocked the presumption of even-
tempered beings and made promises that they would never fear the witch
inside themselves. The women danced wildly as sparks broke away from the
flames and entered the night sky as stars.

And they sang a song given to them by Shoshone grandmothers: 40

Ah ne nah, nah	Consider the rabbits
nin nah nah—	How gently they walk on the earth—
ah ne nah, nah	Consider the rabbits
nin nah nah—	How gently they walk on the earth—
Nyaga mutzi	We remember them
oh ne nay—	We can walk gently also—
Nyaga mutzi	We remember them
oh ne nay—	We can walk gently also—

The women danced and drummed and sang for weeks, preparing themselves
for what was to come. They would reclaim the desert for the sake of their children, for the sake of the land.

A few miles downwind from the fire circle, bombs were being tested. Rab-   41
bits felt the tremors. Their soft leather pads on paws and feet recognized the
shaking sands, while the roots of mesquite and sage were smoldering. Rocks
were hot from the inside out and dust devils hummed unnaturally. And each

time there was another nuclear test, ravens watched the desert heave. Stretch marks appeared. The land was losing its muscle.

The women couldn't bear it any longer. They were mothers. They had suf-   42
fered labor pains but always under the promise of birth. The red hot pains beneath the desert promised death only, as each bomb became a stillborn. A contract had been made and broken between human beings and the land. A new contract was being drawn by the women, who understood the fate of the earth as their own.

Under the cover of darkness, ten women slipped under a barbed-wire   43
fence and entered the contaminated country. They were trespassing. They walked toward the town of Mercury, in moonlight, taking their cues from coy-ote, kit fox, antelope squirrel, and quail. They moved quietly and deliberately through the maze of Joshua trees. When a hint of daylight appeared they rested, drinking tea and sharing their rations of food. The women closed their eyes. The time had come to protest with the heart, that to deny one's geneal-ogy with the earth was to commit treason against one's soul.

At dawn, the women draped themselves in mylar, wrapping long stream-   44
ers of silver plastic around their arms to blow in the breeze. They wore clear masks that became the faces of humanity. And when they arrived at the edge of Mercury, they carried all the butterflies of a summer day in their wombs. They paused to allow their courage to settle.

The town that forbids pregnant women and children to enter because of   45
radiation risks was asleep. The women moved through the streets as winged messengers, twirling around each other in slow motion, peeking inside homes and watching the easy sleep of men and women. They were astonished by such stillness and periodically would utter a shrill note or low cry just to verify life.

The residents finally awoke to these strange apparitions. Some simply   46
stared. Others called authorities, and in time, the women were apprehended by wary soldiers dressed in desert fatigues. They were taken to a white, square building on the other edge of Mercury. When asked who they were and why they were there, the women replied, "We are mothers and we have come to reclaim the desert for our children."

The soldiers arrested them. As the ten women were blindfolded and   47
handcuffed, they began singing:

> You can't forbid us everything
> You can't forbid us to think —
> You can't forbid our tears to flow
> And you can't stop the songs that we sing.

The women continued to sing louder and louder, until they heard the voices of their sisters moving across the mesa:

Ah ne nah, nah
nin nah nah—
Ah ne nah, nah
nin nah nah—
Nyaga mutzi
oh ne nay—
Nyaga mutzi
oh ne nay—

"Call for reinforcements," one soldier said.   48

"We have," interrupted one woman, "we have—and you have no idea of   49
our numbers."

I crossed the line at the Nevada Test Site and was arrested with nine other   50
Utahns for trespassing on military lands. They are still conducting nuclear
tests in the desert. Ours was an act of civil disobedience. But as I walked
toward the town of Mercury, it was more than a gesture of peace. It was a gesture on behalf of the Clan of One-Breasted Women.

As one officer cinched the handcuffs around my wrists, another frisked my   51
body. She found a pen and a pad of paper tucked inside my left boot.

"And these?" she asked sternly.   52

"Weapons," I replied.   53

Our eyes met. I smiled. She pulled the leg of my trousers back over my   54
boot.

"Step forward, please," she said as she took my arm.   55

We were booked under an afternoon sun and bused to Tonopah, Nevada.   56
It was a two-hour ride. This was familiar country. The Joshua trees standing
their ground had been named by my ancestors, who believed they looked like
prophets pointing west to the Promised Land. These were the same trees that
bloomed each spring, flowers appearing like white flames in the Mojave. And
I recalled a full moon in May, when Mother and I had walked among them,
flushing out mourning doves and owls.

The bus stopped short of town. We were released.   57

The officials thought it was a cruel joke to leave us stranded in the desert   58
with no way to get home. What they didn't realize was that we were home,
soul-centered and strong, women who recognized the sweet smell of sage as
fuel for our spirits.

Journal Writing

How do you respond to Williams's decision to go against her ingrained beliefs and to question authority, no longer to tolerate "blind obedience in the name of patriotism or religion" (par. 37)? In your journal, write about a time when you felt compelled to question authority, whether you acted on the feeling or not. Why did you feel as you did? What did you do? What were the consequences? Would you do the same thing today? (To take your journal writing further, see "From Journal to Essay" on the facing page.)

Questions on Meaning

1. Why does Williams say that when it comes to developing breast cancer, "living in Utah may be the greatest hazard of all" (par. 4)?
2. What "deceit" did Williams realize she had been living under (par. 19)?
3. What is Williams's point in recounting the case of *Irene Allen v. The United States of America* (pars. 23–29)?
4. Williams concedes that she cannot prove nuclear fallout was responsible for the breast cancers that afflicted the women in her family (par. 35). On what EVIDENCE does she base her belief in a connection?
5. What was the point of the "act of civil disobedience" by Williams and other women (par. 50)?

Questions on Writing Strategy

1. Williams does not state her THESIS outright. How would you state it? Why do you think she leaves it to her AUDIENCE to INFER her thesis?
2. Why does Williams quote Irene Allen in paragraph 25?
3. Why do you think Williams presents her dream in paragraphs 39–49, especially since she then goes on to tell of the actual civil disobedience in which she participated?
4. **MIXED METHODS.** Where does Williams use NARRATION and DESCRIPTION? What PURPOSE do these methods serve?
5. **MIXED METHODS.** To what extent would you characterize Williams's essay as an ARGUMENT? Why do you think so?

Questions on Language

1. What effect does Williams achieve by referring to herself as one of the "clan" of one-breasted women? What are the associations of the word *clan*?
2. Why do you think Williams quotes the women in her dream singing the words to a Shoshone song (par. 40)?
3. How does Williams use the image of birth in paragraphs 41–42 to help make her point?

4. Why did Williams tell the officer who arrested her that the pen and pad of paper she carried were "weapons" (pars. 51–53)?
5. Consult a dictionary if you are unsure of the meanings of the following words: mastectomies (par. 1); biopsies, malignancy (2); anomaly, stoic (6); reminiscing (12); permeated, buttes, mesas (13); contaminated (19); rampant, regime (20); assuaging (22); plaintiffs (23); leukemia, pancreatic (24); sovereign immunity, absolute monarchs (28); manifest (36); presumption (39); mesquite, sage, smoldering (41); genealogy (43); apparitions (46); cinched (51).

Suggestions for Writing

1. **FROM JOURNAL TO ESSAY.** Expanding on your journal entry (facing page), write an essay about a time when you wanted to or did question authority as a matter of principle. Be sure to make clear what led you to your doubt, what happened because of it, and whether or not you now regret your actions and why.
2. Williams writes that the United States of the 1950s was "red, white, and blue," that anyone who questioned government policies was viewed as unpatriotic and somehow suspect (par. 20). How would you characterize the political mood of the United States today? In an essay, ANALYZE what you see as current attitudes toward dissension and public debate. Refer to specific items from the news media and from your own experience to develop your analysis.
3. **CRITICAL WRITING.** EVALUATE "The Clan of One-Breasted Women" as an argument, focusing on the author's use of APPEALS (rational, emotional, ethical). How well do you think it succeeds?
4. **CONNECTIONS.** Based on what he writes in "The Cancer-Cluster Myth" (p. 427), how might Atul Gawande respond to Williams's beliefs about the sources of cancer in her family and among others in southern Utah? What might Williams learn from Gawande's research? Could she use it to support her beliefs? Why, or why not?
5. **CONNECTIONS.** In paragraph 22 Williams quotes various government officials and publications on the low danger of nuclear fallout. Analyze these quotations as examples of doublespeak, as defined and illustrated in William Lutz's "The World of Doublespeak" (p. 399).

Terry Tempest Williams on Writing

In a 1995 interview on the radio series *Insight and Outlook,* Terry Tempest Williams spoke with Scott London about what it means to her to be a writer. She said that as a writer, she is moved by questions, not answers: "I believe that it is our task, our responsibility, to hold the mirror up to social injustices that we see and to create a prayer of beauty. The questions serve us in that capacity. [. . .] I think that is what the writing process is. It begins with a question, and then you follow this path of exploration."

Williams dislikes calling herself a writer. "It feels so presumptuous, some-how," she told London. "I know the struggle from the inside out and I would never be so bold as to call myself a writer. I think that that is what other people call you. But I consider myself a member of a community in Salt Lake City, in Utah, in the American West, in this country. And writing is what I do. That is the tool out of which I can express my love. My activism is a result of my love. So whether it's trying to preserve the wilderness in southern Utah or writing about an erotics of place, it is that same impulse — to try to make sense of the world, to try to preserve something that is beautiful, to ask the tough questions, to push the boundaries of what is acceptable."

For Discussion

1. Williams implies that her writing serves as a type of mirror. What does she mean by this?
2. What do you think Williams has in mind when she says that her work is motivated by "tough questions"? What might some of those questions be? What questions inform your own writing?

TOM WOLFE

TOM WOLFE, author, journalist, and cartoonist, was born in 1931 in Richmond, Virginia, and went to Washington and Lee University. After taking a PhD in American Studies at Yale, he decided against an academic career and instead worked as a reporter for the *Springfield Union* and the *Washington Post*. Early in the 1960s, Wolfe began writing his electrifying, satiric articles on the American scene (with special, mocking attention to subcultures and trendsetters), which have enlivened *New York, Esquire, Rolling Stone, Harper's*, and other magazines. Among his books are *The Electric Kool-Aid Acid Test* (1965), a memoir of LSD-spaced-out hippies; *The Pump House Gang* (1968), a study of California surfers; *The Right Stuff* (1979), a chronicle of America's first astronauts, which won the American Book Award and was made into a movie; and *From Bauhaus to Our House* (1981), a complaint against modern architecture. Wolfe's two novels, *The Bonfire of the Vanities* (1987) and *A Man in Full* (1998), have been both controversial and hugely popular. Wolfe returned to nonfiction in his most recent book, *Hooking Up* (2000), a collection of essays.

Pornoviolence

This essay, from a collection raking over the 1970s, *Mauve Gloves & Madmen, Clutter & Vine* (1976), is vintage Tom Wolfe. He played a large part in the invention of "the new journalism" (a brand of reporting that tells the truth excitedly, as if it were fiction), and his essay is marked by certain breathless features of style: long sentences full of parenthetical asides, ellipses (. . .), generous use of italics. Wolfe here coins a term to fit the blend of pornography and pandering to bloodlust that he finds in the media. Although not recent, his remarks have dated little since they first appeared.

Wolfe defines the word *pornoviolence* by drawing substantially on several other methods of development as well.

Narration (Chap. 4): paragraphs 10–16, 18, 20, 24
Example (Chap. 6): paragraphs 1–7, 8, 11–15, 18, 21–24, 27, 29–30
Comparison and contrast (Chap. 7): paragraphs 26, 30
Division or analysis (Chap. 9): paragraphs 22–26, 28–30
Cause and effect (Chap. 11): paragraphs 19, 27–28, 31
Definition (Chap. 12): paragraphs 16–17, 25–26, 28–31

"Keeps His Mom-in-law in Chains, meet *Kills Son and Feeds Corpse to Pigs."* 1
"Pleased to meet you." 2
"Teenager Twists Off Corpse's Head . . . to Get Gold Teeth, meet *Strangles* 3
Girl Friend, Then Chops Her to Pieces."
"How you doing?" 4

"*Nurse's Aide Sees Fingers Chopped Off in Meat Grinder*, meet *I Left My*   5
Babies in the Deep Freeze."

"It's a pleasure."   6

It's a pleasure! No doubt about that! In all these years of journalism I have   7
covered more conventions than I care to remember. Podiatrists, theosophists,
Professional Budget Finance dentists, oyster farmers, mathematicians, truck-
ers, dry cleaners, stamp collectors, Esperantists, nudists, and newspaper editors—I have seen them all, together, in vast assemblies, sloughing through
the wall-to-wall of a thousand hotel lobbies (the nudists excepted) in their
shimmering gray-metal suits and pajama-stripe shirts with white Plasti-Coat
name cards on their chests, and I have sat through their speeches and seminars (the nudists included) and attentively endured ear baths such as you
wouldn't believe. And yet none has ever been quite like the convention of the
stringers for the *National Enquirer*.

The *Enquirer* is a weekly newspaper that is probably known by sight to   8
millions more than know it by name. No one who ever came face-to-face with
the *Enquirer* on a newsstand in its wildest days is likely to have forgotten the
sight: a tabloid with great inky shocks of type all over the front page saying
something on the order of *Gouges Out Wife's Eyes to Make Her Ugly, Dad Hurls
Hot Grease in Daughter's Face, Wife Commits Suicide After 2 Years of Poisoning
Fails to Kill Husband* . . .

The stories themselves were supplied largely by stringers, i.e., correspon-   9
dents, from all over the country, the world, for that matter, mostly copyeditors
and reporters on local newspapers. Every so often they would come upon a
story, usually via the police beat, that was so grotesque the local sheet would
discard it or run it in a highly glossed form rather than offend or perplex its
readers. The stringers would preserve them for the *Enquirer,* which always
rewarded them well and respectfully.

One year the *Enquirer* convened and feted them at a hotel in Manhattan.   10
This convention was a success in every way. The only awkward moment was
at the outset when the stringers all pulled in. None of them knew each other.
Their hosts got around the problem by introducing them by the stories they
had supplied. The introductions went like this:

"Harry, I want you to meet Frank here. Frank did that story, you remem-   11
ber that story, *Midget Murderer Throws Girl Off Cliff After She Refuses to Dance
with Him*."

"Pleased to meet you. That was some story."   12

"And Harry did the one about *I Spent Three Days Trapped at Bottom of*   13
Forty-Foot-Deep Mine Shaft and Was Saved by a Swarm of Flies."

"Likewise, I'm sure."   14

And *Midget Murderer Throws Girl Off Cliff* shakes hands with *I Spent Three*   15

Days Trapped at Bottom of Forty-Foot-Deep Mine Shaft, and *Buries Her Baby Alive* shakes hands with *Boy, Twelve, Strangles Two-Year-Old Girl*, and *Kills Son and Feeds Corpse to Pigs* shakes hands with *He Strangles Old Woman and Smears Corpse with Syrup, Ketchup, and Oatmeal . . . and . . .*

. . . There was a great deal of esprit about the whole thing. These men   16
were, in fact, the avant-garde of a new genre that since then has become institutionalized throughout the nation without anyone knowing its proper name. I speak of the new pornography, the pornography of violence.

Pornography comes from the Greek word *porne*, meaning "harlot," and   17
pornography is literally the depiction of the acts of harlots. In the new pornography, the theme is not sex. The new pornography depicts practitioners acting out another, murkier drive: people staving teeth in, ripping guts open, blowing brains out, and getting even with all those bastards . . .

The success of the *Enquirer* prompted many imitators to enter the field,   18
Midnight, the *Star Chronicle*, the *National Insider*, *Inside News*, the *National Close-up*, the *National Tattler*, the *National Examiner*. A truly competitive free press evolved, and soon a reader could go to the newspaper of his choice for *Kill the Retarded! (Won't You Join My Movement?)* and *Unfaithful Wife? Burn Her Bed!*, *Harem Master's Mistress Chops Him with Machete*, *Babe Bites Off Boy's Tongue*, and *Cuts Buddy's Face to Pieces for Stealing His Business and Fiancée*.

And yet the last time I surveyed the Violence press, I noticed a curious   19
thing. These pioneering journals seem to have pulled back. They seem to be regressing to what is by now the Redi-Mix staple of literate Americans, mere sex. *Ecstasy and Me (by Hedy Lamarr)*,[1] says the *National Enquirer*. *I Run a Sex Art Gallery*, says the *National Insider*. What has happened, I think, is something that has happened to avant-gardes in many fields, from William Morris and the Craftsmen to the Bauhaus group.[2] Namely, their discoveries have been preempted by the Establishment and so thoroughly dissolved into the mainstream they no longer look original.

Robert Harrison, the former publisher of *Confidential*, and later publisher   20
of the aforementioned *Inside News*, was perhaps the first person to see it coming. I was interviewing Harrison early in January 1964 for a story in *Esquire* about six weeks after the assassination of President Kennedy, and we were in

---

[1] *Ecstasy*, an early, European-made Hedy Lamarr film, was notorious for its scenes of soft-core lovemaking. Later, paired with Charles ("Come with me to the Casbah") Boyer, Lamarr rose to Hollywood stardom in *Algiers* (1938). —EDS.

[2] Morris (1834–96), an English artist, poet, printer, and socialist, founded a company of craftspeople to bring tasteful design to furniture (the Morris chair) and other implements of everyday life. The Bauhaus, an influential art school in Germany (1919–33), taught crafts and brought new ideas of design to architecture and to goods produced in factories. —EDS.

a cab in the West Fifties in Manhattan, at a stoplight, by a newsstand, and Harrison suddenly pointed at the newsstand and said, "Look at that. They're doing the same thing the *Enquirer* does."

There on the stand was a row of slick-paper, magazine-size publications, 21 known in the trade as one-shots, with titles like *Four Days That Shook the World*, *Death of a President*, *An American Tragedy*, or just *John Fitzgerald Kennedy (1921–1963)*. "You want to know why people buy those things?" said Harrison. "People buy those things to see a man get his head blown off."

And, of course, he was right. Only now the publishers were in many cases 22 the pillars of the American press. Invariably, these "special coverages" of the assassination bore introductions piously commemorating the fallen President, exhorting the American people to strength and unity in a time of crisis, urging greater vigilance and safeguards for the new President, and even raising the nice metaphysical question of collective guilt in "an age of violence."

In the years since then, of course, there has been an incessant replay, 23 with every recoverable clinical detail, of those less than five seconds in which a man got his head blown off. And throughout this deluge of words, pictures, and film frames, I have been intrigued with one thing: The point of view, the vantage point, is almost never that of the victim, riding in the Presidential Lincoln Continental. What you get is . . . the view from Oswald's rifle. You can step right up here and look point-blank right through the very hairline cross in Lee Harvey Oswald's Optics Ordinance in weaponry four-power Japanese telescope sight and watch, frame by frame by frame by frame, as that man there's head comes apart. Just a little History there before your very eyes.

The television networks have schooled us in the view from Oswald's rifle 24 and made it seem a normal pastime. The TV viewpoint is nearly always that of the man who is going to strike. The last time I watched *Gunsmoke*, which was not known as a very violent Western in TV terms, the action went like this: The Wellington agents and the stagecoach driver pull guns on the badlands gang leader's daughter and Kitty, the heart-of-gold saloonkeeper, and kidnap them. Then the badlands gang shoots two Wellington agents. Then they tie up five more and talk about shooting them. Then they desist because they might not be able to get a hotel room in the next town if the word got around. Then one badlands gang gunslinger attempts to rape Kitty while the gang leader's younger daughter looks on. Then Kitty resists, so he slugs her one in the jaw. Then the gang leader slugs him. Then the gang leader slugs Kitty. Then Kitty throws hot stew in a gang member's face and hits him over the back of the head with a revolver. Then he knocks her down with a rock. Then the gang sticks up a bank. Here comes the marshal, Matt Dillon. He shoots a gang member and breaks it up. Then the gang leader shoots the guy who was guarding his daughter and the woman. Then the marshal shoots the gang leader. The final exploding bullet signals The End.

It is not the accumulated slayings and bone crushings that make this 25 pornoviolence, however. What makes it pornoviolence is that in almost every case the camera angle, therefore the viewer, is with the gun, the fist, the rock. The pornography of violence has no point of view in the old sense that novels do. You do not live the action through the hero's eyes. You live with the aggressor, whoever he may be. One moment you are the hero. The next you are the villain. No matter whose side you may be on consciously, you are in fact with the muscle, and it is you who disintegrate all comers, villains, lawmen, women, anybody. On the rare occasions in which the gun is emptied into the camera—i.e., into your face—the effect is so startling that the pornography of violence all but loses its fantasy charm. There are not nearly so many masochists as sadists among those little devils whispering into one's ears.

In fact, sex—"sadomasochism"—is only a part of the pornography of 26 violence. Violence is much more wrapped up, simply, with status. Violence is the simple, ultimate solution for problems of status competition, just as gambling is the simple, ultimate solution for economic competition. The old pornography was the fantasy of easy sexual delights in a world where sex was kept unavailable. The new pornography is the fantasy of easy triumph in a world where status competition has become so complicated and frustrating.

Already the old pornography is losing its kick because of overexposure. In 27 the late thirties, Nathanael West published his last and best-regarded novel, *The Day of the Locust,* and it was a terrible flop commercially, and his publisher said if he ever published another book about Hollywood it would "have to be *My Thirty-nine Ways of Making Love by Hedy Lamarr.*" He thought he was saying something that was funny because it was beyond the realm of possibility. Less than thirty years later, however, Hedy Lamarr's *Ecstasy and Me* was published. Whether she mentions thirty-nine ways, I'm not sure, but she gets off to a flying start: "The men in my life have ranged from a classic case history of impotence, to a whip-brandishing sadist who enjoyed sex only after he tied my arms behind me with the sash of his robe. There was another man who took his pleasure with a girl in my own bed, while he thought I was asleep in it."

Yet she was too late. The book very nearly sank without a trace. The sin 28 itself is wearing out. Pornography cannot exist without certified taboo to violate. And today Lust, like the rest of the Seven Deadly Sins—Pride, Sloth, Envy, Greed, Anger, and Gluttony—is becoming a rather minor vice. The Seven Deadly Sins, after all, are only sins against the self. Theologically, the idea of Lust—well, the idea is that if you seduce some poor girl from Akron, it is not a sin because you are ruining her, but because you are wasting your time and your energies and damaging your own spirit. This goes back to the old work ethic, when the idea was to keep every able-bodied man's shoulder to the wheel. In an age of riches for all, the ethic becomes more nearly: Let him do anything he pleases, as long as he doesn't get in my way. And if he does get in my way, or even if he doesn't . . . well . . . we have *new* fantasies for that. *Put hair on the walls.*

"Hair on the walls" is the invisible subtitle of Truman Capote's book *In*   29 *Cold Blood*. The book is neither a who-done-it nor a will-they-be-caught, since the answers to both questions are known from the outset. It does ask why-did-they-do-it, but the answer is soon as clear as it is going to be. Instead, the book's suspense is based largely on a totally new idea in detective stories: the promise of gory details, and the withholding of them until the end. Early in the game one of the two murderers, Dick, starts promising to put "plenty of hair on them-those walls" with a shotgun. So read on, gentle readers, and on and on; you are led up to the moment before the crime on page 60 — yet the specifics, what happened, the gory details, are kept out of sight, in grisly dangle, until page 244.

But Dick and Perry, Capote's killers, are only a couple of Low Rent bums.   30 With James Bond the new pornography reached a dead center, the bureaucratic middle class. The appeal of Bond has been explained as the appeal of the lone man who can solve enormously complicated, even world problems through his own bravery and initiative. But Bond is not a lone man at all, of course. He is not the Lone Ranger. He is much easier to identify than that. He is a salaried functionary in a bureaucracy. He is a sport, but a believable one; not a millionaire, but a bureaucrat on an expense account. He is not even a high-level bureaucrat. He is an operative. This point is carefully and repeatedly made by having his superiors dress him down for violations of standard operating procedure. Bond, like the Lone Ranger, solves problems with guns and fists. When it is over, however, the Lone Ranger leaves a silver bullet. Bond, like the rest of us, fills out a report in triplicate.

Marshall McLuhan[3] says we are in a period in which it will become harder   31 and harder to stimulate lust through words and pictures — i.e., the old pornography. In the latest round of pornographic movies the producers have found it necessary to introduce violence, bondage, torture, and aggressive physical destruction to an extraordinary degree. The same sort of bloody escalation may very well happen in the pure pornography of violence. Even such able craftsmen as Truman Capote, Ian Fleming, NBC, and CBS may not suffice.

---

[3] Canadian English professor, author of *Understanding Media* (1964), *The Medium Is the Message* (1967), and other books, McLuhan (1911–80) analyzed the effects on world society of television and other electronic media. — EDS.

Fortunately, there are historical models to rescue us from this frustration. In the latter days of the Roman Empire, the Emperor Commodus became jealous of the celebrity of the great gladiators. He took to the arena himself, with his sword, and began dispatching suitably screened cripples and hobbled fighters. Audience participation became so popular that soon various *illuminati* of the Commodus set, various boys and girls of the year, were out there, suited up, gaily cutting a sequence of dwarfs and feebles down to short ribs. Ah, swinging generations, what new delights await?

Journal Writing

Wolfe's essay is almost thirty years old, but it's still relevant to today's media culture. Write about some recent examples of pornoviolence you have seen in the movies, on television, in newspapers, or in magazines. What, if anything, should be done about such instances of pornoviolence? (To take your journal writing further, see "From Journal to Essay" on the next page.)

Questions on Meaning

1. Which of the following statements comes closest to summing up Tom Wolfe's main PURPOSE in writing "Pornoviolence"?

   Wolfe writes to define a word.
   Wolfe writes to define a trend in society.
   Wolfe writes to define a trend in the media that reflects a trend in society.
   Wolfe writes to explain how John F. Kennedy was assassinated.
   Wolfe writes to entertain us by mocking Americans' latest foolishness.

   (If you don't find any of these statements adequate, compose your own.)

2. If you have ever read the *National Enquirer* or any of its imitators, test the accuracy of Wolfe's reporting. What is the purpose of a featured article in the *Enquirer*?

3. According to Wolfe, what POINT OF VIEW does the writer or producer of pornoviolence always take? What other examples of this point of view (in violent incidents on films or TV shows) can you supply? (Did you ever see a replay of Jack Ruby's shooting of Oswald, for instance?)

4. "Violence is the simple, ultimate solution for problems of status competition" (par. 26). What does Wolfe mean?

5. Wolfe does not explicitly pass judgment on Truman Capote's book *In Cold Blood* (par. 29). But what is his opinion of it? How can you tell?

6. "No advocate of change for the sake of change, Tom Wolfe writes as a conservative moralist who rankles with savage indignation." Does this critical remark fit this particular essay? What, in Wolfe's view, appears to be happening to America and Americans?

Questions on Writing Strategy

1. On first reading, what did you make of Wolfe's opening sentence, "'*Keeps His Mom-in-law in Chains*, meet *Kills Son and Feeds Corpse to Pigs*'"? At what point did you first tumble to what the writer was doing? What IRONY do you find in the convention hosts' introducing people by the headlines of their gory stories? What advantage is it to Wolfe's essay that his INTRODUCTION (with its odd introductions) keeps you guessing for a while?
2. What is Wolfe's point in listing (in par. 7) some of the other conventions he has reported—gatherings of nudists, oyster farmers, and others?
3. What is the TONE or attitude of Wolfe's CONCLUSION (par. 31)? Note in particular the closing line.
4. **MIXED METHODS.** At what moment does Wolfe give us his short DEFINITION of *pornoviolence*, or the new pornography? Do you think he would have done better to introduce his short definition of the word in paragraph 1? Why, or why not?
5. **MIXED METHODS.** What do the EXAMPLES in paragraphs 21–23 and 30 (the latter instance developed by COMPARISON AND CONTRAST) contribute to Wolfe's definition of *pornoviolence*?

Questions on Language

1. What help to the reader does Wolfe provide by noting the source of the word *pornography* (par. 17)?
2. "The television networks have schooled us in the view from Oswald's rifle" (par. 24). What CONNOTATIONS enlarge the meaning of *schooled*?
3. Define *masochist* and *sadist* (par. 25). What kind of DICTION do you find in these terms? in "plenty of hair on them-those walls" (29)?
4. How much use does Wolfe make of COLLOQUIAL EXPRESSIONS? Point to examples.
5. What does Wolfe mean in noting that the fighters slain by the Emperor Commodus were "hobbled" and the cripples were "suitably screened" (par. 31)? What unflattering connotations does this emperor's very name contain? (If you don't get this, look up *commode* in your desk dictionary.)

Suggestions for Writing

1. **FROM JOURNAL TO ESSAY.** Write an essay ARGUING why we should or should not try to regulate or otherwise censor violence in the media. Take into account who would set the standards, what the standards would be, and who would enforce the regulations. The issue of censoring media violence has received much attention in recent years, so you should be able to locate opinions and information easily in the *Readers' Guide to Periodical Literature*, on *InfoTrac*, or on the Web.
2. Write an essay defining some current trend you've noticed in films or TV, popular music, sports, consumer buying, or some other large arena of life. Like Wolfe, invent a name for it. Use plenty of examples to make your definition clear.
3. **CRITICAL WRITING.** Analyze Wolfe's distinctive journalistic style. In the note on the essay, we mention parenthetical asides (they appear between dashes as well as parentheses), three-dot ellipsis marks, and italics. Consider also his use of

I, his piling up of detail (as in pars. 7 and 24), his informal diction ("losing its kick," "got his head blown off"), his choice of quotations, and any other features that strike you. What is the overall EFFECT of this style? What does it say about Wolfe?

4. **CONNECTIONS.** What would Tom Wolfe think of the video watched by Don DeLillo's character in the short story "Videotape" (p. 448)? Would Wolfe consider the tape an example of pornoviolence? Why, or why not?

5. **CONNECTIONS.** Spend some time watching one or more "real-life" television shows or videotapes such as *Cops*, *World's Deadliest Car Chases*, or *When Animals Attack*. Then write a two-part essay in which you imagine the responses of Wolfe and then Marie Winn ("TV Addiction," p. 486) to these shows. Would Wolfe describe them as pornoviolence? Why, or why not? How would Winn explain their popularity, even addictiveness, for some viewers?

Tom Wolfe on Writing

"What about your writing techniques and habits?" Tom Wolfe was asked by Joe David Bellamy for *Writer's Digest*.

The actual writing I do very fast. I make a very tight outline of everything I write before I write it. And often, as in the case of *The Electric Kool-Aid Acid Test*, the research, the reporting, is going to take me much longer than the writing. By writing an outline you really are writing in a way, because you're creating the structure of what you're going to do. Once I really know what I'm going to write, I don't find the actual writing takes all that long.

The Electric Kool-Aid Acid Test in manuscript form was about 1,100 pages, triple-spaced, typewritten. That means about 200 words a page, and, you know, some of that was thrown out or cut eventually; but I wrote all of that in three and a half months. I had never written a full-length book before, and at first I decided I would treat each chapter as if it were a magazine article—because I *had* done that before. So I would set an artificial deadline, and I'd make myself meet it. And I did that for three chapters.

But after I had done this three times and then I looked ahead and I saw that there were *twenty-five* more times I was going to have to do this, I couldn't face it anymore. I said, "I cannot do this, even one more time, because there's no end to it." So I completely changed my system, and I set up a quota for myself—of ten typewritten pages a day. At 200 words a page that's 2,000 words, which is not, you know, an overwhelming amount. It's a good clip, but it's not overwhelming. And I found this worked much better. I had my outline done, and sometimes ten pages would get me hardly an eighth-of-an-inch along the outline. It didn't bother me. Just like working in a factory—end of ten pages, I'd close my lunch pail.

For Discussion

1. In what way is outlining really writing, according to Wolfe? (In answering, consider the implications of his statement about "creating a structure.")
2. What strategy did the author finally settle on to get himself through the toil of his first book? What made this strategy superior to the one he had used earlier?

VIRGINIA WOOLF

Generally regarded as one of the greatest twentieth-century writers, VIRGINIA WOOLF earned her acclaim by producing uncommon fiction and nonfiction, the first sensitive and complex, the second poetic and immediate. Born Virginia Stephen in London in 1882, Woolf and her sister Vanessa were educated at home, largely by their father, Sir Leslie Stephen, an author and editor. The two sisters were central to the Bloomsbury Group, an informal society of writers and artists that included the economist John Maynard Keynes and the novelist E. M. Forster. Virginia married Leonard Woolf, a member of the group, in 1912, and the two soon founded the Hogarth Press, publisher of Virginia Woolf and many other notable writers of the day. Woolf's most innovative novels include *Mrs. Dalloway* (1925), *To the Lighthouse* (1927), *Orlando* (1928), *The Waves* (1931), and *Between the Acts* (1941). Her exemplary critical and meditative essays appear in *The Common Reader* (1925), *The Second Common Reader* (1933), and many other collections. Subject to severe depression all her adult life, in 1941 Woolf committed suicide.

The Death of the Moth

One of Woolf's most famous works of nonfiction, this essay was published in *The Death of the Moth and Other Essays* (1942). Though as brief as the life of the moth Woolf observes, the essay is typically evocative, intense, and enduring.

"The Death of the Moth" is a seamless blend of narration (Chap. 4) and description (Chap. 5). It is also implicitly a comparison and contrast (Chap. 7) between the moth in life and in death and between the author's responses to these states.

Moths that fly by day are not properly to be called moths; they do not excite that pleasant sense of dark autumn nights and ivy-blossom which the commonest yellow-underwing asleep in the shadow of the curtain never fails to rouse in us. They are hybrid creatures, neither gay like butterflies nor somber like their own species. Nevertheless the present specimen, with his narrow hay-colored wings, fringed with a tassel of the same color, seemed to be content with life. It was a pleasant morning, mid-September, mild, benignant, yet with a keener breath than that of the summer months. The plough was already scoring the field opposite the window, and where the share had been, the earth was pressed flat and gleamed with moisture. Such vigor came rolling in from the fields and the down beyond that it was difficult to keep the eyes strictly turned upon the book. The rooks too were keeping one of their annual festivities; soaring round the tree tops until it looked as if a vast net with thousands of black knots in it had been cast up into the air; which, after a few moments sank slowly down upon the trees until every twig seemed to have a knot at the end of it. Then, suddenly, the net would be thrown into the air again in a wider circle this time, with the utmost clamor and vociferation, as though to be thrown into the air and settle slowly down upon the tree tops were a tremendously exciting experience.

The same energy which inspired the rooks, the ploughmen, the horses, and even, it seemed, the lean bare-backed downs, sent the moth fluttering from side to side of his square of the windowpane. One could not help watching him. One, was, indeed, conscious of a queer feeling of pity for him. The possibilities of pleasure seemed that morning so enormous and so various that to have only a moth's part in life, and a day moth's at that, appeared a hard fate, and his zest in enjoying his meager opportunities to the full, pathetic. He flew vigorously to one corner of his compartment, and, after waiting there a second, flew across to the other. What remained for him but to fly to a third corner and then to a fourth? That was all he could do, in spite of the size of the downs, the width of the sky, the far-off smoke of houses, and the romantic voice, now and then, of a steamer out at sea. What he could do he did. Watching him, it seemed as if a fiber, very thin but pure, of the enormous energy of the world had been thrust into his frail and diminutive body. As often as he crossed the pane, I could fancy that a thread of vital light became visible. He was little or nothing but life.

Yet, because he was so small, and so simple a form of the energy that was rolling in at the open window and driving its way through so many narrow and intricate corridors in my own brain and in those of other human beings, there was something marvelous as well as pathetic about him. It was as if someone had taken a tiny bead of pure life and decking it as lightly as possible with down and feathers, had set it dancing and zigzagging to show us the true nature of life. Thus displayed one could not get over the strangeness of it. One is apt to forget all about life, seeing it humped and bossed and garnished and cumbered so that it has to move with the greatest circumspection and dignity. Again, the thought of all that life might have been had he been born in any other shape caused one to view his simple activities with a kind of pity.

After a time, tired by his dancing apparently, he settled on the window ledge in the sun, and, the queer spectacle being at an end, I forgot about him. Then, looking up, my eye was caught by him. He was trying to resume his dancing, but seemed either so stiff or so awkward that he could only flutter to the bottom of the windowpane; and when he tried to fly across it he failed. Being intent on other matters I watched these futile attempts for a time without thinking, unconsciously waiting for him to resume his flight, as one waits for a machine, that has stopped momentarily, to start again without considering the reason of its failure. After perhaps a seventh attempt he slipped from the wooden ledge and fell, fluttering his wings, on to his back on the windowsill. The helplessness of his attitude roused me. It flashed upon me that he was in difficulties; he could no longer raise himself; his legs struggled vainly. But, as I stretched out a pencil, meaning to help him to right himself, it came over me that the failure and awkwardness were the approach of death. I laid the pencil down again.

The legs agitated themselves once more. I looked as if for the enemy   5 against which he struggled. I looked out of doors. What had happened there? Presumably it was midday, and work in the fields had stopped. Stillness and quiet had replaced the previous animation. The birds had taken themselves off to feed in the brooks. The horses stood still. Yet the power was there all the same, massed outside, indifferent, impersonal, not attending to anything in particular. Somehow it was opposed to the little hay-colored moth. It was useless to try to do anything. One could only watch the extraordinary efforts made by those tiny legs against an oncoming doom which could, had it chosen, have submerged an entire city, not merely a city, but masses of human beings; nothing, I knew had any chance against death. Nevertheless after a pause of exhaustion the legs fluttered again. It was superb this last protest, and so frantic that he succeeded at last in righting himself. One's sympathies, of course, were all on the side of life. Also, when there was nobody to care or to know, this gigantic effort on the part of an insignificant little moth, against a power of such magnitude, to retain what no one else valued or desired to keep, moved one strangely. Again, somehow, one saw life, a pure bead. I lifted the pencil again, useless though I knew it to be. But even as I did so, the unmistakable tokens of death showed themselves. The body relaxed, and instantly grew stiff. The struggle was over. The insignificant little creature now knew death. As I looked at the dead moth, this minute wayside triumph of so great a force over so mean an antagonist filled me with wonder. Just as life had been strange a few minutes before, so death was now as strange. The moth having righted himself now lay most decently and uncomplainingly composed. O yes, he seemed to say, death is stronger than I am.

Journal Writing

Try thinking from Woolf's perspective, recognizing the struggle and life force within creatures we generally consider insignificant. In your journal, sketch out some ideas. What do you find admirable about turtles, mosquitoes, minnows, or ants? (To take your journal writing further, see "From Journal to Essay" on the next page.)

Questions on Meaning

1. Why does Woolf choose to write about something as insignificant as a moth's death? Does she have a PURPOSE other than relating a simple observation?
2. Why, in paragraph 2, does Woolf say that the moth was "little or nothing but life"? Why is the moth pitiable?
3. What does the moth in his square windowpane represent to the author? How does Woolf's DESCRIPTION in the essay make this clear?
4. How does Woolf's outlook change in paragraph 5? Why?

Questions on Writing Strategy

1. Is Woolf's essay an OBJECTIVE or a SUBJECTIVE description? Give details from the essay to support your answer.
2. What is the EFFECT of Woolf's scene-setting in paragraph 1? How does this description influence our perception of the moth?
3. **MIXED METHODS.** Which of the five senses does Woolf's description principally rely on? Why, do you think?
4. **MIXED METHODS.** This essay is a description in the framework of a NARRATIVE. Summarize the changes in Woolf's perceptions of the moth that occur in the narrative.

Questions on Language

1. ANALYZE the writing in paragraph 5. How do sentence structure and words create a mood different from that in earlier paragraphs?
2. Analyze Woolf's IMAGES in describing the moth and her substitutions for the word *moth*, such as "the present specimen" in paragraph 1. How do these reinforce Woolf's changing perceptions as you outlined them in question 4 on writing strategy?
3. You may find Woolf's vocabulary more difficult than that of some other writers in this book. Look up any unfamiliar words in the following list: rouse, hybrid, benignant, plough, share, down, rooks, clamor, vociferation (par. 1); zest, meager, pathetic, diminutive (2); decking, cumbered, circumspection (3); spectacle, futile, vainly (4); animation, righting, magnitude, minute, mean, antagonist (5).

Suggestions for Writing

1. **FROM JOURNAL TO ESSAY.** Write a brief essay from your journal entry (previous page), using ample descriptive details to depict both the creature and its significance. What lessons does the creature have to offer?
2. Find a place to write, and begin working on this assignment. Examine your surroundings: What could conceivably distract you from your work? Peeling paint? An uncomfortable chair? A funny smell? A noise? The view out your window? Your blinking computer cursor? Write a description of what you see, hear, feel, smell, taste.

3. **CRITICAL WRITING.** Respond to the ideas about life and death in Woolf's essay. First explain what you understand these ideas to be. Then use EXAMPLES from your reading and experience to support or contest Woolf's ideas.

4. **CONNECTIONS.** Human responses to witnessing a death also figure in Barbara Huttmann's "A Crime of Compassion" (p. 112) and Michael Kroll's "The Unquiet Death of Robert Harris" (p. 522). Write an essay in which you explore your perceptions of what happens at death. Draw on the views of Woolf, Huttmann, or Kroll if they seem relevant. If you have been directly affected by the death of a loved one, you might reflect on that experience as well.

5. **CONNECTIONS.** COMPARE Woolf's "The Death of the Moth" with Anna Quindlen's "Homeless" (p. 188). Of these two highly subjective essays, which is more personal? Write a brief essay answering this question, and support your answer with quotations and PARAPHRASES from Woolf and Quindlen.

Virginia Woolf on Writing

A journal keeper from her youth, Virginia Woolf used the form not only to record and reflect on events but also to do a kind of "rough & random" writing she otherwise had little chance for. (See p. 36 for more on journal writing.) Woolf wrote in her journal on April 20, 1919, that "the habit of writing thus for my own eye only is good practice. It loosens the ligaments. Never mind the misses & the stumbles. Going at such a pace as I do I must make the most direct & instant shots at my object, & thus have to lay hands on words, choose them, & shoot them with no more pause than is needed to put my pen in the ink. I believe that during the past year I can trace some increase of ease in my professional writing which I attribute to my casual half hours after tea."

Thirteen years later, Woolf felt just as strongly about the value of writing freely, without censorship. In "A Letter to a Young Poet," she advises against writing solely for "a severe and intelligent public." Follow the excitement of "actual life," she urges. "Write then, now that you are young, nonsense by the ream. Be silly, be sentimental, imitate Shelley, imitate Samuel Smiles; give the rein to every impulse; commit every fault of style, grammar, taste, and syntax; pour out; tumble over; loose anger, love, satire, in whatever words you can catch, coerce, or create, in whatever meter, prose, poetry, or gibberish that comes to hand. Thus you will learn to write."

For Discussion

1. What does Woolf gain from journal writing? What does she mean when she says that such writing "loosens the ligaments"?

2. Do you think Woolf seriously believed that young writers should write "nonsense by the ream"? (A *ream*, incidentally, is about five hundred sheets of paper.) What might the young writer learn from such freedom?
3. These excerpts do not discuss the writer's work needed to turn the loose, private writing Woolf recommends into writing that can be understood and appreciated by others. In your view, what does that work consist of?

USEFUL TERMS

Abstract and concrete   Two kinds of language. *Abstract* words refer to ideas, conditions, and qualities we cannot directly perceive: *truth, love, courage, evil, wealth, poverty, progressive, reactionary. Concrete* words indicate things we can know with our senses: *tree, chair, bird, pen, motorcycle, perfume, thunderclap, cheeseburger.* The use of concrete words lends vigor and clarity to writing, for such words help a reader to picture things. See IMAGE.

    Writers of expository and argumentative essays tend to shift back and forth from one kind of language to the other. They often begin a paragraph with a general statement full of abstract words ("There is *hope* for the *future* of *motoring*"). Then they usually go on to give examples and present evidence in sentences full of concrete words ("Inventor *Jones* claims his *car* will go from *Fresno* to *Los Angeles* on a *gallon* of *peanut oil*"). Inexperienced writers often use too many abstract words and not enough concrete ones.

Allude, allusion   To refer to a person, place, or thing believed to be common knowledge (*allude*), or the act or result of doing so (*allusion*). An allusion may point to a famous event, a familiar saying, a noted personality, a well-known story or song. Usually brief, an allusion is a space-saving way to convey much meaning. For example, the statement "The game was Coach Johnson's Waterloo" informs the reader that, like Napoleon meeting defeat in a celebrated battle, the coach led a confrontation resulting in his downfall and that of his team. If the writer is also showing Johnson's character, the allusion might further tell us that the coach is a man of Napoleonic ambition and pride. To make an effective allusion, you have to be aware of your audience. If your readers do not recognize the allusion, it will only confuse. Not everyone, for example, would understand if you alluded to a neighbor, to a seventeenth-century Russian harpsichordist, or to a little-known stock-car driver.

Analogy   An extended comparison based on the like features of two unlike things: one familiar or easily understood, the other unfamiliar, abstract, or complicated. For instance, most people know at least vaguely how the human eye works: The pupil adjusts to admit light, which registers as an image on the retina at the back of the eye. You might use this familiar information to explain something less familiar to many people, such as how a camera works: The aperture (like the pupil) adjusts to admit light, which registers as an image on the film (like the retina) at the back of the camera. Analogies are especially helpful for explaining technical information in a way that is nontechnical, more easily grasped. In August 1981, for example, the spacecraft *Voyager 2* transmitted spectacular pictures of Saturn to Earth. To explain the difficulty of their achievement, NASA scientists compared their feat to a golfer sinking a putt from five hundred miles away. Because it can make abstract ideas vivid and memorable, analogy is also a favorite device of philosophers, politicians, and preachers. In his celebrated speech "I Have a Dream" (p. 603), Martin Luther King, Jr., draws a remarkable analogy to express the anger and disappointment of African Americans that, one hundred years after Lincoln's Emancipation Proclamation, their full freedom has yet to be achieved. "It is obvious today," declares King, "that America has defaulted on this promissory note"; and he compares the founding fathers' written guarantee — of the rights of life, liberty, and the pursuit of happiness — to a bad check returned for insufficient funds.

In an ARGUMENT, analogy is similar to the method of COMPARISON AND CONTRAST. Both use DIVISION or ANALYSIS to identify the distinctive features of two things and then set the features side by side. But a comparison explains two obviously similar things — two Civil War generals, two responses to a mess — and considers both their differences and their similarities. An analogy yokes two apparently unlike things (eye and camera, spaceflight and golf, guaranteed human rights and bad checks) and focuses only on their major similarities. Analogy is thus an extended *metaphor*, the FIGURE OF SPEECH that declares one thing to be another — even though it isn't, in a strictly literal sense — for the purpose of making us aware of similarity: "Hope," says the poet Emily Dickinson, "is the thing with feathers / That perches in the soul."

In an ARGUMENT, analogy can make readers more receptive to a point or inspire them, but it can't prove anything because in the end the subjects are dissimilar. A false analogy is a logical FALLACY that claims a fundamental likeness when none exists. See page 509.

Analyze, analysis   To separate a subject into its parts (*analyze*), or the act or result of doing so (*analysis*, also called *division*). Analysis is a key skill in CRITICAL THINKING, READING, AND WRITING; see pages 19–20. It is also considered a method of development; see Chapter 9.

Anecdote   A brief NARRATIVE, or retelling of a story or event. Anecdotes have many uses: as essay openers or closers, as examples, as sheer entertainment. See Chapter 4.

Appeals   Resources writers draw on to connect with and persuade readers:

- A **rational appeal** asks readers to use their intellects and their powers of reasoning. It relies on established conventions of logic and evidence.
- An **emotional appeal** asks readers to respond out of their beliefs, values, or feelings. It inspires, affirms, frightens, angers.
- An **ethical appeal** asks readers to look favorably on the writer. It stresses the writer's intelligence, competence, fairness, morality, and other qualities desirable in a trustworthy debater or teacher.

See also pages 502–03.

Argument   A mode of writing intended to win readers' agreement with an assertion by engaging their powers of reasoning. Argument often overlaps PERSUASION. See Chapter 13.

Assume, assumption   To take something for granted (*assume*), or a belief or opinion taken for granted (*assumption*). Whether stated or unstated, assumptions influence a writer's choices of subject, viewpoint, evidence, and even language. See also pages 20 and 504–05.

Audience   A writer's readers. Having in mind a particular audience helps the writer in choosing strategies. Imagine, for instance, that you are writing two reviews of a new movie, one for the students who read the campus newspaper, the other for amateur and professional filmmakers who read *Millimeter*. For the first audience, you might write about the actors, the plot, and especially dramatic scenes. You might judge the picture and urge your readers to see it—or to avoid it. Writing for *Millimeter*, you might discuss special effects, shooting techniques, problems in editing and in mixing picture and sound. In this review, you might use more specialized and technical terms. Obviously, an awareness of the interests and knowledge of your readers, in each case, would help you decide how to write. If you told readers of the campus paper too much about filming techniques, you would lose most of them. If you told *Millimeter*'s readers the plot of the film in detail and how you liked its opening scene, probably you would put them to sleep.

You can increase your awareness of your audience by asking yourself a few questions before you begin to write. Who are to be your readers? What is their age level? background? education? Where do they live? What are their beliefs and attitudes? What interests them? What, if anything, sets them apart from most people? How familiar are they with your subject? Knowing your audience can help you write so that your readers will not only understand you better but more deeply care about what you say.

Cause and effect   A method of development in which a writer ANALYZES reasons for an action, event, or decision, or analyzes its consequences. See Chapter 11. See also EFFECT.

Chronological order   The arrangement of events as they occurred or occur in time, first to last. Most NARRATIVES and PROCESS ANALYSES use chronological order.

Claim   The proposition that an ARGUMENT demonstrates. Stephen Toulmin favors this term in his system of reasoning. See pages 504–06. In some discussions of argument, the term THESIS is used instead.

Classification   A method of development in which a writer sorts out plural things (contact sports, college students, kinds of music) into categories. See Chapter 10.

Cliché   A worn-out, trite expression that a writer employs thoughtlessly. Although at one time the expression may have been colorful, from heavy use it has lost its luster. It is now "old as the hills." In conversation, most of us sometimes use clichés, but in writing they "stick out like sore thumbs." Alert writers, when they revise, replace a cliché with a fresh, concrete expression. Writers who have trouble recognizing clichés should be suspicious of any phrase they've heard before and should try to read more widely. Their problem is that, so many expressions being new to them, they do not know which ones are full of moths.

Coherence   The clear connection of the parts in a piece of effective writing. This quality exists when the reader can easily follow the flow of ideas between sentences, paragraphs, and larger divisions, and can see how they relate successively to one another.

In making your essay coherent, you may find certain devices useful. TRANSITIONS, for instance, can bridge ideas. Reminders of points you have stated earlier are helpful to a reader who may have forgotten them—as readers tend to do sometimes, particularly if your essay is long. However, a coherent essay is not one merely pasted together with transitions and reminders. It derives its coherence from the clear relationship between its THESIS (or central idea) and all its parts.

Colloquial expressions   Words and phrases occurring primarily in speech and in informal writing that seeks a relaxed, conversational tone. "My favorite chow is a burger and a shake" or "This math exam has me wired" may be acceptable in talking to a roommate, in corresponding with a friend, or in writing a humorous essay for general readers. Such choices of words, however, would be out of place in formal writing—in, say, a laboratory report or a letter to your senator. Contractions (*let's, don't, we'll*) and abbreviated words (*photo, sales rep, ad*) are the shorthand of spoken language. Good writers use such expressions with an awareness that they produce an effect of casualness.

Comparison and contrast   Two methods of development usually found together. Using them, a writer examines the similarities and differences between two things to reveal their natures. See Chapter 7.

Conclusion   The sentences or paragraphs that bring an essay to a satisfying and logical end. A conclusion is purposefully crafted to give a sense of unity and completeness to the whole essay. The best conclusions evolve naturally out of what has gone before and convince the reader that the essay is indeed at an end, not that the writer has run out of steam.

Conclusions vary in type and length depending on the nature and scope of the essay. A long research paper may require several paragraphs of summary to review and emphasize the main points. A short essay, however, may benefit from a few brief closing sentences.

In concluding an essay, beware of diminishing the impact of your writing by finishing on a weak note. Don't apologize for what you have or have not written, or cram in a final detail that would have been better placed elsewhere.

Although there are no set formulas for closing, the following list presents several options:

- Restate the thesis of your essay, and perhaps your main points.
- Mention the broader implications or significance of your topic.
- Give a final example that pulls all the parts of your discussion together.
- Offer a prediction.

- End with the most important point as the culmination of your essay's development.
- Suggest how the reader can apply the information you have just imparted.
- End with a bit of drama or flourish. Tell an ANECDOTE, offer an appropriate quotation, ask a question, make a final insightful remark. Keep in mind, however, that an ending shouldn't sound false and gimmicky. It truly has to conclude.

Concrete   See ABSTRACT AND CONCRETE.

Connotation and denotation   Two types of meanings most words have. *Denotation* is the explicit, literal, dictionary definition of a word. *Connotation* refers to a word's implied meaning, resonant with associations. The denotation of *blood* is "the fluid that circulates in the vascular system." The connotations of *blood* range from *life force* to *gore* to *family bond*. A doctor might use the word *blood* for its denotation, and a mystery writer might rely on the rich connotations of the word to heighten a scene.

Because people have different experiences, they bring to the same word different associations. A conservative's emotional response to the word *welfare* is not likely to be the same as a liberal's. And referring to your senator as a *diplomat* evokes a different response, from the senator and from others, than would *baby-kisser, political hack*, or even *politician*. The effective use of words involves knowing both what they mean literally and what they are likely to suggest.

Critical thinking, reading, and writing   A group of interlocking skills that are essential for college work and beyond. Each seeks the meaning beneath the surface of a statement, poem, editorial, picture, advertisement, Web site, or other "text." Using ANALYSIS, INFERENCE, SYNTHESIS, and often EVALUATION, the critical thinker, reader, and writer separates this text into its elements in order to see and judge meanings, relations, and ASSUMPTIONS that might otherwise remain buried. See also pages 19–21, 28, 49–52, 313–14.

Data   The name for EVIDENCE favored by logician Stephen Toulmin in his system of reasoning. See pages 504–06.

Deductive reasoning, deduction   The method of reasoning from the general to the particular: From information about what we already know, we deduce what we need or want to know. See Chapter 13, pages 506–08.

Definition   A statement of the literal and specific meaning or meanings of a word, or a method of developing an essay. In the latter, the writer usually explains the nature of a word, a thing, a concept, or a phenomenon. Such a definition may employ NARRATION, DESCRIPTION, or any other method. See Chapter 12.

Denotation   See CONNOTATION AND DENOTATION.

Description   A mode of writing that conveys the evidence of the senses: sight, hearing, touch, taste, smell. See Chapter 5.

Diction   The choice of words. Every written or spoken statement contains diction of some kind. To describe certain aspects of diction, the following terms may be useful:

- **Standard English:** the common American language, words and grammatical forms that are used and expected in school, business, and other sites.
- **Nonstandard English:** words and grammatical forms such as *theirselves* and *ain't* that are used mainly by people who speak a dialect other than standard English.

- **Dialect:** a variety of English based on differences in geography, education, or social background. Dialect is usually spoken, but may be written. Maya Angelou's essay in Chapter 4 transcribes the words of dialect speakers: people waiting for the fight broadcast ("He gone whip him till that white boy call him Momma").
- **Slang:** certain words in highly informal speech or writing, or in the speech of a particular group—for example, *blow off, dis, dweeb*.
- **Colloquial expressions:** words and phrases from conversation. See COLLOQUIAL EXPRESSIONS for examples.
- **Regional terms:** words heard in a certain locality, such as *spritzing* for "raining" in Pennsylvania Dutch country.
- **Technical terms:** words and phrases that form the vocabulary of a particular discipline (*monocotyledon* from botany), occupation (*drawplate* from die-making), or avocation (*interval training* from running). See also JARGON.
- **Archaisms:** old-fashioned expressions, once common but now used to suggest an earlier style, such as *ere, yon,* and *forsooth.* (Actually, *yon* is still current in the expression *hither and yon*; but if you say "Behold yon glass of beer!" it is an archaism.)
- **Obsolete diction:** words that have passed out of use (such as the verb *werien*, "to protect or defend," and the noun *isetnesses*, "agreements"). *Obsolete* may also refer to certain meanings of words no longer current (*fond* for foolish, *clipping* for hugging or embracing).
- **Pretentious diction:** use of words more numerous and elaborate than necessary, such as *institution of higher learning* for college, and *partake of solid nourishment* for eat.

Archaic, obsolete, and pretentious diction usually has no place in good writing unless for ironic or humorous effect: H. L. Mencken delighted in the hifalutin use of *tonsorial studio* instead of barber shop. Still, any diction may be the right diction for a certain occasion: The choice of words depends on a writer's PURPOSE and AUDIENCE.

Discovery   The stage of the writing process before the first draft. It may include deciding on a topic, narrowing the topic, creating or finding ideas, doing reading and other research, defining PURPOSE and AUDIENCE, planning and arranging material. Discovery may follow from daydreaming or meditation, reading, or perhaps carefully ransacking memory. In practice, though, it usually involves considerable writing and is aided by the act of writing. The operations of discovery—reading, research, further idea creation, and refinement of subject, purpose, and audience—may all continue well into drafting as well. See also pages 35–38, 41–42.

Division   See ANALYZE, ANALYSIS.

Dominant impression   The main idea a writer conveys about a subject through DESCRIPTION—that an elephant is gigantic, for example, or an experience scary. See also Chapter 5.

Drafting   The stage of the writing process during which a writer expresses ideas in complete sentences, links them, and arranges them in a sequence. See also pages 38–39, 42–43.

Effect   The result of an event or action, usually considered together with CAUSE as a method of development. See the discussion of cause and effect in Chapter 11. In discussing writing, the term *effect* also refers to the impression a word, sentence, paragraph, or entire work makes on the reader: how convincing it is, whether it elicits an emotional response, what associations it conjures up, and so on.

Emotional appeal   See APPEALS.

Emphasis   The stress or special importance given to a certain point or element to make it stand out. A skillful writer draws attention to what is most important in a sentence, paragraph, or essay by controlling emphasis in any of the following ways:

- **Proportion:** Important ideas are given greater coverage than minor points.
- **Position:** The beginnings and ends of sentences, paragraphs, and larger divisions are the strongest positions. Placing key ideas in these spots helps draw attention to their importance. The end is the stronger position, for what stands last stands out. A sentence in which less important details precede the main point is called a **periodic sentence:** "Having disguised himself as a guard and walked through the courtyard to the side gate, the prisoner made his escape." A sentence in which the main point precedes less important details is a **loose sentence:** "Autumn is orange: gourds in baskets at roadside stands, the harvest moon hanging like a pumpkin, and oak leaves flashing like goldfish."
- **Repetition:** Careful repetition of key words or phrases can give them greater importance. (Careless repetition, however, can cause boredom.)
- **Mechanical devices:** Italics (underlining), capital letters, and exclamation points can make words or sentences stand out. Writers sometimes fall back on these devices, however, after failing to show significance by other means. Italics and exclamation points can be useful in reporting speech, but excessive use sounds exaggerated or bombastic.

Essay   A short nonfiction composition on one central theme or subject in which the writer may offer personal views. Essays are sometimes classified as either formal or informal. In general, a **formal essay** is one whose DICTION is that of the written language (not colloquial speech), serious in TONE, and usually focused on a subject the writer believes is important. (For example, see Bruce Catton's "Grant and Lee.") An **informal essay,** in contrast, is more likely to admit COLLOQUIAL EXPRESSIONS; the writer's tone tends to be lighter, perhaps humorous, and the subject is likely to be personal, sometimes even trivial. (See Dave Barry's "Batting Clean-Up and Striking Out.") These distinctions, however, are rough ones: An essay such as Judy Brady's "I Want a Wife" may use colloquial language and speak of personal experience, though it is serious in tone and has an undeniably important subject.

Ethical appeal   See APPEALS.

Euphemism   The use of inoffensive language in place of language that readers or listeners may find hurtful, distasteful, frightening, or otherwise objectionable—for instance, a police officer's announcing that someone *passed on* rather than *died,* or a politician's calling for *revenue enhancement* rather than *taxation.* Writers sometimes use euphemism out of consideration for readers' feelings, but just as often they use it to deceive readers or shirk responsibility. (For more on euphemism, see William Lutz's "The World of Doublespeak" in Chap. 10.)

Evaluate, evaluation   To judge the merits of something (*evaluate*), or the act or result of doing so (*evaluation*). Evaluation is often part of CRITICAL THINKING,

READING, AND WRITING. In evaluating a work of writing, you base your judgment on your ANALYSIS of it and your sense of its quality or value. See also pages 21, 31, 49–52.

Evidence The factual basis for an argument or an explanation. In a courtroom, an attorney's case is only as good as the evidence marshaled to support it. In an essay, a writer's opinions and GENERALIZATIONS also must rest upon evidence. The common forms of evidence are **facts**, verifiable statements; **statistics**, facts stated numerically; **examples**, specific instances of a generalization; **reported experience**, usually eyewitness accounts; **expert testimony**, the opinions of people considered very skilled or knowledgeable in the field; and, in CRITICAL WRITING about other writing, **quotations** or **paraphrases** from the work being discussed. (See PARAPHRASE.)

Example Also called **exemplification** or **illustration**, a method of development in which the writer provides instances of a general idea. See Chapter 6. *An example* is a verbal illustration.

Exposition The mode of prose writing that explains (or exposes) its subject. Its function is to inform, to instruct, or to set forth ideas: the major trade routes in the Middle East, how to make a dulcimer, why the United States consumes more energy than it needs. Exposition may call various methods to its service: EXAMPLE, COMPARISON AND CONTRAST, PROCESS ANALYSIS, and so on. Most college writing is at least partly exposition, and so are most of the essays in this book.

Fallacies Errors in reasoning. See pages 508–09 for a list and examples.

Figures of speech Expressions that depart from the literal meanings of words for the sake of emphasis or vividness. To say "She's a jewel" doesn't mean that the subject of praise is literally a kind of shining stone; the statement makes sense because its CONNOTATIONS come to mind: rare, priceless, worth cherishing. Some figures of speech involve comparisons of two objects apparently unlike:

- A **simile** (from the Latin, "likeness") states the comparison directly, usually connecting the two things using *like, as,* or *than:* "The moon is like a snowball," "He's as lazy as a cat full of cream," "My feet are flatter than flyswatters."
- A **metaphor** (from the Greek, "transfer") declares one thing to *be* another: "A mighty fortress is our God," "The sheep were bolls of cotton on the hill." (A **dead metaphor** is a word or phrase that, originally a figure of speech, has come to be literal through common usage: "the *hands* of a clock.")
- **Personification** is a simile or metaphor that assigns human traits to inanimate objects or abstractions: "A stoop-shouldered refrigerator hummed quietly to itself," "All of a sudden the solution to the math problem sat there winking at me."

Other figures of speech consist of deliberate misrepresentations:

- **Hyperbole** (from the Greek, "throwing beyond") is a conscious exaggeration: "I'm so hungry I could eat a horse and saddle," "I'd wait for you a thousand years."
- The opposite of hyperbole, **understatement**, creates an ironic or humorous effect: "I accepted the ride. At the moment, I didn't feel like walking across the Mojave Desert."
- A **paradox** (from the Greek, "conflicting with expectation") is a seemingly self-contradictory statement that, on reflection, makes sense: "Children are

the poor person's wealth" (wealth can be monetary, or it can be spiritual). *Paradox* may also refer to a situation that is inexplicable or contradictory, such as the restriction of one group's rights in order to secure the rights of another group.

Flashback   A technique of NARRATIVE in which the sequence of events is interrupted to recall an earlier period.

Focus   The narrowing of a subject to make it manageable. Beginning with a general subject, you concentrate on a certain aspect of it. For instance, you may select crafts as a general subject, then decide your main interest lies in weaving. You could focus your essay still further by narrowing it to operating a hand loom. You also focus your writing according to who will read it (AUDIENCE) or what you want it to achieve (PURPOSE).

General and specific   Terms that describe the relative number of instances or objects included in the group signified by a word. *General* words name a group or class (*flowers*); *specific* words limit the class by naming its individual members (*rose, violet, dahlia, marigold*). Words may be arranged in a series from more general to more specific: *clothes, pants, jeans, Levis*. The word *cat* is more specific than *animal*, but less specific than *tiger cat*, or *Garfield*. See also ABSTRACT AND CONCRETE.

Generalization   A statement about a class based on an examination of some of its members: "Lions are fierce." The more members examined and the more representative they are of the class, the sturdier the generalization. The statement "Solar heat saves homeowners money" would be challenged by homeowners who have yet to recover their installation costs. "Solar heat can save homeowners money in the long run" would be a sounder generalization. Insufficient or nonrepresentative EVIDENCE often leads to a hasty generalization, such as "All freshmen hate their roommates" or "Men never express their feelings." Words such as *all, every, only, never,* and *always* have to be used with care: "Some men don't express their feelings" is more credible. Making a trustworthy generalization involves the use of INDUCTIVE REASONING (discussed on pp. 506–07).

Hyperbole   See FIGURES OF SPEECH.

Illustration   Another name for EXAMPLE. See Chapter 6.

Image   A word or word sequence that evokes a sensory experience. Whether literal ("We picked two red apples") or figurative ("His cheeks looked like two red apples, buffed and shining"), an image appeals to the reader's memory of seeing, hearing, smelling, touching, or tasting. Images add concreteness to fiction—"The farm looked as tiny and still as a seashell, with the little knob of a house surrounded by its curved furrows of tomato plants" (Eudora Welty in a short story, "The Whistle")—and are an important element in poetry. But writers of essays, too, find images valuable to bring ideas down to earth. See also FIGURES OF SPEECH.

Inductive reasoning, induction   The process of reasoning to a conclusion about an entire class by examining some of its members. See pages 506–07.

Infer, inference   To draw a conclusion (*infer*), or the act or result of doing so (*inference*). In CRITICAL THINKING, READING, AND WRITING, inference is the means to understanding a writer's meaning, ASSUMPTIONS, PURPOSE, fairness, and other attributes. See also pages 20 and 30.

Introduction   The opening of a written work. Often it states the writer's subject, narrows it, and communicates the writer's main idea (THESIS). Introductions vary in length, depending on their purposes. A research paper may need several paragraphs to set forth its central idea and its plan of organization; a brief, informal essay may need only a sentence or two for an introduction. Whether long or short, good introductions tell readers no more than they need to know when they begin reading. Here are a few possible ways to open an essay effectively:

- State your central idea, or thesis, perhaps showing why you care about it.
- Present startling facts about your subject.
- Tell an illustrative ANECDOTE.
- Give background information that will help your reader understand your subject, or see why it is important.
- Begin with an arresting quotation.
- Ask a challenging question. (In your essay, you'll go on to answer it.)

Irony A manner of speaking or writing that does not directly state a discrepancy, but implies one. **Verbal irony** is the intentional use of words to suggest a meaning other than literal: "What a mansion!" (said of a shack); "There's nothing like sunshine" (said on a foggy morning). (For more examples, see the essays by Jessica Mitford, Linnea Saukko, and Judy Brady.) If irony is delivered contemptuously with an intent to hurt, we call it **sarcasm:** "Oh, you're a real friend!" (said to someone who refuses to lend the speaker the coins to make a phone call). With **situational irony,** the circumstances themselves are incongruous, run contrary to expectations, or twist fate: Juliet regains consciousness only to find that Romeo, believing her dead, has stabbed himself. See also SATIRE.

Jargon Strictly speaking, the special vocabulary of a trade or profession. The term has also come to mean inflated, vague, meaningless language of any kind. It is characterized by wordiness, ABSTRACTIONS galore, pretentious DICTION, and needlessly complicated word order. Whenever you meet a sentence that obviously could express its idea in fewer words and shorter ones, chances are that it is jargon. For instance: "The motivating force compelling her to opt continually for the most labor-intensive mode of operation in performing her functions was consistently observed to be the single constant and regular factor in her behavior patterns." Translation: "She did everything the hard way." (For more on such jargon, see William Lutz's "The World of Doublespeak" in Chap. 10.)

Journal A record of one's thoughts, kept daily or at least regularly. Keeping a journal faithfully can help a writer gain confidence and develop ideas. See also page 36.

Metaphor See FIGURES OF SPEECH.

Narration The mode of writing that tells a story. See Chapter 4.

Narrator The teller of a story, usually either in the first PERSON (*I*) or in the third (*he, she, it, they*). See pages 76–77.

Nonstandard English See DICTION.

Objective and subjective Kinds of writing that differ in emphasis. In *objective* writing, the emphasis falls on the topic; in *subjective* writing, it falls on the writer's view of the topic. Objective writing occurs in factual journalism, science reports, certain PROCESS ANALYSES (such as recipes, directions, and instructions), and logical arguments in which the writer attempts to downplay personal feelings and opinions. Subjective writing sets forth the writer's feelings, opinions, and interpretations. It occurs in friendly letters, journals, bylined feature stories and columns in newspapers, personal essays, and ARGUMENTS that appeal to emotion. Few essays, however, contain one kind of writing exclusive of the other.

Paradox   See FIGURES OF SPEECH.

Paragraph   A group of closely related sentences that develop a central idea. In an essay, a paragraph is the most important unit of thought because it is both self-contained and part of the larger whole. Paragraphs separate long and involved ideas into smaller parts that are more manageable for the writer and easier for the reader to take in. Good paragraphs, like good essays, possess UNITY and COHERENCE. The central idea is usually stated in a TOPIC SENTENCE, often found at the beginning of the paragraph that relates directly to the essay's THESIS. All other sentences in the paragraph relate to this topic sentence, defining it, explaining it, illustrating it, providing it with evidence and support. If you meet a unified and coherent paragraph that has no topic sentence, it will contain a central idea that no sentence in it explicitly states, but that every sentence in it clearly implies.

Parallelism, parallel structure   A habit of good writers: keeping ideas of equal importance in similar grammatical form. A writer may place nouns side by side ("*Trees* and *streams* are my weekend tonic") or in a series ("Give me *wind, sea,* and *stars*"). Phrases, too, may be arranged in parallel structure ("*Out of my bed, into my shoes, up to my classroom* — that's my life"); or clauses ("Ask not what your country can do for you; ask what you can do for your country").

     Parallelism may be found not only in single sentences, but in larger units as well. A paragraph might read: "Rhythm is everywhere. It throbs in the rain forests of Brazil. It vibrates ballroom floors in Vienna. It snaps its fingers on street corners in Chicago." In a whole essay, parallelism may be the principle used to arrange ideas in a balanced or harmonious structure. See the famous speech given by Martin Luther King, Jr. (p. 603), in which each paragraph in a series (pars. 11–18) begins with the words "I have a dream" and goes on to describe an imagined future. Not only does such a parallel structure organize ideas, but it also lends them force.

Paraphrase   Putting another writer's thoughts into your own words. In writing a research paper or an essay containing EVIDENCE gathered from your reading, you will find it necessary to paraphrase — unless you are using another writer's very words with quotation marks around them — and to acknowledge your sources. Contrast SUMMARY. And see page 53.

Person   A grammatical distinction made between the speaker, the one spoken to, and the one spoken about. In the first person (*I, we*), the subject is speaking. In the second person (*you*), the subject is being spoken to. In the third person (*he, she, it*), the subject is being spoken about. The point of view of an essay or work of fiction is often specified according to person: "This short story is told from a first-person point of view." See POINT OF VIEW.

Personification   See FIGURES OF SPEECH.

Persuasion   A mode of writing intended to influence people's actions by engaging their beliefs and feelings. Persuasion often overlaps ARGUMENT. See Chapter 13.

Plagiarism   The use of someone else's ideas or words as if they were your own, without acknowledging the original author. See pages 53–54.

Point of view   In an essay, the physical position or the mental angle from which a writer beholds a subject. On the subject of starlings, the following three writers would likely have different points of view: An ornithologist might write

OBJECTIVELY about the introduction of these birds into North America, a farmer might advise other farmers how to prevent the birds from eating seed, and a bird-watcher might SUBJECTIVELY describe a first glad sighting of an unusual species. Furthermore, the PERSON of each essay would probably differ: The scientist might present a scholarly paper in the third person, the farmer might offer advice in the second, and the bird-watcher might recount the experience in the first.

Premise   A proposition or ASSUMPTION that supports a conclusion. See page 507 for examples.

Process analysis   A method of development that most often explains step by step how something is done or how to do something. See Chapter 8.

Purpose   A writer's reason for trying to convey a particular idea (THESIS) about a particular subject to a particular AUDIENCE of readers. Though it may emerge gradually during the writing process, in the end purpose should govern every element of a piece of writing.

In trying to define the purpose of an essay you read, ask yourself "Why did the writer write this?" or "What was this writer trying to achieve?" Even though you cannot know the writer's intentions with absolute certainty, an effective essay will make some purpose clear.

Rational appeal   See APPEALS.

Revision   The stage of the writing process during which a writer "re-sees" a draft from the viewpoint of a reader. Revision usually involves two steps, first considering fundamental matters such as PURPOSE and organization, and then editing for surface matters such as smooth TRANSITIONS and error-free sentences. See pages 39–40, 44–46.

Rhetoric   The study (and the art) of using language effectively. *Rhetoric* also has a negative CONNOTATION of empty or pretentious language meant to waffle, stall, or even deceive. This is the meaning in "The president had nothing substantial to say about taxes, just the usual rhetoric."

Rhetorical question   A question posed for effect, one that requires no answer. Instead, it often provokes thought, lends emphasis to a point, asserts or denies something without making a direct statement, launches further discussion, introduces an opinion, or leads the reader where the writer intends. Sometimes a writer throws one in to introduce variety in a paragraph full of declarative sentences. The following questions are rhetorical: "When will the United States learn that sending people into space does not feed them on the earth?" "Shall I compare thee to a summer's day?" "What is the point of making money if you've no one but yourself to spend it on?" Both reader and writer know what the answers are supposed to be. (1) Someday, if the United States ever wises up. (2) Yes. (3) None.

Sarcasm   See IRONY.

Satire   A form of writing that employs wit to attack folly. Unlike most comedy, the purpose of satire is not merely to entertain, but to bring about enlightenment—even reform. Usually, satire employs irony—as in Linnea Saukko's "How to Poison the Earth" and Jonathan Swift's "A Modest Proposal." See also IRONY.

Scene   In a NARRATIVE, an event retold in detail to re-create an experience. See Chapter 4.

Sentimentality   A quality sometimes found in writing that fails to communicate. Such writing calls for an extreme emotional response on the part of an AUDIENCE, although its writer fails to supply adequate reason for any such reaction. A sentimental writer delights in waxing teary over certain objects: great-grandmother's portrait, the first stick of chewing gum baby chewed (now a shapeless wad), an empty popcorn box saved from the World Series of 1996. Sentimental writing usually results when writers shut their eyes to the actual world, preferring to snuffle the sweet scents of remembrance.

Simile See FIGURES OF SPEECH.

Slang See DICTION.

Specific See GENERAL AND SPECIFIC.

Standard English See DICTION.

Strategy Whatever means a writer employs to write effectively. The methods set forth in this book are strategies; but so are narrowing a subject, organizing ideas clearly, using TRANSITIONS, writing with an awareness of your reader, and other effective writing practices.

Style The distinctive manner in which a writer writes. Style may be seen especially in the writer's choice of words and sentence structures. Two writers may write on the same subject, even express similar ideas, but it is style that gives each writer's work a personality.

Subjective See OBJECTIVE AND SUBJECTIVE.

Summarize, summary To condense a work (essay, movie, news story) to its essence (*summarize*), or the act or result of doing so (*summary*). Summarizing a piece of writing in one's own words is an effective way to understand it. (See pp. 18–19.) Summarizing (and acknowledging) others' writing in your own text is a good way to support your ideas. (See p. 52.) Contrast PARAPHRASE.

Suspense Often an element in NARRATION: the pleasurable expectation or anxiety we feel that keeps us reading a story. In an exciting mystery story, suspense is constant: How will it all turn out? Will the detective get to the scene in time to prevent another murder? But there can be suspense in less melodramatic accounts as well.

Syllogism A three-step form of reasoning that employs DEDUCTION. See page 507 for an illustration.

Symbol A visible object or action that suggests some further meaning. The flag suggests country, the crown suggests royalty — these are conventional symbols familiar to us. Life abounds in such relatively clear-cut symbols. Football teams use dolphins and rams for easy identification; married couples symbolize their union with a ring.

In writing, symbols usually do not have such a one-to-one correspondence, but evoke a whole constellation of associations. In Herman Melville's *Moby-Dick*, the whale suggests more than the large mammal it is. It hints at evil, obsession, and the untamable forces of nature. Such a symbol carries meanings too complex or elusive to be neatly defined.

Although more common in fiction and poetry, symbols can be used to good purpose in nonfiction because they often communicate an idea in a compact and concrete way.

Synthesize, synthesis To link elements into a whole (*synthesize*), or the act or result of doing so (*synthesis*). In CRITICAL THINKING, READING, AND WRITING, synthesis is the key step during which you reassemble a work you have ANALYZED or connect the work with others. See pages 20–21 and 30–31.

Thesis   The central idea in a work of writing, to which everything else in the work refers. In some way, each sentence and PARAGRAPH in an effective essay serves to support the thesis and to make it clear and explicit to readers. Good writers, while writing, often set down a **thesis sentence** or **thesis statement** to help them define their purpose. They also often include this statement in their essay as a promise and a guide to readers. See also pages 38–39.

Tone   The way a writer expresses his or her regard for subject, AUDIENCE, or self. Through word choice, sentence structures, and what is actually said, the writer conveys an attitude and sets a prevailing spirit. Tone in writing varies as greatly as tone of voice varies in conversation. It can be serious, distant, flippant, angry, enthusiastic, sincere, sympathetic. Whatever tone a writer chooses, usually it informs an entire essay and helps a reader decide how to respond. For works of strong tone, see the essays by Barbara Huttmann, Joan Didion, Jessica Mitford, Judy Brady, Russell Baker, and Martin Luther King, Jr.

Topic sentence   The statement of the central idea in a PARAGRAPH, usually asserting one aspect of an essay's THESIS. Often the topic sentence will appear at (or near) the beginning of the paragraph, announcing the idea and beginning its development. Because all other sentences in the paragraph explain and support this central idea, the topic sentence is a way to create UNITY.

Transitions   Words, phrases, sentences, or even paragraphs that relate ideas. In moving from one topic to the next, a writer has to bring the reader along by showing how the ideas are developing, what bearing a new thought or detail has on an earlier discussion, or why a new topic is being introduced. A clear purpose, strong ideas, and logical development certainly aid COHERENCE, but to ensure that the reader is following along, good writers provide signals, or transitions.

To bridge sentences or paragraphs and to point out relationships within them, you can use some of the following devices of transition:

- Repeat or restate words or phrases to produce an echo in the reader's mind.
- Use PARALLEL STRUCTURES to produce a rhythm that moves the reader forward.
- Use pronouns to refer back to nouns in earlier passages.
- Use transitional words and phrases. These may indicate a relationship of time (*right away, later, soon, meanwhile, in a few minutes, that night*), proximity (*beside, close to, distant from, nearby, facing*), effect (*therefore, for this reason, as a result, consequently*), comparison (*similarly, in the same way, likewise*), or contrast (*yet, but, nevertheless, however, despite*). Some words and phrases of transition simply add on: *besides, too, also, moreover, in addition to, second, last, in the end*.

Understatement   See FIGURES OF SPEECH.

Unity   The quality of good writing in which all parts relate to the THESIS. In a unified essay, all words, sentences, and PARAGRAPHS support the single central idea. Your first step in achieving unity is to state your thesis; your next step is to organize your thoughts so that they make your thesis clear.

Voice   In writing, the sense of the author's character, personality, and attitude that comes through the words. See TONE.

Warrant   The name in Stephen Toulmin's system of reasoning for the thinking, or ASSUMPTION, that links DATA and CLAIM. See pages 504–06.

Acknowledgments (continued from p. iv)

Maya Angelou. "Champion of the World" from *I Know Why the Caged Bird Sings* by Maya Angelou. Copyright © 1969 and renewed 1997 by Maya Angelou. Reprinted by permission of Random House, Inc. "Maya Angelou on Writing," excerpts from Sheila Weller, "Work in Progess/Maya Angelou," in *Intellectual Digest*, June 1973. Reprinted by permission.

Barbara Lazear Ascher. "On Compassion" from *The Habit of Loving* by Barbara Ascher. Copyright © 1986, 1987, 1989 by Barbara Lazear. Reprinted by permission of Random House, Inc. "Barbara Lazear Ascher on Writing," excerpt from Barbara Lazear Ascher selection in *Contemporary Authors Online*. Copyright © 1999. Reprinted by permission.

Russell Baker. "The Plot Against People," *New York Times*, January 1, 1951. Copyright © 1951 by the New York Times Company. Reprinted by permission. "Russell Baker on Writing," previously appeared as "Computer Fallout" in the *New York Times Magazine*, October 11, 1987. Copyright © 1987 by The New York Times Company. Reprinted by permission.

Dave Barry. "Batting Clean-Up and Striking Out" from *Dave Barry's Greatest Hits* by Dave Barry. Copyright © 1988 by Dave Barry. Reprinted by permission of Crown Publishers, Inc. "Dave Barry on Writing," excerpts from Dave Barry selection in *Contemporary Authors, New Revision Series*, Vol. 134. Published 1992. Copyright © 1992. Reprinted by permission of the Gale Group <http://www.galegroup.com>.

Bruno Bettelheim. "The Holocaust," excerpt from "The Holocaust" from *Surviving and Other Essays* by Bruno Bettelheim. Copyright © 1952, 1960, 1962, 1976, 1979 by Bruno Bettelheim and Trude Bettelheim as Trustees. Reprinted by permission of Alfred A. Knopf, a division of Random House, Inc.

Judy Brady. "I Want a Wife," copyright © 1970 by Judy Brady. Reprinted by permission of the author.

Suzanne Britt. "Neat People vs. Sloppy People" from *Show and Tell* by Suzanne Britt. Copyright © 1982 by Suzanne Britt. Reprinted by permission of the author. "Suzanne Britt on Writing," copyright © 1984 by St. Martin's Press, Inc.

Armin A. Brott. "Not All Men Are Sly Foxes," first published in *Newsweek* magazine in 1992. Reprinted by permission of the author.

Bill Bryson. "Design Flaws" from *I'm a Stranger Here Myself* by Bill Bryson. Copyright © 1999 by Bill Bryson. Reprinted by permission of Broadway Books, a division of Random House, Inc. "Bill Bryson on Writing," excerpt from "Lost in Cyberspace" from *I'm a Stranger Here Myself* by Bill Bryson. Copyright © 1999 by Bill Bryson. Reprinted by permission of Random House, Inc.

William F. Buckley, Jr. "Why Don't We Complain?" Copyright © 1960 by *Esquire*. Reprinted by permission of the Wallace Literary Agency, Inc. "William F. Buckley, Jr., on Writing," excerpts from *Overdrive* by William F. Buckley, Jr. Published by Doubleday. Copyright © 1981, 1983 by N. R. Resources, Inc. Reprinted by permission of Doubleday, a division of Bantam, Doubleday, Dell Publishing Group, Inc. Excerpt from *Hymnal: The Controversial Arts* by William F. Buckley, Jr. Copyright © 1978 by William F. Buckley, Jr. Reprinted by permission of G. P. Putnam's Sons.

Bruce Catton. "Grant and Lee: A Study in Contrasts." Copyright © 1956 by US Capitol Historical Society. All rights reserved. Reprinted by permission. "Bruce Catton on Writing," excerpts from Oliver Jensen's introduction to *Bruce Catton's America*. Reprinted by permission of *American Heritage* magazine, a division of Forbes, Inc. Copyright © 1979.

Sandra Cisneros. "Only Daughter," copyright © 1990 by Sandra Cisneros. First published in *Glamour*, November 1990. Reprinted by permission of Susan Bergholz Literary Services,

New York. All rights reserved. "Sandra Cisneros on Writing," excerpt from *Interviews with Writers of the Post-Colonial World* edited by Feroza Jussawalla and Reed Way Dasenbrock. Copyright © 1992 by the University Press of Mississippi. Reprinted by permission.

Judith Ortiz Cofer. "Silent Dancing." Reprinted with permission from the publisher of *Silent Dancing: A Partial Remembrance of a Puerto Rican Childhood.* Houston: Arte Público Press–University of Houston, 1990. "Judith Ortiz Cofer on Writing," excerpt from Judith Ortiz Cofer selection in *Contemporary Authors, New Revision Series,* Vol. 115. Published 1985. Copyright © 1985. Reprinted by permission of the Gale Group <http://www.galegroup.com>.

Meghan Daum. "Safe-Sex Lies," *New York Times Magazine,* January 21, 1996. Copyright © 1996 by Meghan Daum. Reprinted by permission of the author.

C. Day Lewis. "The Expulsion: Masaccio" from *The Complete Poems of C. Day Lewis.* Copyright © 1994 by Stanford University Press. Reprinted by permission.

Don DeLillo. "Videotape." Reprinted with the permission of Scribner, a division of Simon & Schuster, Inc., from *Underworld* by Don DeLillo. Copyright © 1997 by Don DeLillo. "Don DeLillo on Writing," excerpt from *Paris Review,* no. 128, Fall 1993.

Joan Didion. "Marrying Absurd" from *Slouching Towards Bethlehem* by Joan Didion. Copyright © 1966, 1968, renewed 1996 by Joan Didion. Reprinted by permission of Farrar, Straus and Giroux, LLC. "Joan Didion on Writing," excerpts from "Why I Write" by Joan Didion. First appeared in the *New York Times Book Review.*

Annie Dillard. "The Chase" from *An American Childhood* by Annie Dillard. Copyright © 1987 by Annie Dillard. Reprinted by permission of HarperCollins Publishers, Inc. "Annie Dillard on Writing," copyright © 1985 by St. Martin's Press.

Chitra Divakaruni. "Live Free and Starve." This article first appeared in *Salon.com.* An online version remains in the *Salon* archives. Reprinted with permission. "Chitra Divakaruni on Writing," excerpt from "Women's Places," interview by Katie Bolick, *Atlantic Unbound,* April 8, 1998 <http://www.theatlantic.com/unbound/factfict/ff9804.html>. Reprinted by permission.

Stephanie Ericsson. "The Ways We Lie," copyright © 1992 by Stephanie Ericsson. Originally published in the *Utne Reader.* Permission granted by Rhoda Weyr Agency, New York. "Stephanie Ericsson on Writing," excerpt from "Amazon.com Talks to Stephanie Ericsson" <http://www.amazon.com/exec/obidos/show-interview/e-s-ricssontephanie>.

M. F. K. Fisher. "The Broken Chain" from *To Be Born Again* by M. F. K. Fisher. Copyright © 1992 by the M. F. K. Fisher Literary Trust. Reprinted by permission of Pantheon Books, a division of Random House, Inc.

Laura Fraser. "Why I Stopped Being a Vegetarian" from *Salon.com,* January 7, 2000. Copyright © 2000 by *Salon.com.* Reprinted by permission of *Salon.com.* All rights reserved. "Laura Fraser on Writing," excerpt from "An Interview with Laura Fraser" on *Randomhouse.com.* Reprinted by permission.

Atul Gawande. "The Cancer-Cluster Myth," *New Yorker,* February 8, 1999. Copyright © 1999 by Atul Gawande. Reprinted by permission of Janklow & Nesbit, agents for the author. "Atul Gawande on Writing," originally titled "The Doctor Is In" by Atul Gawande, from the *New Yorker,* March 12, 2002. Copyright © 2002 by The New Yorker Magazine, Inc. All rights reserved. Reprinted with permission.

Stephen Jay Gould. "Sex, Drugs, Disasters, and the Extinction of Dinosaurs," copyright © 1984 by Stephen Jay Gould, from *The Flamingo's Smile: Reflections in National History* by Stephen Jay Gould. Reprinted by permission of W. W. Norton & Company, Inc. In "Stephen Jay Gould on Writing," prologue excerpts are reprinted from *The Flamingo's Smile: Reflections in National History* by Stephen Jay Gould. Reprinted by permission of W. W. Norton & Company, Inc. Copyright © 1985 by Stephen Jay Gould.

Barbara Huttmann. "A Crime of Compassion," first published in *Newsweek* magazine in 1983. Copyright © 1983 by Barbara Huttmann. Reprinted by permission of the author.

Jean Kilbourne. "'Can An Engine Pump the Valves in Your Heart?'" Reprinted and edited with the permission of The Free Press, a division of Simon & Schuster, Inc., from *Can't Buy My Love: How Advertising Changes The Way We Feel and Think* by Jean Kilbourne. Previously published as *Deadly Persuasion.* Copyright © 1999 by Jean Kilbourne.

Jamaica Kincaid. "Girl" from *At the Bottom of the River* by Jamaica Kincaid. Copyright © 1983 by Jamaica Kincaid. Reprinted by permission of Farrar, Straus and Giroux, LLC. "Jamaica Kincaid on Writing," excerpt from Louise Kennedy, "A Writer Retraces Her Steps," from the *Boston Globe,* November 7, 1990. Reprinted by permission.

Martin Luther King, Jr. "I Have a Dream," copyright © 1963 by Martin Luther King, Jr. Copyright 1991 renewed by Coretta Scott King. Reprinted by arrangement with The Heirs to the Estate of Martin Luther King, Jr., c/o Writers House, Inc., as agent for the proprietor.

Stephen King. "'Ever Et Raw Meat?'" *New York Times,* December 6, 1987. Copyright © 1987 by the New York Times Company. Reprinted by permission. In "Stephen King on Writing," excerpts from "Digging Up Stories with Stephen King" by W. C. Stoby, *Writer's Digest,* March 1992. From "King of Horror" by Bill Goldstein, *Publisher's Weekly,* January 24, 1991. Reprinted by permission.

Maxine Hong Kingston. "No Name Woman" from *The Woman Warrior* by Maxine Hong Kingston. Copyright © 1975, 1976 by Maxine Hong Kingston. Reprinted by permission of Alfred A. Knopf, a division of Random House, Inc. "Maxine Hong Kingston on Writing," excerpt from Maxine Hong Kingston selection in *Contemporary Authors, New Revision Series,* Vol. 13. Published 1984. Copyright © 1984. Reprinted by permission of the Gale Group <http://www.galegroup.com>.

Gina Kolata. "Probing Disease Clusters," *New York Times,* January 31, 1999. Copyright © 1999 by the New York Times Company. Reprinted by permission. "Gina Kolata on Writing," originally titled "Ask a Reporter," from the *New York Times,* January 7, 2002. Copyright © 2002 by the New York Times Company. Reprinted by permission.

Michael Kroll. "The Unquiet Death of Robert Harris," *Nation,* July 6, 1992. Copyright © 1992 *The Nation.* Reprinted by permission.

Jhumpa Lahiri. "Indian Takeout," *Food and Wine,* April 2000. Copyright © 2000 by Food and Wine/Amex Publishing. Reprinted by permission. "Jhumpa Lahiri on Writing" from *Philadelphia Citypaper.net,* September 16–23, 1999.

Christine Leong. "Being a Chink." Reprinted by permission of the author. "Christine Leong on Writing." Copyright © 1996 by Bedford Books.

William Lutz. "The World of Doublespeak" from *Doublespeak* by William Lutz. Copyright © 1989 by Blonde Bear, Inc. Reprinted by permission of HarperCollins Publishers, Inc. "William Lutz on Writing," excerpt from transcript of *Booknotes,* C-SPAN, December 31, 1989 <http://www.booknotes.org/transcriptarchive>. Reprinted by permission of C-SPAN.

Niala Maharaj and Donovan Hohn. "Thorny Truths About Flowers," originally published under the title "Fleurs du Mal." Copyright © 2001 by *Harper's* magazine. All rights reserved. Reproduced from the February issue by special permission.

Nancy Mairs. "Disability," excerpt from *Carnal Acts* by Nancy Mairs. Copyright © 1990 by Nancy Mairs. Reprinted by permission of Beacon Press, Boston. "Nancy Mairs on Writing," excerpt from "When Bad Things Happen to Good Writers" by Nancy Mairs, *New York Times Book Review,* February 1993. Reprinted by permission.

Brad Manning. "Arm Wrestling with My Father." Reprinted by permission of the author. "Brad Manning on Writing," copyright © 1996 by Bedford Books.

John McPhee. "Silk Parachute," originally in *The New Yorker*. Copyright © 1997 by John McPhee. Reprinted by permission. All rights reserved. "John McPhee on Writing," excerpt from "The Strange Case of the Queen-Post Trust" by Douglas Vipond and Russell A. Hunt, *College Composition and Communication* 43.3, pp. 202 and 203–4. Copyright © 1991 by National Council of Teachers of English. Reprinted by permission.

H. L. Mencken. "The Penalty of Death." Reprinted from *A Mencken Chrestomathy* by H. L. Mencken. Copyright © 1926 by Alfred A. Knopf, Inc., and renewed 1954 by H. L. Mencken. Reprinted by permission of Alfred A. Knopf, a division of Random House, Inc. "H. L. Mencken on Writing," excerpts from "Addendum on Aims" by H. L. Mencken in *Prejudices: Fifth Series*. All copyrighted © by Alfred A. Knopf, a division of Random House, Inc. Reprinted by permission.

Jessica Mitford. "Behind the Formaldehyde Curtain" from *The American Way of Death* by Jessica Mitford. Copyright © 1963, 1978 by Jessica Mitford. All rights reserved. Reprinted by permission of the Estate of Jessica Mitford. "Jessica Mitford on Writing," excerpts from *Poison Penmanship: The Gentle Art of Muckraking* by Jessica Mitford. Copyright © 1979. From *A Fine Old Conflict* by Jessica Mitford. Copyright © 1977. Reprinted by permission of Random House, Inc.

Gloria Naylor. "The Meanings of a Word," copyright © 1986 by Gloria Naylor. Reprinted by permission of Sterling Lord Literistic, Inc. "Gloria Naylor on Writing," excerpt from "A Talk with Gloria Naylor" by William Goldstein. Reprinted from the September 9, 1983, issue of *Publishers Weekly*. Copyright © 1983 by *Publishers Weekly*. Reprinted by permission.

Joyce Carol Oates. "Edward Hopper's *Nighthawks*, 1942" from *The Time Traveler* by Joyce Carol Oates. Copyright © 1989 by Joyce Carol Oates. Reprinted by permission of John Hawkins Associates, New York, NY. "Joyce Carol Oates on Writing" excerpts from *Where I've Been, Where I'm Going* by Joyce Carol Oates.

George Orwell. "Shooting an Elephant" from *Shooting an Elephant and Other Essays* by George Orwell. Copyright © 1950 by Sonia Brownell Orwell and renewed 1978 by Sonia Pitt-Rivers. Reprinted by permission of Harcourt, Inc. "George Orwell on Writing," excerpt from "Why I Write" from *Such, Such Were the Joys* by George Orwell. Copyright © 1953 by Sonia Brownell Orwell and renewed 1981 by Mrs. George K. Perutz, Mrs. Miriam Gross, and Dr. Michael Dickson, Executors of the Estate of Sonia Brownell Orwell. Reprinted by permission of Harcourt, Inc.

Emily Prager. "Our Barbies, Ourselves," originally published in *Interview*, Brant Publications, Inc., December 1991. Reprinted by permission. "Emily Prager on Writing," excerpt from "Focus on the United States: Will the Class of 2000 Be Able to Read?" by Emily Prager, *Globe and Mail*, January 14, 1989, p. D5.

Anna Quindlen. "Homeless" from *Living Out Loud* by Anna Quindlen. Copyright © 1987 by Anna Quindlen. Reprinted by permission of Random House, Inc. "Anna Quindlen on Writing," excerpts from "In the Beginning" in *Living Out Loud* by Anna Quindlen. Copyright © 1987 by Anna Quindlen. Reprinted by permission of Random House, Inc.

Richard Rodriguez. "Aria: A Memoir of a Bilingual Childhood," copyright © 1980 by Richard Rodriguez. Originally appeared in *The American Scholar*. Reprinted by permission of Georges Borchardt, Inc., Literary Agency, for the author. "Richard Rodriguez on Writing," copyright © 1985 by St. Martin's Press, Inc.

Lucinda Rosenfeld. "How to Dump a Friend," *New York Times*, April 8, 2001. Copyright © 2001 by The New York Times Company. Reprinted by permission.

William Safire. "On Language: Fulminations," *New York Times*, May 6, 2001. Copyright © 2001 by The New York Times Company. Reprinted by permission. "William Safire on Writing," excerpt from *On Language* by William Safire.

Linnea Saukko. "How to Poison the Earth" and "Linnea Saukko on Writing," excerpts from *Student Writers at Work and in the Company of Other Writers*. Copyright © 1984 by St. Martin's Press, Inc. Reprinted by permission.

David Sedaris. "Remembering My Childhood on the Continent of Africa" from *Me Talk Pretty One Day* by David Sedaris. Copyright © 2000 by David Sedaris. Reprinted by permission of Little, Brown and Company. "David Sedaris on Writing," excerpt from *Me Talk Pretty One Day* by David Sedaris.

Peter Singer. "The Singer Solution to World Poverty," *New York Times*, September 5, 1999. Copyright © 1995 by the New York Times Company. Reprinted by permission. "Peter Singer on Writing," excerpt from "Of Animals and Ethics" by Richard Atcheson, *Princeton Alumni Weekly*, November 15, 2000. Reprinted by permission of *Princeton Alumni Weekly*.

Brent Staples. "Black Men and Public Space," *Harper's*, December 1986. Reprinted by permission of the author. "Brent Staples on Writing," copyright © 1991 St. Martin's Press, Inc.

Shelby Steele. "Notes from the Hip-Hop Underground," *Wall Street Journal*, March 3, 2001. Republished by permission of Dow Jones, Inc., via Copyright Clearance Center. All rights reserved worldwide. "Shelby Steele on Writing," excerpt from *The Content of Our Character* by Shelby Steele. Copyright © 1990 by Shelby Steele. Reprinted by permission of St. Martin's Press.

Amy Tan. "Fish Cheeks," copyright © 1987 by Amy Tan. First appeared in *Seventeen Magazine*. Digitalized with permission of the author and the Sandra Dijkstra Literary Agency. "Amy Tan on Writing," excerpts from "Mother Tongue." Copyright © 1990 by Amy Tan. From the *Threepenny Review*. Reprinted by permission of the author and the Sandra Dijkstra Literary Agency.

Deborah Tannen. "But What Do You Mean?" from *Talking from 9 to 5* by Deborah Tannen. Copyright © 1994 by Deborah Tannen. Reprinted by permission of HarperCollins Publishers, Inc. "Deborah Tannen on Writing," from *Publication of the Modern Language Association of America*, October 1996.

Greg Tartaglia. "The Elusive Butterfly," first published in *Fresh Ink: Essays from Boston College's First-Year Writing Seminar, 1998*. Reprinted by permission of the author.

Gore Vidal. "Drugs" from *Homage to Daniel Shays: Collected Essays, 1952–1972* by Gore Vidal. Copyright © 1970 by Gore Vidal. Reprinted by permission of Random House, Inc. "Gore Vidal on Writing," excerpt from *Writers at Work, Fifth Series* by George Plimpton, editor. Introduced by F. du Plessix Gray. Copyright © 1981 by the *Paris Review*. Used by permission of Viking Penguin, a division of Penguin Putnam Inc.

Sarah Vowell. "Shooting Dad." Reprinted with the permission of Simon & Schuster from *Take the Cannoli* by Sarah Vowell. Copyright © 2000 by Sarah Vowell. "Sarah Vowell on Writing," excerpts from "Sarah Vowell's Topic" from *Transom.org*. Copyright © 2001 by Atlantic Public Media.

Alice Walker. "Everyday Use" from *In Love and Trouble: Stories of Black Women* by Alice Walker. Copyright © 1973 by Harcourt, Inc. Reprinted by permission of the publisher. "Alice Walker on Writing," *New York Times Magazine*, January 8, 1984, p. 24. Reprinted by permission.

Colleen Wenke. "Too Much Pressure," first published in *Fresh Ink: Essays from Boston College's First-Year Writing Seminar, 1998*. Reprinted by permission of the author.

Cornel West. "Race Matters," excerpt from the preface to *Race Matters* by Cornel West. Copyright © 1993, 2001 by Cornel West. Reprinted by permission of Beacon Press, Boston.

E. B. White. "Once More to the Lake" from *One Man's Meat*, text copyright © 1941 by E. B. White. Copyright renewed. Reprinted by permission of Tilbury House, Publishers, Gardiner, Maine. "E. B. White on Writing," excerpt reprinted from *Letters of E. B. White*, collected and edited by Dorothy Lobrano Guth. Copyright © 1976 by E. B. White.

George Will. "The Equity of Inequality" from the April 23, 1995, issue of the *Washington Post*. Copyright © The Washington Post Writers Group. Reprinted with permission. "George Will on Writing," excerpt from "Restoration: Congress, Term Limits and the Recovery of Deliberate Democracy," October 18, 1992, *Booknotes.org*.

Terry Tempest Williams. "The Clan of One-Breasted Women" from *Refuge: An Unnatural History of Family and Place* by Terry Tempest Williams. Copyright © 1991 by Terry Tempest Williams. Used by permission of Pantheon Books, a division of Random House, Inc. "Terry Tempest Williams on Writing" excerpt from "The Politics of Place," interview with Scott London, *Insight & Outlook*, National Public Radio, July 25, 1996. Reprinted with permission of Scott London.

Marie Winn. "Television Addiction" from *The Plug-In Drug*, revised edition, by Marie Winn. Copyright © 1977, 1985 by Marie Winn Miller. Used by permission of Viking Penguin, a division of Penguin Putnam Inc. "Marie Winn on Writing," copyright © 1986 by St. Martin's Press, Inc.

Tom Wolfe. "Pornoviolence" from *Mauve Gloves & Madmen, Clutter & Vine* by Tom Wolfe. Copyright © 1976 by Tom Wolfe. Reprinted by permission of Farrar, Straus and Giroux, LLC. "Tom Wolfe on Writing," excerpt from *The New Fiction: Interviews with Innovative American Authors* by David Bellamy, copyright © 1975. Reprinted by permission of the University of Illinois Press.

Virginia Woolf. "The Death of the Moth" from *The Death of the Moth and Other Essays* by Virginia Woolf. Copyright © 1942 by Harcourt, Inc. Renewed 1970 by Marjorie T. Parsons, Executrix. Reprinted by permission of the publisher. "Virginia Woolf on Writing," excerpts from *The Diary of Virginia Woolf*, copyright © Harcourt Brace Jovanovich, Inc., and The Hogarth Press. From "Letter to a Young Poet," copyright © Harcourt Brace Jovanovich, Inc., and The Hogarth Press.

Visual Images

Page 29: "Trust," advertisement for the Saint Paul Companies. Reprinted by permission of St. Paul Fire and Marine Insurance Company, St. Paul, Minnesota.

Pages 72–73: *Boondocks*, cartoon by Aaron McGruder. © 1999 Aaron McGruder. Distributed by Universal Press Syndicate. Reprinted with permission. All rights reserved.

Page 126: *Doug and Mizan's House, East River, 1993*, photograph by Margaret Morton. © Margaret Morton from *Fragile Dwellings*, Aperture, 2000. Reprinted by permission of Aperture.

Page 166: *Nighthawks* (full painting and detail), 1942, painting by Edward Hopper, American, 1882–1967. Oil on canvas, 84.1 x 152.4 cm, Friends of American Art Collection, 1942.51 © The Art Institute of Chicago. All rights reserved. Reprinted by permission.

Page 174: "Cellular Phones of the Future," cartoon by Barry Blitt, from the May/June 2000 issue of *Mother Jones*. Reprinted by permission of the artist.

Page 212: *American Gothic*, 1930, painting by Grant Wood, American, 1891–1942. Oil on beaverboard, 74.3 x 62.4, Friends of American Art Collection, all rights reserved by the Art Institute of Chicago and VAGA, New York, New York 1930.934 © The Art Institute of Chicago. Courtesy Bettmann/Corbis.

Page 213: *Rural Rehabilitation Client*, 1935, photograph by Ben Shahn. Courtesy of Corbis.

Pages 266–267: *Eagle in Flight, 1884–86*, photographs by Eadweard Muybridge. From *Animal Locomotion* by Eadweard Muybridge. Courtesy of Stanford University.

Page 310: "Deconstructing Lunch," cartoon by Roz Chast, from the *New Yorker*. Copyright © The New Yorker Collection 2000 Roz Chast from *cartoonbank.com*. All rights reserved. Reprinted by permission.

Page 342: Honda Civic Coupe advertisement. Photographer: Michael Rausch. Reprinted by permission.

Page 345: "Valves in Your Heart," Lexus advertisement. Created by: Team One Advertising and Pete Seaward Photography. Reprinted by permission.

Page 346: Advertisement for Honda. Photograph by Michele Clement. Reprinted by permission.

Page 356: "Traditional Values and Quality Return to the Whitey Museum." Copyright © by the Guerrilla Girls 1995, 2002. Reprinted by permission.

Page 410: "Garbage in . . . ," cartoon by Mike Thompson. Reprinted by permission of Mike Thompson, *Detroit Free Press*.

Page 458: "Luxury," advertisement for Lincoln Navigator. Photography by Vic Huber and Olaf Veltman. Reprinted by permission.

Page 498: "Smoking Gun." Reprinted by the permission of the American Cancer Society, Inc.

Page 587: *The Expulsion from the Garden of Eden*, painting by Masaccio (prerestoration). Copyright Alinari/Art Resource, New York. Reprinted by permission.

INDEX

Page numbers in bold type refer to definitions in
the glossary, Useful Terms.